*"I've been reading 'The Liverpool
2001. Dave writes with passion, hc
take himself too seriously. This boc
that have made the fanzine such ar
years. Funny and insightful."*

"Few writers capture the unique humour, sense of hope and relenting frustration felt by Liverpool supporters quite like Dave Usher. His is an authoritative voice on all matters Red, a point of contact for anyone who wants to truly understand the soul of this great club."

Sachin Nakrani, The Guardian

"A brilliant read. Funny, poignant, opinionated and honest, this is the story of Kenny Dalglish's dramatic final season as Liverpool manager as told by a writer at the top of his game. A must read for any Liverpool fan."

Tony Barrett, The Times

"There are two Liverpool writers outside of the mainstream Press whose wit, insight and genuine independence continues to make them enlightening and entertaining reading. Alongside the pioneering Steve Kelly of 'Through The Wind and Rain', Dave Usher of 'The Liverpool Way' has been expertly capturing the mood at Anfield for over decade. That's why this book, just like the fanzine itself, is an essential purchase for all Liverpool supporters."

Chris Bascombe, Daily Telegraph

"Dave Usher's hilarious no-holds-barred account of Liverpool's cup-winning season is essential reading for all Reds fans. Brilliant stuff."

Ben Thornley, Daily Post

"IN all the millions of words expended on football, surprisingly few convey how it truly feels to make an emotional investment in your team, to understand how that commitment really does make it YOUR team. Nick Hornby was the first to offer that insight, but from a sanitised, middle-class perspective. Now Dave Usher has arrived with his searching examination of what it is like to live and breathe Liverpool Football Club in one of the most dramatic seasons in the club's turbulent recent history. This is an entertaining read, funny and furious, enlightening and energetic. Most of all though, it is a brutally honest account of a year that will go down in the history of this great club, from a man who is perhaps the best writer to emerge from the city in the last decade. Forget Hornby and his Islington wine bar perspective, this is the book true football fans should read."

David Maddock, Daily Mirror

"The match reports on 'The Liverpool Way' website are something I always look forward to. Dave Usher not only lives and breathes Liverpool FC, but added to his obvious knowledge of the Reds from Anfield is an eye for detail, understanding of the game and sense of humour. A mix of quality and wit, and with no censorship, it makes for captivating reading. For the fan, by a fan that has the ability to put the view of the terraces into words. A must read for any Red."

Torbjorn Flatin, The Kopite

"From the lows of endless home draws to the relief of a Wembley Cup final win. From hating players who put their first names on the back of the shirt to declaring a never ending love of Steve Kean. From the weekly frustration of not knowing Norwich City's goalscorer to the weekly frustration of there not being a Liverpool goalscorer. Unlike Liverpool's forward line Dave Usher doesn't miss a thing in this highly entertaining, gripping and most of all funny account of the rollercoaster ride that was the 2011/2012 season."

Pete Schulz, TV2 Sport, Denmark

THE KING'S LAST STAND

THE FINAL MARCH WITH KENNY'S ARMY

DAVID USHER

"For me it's a great honour to be back and for the supporters there's no way we're not going to do as much as we possibly can and get some positive results. We've got to get the fans singing, we've got to make them proud of us. And that's what we want to do."

Kenny Dalglish, January 2011

First Published 2012 by David Usher.

Printed in Great Britain by
the MPG Books Group, Bodmin & King's Lynn

ISBN 978-0-9573498-0-3

This book is dedicated to my beloved wife and family, my wonderful parents and all of my friends who have helped and supported me in various ways over the years, with a special mention to my Dad and my good mate John Gallagher for all the hours they've given up selling the fanzine outside Anfield in hail, wind, rain, snow and the all too infrequent rays of sunshine.

Thank you all.

I'd also like to express my gratitude to everyone who has bought this book and/or supported the fanzine and website, as without you... well I'd have to get a proper job.

YNWA

Dave

CONTENTS

The King's Last Stand

Preface

Unlike many reds my age or thereabouts, I didn't grow up idolising Kenny Dalglish. In fact, my first real childhood hero was the man signed to be his long term successor. On the school playground I wanted to be Paul Walsh, not Dalglish. Had I been born a year or two earlier no doubt I'd have been all in on the King, but the truth is I wasn't that big a fan of his back in the day. It wasn't that I didn't like him, of course I liked him, he was Kenny Dalglish for Christ's sake! I just liked Walsh more. What can I say, I was 11 years old, what did I know?

When Dalglish became player-manager, to these young, untrained eyes he was just the fella who kept picking himself instead of my hero. When he stopped playing, he was then the guy who bought Peter Beardsley to replace my hero! So it's fair to say that initially I wasn't the biggest fan of Kenny Dalglish the manager, regardless of the success he had. After all, we were used to success back then, a kid like me didn't know any different. Winning titles was what we did. He was just doing what he was 'supposed' to do, what Bob Paisley and Joe Fagan had done before him. We expected to win the title every year and we usually weren't left disappointed. It was only as I got a bit older and more clued up that my appreciation - and affection - for Dalglish grew.

The disappointment of Walsh's transfer to Spurs eventually subsided as Beardsley found his feet following a slow start, and the football played over the next few years under Kenny's management was as good as anything I've seen before or since. It wasn't just the football either; the way Dalglish conducted himself in the aftermath of Hillsborough was remarkable and inspirational. As we know it took a huge toll on him and eventually forced him to give up the job he loved so much. Twenty long years would pass before he would have the opportunity to sit in the Anfield hot seat again, but sit in it he did and it was a great feeling having him back.

I hold him in a higher regard now than I ever did, even though clearly this second spell in charge didn't go as well as we'd have hoped. He took over at a time when we were at a seriously low ebb and were in need of a lift. He provided that and then some. It felt right having him back in charge, and even in games where things weren't going well for me there was still something comforting about seeing him stood there on the touchline, in his big coat, just like he did back in the day. And how can you not love that beaming smile any time we scored? The man cares deeply about Liverpool Football Club and wanted nothing more than to restore it to it's former glories.

Sadly the team he built second time around didn't compare to the one he constructed in the late 80s. Back then he had Barnes, Aldridge, Houghton. This time it was Downing, Carroll and Henderson. That's where he fell down, but for all the troubles we had in the league he still managed to deliver our first trophy in six years and was within an inch of adding another (had Carroll's header counted I'm convinced that we would have gone on to win that final). We went to Wembley three times, reaching two cup finals whilst knocking out both Manchester clubs, Everton and Chelsea along the way. That's what I'll remember about the King's 'return to his throne'. That and the way he unified a club and fanbase that had been riddled with backbiting, sniping and infighting until he took over.

This book catalogues the roller coaster ride that was the 2011-12 season, 'the final march with Kenny's Army' as it says on the cover. It contains a match report from every one of our league and cup games, as well as a tongue in cheek weekly round up of the rest of the Premier League fixtures from that week. Some of you will have read them on the website at the time, but I found when putting this book together that you get a completely different perspective on things when reading the reports one after another as opposed to having a week or two gap between them. Given the disappointing way we ended the season it's easy to forget how unfortunate we were early on, with the missed penalties, wasted chances and regular hitting of the woodwork. Of course you can argue that's our own fault, and that's true of course. Still, things could so easily have been very different and for me there'll always be a feeling of what might have been about the 11/12 season.

Everything you'll read in this book is as it was written at the time and has not been altered retrospectively. Inevitably that often makes me look like a bit of an arse, whether it's lauding Mick McCarthy's Wolves in August and tipping them to have a good season, or being encouraged by the early form of Stewart Downing. I could have rewritten it to make me look less of a chump, but where's the fun in that? Besides, too many of you will have read them at the time so there's no way I could get away with it.

I've also included chapters on Comolli's departure and on the FA hearing that led to Luis Suarez being branded a racist by all and sundry and banned for 8 games, again as they were written at the time for the fanzine. Given the huge impact that FA verdict had on our season and on the reputation and character of arguably our most important player, I felt it had to be included. Six months later I'm still seething about the injustice. It was outrageous that something like that could have happened, and even more outrageous that the numerous points raised in this book were never publicly used by the club in defence of their player.

So, this is my account of the 2011/12 season as it happened, embarrassing predictions included. Thanks for reading, I hope you enjoy it.

chapter one

With Hope in our Hearts

As usual, I was bitten by the pre-season optimism bug in the summer of 2011. Don't get me wrong, I wasn't under any illusions that we would win the title (admittedly I tipped us to do just that in the first fanzine of the season but I wasn't serious, honest!). I did think that with a bit of luck and a fair wind behind us we could be in the shake up and there was no reason that a top four spot should once again be the 'minimum expectation' rather than the ultimate goal.

There were numerous reasons for that optimism but at the root of it was how we had finished the previous campaign under Kenny Dalglish. We'd looked as good as anybody at times during the back end of 2010/11, which was a far cry from how we'd performed during the first half of the season under Roy Hodgson.

When 2011 began we were a huge mess. Hodgson had been swimming against the tide for six months and he was drowning. A hugely unpopular appointment, some fans had it in for him from the beginning and after a few months his brand of football and penchant for putting his foot in his own mouth had ensured that even those who had tried to get behind him had reached breaking point. Ideally the owners wanted to be able to see out the season with Hodgson at the helm and then implement their own strategy. Results and performances on the pitch combined with the incessant stream of verbal diarrhoea that plagued his every press conference (something England fans are now experiencing) made that impossible however. He simply had to go but finding a replacement in mid-season can be incredibly difficult. Rumour has it that FSG tried and failed to get Didier Deschamps from Marseille and Villas Boas from Porto before eventually sending out the SOS call to the King, who cut short his family cruise to ride in on his white horse.

Whilst his impact wasn't exactly immediate (defeat at Old Trafford in his first game was followed by another loss at Blackpool and a home draw in the derby), as the weeks wore on performances began to improve and 'pass and move' was back in L4 after several years of 'pass and stand still'. We hit five at home to Birmingham and another five away at Fulham; we put three past both Manc teams as well as Newcastle in thrilling wins at Anfield, and although there were some bumps on the road we were playing some terrific football under Dalglish. Throw in the maverick genius of new recruit Luis Suarez and the promotion of several promising youngsters into the first team set up and there was a lot to be excited about. Kenny's time spent in his role at the Academy meant he knew the kids as well as anybody and he had no hesitation in throwing young full backs Jon Flanagan and Jack Robinson into the fray. The performances of 'Flano' and 'Jack Robbo' (both outstanding in a gutsy draw at the Emirates) as well as the exploits of the likes of Raheem Sterling and Conor Coady in the FA Youth Cup gave great cause for optimism, and in Suarez we had a player who in many people's eyes was at least the equal of anyone else in the Premier League. Kenny's man management was evident for all to see, the players loved playing for him and smiles were back on faces.

The best example of it I can remember was when Robinson was suddenly required to go on to replace the injured Fabio Aurelio in that game at Arsenal. For a 17 year old kid to have to go on in such a high profile game and go directly up against Theo Walcott, the quickest player in the Premier League, is a pretty daunting task. A lot of managers would have bombarded the youngster with tactical instructions and advice on how to deal with the jet heeled Walcott. Kenny? He was cracking jokes and making the kid laugh. Jack went on and produced a brilliant display, dealing with Walcott with no problems at all and showing great composure and no nerves whatsoever. Most of the credit for that goes to the player, but the manager played his part too.

After a few years of infighting amongst the fans, and players and management not always being on the same page, things were now completely different. The feel good factor was back at Anfield and the fans were united under the King. Going the game had become fun again. The owners weren't on board as much as the rest of us though. FSG's blueprint from day one had been to have a young coach working under a director of football, but Kenny's impact since taking the reigns had been such that they really had little choice but to hand him the job permanently. It wasn't what they planned, but they played the hand they were dealt and in fairness they made money available for Kenny to put his own stamp on the squad. Konchesky, Jovanovic, Poulsen, Cole, Aquilani etc were all moved out as the new boss sent Damien Comolli out with a shopping list of players he wanted to replace them.

Of the new recruits, the one I was most on board with was Stewart Downing. He'd been desperate to come to Anfield for a few years. I have a tenuous link to him in that a mate of mine is mates with a mate of his. Because of that I knew that Downing was close to coming here in 2008; at one point it looked like it might happen but we signed Albert Riera instead. He was really disappointed it didn't come off but never gave up hope. He'd often speak privately of how much he wanted to come here and he'd watch our European games on TV and comment on how impressed he was by the fans and the atmosphere generated. Knowing how much he wanted to be a

Liverpool player I took more of an interest in his career after that and watched him a fair bit when he moved to Villa. Generally I was impressed with what I saw. He was named Villa's player of the season in 2010/11 and scored the winner against us on the final day of the season. Another mate of mine was told by a Villa player that Downing was easily the best player at the club, and I remember when Capello first took the England job it was Downing he singled out as the most impressive player in the squad. Carragher and Gerrard spoke highly of him based on their experiences training with him with England and Kenny had been chasing him ever since he got the job. The problem was that Villa were making things difficult and were demanding a big fee having already lost Ashley Young to the Mancs. They were desperately hoping to keep hold of Downing and even after he refused to sign an extension to his contract they still hoped they could persuade him to stay. Kenny was undeterred. Downing was the player he'd identified to solve our perennial left wing problem and not even a £20m price tag would put him off.

The deal eventually went through after Downing burnt his bridges with Villa when he was pictured in a Spanish bar with Andy Carroll holding a Liverpool scarf over his head. His club made Downing put out a statement saying the photo was fake to save face, but it was genuine (like I say, tenuous link to him!) and Villa bowed to the inevitable and accepted our offer. I thought we'd paid around £6m too much, but I can't say I was bothered by it as I thought he'd fit in perfectly. We needed someone to provide crosses for Carroll and Downing was right up there in that department. Kenny won the title at Blackburn with Wilcox and Ripley supplying crosses for Shearer, and Downing is more talented than both of those ever were. Of course £20m was too much. We paid extra for a player that Kenny wanted rather than get someone he wasn't as keen on just because he's cheaper. I was ok with that. At the time anyway.

Charlie Adam and Jose Enrique were both signed fairly cheaply and both filled gaps that needed filling. We had no recognised specialist left back at the club other than the perma-crocked Fabio Aurelio (injured again in the first week of pre-season training!) and the inexperienced Robinson. I didn't know much about Enrique and didn't have any real expectations of him. After all, Newcastle haven't exactly been known for the quality of their defenders. It's not like there's loads of quality left backs out there though and the reports on Enrique from people who had watched him were encouraging.

Adam was an intriguing one. He'd been a revelation at Blackpool, providing goals from midfield and developing a reputation as arguably the best dead ball specialist in the land - two qualities we really needed adding to our squad. Kenny had wanted him in January when Suarez and Carroll had arrived but Blackpool wouldn't sell as they were in a relegation battle that they would eventually lose. Tottenham and Manchester United were both strongly linked to him back then as well, with 'Arry winding down his car window to tell SkySportsNews what a 'triffic player he is and how he'd love to take him to Spurs, whilst Ferguson made some comment about Adam's corners alone being worth £10m. In short, I was happy to see him at Anfield and was confident he'd be a good addition to the squad. His lack of defensive ability and habit of giving away stupid fouls was a concern, but he probably wasn't going to be playing every week and would be a real asset in games where the attacking onus was on us.

Jordan Henderson however, I didn't get at all as he didn't fill a position of need. Well technically he did fill it for much of the season, but he shouldn't have, if that makes sense? I know what I'm trying to say even if you don't. We needed a right sided midfield player, and although he has played in that role he's not very good at it as he's clearly more of a central player. So why not just sign a specialist right sided player instead? My brother-in-law is a season ticket holder at Sunderland but he'd never really spoken much about Henderson. That alarmed me, especially given how he'd wax lyrical about the distinctly average Darren Bent. He was like a bear with a sore head when Bent went to Villa, but when we signed Henderson he wasn't arsed at all. His assessment was 'can't tackle, doesn't score, got a decent cross on him. You've paid for potential'. So I wasn't particularly excited by that signing, especially as Henderson's arrival seemed to confirm the rumours that the club wanted rid of Raul Meireles. The Portuguese midfielder had been the one Hodgson signing who'd actually been any good. A classy footballer and a versatile performer, he was popular with the fans especially after hitting a bit of a purple patch of goalscoring under Kenny. He'd been promised a pay rise by the previous regime and FSG didn't want to honour it given he was approaching 30, especially as Kenny didn't really fancy him. Henderson looked to be a direct replacement for Raul, and so it proved as Meireles rejoined his old Porto boss Villas Boas at Chelsea on deadline day.

Although he'd joined the previous January, Andy Carroll was effectively a new recruit too. He was injured when he arrived, and by the time he was back playing he never looked fully fit and seemed to be carrying a bit of weight. With a full pre-season behind him and having had time to get to know the club and his new team-mates, big things were expected of the powerful frontman. We also had the return of Steven Gerrard to look forward to, the skipper having been sidelined for much of Kenny's tenure to that point with a nagging groin injury that required surgery.

The one major concern I had going into the season was the fitness of Suarez. Or more specifically, the freshness of Suarez. Whereas most of his team-mates had a rare summer off, Luis had been tearing it up at the Copa America, where he finished as the competition's top scorer as well as being voted best player as Uruguay lifted the trophy. He'd be on a massive high coming back which was obviously good for us, but he might be knackered, which would not be so good for us. His minutes would have to be managed but on the plus side we had no European football to contend with, and playing just one game a week makes it a lot easier to keep picking your best players. Not being in Europe didn't bother me in the least. Yeah, the Champions League is where you want to be, but if you aren't in that then the Europa League can be a real chore. It's fine when you reach the latter stages and you're playing some of the big boys, but let's face it those early group games are fucking grim. Last season's games were just brutal, seeing the likes of Ngog and Jovanovic stinking it up against some Lithuanian pub team. No, I was glad to be out of it in all honesty, especially as in theory it should really help us have a better season domestically. I couldn't wait for the season to get started, the Return of the King had really whetted my appetite for the game again, the enthusiasm and passion he brings is just infectious. You'd see the huge grin on his face after we'd scored a goal in a pre-season game against some Thailand Select XI or someone and it'd make you feel all warm and fuzzy inside. It just felt right having him back in charge again.

Even in the worst of times I always find that pre-season is the time when things look their rosiest. The new signings haven't had the chance to show how bad they are yet and we aren't looking up at how many points we need to claw back on those teams above us. That optimism took on new levels due to the Dalglish factor and going into 2011/12 the squad looked to be much stronger than it had been in some time. We were short of cover at centre half but the highly regarded Sebastian Coates would arrive before the window closed and we seemed to have two players in each position and looked in good shape to pick up where we'd left off at the end of the previous campaign.

We had Kenny back at the helm and we had hope in our hearts....

chapter two

August

LIVERPOOL 1 SUNDERLAND 1

Competition - Premier League
Date - Sat 13 Aug 2011
Venue - Anfield
Scorer(s) – Luis Suarez
Half Time - 1-0
Star Man – Daniel Agger

Team: Reina; Flanagan, Carragher, Agger, Enrique; Henderson (Kuyt), Lucas, Adam, Downing; Suarez (Meireles), Carroll:

Rarely has the old cliché of 'a game of two halves' been more appropriate. For 45 minutes it was all going according to plan. The returning Suarez had overcome an early penalty miss to carry on where he left off last season (and indeed in the Copa America), Charlie Adam had displayed the prowess from set pieces that had helped get him here, Downing had the fans on the edges of their seats with a stunning run and shot against the crossbar and all in all we were pretty happy at half time. And then it went tits up.

The second half was terrible and in the end we were probably a little fortunate to hold on for a point as they had a couple of chances on the break that they didn't make the most of. Better opposition and we may have paid a heavy price for that.

It's difficult not to look at this and say 'here we go again'. Since our last title win, the thing that has held us back the most is the inability to take maximum points from the games we should be winning. Equally, this is the thing that has separated the Mancs from the rest in recent years. If you win the games you should be winning, you won't be far away at the end of the season. After one game, we're already two points down on what we should be, and you could see the disappointment on the fans faces coming out of Anfield today. Our chips were well and truly pissed on.

But it is just one game, and perhaps it shouldn't be much of a surprise. After all, we had four debutants in the side and we've had a disjointed pre-season where the team has not really had a proper chance to gel as we've been giving run outs to a number of players who have no future here. It's going to take some time for it all to come together, and we still have to overcome the problem of how to utilise Andy Carroll properly, without resorting to the lazy 'hit up to him and hope' approach that blighted some of the games he started last season and reared it's ugly head again in the last half hour of this game.

Also, you have to give some credit to Sunderland for upping their own game and making things difficult for us. Steve Bruce's record against us is seriously starting to get on my tits now. We've won just five out of 18 league games against sides he's managed. It's not like he's managed Chelsea, United and Arsenal either. With a record like that, there's a danger he'll develop a big head....

We just need to get better, and dare I say fitter too? There seemed like a significant drop in the energy levels of the side during the 2nd half, and that for me was what allowed Sunderland to get back into it. That and Phil Dowd. I'm loathe to start on referees after just one game of the new season, but it's impossible not to point to the massive helping hand the Mackems got from Dowd and his assistant in the first half. The decision not to send Richardson off for the most blatant of red card offences was infuriating, especially as Suarez then compounded it by producing arguably the worst penalty I can remember seeing at Anfield. His run up was reminiscent of a rugby player kicking a penalty, and the outcome even more so. I assume I wasn't the only one wondering why Charlie Adam wasn't taking it? In the absence of Kuyt and Gerrard, I'd imagine Adam will be next in line from now on.

Suarez had won the penalty with all his own work, charging down a clearance and running through on goal. I thought he should have shot early rather than go round the keeper, but that doesn't alter the fact he was tripped from behind by the last defender. He'd gone round the keeper, and his next act would have been a shot at an empty goal. Richardson's trip prevented that, but Dowd presumably didn't want to be the ref who sent a player off five minutes into a new season. Suarez had scored from the spot at least once for Uruguay in the Copa America, so confidence won't have been an issue, but that kick was truly woeful. He looked both stunned and gutted.

You can't keep a good man down though and he wasted little time in making amends, nipping in to convert a dangerous ball in from Adam. Much has been made of the extra quality Adam will bring to our set pieces, and this was the first of what will hopefully be many assists by the former Blackpool man.

All good at this stage, despite Sunderland wrongly still having eleven men on the field. The officials would intervene on Sunderland's behalf again before the break. Carroll brought the ball down and finished superbly, and it should have been 2-0. But no, the linesman decided Carroll had fouled the human baked bean, Wes Brown. Absolutely nothing wrong with that goal, and had it stood then I doubt Carroll would be getting scrutinised as much as he has been on the forums/phone ins etc since this game ended.

I thought Carroll played quite well overall given the way the game went. I don't blame him for what happened in the second half, and like I say if you take away that stupid decision by the linesman then we're all talking about what a great goal that was. I'm more annoyed by that than I am the lack of a red card for Richardson to be honest. Had it gone 2-0 I wouldn't have bet against four or five, but at 1-0 it's always on a knife edge. Carroll needs to get amongst the goals early and this would have been a great start to the season for him.

Speaking of great starts, imagine had Downing's shot been two or three inches lower? What an early impression that would have been. He'd not had much joy on the left because Sunderland had clearly decided they would double up on him any time he got the ball. After switching to the right though he collected the ball in his own half and saw he had plenty of space in front of him so he took off. He went past two or three would be tacklers and then thumped a shot from 20 yards against the bar. Had it gone in, there's your goal of the season right there on opening day.

It was an enjoyable first half, as despite being under pressure Sunderland did look to get numbers forward when they had the ball and their front two of Gyan and Sessignon were very busy and battled for every ball. Carragher and Agger had to be on their games to keep them quiet, and Carra was booked for catching Gyan high and a fraction late. Flanagan was fortunate not to escape a booking too for a mistimed challenge, whilst for the Black Cats Cattermole was predictably yellow carded after a typically 'robust' challenge. He'd gotten away with a worse one earlier on as Dowd waved play on after he'd gone through Adam.

There were other bookings too, but there were so many I lost track of them and what half they came in. I think Lucas and Adam both got booked, and Adam in particular seemed to struggle without the ball. It wasn't too much of a problem 1st half though as we were on top and playing well. It was interesting to see that the side was made up of five left footers and five right footers too. I can't remember the last time that happened.

The single negative from the opening 45 minutes was that we only had a one goal lead to show for our efforts. You can never feel comfortable with only a one goal advantage, no matter how 'on top' you are. A set piece, a deflection, a refereeing error or just a rare attack from the opposition and you can see all your hard work wiped out in a flash. Our play had merited at least a two goal cushion, which we would have had but for the incompetence of the officials. I don't want to use that as an excuse though, as it wasn't the officiating that caused us to stop playing at half time. As good as we'd been in the first half, we were equally as bad in the second.

Why was that? I don't think there's any one specific thing that can be pinpointed, it just looked like the wheels completely came off physically and mentally. We started to look leggy, players stopped showing for the ball as much, we stopped closing them down and allowed them to play. We also seemed to lose confidence - especially after they scored - and didn't appear to have any idea what we were trying to do. It was alarming how clueless we suddenly looked. Downing was used in about four different positions during the game, and I don't think that particularly helped him or the side.

Suarez going off really hurt us too, because he was the outlet ball down the channels whilst he was on the field. When he went off, that outlet ball then became the big punt to Carroll, as he can't run the channels in the same way Suarez does and shouldn't be expected to. It's easy to criticise the defensive players for going that route, but for me it's more on the midfield as they just weren't showing for the ball and dictating the game as they were in the first half. Lucas was very good before the break, and non-existent after it. Adam was similar, he seemed to run out of steam a little to me but maybe I'm reading too much into that because I've heard so much about how he would fade in the last quarter of games for Blackpool? He didn't disappear completely and still had some forward runs late in the game, but it looked to me like he had spells where he was 'catching a breather' maybe and wasn't coming to show for the ball quite as much as in the first half.

I felt we lost the midfield battle after the interval, and personally I'd have got Spearing on there early in the second half. He demands the ball, he closes people down and harries them in possession. Lucas does that too, just not in this second half for whatever reason. Having Speo in there to share the load would have helped both Lucas and Adam. Jordan Henderson was not contributing anything and may as well not have been there. He was like an extra in a soap opera. Stood at the bar in the Rovers or playing the fruities in the Queen Vic, supping his pint whilst the viewers are focusing on what the main characters are doing. He didn't stand out for anything he did wrong, but he just didn't do anything. I didn't really expect much else to be honest. Had he been been playing central I'd have been looking forward to seeing what he was capable of, but when I heard he was playing on the right it's fair to say I had little expectation. It's difficult enough making your debut for a new team, but when you are just 20 years old and cost a lot of money, and you are playing against the side you have just left (and the team you've supported all your life) then it's even more difficult. You really want to be playing in a position that you are completely comfortable with, and Henderson didn't have that luxury. I know he's played on the right before, but that's not the same as actually being a natural wide player. He was just ultra cautious when he had the ball and didn't try to do anything remotely positive.

Apparently some Sunderland fans were chanting *"Thank you very much for buying Hendo"* as they made their way back to their coaches. From their point of view I understand that, especially as many of them will be under the illusion they got £20m for him. He wasn't a player that they felt they couldn't afford to lose, but I imagine it was a bit tongue in cheek as he's one of their own and I'm sure they'd like to see him go on to do well (especially as there are plenty of 'addons' in the deal!). I'm surprised he started actually, and I was a little shocked to see Dirk on the bench and Maxi not even in the 18. For me, in a 442 Maxi is the best option we have on the right, especially at home. Even more surprising was the inclusion of Flanagan over Kelly. I don't think many expected that, but Kenny has a lot of faith in young Flanno. He didn't have the best of afternoons though, and the second half was pretty torrid for him. He'd done well enough before the break, but like most of his team-mates he fell off a cliff after half time. This is all part of the learning curve and I'm sure he'll be better for the experience. We all want to see young players brought through and given a chance, and Kenny has shown he is willing to do that. The trade off though is you have to be prepared for them to have the occasional bump on the road and that's what this was for Flanagan.

When it went to 1-1, we seemed to panic, especially when Suarez departed. Kuyt replaced Henderson but went to the left initially as Downing moved over to the right. Meireles came on for Suarez and he was then sent out to the left, as Downing went to play behind Carroll and Dirk went to the right. At one point it even looked like Downing was briefly playing in a midfield three with Lucas and Adam. Kenny certainly wasn't afraid to examine all his options, but nothing he tried made any difference.

Our confidence and belief seemed to have drained away, and Carroll was cutting an increasingly frustrated and isolated figure up front. I just felt that Raul was not going to give us anything from the left wing. I'd have preferred to see him trying to get up in support of Carroll and Downing told to just stay out on the left and whip crosses in. Carroll was feeding on scraps, whatever crosses did come in were usually a bit behind him where he had to generate his own power. In those situations, even small defenders can make it difficult just by leaning into him as he's in the air. There was one header late on where I felt he should have done much better, but he headed it wide of the far post. In general though, the service he got from out wide was piss poor.

So clearly we have work to do, but it was probably naive of me and anyone else to think we'd hit the ground running and sweep Sunderland away with a display of free flowing football. With new players generally comes some teething trouble, and we had four of them, plus Carroll and Flanagan who'd not played too much either. The result and second half performance were disappointing, but there's a long way to go and plenty to be positive about. Suarez is back and scoring, Downing has the kind of pace and directness we've been lacking and that should be particularly useful away from home when he'll have space to run, whilst Enrique looked very steady and solid at left back.

Next week's trip to Arsenal gives us a good chance to claw back the two points we dropped here. We're certainly capable of doing it, but we'll need to see more of the first half football and a lot less of the second.

Star man was far from easy. Suarez was dangerous until he got tired, Enrique was pretty good and Downing did well. Carragher and Agger both defended stoutly and I reckon I'll go for Agger just ahead of Downing.

Premier League Round Up (13-15 August 2011)

Football was back, but not exactly with a bang. As far as opening weekends go, it was a bit shit. Perhaps my view on that is tainted because we didn't win, but even leaving aside our own disappointment I thought it was a fairly dull, and sadly predictable weekend. The Mancs came from behind to win with a late, spawny, deflected goal, there were some diabolical refereeing decisions, Fernando Torres drew a blank yet again, Kieran Dyer went off injured and Joey Barton got into a scrap. Same old same old.

QPR were back in the big time, but Neil Warnock got his arse handed to him as Bolton hit four at Loftus Road. This despite QPR having Jay Bothroyd in their side. He's apparently better than Andy Carroll according to Warnock. Presumably DJ Campbell is better than Aguero too. He's a bad whopper is Warnock, but it's good having him back in the Prem as it's funny watching his constant bitching on MOTD every week. *"After 40 years in the game Neil Warnock is approaching this season like a little boy at Christmas"* declared Jonathon Pearce during his commentary. Kinell, can you imagine what that obnoxious oik would be like if he was a kid? No matter what present he got, he'd find a way to complain and point out that the richer kids down the street always get preferential treatment at Christmas time. Then he'd brag to anyone who'll listen that his Fuzzy Felt is actually better than an xbox 360. He's such a dick, but it's going to be fun watching him this season as his interviews are always amusing in a 'point and laugh at him' kind of way.

One person we won't be watching much of though is poor old Kieran Dyer, who lasted two whole minutes before going off injured. Fair play, that's longer than I'd have predicted. He's a shambles, he makes Aurelio look like Brett Favre or Cal Ripken Jr (little US sports reference there for any readers across the pond). QPR gave it a good go until Gary Cahill opened the scoring with a brilliant goal. Made up with that, he's in my fantasy team. Bolton ran out comfortable winners in the end, coming away with a 4-0 victory that flattered them a bit as two of the goals were on the spawny side. Can someone keep Kevin Davies off the TV though? I'm perfectly comfortable in my dislike of him and I don't need anything to make me question it. My stance is well entrenched, he's a rugby ball headed, barrel chested, elbow throwing tit. I can't stand him, he's a twat, but then I see him on Goals on Sunday and start thinking he's a sound fella who talks a lot of sense. Kind of like Gary Neville, apart from the being sound and me questioning whether he's a twat or not. So not like Gary Neville at all really.

Had to laugh seeing Clint Hill getting sent off for a ridiculous attempted head butt into the chest of Petrov. I can't believe he's still playing, he must be 45 now surely? I remember years ago when Tranmere were actually significant and most of us here on Merseyside took an interest in them. Back then Hill was getting sent off on a fortnightly basis, he was a proper head the ball. I guess I shouldn't be surprised he's ended up playing for Neil Warnock.

Speaking of 'head the balls', Joey Barton was in the news again. He was more sinned against than sinner this time, but there's always something isn't there? The stamp by Song was snide, and Gervinho had to go for the slap (he should have been red carded for that fucking obscene head of his. Seriously, WTF????), but that flop by Barton was ridiculous, as was the 'he punched me' claim to Van Persie. Barton sees himself as a crusader against cheating, so he should be embarrassed by the way he hit the deck and clutched his face like that.

It was also bit surreal seeing him tweeting about MOTD and then Lineker reading out the tweets, erm on MOTD. Funny that they didn't read out the one where he slated Shearer's dress sense as well as his opinions, before demanding 'sort it out slaphead'. Don't think he likes his former boss much. As for Arsenal, same shit different season. Lack of discipline, lack of spending, points dropped away from home, Wenger not seeing selected incidents. At least we don't have to listen to the annual Fabregas to Barca crap anymore. Good riddance, and hopefully I will no longer have to listen to non-Arsenal fans referring to him as 'Cesc' as though he's their mate. Winds me right up that. If you're not an Arsenal fan, then it's fucking FABREGAS, ok? What's next, calling Rooney 'Wazza'??

Moving on, Wolves won at Blackburn, and they could have a decent season I reckon. 'Sam the Eagle' has built a decent little side there and Roger Johnson will be a really good addition for them. They came from behind in this game, Formica with a nice finish (yeah I know, fish in a barrell etc) to put Rovers in front, but Jarvis set up Fletcher for the equaliser and Ward hit the winner after Doyle had missed a pen. They've bought well in the last couple of years, players like Fletcher, Jarvis and Doyle would get a game for most sides outside the top six. As for Blackburn, they're shite and may well go down. If they do there'll be few who'll miss them. They've got a striker called Goodwillie though. *sniggers*

Norwich are back in the top flight after successive promotions under the highly rated Paul Lambert, but probably not for long. Zak Whitbread is there, so I hope they do surprise people and stay up. I say that even though Zak once 'merked' me good and proper with a prank phone call when he was on a night out with some of his Liverpool team-mates. No hard feelings though, Zak. I'm happy to see you back at the top level and hope you have a great season. Honest.

They got a point at Wigan thanks to a goalkeeping error by Al Habsi. Gonna be a long season for the Latics too I think, there's not too much Premier League level quality in that team. They'll be heavily reliant on Moses, but he may find that parting the red sea is a lot easier than helping these chumps avoid relegation.

Great to see Martin Jol back in England, I can't help but like that crazy bashtard. Also nice to have Riise back in the Premier League too. He was re-united with Super Dan as Fulham went to Villa Park. The pair combined well early on but Riise unusually ballooned his shot over. Pity, I'd like to see him do well and I also want to see Villa struggle just to see what the fans will do about it. Lot of unrest there, those fans really didn't want the man affectionately referred to as 'Big Eck' (probably by many of the same people who say 'Cesc'). Could get ugly that one, and I mean the situation in general rather than the pink skinned McLeish. That particular ship sailed to Ugly Island sailed a long time ago with him at the front of the queue of passengers.

Onto Sunday now, and the Mancs visit to the Hawthorns. I watched this on MOTD2 on BBC HD. Have to say, HD really isn't all that it's cracked up to be at times. Seeing Rooney's new 'do' in not so 'glorious high definition' is a definite drawback. He didn't even look real, I felt like I was watching someone playing FIFA or Pro Evo on my telly, especially as it looked like someone had edited the stats on United's new keeper. "Diving 3; Command of area 1; Shot stopping 0;" So how about that De Gea, eh? Watching him the last couple of weeks makes me think back to Mick McCarthy commentating in the 2006 World Cup. "Keeper's gone down like a roll of lino" That line could have been written for De Gea. Teams should be shooting on sight from now on until he shows he can actually move a little bit quicker than Pavarotti getting off the couch.

As for the game, much like the Arsenal one it was a case of same shit different season. Late winner from a cross that took TWO deflections on it's way in? Really? That shit is starting already, on the opening weekend? Ashley Young fits right in there already as he looks like a proper United player. By that I mean the kit just looks right on him, and he's a complete cunt that you'd never tire of smacking. Speaking of which, Phil Neville was there in the away end. Let me elaborate slightly on that. Everton's captain was sat in the Manchester United end at a Premier League game. The saddest part is Evertonians won't care. Once a blue always a manc etc I just found it distasteful and inappropriate, a bit like Mike Phelan's beard.

Chelsea were held to a goalless draw by Stoke, thanks in part to some very shoddy refereeing from Mark Halsey, who denied them two clear penalties. The most interesting thing to note in this game was that Torres actually looked like a footballer again. He was very good, sadly.

There was also a Monday night game, which I didn't see and have no desire to. As a mate of mine said, "If I ignore City hopefully they'll just go away". I had no desire to watch them, so I went the pictures to see 'Planet of the Apes' instead (insert your own Gareth Bale joke here). The whole City thing just makes me sad, it's beyond wrong what they are being allowed to do and I hate it. Teams shouldn't be allowed to spend this kind of obscene money unless they raise it themselves (and not by some dodgy fucked up stadium naming rights thing either), and if this kind of shit is going to happen then FIFA need to impose some kind of handicap, and I don't mean having Mancini as manager or Lescott at centre half.

A lot of people are raving about City after this, especially after the impact made by Aguero (or 'Kun' to all you 'Cesc' lovers out there!), but let's not crown them yet. It was only Swansea after all (this years Blackpool?). The only teams not involved this weekend were Spurs and Everton, who of course weren't allowed to play because of the riots in London. Ifithadnerbinferdemrioterswedbetopoftheleague etc. On the bright side, the blues not playing meant I didn't have to listen to them bitching about being shown last on MOTD again.

ARSENAL 0 LIVERPOOL 2

Competition - Premier League
Date - Sat 20 Aug 2011
Venue - The Emirates
Scorer(s) – Aaron Ramsay O.G., Luis Suarez
Half Time - 0-0
Star Man – Jose Enrique

Team: Reina; Kelly, Carragher, Agger, Enrique; Lucas, Adam; Kuyt (Meireles), Henderson, Downing; Carroll (Suarez):

They say good things come to those who wait and also that good things often come in threes. Well we had to wait 70 minutes but then got the triple whammy; A long overdue red card for Frimpong closely followed by the arrival of Luis Suarez and Raul Meireles. I felt the game was always tilted in our favour on the balance of play anyway, but those three things were too much for Arsenal to overcome and ensured we came away with our first ever victory at the Emirates.

Perhaps some of the shine is missing from the win due to the number of absentees from the Arsenal ranks, but I don't really care about that. A win is a win, and Arsenal are one of the sides we'll have to overhaul to get back into the top four, so this was very important. We played well, we got three points, that's all that matters. I'd have been disappointed had we taken anything less than three points given the state Arsenal are in right now, but that doesn't mean I'm not thrilled about the win. It wasn't perfect and there were still some things we should be doing better, but we never looked under any pressure and overall I'm sure Kenny will be very pleased.

This represented our best opportunity in many a year to get a win at their place, even allowing for the fact we are still bedding in several new players to the team. With that in mind, it was very frustrating to see Suarez starting on the bench. Is it because he's not fully fit right now, or because they are being careful to ensure he doesn't have problems later in the season? Given what we've seen from him so far it looks to be the latter to me. Put it this way, if he's not fully fit now then God help the rest of the league when he is.

There's two schools of thought on what to do with players who you don't think can play 90 minutes. One is to start him and hope that he wins you the game so you can then bring him off after an hour and give him his rest that way. The other is keep him on the bench and bring him on late if you need him. Last week Kenny opted to start him. It didn't work out, mainly because Phil Dowd didn't do his job properly. Suarez scored and he also won a penalty that should have seen the opposition reduced to ten men. A red card for Richardson so early in the game probably puts us in a position where we could get two or three goals and give Luis a rest with the points in the bag. It didn't work out that way though, and we had to bring him off with the game still in the balance.

This time Dalglish went with the second option and it worked perfectly. Carroll didn't have too much joy - largely due to Vermailen turning in a fantastic performance - but what defender is going to want to battle with Carroll for 70 minutes and then have to chase Suarez around for the last twenty? Carroll did go very close with a good header that was well saved by the Szcziesny, and for the second week in succession we had a goal ruled out after he was penalised for the crime of putting his hand on an opponent who was about to collide with him. Last week's decision was bad, but this was even worse. The defender was moving backwards and was about to bump into Carroll, who simply put his arm up to prevent the contact. He nods it down, Stewart Downing drills the ball into the net and once again we see a cheap foul given against the big forward. Carroll doesn't get free-kicks when defenders do that to him, but the second he touches anyone he's penalised. Same thing used to happen to Crouch too.

Funny thing is, I remember listening to someone who worked with him at Newcastle (either a former manager or coach, can't remember who it was now), and he was asked what are Carroll's best attributes. One of the things he said was that unlike most big strikers he hardly ever gives away free-kicks when he challenges for the ball in the air. Maybe he didn't get penalised at Newcastle, but you can see already here that the second he even farts in a defender's direction the whistle comes out, and it's cost us two goals in as many games. Having said that, Szcziesny didn't appear to make much of an effort to save Downing's shot as he'd clearly heard the whistle.

Overall Martin Atkinson wasn't too bad, but he got that wrong and he also could have cost us a goal when he allowed Arshavin to throw Kelly to the ground before rolling the ball to Van Persie who's shot was just about kept out by a furious Reina. Look at the Carroll incident and then look at that. Ridiculous. It doesn't matter because we won, but it could easily have cost us the game had Van Persie not scuffed his shot and allowed Pepe to make the save.

The biggest decision Atkinson had to make of course was the sending off. Clearly he got that right unless you want to argue that he should have produced a straight red and not just a second yellow, but that could have gone either way and he probably went with the more lenient option just to be on the safe side. He knew the player was having an early bath so if he had any doubt as to whether it was a straight red he'll have just gone with the second yellow.

This is was the first time I've ever seen that Frimpong and it took about 90 seconds for me to mark his card as a bad knobhead. The reckless foul on Agger with just over a minute gone, and his 'hard done to' reaction to it pissed me right off. He then got into a little spat with Henderson that earned him the yellow card he should have got earlier, before yelling 'FUCK OFF!!' in a linesman's face despite the fact the decision was clearly correct. I can sympathise with players who show dissent when they know they are in the right, but when you see player's going nuts at an official when they are completely in the wrong, that's unacceptable. Remember that Fulham player giving it the v's to the ref last year after he blatantly hacked down one of our players on the touchline? I can't be doing with that shit.

There won't be a bigger inevatability in the Premier League all season than Frimpong getting that red card. I knew after about ten minutes there was no way he was getting through the game. I'm surprised it took as long as it did, but the tackle on Lucas was awful, and dangerous. He's not going to be a stranger to the referee's notebook that lad. Another twat off the production line, you have to hand it to Wenger he keeps churning them out.

We had players booked too, but they smacked of Atkinson trying to appease the home crowd who were annoyed at Frimpong's early yellow. Carroll was stupidly booked for putting the ball in the net after the whistle. It's a soft booking, as he wasn't attempting to waste time or gain any advantage, but the rule is there and Carroll knows about it so he shouldn't be putting refs in the position where they have to punish him. Lucas was also booked for what may have actually been his first foul. It's a sad indictment of the standard of refereeing these days that this may well prove to be one of the better displays of officiating we'll see this season.

We started quite well and at no point did I ever think Arsenal were on top. The problem for us was we were often poor in the final third. This was especially frustrating given that Arsenal had to send on a rookie centre half when Koscielny hobbled off. We never really tested him, largely because Vermailen was just so damn good. He cleared virtually every ball played into the box. We kept the ball well, we defended stoutly, but we just didn't create enough chances until Suarez came on. The first half was relatively even, but we looked more dangerous. Carroll's header from Enrique's cross was the first threatening moment from either side, whilst Henderson also had a header saved after good work by Kuyt. Charlie Adam hit a shot from halfway that had Szcziesny scurrying back towards his goal, but the ball sailed just over.

At the other end, Arsenal's best moment was a shot by Frimpong that Reina dived full length to tip around the post. World class save that. Nasri also had a shot from outside the box that went narrowly wide, but for the most part our back four kept the Arsenal frontline in check. Enrique was especially impressive in dealing with Walcott, who was completely anonymous. The

Spanish full back looked good going forward too, and the early signs are very encouraging from him.

The second half began with Adam trying another shot from his own half, this one was clutched by Szcziesny underneath his crossbar. He'll probably score from his own half this season if he keeps striking them as well as the two he hit in this game. Adam was a whisker away from playing Carroll in following a quick breakaway by the reds, but the pass sent the striker a little too wide. He did well to cut it back into the path of the marauding Kelly though, but his drive smacked against the outside of the post. I thought Adam played well. Not outstanding, but good. Our midfield play in general was impressive, we kept the ball and knocked it around well. Lucas had a fantastic second half, whilst Henderson was efficient if not spectacular. The game was screaming out for Suarez, especially when Frimpong got his walking papers. The question was who would make way. Most people probably felt it would be Henderson, but Kenny opted to bring off Carroll. He also replaced Kuyt with Meireles, and the impact was instant.

Suddenly we were swarming all over Arsenal. We were more incisive, we were finding space and Suarez was getting on the ball and causing problems. I'm sure the extra man advantage played a part in that, but there's no denying the improvement that the substitutes brought to us. It was exciting to watch, and you could sense a goal was coming. Downing brought a smart save out of Szcziesny after a lovely Adam pass set him in, and the former Villa man was a livewire throughout. He put some good crosses in and was always looking to get on the ball. He's a good outlet and there is a lot of promise in his partnership with Enrique on the left. His first goal won't be long in coming on the evidence of what he's shown in his first couple of games (Update: Hahaha!)

Meireles should have broken the deadlock when he found space on the right of the box but sliced his shot wide when he should have at least made the keeper work. You expect better from him as he's such a clean striker of the ball usually. With 13 minutes left the goal finally arrived. Suarez showed remarkable awareness to play a reverse pass into Meireles, and immediately set off looking for the return. Meireles' attempted ball was snuffed out by the covering Arsenal defenders, but the young Spanish centre half's clearance hit Ramsay in the chest and looped over Szcziesny. A fortunate goal, but not undeserved. Wenger claimed it was offside, and he may be right. However, if it was off it was literally by inches, and given that officials are supposed to side with the attackers when decisions are that tight, the linesman got it right. Meireles missed another opportunity before Suarez made the game safe in the last minute. His deft flick and turn left Miquel blowing for tugs as he tried to stay with him, and although the initial pass didn't go to him Meireles rolled it back across goal where Suarez had a simple finish. Again, Wenger says it's offside, but he would, wouldn't he? Straws. Clutching. At.

The travelling fans were buzzing and could be heard loud and proud all the way through. The Arsenal fans on the other hand were even more silent than usual. They couldn't even be arsed with that annoying 'Hoof' crap we normally have to put up with from them. It looks like Arsenal have no fight left in them, they're in a bit of a mess. Half of them fucked off because it was raining and they were getting wet. Wenger probably wished he could do likewise, as he sat there like a drowned rat furiously rubbing his head like Roy Hodgson.

Arsenal clearly have problems at the moment, but this is still a big win for us. After dropping two points last week in a game we'd expect to win, we're back on track now having picked up three points from what is traditionally a difficult fixture. We're still a work in progress though and there is plenty of room for improvement. The good thing is that the new signings are bedding in nicely, with Enrique and Downing especially having fitted in seamlessly so far. Martin Kelly was back in the side too and caught the eye at both ends of the field. Capello was watching and made some favourable comments about Kelly afterwards. Good for the player, not so much for us given the injury history Kelly's had. The fewer 'unnecessary' games he has the better for me, but it's going to be interesting to see what happens - for club and country -when Glen Johnson is fit again.

Premier League Round Up (20-22 August 2011)

Fair play to MOTD for making it look like Arsenal were hard done to. Some feat that, and if someone can explain the offside rule to Jonathon Pearce (and Arsene Wenger for that matter) that would be very helpful, thanks.

Moving on, and Everton were in action for the first time this season. Whatsmore, they were the SECOND game on MOTD, which will no doubt have meant half the blues missed it as they don't usually tune in until midnight to catch the 30 seconds or so they usually get. Probably for the best actually, as had they tuned in from the start not only would they have had to see us win at Arsenal but they'd have then seen their team humbled by QPR followed by Moyes having a go at the fans who exposed Kenwright. More on that shortly.

This was bad for Everton. QPR were without both their strikers after being hit by a flu bug and they had former Wimbledon yard dog Patrick Agyemang leading the line yet still managed to win. Lucky for the blues QPR didn't have any capable strikers or this could have been even more humiliating for them. Just to add even more humour to the proceedings, the winning goal was scored by 'Tommy Smith'. Last time the blues saw a Tommy Smith 'goal' the bastards shopped him to the DSS and the Anfield Iron had his invalidity benefits stopped. No doubt the DSS switchboard was lit up again after this game, fucking grasses.

Cahill missed a sitter, and Beckford was taken off much to the angst of the fans who were frothing at the mouth even more than usual as Moyes opted to go with no strikers. Youngster Ross Barkley looked pretty good, so there's one sliver of hope for them there as Kenwright might be able to use him as collateral to get another loan. Either that or sell him to the Mancs to appease the banks. Lineker said afterwards *"we've all heard about Ross Barkley for some time"*. Have we? I watch our reserves and u18s, and I've seen us play the blues several times but I've honestly never heard of the kid until this weekend. The last blue I remember being really hyped up was John Paul Kissock and he's now playing at Southport.

It was funny watching the two managers afterwards. Warnock was buzzing about making four or five new signings this week. Moyes was bitching about how underhanded those fans were for recording Kenwright. Never mind the fact that everything they reported back to their fellow Evertonians was actually word for word what the chairman said, apparently they're the bad guys here. Still, as Blue Rinse Bill told those fans upset about them being the only team in all four divisions not to sign anybody, *"if that's what we've got to worry about guys, considering what's going on in the world, Norway, East Africa......"* Wow, you really went there, eh Bill? Poor, poor form that.

Onto the North East derby now. Watching the teams come out the first thing that caught my eye was Howard Webb and his stupid smug face. You know how there are certain people that just the sight of them can make you want to go out and find a little guy to beat up (or a regular sized guy if you're not soft like me)? Webb would be top five on that list for me. I hate his shiny bald head and his smarmy smile, his popeye forearms and the way he wraps his whistle around his stupid fucking wrist. He's the kind of knobhead you see at the gym, working out in front of a mirror and then drinking his protein shakes in the hydropool. I really hate that twat. He's right up there with John Terry and Ferguson for me.

Anyway, as you'd expect, it was a lively game. Sessignon and Gyan looked sharp, they're like the terrible twins those two. They run the same, have the same haircuts, same build, same playing style... Decent players, and they'll be a handful for a lot of teams this year.

Joey Barton took time out from the sterling work he's been doing all week getting people to sign the Hillsborough petition, and as usual he was in the thick of the action. He understandably went nuts after Webb failed to spot Larsson handle his goalbound header on the line. He also got chopped down by Cattermole but Webb didn't produce a card. There was a bad tackle by Cabaye on Bardsley too and you could tell it was going to go off at some point. Pardew was stood on the touchline busily writing notes, presumably for his half time team talk.... *"A princess is protected by a well fortified castle, this being Bardsley, Ferdinand, Brown and Richardson. The bodyguard is Mignolet who has made mistakes with his handling before now. The gatekeepers are Cattermole and*

Colback. This is the tricky part, they rarely move, just sit in front and make sure that the castle is never short of numbers. From this base their offensive warriors are sent out to rampage amongst the would be suitors. Their best warrior is Gyan and he has licence to roam, making him difficult to pin down. Of course stopping their attacks is one thing but how to score and capture the princess? Our plan is to target Ferdinand. To do that we must attract Richardson by giving him room to come out of his position, thus exploiting the space down the side of Ferdinand with our best and fastest solidier Ameobi. However, our best chance to score will be to time a perfect thrust when the defenders rush to the castle walls, trying to catch us offside. THEY ARE VERY EFFECTIVE WITH THIS TACTIC but if we get it right just once it may be enough to steal the princess!!" I expect that's jibberish to most of you and unfortunately I'm not at liberty to elaborate further. To, those of you who do get it... *High Five*

Ryan Taylor got the winner with a great free-kick, he's always been boss at set pieces going back to when he was at Tranmere. Cattermole was eventually booked for another wild challenge that prompted a confrontation resulting in bookings for Barton and Bardsley, even though Joey tried to kiss and make up before Webb got his card out. Progress that, a year ago he'd have sparked the ref as well as Bardsley.

The Sunderland full back was then given another yellow card for a horrific tackle. Only a yellow, Howard? Really? We may not see a worse tackle than this all season, yet Webb only gave a yellow card. This is the man who gave Gerrard a straight red at Old Trafford last season for a tackle nowhere near as bad as this. Just a really shit ref, I hate him. Fuck you Howard Webb.

You can see how hard Barton is trying to change though, but he's probably fighting a losing battle. When Bardsley went off he was over there commiserating with him and patting him on the head, and you'll often see him acting as peacemaker these days. He's on such a short fuse though he's always going to run into trouble, I compare him to Samuel L Jackson in Pulp Fiction. He's like the tyranny of evil men, but he's trying, Ringo, he's trying real hard to be the shepherd. More than you can say for Cattermole. We get linked with him every summer for some reason, regardless of who our manager is. I wouldn't touch him with a shitty stick, he's probably the dirtiest player in the league and he's not so good that you'd put up with it. Unless you're Steve Bruce, obviously.

Moving on, and Premier League action was back at the Bridge, meaning plastic flags and the campest entrance music in the league. Seriously, what the fuck is that? It's proper shit, with all the knobs clapping and then chanting "Chewwwwwlsea". I just shake my head whenever I hear it, but it's kind of fitting for them really. Sums them up perfectly. Hodgson and Villas Boas seemed really happy to see eachother and had a long chat beforehand. You could then read AVB's lips as he said *"I'll talk to you after the game"* By all accounts Vilas Boas is a bit dull with not much of a personality. If I was a fly on the wall in that room I think I'd be out the nearest window looking for a turd to hang out on. Wouldn't have to go far actually, that Chelsea dressing room is full of them.... Ba dum tish.

West Brom took the lead with a brilliant goal by Long, he just bullied Alex and shrugged him off the ball. Impressive that, as Alex is a big old bruiser. Scharner could have made it 2-0 and they also blew another great opportunity when Long overhit a pass for Tchoyi. Can't waste opportunities like that against the better sides, as you'll always pay the price and that's what happened as Anelka equalised early in the second half and Malouda got the late winner after some awful defending down the left side of the Baggies. Not a good day for Torres again though, who was subbed midway through the second half after drawing another blank. Odemwingie could have equalised at the end but it wasn't to be, prompting Roy to bemoan his luck and set a world record for the amount of times he referred to himself as 'one' in a 30 second period. I'm paraphrasing but it was basically *"One can't help but bemoan ones luck when one sees a deflected goal go into ones net two weeks in a row, and then one has to feel hard done by when one's team twice concedes late goals like that"* Shut up man, you aren't Prince Charles you know, although you do bear an ever so slight resemblance to Camilla Parker Bowles when one thinks about it.

Off to Villa Park now, and Agbonlahor scores a cracker as Villa turned over hapless Blackburn. Heskey scored too, his first goal in six and a half years. Or maybe it just seems like it. Pedersen pulled one back after great play by the impressive Junior Hoilett, but Darren Bent wrapped it up with a typically messy goal. Blackburn are dog dirt, it's early days but I could see them finishing bottom. Steve Kean just looks like he shouldn't be there, he's got 'caretaker' written all over him and if they're gonna have a caretaker manager they may as well go back to that other fella who had about six spells in charge. Tony Parkes was it? I don't like Kean at all, but I'm not sure why. Kind of like how I always felt about that Billy Davies knobhead.

Wigan drew 0-0 at Swansea, and there's not much more to say about that. A few years ago this would have been a third division fixture, and that's probably where it belongs. I'd like Swansea to stay up, but they probably won't. They wheeled out Max Boyce before the game, so it's probably for the best that they go back where they came from. Max Boyce? C'mon man. They were lucky not to lose this, Wigan hit the woodwork twice and missed a pen.

Onto Sunday, and City were just about too much for a plucky Bolton side. Aguero was in the starting line up after his impressive cameo last week but he did fuck all and missed an early sitter. He would do wouldn't he, given that I put him in my fantasy team this week. Typical. And how come he's allowed to have *'Kun Aguero'* on his shirt?? That's not your name, dickhead. What are the league doing allowing this shit? You've got that Mexican prick at United, and now this. English players aren't allowed to have nicknames on their shirts, so how come these two are? I'm serious, it's pissing me off. It would be interesting to see what happened if an English player asked to do it. Would they allow 'Worf Lescott' No chance, so fuck this 'Kun' and 'Chicarito' shite off.

As for the game, Silva made it 1-0 after a mistake by Scruffy Jaaskelainen. Gareth Barry then made it 2-0 with a screamer, but Klasnic pulled one back almost immediately. I like him, the guy can finish. Don't know why they want Ngog when they've got him, as there's no comparison. Not that I'm complaining like, if they want to throw some cash our way for the Gog that's fine by me. Dzeko made it 3-1 after awful play by Knight and although Kevin Davies scored a great header to keep them in the game City held on for their second win of the season.

Stoke and Norwich now. Daniel Ayala was on the bench, but Zak Whitbread was nowhere to be seen this week. May have been injured, I don't know. Or maybe he finally picked the wrong person to phone prank.... On loan manc Richie De Laet gave Norwich the lead, but then their other centre half was sent off for what looked like nothing as Stoke were awarded a pen. It wasn't even a foul and it was outside the box anyway, but Norwich ended up down to ten men and facing a penalty kick. Former Everton keeper John Ruddy saved the pen, but just when it looked like the Canaries would hold on for three points Kenwyne Jones popped up in stoppage time to earn Stoke a draw. As a footnote to this game, Tony Pulis used the expression "suck it and see" in his post match interview. I don't know what to say about that, other than much like him wearing a baseball cap it made me feel a bit uncomfortable.

The other game on Sunday saw Wolves comfortably see off Fulham. Pjatim Kasami started for Fulham, he was actually in our u18 squad a couple of years ago but we couldn't get a work permit for him and he ended up in Italy. Be interesting to see how he does. Kevin Doyle scored and was then booked for taking his shirt off. Well deserved yellow that, and he should have got a second for the shit dance he did too. White footballers can't dance, it's science. Apart from Crouchy, obviously. Jarvis then made it 2-0 as Mick McCarthy's side maintained their 100% record to go joint top.

The final game of the 'weekend' saw Spurs perform their usual capitulating act at Old Trafford on Monday night. So predictable, and I'm happy to say I didn't watch any of it. Modric didn't play and is almost certainly off, whilst 'Arry has not been able to do any of his usual wheeler dealer stuff and they look a bit stale now. Who's in the deepest shit, Spurs or Arsenal? Don't know, but it has to be good for us so let's hope both of their woes continue.

EXETER CITY 1 LIVERPOOL 3

Competition - Carling Cup
Date - Wed 24 Aug 2011
Venue - St James' Park, Exeter
Scorer(s) – Luis Suarez, Maxi Rodriguez, Andy Carroll
Half Time - 0-1
Star Man – Luis Suarez

Team: Reina; Kelly, Carragher, Agger, Enrique; Lucas, Adam; Kuyt (Meireles), Henderson, Downing; Carroll (Suarez):

Job done. This is how it's supposed to be. A far cry from the shambolic exit to Northampton last season and other cup horror shows like Barnsley and the battering we took at the hands of Spurs' second string. Kenny got the balance right and picked a strong side - including our most important player - but he was still able to give run outs to a couple of youngsters and to other key members of the squad.

Good job he did play Suarez actually, as without him who knows what the outcome may have been. The talismanic Uruguayan scored one and made two. He's been involved in every goal we've scored so far this season. There are some star players who may look at a wet night at Exeter in the League Cup as being a bit beneath them. They mightn't fancy it. Not Suarez though, it doesn't matter who he's playing or where, he just approaches every game the same way, whether it's the Copa America Final or the 2nd round of the so called 'Micky Mouse Cup'. He's just fucking boss, I love watching him and his importance to our chances of doing anything this season just can't be underestimated. With him on the pitch we can look great. With him off the pitch.... well, we don't look great. Our play dropped off significantly when he left the field, but then we were 3-0 up and cruising so that's understandable. I'd have liked to have seen us bang a couple more in without Suarez though just for peace of mind, as I do worry a little about how we'd look if we had to do without Luis for any period of time.

That's why the prospect of a return to Anfield for Craig Bellamy really appeals to me, in fact I'd be absolutely made up with that. We need another option up front, someone with pace who can work the channels, and the narky little Welshman fits the bill perfectly. Kenny is interested and Bellamy wants to come here but I can't see City making it easy as I'm sure they'd much prefer he went abroad or back to Cardiff. Fingers crossed though as I'd be a lot happier if we had another forward on board.

At least Carroll is off the mark for the season. Great goal too, he's got a real sledgehammer for a left foot hasn't he? Apart from that strike though, his performance was, shall we say, patchy. That's probably being generous, but I'm an Andy Carroll guy and believe he's going to be a real asset to us. He did some good things, but also some really sloppy things too. Once again he hardly had any decent crosses to attack and we still need to figure out how to play more to his strengths. He has to be better too though, there's no question about that and I'm sure he will be. Fitness wise he's looking much better this season than last and whilst I can understand why a lot of people are worried, I'm still a believer.

Whilst it wasn't the plan, I'm glad Carroll got such a long run out as the more games he plays the better in terms of getting him sharp. I'm sure Kenny wasn't planning on him coming on until the last half an hour, probably for Suarez, but the King's hand was forced when Meireles went off with an injury to his collar bone. A real shame that, he was looking lively and had played some lovely one touch passing early on. Maxi is more than capable of stepping in to take the minutes that Raul has been getting so it's not a huge concern.

The squad is steadily starting to look much stronger now. The deadwood is being shifted, not much left now actually, and in people like Maxi and Spearing we have good players who can step in without any real drop off in the quality of the side. In recent years when we've rested players and given the 'squad men' a run out, there'd be a few players in the side who realistically shouldn't have been anywhere the team. Degen, Ngog, El Zhar, Kyrgiakos etc

This time there wasn't one player in the 18 who I looked at and thought *"I wish he'd fuck off"*. We had a lot of first choice players in there, but there was also Skrtel, Wilson, Maxi, Spearing, Flano and Jack Robbo. Then you have Raheem Sterling sat in the stands (and complaining about it on twitter, silly boy) and people like Johnson and Gerrard still to come back from injury. Things are looking up, especially with another centre half on the way in and hopefully Bellamy before the window shuts.

Exeter gave it a good go though and tried to play football rather than just launch it and defend in numbers. That played into our hands a bit, and the first half saw us play some lovely stuff. The goal came from a well worked move that ended with Henderson trying to pick out Carroll in the centre. The keeper got a hand to it to take it off the striker's head, but Suarez collected on the back post and drilled a low shot through the legs of the keeper and also the defender on the goal-line.

Suarez then broke away superbly down the right and produced a wicked low cross that Maxi just couldn't get anything on. Brilliant play by Suarez though, who was running poor Exeter ragged. Far better defenders than theirs have been and will be put to the sword by our number seven though, and they have nothing to be embarrassed about as they actually played pretty well. Just before half time Luis showed he is human after all by putting one over following great set up play by Spearing and Maxi. Would have been a fantastic goal if he'd finished that off, as it was terrific football.

Exeter hadn't really been able to threaten at the other end, but within seconds of the restart ex manc Nardiello got away from our defence and forced Reina to come charging out of his goal. Nardiello got there first and lobbed the ball over Pepe, but thankfully it went wide of the post. A let off, and a reminder that 1-0 is nothing and can be wiped out in a second.

Within ten minutes, 1-0 became 2-0 and we had our cushion. Henderson broke and released Suarez, but his initial attempted cut back to Carroll was blocked. Suarez showed great awareness to collect it again and pull it back to the onrushing Maxi who slotted it home. Aside from Suarez, Maxi may just be the biggest goal threat we have these days (with the possible exception of Kuyt I guess). He's had a new lease of life under Kenny and always seems to pop up in dangerous areas.

It was soon to be 3-0. Suarez megged an opponent for what seemed like the tenth time in the game, and then found Carroll on the edge of the box. Suarez wanted a return pass but Carroll was unable to play it early enough and was almost dispossessed. He adjusted his feet well though and leathered an unstoppable shot into the top corner. He didn't look particularly happy about it mind, and he seemed agitated all night actually. He's probably a little low on confidence, but hopefully this helps and he can build on it.

Suarez was immediately withdrawn with the game won and Downing came on to replace him. He's gone close to scoring in both games so far, and will have fancied his chances of getting off the mark in a game that the reds were now in total control of. But for a good save by the keeper he would have, as he cut in from the right and hit a rasping low drive that was parried behind for a corner. He had another chance late on too, as a counter attack from a corner saw him sent clear. It looked like he would just run through and get his shot away, but he somehow didn't get properly into his stride and was caught from behind, forcing him to try a chip that was easily saved.

With the reds now in cruise control, Exeter came back into it a bit more and grabbed a consolation goal when the otherwise dominant Skrtel stuck out a leg and needlessly tripped Nardiello. He picked himself up and drilled the penalty down the middle as Pepe dived to his right. Seems a long time since Pepe saved a pen now. Can we not bring back his old coach who used to tell him where all his opponents like to put their pens?

The rest of the game was fairly uneventful and there were no further dramas as we booked our place in the next round. Overall, a good performance with some players really excelling. None more than Suarez of course, who was head and shoulders above everybody. Take him out the equation though and Speo would have been my star man, I thought he was really good and kept things ticking over nicely.

Henderson was ok, a bit up and down again I thought. He did some nice things but still plays it a bit too safe too often for me. He was also involved in the most contentious incident of the match, when it looked like he'd been brought down for a penalty only for him to be yellow carded for diving. Weird one that, as there was definitely contact even though Henderson left his leg in there waiting for it. That kind of thing usually gets you a pen, but Henderson had no complaints about it and accepted his booking with good grace, which suggests he knows he was in the wrong. I was pissed off about it, not because I thought it was a pen, but because he should have been looking to score. Trying to win a penalty was a cop out, he should have been confident enough to just go on and score, but you can see that he isn't totally confident yet and is still feeling his way into the side. I'm not as confident about him coming good as I am with Carroll, but there is definitely a player in there and technically he seems very sound. He just needs to be more assertive I think, and hopefully that will come as he begins to feel more comfortable here. It was good for the two young full backs to get more playing time, and Robinson had a fine game I thought. Flanagan wasn't at his best again though and was sloppy in possession a few times. Up until the second half of the Sunderland game 'Flano' had been pretty much flawless, but all young players go through this and it's all part of the learning curve.

Nice for Wilson to see some playing time at centre half rather than left back. As a full back, he's pretty poor I think, but I like him in the middle. There's shades of Agger about him in his style of play, but he really needs to get out on loan somewhere and play some games if he's continue his development. A good Championship side, or even a lower Premier League one would be ideal for him, especially with Coates coming in.

The longer we stay in the League Cup the better it is for people like Wilson and Shelvey, but I get the impression that Kenny will pick his teams based on the level of opposition. If we get a strong opponent, I don't see Kenny picking too many of the younger players as he'll be as desperate as we are to win a trophy this season.

LIVERPOOL 3 BOLTON WANDERERS 1

Competition - Premier League
Date - Sat 27 Aug 2011
Venue - Anfield
Scorer(s) – Jordan Henderson, Martin Skrtel, Charlie Adam
Half Time - 1-0
Star Man – Lucas

Team: Reina; Kelly (Skrtel), Carragher, Agger, Enrique; Henderson (Maxi), Lucas, Adam, Downing; Suarez (Carroll), Kuyt:

Looks like we learned from the Sunderland game then. Just like on opening day, we produced a wonderful first half performance but had just a one goal lead to show for it. Thankfully there was no second half horror show this time. We stepped it up even more and made the game safe with plenty to spare, ensuring that when a defensive lapse occurred this time the only damage it caused was to the pride of the captain.

It's difficult not to get carried away after this, as it was really, really good. Bolton are one of those middle of the road sides who can cause you problems if you aren't on top of your game. A bit like Sunderland really. If a top six side plays well, they'll always beat a Bolton, Stoke or a Sunderland etc, but if they aren't at it then it's very easy to drop points against them. Owen Coyle's men were completely out-matched at Anfield though, as every one of our players hit form and some of the football produced was scintillating. They didn't stand a chance, and unlike Sunderland they didn't have Phil Dowd to bail them out. Having said that, this ref was shite too and we're fortunate that his errors didn't cost us.

There was one surprise when Kenny's team was named, only a mild one, but I'm sure there will have been the odd Ancelotti style eyebrow raised when Andy Carroll's name was omitted from the starting XI. I don't think it's unfair to say that Carroll's absence from the side and the wonderful football we produced on the day are not entirely unrelated. As I've said before I'm an Andy Carroll guy, but since he's been here we've played most of our best football with him on the bench or in the stands and Kuyt in tandem with Suarez.

I don't think it's Carroll's fault as such, but it is a fact. Ideally I want to see Carroll in the side, but I can't really put up much of argument with anyone who says it should be Kuyt alongside Suarez. It's up to Andy to do enough to prove he's got more of a claim to the shirt than Dirk, and right now he hasn't done it. It's that simple. I think he will eventually do that, but the great thing for us is that we can wait because we aren't reliant on him.

At the back end of last season when we had Kuyt and Suarez paired up top we began to look really good. When Carroll came back in, we didn't look quite as free flowing (the one notable exception being the Man City game). Since then we've added people like Downing, Henderson and Adam to the mix, and whilst it's going to take time for that to gel properly it's impossible not to be excited by how all of those players performed against Bolton. Two of them scored, and Downing has done just about everything but get on the scoresheet so far. Every game he's gone close and he's slotted into the side seamlessly, forming an exciting combination down the left with the mightily impressive Enrique. That left hand side was just too much for Bolton to deal with, especially when Suarez joined the party with his regular forays out there. He and Downing linked up very well on a number of occasions, and it's very encouraging to see those two starting to strike up such an early understanding.

The opening goal was a thing of beauty and originated down that left flank. Downing moved inside taking the full back with him whilst Suarez ran into the space down the channel dragging Cahill out of the centre. Suarez received the ball from Enrique and then played possibly the pass of the season so far in to Downing with the outside of his right boot. Downing's first time volley was top drawer and deserved a goal but that tramp Jaaskelainen made a fine save. Kuyt picked up the loose ball and fed Henderson and although his first shot was blocked he then curled one into the top corner with his left foot. Great finish.

Henderson has improved with each game so far. This was easily his best performance, and it appears that Kenny is going to keep playing him even though a lot of us would still have Meireles or Maxi (who'd be my personal preference) in the side over him. My Mackem brother-in-law text me after the goal saying *'enjoy it, he doesn't get many'*. Fucking killjoy. That's the challenge facing 'Hendo' though, he needs to find the net regularly because both

Maxi and Raul have shown they can do that.

I still think he has been playing things safe a bit too much when he has time to try and do something more positive (understandable for a young lad in a new team), but there were definite signs of that changing in this game. He was demanding the ball much more than he has previously and he clearly enjoyed himself. If he plays like this every week then he'll more than justify his place in the side. It's only one game though so let's see, but it's great for him to break his duck so quickly.

Henderson was involved in most good moves in the first half, including the first real opportunity of the game that started when a Bolton corner was cleared to Suarez in the centre circle. He wriggled away from his marker and was cynically taken out of the game but play was correctly waved on as Henderson seized on the loose ball and released Downing. Unfortunately the winger's touch was too heavy and a defender got back to clear. No yellow card for the defender who took Suarez out however.

Great to see us hitting teams like that though, and it's a direct result of a change that Kenny has made that I've been calling for since the days of Evans. Evans, Houllier, Benitez and Hodgson all brought everybody back for corners, and it did my fucking head in. If you leave one up, not only do they have to keep two - sometimes three - back, but you also have someone to hit when you clear the ball which means it doesn't always come straight back. Kenny leaves Suarez up, and we're much better for it.

Henderson created another opportunity for Kuyt with an absolute peach of a cross that the Dutchman just couldn't get anything on. A corner was awarded so perhaps a defender got a slight nick on it to take it away from him. It was great to watch though, fast, incisive attacking football and we were coming at them from all angles. Adam was heavily involved too, and he picked out Suarez with the kind of pass that helped persuade Kenny to sign him, but Luis couldn't quite gather it when any touch would almost certainly have led to a goal either for him or the supporting Kuyt who was all alone in the centre.

Suarez then should have done better when he was put through by the influential Henderson, but his audacious chip landed on the roof of the net. The only criticism that can be levelled at Suarez - and I hate levelling any criticism at him at all as he's rapidly becoming one of my all time favourite players - is that he isn't always as clinical as he should be. Having said that, if he was then he'd be in the top three players in the world as everything else is ridiculously good.

We had strong appeals for a penalty when Downing collected another brilliant Adam pass and knocked the ball past Steinsson who deliberately handled. The ref gave a free kick right on the edge of the box and booked the Bolton full back. I couldn't tell if it was inside from where I was sat, but turns out the ref got it right. Probably more through luck than good judgement based on his second half display. Kuyt then blasted a shot just over following another good build up.

Bolton's only effort of the first half was a stinging volley by the lively Petrov that was punched clear by Reina. The only negative of the opening 45 minutes was another injury to Martin Kelly. It didn't look too serious, but it's a further indication that the lad has a touch of the 'Daniel Aggers' about him. Thankfully he's not quite a 'Fabio Aurelio' (not yet anyway), but he does tend to pick up a lot of injuries and it's the only knock on him as otherwise he's a top, top prospect.

With Glen Johnson still not fit and Jack Robinson preferred to John Flanagan on the bench, Kenny had no other right back to call on. When Skrtel was brought on I imagine that like me most people assumed that Carragher would be moved to full back. That's what would have always happened in the past so it was therefore surprising to see Skrtel go to full back, especially given what happened the last time he played there when he was given a chasing by Downing at the Riverside.

It proved to be an inspired move as Skrtel was outstanding. Carragher and Agger are playing well as a pair and keeping them together meant that there was very little disruption to the backline, especially given how well Skrtel slotted into right back. With the impending arrival of the highly rated Sebastian Coates (who was watching from the stands), Skrtel has done himself no harm here by showing another string to his bow.

The first half had been brilliant and the crowd were well into it. I've just realised that I haven't even mentioned the best player on the pitch yet either. Whilst Suarez, Kuyt, Adam, Downing and Henderson were posing Bolton all manner of problems, Lucas was earning most of the plaudits from the crowd as his constant pressurising and strong tackling set the tone for our dominance. Whether he was winning headers against Kevin Davies, or snapping into challenges against Re-Coker, Lucas seemed to be everywhere in the first half.

He wasn't as dominant after the break but he didn't need to be as we put the game to bed fairly early on. This kind of display is becoming the norm for Lucas under Kenny's management. He'd been playing well for a while before Kenny took over but he's gone up quite a few notches since.

For all our dominance and flowing football though, there was only one goal in it and I couldn't help but think back to that Sunderland game a couple of weeks ago. Would Kenny be telling them not to make the same mistakes as last time, where we came out flat after the break and just got flatter? How would we approach the second half? And would Scruffy Jaaskelainen snub the applause of the Kop like he usually does? Well yes, he did, the fucking skidmark. Can't stand him. Him and that Dean Kiely gobshite who used to play for Charlton. Ungrateful turds.

Whatever Kenny said in the dressing room worked, as if anything we raised the tempo even more from that impressive first half. Bolton just got blown away as wave after wave of attacks descended on the Kop end goal. Adam had a shot deflected just wide, Downing cut inside but shot well over and there was a real momentum building. Bolton couldn't get out of their own half, and the crowd were right into it too. It was great stuff.

Suarez continued to torment poor old Zat Knight and should have had a penalty when he went past him on the right flank as he entered the penalty area. He looked to have ridden Knight's attempted tackle but then crumpled in a heap after he'd seemingly gotten away. My first reaction was it had to be a penalty as why would Suarez have gone down when he was in the clear? My second was that I didn't really see much contact and it looked like he'd gone down a bit easy.

From my seat in the Main Stand my view of what happened was obscured by the large frame of the prone Bolton defender, and it was only after the game I heard that Knight had grabbed Luis' foot and pulled him down. Given that the linesman had a similar view to me I can't blame him for not seeing it, but the ref needs to be in position to give that. He got it wrong, but if he thought it was a dive then why didn't he book Suarez?

Thankfully we didn't have much time to dwell on that injustice as Adam whipped in a delicious corner that Skrtel gleefully powered into the net. He's usually got a head like a 50p coin but he met this one perfectly and it was a cracking goal, the kind of which we rarely seem to score. Adam's delivery was so good though it was just begging to be finished off.

We were on a roll now and Anfield was rocking. Within no time it was 3-0, as Kuyt fed Adam and he fooled everyone by not cutting back onto his left foot, instead rolling a shot into the bottom corner with his right peg. That's what he brings to the side, goals and assists from midfield. We haven't had enough of that down the years, and if Adam could notch double figures from the middle of midfield that would be massive for us.

He's started his Liverpool career quite well without being especially spectacular, and like Henderson this was his best game so far. It's really exciting to see the new players all settling in and making their mark so quickly. It's even more exciting to think how good we should be when they've had more time to bed in properly and when we have Gerrard and Johnson back on the pitch.

Mind you, could Enrique 'bed in' any more than he already has? He looks like he's been here for years. He's been flawless so far, at both ends of the pitch too. Often full backs are either good going forward and suspect at the back, or good defenders who offer little going forward. On the evidence so far, Enrique is one of the few that is equally good at both. It's still early days and it's probably best to wait a dozen games or so (I still remember being fooled by Josemi), but he really looks the part doesn't he?

He's as strong as an ox and I didn't realise how fast he was until the second half of this game, when twice he turned on the afterburners and blew by Bolton players who had several yards start on him. Given the fee we paid, he might be the best bit of business we did this summer, and he's probably the one I had the least expectations of too. He looks way better than I thought he'd be, I just hope he keeps it up.

At 3-0 Bolton were all over the place, and Suarez was causing mayhem. He was desperate to score and started getting really pissed off with himself and his team-mates. He went mad at Henderson when the midfielder broke clear but didn't play the pass early enough. Suarez had pulled off into space and had been screaming for a pass that didn't come, and he was livid.

If he was angry then, I thought he was going to assault someone when Jaaskelainen picked up a backpass from Robinson and wasn't penalised for it. Suarez had been chasing it down and almost got there too, but the keeper just bent down and picked it up. It was the most clear cut decision of the game, yet the ref and liner both let it go. I was dumbfounded by it, and still am now. Even if they thought that Suarez possibly got the first touch on it before the keeper handled, there's no way they could have been sure of that and given that the keeper made no attempt to go for it with anything other than his hands, why would you give him the benefit of the doubt there? Replays confirmed Suarez didn't touch it, and this might be the worst decision we'll see at Anfield all season. Thankfully it didn't matter.

The linesman also showed he wasn't paying proper attention to what was going on when Henderson and Adam worked a clever corner only to have it pulled back. Henderson went over to take the kick, but then made out he was leaving it to Adam who was walking over. Henderson had actually taken it though as he nudged the ball out of the corner box, and Adam collected it and ran towards goal before being pulled back because of the linesman's flag. Adam and Henderson weren't impressed, as it was clearly a training ground move. Good to see us trying that kind of innovative stuff.

Suarez was becoming increasingly agitated as he tried to maintain his record of having scored in every game. He overhit the ball as he tried to go past a defender and then berated himself even more than he'd done Henderson. It was funny watching him. Funny and endearing. He's just so desperate to do well, and Kenny must have been tempted to leave him on so he could get his goal. Zat Knight will have been desperate to see Suarez depart, the poor fella was run ragged all afternoon, to the point where he almost tied himself in knots as he controlled the ball by the Main Stand touch-line simply because he knew Suarez was in the vicinity.

Much as I'm sure we all wanted him to stay on, the prudent thing to do was to bring him off. The game was won, and although we don't have another game for a fortnight, Suarez has been called up by his country I believe so any rest we can give him will hopefully see us rewarded later in the season.

He was replaced by Carroll and once again we didn't look as good with Suarez off the field. Of course in the interests of fairness you have to factor in that the team eased off a bit at 3-0 up, but still, it would have been nice to see us knock in a couple of goals with Luis on the bench. In truth we probably should have. Downing put a sensational cross in that flew across the goal-mouth just begging to be finished off, and then Enrique produced two more similar efforts.

All three came to nothing as Carroll - and to a lesser extent Kuyt - failed to get in there to finish them off. I've regularly defended Carroll due to the lack of service he's had, but I can't complain about service this time as he could have had a couple of tap ins today if he'd gone into the areas a centre forward is supposed to go into. John Aldridge made a career out of getting on the end of the kind of crosses that Carroll stood and watched yesterday.

Kenny could do worse than put on a DVD of all Aldo's goals and show Carroll how it's done. Aldo is the player Carroll should be looking to emulate. Comparisons between Carroll and Drogba are unfounded, as Drogba has much more pace than Carroll. Aldridge was a different type of player to Carroll too, he wasn't as physically imposing or technically adept as Carroll, but the big man could learn a lot from the positions Aldo would take up and how he led the line in a side containing the likes of Barnes, Beardsley and Houghton.

Comparison's between Suarez and Beardsley are obvious, whilst Henderson's current role isn't too dissimilar to that of Houghton in that he doesn't have to stick to the touchline and has freedom to play further infield and get into the box. Downing is no John Barnes (who is?), but against Bolton he was playing the same role that 'Digger' excelled in and that ball he whipped across the face of goal late on was vintage Barnes to Aldridge, except 'Aldridge' was caught on his heels and didn't anticipate it.

I'm not suggesting Kenny is trying to replicate that side, but there are certainly some comparisons that can be made in how the team is set up and the style of football they are trying to play. Carroll can be a big part of it, but he has to do better and he also looks like he needs a confidence boost too. He's about the only one you can say that about, as the rest of the side look very assured and confident in what they are doing.

The goal at the end was frustrating, and only happened because we were 3-0 up and cruising. 99 times out of 100 Carragher clears that ball with his right foot into the back row of the Main Stand. With a comfortable lead he decided to try and bring it down with his left foot and let Petrov in. Carra did remarkably well to get back at Petrov and nick the ball off him, but could only divert it into the path of the clinical Klasnic who buried it past a furious Reina.

I don't think I've ever heard a goal at Anfield greeted by complete silence before. Even when we're playing some tinpot Eastern European side who only have 20 fans in the upper Centenary, you still hear SOMETHING. Bolton's fans are a joke. They took a pitifully low allocation anyway for a fixture that's only 45 minutes up the road, and they didn't even sell that. Their corner looked about half full, and those that had bothered to stay til the end couldn't even muster an ironic half arsed cheer. Awful fans.

As for us, we've started the season well and given the complete mess both North London clubs seem to be in, a top four spot looks to be there for the taking. We look like a good side now, and there's every reason to think we will improve further when everybody gets to know eachother better through playing together more often. Unfortunately we've now got to wait two weeks to play again because of yet another shitty international break.

Premier League Round Up (27-28 August 2011)

Norwich kicked things off on MotD with a trip to the Bridge. If ever there was a game that I should have put on mute it's this one. If that shitty 'Birdie Song' entrance music wasn't bad enough, John Motson was doing the commentary.

Every year we hear that he's hanging it up, but then the new season starts and irritating fucker is still there with his stupid over pronunciations of players names (Drogbaaaarrr) and his high pitched, over dramatic shitty comments. I genuinely hate John Motson, have done for years. Funnily enough I can trace that hatred back to it's exact origins too. We drew 2-2 at Stamford Bridge and McManaman got both our goals. Motson sounded devastated when they went in, but went completely overboard for Chelsea's goals. He may as well have been singing 'one man went to mow' whilst waving a cheap plastic flag. When Chelsea scored (think it was that little rat John Spencer) 'Motty' was as excited as David Pleat in a traffic jam in a red light area.

Anyway, Bosingwa gave Chelsea the perfect start with a screamer from distance, but Norwich were always in this and gave as good as they got by the looks of it. Chelsea aren't looking particularly impressive at the moment, and based on the highlights they looked fortunate to win this as Norwich had plenty of chances. Still, BBC have a tendency to edit their highlights to make even the most one sided game look even so maybe I'm under-rating Chelsea a bit. From what I've seen of them so far though, I'm not seeing much to concern me as a Liverpool fan.

Norwich drew level after a typical blunder by Hilario(us) allowed Grant Holt to hook the ball in impressively. Motson described it as a howler by Ivanovic, the fucking clueless idiot. Then Drogba got knocked spark out. I'd heard before I watched it that Drogba was ok and just had a bit of a concussion, so knowing it wasn't a serious injury I have to admit I laughed my fucking head off when I saw it. It looked bad, and you could tell he was genuinely hurt as he didn't do 13 roll overs. Replays showed he was out cold before his head smacked against the turf, the glass jawed little bitch. The keeper didn't hit him that hard and besides, those goalie gloves have plenty of padding in them. Big, strong fella, but definitely a bit 'chinny' as they say in the boxing world.

Torres was booked for a high foot and some will say he was lucky not to get a second yellow after a petulant trip on a defender after he lost the ball. As funny as that would have been, I don't actually think either of them deserved a yellow card. He's got more bookings than goals so far for his new club, and he was subbed once again in this game. One goal in 18 games now. I'm not kidding when I say I think I could match that tally given the opportunity. Don't get me wrong, I'd look shite and contribute absolutely zero to the game, but I reckon if I had 18 games in that

Chelsea side I could find the net at least once, assuming I managed to avoid the temptation of stabbing John Terry.

Chelsea were struggling badly until they got a helping hand from the ref. The penalty was fair enough even though Ramires was looking for it, but the red card for the keeper was well harsh as there was a defender on the line. That killed the game, and Mata scored on his debut in the 11th minute of stoppage time.

Villas Boas' interview afterwards was an eye opener. His comments on Paul Lambert were really, really smug, and it seems he's got a chip on his shoulder already even though he's only been here five minutes. Jumped up little shitbag, trying to be the 'new Mourinho'. Sorry lad, not going to happen as Jose is in a league of his own when it comes to that kind of obnoxious shite. He'd have me wanting to my foot through the TV, but Villas Boas just had me raise an eyebrow and mutter 'fucking tit'. He's not 'Special', he's just some beaut with 'Roy Hodgson hair' in a designer suit. Go and play with your fucking pokemon cards, junior.

I have to admit I was actually made up with that interview, as until this weekend I didn't really know what to make of him. He seemed to be a fairly inoffensive nerd, so I was happy to discover he's actually a mildly offensive nerd, with the potential to be an extremely offensive one.

I much prefer Chelsea managers to be twats, as everything else about the club reeks of twattishness so it's only right that the manager should too. I always liked Ancelotti though, he was a good guy and it didn't sit well with me him being in charge of that club. Avram Grant wasn't a bad guy either actually, but it looks like they've got themselves a keeper here.

Speaking of gobshite managers with chips on their shoulder, David Moyes took his Everton side to Ewood Park this weekend. 17 year old Ross Barkley kept his place in the side but it was not a good day for him as he conceded a soft pen when he left a leg out on Formica, who gleefully took advantage with a blatant piece of gamesmanship. Hoilett's pen was poor and was saved by Howard. I guess I jinxed Hoilett by bigging him up last week. Blackburn may be shite, but they battered Everton here. They hit the post through Dunn, and also saw an effort by Goodwillie *sniggers* hit the crossbar. Formica won a second penalty with another dubious fall, but the tit then went and missed it. You waste two penalties in a game you don't deserve anything, and that's exactly what they got when the perrenially woeful Lee Mason made his third bad penalty call of the game by punishing Samba for what was just a great header. Legohead Arteta put the pen away and Everton had their first three points of the season, despite looking proper shite again.

Wigan / QPR was next. New QPR signing Joey Barton watched from the stands looking like the school bully from Grange Hill in the 80s. Denim jacket and that barnet of his, right out of the 'Tucker Jenkins' fashion catalogue that. His first game for QPR is going to be against Newcastle at St James' in two weeks. Should be fun that. I don't like QPR keeper Paddy Kenny but I'm really not sure why. Do we have some kind of history with him from when Sheff Utd were in the Premier League, or is it because he reminds me of that twat Dean Kiely?

Wigan won it with Franco Di Santo getting both goals via off target shots that were deflected in. I've seen him play a few times, including when he was at Chelsea and he played against our youth team at the Academy. I'll go out on a limb here and say he's absolutely fucking garbage. He looks the part, fancy boots, exotic name, powerfully built, nice tan etc. He's like a young Roque Santa Cruz, apart from the being able to play football part. Like I say, crap. I've decided I want Wigan relegated. Sick of the empty seats, the fucked up pitch that they also use for Rugby League and most of all the music they play after goals. There's a few teams guilty of that, Bolton have done it for years and they can fuck off too, but that song Wigan play is the very definition of small time and belongs in League Two. Plus their chairman is evil. Hope they go down this year.

Sunderland took on Swansea at the Stadium of Light. John O'Shea made his debut and hit the bar, whilst Scott Sinclair did likewise at the other end with a piledriver from 25 yards. Sinclair was really highly rated a few years ago and it will be interesting to see what kind of season he has. Swansea held their own again, and they do play some nice stuff. Their keeper looks decent too, but there's definitely shades of Blackpool about them.

Villa - Wolves was the final game on Saturday. Bit crap, ended 0-0. Villa's full back Chris Herd ran head first into the goalpost but remained conscious. Guess those metal posts aren't as hard as a goalkeeper's glove, eh Didier? Or maybe Herd doesn't have a glass jaw.

Saturday's MotD ended with Lineker saying *"Can King Kenny win the crown? Calm down, calm down"* Fuck off Jug Ears.

Onto Sunday now, and before I get to the big games I'll deal with the boring ones first. Newcastle beat Fulham 2-1 in a game that could have gone either way. Fulham played alright and had their chances, but a double from Leon Best gave the Geordies the three points. He must feel like he's won the lottery as no way is he a Premiership striker. That's the Mike Ashley effect right there. Replace a £35m striker with some cheap nobody. I see that Gabriel Obertan is at Newcastle now, I always have a chuckle when I see this odd looking creature. I always say that Franck Ribery looks like the Neville brother who'd be forced to live in the cupboard under the stairs as he's so ugly. Well Obertan would live under the stairs in Mickael Silvestre's family home. One final point from this game, add 'Jonas' to the twat list alongside 'Kun' and 'Chicarito'.

Meanwhile, West Brom went down 1-0 to a controversial late goal to Stoke. For me that goal shouldn't have stood, the striker went in studs up and the keeper had two hands on the ball. I didn't even know Ben Foster was at West Brom. What's happened to Carson then, dropped or has he left? Good three points for Stoke, but that's no points from three games for Hodgson's Baggies. The facerub is imminent, I can feel it coming.

Those two games were being played on Sunday because Fulham and Stoke have been playing in the Europa League. I keep forgetting about that, and I can honestly say I have no idea how either of them have done or who they've been playing. I doubt I'll watch a single Europa League game this season, I'm just really glad we aren't in it.

Onto the 'Super' Sunday clashes now, and it was North London v Manchester. Complete mismatch, we're talking Mohamed Ali in his prime against Glass Jaw Drogba here. Tottenham was the scene of another riot as City absolutely trashed 'Arry's boys. Spurs were actually doing alright until they went behind. They'd had several chances to take the lead, the best falling to Gareth Bale who ballooned it. Nine months ago he was the hottest property in English football, but he's done fuck all for a good while now. Needs to up his game. Spurs paid the price for that miss as Dzeko put City in front shortly after and then added a terrific second before half time. He bagged two more in the second half - one of them was an absolute belter - and Aguero scored a cracker as well. I liked Dzeko much more when he was shit.

Tell you what's weird about City though, they have Patrick Viera sat in the stands as 'an ambassador' for the club. He was there five minutes and hardly played, what's with that? It's the equivalent of us bringing in Jan Kromkamp to be our ambassador. It's just wrong, but then everything about that set up at Man City is wrong. As people have pointed out, it's like they're playing footy manager but using the editor to cheat. Manc pricks.

Spurs' humilation would have been the big story on Monday morning, but then Arsenal got them off the hook by letting in EIGHT goals at Old Trafford. Let's put this in perspective here. This is Arsenal we're talking about, not Watford, Ipswich, Swindon or some other team that was in over their heads. There is no excuse for a team of Arsenal's standing to ever let in eight goals to anybody. I'm not taking anything away from the Mancs' performance, you have to acknowledge that its pretty fucking amazing to put eight goals past a top four side. But seriously, Arsenal's players need punishing for that. I don't care what's in their contracts, if I was running that club they'd all be fined two weeks wages. If they complained about it, I'd transfer list the fuckers. If they had any professional pride they'd accept the fine.

They were always going to be up against it as they had several players missing (some of them self inflicted because they have no discipline), and no-one could have complained about them losing as it was to be expect-ed. But eight goals? EIGHT fucking goals? They just gave up, and although to the rest of us it's pretty funny seeing an Arsenal side let in eight goals, the fact is that those players showed absolutely no pride in their shirt and they should be ashamed of themselves. Wenger will be the one who carries the can for it, and he is now being linked with dozens of names as he has finally realised that the only way out of this is to actually buy some fucking players, but some of those on the pitch at Old Trafford are bad shithouses who are stealing a wage. Walcott had a blazing row with their young right back Jenkinson, Arshavin was recklessly flying into tackles and should have been red carded, Van Persie bottled the penalty and then had a bust up with some of his team-mates who didn't applaud the fans at the end. Traore was actually smiling at the end, and people like Djourou, Rosicki and Arshavin aren't who you want in the trenches when things are going badly.

Arsenal have offered a free ticket for their next away game to all those fans who went to Old Trafford. Yeah, that's nice of them isn't it? Tell you what Arsenal fans, how about you pay me £50 and I'll repeatedly kick you in the balls for 90 minutes. Then to show you how sorry I am, I'll do it for nothing next time. Fuck me, what kind of warped logic is that Arsenal? Just give them their money back if you want to do something for them. Actually, you know what, don't. Fuck 'em. Arsenal fans do my head in anyway, they used to be ok but then they got all up their own arses and obsessed with how they play the 'most beautiful football in the league'. I quite like the idea of kicking them in the balls for 90 minutes, and just for good measure I'd yell 'HOOF!!' every time I did it. Just remember, you can't spell Gooner without the word Goon.

chapter three

September

STOKE CITY 1 LIVERPOOL 0

Competition - Premier League
Date - Sat 10 Sep 2011
Venue - The Britannia Stadium
Scorer(s) –
Half Time - 1-0
Star Man – Charlie Adam

Team: Reina; Skrtel (Johnson), Carragher, Agger, Enrique; Henderson (Bellamy), Lucas, Adam, Downing; Kuyt (Carroll), Suarez:

"I think we have been respectful to the referees. But more important than being respectful to the referees in their campaign is having respect for Liverpool Football Club. And if I feel they are suffering in any way, shape or form, then I think I'll just need to go the same route as some other people go and see if we can gain some benefit from that. I'll speak to the owners first and see what they say, because the last thing I want to do is have my behaviour to impinge on the club's success in any way, shape or form."

Very strong words from the King, justified too as this was really hard to take. Usually when we go to Stoke we're garbage but this time we went there and basically dominated the game. Not quite from start to finish, but certainly for at least three quarters of it. I don't like using referees as an excuse, but sometimes it's impossible to ignore it. Kenny's right, the difference between the two sides was Mark Clattenburg. I'll certainly concede that we didn't help ourselves with some poor finishing, but essentially we lost this because of a penalty that never was, and two or three that probably were but Clattenburg ignored.

It's not sour grapes, it's a fact. If you're going to give a soft penalty like the one awarded when Walters dramatically flung himself to the floor the second he felt Carragher's arm go around him, then you can't suddenly become Mr Lenient when Stoke's players decide to start playing basketball in their own box. Three times there were strong appeals for handball. One was an absolute stonewall penalty, one could have gone either way and I haven't seen any replays of the third one so cant really comment.

Dalglish has every right to feel aggrieved. His comments were basically a case of *"I've tried keeping a dignified silence, but that's not working. If the owners are ok with it maybe I'll go down the Alex Ferguson route and just bully officials to the point where this doesn't happen to us anymore"*

Stoke never looked like scoring, they didn't cause us any problems and they couldn't even get out of their own half after the break. It was completely one sided, but until the final twenty minutes or so we really didn't do enough in the attacking third. Clattenburg is the reason we lost, but he isn't the reason we didn't win, if that makes any sense? That's on ourselves I'm afraid, for leaving it too late to really turn the screw and for wasting the clear opportunities we created. I guess what I'm saying is Stoke wouldn't have scored without that gift from the official, but it's our own fault that didn't then do enough to get back into it.

I didn't particularly agree with the side we went in with, but I understood it. The team played so well last time out against Bolton that it's understandable Kenny chose to stick with them. That included Skrtel at right back, and once again I thought he did pretty well. Defensively he was fine, and he did his best to get forward whenever possible. The end product wasn't always there, but that's ok as to be fair he's no Steve Nicol or even a Glen Johnson. He did about as well as could be expected I'd say.

My main gripe with the team was up front. I thought Andy Carroll was a certainty to start this one. Firstly there's the height aspect. Him coming back for set pieces would have helped neutralise their main goal threat. Secondly, after the week he's had in terms of bad headlines (through no real fault of his own this time) it would have been just like Kenny to put him in there and say 'go and show 'em son'. Instead Dirk kept his place alongside Suarez. As it turned out, we didn't need Carroll to deal with their set plays as they hardly had any and those they did have we dealt with comfortably. In an attacking sense though, it didn't work. Usually as a pair they combine really well, but it just didn't happen for them in this game and Kuyt was fairly anonymous before he eventually made way for Carroll.

The first half was scrappy, as you'd expect against Stoke. They don't play football, and it's difficult to play any against them. Not because of their style of play, but because of the pitch. Funny how teams only seem to have difficulty passing the ball against Stoke in games at the Brittannia. We don't have problems at Anfield, but going to their place is usually a different story. I lost count of the number of times passes played into the feet of our players came up just short and were intercepted. I didn't think anything of it at the time, I was just frustrated with the team. It was only afterwards when I heard it mentioned that they deliberately allow the grass to grow longer to make it difficult for passing sides that it clicked. Enrique, Lucas and Adam in particular struggled with this a lot before the break I thought, and there were far too many for it to be a co-incidence. The second half was better as the player's adapted and put a bit more fizz into their passes.

We started brightly enough, Suarez put a shot over from 25 yards early on and we were on the front foot in the opening exchanges. Stoke were looking for Crouch at every opportunity but he wasn't really getting any kind of decent service and Agger and Carragher were coping easily enough. Then out of nothing they were awarded a pen. The way I saw it from behind that goal, Walters barged Carra who lost his balance as a result and put his arm around the player in an attempt to steady himself and stay on his feet. Walters flung himself to the floor, and my first reaction was that the ref would blow for a free-kick in our favour. I couldn't believe it when he pointed to the spot.

Having seen the replays, I stand by that view. It wasn't a penalty, it was either a free-kick to us or 50-50 and you let it go. Walters is a big lad, it should take a hell of a lot more than that to put him on the floor. A clear dive, and I hate all this justification of it by commentators and pundits. *"He felt the contact so he's entitled to go down"*. Really? That's acceptable now is it? If players are 'entitled' to hit the floor any time a defender puts a hand on them, then we're going to see fifty penalties every game, half of them against Martin Skrtel.

Walters is one of those players who seriously grates on me, but until this game I had no particular reason for it other than I think he's dogshit and I don't like his face. He's just a big bruiser, a less shit version of Shefqi Kuqi if you like. I didn't appreciate him shushing the away end after scoring a pen that he'd cheated to win, and it offends my footballing sensibilities that he now has a winning goal against Liverpool on his CV. He joins a not so elite club that includes such luminaries as Ian Marshall, Helder Postiga, Tommy Mooney and Kevin Lisbie amongst others.

Clattenburg may as well just have awarded a goal instead of a pen, as the days of Pepe saving spot kicks are in the distant past. Players are clearly now just smashing them up the middle as they know he's diving before they take it. There was a time when his goalkeeper coach would be pointing that out to him. Not any more it would seem. It's too easy these days. I say again, can we not bring back Xavi Valero?

We didn't deserve to be behind, especially due to the nature of the goal, but there was still plenty of time to turn it around so I wasn't unduly worried. We lost our way a little bit after the goal though and passes were going astray too often. Charlie Adam was one of the biggest culprits, but I was ok with it as it was Adam that was constantly trying to get on the ball and get us playing. He never hid and became more and more influential as the game wore on.

One thing I have to give Stoke great credit for is the blocking by their defenders. Every time it looked like we had a clear opening a body would appear from nowhere to charge down the shot. The best opportunity we had before the break was a shot over the bar by Skrtel when he arrived late in the box to get on the end of a Suarez cut back. Apart from that, every other shot we had seemed to be blocked and they really did defend superbly.

There was also a clear handball that wasn't given. I couldn't see it at the time as it was down the opposite end, but when you see the replay it was a definite pen. There's always that grey area of ball to hand and whether it was 'deliberate' or not, but you can't stick your arm out and then palm the ball with your hand. Penalty all day that. Clattenburg didn't want to know though.

I felt it it was obvious at half time we needed to change things, as did most of those around me. Kuyt had not done anything, neither had Henderson and Downing had been largely disappointing too. In Downing's case I felt we just weren't getting him enough of the ball. He was up against Huth, and that's a match up I'd expect him to win more often than not. He can't do it if he doesn't have the ball though.

Kenny did it change it at the break, but not with the use of substitutes. He switched Downing and Henderson, which was a bit puzzling. It was probably worth having a look at Downing on the right, but I couldn't see Henderson doing much on the left other than cutting inside or passing the ball backwards to Enrique. For the most part that's what he did, but there was one break through the centre that should have turned the game on it's head. I don't know how come he ended up in so much space but when Enrique sent him clear he simply has to score in that situation. I didn't have any confidence that he would though, and when I asked a few mates afterwards they said the same. I don't know why, but I just expected him to miss. Too much time to think about it, and he just bottled it. The tame shot straight at the keeper was straight out of the Emile Heskey handbook. Henderson was fortunate in that he got a second bite at it as the rebound fell nicely to him. He missed that one too, not getting enough height on his shot and allowing the keeper to save again. The third effort was well blocked by a covering defender but Henderson then did well to get the ball to Adam. His first shot was blocked yet again but he showed great composure to take the ball goalwards and looked to have done everything right until the finish, which was saved by Begovic and scrambled to safety.

Part of me knew then we weren't going to get anything from this game. There was still plenty of time and we were well on top, but when something like that happens you do start to wonder if it's one of those days. Henderson put another presentable opportunity high over the bar from 18 yards, and was hooked shortly afterwards. He probably felt like shit, I felt sorry for him. Kuyt went off too as Carroll and Bellamy entered the fray.

Bellamy made an immediate impact, twice playing Enrique in on the overlap as the reds piled on the pressure. One Enrique cross found Downing on the far post but his header was saved. The other was looking for Suarez but was cut out by a defender. Suarez wanted a corner and flipped when he didn't get it. He was getting more and more frustrated and had earlier gone nuts at Henderson when he missed that great chance. Suarez's temper snapped completely when his cross struck Upson's outstretched arm but no penalty was awarded.

From behind the goal it looked a blatant penalty and the travelling fans went nuts. So did Suarez, who ran over to harrass the linesman, cursing and baring his teeth like a rabid dog. A yellow card was inevitable but merely rubbed salt into the wounds. The move that had led to the 'handball' was superb, as Suarez and Downing combined to slice through Stoke. Downing was becoming more and more involved, and was very good in the last half hour of the game. He produced a series of good crosses that came to nothing, but he also blazed a shot over when he should have at least hit the target.

Johnson also came off the bench to replace Skrtel but had only been on the pitch about a minute when it appeared he'd injured himself again. He was running back but seemed to be treading water and got completely left by Kenwynne Jones. After that he wasn't going forward much and it was clear he'd done something. He tweeted after the game his hamstring went again. Looks like Skrtel will be keeping that job next week then.

Bellamy headed wide from a Downing cross and Suarez went close when he ran through several challenges and dragged a shot just wide. The final opportunity of the game fell to Suarez as Begovic flapped at an Adam cross and the ball dropped at the feet of the Uruguayan, but he failed to hit the target as the ball rolled agonisingly wide. He was distraught, as were the fans behind that goal.

This was our first defeat of the season and it was an undeserved one. It was really difficult to take and it was just an incredibly frustrating afternoon. *"We're Stoke City we'll play how we want"* sing their fans. Fair enough, I don't mind them going long ball and playing for set-pieces. Doesn't bother me if that's how they want to play. Letting the grass grow bothers me, as does the gamesmanship shown by Upson when he went down with an 'injury' a yard from the goal-line just to try and kill our momentum. Clattenburg should have told him to roll off the pitch for treatment, instead he stopped the game and let the physio on, the dick. No surprise that Upson was fine to continue. I hate him too, he looks like a head on legs.

Begovic also feigned injury to try and get Lucas in trouble. There was minimal contact - if any - but he went down clutching his face demanding the referee do something about it. Shithouse. I don't know if I'd have rather we'd been outplayed or not. It would have been easier to accept the result but then there wouldn't have been anything positive to take from it. Not that it's easy to take anything positive from a kick in the bollocks, but all I can say is compare it to the game at the Britannia last season. We lost that one too, but the difference in the performances was night and day. We weren't great this time and we can certainly improve on what we saw, but to go to Stoke and completely dominate them as we did is not something you'll see too many teams do. Take away Clattenburg's contribution and the wastefulness in front of goal, and we win this easily. Look at the stats for possession, shots on goal etc Completely one sided game. We just didn't make our superiority count.

You have to be pleased with how comfortably we dealt with their aerial threat. That was in large part due to not letting them get near enough to the goal to pose any problems, and I can barely remember them having any long throws either. That was encouraging, the lack of end product wasn't. You can't miss chances like those Henderson and Suarez had and expect to win games away from home. Having said that, it wouldn't surprise me in the least if we went to Spurs next week and won comfortably. Hopefully this result was just a little bump in the road. An undeserved bump, even if some players will feel they weren't at their best and didn't perform to the levels they did against Arsenal and Bolton for example.

Enrique's standards certainly slipped from what he's shown so far, although I thought he was much improved second half. Carragher had a day to forget too. The penalty was unfortunate, but he hit too many long balls and more to the point, they weren't particularly accurate, especially in the 1st half. Lucas wasn't himself either, at least not in the 1st half. Usually he rarely wastes a pass, but a few went astray in the opening 45 minutes. Carroll was frustrating when he came on as too often he wasn't getting in the box when the ball was out wide. We don't want you showing for a five yard pass from Downing out wide, we want you busting a gut to get on the end of the crosses he'll be putting in!! Kuyt was poor, Henderson didn't play well and looked devastated when he went off, yet despite all this we still dominated for most of the game. I guess that is a positive, even if it doesn't feel like it right now. I mean if we can completely boss a game against Stoke despite having numerous players below their best, we should be pretty good when everyone plays well. Referee's permitting, of course.

Update: Turns out that Walters is a bitter: *"My dad is from Liverpool, but it's a Blue family so we're all happy. My brother was up there in the stand, and he's a Blue as well. Most of my family are Evertonians apart from the wife's father who is a red, but most of them will be happy and so will I because I'm a blue"* Suddenly it all falls into place. That'll be why I couldn't stand the fucker despite not having any really good reason for it. I can smell them a mile off, it's like a sixth sense.

Premier League Round Up (10-12 September 2011)

It was hard work watching MOTD this weekend. Big wins for City and United, a frustrating defeat for us and wins for Spurs, Chelsea and Arsenal. There wasn't even a loss for the blues to cushion the blow. If Carlsberg made weekends, they sure as hell wouldn't be anything like this shitty one.

To compound my misery, that irritating old goat John Motson was assigned to our game. Great, just great. Usually I wouldn't even watch, but I've made a commitment to writing this so had to grit my teeth and get on with it.

City kicked things off at home to Wigan. Aguero stole the show again, bagging himself a hat-trick as City stuffed Roberto Martinez's side. 3-0 flattered Wigan a lot, they're lucky it wasn't a repeat of the whupping they got at Spurs a few years back. City are looking pretty scary these days, and I'm not talking about Carlos Tevez's mush either. Actually should I even be saying that given the amount of times I've had people tell me I look like him? Bastards.

Since Mancini stopped being a massive shithouse and started picking attacking players rather than selecting eight holding midfielders they've started hammering teams, and it's got to be a worry for those of us with aspirations of competing with them. Mancini's cowardice was the main hope I had, but if he's grown a pair then fuggedaboutit.

Aguero opened the scoring with a well worked team goal, but Di Santo should have equalised for Wigan when he went clear. He toe poked it miles wide and this week there was no deflection to save him, the useless turd. I told you all he was crap last time didn't I? Mind you, I've also said Silva was over-rated and no better than Benayoun (not in print, but nevertheless I can't deny I've said it). File that one away with *"Joe Cole is gonna be a great signing"* and *"If we sign Gary McAllister this summer I'll show my arse at the first home game"*. Tevez missed a pen and Richards and Kompany both hit the bar as City completely pummeled the Latics, yet it was only 1-0 at the break and Rodallega almost levelled it early in the second half. Aguero then grabbed his second before completing his hat-trick after more brilliant play by Silva. Astonishingly Dzeko was left on the bench despite scoring four in his last match. Talk about spoilt for choice. Makes you sick doesn't it?

Other observations from this one. I really hate that Poznan crap and the Premier League should invoke a new rule that states Balotelli has to play in every minute of every game (red cards notwithstanding), as he's compulsive viewing and you just never know what the mad bastard's going to do next.

As for the other Mancs, not much to say other than they looked depressingly devastating. I can't help feeling things would have been different if Bolton had unleashed the Gog instead of leaving him on the bench though. Missed a trick there. Obviously erm Rooney is erm, obviously, erm in the form of his erm, life and that Phil Jones looks promising too. I can't forgive BBC for going crawling back to that twat Ferguson though. The last few years of him not talking to them have been bliss. I miss Mike Phelan. Thats a sentence I bet nobody has ever written before, anywhere, ever.

Next up was Chelsea at Sunderland. Torres was on the bench watching his *'old and slow team-mates'* and Gyan was on his way to the UAE yelling *"SHOW ME THE MONEY!!"*. If there was a poster boy for bad career choices then these two would be fighting it out to be front and centre. Knobheads.

Mata hit the post with a free-kick and seconds later Mongo opened the scoring from a tight angle with a smart finish. He may be a repugnant, ugly, vile, huge foreheaded chav gobshite who is completely lacking in any kind of moral fibre and human decency, but.... actually I don't know where I'm going with this.

Meireles then set up the second for Sturridge, who's finish was outrageous. Personally I'd put it down as an own goal though, firstly to piss on Sturridge's chips because of the shitty dance he did afterwards, and secondly because it was Wes Bean, sorry Brown.

Loads of empty seats there though, the Mackem fans are really disgruntled at the moment. No wonder, they've lost eight out of nine home games and Steve Bruce is getting fatter every week. I don't think those two facts are connected, but both were worth mentioning I think. I felt sorry for Bruce watching that post game interview. Then I remembered those two goals he scored thirty six minutes into stoppage time against Sheffield Wednesday that basically won the title for the Mancs, and I laughed at his stressed out, bloated red face. Where's your beach ball now fathead? Up your jumper by the looks of it.

Over at Goodison, the Everton fans were revolting. They also had a protest (never gets old!). Yet Kenwright's face appeared on the big screen and he was applauded. I honestly don't know what to say about that. The blues were denied a stonewall pen at 1-0 when Baines was tripped. The ref was stood about five yards away and saw it clearly. It's funny coz it's Everton, but seriously, how shit are these fucking refs nowadays? They're defo getting worse and that was outrageous. Petrov equalised with a pearler before Everton were eventually awarded a pen in comical circumstances. The ball was in orbit when Delph went up for it. There's jumping early, and then there's this. He'd already flattened the Everton player before the ball had even come down, it was amazingly stupid. Baines put the kick away, before Agbonlahor equalised with a good header and then took his shirt off and got booked, the blert. If you take your shirt off when you score, you're a moron. It's as simple as that. You know it's an automatic yellow card, and if you get five yellows it's a suspension. So why fucking do it? You have to be braindead to do it now, and if I was a manager I'd fine any player who did it and if he did it more than once I'd transfer list the fucker. Unless it was Suarez, I just love him too much, I'd forgive him anything.

Moving swiftly on, Swansea almost took the lead early on at the Emirates but were denied by a fantastic save by Szczesny. For all the goalkeeping problems they've had in recent years, I think this lad is decent. Speaking of keepers, Swansea's has been getting plenty of good press up to now, but the goal he gifted Arshavin is something that will be shown on blooper videos for years to come. Arsenal needed that helping hand, as they're a bit shit right now. Sinclair hit the bar for the Swans whilst Van Persie hit the post for the Arse. Swansea had a great chance to snatch a point in stoppage time but Graham put it over. Swansea haven't scored yet, and with finishing like that's it's not surprising. They've played some nice stuff though and as I keep saying they look like being this year's

Blackpool. Neutrals will root for them, and Norwich too I guess who also have a touch of the 'Blackpools' about them.

Spurs and Wolves wrapped things up for Saturday, and I don't think I'll ever get used to Adebayor in a Spurs kit. It just looks weird, and I'm surprised he'd go there given that 'Elephant' song the Spurs fans used to taunt him with. They love him now, obviously, especially after he scored on his debut to set them on their way to three points. He's a good player when he can be arsed, which is about 50% of the time.

Onto Sunday, and Roy Hodgson's Baggies were looking for their first win. There was a minute's silence for 9/11 and for a West Brom youth player who passed away this week. You know what I hate about these silences? There's always one dickhead who has to be the first to shout the second the referee's whistle blows. No matter where it is, there's always one. Their eyes must be glued to the ref just waiting for him to put the whistle to his mouth. Losers. Odemwingie opened the scoring after two minutes. They've missed him, he's vital to them and looks a good player. How good is he though? He's been linked with some of the big boys, but is he that good or would he just be one of those players who can't step up? I'm not convinced at all he's top drawer, but a team like West Brom is fortunate to have him.

For Norwich Grant Holt missed a sitter before Dorrans hit the post at the other end. WBA were awarded a penalty after a dive by Reid. Poor decision. Justice was done as Odemwingie missed. Then James Vaughan was elbowed in the face by Tamas. The replays suggested it was deliberate and he knew what he was doing. Paul Lambert certainly thought so, naturally Hodgson disagreed. No pen for Vaughan though, and no sympathy from me either. He's a dirty blueshite bastard who isn't averse to roughing people up with elbows himself, just ask any of our reserve team defenders who came up against him and his partner in crime Victor Anichebe. I still haven't forgotten their antics against Dudek in a reserve game a few years back when Jerzy was eventually sent off for retaliation. I'm made up Vaughan got a taste of his own medicine.

Fulham / Blackburn was the other Sunday game. It ended 1-1 and that looked a fair result. Blackburn look to be getting a bit better. They should have beaten the Blues last time out, and they gave a decent account of themselves here. There was a great overhead kick by Goodwillie *sniggers* that went just over, before Rochina put them ahead with a superb strike. Looks a decent player him. Zamora felt he should have had a penalty when he was barged over by Salgado. Howard Webb gave a free-kick against him as he handled the ball when he fell to the ground. I look at that and then look at the pen given against us, and just have to shake my head. These refs are just shite and getting worse.

Zamora eventually equalised, a week after I jibbed him from my fantasy squad. Cheers for that Bobby. Hoilett got completely laid out by Schwarzer. It wasn't exactly Harold Schumacher / Patrick Batiston, but it was painful even just looking at it. The keeper got a yellow card, Blackburn wanted a red. Difficult one as I don't think he deliberately took Hoilett out, he went for the ball but was beaten to it. The covering defender would have cleared the ball had Hoilett not been fouled, so Howard Webb got one right. I guess it's true what they say, the sun does even shine on a dog's arse somedays.

Finally there was the Monday night game. No goals, not much incident. Wright-Phillips looked good, Taraabt is extremely skilful if a little erratic and QPR should have won. Joey Barton was applauded by both sets of fans, which may be a first for him. It shouldn't be the last time though, I'd expect him to get a good reception at Anfield after the great work he did pushing the Hillsborough petition on twitter. He also referred to Anton Ferdinand as 'Scooby Doo', and that too deserves applause.

TOTTENHAM HOTSPUR 4 LIVERPOOL 0

Competition - Premier League
Date - Sun 18 Sep 2011
Venue - White Hart Lane
Scorer(s) –
Half Time - 1-0
Star Man – Nobody

Team: Reina; Skrtel, Carragher, Agger (Coates), Enrique; Henderson, Lucas, Adam; Downing (Spearing), Carroll, Suarez (Bellamy):

Ouch. Woeful from start to finish. It was torturous to watch and there was no respite from it at any stage during the game. No-one played well, no part of the team functioned even remotely close to an acceptable level and we got our arses handed to us by a Spurs side who aren't even that good and who have been spanked by both manc teams already.

White Hart Lane is becoming a seriously unhappy place for us, bad things always seem to happen to us when we go there. The score looks bad, but the performance was even worse. The only surprising thing was that up until Skrtel stupidly got himself sent off the score was only 1-0. It's understandable that the floodgates opened after that as playing with nine men is nigh on impossible. What went before that though was completely unacceptable.

Both red cards were justified, the referee clearly wasn't in any mood for leniency and was certainly a bad jobsworth but much as I'd like to I can't complain about the two dismissals (had he seen an off the ball kick by Parker on Lucas then Spurs would also have found themselves a man down, but unfortunately he missed it). The ratio of fouls to yellow cards gives cause for complaint, but looking at the incidents in isolation I can't say I feel particularly hard done to. Adam's first yellow was possibly a little on the harsh side but having already been booked he was stupid to then go in with his foot up. He didn't even see Parker coming and it wasn't a deliberate foul, but you've got to be careful when you're on a yellow and he was reckless. It could even have been a straight red under the letter of the law as it was studs first and knee high. Certainly a yellow and I have no complaints.

Defensively Adam is poor, it was a concern for me before we signed him and I've seen nothing to ease those concerns. He's a good player and he'll be an asset for us in 75% of our games but he might turn out to be a liability in the remaining 25%. Better teams can play around him as he's not the quickest, can't tackle and gives a lot of free-kicks away. The Skrtel red card was similar. First booking looked harsh (very harsh in fact but I've only seen one replay of it) but the second one was fucking idiotic and he needs his arse kicking. There was just no need to make that challenge, he just couldn't help himself though. It's his biggest weakness and it's something he's never been able to eradicate from his game. Playing out of position is not an excuse and minutes before it he'd allowed himself to be outmuscled by Jermaine fucking Defoe. Pitiful. To make it worse, he then stayed down on the floor as Spurs attacked. That's our hard man?

His red card didn't really affect the result, only the margin of our defeat. Going down to nine men made it easy for Spurs to run up the score but it was Adam's dismissal that really ended our hopes of getting anything from the game. We were already 1-0 down and playing awfully. Even with eleven men there was little to suggest we'd get back into it, but going a man down ended any slim chance we had.

We'd been sloppy right from the opening whistle and Spurs were right at it. They could have scored a couple in the first few minutes as we were all over the place. When the goal eventually came it was one of those you can't really legislate for. It was an amazing strike from Modric, you just have to take your hat off to him for that. The goal was just one of those things, but I was more concerned with how bad we were when we had the ball, and how easily Spurs were playing through our midfield. We'd started with a 433 formation, yet our three central midfielders were being outplayed by Spurs' two. That simply can't happen. You have three in there so you control the middle of the park, but Parker and Modric took the piss and we didn't get near them. Lucas, Adam and Henderson were beyond useless. That's where our problems started. We weren't great anywhere else either, but it was in the midfield where we lost this game. They didn't protect the defence, they didn't support the attack, and they didn't keep the ball. They didn't do anything.

Carroll was rubbish too, even if once again he can point to a shocking lack of any kind of service as a reason for his ineffectiveness and I have some measure of sympathy when I see him sent to the right wing. What's he gonna do out there other than look slow and shit? Completely self defeating having him out there.

Suarez looked to be the only hope we had, but he didn't get any kind of support either and eventually became so frustrated it looked like he'd be sent off for dissent. He was booked for sarcastically applauding, and then continued to rant and rave in Spanish at both the ref and linesman. The half time whistle came at a good time for him.

It was just brutal all round, topped off by an injury to Agger sustained when trying to prevent Modric's goal. He tried to stay on but eventually had to make way for Coates. Not the kind of situation you'd want a new signing to make his debut in. Coates didn't stand out much either positively or negatively. The only thing I really noticed him do was get done for pace by Adebayor and collect a yellow card for bringing him down.

The most alarming thing about this for me is that I had been very confident when I saw the starting eleven. A narrow three in midfield with Downing and Suarez either side of Carroll looked good to me. Skrtel was a concern up against Bale, but Kenny had little choice but to use him there as Kelly and Johnson were ruled out. Skrtel had done well in the previous two games and deserved to stay in. He hadn't been up against Gareth Bale in those two games though, and this was a big test. He failed it.

Not that he was given much protection. I say 'much' but I should probably say 'any'. I don't know who's job it was to help the full back out, whether it was Downing or maybe Henderson, but whoever it was they didn't do it. After the sending off, we then had Andy Carroll playing right wing. I just couldn't get my head around that at all. Carroll is big and lacks pace. His technique is decent enough for the kind of player he is (a target man) but he doesn't have the skillset to be able to play on the flank in tight spaces. It reminded me of Egil Olsen's Norway with Jostein Flo on the wing. Why was he out there, it made no sense? It wasn't helping us in any way, and certainly did Carroll no favours. Speaking of which, the white boots don't help either Andy. Try banging in a few goals before you go down that road.

Surely Carroll either had to be left up top as the lone forward with Suarez dropping wide, or get him off and put Kuyt or Bellamy on who can both actually play that role. Having Suarez central was probably the most logical move as he was basically the only hope we had of doing anything, so that being the case just get Carroll off. Don't stick him on the right wing and let him struggle. Henderson should have gone off too as he was a total passenger. No-one was getting amongst their midfielders and pressurising them when they were on the ball. The same thing happened at Anfield towards the end of last season actually.

I assume the reason Kenny didn't make changes earlier was because there were so many players worthy of getting the hook and he was spoiled for choice. I can't think of any other justification for not doing anything as we struggled so badly. Eventually Suarez and Downing went off, more to protect them for the games ahead than anything else. Downing was anonymous, but then we weren't getting the ball to him because our midfield was so bad. Doesn't excuse his performance, but it does explain it somewhat.

There isn't anything remotely positive to take from this. It could easily have been even worse than 4-0, as Spurs had numerous opportunities they didn't take. As for us, it took an hour to even produce some kind of shot. The only effort on target I can remember was a long range effort from Downing. We did have a goal disallowed in the 1st half but Suarez was a yard offside and we can't complain about that. Worth mentioning that had Carroll's touch been better he could have gone himself and Suarez wouldn't have even come into the picture.

After three games we were flying and hopes were high. After five games, not so much. Seven points from five games isn't a good start (we're even below Everton who have a game in hand too), but it's still far too early to be judging the side or the new players. What worries me a little is that the teams we have beaten have since been proven to be garbage. Arsenal let in eight to the Mancs and just let in four at Blackburn. Bolton shipped five at home to United and just lost to Norwich.

We played well and lost at Stoke, but they just got caned by Sunderland. Whilst you can twist these things to suit whatever point you are trying to make, I can't help but be a little concerned. I thought the days of these kind of performances were over, and this was a shock to the system. The two red cards obviously didn't help, but they don't explain the complete ineptitude we witnessed. There are clearly some things that need working out, and the next few games will tell us more about where we actually are as the sample size at the moment is still too small. A couple of weeks ago Spurs were in disarray and we were looking good. Look how quickly things can turn around.

One thing that occurred to me whilst watching the game was that when we were playing that great stuff towards the end of last season, some of the players who were influential in that are no longer in the side. Spearing, Kuyt and in particular Maxi all contributed greatly to those performances. I'm not saying we need to bring them all back in and we'll suddenly start hammering teams, but the players who are in the side ahead of them haven't done much to warrant it yet.

Two consecutive defeats is worrying at the best of times, but it's the manner of this one that's really dragged me down. Still, it's a long season and even the best teams can have days like this one. I remember thinking just how bad the Mancs looked when we battered them at Anfield last season but they still ended up winning the title. Any team can have a really bad day, the important thing is to make sure they don't happen often and when they do you bounce back quickly.

It's up to the players to show that this was just a bad day at the office and to get back on track against Wolves next weekend. That's a game we have to win as the buzz that was surrounding the team after those consecutive wins over Arsenal and Bolton has all but been wiped out now. As we've seen though, things can turn around in a couple of games and if we win our next two then we can put this nightmare display behind us.

Premier League Round Up (17-18 September 2011)

Jeez, I thought last weekend was bad!! This was brutal. A bumming for us and wins for the Mancs and blues. Not even that amazing miss by Torres could put a smile on my face. Well ok, it did, but only a little one and not for long. May as well start with Sunday's games this time as that's when all the relevant sides were in action (Arsenal stopped being relevant when 1) they became a selling club and 2) when they bent over at Old Trafford).

The game at Old Trafford was just weird. I thought Chelsea were the better side in the first half yet they found themselves 3-0 down at half time. The first goal from Smalling was offside, the second from Nani was brilliant (although what was Meireles doing showing him onto his right foot?) and the third from Rooney was bad defending and positioning from Chelsea (Meireles again didn't cover himself in glory). Was it lucky the way it bounced to Rooney? Yes, but when you have five men in the box against four defenders, the odds of something dropping to you are pretty good and those fuckers do that better than anybody unfortunately. In between, Ramires missed two great chances, one of them an absolute sitter put on a plate by the lively Torres. Chelsea had plenty of other chances too but somehow found themselves down by three at the break. Villas Boas brought on Anelka at half time and within seconds he'd created a goal for Torres, who finished really well. He looked like the old Torres there. His goal drought has been funny, but it was never going to last and if it was going to end anywhere I'm glad it was here. Nani hit the bar and was then brought down as he went for the rebound. Rooney's pen was boss, pissed myself at that. Reminiscent of Mongo in the CL final. Torres then put one over after he'd conjured up more great approach play, and Rooney scuffed one against the post. Laughably, the gobshite Mancs chanted 'you scouse bastard' at Torres. There was only one scouse bastard on that pitch, and he's your hero you fucking whoppers.

Ashley Cole was booked for a late tackle on Hernandez, yet no penalty was given. Apparently Phil Dowd reckoned the ball was out of play when Cole clattered him. It's easy to not give United pens when they're 3-1 up though. It'd have been a different story at 0-0. Chelsea kept plugging away and looked to have cut the deficit to 3-2 when Torres effortlessly went round De Gea and was faced with an open goal at the Stretford End. I still can't believe what happened next, and each time I see it it gets worse. Ronny Rosenthal is probably the happiest man on the planet right now. Of course it was funny and I have no sympathy for him, but I wish it hadn't happened THERE. Any other ground but there, preferably Anfield or even Stamford Bridge. This was just a case of feeding the animals, and the glee on those manc faces takes the edge of the hilarity for me. My contempt for the knobs in the Stretford End eclipses that for Torres by some distance and to be honest I'd rather he'd scored.

There's nothing worse in football than smug, celebrating United fans, and this was a great weekend for them as everything went their way. They beat one of their main title rivals, we got spanked and City threw away two points down at Craven Cottage. Mancini's side had flown out of the traps against Fulham, Silva teeing up Aguero to make it 1-0. Seconds after the break Aguero bagged another and City were cruising to a fifth successive win. And then they blew it. Bobby Zamora started the comeback with a great finish. Have to say I like Zamora, very underrated player and Dembele looks decent too. Joe Hart made great saves to keep out Dembele and then Dempsey before SuperDan bagged the equaliser with a deflected shot. Danny's always been a mancbuster, shame these were the wrong Mancs. There was a blatant foul on Dzeko in the build up to that goal, and you have to wonder how the ref can see that and not give a foul. I say it every week, but they really are getting worse every year. One final note from this game. Carlos Tevez has grown a weird looking beard. Great news, if he keeps that then the days of people saying I look like him are long gone as I couldn't grow a proper beard even if I tried.

The final Sunday game saw unbeaten Stoke go to Sunderland. Stoke beat us last week but they looked proper shite in the process, and it was no great surprise to me they lost in the North East. The margin of victory was surprising though, I doubt even the most optimistic Mackem (are there any optimistic Mackems these days?) dreamed they'd win 4-0. Did you see all those empty seats though?? Damn, the whole end behind one of the goals looked like it had about ten people in it. That place used to be packed out every week, I remember them even getting something like 40,000 for a ressies game against Newcastle once.

Stoke should have known they were in trouble when Titus Bramble scored against them. As if that wasn't bad enough, Woodgate then scored an oggy to make it 2-0 with only ten minutes gone. Gardner got the third with the aid of a wicked deflection, and Tony Pulis must have been cursing his luck at this stage. Newsflash, you used up all your good fortune last week numbnuts. Where's Mark Clattenburg when you need him, eh Tony?

Seb Larsson wrapped things up with a nice free-kick, and it could have been more if Bendtner had been born with even the tiniest modicum of footballing ability. Think I'm gonna snap Larsson up for my fantasy team and ditch Downing. Hopefully that will get Stewy firing the way it did when I dropped Zamora.

Swansea have been playing well but haven't been able to score up to now. A home game against struggling West Brom gave them a great chance to put that right, and they did in some style. Sinclair opened the scoring with a composed penalty, which sadly was the cue for celebration music, the same crappy song that Wigan play when they score. I suppose I should be grateful they didn't wheel Max Boyce out again.

Leroy Lita added a second and promptly took his shirt off, the knobhead. Why do they do it? Why? It must just be to show off their physique, but come on, they're footballers and they supposed to be in good shape. No-one is impressed. Some say it's a stupid rule that forces refs to produce a yellow card any time someone removes their shirt. I agree with that, it is stupid. It should be a fucking red. Vain bastards. Nathan Dyer wrapped this one up in the second half, picking up ten fantasy points for me in the process. He looks a little bit like Omar from the Wire, which is no bad thing.

It's been a bad start for the Hodge though, and it could be a long season for him. Mark Lawrenson reckons West Brom will be fine as Hodgson is 'a wily old fox'. As with a lot of things that come out of Lawro's mouth, that's a statement that many Liverpool fans would disagree with. Certainly the 'wily' and 'fox' part anyway.

Albion's Black Country rivals Wolves had a bad day too, as a Joey Barton inspired QPR went to Molyneux and won easily. Ten minutes in and they were 2-0 up, prompting that dickhead Motson to hysterically squeal "QPR are 2-0 up, can you believe this?" Well yes I can, they were playing Wolves, not Barcelona you irritating, gibbering fuck.

It finished 3-0 but it could have been more. Barton was excellent, Taraabt is talented, Faurlin looks good and SWP is looking very sharp so far. He's always been a good player but he's wasted years of his career by being at clubs where he never got a game. I often wonder how things would have turned out had we signed him before he went to Chelsea. Same with Damien Duff actually.

The story of the game once again though was Barton and his running feud with Carl Henry, or 'Kelvin' as Barton keeps calling him. I have to say I can't help but be fascinated by Joey Barton, I find his antics and his brutal honesty hilarious. He says what he thinks, which is not always the smartest thing to do and that's why hardly anybody in football does it. After the game he was calling 'Kelvin' Henry a Sunday League player. As well as it being funny, it's right too. Henry is a fucking dog, one of the dirtiest players in the top flight. Of course Barton is no angel either and it's amusing listening to him talking about other players being overly physical given some of the shit he's pulled, but at least he can play. His '3-0' gesture and kiss blowing to the Wolves fans was boss as well. He topped it off by going on Goals on Sunday and ripping into Henry again. He's a bit of a knob but he's probably the most entertaining character in English football right now, along with Balotelli of course.

Bolton tried to halt their slump at home to Norwich. They made a change up front but it wasn't their recent recruit from Anfield who came into the side, it was Stoke reject Tuncay that got the nod. When will Owen Coyle learn??? For God's sake man, UNLEASH THE GOG!!

Klasnic was flattened by a shockingly high challenge by Leon Barnett but Howard Webb failed to produce even a yellow card when it probably should have been a straight red. Reckless, dangerous, wild assault that could have had serious repercussions, but Webb let it go, the useless bald turd.

Norwich went in front with a scrappy goal from Pilkington and then Johnson made it 2-0. Klasnic was red carded for barely touching Tierney with his head. The Norwich player flung himself to the floor and Webb did the rest. Whilst under the letter of the law you can say Klasnic had to go, it must be pretty difficult for the lad to accept when you look at the challenge on him from Barnett and compare it to what he did. Tierney is a shithouse for doing that. Klasnic will get banned for three games, but if it was up to me I'd ban Tierney for ten. And Howard Webb for life. At 2-0 behind and a man down, Bolton needed a hero, a superhero in fact. Finally 'the Gog' was unleashed. It was like watching tag team wrestling on ITV in the 80's. Big Daddy's partner would be getting pummelled but couldn't get over to tag his partner in. Then eventually he manages to crawl over and make the tag to Big Daddy who cleans house and lays a beat down on everybody. David Ngog is 'Big Daddy'.

He tagged in and immediately won them a penalty that was converted by Petrov and he almost earned them a point at the end but was denied by a great save from Ruddy. You'd have thought Coyle would have learned from last week's mistake of not picking him against the Mancs, but clearly not. Put him in the starting line up, dummy.

Elsewhere, Everton overcame Wigan in a game that was a lot closer than the 3-1 score suggests. Before watching the highlights, I'd seen that Di Santo had scored. *"I hope it wasn't a screamer"* I thought. Having caned him for the last few weeks for being shit and only able to score with the aid of wicked deflections the last thing I wanted was to have those words shoved down my throat, although I could have lived with it given the opposition I suppose. I was pretty damn smug when I saw the goal though, it took not one but TWO deflections for his shot to beat Tim Howard. Hey, I know my shit players, I've seen enough of them in red shirts recently that I've become something of a connoisseur.

Anyway, Jagielka equalised but Wigan were looking the more likely winners until some Greek kid I've never heard of came off the bench and put the blues in front with a nice header from a Tony Hibbert cross (yes, Tony Hibbert is STILL getting a game. I was shocked too). Dave Jones hit the bar and Rodallega almost buried the rebound before Drenthe made it 3-1 in stoppage time. Why does he have "R R Drenthe" on the back of his shirt though? I thought his name was 'Royston', so what's the second 'R' for? Does the Everton kitman have a stutter? Given Drenthe's reputation for being a bit full of himself, maybe he's calling himself 'Rolls Royston'? I need an explanation for this, otherwise he's on the twat list with 'Kun' 'Chicarito' and 'Jonas'. I just realised, do I need to add

'Maxi' to that list as essentially he's doing the same thing as Gutierrez. I'll just remove 'Jonas' I think.

Newcastle and Villa were both unbeaten going into this, and were both unbeaten coming out of it too. That tells me that neither of them have played anyone decent yet as they are both the very definition of average. Agbonlahor opened the scoring with a Djibril Cisse / Darren Bent kind of goal. By that I mean he hit it straight at the keeper and somehow it found it's way through. Cisse and Bent have both made careers out of that kind of crappy goal. Agbonlahor has started the season well, but I don't like his face, he seems like a bit of a wrong 'un. The kind who'd eat crayons and bogeys when he was junior school. Leon Best equalised with his third goal in five games. Honestly, I'll be surprised if he gets another three all season. Cabaye looks a very good player though, Mike Ashley is probably shopping him around already.

Finally to Ewood Park and another Arsenal away day horror show. Jonathon Pearce began his commentary by saying Arsenal had started to turn the corner. On what basis, a fortunate win over Swansea last week? Ha! Gervinho gave them the lead and it was all Arsenal early on. Then, out of nothing Yakubu drew the home side level with a quality finish. Fair play to the Yak, who broke his own record as the Premiership's oldest goalscorer at 67 years young. That all you can eat incentive based contract Venky's have given him is paying off already. As the chant goes, feed the Yak.... Yakubu's former Goodison team-mate Legohead Arteta put Arsenal back in front but Alex Song put through his own net to level it up again, and the Yak added another one before Koscielny chipped in with another oggy. Arsenal's defending was abysmal, especially Djourou who is so bad Arsenal fans may soon be longing for the days of Igor Stepanovs. Chamakh pulled one back with a collectors item, as goals from him are as rare as rocking horse shit these days. I saw something on twitter about Chamakh that made me laugh, someone asked how come he always looks like he's just been hit with a water balloon. Great question, I don't have the answer though sadly.

Arsenal then laid siege to the Rovers goal looking for an equaliser but it wasn't to be and they crashed to yet another defeat. One final note on this game. Allow me to refer you to a paragraph from a previous round up after they got wallopped by the Mancs: *"Arsenal have offered a free ticket for their next away game to all those fans who went to Old Trafford. Yeah, that's nice of them isn't it? Tell you what Arsenal fans, how about you pay me £50 and I'll repeatedly kick you in the balls for 90 minutes. Then to show you how sorry I am, I'll do it for nothing next time. Fuck me, what kind of warped logic is that Arsenal?"* For the record, **THIS** was their next away game. What's next Arsenal? *"Hey Gooners, come down to the training ground and watch us trying to defend set pieces whilst we repeatedly jab you in the face with a cattle prod. And we'll do it for FREE!!!"*.

BRIGHTON & HOVE ALBION 1 LIVERPOOL 2

Competition - Carling Cup
Date - Wed 21 Sep 2011
Venue - Amex Stadium
Scorer(s) – Craig Bellamy, Dirk Kuyt
Half Time - 0-1
Star Man – Craig Bellamy

Team: Reina; Kelly (Flanagan), Carragher, Coates, Robinson: Kuyt, Lucas, Spearing, Maxi; Suarez (Gerrard), Bellamy:

We're in the hat for the next round and the Spurs game is out of our system, Bellamy is back amongst the goals and Gerrard was back on the field. All in all, a satisfactory night despite being outplayed for long periods of the second half by a Championship side.

The first 40 minutes were superb, we played some great stuff and should have been out of sight. We didn't take our chances though and to be fair Brighton were fantastic after the break.

Whilst it is a little disconcerting seeing a Liverpool side being outpassed by a team from a division below, the important thing is we got the win and progressed to the next round. We're taking the competition very seriously and once again Kenny named a strong side. He was still able to give some bench players some much needed game time, but the core of the team was still there with Reina, Carragher, Lucas and Suarez all starting. Bellamy and Suarez hit it off immediately, ably assisted by Kuyt who was heavily involved in the first half when we were so dominant. The movement of the three was great to watch, as was some of the one touch passing between them. We played very well early on and the opening goal was a cracker. Great movement by Bellamy, perfectly weighted pass by Suarez and a nice finish.

Suarez should have added a second not long after when Kuyt's brilliant first time ball round the corner sent him in but he put his shot inches wide of the far post. Should have scored though, his finishing is possibly one of the weakest parts of his game. Not that it's bad, but it isn't as good as other areas of his play.

The only thing keeping this from being a rout was the woodwork. Suarez saw a header clip the post, Bellamy smacked the bar with an amazing strike from distance and Spearing saw a fine low shot tipped onto the post by the keeper. At the other end Brighton hadn't done much at all until half time drew near and suddenly they came to life. Their left winger Craig Noone had gotten a fair bit of publicity prior to the game as he's a lifelong Liverpool fan and he'd done some work on Gerrard's house when he was a part timer playing non-league. He looked useful throughout and had a great chance to score five minutes before the break but he hit his shot too close to Reina. Pepe made a meal of it though and it looked like their centre forward would have a tap in but Kelly came to the rescue with a terrific clearance. That gave Brighton hope and they never looked back from that.

The second half was all the home side, they were outstanding to be fair. Not the usual 'up and at 'em' lower league stuff either, they just passed us off the park. At one point a stat flashed up on the screen showing they had 61% possession in the 2nd half. I doubt Spurs even had that on Sunday when we were down to nine men! Really impressive stuff from Gus Poyet's side. Noone was superb and was within a whisker of scoring a dream goal when his dipping effort from 25 yards hit the bar. That came after an inexplicably bad pass by Coates across his own box. I wasn't overwhelmed by him, but I'm not particularly bothered about it as it was always going to take him time to adapt. He did ok, but missed a few challenges and positionally seemed to be too close to Carragher a few times. Very early days though and the outing will have done him a lot of good.

As well as Brighton played, you still have to look at how we allowed it to happen. It's difficult to pinpoint exactly what our problem was. It looked like we just stopped doing the things we'd been doing well in the first half. Lucas and Spearing had bossed the game before the break, but they were barely in it 2nd half. Maxi all but disappeared until he had a hand in the second goal, and Suarez was way below his best. Defensively we were did ok and Bellamy looked sharp all night. We needed that second goal though, especially as Gerrard's introduction was dependent on the game being safe. Had we got a second or third goal the skipper would have come on sooner, but Dalglish had to be cautious if there was any possibility of extra time. Eventually it was time to send him on, and it was no surprise that it was Suarez who made way. It makes sense to rest him any time it's possible, and besides, he was playing second fiddle to Bellamy on the night anyway.

The crucial second goal eventually came from a quick counter attack. Bellamy collected it down the left and played an inch perfect ball into the path of Maxi who didn't have to break stride. A defender got back at him so he couldn't go on his own, but the ever willing Kuyt had made a great supporting run to his right and collected the pass before finding the far corner with a perfectly placed finish.

As it turned out, that goal would prove decisive as Brighton got the goal their performance deserved when a mistake from Spearing resulted in Carragher bringing down Vicente in the box. Pepe's run without saving a pen continued but this was a perfect penalty, you don't save those no matter who you are.

The late goal took the shine off things somewhat, especially for Spearing who will be kicking himself over the error. We are making too many mistakes in defensive areas, but I don't expect that to continue and I'm sure we'll tighten things up as the season progresses. Kenny will have some selection headaches ahead of the game this weekend though. Bellamy has surely played himself into the starting line up and it would be harsh on Kuyt if he had to drop back to the bench too. It's also going to be interesting to see who makes way for Gerrard when he's ready to play a full game again.

Overall, more positives than negatives but we can't afford a repeat of that second half when we're playing Premier League opposition as we'll be made to pay. Star man was Bellamy, he was head and shoulders above everyone else (insert your own 'no neck' joke here).

LIVERPOOL 2 WOLVERHAMPTON WANDERERS 1

Competition - Premier League
Date - Sat 24 Sep 2011
Venue - Anfield
Scorer(s) – Roger Johnson O.G. Luis Suarez
Half Time - 2-0
Star Man – Luis Suarez

Team: Reina; Kelly, Carragher, Skrtel, Enrique; Henderson (Kuyt), Lucas, Adam, Downing; Suarez (Gerrard), Carroll:

Much closer than it needed to be. We played well today but when you miss as many chances as this you're asking for trouble. Still, there seems to be far too much negativity surrounding this one, no doubt because the Spurs game really shook people's confidence in the side. I just think had we put away just two more of the numerous clear chances we created, people would be buzzing about this.

Instead, there's a lot of doom and gloom. Not for me though, we played some good stuff. The first half was one way traffic and after a brief early flurry Wolves simply weren't in the game at all. They'd had a succession of free-kicks around our box early on mainly due to Lucas and Adam giving away silly fouls. They came to nothing but O'Hara had a good early chance when they got in behind us, thankfully his shot was tame and straight at Pepe though.

After that we took control and Suarez was electric. A great turn from him set up Adam for a crack from 25 yards that was deflected behind for a corner off Roger Johnson. Soon after Johnson would deflect another shot from Adam, only this time the ball flew into the bottom corner. Wolves were unhappy about it and wanted a free-kick for what they claimed had been a foul on Johnson by Carroll in the build up. May or may not have been, I'd lean towards a big fat no, and besides, Carroll has been penalised twice already this season for nothing incidents that have chalked off goals, so he deserved a bit of a break.

Having gone in front we stepped things up and had Wolves on the ropes. A brilliant first time ball from Adam sent Suarez away down the left. He won a corner that Carroll rose to meet but his header was saved by Hennesey. Carroll was looking lively and great pressure from him saw him win possession and set off into the box. He tried to cut the ball back for the supporting Lucas but Wolves snuffed out the danger. Good stuff from Andy though. Suarez then latched onto a huge clearance from Reina and a wonderful first touch saw him take the ball in stride but he was driven a little wide and appeared to be hemmed in by Johnson. Out of nothing he produced a backheel nutmeg and was away but his attempted pull back was cleared by the Wolves defence. Simply wonderful skill though, it had the crowd on their feet. What a nightmare he must be to play against. Suarez was then inches away from converting a delicious left wing cross from Carroll and then dragged a shot wide after a lovely one-two down the left involving Enrique and Downing created the opening for him. Carl Henry and Lucas were both booked for innocuous fouls as referee Kevin Friend did his best to ruin what was a good half of football.

Suarez eventually got the goal he'd been threatening when he timed his run perfectly to beat the offside trap and collect Enrique's fine pass without breaking stride. He turned the defender inside then out then in again before powering a shot in at the near post. Great goal, but it's a good job for Suarez it went in as Carroll was unmarked in the centre and would have had a tap in. The Uruguayan went close to a second just before half time when more good play down the left involving Downing and Enrique created an opportunity for him, but his toe poked effort went across the face of goal and wide.

Wolves needed to change it as they were offering nothing. Kevin Doyle is a willing runner but he was far too isolated and it was surprising that Fletcher didn't start the game. He was introduced at half time and within no time he'd made his mark, blasting in from eight yards after Hunt had been fortunate to collect a ricochet off Enrique and deliver a cutback. Having been 2-0 up and cruising that goal came right out of the blue and really lifted the visitors who had looked completely dead in the water at the end of the first half. Now they had a spring in their steps and we had a game on our hands. To our players' credit they responded immediately and created three glorious opportunities in a short space of time. Hennesey flapped at a high ball under pressure from Carroll but then redeemed himself by making an amazing save to keep out Suarez's follow up. That was a close call, but we'd go closer shortly after following some terrific football. Adam found Carroll who swept the ball out to the left to Enrique. Downing ran on past him and the full back rolled it into his path. The cross from Downing was a good one but Carroll just couldn't get in front of the defender who partially cleared the danger. Downing collected and then delivered a brilliant ball that Carroll attacked at the back post and planted a header against the post. Desperately unfortunate but that link up is what we expected when Kenny brought Downing to the club. We haven't seen enough of it yet but it's early days.

We were piling on the pressure and it seemed like only a matter of time before we restored the two goal cushion. Wolves were having a go too and that meant they were vulnerable to counter attacks. From one such counter Downing really should have scored. It was a great move, as Carragher cleared from inside his own box towards Carroll, who hooked the ball inside to Suarez. Luis did superbly to win the ball and lay it into the path of Adam who had space to run into. He carried it forward and draw the last defender before sending Downing clean through with a perfectly timed pass. The winger's shot was turned around the post by Hennesey and the chance was gone. For me he simply has to score in that situation.

With so many chances going begging, we began to get edgy and Wolves began to get plenty of balls into the box. It wasn't quite panic stations, but it was getting pretty hairy. Reina completely whiffed at a high ball as he was beaten to it by Doyle, but luckily his header drifted just wide. Huge let off. Lucas was then inches away from making the game safe with a low shot from 20 yards the drifted just past the post with the keeper beaten. Nice lay off from Carroll to set that up. More brilliance in a confined space from Suarez almost set up a goal for Carroll but just as the striker was ready to pull the trigger Roger Johnson got the faintest of touches to deflect the ball away from him.

Kuyt replaced Henderson and Gerrard came on for Suarez, who didn't look happy about it. Gerrard almost made an immediate impact when he surged onto a flick by Carroll and blasted a shot just over. Would have been a great way to mark his first Premier League appearance since March. There was one more scary moment when Kuyt needlessly gave the ball away and Jarvis took off down the left. He made up a lot of ground and we could have been in trouble but Lucas got across and overpowered him. Had he got that even the slightest bit wrong he'd have been off, but thankfully he timed it right and averted a potential problem for us.

With the last action of the game Carroll seemed certain to score the goal his performance deserved. He just couldn't get a shot away as he tried to walk the ball in. He showed good footwork to be fair, but he overdid it and it was frustratng that he didn't take the chance as he really needs to start finding the net. I thought he played well today though. His link up play was good, he worked hard and the only thing missing was a goal. He should have buried that header and the chance he had at the end but that's how it's going for him at the moment. He just needs to keep doing what he did today and he'll come through it.

Suarez was the star turn again though, just different class. Some of the things he did in this game were borderline genius, although bizarrely MOTD didn't deem them worthy of broadcast for some reason. People watch football to see things like that backheel turn Suarez did in the first half. They don't tune in to look at Mark Lawrenson's dodgy barnet.

Premier League Round Up (24-26 September 2011)

It was with a sense of relief that I settled down to watch MOTD this weekend. The previous two weeks hadn't been much fun, but we were back to winning ways and not even the return to the MOTD studio of Mark Lawrenson and his fashion sense that makes my arl fella seem like David Beckham was going to put a downer on this weekend.

First up was the Mancs at Stoke. Tony Pulis is one of those managers who Ferguson seems pally with, so add that to the long list of reasons not to like him. The Mancs were without Rooney and so was I, as he's the captain in my fantasy team. Hey, I'm not proud of it, but what can I say, I wanna win. They lost Hernandez too, he was hurt in a collision with the keeper and thought he should have had a penalty for a shove in the back by Woodgate. Looked to me like he took a bad first touch and just fell over. Admittedly I may be seeing that through scouse tinted glasses.

Regular readers will know how I feel about that whole 'Chicarito' bollocks and how he shouldn't be allowed to have that on his shirt. Well you know what's even worse than him having 'Chicarito' on his shirt? Ferguson referring to him as 'Chicarito'. And you know what's even worse than that? He pronounces it 'Cheecharito'. Turns my stomach, bring back Mike Phelan.

The latest brilliant goal from Nani gave United the lead and he should have scored another after an awful mistake by Begovic, whilst at the other end De Gea made great saves from Wilkinson and Walters. Probably for the best that Walters didn't score, after all he wouldn't want to ruin his family's weekend now would he. Bluenose twat. Crouchy did score though, the big leg. He should have had a second not long after but De Gea made another top save, and right at the end he had another chance when he chested the ball down but put his shot wide. The final act of the game saw Ryan Giggs slice a great chance wide. Might just be the first time in his life he's not taken advantage of an 'open goal'. Ferguson wasn't pleased about the penalty that wasn't given; *"A lot of referees would have given it but it was just too early in the game"* Too early in the game eh? Weren't saying that when your pet ref Howard Webb gave a pen against Agger in the Cup last season were you? When you say 'a lot of refs' would have given it, what you mean is the ones you've got in your pocket. Don't expect to see Peter Walton refereeing United again any time soon.

Onto Chelsea and I'm sure I spotted Jon Obi Mikel in the opposition half at one point. Must have got lost, they need to get him a satnav he can carry round with him so it doesn't happen again. Maybe one that electrocutes him if he crosses halfway? Or preferably one that just electrocutes him regardless, the shit bastard. Torres opened the scoring with a good finish and he then had a hand in the second goal that was scored by Ramires. Can't be a co-incidence that he went shite when he stopped dying his hair and he's suddenly become boss again since he dusted off the peroxide bottle and grew his locks again. Wish he'd get back down the barbers and chop it all off again to be honest. Thankfully Wirral based Mike Dein cut short the Torres revival by sending him off after a two footed lunge that didn't actually make contact but looked ugly. Well in Mike lad.

The lively Dyer hit the bar for the Swans, whilst Anelka did likewise with a screamer before Ramires grabbed his second. Flat track bully him, his arse went on the two chances he got at Old Trafford last week, but he put both of these away at home to little old Swansea. Ashley Williams bagged a late consolation with a good header, and he nearly repeated the feat shortly after before Drogba wrapped it up in stoppage time.

Everton went to the Etihad Stadium with no attacking intent and Tim Cahill up front on his own. Tell you what, that Everton tracky that Moyes wears is absolutely horrible. It's that shiny material that's really cheap and nasty looking but was big in the 80's. Quite apt really, given who he manages. Hope he dusts off his best suit for the derby next week as I don't wanna see that monstrosity again. It's the football manager equivalent of white socks and sandals. Cahill was booked and then carried off after a challenge on Kompany. Not sure if the yellow card was for the foul on Kompany or for making Lescott look like Alan Hansen seconds before it. Louis Saha took time off from bitching on twitter to replace the injured Aussie, but it was City's subs that turned the game as crazy Balotelli side-footed home from the edge of the box before Milner made it 2-0 after an error by R R Drenthe. Really Rubbish? Moyes commented afterwards that Kompany had 'done' Cahill. The video backs that up, but I defy anyone to look at that incident without a replay and see anything other than a lunge by Cahill. Can't blame the ref for not seeing that sneaky stamp by Kompany. Hopefully Cahill misses the derby next week as he's just about the only Everton player that frightens me.

Under fire Arsenal had the perfect fixture to try and get them back on track. Bolton are probably the only side in worse form than the Gunners. Owen Coyle finally unleashed the Gog but was without Gary Cahill. Motson was commentating, and talking shite as usual. Koscielny nutted Ngog as the striker went for a header, both players were down but the Arsenal player came off worst and had to stay off the field while Bolton took the free kick. *"This is where I think this law is very unfair on the defending side because Arsenal through no fault of their own are deprived of a back four player as Bolton take the free-kick"* Erm, 'Through no fault of their own'? Really, Motty? The clue there is in the words *'Bolton take the free-kick'* you dribbling idiot. And why does he always run out of the breath at the end of his stupid high pitched whiny sentences? I hate him I tells ya!

Many will say the game turned on the sending off of Wheater for a silly tug of Walcott's arm as he ran clear, but they would be wrong. Bolton's hopes of getting anything from the game were dashed when 'the Gog' had to go off injured after just 20 minutes. Game over. Van Persie scored a couple of nice goals and could easily have had three or four more. He's a class player, Arsenal are going to be screwed when he takes his annual three month injury lay off shortly. Song added a nice third to take some pressure of the Gunners ahead of next week's North London derby.

Meanwhile, Newcastle are still unbeaten and picked up three points against Blackburn. Is it possible that Pardew is actually a good manager? Surely not. It's a leap I'm certainly not prepared to make yet, if ever. Two goals in three minutes for Demba Ba set the Toon on their way. Decent player him, he was a nice pick up for the Geordies. Hoilett pulled one back for Rovers and every time I see him I'm impressed. Ba completed his hat-trick in contentious circumstances when Best appeared to shove Dann. Olsson was booked for protesting and was then sent off for an unforgivably stupid foul that earned him a second yellow shortly after.

Spurs were at Wigan and the commentator was trying to big up Franco Di Santo and his three goals before the game. *sighs* THEY WERE ALL DEFLECTIONS - HE'S GARBAGE. A blunder from Figueroa allowed Adebayor to set up Van Der Vaart to make it 1-0. Adebayor should have doubled it shortly afterwards, but Gareth Bale did with a near post header from a corner. Diame pulled one back for Wigan with a nice finish but Spurs held on and Wigan were reduced to ten men when Gohouri 'did a Skrtel' and got himself two yellow cards for fouls on Bale, the second of which was plain stupid. Adebayor has transformed Spurs, but how long will it last? He seems to start every season like a house on fire and then come December/January he loses interest. Let's hope that continues.

West Brom v Fulham saw Roy Hodgson's new side up against one of his old ones. Somehow it ended 0-0 despite both teams having plenty of chances. Hodgson continued his impressive run of 273 consecutive TV interviews in which he has touched his ear and scratched his nose.

Onto Sunday, and QPR entertained unbeaten Villa at Loftus Road. Taraabt was inches away from a goal of the season contender for the home side, whilst youngster Barry Bannan went close with a nice free-kick for Villa. Alex McLeish's side were awarded a controversial pen when Traore pulled Agbonlahor's shirt. Looked a soft pen, but the ref had a good position and from where he was he clearly saw the tug. Bannan rolled in the spot kick as Neil Warnock's blood began to reach boiling point. His main argument for it not being a pen was that none of the Villa fans behind the goal appealed for it. Hmmm, maybe because the tug was on the back of Agbonlahor's shirt so they couldn't see it but the ref could? Just a thought. Two unsuccessful handball appeals against Hutton further added to Warnock's ire, until eventually Traore was sent off for a stupid foul and Warnock threw him under the bus by bollocking him at pitchside and then slaughtering him on MOTD. This is the kind of thing he does, he's great entertainment I think and I'm glad he's in the Premiership again, even though everyone can see he's a bad whopper. He was right about Traore too. You can make a case that a manager should keep that stuff in house, but that makes for shit TV so I say good on him. Fortunately for Traore his team-mates bailed him out by forcing a late equaliser when Ste Warnock's goal-line clearance struck Richard Dunne and ended up in the back of the net in the 4th minute of stoppage time. Honours even, Villa still unbeaten and QPR happy to pick up a point. And for once, no-one is talking about Joey Barton, not even me. Oh wait, I just did.

Onto Monday night, and another defeat for Sunderland. Good three points for Norwich though. Aside from Zak Whitbread and Danny Ayala, I don't think I'd recognise any of their players even if they knocked on my front door dressed in full kit. I know their names, Morrison, Tierney, Bennett, Barnett, Holt, Johnson etc but as for their faces? They might be the most unrecognisable team in the history of the Premiership. Or maybe it's just me not paying attention? I'm lost without my Panini Sticker Albums to be fair. I still buy them for World Cups though.

chapter four

October

EVERTON 0 LIVERPOOL 2

Competition - Premier League
Date - Sat 1 Oct 2011
Venue - Goodison Park
Scorer(s) – Andy Carroll, Luis Suarez
Half Time - 0-0
Star Man – Jamie Carragher

Team: Reina; Kelly, Carragher, Skrtel, Enrique; Kuyt, Lucas (Henderson), Adam (Gerrard), Downing (Bellamy); Suarez, Carroll:

Merseyside derbies eh? Never a dull moment. It was a pretty safe bet Martin Atkinson would be the name on most people's lips after the game, I'm just glad it wasn't us getting shafted by him this time. The red card was clearly a contentious decision, in fact it was equally as controversial as the decision to not show one for a typical Tony Hibbert lunge. I'm sure David Moyes will have pointed that one out too, being the fair minded good egg that he is.

What's that you say? He didn't mention the Hibbert challenge? Well I'll be damned. In fairness, he does have a blind spot where 'Hibbo' is concerned. Selecting him over Phil Neville is proof of that. As my cousin Al said the other day, *"Hibbert is Moyes before he found the ring"*. He's right you know, just look at his face, Hibbert is the Smeagol to Moyes' Gollum. Moyes accused Atkinson of ruining the game with the sending off of Rodwell. Speak for yourself bogeyes, it didn't ruin it for me, in fact I'd say it contributed greatly to my enjoyment of the occasion.

I think he got it right too. It was a bad challenge and Suarez is fortunate he wasn't injured by it. Hopefully the FA look at it and increase the ban from three games as frankly that's isn't enough. If the FA are serious about stamping out violent, dangerous play then they need to start handing out stiffer punishments.

Of course, I'm taking the piss. Much as I'd like to try and justify the red card, it was clearly an awful decision. It might actually turn out to be the worst sending off decision we'll see all season in fact. It may have cost them three points or it may not have. No-one knows how this game would have turned out had Rodwell stayed on. No-one.

At the time, it was an even contest, a typical derby in fact. Most of these games are like this, high tempo stuff with not much in it until one team scores. Neither side were on top, but that doesn't mean it would have stayed like that. Of course we'll never know because Atkinson's mistake put Everton on the back foot and they remained there for the rest of the game. Did it help us win the game? Hell yes it did, and it makes the win even sweeter just for the comedy element of it. We'll be hearing about this for the next twenty years I expect. Poor old Clive Thomas might start feeling a little neglected. And don't forget about Collina the Kopite.

It's not easy having to play in derbies a man down, we should know as we had to do it two seasons back when Atkinson harshly sent off Krygiakos (we still won, so it's not quite the 'game ender' that Moyes would have you believe). As I said in the opening paragraph, I'm just glad we weren't the ones on the receiving end of his incompetence for once. These games are very difficult to referee, but until that decision the game was nothing out of the ordinary with not a bad tackle in sight. He made a rod for his own back after the red card though, as it whipped the mob into a frenzy and they were baying for our blood even more than usual.

I thought our players then did a great job of not allowing Atkinson to even up the score. There were a few moments where it looked like one of our lads would go into a 50/50 before they thought better of it, and I'm sure there will have been instructions from the bench for them not to take any risks by going into tackles that could give the ref the chance to 'rectify his mistake'.

Atkinson couldn't nail any of our players, so instead he opted for leniency on theirs. Fellaini caught Lucas with a studs up challenge on the edge of the box that was far worse than Rodwell's, whilst Hibbert's lunge on Adam didn't even result in a free-kick, let alone a red or yellow card or even a talking to. That was a potential leg breaker, whereas I didn't even think Rodwell's was a free-kick let alone anything else. That's Martin Atkinson for you though. In fact, that's referees for you. They're all terrible these days.

Before Rodwell's dismissal it was shaping up to be an interesting game. We should have scored through Suarez following outstanding play by Kuyt, but seconds later Reina had to acrobatically tip over a header from Cahill. The Aussie is a one trick pony who offers little else other than an aerial threat, but he is unbelievably good at that 'one trick'. Never ceases to amaze me how good he is in the air. Great save by Pepe too.

Distin then shot over after showing nifty footwork to go past Skrtel and Enrique, and Saha curled a low shot a foot wide. It was a good even contest at that point, then Rodwell flew in on Suarez and all hell broke loose. I don't know what Atkinson thought he saw but his reaction was immediate, there was no hesitation. Lucas and Adam were both on the spot complaining, but they weren't demanding a red card. It was a typical reaction to a strong challenge on a team-mate, I'm sure they were as surprised as everybody else when Rodwell was sent packing. They did nothing wrong, but I can see why Evertonians would be upset about it.

I've noticed Suarez getting criticism too for his part in the incident, but the bottom line is nobody knows how much or how little that hurt. There was certainly contact as Rodwell's knee caught Suarez's ankle on the follow through, and Suarez was limping around for a bit afterwards. He may or may not have been milking it, I don't know and neither does anyone else. The only person to blame for that red card is the referee, it's not the fault of Lucas, Adam, Suarez or Rodwell for that matter.

He went in hard and got the ball. His follow through caught Suarez, but it wasn't with his studs it was with his knee. In terms of being dangerous, I don't think it was. Hard, yes. Dirty, absolutely not. Evertonians don't need much to send them into a seething mass of frothing at the mouth, bile spewing, booing neanderthals, and Atkinson's action was the equivalent of waving a red rag to a bu... well, to an Evertonian.

The rest of the game saw them booing, screeching 'aaaaayyyyyyyyyyyy' any time one of our players went within five yards of a blue shirt, and of course the usual demands for 'handball!!!!!!!!' whenever a Liverpool player controlled the ball with any part of their anatomy that wasn't their foot, and sometimes even when it was. And that's without even mentioning the 'corner flag mob' and their contorted with rage, hate filled faces (more on them later).

Their players were losing their heads too. Cahill was booked for catching Adam (I didn't think it was too bad but was worthy of a booking), Fellaini did Lucas (nasty challenge) and there was the shocking Hibbert assault. They couldn't get on the ball and we were completely bossing it now in terms of possession but they were defending well, especially the centre backs. Suarez shot into the side netting instead of trying to cut it back to Carroll and Adam hit the bar with a terrific strike. The best chance of all came from the penalty spot when Suarez was clumsily chopped down by Jagielka. Stonewall pen, didn't stop the blues from chanting 'cheat' at Suarez though. Dirk is normally the main man from the spot, especially against the blues. Not this time though. It wasn't an awful pen, he just didn't hit it hard enough and Howard got down to make a superb save. Unfortunate for Dirk, he played well I thought.

By and large we weren't creating as much as I'd have liked. What we did do was keep the ball and make them work. That would pay off later on. It's not easy when the opposition have nine men behind the ball, but it was difficult to imagine Everton being able to keep us at bay for the entire game a man down and on such a sweltering hot day. They were going to run out of steam, and we had Gerrard and Bellamy to call on.

At half time it was difficult to see anything other than a Liverpool victory, but the penalty miss and the shot hitting the bar was weighing a little heavy on my mind. One of those days? The way the second half began did little to ease those concerns. Everton looked to have regained their composure during the break and they did ok for a while. More than ok actually, they did about as well as could be expected I thought. Saha had a couple of shots and they got some decent crosses in too. Our back four held firm though, every one of them performed well with Carragher and Enrique especially good.

For us, Andy Carroll twice went close with towering headers from corners. One was cleared off the line, the other was deflected and brought a good save out of Howard. It was starting to have stalemate written all over it until Kenny played the aces up his sleeve. Bringing on Gerrard and Bellamy was a no brainer, the only decision to be made was who should go off. Downing was an obvious choice as he'd done nothing. He wasn't doing much wrong, he was just anonymous. I've been saying that most of the season about Henderson, but this time it was Downing who was Mr Invisible. Very disappointing, especially as he was up against the awful Hibbert. I think he's played quite well so far for the most part, but this wasn't good enough and he has to contribute more. Did he even put in a single cross? I can't remember any.

The other change wasn't as straightforward. I guess most people would have taken Carroll off, and if it had been 11 v 11 then maybe Kenny would have, we'll never know. Looking at it now, it was a masterstroke by Dalglish leaving Carroll on as obviously he scored. More than that though, I like it because of the intent it showed. I don't think Adam did anything wrong, he played fairly well but they were down to ten men so we got as many attacking players as possible on there.

They'd have been happy to see Carroll go off as it would have been one less attacking threat for them to worry about. The Mancs have won so many games with that approach, keep sending on attacking players until you break them down. Suarez, Carroll, Kuyt, Bellamy and Gerrard. That's a lot for ten men to handle, especially in that heat. It didn't take long to pay off either. Bellamy and Enrique had shown some good signs of an understanding at Stoke, and it was evident again here as the Welshman collected the ball and the Spaniard flew past him on the overlap. Bellamy's pass was perfectly weighted, Enrique's cut back was cleverly ducked under by Kuyt and Carroll buried it in front of the Gwladys Street.

Massive relief, not just because we'd finally broken the deadlock but also because it will hopefully get Carroll going and silence the ever growing number of doubters. Those doubts are justified as he has struggled for the most part but some of the things written about his 'lifestyle' certainly aren't justified. Kenny probably went a bit overboard afterwards and he's more than a little defensive about any questions relating to his number nine. If it helps to get Carroll firing and playing well I don't care how prickly he is in interviews and I'm sure Carroll really appreciates the backing he's getting.

The goal was a relief, but we needed another to make it safe and it came when Suarez took advantage of a mix up between Baines and Distin to gleefully side foot past Howard. That tipped some Evertonians over the edge. The goons by the corner flag had earlier been hurling abuse at Adam whenever he took a corner, but now they were yelling more than insults, they were throwing whatever they could get their hands on. Coins, plastic bottles, pies...

We're no angels and you occasionally see this from our fans too, usually when Rooney comes to town. It also used to happen to Gary Neville (who brought it on himself and in fairness never complained about it) and I remember some dickhead spitting on Phil Neville when he was taking a throw. Generally it's a rarity however and it's reserved for only the most reviled of opponent. Not excusing it by any means, but as a rule there has to be some history there with the player and it simply doesn't compare to the gauntlet ALL of our players have to run at Goodison. It's just weird I think. I can't imagine being driven to that kind of rage just at the sight of say, Seamus Coleman or Bilyadel… Billyaladi.. Bil.. that Russian lad.

I can understand their hatred for Gerrard and Carragher, I can see why they despised Torres and now Suarez as they are/were all seen as symbols of the club. I can't relate to how they can get themselves into a slobbering vitriolic mess over Charlie Adam though, who's only been here five minutes and has done nothing so far to offend their sensibilities other than don the red shirt. Just look at the faces in the crowd when Adam is taking a corner. So much hatred. I've been at Goodison and sat in with the home fans whilst they were hurling all kinds of insults at people like Josemi, Diao, Pongolle etc. It's anyone in a red shirt, no matter how crap or inoffensive they are. I mean Josemi??? Really blues fans?? You want to abuse Josemi? You should have been buying him drinks, not yelling abuse.

With Adam off the field, their new target was Craig Bellamy who just stood there laughing at them. He loves that kind of shit, he's in his element. One whopper was screaming insults at Bellamy whilst filming him on his phone. Bizarre. It probably made Bellamy's day seeing how they reacted to him. Suarez also had to deal with it and was hit by a coin (insert your own joke about David Moyes' transfer kitty). His response was to take a brilliant quick corner to Kuyt who was desperately unlucky to hit the post. Would have been a memorable goal that, brilliantly worked between them. Gerrard had also come within a whisker of scoring, pity that didn't go in as I'd have loved to have seen his celebration. Kenny gave Lucas a well earned rest late on, sending on Henderson to partner Gerrard in the middle. Lucas was on a yellow card so it made sense to get him off. His little fist pump to the away end was class too.

We won 2-0 at Goodison with a team that is still bedding in. It wasn't perfect, but we're only seven games in and we're doing ok. We've got 13 points which is decent but should be better, and we've got four of the most difficult away fixtures out of the way. We've got Gerrard back and Carroll is off the mark for the season. And of course we've got Suarez. I thought this was his worst performance of the season, but he still scored and won a penalty.

All in all, I'm happy. I know there's things that weren't especially great but I'm not going to nit-pick over it. I'd rather just savour the moment than worrying about how many times Andy Carroll touched the ball in the opposition half or what Charlie Adam's pass completion ratio was or why Craig Bellamy isn't starting etc I understand a lot of the concerns people have, and those concerns may well prove to be justified. I just think it's far too soon to tell and I'm trying to stay positive as on the whole things look promising. Certainly a lot more promising than the last time we visited the Pit anyway.

So those concerns can wait for another day. We've got a two week lay off, so for now I'd rather just enjoy the win. We got the three points, Everton got a ready made excuse for losing and something to complain about, so as Del Boy would say, *'Bonet de Douche, everyone's a winner'*. My glass isn't overflowing, but it's definitely half full.

Premier League Round Up (1-2 October 2011)

I think I'll start with Sunday's games this week. The North London derby was the big game of the day, and it didn't disappoint. There was a contentious goal, Wenger offered Clive Allen out in the tunnel and Redknapp took a swipe at Arsenal fans for chanting about Adebayor. ***"It was disgusting. How do you chant something like that to someone? You can't be right mentally. You need help. There are kids up there as well. It's got no place anywhere in life, that sort of stuff."***

Hmmm, not condoning what Arsenal fans did (chanting *"It should have been you, the Togo shooting, it should have been you"*) but they've had to listen to a lot of that kind of shite from Spurs down the years. Two wrongs don't make a right of course, but where was Redknapp's outrage on Adebayor's behalf when Spurs fans were singing that his dad *"washes elephants"* and his mother's *"a whore"*? And how many years have Spurs fans been singing about Wenger being 'a paedophile'?? If Redknapp had been as vociferous about that and called Spurs' fans 'disgusting' then his words now would count for something. Maybe he did and I missed it? If so then fair enough. If not he can stick his moral indignation up his arse.

As for the game, the opening goal was a great finish by Van Der Vaart, but Wenger insists it shouldn't have stood as he used his arm to control the ball. I've seen about ten replays of it and still can't be certain if it hit his arm or not. The angle of his body and the way the ball dropped suggest it did, but even a referee hater like me can't pin that one on the official. How could he possibly tell when numerous camera angles aren't even conclusive? Arsene sees what he wants to though doesn't he? He's understandably going to be unhappy about it as he's under pressure. Their season has been wretched up to now and they look to be in real trouble. Not relegation trouble, obviously, but their run of top four finishes is under serious threat. Arsenal rallied after the break though and scored a nice equaliser. They were looking good at that stage but they didn't kick on from it and Spurs deserved their win in the end. The deciding goal looked like a goalkeeping error, but I have sympathy for the keeper as that ball was moving all over the place. Szczesny was actually the only thing standing between Arsenal and a bumming and he's the least of their problems right now.

Gareth Bale seems to be coming back into the form that made him the best player in the country for a spell last season. Sagna was coping with him relatively well but then broke his leg in a freak incident. Arsenal seem to get more serious injuries than everybody else year in year out and this is a big one, they can't replace Sagna as the other lad they have (Jenkinson?) is crap. After the game Wenger apparently got into a row with Clive Allen and reportedly asked him to come down the tunnel to sort it out. I have a confession to make, I quite like Arsene Wenger. I know it's not a popular view, but I can't help it. He doesn't back down to anybody. When he looks in the mirror he must see a big meathead looking back at him and not the scrawny, pencil necked dweeb that the rest of us see. The man tried to pick a fight with big Martin Jol for God's sake, how can you not respect that?

Speaking of Martin Jol, Fulham had a good day didn't they? I don't think anyone saw that coming, least of all Neil Warnock. Fulham scored after a minute and never looked back. I'd completely forgotten how much I used to despise Andy Johnson when he was at Goodison. He's been such a non-entity since he left, but apparently he's scored six goals in Europe this season. Ngog did the same last season so it takes more than that to impress me. Mind you, he bagged a hat-trick in this game, helped set up another and also won a penalty, so fair play. He still looks like a giant penis though.

Bolton's woes continued as they got whalloped by Chelsea at the Reebok. Lampard was back in the side after being dropped and responded with a hat-trick. Sturridge scored two and refused to celebrate either out of respect for former club Bolton. Classy that, he'd better knock that shit off though as there's no room for anything classy at Chelsea. Silly boy.

Bolton are woeful at the back, they're actually so bad defensively that they are negating the genius of The Gog at the other end. He still managed to boot Mongo in the nuts though. Good lad. Bolton gave it a bit of a go 2nd half. They scored one and should have had a second through Kevin Davies who's shot was well over the line before Ivanovic cleared. The linesman didn't spot it, but it didn't really matter anyway. The only people who'll be bothered are those who have Davies in their fantasy team, and let's face it, anyone who is stupid enough to select Kevin Davies in their fantasy team probably has a lot more to worry about in their life than this. One final note from this one. Bolton left back Paul Robinson rivals Tony Hibbert for the worst player in the Prem award. They'd be better off with Paul Robinson the keeper playing there. Or Paul Robinson from Neighbours for that matter. Or Mrs Robinson from the song. Or a bottle of Robinson's Barley Water. Or... well you get the picture.

The other game on Sunday saw Swansea's impressive home form continue with a 2-0 win over Stoke. That's two wins and two draws at home for the Swans now and no goals conceded. That Wilkinson from Stoke might just be the dirtiest player in the league, he's a fucking dog him. He's crap too, and I may have been a bit hasty proclaiming Robinson as Hibbert's main competition. Pleased for Swansea, if they can promise to stop wheeling out Max Boyce then I'll be more than happy for them to stay up.

Onto Saturday, and Newcastle are STILL unbeaten. This is getting weird now. Wolves are slumping after their bright start, but fair play to the Geordies as they are surprising a lot of people up to now, even though they were incredibly lucky to win this game. 'Jonas' - no longer on the twat list as I didn't want to add 'Maxi' to it - scored a cracker. Tiote is a really good player, and Demba Ba will definitely score goals for them. They still have a lot of shite in their side but Pardew clearly knows how to polish turds. One of those turds, Steven Taylor, was very lucky not to concede a penalty when he flattened O'Hara about two yards inside the box but Mark Halsey said it was outside. When it's borderline it's difficult for refs to know if it's inside or not, but this wasn't even close. Awful decision. Fletcher pulled one back after some good play by my boy Adam Hammill, and Doyle thought he'd equalised after another cross by Hammill was headed back by Jarvis. The linesman had other ideas and ruled that the ball had gone out of play. He was wrong, but in his defence he probably didn't want to have to listen to that dreadful, smalltime music Wolves play after a goal, so I'll give him a pass.

City went to Blackburn without Tevez and they also left out Dzeko. Aguero started and went off injured, so Balotelli ended up playing through the middle. Makes me sick, it wasn't too long ago they had Darius Vassell and Benjani playing up front. Blackburn kept City out until the 2nd half, but then the floodgates opened. Johnson, Balotelli and Nasri scored, before some fella I've never even heard of made it 4-0. Savic? Who dat? I bet they paid about £20m for him, didn't they? Blackburn's fans staged a sit in protest against Steve Kean. I'm not going to sit in judgement of them, as I wouldn't want him managing my team either. He just doesn't inspire any confidence and has 'caretaker' written all over him. He's Les Reed with a Scottish accent.

Villa are still unbeaten and Agbonlahor is in great form at the moment. Pace, power, directness, he's a real handful. He just comes across as being incredibly thick though, he's just got that look about him and have you ever heard him talk? Jesus Christ. Can't help thinking he might just be the only player in the league who's IQ is lower than his shirt number. He may even be borderline special needs. Good player though, very exciting when on form.

Sunderland had been having a bad time of it aside from that 4-0 win they had last week, and they found themselves 2-0 down after five minutes at home to West Brom. The boos were ringing out when that second goal went in, but the Mackems rallied and were back level before half time. They couldn't find a winner though and the natives are restless. As for West Brom, well Hodgson's post match interview was awesome. Comedy gold. *"There were 90 minutes left to play when we were 2-0 up, so the game starts all over again. I think we should give credit to Sunderland for really mounting a strong challenge and getting over the disappointment of a poor start both in terms of conceding goals and maybe giving the ball away far more than Steve would like in that early spell. We mustn't be too upset with ourselves, if they'd have gone 2-0 up and we'd have got two goals and come away with a 2-2 after coming back from 2-0 down we'd be turning cartwheels and congratulating ourselves. When you go 2-0 up and the other team comes back you can be harsh on yourself and say you've squandered a lead. I don't think it was a question of that"*

There's a David Brent like aspect to his interviews, they're uncomfortable to watch but can be side splittingly funny (when he's not your manager, obviously. I doubt West Brom fans were laughing about it). Roy Hodgson and interviews are like Superman and Kryptonite, or Jussi Jaaskelainen and a bar of soap. At least Superman and Jaaskelainen know to avoid Kryptonite and soap, Roy should follow suit and just stop talking.

The other Mancs were far less impressive but still collected three points. Based on the highlights Norwich looked like they should have won. They wasted loads of good openings and paid the price by conceding a soft goal from a corner to that twat Anderson before a late Wellbeck goal made it safe. De Gea was left on the bench in favour of Lindegaard. I don't know why as BBC didn't say and never had the balls to ask Ferguson afterwards. Ferguson and Motson were too busy giving each other handjobs to bother with any serious questions though. That little exchange between them afterwards made me throw up in my mouth a little. The King's daughter should conduct every interview with that bully. He saw his arse when she asked if Lindegaard had given him a selection headache. Two weeks later De Gea is on the bench and Lindegaard is playing. Kelly knows. Apparently De Gea was caught on CCTV through the week eating a doughnut in a shop and not paying for it. He says it had nothing to do him being left out of this game though: *"Absloutely not true. They're not going to drop me for a doughnut."* Not sure Lindegaard will appreciate being called a doughnut, especially by the Spanish Massimo Taibi.

Before I forget, it seems I may owe Ferguson an apology over something written in last week's round up. Turns out that his pronunciation of 'Cheecharito' is actually correct, so my bad. It still makes him sound like a lovestruck teenage girl though, and it's bad cringeworthy stuff. He's 70 years old for God's sake. He's not much older than my dad, and the idea of my arl fella calling a player by their nickname seems more alien to me than Robert Earnshaws head. *"That 'El Pistolero' is a great player isn't he son?"* Haha. Kinell, my old man is doing well if he actually remembers a player's name, never mind pronounces it properly. I still rip the piss out of him over 'Cesc

Fibreglass' and to this day I'm sure he doesn't know Voronin's name, he just used to call him 'Ponytail'.

Great stuff from the Norwich fans who responded to that tedious *"We'll do what we want"* chant with *"We're Norwich City, we've come for our scarves"* Brilliant that. On the subject of all that green and gold garbage, whatever happened to all that protesting stuff? Oh yeah, they won something, that's what happened. Knobs.

MotD ended with a tribute to 'Motty', who was celebrating 40 years stealing a wage from the TV licence payer's money. The montage got me quite emotional to be fair. Even the coldest of hearts would find it difficult to look back and not get upset at the amount of fantastic goals and iconic moments absolutely fucking ruined by that twat's whiney, hysterical voice.

LIVERPOOL 1 MANCHESTER UNITED 1

Competition: Premier League
Date - Sat 15 Oct 2011
Venue - Anfield
Scorer(s) – Steven Gerrard
Half Time - 0-0
Star Man – Charlie Adam

Team: Reina; Kelly, Carragher, Skrtel, Enrique; Gerrard, Lucas (Henderson), Adam; Kuyt, Suarez, Downing:

It looked like a golden opportunity to turn them over when the teamsheets were handed in. No Rooney, Nani or Hernandez and a midfield of Giggs, Jones and Fletcher? Happy days. The seven on United's bench would probably beat the eleven they put on the field, so there seemed to be a great chance for us to get the win. As it turned out, that team selection did us no favours. Ferguson came to park the bus, and that's what they did.

We found it very difficult to play through them and the game only opened up late on when they had to come out of their defensive shell and introduce their attacking players. When that happened, we created a load of chances. We couldn't put them away though and had to settle for a point. Frustrating, and yet at the same time encouraging.

Steven Gerrard's return was always going to make Kenny's team selection interesting. I was happy to see us go with a three man midfield as I believe that plays to the strengths of all three. Lucas and Adam as a pair hasn't really convinced even though I'd say both have played fairly well individually. Adding Gerrard to the mix should, in theory, help both of them as well as the skipper. The problem is that if you go with the extra man in midfield, someone further forward misses out. Suarez is an automatic selection, so it's any two from Downing, Kuyt, Carroll and Bellamy. This time Kenny opted for Kuyt and Downing, with Carroll unfortunate to sit it out after scoring in the derby last time out.

United went with the same system, and both teams cancelled eachother out for most of the first half. They only had one chance, when Evra got to the byline and crossed to the back post where Jones headed wide. We only had one clear chance ourselves, Suarez shooting straight at De Gea after collecting a ricochet following Adam's driving run and shot.

Basically the first half was crap, there weren't even any tasty challenges going in. It was pretty dull stuff, and I'd put the blame for that squarely at the door of the Mancs. They set out to stifle us, their team selection proved that and the way they played was further evidence. And we weren't good enough to overcome it.

When Reina was in possession, they pushed up to mark all of our players and prevent us building from the back. Adam and Gerrard were man marked whenever they dropped deep to try and get on the ball, and United showed virtually no ambition other than to keep us in check. Of course it's up to us to get past that, and for the most part we didn't look capable of doing it, so Ferguson will feel his shithouse approach did the business for them.

We knocked the ball around a bit but we didn't get enough from wide areas and most of our play was in front of their defence. Suarez should have done better when he failed to get on the end of a brilliant ball in from Gerrard and he then tried his luck with a shot from inside the centre circle that he didn't quite catch flush and it drifted wide. Not particularly threatening though, and I wouldn't even describe them as half chances. The one time we did get a good sight of goal was from Adam's surging run from deep that took him past a couple of players, but even then it took a fortunate rebound to create the opening for Suarez. He dummied well to make space, but his left foot shot was straight at De Gea.

The biggest disappointments of the first half for me were Lucas and Downing. This is the kind of game that Lucas usually thrives in. Not this time, he looked a bit off the pace right from the start, perhaps due to the travelling he'd done in midweek. His passing wasn't as crisp as usual and he just didn't seem to be himself. The harsh booking he collected didn't help either, and he'll now miss our next game through suspension. The rest might not do him any harm actually.

As for Downing, he wasn't terrible, but he just wasn't assertive enough. He wasn't trying to get by Smalling on the outside enough, and his understanding with Enrique was off for most of the first half. If Kenny sticks with the 433 system, Downing will have to step it up quite a bit as Bellamy has done well on the left whenever he's had an opportunity. In fairness, Downing got better after the break though I thought. As did the rest of the team.

The second period started in much the same vein that the first had. Very tight, not much in the way of chances and stalemate written all over it. As so often happens though, once you get to around the hour mark, the game starts to get stretched and you get chances. Kenny acted fairly swiftly to change things, bringing off Lucas after 57 minutes and sending on Henderson in his place. Lucas had conceded a couple of free-kicks early in the second half (one of them incredibly harsh when Young ran into him) and that may have had a bearing on the decision, as he was probably one more foul away from a red card for persistent offending. Spearing would have appeared to be a more logical replacement, but Kenny went for the more adventurous option of Henderson, with Gerrard dropping a bit deeper to fill the gap vacated by Lucas. It worked well, with Henderson and Adam both getting forward to good effect.

We had a decent penalty shout when Kuyt's header struck the arm of Evans. Seen them given, but it's not one I can kick up a stink about as you can't just make your arm disappear. Not much Evans could do about it as his arm was more or less by his side, but if it had been at Old Trafford and it was a Liverpool player….

The deadlock was finally broken with a little over 20 minutes left. I'm not going to say it came in contentious circumstances, because I don't believe it did. The only thing contentious about it was whether Ferdinand should have been sent off for a second yellow. He probably should have but again I'm not overly upset about it. I've got no doubt he caught Adam and despite a lot of talk to the contrary I don't think Adam went down too easily. Why would he go down? His next act would have been to get a shot away as he still had control of the ball and was running into the area. I don't see why he'd go down unless he had to. The contact was minimal, but it looks like he stood on Adam's standing foot which will usually bring you down when you're running. His fall looked pretty natural too, and if it was a dive (and only Adam will know) then he must practice that a hell of a lot as it looked convincing enough to me. Ferdinand's sense of injustice was compounded when Gerrard stepped up and put the ball through the wall and into the bottom corner. Great to have him back, the big fucking leg.

Ferdinand was bitching about it on his twitter afterwards, but fuck him. For years he's kicked lumps out of our strikers without any recourse. Torres got some terrible stick from him that usually went unpunished, and the camel faced twat was trying the same shit with Suarez all day as well. You look at some of the cheating bastards he's lined up alongside over the years, and he's got some balls on him calling Charlie Adam out. He should be calling out Giggs, who moved out of the way of the free-kick like a little girl who didn't want to get hit by the ball. Fanny.

Ferguson responded by sending on Nani and Rooney. Strangely, Rooney went to a centre midfield position. He was taunted unmercifully by the Kop. *"Who's the scouser in the wig?"* and *"your hair isn't yours, you baldy bastard you hair isn't yours"* Whilst I admit I was pissing myself, I was also thinking it might be tempting fate a bit, especially as we had started to sit off them and looked like we were just trying to hold what we had. They came right into it and were seeing much more of the ball than they had been previously. Ferguson played the final ace up his sleeve, sending on Hernandez as they threw everything they had at us. They forced a few corners, but Pepe hadn't had to make a save and we were defending well. Then from one of those corners, Wellbeck got away from Carragher to flick the ball across the face of goal, and Hernandez escaped the attentions of Skrtel to head it in from close range.

It's easy to point the finger at our centre halves, but it's incredibly difficult staying with people who are moving around in a crowded penalty area. Wellbeck cleverly shoved off on Carra to give himself some space, and the only way Skrtel would have been able to stick with Hernandez would have been to grab hold of him, which he tried to do and ended up falling over and losing him. How do you stay touch tight to a player who is running around in between other bodies in the box? It's nigh on impossible, you just have to get as close as you can and hope the ball doesn't fall to them. Unfortunately for us, it fell perfectly for United.

It was a soft goal to give away, but we had lost the momentum we'd been building before we scored and we paid the price for that. Maybe Kenny should have made some changes, but I could see why he didn't. At 0-0 I'd have definitely been looking to get Carroll and Bellamy on for Downing and Kuyt, but once we went in front suddenly Kuyt becomes much more valuable. I'd have still sent Bellamy on for Downing, mainly because United were having to commit men forward which meant space to counter attack. Kenny opted to stick with what we had, and once United drew level he may have felt changing things then could have unsettled us. I don't know why he didn't change it, but given how the rest of the game played out I'd say he got it right because we pummelled them after that equaliser.

I had feared the worst when they equalised and expected us to go on and lose. But we regrouped and looked like the only team trying to win it by the end. Almost immediately after they scored Downing whipped in a stunning cross that Kuyt did well to get on the end of, but his shot went straight at the diving De Gea. Henderson was next to be denied by the keeper, his clever lob being clawed away when it seemed headed for the top corner. Just needed another six inches on that and he's a hero. We then went close from a couple of corners. First when Downing did well to turn the ball back into the middle from the back post only for United to just about scramble it away. Then another when United failed to clear the danger and Adam found himself in behind and nodded the ball across goal towards Suarez. It looked a certain goal but Rooney managed to outjump him and nod it away as far as Skrtel, who ballooned his volley high over the bar. That seemed like it would be our last chance of the game but it wasn't. We continued to pile forward and Downing put in another great cross that found the head of Henderson, but he couldn't direct his header well enough and it dropped onto the roof of the net. Should have done better, but I liked what I saw from Henderson in this game. Playing central with the freedom to get forward, he did very well.

We really should have won the game as we were the better side and De Gea was by far the busier of the two keepers. It's frustrating that we couldn't take the three points, but we need to take heart from the performance and make sure we go on to beat the teams we should be beating. If we do that then we'll be in good shape. Having Gerrard back will hopefully give us a huge boost in the coming weeks, it's fantastic having him back and fitting that he scored on his return.

Star man was a toss up between Adam, Kelly, Carragher and Suarez. I'm going for Adam as this was his best game for us and I thought he was excellent in everything he did. The way he'd shield the ball when in possession to compensate for not being the quickest was very impressive, and I'd like to see more of him carrying the ball forward like he did on a couple of occasions in this game. Good to see him playing like this and hopefully now that Gerrard is back we'll see more of the three man midfield and therefore more of Adam as an attacking force.

I've not mentioned the Suarez / Evra thing as far too much is being said about that at the moment. Let's see how it plays out, I've got my thoughts on it but I'd rather wait and see how this all comes out in the wash before commenting. I will comment on Evra's manager though, the purple nosed, bacon faced cunt. Hate is a word that is much overused in football. I use it far too often myself about people who in reality I don't actually give two shits about in the grand scheme of things. We all do it, *"I hate that Jon Walters dickhead"* or *"I can't stand that Neil Warnock"*. Really though, it's bollocks isn't it?

I do actually genuinely hate Alex Ferguson though. With a burning passion. I despise the man. He's just a massive, malignant, spiteful twat. Hearing him talking afterwards about *'the boy Suarez diving all over the place'* wound me up no end to the point where I was wishing things that I'm really not proud of. I guess I'm not alone in that either. He brings out the worst in people. Just why did BBC have to inflict him on us again, that's what I want to know. Non-Utd fans have been perfectly content not having to look at him and listen to his warped, hypocrital, one eyed views for the last few years, but now they go crawling back to him and we have to suffer that kind of attack on a player who actually did nothing wrong whatsoever in that game. There was not a single dive from Suarez in that game. Not one. So why that attack on him? The vile old bastard is jumping on this bandwagon that was started by Everton a couple of weeks ago. Make sure Suarez gets a reputation so refs think twice about giving him decisions. It's obvious what he's up to, and I bet it works too as most refs are so weak they are influenced by that bullying scumbag. He's got previous too, as he did it last year when he had a go at Torres and called him a diver. Torres had become a big thorn in United's side and they'd had people sent off for fouling him. It was obvious what he was up to then, and it's obvious what he's up to now. Roy Hodgson was pilloried for not sticking up for his player, and rightly so. I doubt that Kenny will allow this to go without response, and nor should he. Tell Ferguson to get his own house in order before sticking his purple nose into our business.

Premier League Round Up (15-16 October 2011)

After a week of international football that I can honestly say I didn't watch a single minute of, it was back to the proper stuff this weekend. Jonathon Pearce was the commentator on the biggest game of the day, which was of course us taking on the Mancs at Anfield.

Ferguson described it as 'the biggest fixture in world football,' and then did his best to ruin it as a spectacle by leaving out of all his attackers and playing for a point. Pearce offered an explanation for Ferguson's negative team selection by revealing; "*Rooney took his international suspension hard, according to his manager.*" Hahaha, took it hard did he? Shouldn't go around randomly booting people then, the soft twat. You can get away with that in a United shirt, but that shit don't fly in international football when you can't hide behind your club and your bullying manager. And what of Nani and Hernandez? Were they hurting for poor little, hard done by Shrek too? It's bullshit anyway, as if Rooney wouldn't be in the right frame of mind to play against Liverpool. He's one of the most mentally resilient players in the league, he needs to be given the shame he's brought on himself and his family over the years. It's pretty insulting actually to suggest he couldn't play at Anfield because he was upset about being banned by UEFA. He didn't play because Ferguson was probably scared he'd get sent off again, and because after three successive losses at Anfield he decided to park the bus. "*Phil Jones unlucky,*" said Pearce. Wait, I thought having a bird shit on your head was supposed to bring good luck? Guess that is just an old wives tale after all then. Hey Phil, 1995 called, it wants it's hair style back. I know a lot of people find Pearce annoying but he's fine by me, mostly on the basis that he isn't John Motson.

Next up were unbeaten Villa at Manchester City. They gave it a good go early doors but they aren't unbeaten anymore. Agbonlahor and Warnock both went close as City struggled to get going without Aguero and Silva. Balotelli then slipped over right in front of the Villa fans, who naturally laughed and took the piss. He just stood up, stern faced and put his finger to his lips to shush them. He was deadly serious too, it wasn't banter. He was on a one man crusade to shut them up after that and almost did the next time he touched the ball, forcing a good save out of Shay Given. Not long after he was stood in front of the Villa fans again, giving them the stink eye after burying an overhead kick to give City the lead. He's strange and a little disturbing, but he's compulsive viewing. Like the football equivalent of the Jerry Springer Show. Adam Johnson made it two after a howler from Ste Warnock and the ever impressive Vincent Kompany added a third before Warnock pulled one back. Milner wrapped it up for City with a belter to send Mancini's side top of the table and set themselves up nicely for next weekends manc derby.

Milner was interviewed afterwards and he's clearly stolen Michael

Owen's voice. I guess Owen doesn't need it anymore as let's face it who wants to talk to him these days? If you're gonna rob someone's voice though, surely a James Earl Jones or Patrick Stewart would be a better choice than Michael Monotone Owen?

Swansea went to Norwich in a battle of the new boys but the home side scored in the first minute through Pilkington. Cue celebration music. Why do they do it? No need for it. They added a second through some fella I'd never heard of until now (Russell Martin). Cue stupid music again. Danny Graham pulled a goal back for Swansea and chances were now coming at both ends. Cracking game, and both of these sides have provided good entertainment so far this season, especially Norwich. Pilkington's second of the game made it safe and was the cue for that crap music yet again.

Clubs that play music after goals are basically admitting 'yeah, we know we're smalltime but this is who we are and it's what our knobhead fans want'. Liverpool, Arsenal, City, United, Spurs, Chelsea.... none of them play music after goals. Hell, even Everton don't do it, so there's no excuse for anyone else to. When you look smalltime even in comparison with the blues, you know you're doing something wrong. As for Pilkington, he can fuck off. He missed a great chance against the Mancs in their last game when it was 0-0. He put both chances away in this one and later said it was because he'd been working on his finishing in training this week. Why didn't you work on it before you went to Old Trafford then, soft shite? Stable door. Bolted. Cart Horse. He's a lifelong United fan and was a trainee there too. I'm just saying.

Speaking of United fans, Everton went to Stamford Bridge in the evening game, a ground that amazingly they hadn't tasted defeat at in six league games. Very strange anomaly that, a bit like Leighton Baines' barnet. Everton looked to be the better side early on but Sturridge eventually put Chelsea in front after half an hour. No crap celebration music, but they do have Abramovich clapping like a demented seal and Villas Boas doing the Mourinho fist pump. He'll be sliding on his knees and shushing the crowd whilst wearing a shit coat next, the little wannabe gobshite. Speaking of gobshites, Mongo added a second just before half time when the ball was sucked into the gravitational pull of his forehead. Not fair really is it, Tim Howard had no chance as the ball was orbiting Terry's head like a small moon and the Everton keeper had no idea where it was going to end up. Ramires made it 3-0 and he seems to get his fair share of goals despite giving off a very good impression of somebody who is pretty shite. Is he actually any good? I can't make my mind up on him at all. I think he might be really good, but there is definitely room for some doubt there. And where the fuck is Essien these days? Is he injured again? There's even been a couple of Aurelio sightings since the last time I saw Essien.

That Greek kid came off the bench and scored within eight seconds. You could tell he really wanted to go mad with his celebration but then realised they were 3-1 down and it wouldn't be appropriate. They've got absolutely nothing up front and this lad might be their best hope as he's just about the only forward they have that looks like he can find the goal without the aid of a map. They've got a bad run of fixtures coming up and they're only a point above the relegation zone at the moment. Still, they've brought James McFadden back now so I'm sure they'll be fine. Like when Neighbours brought back Harold Bishop thinking it'd improve ratings.

Two other teams down there in the basement met at the DW Stadium. Scruffy Jaaskelainen was back in goal for Bolton after losing his place to that crap ginger kid the other week, whilst Owen Coyle unleashed the Gog again. As ever, the Gog delivered. He was involved in the first goal for Reo-Coker and he scored the second himself. Sandwiched in between those goals was a cracker from Diame that drew Wigan level. Good player him, he'll be snapped up by someone when Wigan go down. Yeah that's right, I'm calling that already. Wigan will go down. Bolton were awarded a penalty when Mike Dean adjudged Caldwell to have shoved Boyata. He did do, but only because Kevin Davies had shoved him in the back and he couldn't avoid barging into Boyata. Justice was done as Al Habsy saved the pen, but Chris Eagles managed to 'Escape from Alcaraz' to make it 3-1. See what I did there? Every week Roberto Martinez has to put on a brave face and come out saying that they will keep playing their football but need to stop making mistakes. And each week they come out playing their football but making stupid mistakes. All three of Bolton's goals came from Wigan defenders fannying about and getting caught in possession, with Alcaraz being the guilty party for two of them.

Matthew Etherington had a sugar injection in his back to help him recover from a hamstring injury as Stoke played host to Fulham. Sugar injection eh? Hardly a new thing, Emiliano Insua used to have those before and after every training session. And before and after every game. Or if he was just sat at home watching TV. Or if he fancied a midnight snack. He didn't have a needle shoved into his back either, he'd simply peel off the wrapper and scoff down that bad boy, which is why he was dubbed 'the Mars Bar kid' by some at Melwood.

On the subject of former Liverpool players, there were four of them on show in this game, two on each side. Some great play by Pennant and Crouch looked to have unlocked Fulham early on, but the finish by Pennant was awful. No surprise there, if he could score goals he'd probably still be at Anfield, but wingers who score one goal a season aren't really much use when you have ambitions that stretch further than finishing in the top half. That kind of miss was all too frequent when Jermaine was in the red shirt. There was another blast from our past as Riise crashed a free-kick against the bar in typical fashion. This was a bit like the one he buried against the Mancs at Anfield only this one hit the underside of the bar and bounced out rather than in. That Jon Walters tool opened the scoring and Delap wrapped it up when Riise failed to pick him up properly at the back post (deja vu again) and Stoke ran out comfortable winners. Why are Fulham so shite away from home and yet they're a match for anyone at the Cottage? It's a weird one that, as it's been the case under their last three managers. Last time out they put six goals past QPR, but they were pretty toothless at Stoke. Hopefully they win their next home game, which is against Everton.

Speaking of QPR, they entertained Blackburn and their beleaguered boss Steve Kean on Saturday. Heidur Helguson put QPR in front with a cross that beat everyone and dropped into the far corner. Pretty sure they played some crappy music after it too. Knobs. Chris Samba equalised for Rovers with a towering header. I like Samba, he's far too good for Blackburn and I can't understand why Arsenal didn't take him as he's exactly what they've needed for some time. He's big, he's nasty, he dominates people and he's an aerial presence at both ends of the pitch. Samba and Hoilett will both be playing for bigger clubs sooner or later. I'm half tempted to lump them in with Wigan in my relegation prediction, but they might still sack Steve Kean so I'm not going to write them off completely yet.

Onto Sunday's games now, and first up were unbeaten Newcastle (just how long am I going to have to keep writing that, it's getting out of hand now) taking on Spurs at St James'. With one side just ahead of us and the other just behind, a draw was the best result for us and that's what we got after a pulsating game. Van Der Vaart gave Spurs the lead from the penalty spot after that dick Steven Taylor brought down Adebayor. Demba Ba equalised after brilliant play by Gutierrez, but substitute Defoe put Spurs back in front with a great strike. Fair play to Newcastle though, they didn't let their heads drop and you can see the sense of belief they have in themselves right now. It's like they are completely blind to how shit they actually are. Does Pardew have some kind of mind control over them? I watched 'Shallow Hal' on TV the other day, I reckon Pardew must have bumped into that 'self help guru' on one of his *ahem* 'scouting trips' to the USA a few years back. Those Geordie players look up front and they don't see Leon Best, they see Alan Shearer. They look to the right wing and they don't see the weird looking alien that flopped at Manchester United, they see Cristiano Ronaldo. They don't see Steven Taylor as the error prone, arrogant whopper the rest of us see, they see Bobby Moore in his pomp back there. Pardew has somehow got them believing they are much better than they should be, but surely reality will kick in sooner or later?

For now though they are riding the crest of a wave and Ameobi produced a brilliant finish to get them level. When he first burst onto the scene I thought Ameobi was going to become a really good player (I remember seeing him and Lua Lua destroying our reserves at Knowsley Road), but it's never happened for him for whatever reason. Whatever reason actually being that in reality he's just not very good. He was class as a youngster but he's never fulfilled the potential he had despite clearly having talent. On his day he's a handful, but he doesn't have enough of those days which is why he's being kept out of the side by Shear... I mean Leon Best. Defoe could have won it for Spurs and Collocini should have won it for Newcastle but it ended all square, and yes, Newcastle are STILL unbeaten. The day I have to acknowledge that Pardew is a good manager isn't here yet, but it mightn't be far away. Unless of course that guy from Shallow Hal shows up and reverses whatever he's done to that bunch of deadbeats.

It was the Black Country derby on Sunday and Wolves went into it on the back of four straight defeats. It's now five. Chris Brunt's first goal of the season put the Baggies in front after just eight minutes. It was end to end after that with chances for both sides, the best of which was wasted by Roger Johnson when he headed wide from close range. Shortly after, Odemwingie made the game safe for West Brom with a good finish. Wolves probably deserved at least a point, and I still think they're a decent side who'll finish around halfway up the table. Fletcher, Jarvis and Doyle should give them enough to turn things around, but they need to stop this rut they're in, and sharpish. As for West Brom, wasn't really impressed with them other than Shane Long who looks like one of the best signings of last summer.

Finally on Sunday, Arsenal played host to Sunderland in a game they really needed to win. They did, but only just. Where would they be without Van Persie though? He scored in the first minute, hit the post with another stunning effort and then he got the winner late on after Larsson had equalised for the Black Cats with a brilliant free-kick. The only knock on Van Persie was he let himself down by taking his shirt off after he scored. It's not cool, especially when you're wearing a vest that looks like it was bought from 'George at Asda'. He picked up a yellow card, and if he reaches five yellows he'll be suspended, and for what? So he could show off his old man vest. Absolutely stupid. Van Persie is brilliant though and he's too good for Arsenal now. Look at the team they had a few years ago and compare with the side that started this game. They are weaker in every position except goalkeeper. They could easily have lost this game but for Szczesny. The save he made from Cattermole was superb, he's the best keeper they've had in donkey's years, or since donkey's years if you like, as the last time they had a good keeper Tony Adam's was eee-awwing his way around Highbury. Szczesny might even prove to be better than David Seaman actually, as I always thought he was seriously over-rated and not just because I hated his 'tache and unnaturally deep voice.

I can't end this round up without referencing Neil Warnock's brown corduroy shirt that he was sporting on MOTD2. Did he lose a bet? That might just be the worst item of clothing I've ever seen anyone other than Barry Venison wear on TV. Seems his fashion sense is as nasty as his post-match demeanour. And guess what, no Motty this week! Bonus.

LIVERPOOL 1 NORWICH CITY 1

Competition - Premier League
Date - Sat 22 Oct 2011
Venue - Anfield
Scorer(s) – Craig Bellamy
Half Time - 1-0
Star Man – Luis Suarez

Team: Reina; Johnson, Carragher, Skrtel, Enrique: Downing (Carroll), Gerrard, Adam, Bellamy (Henderson); Kuyt, Suarez:

Is there a more wasteful team in the Premier League right now than Liverpool? Poor finishing cost us two points against Sunderland, three at Stoke, another two against Manchester United and two more here against Norwich. We should have won every one of those games based on the ratio of chances created compared to our opponents.

The only points we've dropped that can't be blamed on missed chances was the drubbing we suffered at Spurs. We're playing pretty well overall, but we aren't finishing off the good work and we're leaving points on the field far too often. Suarez is the biggest culprit, but he's by no means the only one. Carroll and Downing both squandered excellent opportunities against Norwich, Henderson missed chances against Stoke and Manchester United, Skrtel and Kuyt also didn't put chances away in that game with the Mancs… I could go on but I won't. Basically it's been the same story every time we've dropped points. Some misses were obviously worse than others, whilst we've also hit the woodwork more often than any other side. It's part bad finishing and part bad luck. Someone is going to get a severe beating from us soon, but that won't bring back the points we've already thrown away unfortunately.

This was just incredibly frustrating. Actually no, it was more infuriating than frustrating. We started brilliantly, played some wonderful football early on and created chance after chance. It was ridiculous that we had to wait so long to eventually score, more or less with the last kick of the first half. Suarez, Kuyt and Bellamy in particular were just cutting through the Norwich backline with some incisive football, but the end product just wasn't there. Glen Johnson was back in the side and he got forward well before the break before disappearing in the second half.

The chances came regularly early on. Skrtel hit the bar with a good header from an Adam corner, but most of the chances fell to Suarez. The only weakness in his game is that he just isn't clinical enough and fails to convert a high percentage of the chances that come his way, and this game was a perfect illustration of that. He makes a lot of those chances himself through his sheer brilliance and persistence and for that reason it's difficult to be critical of him. The turn he produced to leave two defenders completely bamboozled was genius. The shot he then dragged wide was anything but. You simply have to score there.

He was unfortunate with another effort that was pushed onto the post by impressive City keeper John Ruddy. That came at the end of an electrifying move that started with Adam's stunning ball out to Bellamy on the left. Bellamy escaped the full back and cut the ball back to Suarez, and I can't fault his finish as he did everything right. Just a great save by Ruddy. That said, Downing's follow up effort was horrific, he needs to be putting that in the back of the net.

Suarez had another chance when Johnson's first time pass found him in the box. He let the ball roll across his body but then dragged his shot across the face of goal. Not an easy chance but he'll feel he should have hit the target. Then he should have done better with a header from a nice Downing cross but he didn't get any power on it. Another chance went begging when Suarez and Bellamy caused confusion in the Norwich rearguard, and Suarez did well to win the ball and drill it across the face of goal but Kuyt hadn't anticipated it and nothing came of it.

The goal eventually came just on the stroke of half time. Suarez managed to get in behind the Norwich defence and appeared to have been held back, but Bellamy had ran onto the loose ball and advanced into the box to just about find the net at the Kop end. Not a convincing finish, it went on off the boot of a covering defender, but no-one cared as we'd finally got our noses in front and Bellamy had his second goal in as many starts since his return to the club. Downing's place is surely under threat now, as Bellamy's understanding with Enrique is much better than Downing's at the moment in time.

That goal should have given us the platform to go and finish the game off in the second half, but as we've done so many times already this season we ended up making hard work of things due to our inability to put the ball in the net. Even some of the games we've won have been closer than they should have been because of our inability to convert a decent percentage of our chances.

Had we put away one of the early chances we created in the second half this would have ended up a comfortable win. We didn't, but there was an element of misfortune involved and we really aren't having any luck at the moment. Suarez produced another breathtaking piece of skill to bring the ball down and nutmeg a defender, but he had no time to set himself as another defender was coming in to challenge. He tried to toe poke it into the far corner but the defender got a touch on it and it hit the post. Can't blame Suarez for that, he was desperately unlucky but it's typical of our season really.

Gerrard then went surging through after a one-two with Suarez but his left foot shot was weak and straight at Ruddy. We were getting into some very promising positions but we just weren't taking advantage of them. Bellamy tried to pick out Kuyt with a left wing cross but a defender cleared. He tried again, and this time Downing arrived at the far post and did very well to turn the ball back into the six yard but neither Kuyt nor

Suarez were in position to capitalise on it.

Norwich were under the cosh but they kept trying to play their football. They knocked it about when they could and had a real pace and purpose to everything they did. They are an extremely well coached team and based on what I've seen so far I don't see any danger of them being relegated. I was very impressed with them, even in the first half when they were getting battered they stuck to their gameplan and kept their shape. They'd had a few half decent attacks without looking overly dangerous, but they certainly looked like they had a goal in them. It wasn't until they sent on Grant Holt that they really offered any serious threat though. Morrison had done his best up there on his own, but he needed help and when Holt came on that the Canaries looked a much more potent threat.

At this point it's worth mentioning that aside from our inability to convert chances, the other big problem we've had is making silly errors at the other end. That reared it's ugly head once again, this time Pepe Reina was the culprit. Pilkington's cross was a cracker, and Reina was never getting anywhere near that as it swung away from goal. He shouldn't have come for it, and by coming out like that all Holt had to do was get his head on it and it was a goal. Credit to the striker, he attacked the ball and Carragher and Johnson were powerless to stop him. Pepe should have stayed put though. Maybe he still wouldn't have saved it, but at least he'd have had a chance. We need to cut out these errors, but that's not our biggest issue. You'll always have mistakes, it's impossible to play the perfect game. With better finishing, the mistakes aren't costly. I also think there's an element of bad luck involved here too, we seem to be getting punished for every error at the moment.

Norwich's tails were up now though and they could see that Holt was giving us problems with his physical presence. He almost gave his side the lead from another superb Pilkington cross, but this time Pepe had stayed put and was in position to make a smart save. We quickly regrouped and regained control of the game, but we just couldn't put the ball into the net. Kenny replaced Bellamy with Henderson, a move I didn't understand and one that I think weakened the side. Why is Henderson being brought on ahead of the striker we paid £35m for? It doesn't reflect well on Andy Carroll at all. And then when Carroll was brought on, Kenny took off the player who had been signed to provide the ammunition for him!

Downing can have no complaints about being hooked, he didn't do enough again and continues to frustrate. He wasn't awful and he still managed to put in three or four very good crosses, but he simply has to do more. He looks a little short of confidence to me and isn't being assertive enough, but that said I'd have taken off Kuyt and told Downing to hug the touchline and bombard Norwich with crosses aimed towards Carroll. Kuyt played well in the first half, but was very poor in the second. Nothing typified that more than a break we had late on when we had three against three. Suarez went to Dirk's left, and Carroll was all alone on the right edge of the box as two defenders converged on the Dutchman. All he had to do was roll it across to him but instead he tried to shoot and the ball looped up into the air. Carroll managed to nod it to Suarez but he put the ball wide. The linesman flagged anyway so it wouldn't have counted, but still, come on Luis put it in the fucking net.

Carroll hasn't had particularly good service for much of his time here, but Gerrard whipped in a great ball that should have been meat and drink to the big fella. He seemed to get a little bit ahead of it though and as a result was unable to get his header on target. He has to score in that situation, and when that didn't go in I knew we were done. There was time for one more opportunity when another great Gerrard cross found Suarez, and although he did everything right and produced a great volley, Ruddy was on hand to make another fine save.

It's difficult to take, and it's incredibly frustrating. I was really pissed off after the game, not at the performance but just at the wastefulness we keep showing. I'm enjoying how we're playing and I certainly think we're going in the right direction, I just wish we could put the fucking ball in the net. Is it something we will be able to correct with the group of players we have, or do we need to bring in an out and out goalscorer? That player isn't Luis Suarez, it needs to be Andy Carroll and if it isn't then we're going to have to get someone else in. We could quite easily score six next time out, but the concern for me is that the game after we'd end up wasting a load more chances and drawing a blank. Luck is playing a part too, and if that turns then results like this won't happen. It's incredibly frustrating, but it's not the time to panic. The time to panic is when we stop creating chances and stop playing our football.

Still, it's impossible not to look at the points we've dropped at home already, as you just can't do that if you want to be competitive. You have to win at home and you have to beat the teams you're supposed to beat. We've got Chelsea and City coming up soon and we needed to take the three points here to keep pace with the top four as it's not inconceivable that we get nothing from those two games. Dropping points at home to Norwich means you have to make them up somewhere else, against a side that maybe you wouldn't expect to beat. I wouldn't be surprised if we beat City at Anfield or Chelsea at the Bridge, but you certainly can't bank on it and we aren't going to beat anyone unless we start putting away our chances.

Star man was Suarez, despite the fact he failed to convert any of the numerous chances that came his way. He made most of them himself anyway, and was a constant menace to the Norwich defence. He also got nothing at all from the referee, and I don't think that is unrelated to the comments made by Ferguson last week. Again, much like last week I didn't see Suarez doing anything wrong and he wasn't 'diving' at all, but Peter Walton just didn't want to give him any decisions.

Premier League Round Up (22-23 October 2011)

I was walking around London in the early hours of Monday morning with five mates, it had been a great day at Wembley watching the NFL and now we were looking for a taxi to take us back to our hotel. Not just any taxi though, we needed a 'David De Gea', one that would let six in. Boom!!

I'll get to City's GBH on their neighbours all in good time, but let's kick things off with the other unbeaten side in the league. Newcastle's fixture list hasn't exactly been challenging so far, and they had another easy looking fixture as they played host to struggling Wigan. They won, but they didn't play well. You don't need to play well to beat Wigan though, they just aren't very good at either end of the pitch.

Newcastle's flesh coloured goalie kit is absolutely brutal. When you see Tim Krul running to his goal at the start it looks like there's a streaker on the field. Not a Geordie streaker, obviously, they'd need to incorporate man-tits and several tattooed spare tires into the kit to pull that look off. Cabaye got the only goal of this game and he's been one of the most impressive players in the league up to now. Wigan were unlucky on the day, they created the better chances but they didn't put any of them away. Pardew's post match interview made my skin crawl. He's just a creepy, slimy bastard isn't he? A mate of mine reckons if you shook hands with him he'd leave one of those slimy snail trails on your hand. He is a bad wrong 'un, but fairs fair, he's doing well there at the moment. Realistically though, it's not going to last though is it? Is it???? It better not.

The Midlands derby at Villa Park was a feisty affair but it was Roy Hodgson's West Brom who came out on top after a large helping hand from referee Phil Dowd who sent off Chris Herd. Mind you, Villa can't complain too much as Alan Hutton should have been off earlier for a wild, out of control lunge on Shane Long. Long came back on and then got the better of him with a shoulder charge, so Hutton responded by hacking him down again and belatedly went into the refs notebook. He's shite that Hutton, and he's a clogger. Scottish Tony Hibbert.

Villa went in front from the spot after Agbonlahor had done well to capitalise on hesitation between defender and goalkeeper. Albion were then awarded a ridiculous penalty and it was a double whammy for Villa as Herd was red carded for the incident. I've watched it about ten times now, and there was no foul from Herd and there was certainly no stamp either. I said after the derby at Goodison that the Rodwell sending off might be the worst red card decision we'll see all season. Well it wasn't, this one was much worse. Can't blame Dowd though, he was only acting on the advice of a linesman who claimed to have seen it clearly. Difficult to pin that on the ref in fairness, as what's he supposed to do? Brunt missed the pen, but Villa's goose was cooked and West Brom went on to beat the ten men through goals by Olsson (who up until the red card had been picked up at set pieces by Herd) and Scharner.

Next up was Wolves taking on Swansea at Molyneux. Based on the highlights it looked pretty even to me with chances for both teams. Swansea put theirs away though and went into a 2-0 lead. Highlights can sometimes be deceiving and by all accounts Wolves were awful. There was a hilarious shot of some girl crying her eyes out. She was wearing a Koala Bear on her head, so I'm not sure I should be laughing at her as maybe she's got more problems than Wolves being a bit poo? Mick McCarthy made a double substitution, taking off both his wingers much to the displeasure of a crowd now in open revolt and baying for his blood. They booed and chanted *"you don't know what you're doing"*. Mick turned around and said *"Ah fuck off!!"* and you know what, seems he did know what he was doing as they came back to draw 2-2. The weird thing was that some fans didn't appear to even celebrate the equaliser, one of them was stood there shaking his head and others weren't even bothering to applaud let alone cheer. Strange times at Wolves, and a far cry from the opening two games when they took maximum points. Still think they'll be ok though, they've got good wide players and strikers, and eventually they'll break out of this slump. McCarthy is ace I reckon, he's a bit of a tool but he's dead funny. His post match interview was hilarious: *"Do you know me?? Have you ever known me to give up hope? Do you know me at all?"* Hahaha he loves playing up to the 'straight talking, no nonsense Yorkshireman' image doesnt he? I like him though.

Hapless Bolton were at home to Sunderland. On paper it was a good chance for them to halt a run of six straight home defeats but they couldn't do it. Here's the thing though, the Gog played and did fuck all. Have I been had? Could it be that he's actually not very good at all? I don't know what to believe anymore, this is like when I found out that Star Wars didn't really happen *"A long time ago in a galaxy far, far away"*. Say it ain't so somebody.

Sunderland were good value for their win. Sessegnon opened the scoring (I'm really warming to him, he's a good player) and Bendtner wrapped it up with a nice finish as the Mackems hit Bolton on the break. The Trotters look doomed, they're terrible at the moment, especially at the back. I've already gone out on a limb and said Wigan are going down, and now I'm doing the same for Bolton. They're actually worse than Wigan, if they don't improve they'll finish bottom. They're a complete mess. Owen Coyle's reputation is taking a real hit at the moment, 12 months ago he was being touted for big things but he's looking like a flash in the pan now. And Gary Cahill's transfer value is plummeting faster than the X Factor's viewing figures.

Onto Sunday now. Everton made the trip to Craven Cottage for a grudge match with Fulham. These two teams really dislike eachother, it's one of those weird irrational rivalries that have nothing to do with long standing history or location. I'm not even sure what sparked it off, but from what I remember they had a few feisty encounters and Luis Boa Morte biting David Weir's ankle during a mass skirmish definitely escalated the bad feeling to a new level, especially when the Fulham player had to go for a tetanus jab afterwards in case he caught something off that rabid old dog.

Drenthe opened the scoring with a great shot from distance and then Rodwell missed an easy header, which was surely down to the lingering sense of injustice felt from Martin Atkinson's decision to send him off in the derby. SuperDan hit the post before Bryan Ruiz equalised with a brilliant chip. Have to say that man has the most stunning locks the Premier League has seen since Sebastian Leto departed these fine shores. It really is a truly magnificent mane, the shine and bounce is breathtaking. I'd love to touch Bryan Ruiz's hair. In a completely non-sexual way of course, I'm a happily married man. That hair though, it's beautiful. He's like a walking shampoo commercial. It therefore saddens me that I've had to add him to the twat list due to him having 'Bryan' on the back of his shirt. What the fuck are the Premier League doing allowing that? Bryan??? Really?? Fuck off. May as well have 'Wanker' on the back of your shirt as that's what people are thinking when they see 'Bryan' on there. Great hair or not, that shit isn't acceptable. Anyway, Fulham are good at home and you'd have expected them to go on and win once they got level. They should have too when Zamora went round Howard in the last minute but then blazed over the empty net. Terrible that, and Everton made them pay with two goals in stoppage time. One of them was scored by Rodwell which begs the question; how many goals could he have had in the last couple of games ifithadnabinfermartinatkinson?

Arsenal were unconvincing again, but once more Van Persie bailed them out as they just about overcame Stoke at the Emirates. Dwayne Dibley opened the scoring for the Gunners, but Crouchy levelled things with a tap in. Arsenal were going nowhere until they brought Van Persie on, but even then they had Begovic to thank for two errors that allowed Van Persie to claim two more goals. Begovic is one of those twats who always has the game of his life against Liverpool and is always shite against any of our rivals. The 'new Mark Schwarzer' if you like.

The other North London club were also in action on Sunday, and it was a narrow win for them too. Van Der Vaart got both of their goals, the first a cool finish after great play by Kyle Walker. Blackburn equalised with a smooth finish by Formica (like shooting fish in a barrel), but Van Der Vaart's second was just reaking with awesomeness. Great finish, great player. I don't like him though, something about him rubs me up the wrong way. It might be the over the top celebration he did after scoring at Anfield last season, although I think I had beef with him even before that. I don't even remember why, might just be that he comes across like a bit of an arrogant cock.

I'm almost starting to feel sorry for Steve Kean now. Those fans who stayed behind protesting about him seemed like bad knobheads. I've got no problem with fans wanting rid of their manager, or even protesting about it, but those Blackburn fans just looked like gobshites who wanted to be on the telly. Especially the whopper who'd gone to the trouble of making a giant P45. Ideal scenario for me now is they sack Kean and then still finish bottom. He's handling himself with a fair bit of dignity, and his side are probably playing as well as can be expected given the lack of talent there. The first few weeks of the season they looked hopeless, but they're pretty competitive at the moment and certainly better than the likes of Bolton and Wigan and arguably a few other sides too. I'm on the verge of starting to root for Steve Kean now, which I accept makes me a fickle fucker but I don't care.

Chelsea made the short trip to Loftus Road to take on QPR. They got off to a bad start when David Luiz conceded an early pen. Great footballer, shite defender. He's Franck Leboeuf in a curly wig. It got worse for Chewwwwwlsea when Bosingwa was red carded for pulling down SWP. Mongo was livid, and is there a funnier sight in football than seeing his stupid, mouth wide open gape when a decision has gone against them? It got better, as Drogba then saw red for a two footed tackle. A clear sending off, but Mongo tried to admonish the referee by saying *"it was his first one"*. Hahahaha fucking dickhead. Still, I'm impressed he can actually count that high. Not like Drogba that though, he may be a diving, over dramatic, hysterical, crying cheating fuck, but he's.... erm... can someone help me out here?

It says a lot about QPR that despite playing against nine men for such a long time, they only just managed to hang on. Credit to Chelsea, being down to nine men puts you in an almost impossible position, but it looked like they were the better side and they certainly had chances to equalise. I thought they should have had two penalties and Anelka should have scored at least once, probably twice. Luiz went close with an overhead kick, but it hit Lampard and bounced over the bar. Irony of ironies there, as that's a man who has built a career on deflected goals.

Motson was the commentator, and whilst if I had my way I'd ban him from commentating on any game of football ever again, I'd be willing to compromise on that and settle for him never being allowed to cover any games in which there are Portuguese players or managers involved. The over pronunciation of names get right on my tits. Meirelessshhhhhh and Villasshhhh Boasshhhhh. The twat sounds like a pissed up Dutchman with a speech impediment. Fuck off Motson.

Speaking of Villasshhhh Boasshhhhh though, as a connoisseur of fine hair I have to say; for christ's sake, can someone please buy that man a pot of Bryll Cream or hair gel, as his Roy Hodgson style fluffy bouffant is seriously offending my sensibilities. He's the antithesis of Bryan Ruiz.

After the game John Terry issued a statement denying making a racist slur against Anton Ferdinand after lip readers adjudged him to have shouted something after an altercation between the pair. Now John Terry may be a repugnant, ugly, vile, huge foreheaded chav gobshite who is completely lacking in any kind of moral fibre and human decency, but.... no sorry, dunno where I was going with this one either. There's no end of insults you can hurl at Anton Ferdinand without having to stoop as low as racism. The whole thing seems to have blown up on the internet after a clip was posted on youtube by someone in the Manchester area with the handle 'Patrice_3_utd_4ev(r)a'.... What, too soon?

Speaking of everyone's least favourite boy who cried wolf, it wasn't a good day for Patrice and his United chums, as they were completely humiliated by their neighbours and main title rivals. I didn't get to watch this game live as I was at Wembley, but oh how we all laughed as the texts kept pouring in. Before all the fireworks started - the on pitch ones I mean, not the ones that Super Mario set fire to his house with the other night (he says his mate did it, yeah right, just like Shelvey's 'mate' posted the picture of 'little Jonjo' on twitter), I got a couple of texts telling me about a shocking dive by Ashley Young and how the sky commentators completely glossed over it. It wasn't just Sky. I watched it on MOTD2 and it was greeted with silence by the BBC commentator too. Milner didn't touch him, he wasn't even close to touching him and the replays showed it as clear as day. So how come the commentator said fuck all about what was a case of blatant cheating? Not exaggerating contact, or playing for a free-kick, just an out and out dive. I want to know why it was ignored, and I want to know why no-one has the balls to confront Ferguson with it after his unwarranted attack on Suarez last week. Shithouses.

Anyway, Balotelli gave City the lead with a finish that was just brilliant in it's simplicity. Great technique and great confidence in himself to do that. His celebration was hilarious too, didn't move from the spot and just lifted his shirt up to reveal *"Why always me?"* Erm, maybe it's always you because you're a mad bastard who is always pulling crazy stunts? Please don't ever change though because you're fucking ace. What was particularly impressive about this celebration was the attention to detail that had gone into its planning. None of this 'marker pen on a plain white t-shirt' crap for Mario. No sir, this was official Premier League lettering on what looked like an 'under armour' shirt and my guess would be he even had it printed in the club shop. Top work. I'm sure you'll all know by now my feelings on players taking their shirts off but in case you haven't been paying attention, I'd give them a straight red, never mind a yellow. This is different though, I've got no problem with players showing off something that's written on a t-shirt underneath, in fact I'd actively encourage it as long as it's something original. There's a world of difference between that and some knobhead wanting to show off his six pack. Mario got booked for his 'celebration' and for me that's just a stupid rule. It did raise the question of whether he'd do it again if he bagged another goal. When the text arrived saying he'd scored a second, I was half expecting it to be quickly followed by 'and he's got a second yellow for showing his t-shirt again'. Thankfully he showed some restraint, unlike the following morning when he was reportedly driving around Manchester with the roof down on his convertible, high fiving City fans.

By the time he'd scored his second, United were down to ten men after Johnny Evans had been sent off for a foul on the edge of the box. It could have been even worse for United as City then should have had a pen when Anderson barged into Richards. Clattenberg daren't give that though, he knew he'd already be in 'Fergie's Doghouse' after the red card. Aguero added a third before Mancini decided to give him and Balotelli a rest as United fans left in their droves. *"We're Man United, we'll leave when we want"*. Fletcher pulled one back and City wasted several good chances to increase their lead until Dzeko eventually made it 4-1 with a minute to go. They weren't done there though, as the brilliant Silva made it five and Dzeko wrapped it up with his second. He should have had four as he missed two great chances. Imagine how it must have felt to be a City fan in that away end? They've had to endure a lot of shit down the years, so I can't begrudge them a day like this. Seeing United getting bummed like that must have been hilarious for the whole country. They've had this coming all season though, they give up loads of chances to the opposition in virtually every game but always seem to get away with it, the jammy bastards. Not this time. They're lucky it was only six as it should have been ten. Pity it wasn't.

The only sour note for me was I'd been looking forward to giving Rio Ferdinand shit when he took the field at Wembley as an 'honourary captain' for the Tampa Bay Buccaneers against my Chicago Bears. Having seen the score at Old Trafford I suspected he wouldn't show up and it was no surprise when he didn't. He probably wishes he'd stayed away from Old Trafford too, and I expect a lot of United fans agree, the washed up loser.

STOKE CITY 1 LIVERPOOL 2

Competition - Carling Cup
Date - Wed 26 Oct 2011
Venue - The Britannia Stadium
Scorer(s) – Luis Suarez (2)
Half Time - 1-0
Star Man – Luis Suarez

Team: Reina; Kelly, Carragher (Skrtel), Coates, Agger; Henderson, Spearing, Lucas, Maxi (Bellamy); Suarez (Kuyt), Carroll:

Have that you pitch shrinking, time wasting, ball wiping, alehouse bastards. Stoke had stolen a win from us once this season and at half time it looked like they might do it again. We battered them, but chance after chance went begging and as soon as we made an error at the other end it was punished with a goal. Story of our season so far that.

Then Luis Suarez took matters into his own hands and ensured we got what our impressive performance deserved. Suarez has been guiltier than anybody when it comes to the wastefulness we've shown in front of goal this season, and he'd had several chances in the first half of this game too. It's difficult to hold it against them though, as he's just so fucking ace and he never stops trying. Eventually he was always going to get his reward, and there have surely been few more deserving matchwinners than Luis Suarez in this game, as he just refused to accept defeat and put the team on his back and carried them home.

Stoke can fuck off. They deserved NOTHING from this game, and something needs to be done about the amount of playing time that is lost every time they get a fucking throw in. Absolutely ridiculous it is. Throw-in is awarded, their defenders slowly make their way into the box, Delap strolls over and then spends a good 30 seconds wiping the ball with a towel and deciding where he's going to throw it. And this happens over and over. If I wanted to spend half an hour watching a big ugly grock towelling his balls, I'd go the gym. Rory Delap simply can't play football, he only gets a game because of his freakish throw ins, the shit bastard.

We were outstanding in the first half. Chance after chance was created, but we just couldn't put the ball in the net. It's been a problem all season, but as I wrote after the Norwich game, part of it is down to bad luck. Little breaks not going our way, like when Carroll's shot was parried by the keeper but just didn't fall right for Suarez and he couldn't direct his follow up effort on target. When things are going well, that falls right into the path of Suarez and he scores. It's also partly down to bad finishing of course. Carroll should have done better with a close range chance on his right foot, but his shot was weak and Sorensen saved.

Suarez also should have done better when he burst through the inside right channel just before half time. He was fouled but stayed on his feet and then dragged his shot wide. If he'd looked up Carroll had found acres of space in the centre and would have had a tap in. Some of the football we played was brilliant though, not least the move that ended with Lucas getting in behind and playing a perfect ball across to Suarez who's shot was magnificently kept out by Sorensen. It looked a certain goal, but I'm not sure what Suarez could have done differently. The keeper was on him as soon as the ball arrived and again, this was more bad luck than bad finishing. More specifically, it was great goalkeeping.

Stoke had not really done much. There were a few hairy moments from set pieces, including a disallowed goal when Walters flicked in a Delap throw in. I don't know what happened but I do know I heard the whistle before Walters even got his head on the ball. Pulis wasn't happy, but tough shit. He was also upset that Carragher wasn't given a red card for a lunge on Etherington after Spearing had played him into trouble with slack pass. Could have gone either way that one, I'd describe it as a bit worse than a yellow but not quite bad enough for a red. Pulis should just be thankful for the decisions that went their way in the league game and shut the fuck up, the tramp.

Stoke were absolutely shocking. Their entire gameplan was about getting the ball into the channels and trying to win throw ins. I accept they have to play to their strengths, and I don't care if they want to play it long or base their whole style around getting set pieces. It's the other shit they do that I don't like. The time it takes them to get the ball in and the way they make sure the game doesn't flow by stopping it as much as possible.

Whenever we were building up any kind of momentum, they'd win a set piece and take about two minutes to get the ball back in play. It's so difficult to get into a rhythm against them as they do everything they can to ensure the game doesn't flow and is constantly stopping and starting. And then there's the constant grabbing and holding they do when defending corners. It was happening all night and despite the ref constantly talking to them about it prior to ball being played in, they carried on doing it and he let it go. Having said that, Coates got away with the most blatant one of the game late on when he grabbed Crouch by the arm and hauled him down. The ref saw it, as did all of us behind that goal. He didn't give it though, and whilst he got that wrong at least he was consistent as Woodgate, Huth and Shawcross had been doing that all night.

It must be incredibly frustrating to have to play against them but we remained patient, kept playing our football and this time we were eventually rewarded. I'm made up with how we played, I thought we were terrific and on another night we'd have been out of sight by half time. We don't make it easy for ourselves though do we? Aside from the missed chances, we seem to be throwing in one defensive error every game and whenever we do it costs us a goal. Coates clearly should have put the ball into the stands instead of letting it bounce and allowing Walters to dispossess him. That being said, most of the time that leads to nothing. At the moment though, any time we do something like the ball ends up in our net. Walters picked out Jones and his header gave Reina no chance. Right before half time too, a real hammer blow.

Presumably Kenny's teamtalk will have been along the lines of *"Don't let your heads drop, keep doing what you're doing and you will win this game"*. We had to do it without Carragher though, who had picked up a calf injury and didn't come back out after the break. Skrtel came on to replace him and I thought he was fantastic, I was really impressed with him. Coates was decent too, he put his mistake behind him and was solid for the rest of the game aside from the grab on Crouch that he got away with. Everyone played well I thought. Agger was very good at left back, Spearing was superb in midfield (that one sloppy pass to Carra aside) and Henderson was purposeful throughout. The front two were the pick of the bunch for me. Carroll led the line excellently, his link up play was very good and he worked his arse off. He deserved a goal but if he keeps playing like this the goals will come. I hope he keeps his place for the weekend as for me he needs a run of games to get into a groove, and he's starting to show signs of settling in.

As for Suarez, what can you say about him? He's just fucking boss, he ran Stoke ragged and that first goal was out of this world. You look at some of the chances he's missed this season and then you see him produce something like that. If he could score the easy ones he'd be scoring 30+ a season easily. The nutmeg was class, the finish was just ridiculous. The ball started out about five yards outside the width of the posts and curled back in. The keeper had no chance, and that's the best goal I've seen a Liverpool player score in years. Probably since Fowler. Genius. We kept pressing looking for the win, and Kenny sent on Bellamy for Maxi. In the first half Maxi had been very influential, but he wasn't as effective in the second. Bellamy wasted no time getting involved, racing past a defender and laying the ball into Carroll's feet. The big man held it up and gave it back to him, but the shot hit the post. The latest in a long line of shots we've had against the woodwork this season. We kept going but it was looking like extra time was on the cards. Then Henderson spotted Suarez unmarked on the back post, and delivered an inch perfect ball onto the striker's head and we had the lead we deserved.

Stoke threw everything they had at us in the last few minutes, forcing numerous throw ins and corners, but we held firm and defended them very well. Admittedly we got away with a blatant pen, but as I said earlier Stoke do that kind of thing all the time. Besides, they were diving all over the place late on whenever there was a set piece so maybe the ref didn't want to give them the benefit of any doubt as he couldn't be sure? I don't care, we got shafted in the league game so if it's balanced out after this then fucking great. We were by far the better team and deserved the win (as I think Pulis actually admitted in fairness). For the most part this season we've played very good football and I'm happy with where we are headed. There's room for improvement, but if our finishing had been up to scratch we'd be riding high in the league despite the lack of clean sheets. There's not much wrong with us that a little change in fortune won't fix. Someone is going to get a mauling from us soon, hopefully it will be West Brom this weekend.

As for the League Cup, the draw is on Saturday and the chances are we'll get a tough draw as all the big guns are still in there. Ideally you'd want Cardiff or Palace, but as long as we get a home draw I'll happily take on anyone. I love how we've approached this competition, we've put out a strong team every round but Kenny has still been able to give the likes of Maxi, Spearing and Coates some much needed game time. Whether he'll continue to do that if we draw Chelsea, United or City remains to be seen, but those who have come in have played very well and the side certainly hasn't been weakened by it.

WEST BROMWICH ALBION 0 LIVERPOOL 2

Competition - Premier League
Date - Sat 29 Oct 2011
Venue - The Hawthorns
Scorer(s) – Charlie Adam (pen), Andy Carroll
Half Time - 0-2
Star Man – Luis Suarez

Team: Reina; Johnson, Skrtel, Agger, Enrique; Henderson, Lucas, Adam, Downing; Suarez (Bellamy), Carroll:

It's doubtful we'll have a more comfortable away game all season than this and it's a little worrying that we only beat them 2-0 given just how completely one sided this was. Still, the performance was good and encouragingly we've won this game at a canter despite having plenty of room for improvement.

Three points away from home is never anything to sneeze at. Once again we were guilty of missing easy chances but we did manage to put the ball in the net twice and we didn't make any of the costly errors at the other end that have plagued us so far this season. We were solid at the back, totally bossed the midfield and the front two linked up well throughout. I'd rather us be wasteful in front of goal than not be creating chances at all, but it is still frustrating to watch so many opportunities go begging.

One day it will all click into place and we'll batter somebody. I had a feeling it was going to happen today but it wasn't to be. Thankfully the Baggies were so inept that they couldn't capitalise on our profligacy. A goal in the last ten minutes would have really made things uncomfortable for us, and that's the concern for me. A game this one sided needs to be put to bed by half time, and Kenny would have been able to then use his subs to give players a rest. He couldn't do that because the game wasn't completely safe even though it was complete dominance from the reds from start to finish. It isn't solely a case of poor finishing, in fact a bigger problem in this game was not taking the right option when we were in promising situations, especially in the second half.

The first half was good. We started well and as early as the first minute it was obvious West Brom's defence was going have problems keeping us out. Enrique's superb pass found Suarez in acres of space behind their back four, but for once his touch was off and the ball ran to safety. It was encouraging to see how much space he'd found though. Their defence looked stretched any time we attacked. We had loads of time on the ball, and it was just too easy for us to pass our way down the field into their final third. There was no pressing of the ball, and they were defending too high up the pitch which is a recipe for disaster. You either defend deep and don't press, or press and defend a high line. You don't do what West Brom did, as it's suicide. Hodgson was very agitated and unhappy on the sideline all evening, but he only has himself to blame for how his team approached this game. Referee Lee Mason was the main focus for Hodgson's ire, but I'm not sure why as really he should have been thanking the useless baldy bastard for ensuring the game wasn't over by half time.

Mason missed three blatant Liverpool penalties in the first half. Thankfully his linesman spotted one of them and ensured it was given. Hodgson was livid about it, but tough shit. It was a penalty, no doubt about it. It was a very soft penalty, and on first viewing I wasn't even appealing for it. When you look at it again though, there's no doubt. Suarez didn't make a meal of it and he didn't even appeal for a penalty, but he was fouled by Thomas and the linesman got it spot on. It's worrying that Mason needed his assistant to give it though.

In the absence of Gerrard and Kuyt, and with Suarez having missed against Sunderland, Charlie Adam seemed the obvious choice to everybody to take the kick. Everybody except Andy Carroll that is, who did his best to get the ball from the midfielder. Adam would not be swayed though, and despite having to wait like what seemed an eternity he eventually stepped up and sent the keeper the wrong way. I like that Carroll had enough confidence to want to take it and if Adam hadn't been on the field I'd have no qualms about him stepping up as he's got a left foot like a cannon. He was excellent at Stoke the other night, and he played well again in this game. He was unlucky not to win a couple of penalties himself. First when he was shoved in the back by Olsson when attacking a corner, and then when his header from a superb Suarez cross was blatantly handled by a defender. I'm not one to usually claim penalties for 'ball to hand' incidents, but when the guy's hand is up in the air and blocks a goalbound effort like that, it's a penalty, intentional or not. Shocking decision by Mason as when you look at his positioning he had a perfect view of it. Despite these favours from Mason the home crowd and indeed Roy Hodgson were baying for the official's blood. Every little decision that went against them was greeted with mass derision in the stands and a temper tantrum on the bench. It was like watching a game at Goodison.

Hilariously, at one point Hodgson ripped off his coat in frustration and threw it on the floor only to then realise it was a actually a bit nippy and he was going to need it, so he sheepishly picked it back up and put it on again. Fantastic. This year's face rub.

Carroll eventually got the goal he deserved just before half time. West Brom had committed men forward for a set play and then gave the ball away cheaply. Lucas released Suarez who played a perfect first time ball into the path of Carroll in the centre. His first touch looked to be a little heavy and Foster was suddenly on him, but Carroll showed good footwork to stroke the ball past the keeper with the outside of his left peg and the ball nestled in the corner.

Coming at the time it did it was a real killer for West Brom and it should have given us the platform to run riot in the second half. It never happened though, and not because the home side came out with fire in their bellies and made it difficult for us, because they didn't. They were just as poor in the second half as they were in the first and we were in complete command of the game. We were just so damn wasteful though. Suarez ran amok but didn't have the finish to go with the brilliant approach play. He was unlucky to have a shot blocked after being teed up nicely by Carroll, and he put another couple of efforts off target when he should have done better.

Carroll had one fantastic effort beaten away by Foster and another less than fantastic effort go several yards wide when he should have played in Henderson. Enrique had a shot saved and Downing hit the post late on, and there were probably other chances I've forgotten about. In addition to those, there were so many opportunities that went begging due to a poor cross or the wrong decision being taken. Had we been more clinical West Brom were ripe for a proper bumming. We let them off the hook and on another day we could have been punished for it.

I'm moaning a lot more than I intended to, as believe it or not I'm actually very happy with things at the moment. We're playing very well, and we're nestled in nicely just one point behind 3rd placed Chelsea. It can't be easy for Kenny picking his team at the moment as there are so many players who will feel they deserve to be in the side. There was no Gerrard, Carragher or Kelly for this game and Bellamy and Kuyt were only on the bench. Skrtel and Agger looked solid despite not really being tested by a feeble West Brom attack sorely missing the talismanic Shane Long. Johnson and Enrique were both very good and supported the attack well. Lucas and Adam bossed the middle of the park and Henderson had another quietly effective game and seems to be growing in confidence. The front two did well, and the only negative for me was Downing who once again just didn't do enough. He could really have done with that late chance going in as he looks like he's in need of a confidence boost right now.

Star man is Suarez, who continues to dazzle despite the shite being thrown at him by commentators, media and opposing managers and players. He got booed by West Brom fans for being fouled. He didn't throw his arms up and demand a pen, he was just bundled over and then got up. Yet he was public enemy number one at the Hawthorns (ok, number two behind Mason). It's a joke. Those West Brom fans were in full on Evertonian mode. They booed his every touch and then screamed blue murder wanting him sent off for the crime of slipping over and accidentally colliding with one of their players (who he repeatedly apologised to and kept checking to see if he was ok), and there were several snide remarks by the commentators on ESPN. Then there was the disgraceful hatchet job in the Sunday Mirror today. Bang out of order that, and the club need to come out firing over the shit being flung in Suarez's direction. This all started after the manc game, with Evra's accusation and then Ferguson's snide jibes about 'diving all over the place'. Now every smalltime knobhead is jumping on the bandwagon.

Like Paul Scharner for example; *"It was a nice dive for the penalty and that got Liverpool well started for the game. He (Suarez) is very good at winning penalties. He's one of the best on the planet, in fact. I had a good view of it. If that's a penalty, then you will find 1,500 penalties are given in every match"* Bollocks. Absolute bollocks. LFC should report the knobhead for that. And the PFA need to get a grip of him too, as last time I checked Suarez was one of their members and that's a fucking outrageous comment given that it's clear for everyone to see it wasn't a dive, and it wasn't even making a meal of contact. I don't expect any statement from Gordon Taylor though, it can't be easy to talk when you're permanently tonguing Ferguson's balls.

As for Paul Scharner, he's a fucking tit. Trying too hard to be 'cool' with his stupid hairstyles. Newsflash soft lad, you're from Austria, it's impossible for you to be cool. I don't wish to offend any Austrians who may be reading this, but it's true. Germany has a reputation for being really uncool, but Austria is Germany's even more uncool little brother. Those multi coloured hairstyles just make you look like you're trying too hard, Paul. People laugh at you. You're like the pensioner in jeans and a baseball cap. Loser.

Premier League Round Up (29-31 October 2011)

And so the madness continues. There's been some crazy games between the big teams this season and Arsenal's visit to Stamford Bridge was as wild as any of them. Absolutely amazing stuff, not to mention funny as fuck. The defending from both teams was abysmal, but it made for a great spectacle. We've all made jokes at Arsenal's expense, usually about a lack of bottle, but credit where it's due, they showed great character in this game to come from behind twice and then go on and win it after they'd been pegged back late on.

Walcott was tremendous, he tormented Ashley Cole throughout and put numerous chances on numerous plates for wasteful team-mates. From one delicious cross Gervinho's finish was as shocking as his hairdo, and the usually clinical Van Persie also wasted a great chance from another Walcott centre early on. There were more chances in the opening ten minutes of this than you see some sides create in ten games (yes Stoke, I'm talking about you, you dull, alehouse bastards). Chelsea went in front when Lampard headed in a cross by Mata. Sturridge then missed a sitter and Arsenal made him pay when Ramsay and Gervinho combined to give Van Persie a tap in. Sturridge did put the ball in the net shortly after, but it was disallowed for offside. The defending from both teams was as bad as I think I've ever seen from two 'top four' sides. You'll get days when one team has a mare, like Arsenal at Old Trafford or United last week against City, but rarely do you see two good sides so utterly inept at the back. Warms the cockles of the heart doesn't it?

I don't see it as just an off day either, Arsenal and Chelsea are just shit at the back right now. They're both terrific going forward though, and this was a fantastic game. 'Mongo' put Chelsea 2-1 in front, prompting the commentator to yell *"John Terry, who else"*. Who else? Erm, how about Lampard, Sturridge, Ramires, Drogba, Mata, Torres.... ok not Torres, but you get the picture. It's not like Terry is the first player you'd think of when you hear Chelsea have scored a goal. Oh right, I get it, he means because of all the publicity he's had this week, and how 'big brave JT' puts all that behind him and doesn't let any of that negative press affect his game. Righto.

We had the same shite when he was exposed for knocking off Wayne Bridge's tart. *"Oh look how he doesn't let any of that affect him, he's so brave blah blah blah"* Yeah, he's a real fucking hero isn't he. A national treasure. We should all be proud of him according to his manager. Why, just because some idiots chose him to lead a country. So tell me Mr Villas Boas, should Austria be proud of Adolf Hitler? Local boy made good and all that. Proud of John Terry??? He's a despicable turd who happens to be quite good at football. When he's no longer able to play football to a high level, he'll just be a despicable turd. What exactly is it we should be proud of again? The mocking of American tourists after 911? The spitting at opposing players (Carlos Tevez)? The snide stamps on smaller opponents when the ref's back is turned (Luis Garcia)? Touting out his box at Wembley? Shagging his mates girlfiend? Threatening to leave Chelsea for Man City because a measley £100k a week isn't enough to get by on these days? Trying to lead a mutiny in the England World Cup squad because he was no longer captain?

There's probably countless other things I've forgotten about too, even leaving aside this whole Anton Ferdinand business (can't hang him for that until the full story comes out). Suffice to say, on a list of Englishmen to be proud of, John Terry ranks near the bottom, sandwiched in between Peter Sutcliffe and Simon Cowell. That Villas Boas is a proper tit though. Amazing that there are people saying the same kind of stuff about him that they did about Mourinho... *"he's got great hair, he's so suave, he's the housewives favourite etc"* He's Portuguese, he manages Chelsea, he's quite young in managerial terms, he wears a fancy suit and he's a bad knobhead. There endeth the Mourinho comparisons. Great hair???? Ha! Said it before and I'll say it again, he's got Roy Hodgson hair. If he had great hair, I'd have pointed it out ahead of everybody, let's be honest here, that kind of thing doesn't get past me very easily does it? He hasn't though, he's got crap hair. And he's a fucking bore. Along with the Hodge and Moyes, he's probably the least charismatic manager in the league. He's no Mourinho and he's no Mancini either for that matter. Mate of mine said on Saturday that Villas Boas is what would happen if Arnold Rimmer tried to be Pep Guardiola. I think that's a little unfair on Arnold Rimmer, but I see where he's coming from. Joachim Loew was in the stands for this one, he's more suave than Villas Boas and he eats his own bogeys in the dugout and has massive sweat rings under his arms. Got much better hair too.

Anyway, back to the game. The second half was even more open than the first. Arsenal had two great chances in the first minute after the break, and it wasn't long before they'd equalised. Song played in Santos and he finished nicely. Then came the most contentious moment of the game when Szczesny fouled Cole on the edge of the box. Andre Marriner gave a yellow, the crowd wanted a red. Could have gone either way, I'd say he got it right largely based on the fact that Ashley Cole is a massive twat. Arsenal then took the lead in bizarre fashion as Walcott fell over when surrounded by four Chelsea defenders, yet somehow managed to get up and take the ball through all of them and run through and score. Great goal from Walcott, embarrassing defending from Mongo & co. Dead funny though.

Having worked so hard to get in front, Arsenal couldn't hang on and Mata equalised with a deflected shot from distance. The stage now seemed set for Chelsea to go on and win it, but out of nothing Arsenal were back in front in side-splittingly funny circumstances. Malouda's pass intended for Terry was truly shocking and sent Van Persie clear. The funny part was Mongo inexplicably just falling over, which on first viewing looked like he slipped. I've watched it over and over now, mainly because it was so funny, but the more I watched it the more I couldn't see any reason for him to go down. His foot didn't get caught in the turf, he didn't appear to slip or lose his footing, it just looks like he threw himself to the floor as he knew he wasn't getting there. Big, brave JT taking the shithouse way out? Surely not. Chelsea threw everything forward trying to draw level but they were caught on the counter attack as Van Persie completed his hat-trick with a typical finish. Van Persie is up there with Suarez and Silva as the best player in the league at the moment and Arsenal have put their bad start behind them to get right back into contention for a top four spot. They've not looked good up to now and some of the wins have been unconvincing, but Van Persie has put them on his back and carried them. Great player, but will they be able to keep hold of him? Hopefully not from our point of view.

Norwich / Blackburn was a belter as well. It's typical of our season that a keeper who had a worldy against us last week turns into Krusty the Clown the next week. John Ruddy was inspired at Anfield a week ago, but he was all over the place as Blackburn beat him three times. He had no chance with the first goal, a cracker from my boy Junior Hoilett, but the second from the Yak was an inexcusable piece of goalkeeping. In between those two strikes, Morrison had scored a cracker for the home side and the more I see of Norwich the more I like him. I had him pegged as a bit of a yard dog at first (the skinhead and number five on his back gives off a Matt Elliot kind of 'defender sent up front' vibe), but he's not, he's half decent. Pilkington is a decent player too, looks to have two good feet and he's got great delivery from out wide. I still can't forgive him for that sitter he missed at Old Trafford though. Knob. Samba made it 3-1 to Blackburn and Steve Kean looked like he was on his way to a much needed three points. Then a flukey deflected goal gave Norwich hope and in stoppage time they were given a ridiculous penalty which was converted by Holt to make it 3-3. Harsh on Rovers that, but at least Kean's Ewood fanclub will be happy.

Moving on, and after their huge win at Old Trafford last week there was always the danger City might suffer a bit of a letdown at home to Wolves. That proved to be the case as John Motson was assigned to their game. Nevertheless City overcame that setback and ended up with a fairly routine victory. It took them a while to break Wolves down and it was 0-0 at half time, largely due to a string of saves by Wayne Hennessey. The keeper would go from hero to villain early in the 2nd half though as he dawdled on the ball and Dzeko had a simple finish. Kolorov made it 2-0 before Kompany was sent off for fouling Doyle in the box. Hunt scored from the spot to make it interesting but substitute Adam Johnson wrapped it up for City. Is he the whitest man on the planet? He always looks like he's been up all night spewing his ring up, the lad has no colour in his cheeks and just looks permanently ill. I guess growing up in Middlesbrough will do that to you, poor lad probably didn't see the sun until he played his first away game.

Darren Bent was back at the Stadium of Light this weekend. He predictably got dogs abuse but said he was surprised by it. Really? Are you that removed from reality? Aside from the Mancs getting three points at Goodison, the biggest certainty of the weekend was Bent getting booed by the Mackems. He said he wanted to leave so he could win things. Fair enough, one small flaw in that though. He signed for Aston fucking Villa. Just how thick do you think Sunderland fans are, Darren? Your move was as much about winning things as Asamaoah Gyan's was. Villa took the lead with a cracker from Petrov, but Connor Wickham levelled for the home side. Bent had a great chance to silence the crowd but hit his shot at the keeper. Richard Dunne put Villa back in front but Sessegnon earned a point for Steve Bruce's side late on. Both teams are headed for mid-table mediocrity this season, but Sunderland will be the happier of the two after this, mainly because Bent didn't score.

Coming off the mauling they got at home by City last week a trip to Goodison wasn't the easiest game United could have faced, despite the affection they are held in by the majority of the home crowd. The blues used to happily take one for the team when they faced United, but Rooney's defection and subsequent antics whenever he has returned changed all that and for the most part they have given it a good go since then. This was no exception. A solitary goal by Hernandez settled it, but Everton definitely deserved something from the game and played pretty well. Frodo Baines hit the bar and they had numerous other chances but couldn't score. So Everton play well and United get the three points, meaning Evertonians get the best of both worlds. They even got a nice little patronising pat on the head from Ferguson afterwards in his post match interview, the smug twat. So, a lot of happy bluenoses on Saturday evening, until we won at the Hawthorns of course. Fuckin redshite bastards.

Also on Saturday, Swansea played host to struggling Bolton. The Welsh side hadn't conceded a goal at home all season and you wouldn't have bet on that changing against this dreadful Bolton team. The Gog went close with a snap shot on the turn that was well saved by Vorn, but the game changed when Gardner was sent off for two bookings, both of which seemed on the harsh side to me. Joe Allen has been making a bit of a name for himself this season, and he opened the scoring with a nice finish after being given far too much time and space by Bolton. Sinclair added a second from the spot after Pratley had clumsily brought down Graham, but Bolton were given a lifeline when Graham then put through his own net. That's what happens when strikers come back into their own box to defend. It's why I don't ever do it, and next time I get pulled up on it by less gifted, moaning team-mates I'm gonna use Graham's own goal as the case for my defence. The striker atoned for his error by making it 3-1 late in the game. Can't score those when you're back defending can you? Lesson to be learned there.

Wigan are desperately in need of points and a home game against Fulham is as good an opportunity as you'll have to get a win. The Londoners are awful on their travels and it says a lot about Wigan that they managed to lose this game. Once again, abysmal defending cost them as they tried to play offside and failed miserably. Zamora teed up Dempsey to open the scoring, and although Wigan hit the post through Rodallega and Figueroa, Dembele then added a second to make the game safe after more awful defending by the Latics. Alcaraz, how bad is he? Poor old Roberto Martinez was talking about how the stats show how well they played. There's an expression commonly used by NFL coaches; 'stats are for losers'. Very apt. Wigan will be playing in the Championship next season and Martinez is probably wishing he'd taken the Vila job now. Fair play to him for being loyal I guess. He's no Darren Bent that's for sure.

MOTD2 was proper shit this week. There was only one Sunday game, Spurs taking on QPR at the Lane. Not a game I had any real interest in, but these round ups mean I had to watch it anyway. It was always going to be a home win as QPR are really not very good. I thought they would be a bit better than they are, especially after they won at Goodison and then signed Joey Barton. Of the newly promoted sides they look comfortably the worst up to now, that may change in January if they spend some cash though. Having barely been able to hang on against nine man Chelsea last week, I didn't hold out much hope for them to do us a favour by taking something off Spurs. Any team that has Heidur Helguson playing regularly is in trouble. I notice that Jay Bothroyd has only been on the bench recently. Didn't Warnock say he's better than Andy Carroll? And he's being kept out the team by Heidur Helguson? Sorry, but Andy Carroll after 12 pints would still be a better bet than Helguson, so what does that say about Bothroyd? Nothing actually, it says a lot about Warnock though.

Gareth Bale opened the scoring, and then did a weird little jig. If you didn't see it, then type 'dancing chimp gif' into google and you'll get the picture. Van Der Vaart made it 2-0, and 'Bernie Mac' Adebayor had a few chances he was unable to convert. Warnock made changes at half time, taking off the woeful Taraabt and 46 year old Shaun Derry, and they got themselves back into it when Bothroyd nodded in from close range after Helguson had nodded the ball across from a corner. Took two of them to head that corner in, Carroll would have done that on his own. Just sayin' like. Lennon and Bale combined superbly for the third goal, the Welshman curling in a fine shot for his second of the game. QPR had a few more chances to pull another one back but it ended 3-1. Final observation from this, it dawned on me that I don't like Scott Parker anymore. Not sure why, as I was a big fan of his until recently. Suddenly I don't like his cockney looking face and 1930's head, whereas I never noticed them before. I guess I liked the plucky underdog playing for struggling West Ham, but now that he's a threat to us he can fuck off. Not his fault, but whaddayagonnado. Neil Warnock was laughing his head off afterwards, saying he couldn't stop clapping when Spurs scored their third goal. I think he may have been drunk, as he was far too happy for someone who's team had just been whooped, especially as he's normally a narky bastard when he isn't winning. He's never dull though.

Finally, unbeaten Newcastle went to Stoke on Monday night. I'd have put good money on them not winning this game, but luckily I didn't as I'd have lost it. They won at a bit of a canter as Demba Ba hit a hat-trick in a 3-1 win. Not many teams will go there and win, and it pisses me off that Newcastle are one of them. Stoke are garbage but they're difficult to play against on their subbuteo sized pitch and I didn't see the Geordies getting any more than a point at best. They keep proving me wrong though and they're third in the table now, what the fuck's going on there? They've conceded less goals in ten games than Arsenal let in at Old Trafford. This is Newcastle we're talking about here. Over the years their defence has been more charitable than UNICEF, and that was with far better personnel than they have now. It's the same all over the park (with the exception of the middle of midfield where they have two very good players), but sometimes their shitness works in their favour. Take the second goal for instance. If Leon Best was any good he'd have brought the ball down and got a shot on target. He brought it down ok, but his shot was feeble and off target yet ended up as a perfect pass to give Demba Ba a tap in. Pardew may be onto something here. Is shit the new good?

Shitness isn't restricted to Newcastle though. Take Stoke's goalscorer for instance. Walters was making his 50th appearance in the Premier League, and that was his 9th goal. How many have been pens? At least two, probably more. A quick look at wikipedia says he has 60 career goals in 309 games. He's a striker, he's spent most of his career in the lower leagues and still can't do better than 1 in 5. Shit blueshite twat.

The more I think about it the more I'm glad Newcastle won as I've got a massive downer on Stoke right now. Their fans are dicks, chanting *"Demba Ba, you're a wanker"* and booing his every touch. His crime against Stoke? Failing a medical because of a dodgy knee. Knuckle dragging morons. Newcastle will eventually find their level, but the more Stoke get beat the better as far as I'm concerned.

Finally, David Ginola has really let me down. For years my missus has been giving me grief about my ever greying barnet. *"Why don't you get some 'Just for Men'?"* she'll say. *"Hey, David Ginola's got longish grey hair and I don't hear anyone on his case about it"* I'd respond. Well not any more, thanks for that Daveeed. Now the only other example I can use is the gnarly old bastard from roadhouse, which is hardly the same is it? Fucking sell out. I hope it was 'worth eeet'.

chapter five

November

LIVERPOOL 0 SWANSEA CITY 0

Competition - Premier League
Date - Sat 5 Nov 2011
Venue - Anfield
Scorer(s) –
Half Time - 0-0
Star Man – Jose Enrique

Team: Reina; Johnson, Skrtel, Agger, Enrique; Henderson (Kuyt), Lucas, Adam, Downing; Carroll (Bellamy), Suarez:

Every time it looks like we've cracked it, there's a kick in the nuts just around the corner. This was the worst yet. You can't get these points back, they're gone and they usually hurt you at the end of the season when you look back and see where it all went wrong. Every year we drop points to newly promoted clubs or teams who go on to finish in the bottom three. Every fucking year.

It's not just the two points we dropped that hurts this time, it's that we can't even say we deserved to win or were unlucky. Barring the odd exception, we've been the better side in most games this season and it's been poor finishing and bad luck that's been our problem. Not this time. We certainly weren't better than Swansea, and whilst bad finishing was again in evidence there was nothing unlucky about it. This wasn't like the Norwich game where we should have won 5-2. Games like the Norwich one are frustrating but some days the ball doesn't roll for you. This was different, this was an even contest that we could just as easily have lost as won (both teams missed Kop end sitters).

Worryingly, it seemed to me that we were out-thought by Swansea. Tactically they got it spot on and the extra man they had in midfield meant they were able to keep the ball and at times we were chasing them around like a dog in a park. It was embarrassing, it felt like we were playing Arsenal (only without the crap defending). What went wrong? Quite a bit. Kenny named the same team that beat West Brom so comfortably last week, but it's clear now that Swansea are a completely different proposition to the dis-organised mess that Roy Hodgson sent out against us last week. Any criticism of our own performance needs to be tempered with praise for the Swans. I can't speak highly enough of them, I thought they were fantastic and I don't think they'll have any problem staying up based on what they've shown so far. Having said that, we have to look at ourselves and regardless of how impressive Swansea were, the bottom line is this wasn't good enough. It's partly on the players, but also on Kenny and Steve Clarke for me as I don't think we gave ourselves the best chance to succeed with our tactical inflexibility and use of substitutes.

It's difficult to fault the starting line up, those players had a good win at West Brom so Kenny kept faith with them. Can't really argue with that too much, and maybe if Carroll buries that sitter early on we go on to win the game comfortably. The starting line up was understandable, but it was obvious by half time that we needed to change it. We'd played some good stuff but the longer the half went the more comfortable and confident the visitors started to look. Swansea's three man midfield were just passing their way around our two with embarrassing ease. We changed a player at the break, but not the system and the problems we had before the break intensified after it.

Lucas and Adam have regularly had problems with this, sometimes when they've only been faced with two opponents so against three they have no chance. It's not a knock on either of them especially, it's just blatantly obvious that when a team has an extra man in there it's easy for them to dominate the midfield area against us. They needed help in there, but it never arrived. I actually thought Adam played pretty well, certainly with the ball anyway. His passing was good and there were two or three beautiful defence splitting passes he played inside the full back to Downing (including the one that led to Carroll's miss). Without the ball he struggled and so did Lucas. It's hardly a surprise though, Swansea's midfield three are all good in possession and very busy. The little number seven was superb, I didn't even know who he was initially. I thought he must have been some Spanish lad who was left over from when Martinez was manager there, especially as he was playing like Xavi. Turns out it was Leon Britton, a journeyman type who has played most of his career with the Swans but has had spells at West Ham and Sheffield United too. So he isn't Xavi, we just made him look like it. Joe Allen was very good too and those two and Gower just passed their way around Lucas and Adam with ease. In addition to that, both of their wingers were lively and gave us problems and if they had a better striker they'd probably have won the game.

What struck me more than anything was how willing Swansea were to knock the ball about even in tight spaces. Hitting it long wasn't an option, they just refused to do it and everything was short and in to feet. Often they'd be passing it around the pitch from one side to the other and we couldn't get it off them. Every time it looked like we were about to force a mistake or a hurried clearance, they'd find a team-mate. They were very impressive.

It obviously needed changing at half time, but the problem Kenny faces is how to set up his team whilst keeping Andy Carroll on the field. With him on the pitch we have to play two up front, and therefore one less in midfield. To have the extra man in midfield, one of the forwards has to be left out and it isn't going to be Suarez. The problem is that not only did Carroll cost a shedload of money, but he is now starting to play quite well. Whilst he's in decent form you want him in the side so he can maybe get on a bit of a roll and justify the massive investment in him. I want to see him in the side playing well and scoring goals and I really like him as a player. However, the balance of the side is often better when he isn't in it. It's an issue at times mainly because the midfield isn't strong enough to just have two in there, unless we're up against old school 442 sides like Stoke or the tactically inept West Brom (games in which Carroll did very well). Leaving Carroll on the bench isn't going to do him any good, but having him on the pitch sometimes upsets the balance of the side as it makes our system very rigid, which is ok against some sides (see Stoke and West Brom) but hurts us against others. Having Kuyt or Bellamy in the team alongside Suarez gives us various other options to change the system during the game, and I keep thinking back to some of the games at the back end of last season when the movement of Suarez and Kuyt was running defences ragged. We can't do that with the big fella, but having paid so much money to bring him here what do you do?

When Bellamy replaced Carroll late on in this game, we ended up piling on the pressure and had several chances. Co-incidence? Maybe. We certainly stretched them a lot more though with Bellamy moving around all over the place. Carroll did his job to a reasonable standard, he won flick ons and knocked the ball down at the back post a few times, albeit to nobody as we didn't have anyone breaking into the box (not Carroll's fault). The job he did wasn't really beneficial to winning the game though, especially given that he failed to do the main thing he was bought to do - score. The bottom line is he HAS to put that chance away. Just has to. Regardless of whatever else he does or doesn't do in the game, a centre forward has to put that ball in the net in that situation and Carroll didn't do it.

I've defended him all season and will continue to do so, but he isn't going to win over his detractors missing chances like that. There are a lot of doubters out there, most of my mates included actually. I rate him, but at the back of my mind is the fear that he's a square peg in a round hole. Speaking of which, Jordan Henderson has been doing better of late but this game saw him go back into his shell and revert to the 'safety first' football we've generally seen from him when he plays on the right. He did nothing in the first half and bringing him off was an obvious decision. He's a player with potential, but he should not continue to start games on the right of midfield as even in the games he's played well there he's hardly pulled up any trees. Play him in the middle or not at all, as this is doing him no favours. He's extremely fortunate to be in the side ahead of Kuyt and Maxi as his performances haven't justified that selection. I don't think anyone can dispute that at this moment in time. It's a recurring theme throughout the side actually. I like Downing, but he's not done enough to keep out Bellamy or Maxi, and how many people would select Johnson over Kelly right now? Spearing can also consider himself unfortunate to never be getting on the field given how good he was last season. It's frustrating and I can understand people being baffled by some of the selections. Having said all that, and as bad as this was at times, I still feel we are playing good football and on the whole I'm enjoying watching us. Even in this game I thought we played some good stuff. Not enough of it, but there was still some good football.

There was a really bad spell in the middle of the second half when we completely lost our way, but aside from that our main problem was when we didn't have the ball and how easy it was for Swansea to play football against us. It's happened before too. The second half against Sunderland for example, whilst despite being fortunate not to get hammered even Norwich were also able to get the ball down and play against us, and Brighton dominated possession in the second half of that cup tie. With the ball we're pretty good (until it comes to actually putting the ball in the net of course) but without it we often struggle, even against the 'smaller' teams. I worry about our fitness levels too. Are we so easy to play against because we don't press the ball enough? Or is it just a tactical issue? It's not all doom and gloom and I'd like to think it's fixable, but we need to be more flexible and most people seem to think we need to go with an extra man in the middle of the park, at least until Gerrard is able to return. That probably means Carroll missing out which is unfortunate for him, but unless Kenny can find a way of strengthening the midfield without sacrificing the big man then I don't see any other choice as we can't carry on with Lucas and Adam regularly being outnumbered in there.

Despite the points we've squandered at home, I don't feel anywhere near as disillusioned with this team as I did under Hodgson or in the latter part of the Benitez era. Frustrated, yes. Disillusioned? Not yet, it's far too early for that and at least I can see us trying to play pass and move, attacking football. The missed chances are doing my head in and teams seem to have a lot more possession against us than we've become used to, but there have been games in recent years where we've seemed incapable of putting more than three passes together. That's not the case anymore. The problems we have are fixable. I think. I hope. Clearly there are some things that need sorting out. The main one being the lack of goals. We've been unlucky with a lot of the efforts that have hit the woodwork, and we always seem to run into keepers who decide to make a name for themselves at our expense. Look at the lad at Norwich, pulls off some great saves against us and then gets beaten at his near post by fucking Yakubu a week later.

Expect the Swansea keeper to fuck up next week too. He turned into Superman in the closing stages of this game, but he'll throw one in next week you watch.

Still, even allowing for all that, 14 goals in 11 games is not good enough. Scoring goals wasn't a problem at the back end of last season, but two of the main contributors aren't getting many starts and one of them has been sold to Chelsea. I'm not arsed about Meireles leaving, but I can't help thinking that Maxi is very unfortunate to be getting constantly overlooked and Kuyt is missing out because of the need to get Carroll integrated into the side. Downing, Carroll and Henderson have three goals between them in a combined 29 Premier League starts. Pitiful. Let's say Bellamy, Kuyt and Maxi had replaced them in the side for those games. I'd bet my house they'd have chipped in with more than three goals, and there's a decent chance they'd have that many apiece let alone combined. Of course it's not as straightforward as that and there are other things to consider, but neither Downing or Henderson have done too much else either (Downing has put some good crosses in that should have been converted, just not enough of them). The flip side of it is that they are new signings and it usually takes time to build a team. Kenny put his faith in those players when he signed them, as he did with Carroll. He has to give them the chance to bed in and for the team to gel, but the fans are not all going to like that, especially when there are players on the bench more deserving of a starting place. That's why there's a bit of unease at the moment.

A lot of people would like to see Maxi and Kuyt back in the side linking up with Suarez, and personally I'd like to see Spearing drafted in to help out Lucas and allow Adam to get forward more as he's shown he's got goals in him. But Kenny is trying to build a team and he bought those players for a reason. He's in a bind now because he can't drop them and go back to what was working last season, as how will he explain that to the owners? They backed him with money, and he now has to back the players he spent it on.

There's a growing number of fans who think a lot of the money spent has been wasted. They may be right, there are certainly alarm bells ringing but I feel it's too soon to make that call. Teams don't always gel right away and it can take time. There will be bumps on the road and we've had a few already. Those bumps might end up costing us our chance of a top four spot, and right now it is looking an increasingly difficult task. Things can change very quickly though, look at Arsenal. After their horrendous start they are now level with us. The worrying thing for me is that this was a run of three games that we should have taken nine points from. We managed just five and now we have Chelsea away and City at home. The table doesn't look great right now, and it could look a hell of a lot worse after the next two games. The more difficult fixtures may actually work in our favour though, and the international break may give Kenny and his staff the opportunity to take stock and come up with a way to solve the problems we've been having. I'd be staggered if Kenny went to Stamford Bridge and played 442 with Carroll up front. He'll draft in an extra midfielder and Suarez will be up front in a 433/451. I wouldn't bet against us taking four points from the next two games, but equally I won't be betting on us beating QPR at home after that.

After the way we ended last season and the money spent in the summer, I'm sure most of us expected better than the results we've had. There were boos at the final whistle, and it seems that patience is in short supply these days. As early as 15 minutes into this game there were rumblings of discontent whenever a pass went astray. I guess that's a result of the Sunderland and Norwich games, but I was a little surprised as how edgy people were so early into the game. The atmosphere in general was shite all day. Just goes to show that those early kick offs and Sunday games weren't the reason for it, as even 3pm Saturday games are terrible too these days.

Premier League Round Up (5-6 November 2011)

Jesus Christ, I thought the Motson tribute the other week was nauseating, but congratulations BBC you've outdone yourself. The Ferguson cock munching this weekend was hideous and capped off another shit weekend for LFC fans.

And what the fuck was he doing on the pitch with a microphone, the attention seeking arl bastard. The Mancs named a stand after him, but he reckons he had no idea that's what was happening. Yeah right, so why was your nose going a deeper shade of purple with each and every filthy lying word that came slurring out of your mouth? And shove that false modesty up your wrinkly old hoop, Taggert. Fuck him and his 25 years, at least we can take comfort that there won't be 25 more.

The game had a testimonial feel to it, as a load of his old boys returned to pay their respects. He couldn't have hand picked a better opponent for his big day than Steve Bruce and his band of United rejects. Hernandez was guilty of a blatant dive to try and win a penalty early on. Must have learned that from Suarez, eh Alex? Astonishingly that moron Lee Mason didn't point to the spot. Still, you don't need favours from refs when you've got so many loyal foot soldiers in the opposing ranks. Sunderland were about to go in to the break all square until Wes Brown took matters into his own hands by planting a great header past his own keeper. The Mackems offered virtually nothing in attack but it looked like they'd been handed a lifeline when the linesman spotted an arm go up and handle the ball. The arm belonged to a Sunderland player, but clearly the linesman didn't know that as he flagged for a pen. Mason didn't know either, but after a quick conversation with the lino they reversed the decision. No doubt that conversation went a little like this:

Lino: *"Yeah, his hand went up and deflected the cross, it's a pen"*
Mason: *"But it's Alex's big day, we can't spoil the party, we'll never be invited back. You know what happened to every other official that upset him."*
Lino: *"Yeah, you're right. Best to just ignore me."*

Of course it wasn't a penalty, but neither of them knew that so how did they come to the decision to reverse it? I'd love to know, but we never will.

The other Mancs were also in Saturday action, taking on QPR at Loftus Road. It had rout written all over it, but surprisingly Neil Warnock's side actually gave it a right good go and were unlucky to lose. Bothroyd put them in front, Helguson almost made it 2-0 and then Bothroyd hit the post as QPR dominated. Predictably City came back into it and Dzeko equalised. Silva put City in front after a wonderful first touch set him up for an easy finish, but Helguson equalised after a header by Bothroyd hit him on the back as he stood on the goal-line. City wanted offside, but one of their defenders was playing him on and the linesman was correct. City won it with a header by Yaya Toure, but Helguson hit the post late on and QPR will feel a little hard done by not to have come out of this with a point as they were excellent. I'm actually glad City won, but that depresses me. I'm fed up of having to root for other teams just because we aren't good enough to stop United winning the title. It's been going on for far too long, and I wish I didn't have to do it. I don't want to root for City to win games, just as I didn't want to be rooting for Chelsea and Arsenal in previous years. As it stands though, the only thing that will stop United pulling further ahead of us in terms of titles is City. I wish it wasn't the case, but it is. So whilst I'm not going to sing Blue Moon or put my arm around the missus and turn our backs to the TV whilst jumping up and down like dickheads, I am going to hope City win every game except when they are playing us. I'm not proud of it, but needs must. Having said all that, if City keep sending the moonfaced bore David Platt out to do the post match interviews I may have to have a rethink on that. I know it was after 10pm, but seriously, some warning of what was about to come would have been nice. He's like a giant helium balloon with a face drawn on it. He shouldn't be on MOTD, he should be 'In the Night Garden' with the rest of the 'Haahoos' (one for those of you with little kids there).

'In the Night Garden' is actually Gabby Agbonlahor's favourite TV show. Not a lot of people know that, but he loves it, bless him. He loves to run around the training ground pretending to be Iggle Piggle. Which brings me nicely to Aston Villa v Norwich (I believe that's whats known in the writing game as a perfect seguet). Pilkington put the Canaries in front with a brilliant free-kick. He reminds me of Beckham the way he strikes a ball, his crossing and shooting have really caught the eye this season (except that shot when he was clean through at Old Trafford, the shithouse). Bent equalised following a brilliant cross by Agbonlahor although Norwich were furious that a handball by Warnock hadn't been spotted by the ref. Agbonlahor's persistence put Villa in front when he latched onto Barnett's awful backpass to beat Ruddy, and Bent made it 3-1 with a tap in from another Agbonlahor cross. Norwich kept going though and pulled one back through Morrison who headed in a superb cross by Holt, but Villa held on for the win. The brummies seem to be totally reliant on Agbonlahor at the moment, he really is in fine form. I thought N'Zogbia would be a great signing for them but he's been shite up to now. Surprising that as I think he's a good player. As for Norwich, they need to tighten up at the back or they will undo all the good work they're doing at the other end.

Chelsea were looking to bounce back from last week's humbling by Arsenal and they just about overcame plucky Blackburn. Yakubu missed a sitter early doors and almost smashed Cech's face in in the process. The keeper ended up with plugs up both nostrils, which in tandem with his headguard made him look even more 'special' than usual. Reminded me of when Black Adder was trying to convince people he was round the bend so he could get discharged from the Army. The only goal of the game came from a Lampard diving header, which apparently measured 3.5 on the richter scale and could be felt as far away as Preston. Is it still ok to still make fat jokes about Lampard? No-one seems to do it these days, probably because he's about as far from being overweight as John Terry is to being likeable. That just makes it even funnier though I reckon. The fat fuck. Yakubu and Frank Lampard were in the player's lounge afterwards. Frank says; *"Your round"*. The Yak replies *"Look who's talking, you fat twat."*

Blackburn had several great chances but couldn't score, and Chelsea should have made it safe at the end but Torres embarrassingly missed from a couple of yards. He's back to looking shite again after briefly threatening to get his form back. The pass he played in the build up to that chance was brutal too. His form is more up and down than John Terry on a teammates missus. Blackburn fans were banned from taking banners into the ground because of all the 'Kean out' stuff, so they hired a plane to fly overhead instead. Kean should hire his own plane saying *"fuck you, losers"* with a big picture of him giving it the middle finger. Or I guess he can just keep losing games whilst taking a good wedge, that works too.

Speaking of losers, Roy took his Baggies to the Emirates to face 'the Arsenal'. Why do people insist on putting a 'the' in front of Arsenal? They may as well walk around with a sticker on their forehead that says *"Hey everyone, look at me, I'm a bad tit"*. Van Persie scored the first and then made the second for Vermailen and the third for legohead. Arsenal will still drop points fairly regularly, but they're over their terrible start and Van Persie is as good as anyone in the league right now. Hodgson said afterwards *"With 'the Arsenal' in their current mood and current form, they were obviously able to play on that and relax, and I thought they could have made life more difficult for us than they actually made it."* 'The Arsenal' eh? I'm saying nothing. Maybe Roy should do likewise, especially if that was the kind of thing he was saying to his players before the game. Jesus, talk about beaten before you even start.

Meanwhile, 'unbeaten Newcastle' won again. Not good for us, but at least it was the blueshite they turned over this week. They took the lead when Heitinga turned a right wing cross into his own net, and the blues fell further behind when Ryan Taylor scored a screamer from 25 yards. His second Premier League goal of the season, which is the same as Carroll and one more than Torres I believe. The commentator said Newcastle are one of Saha's former clubs. When was that then? I've actually got no recollection of that whatsoever, although I'm not doubting the commentator's accuracy. If Saha was at Newcastle he can't have made much of an impact there. Probably spent most of his time injured, just like he has everywhere else he's been. Everton had poppies on their shirts. Red poppies. Is it wrong that I'm shocked by that? I'm surprised they didn't insist on wearing blue ones, as that's how they usually roll, the bitter bastards. Taylor pointed out afterwards that the goal was extra special for him as it was against Everton and he grew up a Liverpool fan. I love these little human interest stories, it's always nice to see players score against sides they hated when they were kids, and I'd never begrudge a player that kind of special moment. Good lad Ryan, well done son.

Onto Sunday's games now, and that blueshite twat Jon Walters and his Stoke side got their arses handed to them by lowly Bolton. Nothing has gone right for him since he embarrassed himself on MOTD, gloating about being an Evertonian scoring the winner against the Reds. Spiteful, petty bastard, I hate that sort of cringeworthy shite. I'm made up Stoke got battered, I'd happily see them relegated even though it's extremely unlikely. They just can't cope with the demands of playing in Europe in midweek and then having to play again on the Sunday. It's killing them. It's funny really, as we always hear about how difficult it is to compete on two fronts, but I've never really taken it that seriously as most of the big clubs seem to manage just fine. It's completely new to Stoke though and they're floundering badly. Good, the pitch shrinking, alehouse bastards. Bolton's opener was hilarious. Howard Webb decided that Whelan's sliced clearance was in fact a backpass, and whilst Stoke were arguing about it Klasnic ripped the ball out of the keeper's hands and teed it up for Davies to tap it in. Stoke were furious, but Webb was having none of it and allowed the goal to stand. I just think it's funny cos it's Stoke. Chris Eagles made it 2-0 with a brilliant strike with his left foot. Good player him, not Premier League good, but in the Championship he'd comfortably be the best player in the division. He may get to prove it next season too, as despite this win I'm not buying into Bolton one little bit. Eagles added another nice goal and Klasnic bagged a couple as well. He's a proper goalscorer that Klasnic, I like him a lot. Always in the right place at the right time and he's a good finisher. It could easily have been seven or eight in the end as Stoke really shit the bed in this one. Fair play to Pulis who refused to complain about the opening goal and instead pointed out how bad his team were. Took me by surprise that did.

Spurs went to Craven Cottage without the convalescing Harry Redknapp, meaning assistant Kevin Bond was in charge, the horrible spitting twat. Younger readers won't remember, but back in the 80s when he was playing for Southampton, he grebbed in Paul Walsh's face during a game at the Dell. Walsh wiped the spit away, followed him downfield and then laid him out with a stunning right hook to the face. It was beautiful, but it earned Walshy a three game suspension from what I remember. He'd get three years in Walton nick if he did it now, as football has gone too soft. The worst thing for Bond was he had to come and play at Anfield a few days later sporting a massive shiner. At full time, a fan ran on from the Kemlyn and laid him out again. Bond looked like a fucking panda afterwards. Those were the days, imagine someone running on and decking John Terry now? If only.

Anyway, Spurs somehow managed to get three points despite being pummelled by Fulham for most of the second half. Brad Friedel was sensational and Fulham were also denied a blatant pen when they were only trailing 2-1. Bale had scored the first and then did his dancing chimp routine again. Lennon added the second, a superb solo goal the kind of which he really should be doing much more frequently, but doesn't because he's actually a bit poo. Fulham pulled one back and then laid siege to Friedel's goal but got no luck at all, and Defoe wrapped it up with the aid of a huge deflection in stoppage time. Spurs probably should have had a pen of their own to be fair when Parker was bundled over by Sidwell. Tottenham are getting right on my tits at the moment I have to admit.

Finally, Wigan went to the Black Country to face Wolves. I watched the entire game believe it or not. I think this might be the first full game I've seen all season that didn't involve LFC. I could be wrong on that though as my memory is diminishing faster than John Terry's talent. I enjoyed this game, it was pretty open as...well... Wigan were playing so it's hardly going to be anything else is it. They aren't capable of playing it cagey as they're abysmal at the back. There was a 30 second spell that was just Wigan in a nutshell. Some lovely football saw them carve Wolves open but Rodallega inexplicably put the ball wide. Wolves went right up the other end and scored after Alcaraz was turned inside out by Doyle and O'Hara put the ball in the net. That's who they are.

I wrote a few weeks back that Bolton's Paul Robinson is the worst player in the Premier League not named Tony Hibbert. Well I'm having a rethink, as Alcaraz is a complete train wreck. Every goal Wigan concede, he seems to be right at the heart of it. He's slow and error prone, yet he's the captain. He also spat at a Wolves player, the dirty snide bastard.

Where's Paul Walsh when you need him, eh?

Another observation from this game, maybe Di Santo isn't quite as crap as I've been saying. He's not good by any means, he's scored five goals in 66 games in English football, and at least three of those were deflected!! You know what he is though? He's the white Ngog. Watch him play, the resemblance in style is uncanny. The similarities are there, but the one big difference is that Ngog can put the ball in the net, this chump can't. Unless it goes in off a defender's arse, obviously. Oh, and Steven Hunt, lose the alice band, son. You lost your hairband priviledges when you cut your hair, so let it go. It's like when Fabregas used to wear one despite having a short back and sides. Pisses me right off. You have to earn the right to wear a hairband, and you earn it by, ya know, growing your hair. At least Hunt used to have long hair, so I guess he's just having trouble coming to terms with his shit new look. Fabregas though, what was that all about? Him sporting a hairband was the equivalent of some shitkicker strutting around in an Augusta 'Green Jacket' having never picked up a golf club, let alone won the Masters. Shit just ain't right.

CHELSEA 1 LIVERPOOL 2

Competition - Premier League
Date - Sun 20 Nov 2011
Venue - Stamford Bridge
Scorer(s) – Maxi Rodriguez, Glen Johnson
Half Time - 0-1
Star Man – Charlie Adam

Team: Reina; Johnson, Skrtel, Agger, Enrique; Kuyt, Lucas, Adam, Maxi (Downing); Bellamy (Henderson), Suarez (Carroll):

If only there were more teams like Chelsea eh? Not only are they generously bankrolling our transfers by signing players to sit on their bench, but Kenny simply can't lose against them. He's never lost against them as a Liverpool manager apparently. Impressive stuff.

This was a deserved victory, just about. First half was superb, the second was much more difficult but we withstood whatever they could throw at us (which wasn't much really) and then we kicked on again and won it late on. Made up with this, it's always nice beating them as they're just such massive twats aren't they?

I loved the intent in Kenny's starting line up. I can't deny that I was concerned about how Lucas and Adam would do against the three man midfield Chelsea employ, but how can you not be excited about what Suarez and Bellamy could do to Chelsea's dodgy backline? As it turned out, the midfield did just fine for the most part and Bellamy helped with that by dropping off and sitting on Mikel to negate their extra man. The most interesting selection was Maxi who hadn't started a league game all season. It was the right call as we've been struggling for goals all season and Maxi is more of a goal threat than those who have been getting selected ahead of him. He showed that once again, and surely he has to keep his place now? Henderson, Downing and Carroll were all left on the bench as Kenny reverted to what had served us so well last season. Maxi was a big part of that with his clever movement and neat short passing game. He's on the same wavelength as Suarez and we play some lovely football when he's on the field. And he scores goals of course.

It was a brave decision for Kenny to leave out three of his big money purchases. The two signings who started were the 'bargain buys', meaning £70m worth of Dalglish recruits weren't on the field. It was the correct decision, and until those who were left out do enough to suggest they should be playing ahead of people like Maxi and Bellamy, the bench is where they should stay, regardless of how much they cost. That will bring it's own criticism even if the team are winning, but the results are more important than persevering with players in an attempt to show they are worth the money paid for them.

The first half of this game was just like some of the impressive performances of last season. Quick, sharp passing, lots of movement off the ball and great pressure when the opposition have the ball. Maxi was a key component in that last year and Bellamy has shown in his limited opportunities this year that he's another who helps us in that regard. Chelsea couldn't deal with it in the first half. It looked as though we targeted Luiz and Mikel in particular. Any time they were in possession, we pressed them. Luiz is a really good footballer, but defensively he's a major liability and always looks like he has a mistake in him. He's a snide too, he got Lucas booked by making a meal of a nothing challenge (they're mates too) and he tried to pick fights with Kuyt and Suarez as well. Sideshow Bob looking blert. As for Mikel, he's shite, always has been. He's a fucking crab who brings nothing to the game whatsoever. It's always amazed me how Chelsea have stuck with him all these years. You look at the top midfield players they've had (and still have), and then you look at his big dope. How does he get a game? I don't know, but I'm glad he does as it benefits us. The first goal came about as a result of us pressing him. In Mikel's defence, why is Cech playing the ball to him in that position? Cech trains with him every day, he surely has to know the lad is shite? You don't put him in that situation as it's asking for trouble. Charlie Adam closed him down and applied pressure (probably fouling him in fairness), Bellamy collected the loose ball and exchanged passes with Suarez before fooling everybody by feigning to shoot only to roll it to the unmarked Maxi who's scuffed shot beat Cech.

No more than we deserved based on the run of play, although it probably should be said that we didn't test Cech at all despite getting into several promising positions. At the other end Chelsea had toiled without ever looking comfortable, but we did have two close shaves when Mata and Drogba both went close. Mata's cross-shot went right across the face of goal but there were no Chelsea players on hand to convert. Then Drogba's deflected free-kick looked like it had gone in, as it hit the back stantion and rebounded along the back of the net. Chelsea's fans celebrated, and Gary Neville and Martin Tyler both continued to think it had gone in seconds after everybody else had realised it hadn't. Knobs. I have to wonder if they were even in the stadium or whether they were watching on a portable black and white telly somewhere as they got other things wrong too, such as blaming Suarez for a foul on Luiz that was clearly committed by Lucas. Maybe they were sat in the section where Chelsea used to put the away fans? The worst view you'll find in any stadium not named Goodison Park. Unless you're unfortunate enough to be sat in the ten rows behind Steve Bruce's head that is.

Despite the lack of goalmouth action, I thought it was an intriguing first half. We played very well, especially the midfield duo of Lucas and Adam who bossed it I thought. Adam was all over the place, winning tackles and putting himself about. He was surging forward too and this might be his best performance in a red shirt. I've said that a few times lately so clearly he's doing well. The only criticism I have of the first half display was our passing in the final third wasn't always the best. Suarez was culpable of this a few times, he was a bit up and down in this game. He must have had about five or six nutmegs on Chelsea players and he never stopped running, but he didn't make the most of some really good situations. The movement with him and Bellamy was giving Chelsea's defence plenty to worry about, and at half time it was looking really good for us as surely we'd get chances on the break as they would have to come at us? Didn't work like that though.

Villas Boas withdrew Mikel who'd been one of our best players, and sent on the dangerous Sturridge. That freed up Mata to move inside and get on the ball more, and the midfield mismatch I'd been worried about prior to the game was now starting to happen. We still looked comfortable at the back as Skrtel was all over Drogba like a cheap suit, but they were having more of the ball and when we did manage to get it we weren't keeping it. The pressing game that had been so evident in the first half disappeared, and we started to look a bit passive. I don't know if that was a conscious thing, or whether we didn't have the legs to keep playing at that tempo, or if it was simply a case of Chelsea doing a better job of moving the ball. We were starting to get a bit penned in though, and it wasn't a shock when Chelsea equalised. The goal was spawny, a mis-hit shot by Malouda squirmed across the goalmouth and was put in by Sturridge at the back post. Not great defending, as Malouda had too much time and Sturridge wasn't picked up as our defence appealed for an offside they were never going to get. We had to weather a bit of a storm for the next few minutes, they had their tails up and it needed a great save by Reina to keep us on level terms.

It needed changing, and Kenny brought off Bellamy to shore up the midfield by getting Henderson in there. I'll admit I wasn't thrilled about it, as firstly I'd have taken Maxi off before Bellamy as he wasn't getting a kick now with the way the game had gone. Secondly, I'd have put Spearing on rather than Henderson. Kenny got it right though, we began to keep the ball better and were no longer getting over-run. Adam was able to get on the ball more now that he wasn't chasing shadows, and the game became more of even contest again. Chelsea made two more changes, sending on two players who are very familiar to us. The stage looked set for Torres to come on and score the winner, probably from a Meireles pass. Things like that tend to happen in football, and it was indeed an old boy who came back to haunt his former club with the winning goal, but you'd have got long odds on it being Glen Johnson. It's easy to forget that Johnson even played for Chelsea. I never associate him with them at all. A bit like Scott Parker really. You don't think of him as a former Chelsea player, at least I don't. The only memory I have of him playing for Chelsea was being torn a new one by El Hadj Diouf at Anfield. Not really something you want on your CV.

The goal was great though. Lovely raking pass from Adam, great first touch and then a meg on Cole before keeping his composure and rolling it in the corner. There were still a couple of minutes left plus stoppage time, but this was in the bag. I wasn't the slightest bit worried that we wouldn't win, which is a strange feeling. We could even afford the luxury of taking off Suarez. Carroll replaced him and did himself no favours with an awful cameo in which he repeatedly gave possession away. Thankfully it didn't matter. This was a great win, but it also highlights just how costly our inability to beat the smaller clubs at home has been. We should be six points better off right now, with away wins over Chelsea and Arsenal under our belts. That would be a seriously impressive start. Instead, we're in a four way tie for that fourth spot (although Spurs have two games in hand). Our away record is very good and we're not conceding many goals. Interestingly, nine of the eleven that we have conceded have been in the second half. An anomaly, or an issue with fitness? Something to keep an eye on as the season progresses maybe.

Star man is Charlie Adam, just ahead of Skrtel and Lucas. Everyone played their part though, even the subs (not counting Carroll). Henderson helped steady the ship and had one fantastic run down the right that led to another sub, Downing, cushioning a lovely ball into the path of Kuyt who made a pigs arse of it. Typical of Downing's LFC career to date as any time he's done something good to create a chance, one of his team-mates has failed to convert it. He has a fight on his hands to get back in the side and whilst ideally you'd want a £20m signing to be in the side and justifying his selection, the flip side of it is look how strong our bench is at the moment. It wasn't that long ago we were sending on people like El Zhar and even Degen to play on the wings in important games.

City are up next, and I'm more confident of us winning that game than I would if we were playing QPR or Wigan. We battered City at Anfield last season but they are a much better side now than they were then. Andy Carroll was the star that night and I remember how excited everybody was about him afterwards. He scored twice that night, and has only scored two more league goals since.

Still, it's more than the man he replaced. If I were a Chelsea fan I'd be pretty pissed off seeing Torres laughing and joking with some of our players afterwards. Mind you, if I was a Chelsea fan I'd have to kill myself.

Premier League Round Up (19-21 November 2011)

The MOTD crew were in a snazzy new studio this week. Shearer looked different somehow, I can't put my finger on what it was but I suspect some kind of plastic surgery. His head and face looked very shiny, I know that much. Botox maybe? Personally I'd say he'd have been better off spending his cash getting the Rooney treatment. By that I mean hair transplant, not hookers.

Anyway, first up this week was Saturday's big game, 1st v 3rd and the league's only two unbeaten records on the line. At least I can stop saying 'unbeaten Newcastle' now, that was becoming more and more surreal by the week. They've done well, but this was the first really big test and let's face it, not many teams are going to avoid defeat against City this season. Newcastle never had a prayer of getting anything from this. The difference between City and everybody else is they can leave out arguably their best player (Silva) and bring in the likes of Aguero or Nasri in his place. Next week they'll probably leave out Balotelli and bring in Dzeko. And whilst they are doing all this, Carlos Tevez is on strike and it's not hurting them in the slightest. Imagine how screwed we'd be if Suarez pulled a Tevez on us, or if Van Persie did it to Arsenal? That's without even mentioning the multi million pound mistakes they've had to loan out. No-one can compete with that, certainly not Newcastle with their squad of rejects and misfits. Mind you, Demba Ba should have scored when it was still 0-0. He actually missed two great chances before City were awarded a penalty. It wouldn't have made much difference as City always looked in control, but it may have made things interesting for a while had Ba put one of those away. He didn't though, and Balotelli nonchalently converted the pen and then strolled towards Krul with his arms folded. Don't normally like to see that kind of thing, but because it's Balotelli it was hilarious. I read somewhere that Krul had tried some gamesmanship to try and put him off before he took the pen, if that's true then that backfired pretty spectacularly.

Richards made it 2-0 just before half time and that was it for the Geordies. Ben Arfa hit the post but they weren't coming back from two down away at City. The home side then got a soft pen to make it 3-0 when Richards slowed down in the box to initiate contact with Ben Arfa who'd gotten wrong side. Technically it was a pen, but Richards defo played for it.

Newcastle got a late consolation through Gosling. This is the kid who scored for Everton against us in the FA Cup. That was the goal that was missed by millions of TV viewers as ITV hilariously cut to an advert during the game. Nevertheless, it was voted Everton's goal of the season. Don't need to see it when it's against der redshite, it could have gone in off his arse from a yard out and it was still their goal of the season. That should have immortalised Gosling in the anals of Everton history. He could have been sharing a throne with other Evertonian derby winning luminaries such as Danny Cadamarteri and Andrei Kanchelskis, but he threw it all away to join Newcastle. The circumstances of his departure were comical. With his contract expiring, Everton made him an offer of a new deal. To prevent players under the age of 23 leaving for nothing, you have to offer them at least the same wage they are on. He was on a reported 8k a week at Goodison, and they made him a verbal offer of 15k. All well and good, except Blue Rinse Bill seemingly forgot that a verbal contract ain't worth the paper it's not written on, and the blues never put the offer in writing, meaning he could walk away for free (or hobble away in his case as it turned out he had a bum knee). Had they done so, they'd have gotten around £4m from Newcastle. Instead, they got nothing. The real victims were Gosling's former club Plymouth, who had a sell on clause in the deal that took him to Goodison, but Everton's incompetence shafted them too and they ended up going into administration. Gosling has been injured for most of the time since, which let Everton off the hook really as imagine if he'd actually turned out to be any good? That would have been the biggest transfer embarrassment since they flew Brazilian World Cup striker Muller in and made a big deal of his impending capture, only for him to jump on the first plane out of there when he discovered he had to pay tax on the salary they'd promised him.

I see Steven Taylor was wearing one of those 'Phantom of the Opera' masks for some reason. The commentator didn't explain what happened to him, presumably he's been texting one of his team-mates' birds again, the daft bastard. If he wasn't a footballer he'd be nailed on to be in Big Brother or Geordie Shore that lad. Massive whopper.

Wigan v Blackburn was next in the "Battle of the Basement". The Yak bagged himself another goal after typically shocking Wigan defending. Not by Alcarez this time, that turd was serving a suspension. Caldwell was the guilty party this time. Yakubu is still banging them in though to be fair to the old fella. Wigan were denied a stonewall pen when Moses was hacked down right in front of referee Andre Marriner, but Jordi Gomez scored almost immediately after. Caldwell showed he's better in the opposing box than he is in his own (not good when you're a centre half) with a fine header to put Wigan in front, and then David Dunn was sent off for a second booking. That sparked the travelling Rovers fans into a 'Kean Out' chant. Didn't the Venky's just give him a new contract, or did I dream that? He ain't going anywhere. You can just tell those Rovers fans are wanting their team to get a proper hiding so maybe Kean will get the bullet, but the players are still digging in and fighting for the shirt every game. They aren't very good, but they are trying.

Whilst that is happening Kean is safe I reckon. Hope so, as I want to see what those fans do next. They've had protests in the ground, they've hired a plane to fly over with a 'Kean Out' banner, what's next? My money is on them releasing a song for Christmas, the fucking losers. *"Jingle Bells, Steve Kean smells, David Dunn's a twat. Yakubu is a pensioner and he's also somewhat fat"* Needs a little work but I'd buy it, if only to keep whatever shite X-Factor churn out from reaching number one. Rovers equalised in bizarre circumstances when Pederson took a corner to himself and then crossed for my boy Junior Hoilett to nip in and score at the back post, but a howler by Robinson looked to have gifted Wigan the points late on. The keeper let a weak shot by Wigan substitute Crusat squirm under his body and the home side thought they were home and dry. Crusat is only about three foot two, and a good six inches of that is his hair. He seems more suited to Willie Wonka's chocolate factory than Premier League football. Robinson made amends in some style though, going forward from a corner and putting his head in where it hurts to win a pen that the Yak showed great nerve to convert. Great point for Blackburn, another bad day for Wigan who look certainties to go down at this moment in time. They've every right to feel hard done by here though, Marriner's performance was pitiful. Pleased for Paul Robinson though, he seems like a good lad and always applauds the Kop when he plays at Anfield. He's also a better left back than his namesake at Bolton.

Swansea entertained the Mancs at the Liberty Stadium. Giggs was playing, presumably after United had pulled a BA Baracus 'sleeping pills in the milk' routine on the fucker, as trying to get that bastard to play in Wales is nigh on impossible, just ask John Toshack, Mark Hughes, Bobby Gould et al. Unpatriotic, sister in law shagging, hairy twat. Hernandez scored after Swansea got caught trying to be too clever on the edge of their own box. Sinclair missed an absolute sitter and Swansea had other chances too but United held on.

Robin Van Persie FC travelled to Norwich to take on the Canaries. VPFC fell behind when Mertesacker's dawdling allowed Morrison to nip in and score. Van Persie equalised before half time and then grabbed the winner after the break.

QPR went to Stoke in what was probably the least attractive looking fixture of the weekend. The game was notable for one thing, Jonathon Walters scored a goal from open play. Heidur Helguson equalised with a great header and Luke Young put Rangers in front with a good finish from a lovely passing move. Helguson stole in at the back post to convert a teasing Barton cross to make it 3-1. Stoke pulled one back with a typical Stoke goal bundle in by Shawcross and they also had a couple of penalty appeals turned down. Pulis reverted to type and was back to crying about the ref again. I'm loving seeing Stoke's troubles, long may they continue. Fuck off Stoke.

Next up was Everton v Wolves. The Evertonians were revolting again and they also had another pre-match protest (like I say, never gets old). Wolves took the lead from the penalty spot after Fellaini left one of his canoe feet in and tripped Edwards. Boyhood red Steven Hunt tucked the penalty away, but Jagielka levelled for the blues shortly after. Another boyhood red settled the game from the spot, Leighton Baines rolling the ball in calmly after Saha had been shoved in the back. McCarthy was furious about the decision, and even Moyes said it was a bit soft. I thought the ref got it right, whoever he was. I've never seen that ref before and have absolutely no idea who he is. Doesn't really matter, they're all pretty much as shit as eachother these days.

West Brom beat Bolton at the Hawthorns. Jerome Thomas opened the scoring when he beat the offside trap and rounded the keeper. Motson saw the replay and said *"it's one of those you could see two or three times before you call it"*. Yeah, you could if you're a dribble chinned, jabbering idiot who should have retired years ago. Most of us just saw one replay and could tell he was onside. Fuckin' Motson. This was another ref I've never seen before, and he gave a pen when he adjudged Thomas to have fouled Muamba. I await Paul Scharner's attack on the sportsmanship of Muamba. Oh wait, he won't do that as there's no Alex Ferguson started 'Muamba is a diver' bandwagon for him to jump on, the fucking uncool geeky bastard. Klasnic buried the pen, but Long put the Baggies back in front with a smart header and he should have been awarded a pen when he was hauled down by Wheater. Good player that Long, if he keeps this up he'll be playing for a better side than West Brom next year. Bolton stink though.

Finally on Saturday, Fulham and Sunderland played out a goalless draw in the North East. Sunderland hit the bar twice, and both sides could have won it in the last couple of minutes. Apart from the fans of both these teams, no-one cares really. That's why they were on last.

Onto Monday, and Spurs had a comfortable 2-0 win over Villa. I didn't watch it and I've only seen the goals. Adebayor has been a great signing so far for Spurs, but you can go back to what I was saying earlier about City. They paid a fortune for him, gave him stupid wages and then decided after a year they didn't want him. No-one could pay the fee AND his salary, so essentially Spurs get a player for nothing who they would not normally have been able to sign. They'll probably have to do the same with Tevez, and no doubt 'Arry will be first in line with his grubby hand out there too. Modern football stinks, it just stinks a bit less when you win.

LIVERPOOL 1 MANCHESTER CITY 1

Competition - Premier League
Date - Sun 27 Nov 2011
Venue - Anfield
Scorer(s) – Joleon Lescott O.G.
Half Time - 1-1
Star Man – Lucas

Team: Reina; Johnson, Skrtel, Agger, Enrique; Kuyt (Carroll), Henderson, Lucas, Adam, Downing; Suarez:

We've had five draws at home so far this season, but this was probably the least disappointing. We were a little unfortunate not to win the game but if I'm honest I'd have taken a draw beforehand so I'm not too downhearted about having to settle for one point rather than three.

The performance gives great cause for optimism, and I live in hope that one day a keeper is going to come to Anfield and not turn into some kind of hybrid of Gordon Banks and Lev Yashin. Seriously, can we not just have a keeper come here and make a fucking mistake instead of repelling everything that's thrown at him? Just once?

Look at the last four home games. De Gea makes a string of saves late on to prevent us beating United. John Ruddy has the game of his life for Norwich, Vorm produces stoppage time heroics to win a point for Swansea and now Joe Hart does it for City. The save late on to deny Carroll was ridiculous, but summed up our season. Games are won and lost on fine margins, and we could so easily be at least eight points better off right now. An inch here, a couple of inches there, and those draws turn into wins. The important thing is we keep doing what we are doing and hopefully we'll eventually get our reward. City will be delighted to be still unbeaten after this, as despite an excellent start by them they were hanging on desperately in the second half. They were penned back in their own half for long spells, and even before they were reduced to ten men they were second best. We have to be encouraged by that, especially coming off the back of a win at Chelsea. Four points from those two fixtures is an excellent return, but it means nothing if we can't go on and beat the likes of Fulham and QPR.

It would have been interesting to know what side Kenny would have picked had Bellamy been available. It was perfectly understandable that he wasn't of course, he'll have been affected more than most by the tragic death of Gary Speed. I don't know if the decision was taken by Bellamy or by Kenny, either way it was completely understandable. Given how well we played last week at Chelsea a strong case could be made for going with an unchanged side, but I always felt that we'd see an extra midfielder brought in for this game as going up against City with just Lucas and Adam in the middle is asking for trouble. Silva would have run amoc, so it was no surprise to see Henderson brought in to replace Bellamy. Personally I'd have preferred Spearing in there - he and Lucas were outstanding in this fixture last season - but if Henderson is to play then much better if it's centrally rather than out wide. Downing getting the start over Maxi surprised me a little though and the little Argentinian must be wondering what he has to do to get in the side. The presence of Micah Richards might be a factor in that, he's been playing like a right winger of late and Maxi may have struggled to deal with him? I don't know, there must be a reason for it though. From that perspective, Downing actually did well as Richards didn't get forward much at all and was penned back completely in the 2nd half as we dominated. That was quite a turnaround from the opening period of the game when City looked ominously good. They were moving the ball quickly and the movement of the front players was excellent. It reminded me a little of some of the games we've had at Anfield against Arsenal when they were good. We were struggling to get near them early on as Silva, Nasri and Aguero were all very prominent as City attacked the Kop end. We were living dangerously in the opening 20 minutes. Reina had to be alert to dash off his line and tackle Aguero after an awful backpass from Enrique. Aguero was appealing for something, at the time I thought he didn't like the challenge from Reina but having seen the replay he wanted a handball. The ball did seem to hit Pepe's arm and we maybe caught a bit of a break there, although it was one of those calls that could have gone either way.

City were menacing though, and got down the left hand side a couple of times to get dangerous balls into the box that we did well to deal with. Aguero then dropped the shoulder and completely blew by Skrtel, but Agger did enough to put him off and he ran the ball out of play. That came after Adam looked to have been brought down in City's half right in front of referee Martin Atkinson. City were well on top and it wasn't a shock when they took the lead through Kompany. Initially it looked like a great near post header, but the replay showed he was very fortunate to score as he missed it with his head and it glanced off his shoulder and into the far corner. Had we put someone on the post he'd probably have cleared it, but for whatever reason we don't seem to do that. At least we don't bring everybody back anymore and always have someone on halfway. Maybe that's why there's no-one on the back post though.

City's fans were in gloat mode now, no doubt expecting the floodgates to open as they have in so many of their other games this season. Who knows, they may have done had we not hit back almost immediately with a fortunate strike of our own. Adam's shot was going wide, but just like against Wolves earlier in the season, it struck a defender and deflected in. From that moment on the game changed I felt. City seemed to lose a bit of their swagger whilst we grew in confidence. We were the better side after that, and Adam was very unlucky not to make it 2-1 shortly after when Suarez and Kuyt combined to create an opening which the Scot sidefooted goalwards only to have Hart make a great save with his foot.

The second half was really impressive. Aguero's influence on the game all but disappeared, he was anonymous as Agger in particular did a great job on him. We were enjoying a lot of possession as Lucas and Adam took hold of the middle of the park, and Enrique and Downing began to enjoy a lot of success down the left. I thought we were terrific 2nd half, really impressive. We played at a high tempo and City were knocked out of their stride. When we had the ball we moved it quickly and incisively and all that was missing - again - was the finish at the end of it. Downing almost teed up Kuyt twice. First when his purposeful run and cross was deflected by Kompany and Kuyt misjudged the flight of it slightly and was unable to direct his diving header on target, and then when he met Henderson's deep cross with a volley that flew across the face and just in front of Dirk. He hit that too well, if he scuffed it Kuyt would have had a tap in. He did scuff another effort that looped up and brought a good save from Hart, whilst Suarez almost created a goal when he skinned Kompany and forced a panicking Lescott into a poor clearance that rebounded off Kuyt and nearly into the net.

City weren't doing much at all, and it was no surprise when Balotelli was introduced midway through the 1st half. He didn't look interested from the minute he slipped over when it looked like he was going clean through. After that he was just standing around looking miserable, giving the ball away cheaply and conceding free-kicks. His first booking was stupid. He had to know he'd be booked for such a blatant pull back. As soon as that happened I knew he was going to get sent off, I haven't seen anything more obvious all season. I'm just surprised it took so long to happen. The second yellow was beyond stupid. He barged into Skrtel with his arm raised and his elbow struck Skrtel on the side of the head. I've seen it suggested that Skrtel made a meal of it, and Mancini went as far as to say the ref didn't want to book him but the reaction of our players forced him into it. Firstly, those who say Skrtel milked it, maybe he did a little but when someone runs into you and hits you in the head with their elbow raised, there's a decent chance it's going to fucking hurt a little bit, whether it's a swinging elbow or a straight arm. Secondly, Atkinson's hand was going to his back pocket before any of our players got near him, and so it should have as that's as blatant a yellow card as you'll see. It wasn't a malicious foul, but it was a completely braindead one that was begging for the punishment it got. If you're already on a booking why would you make a challenge like that? Why does Balotelli do any of the mad stuff he does? Because he's batshit crazy that's why. I really disliked him when he first came over here, but this season I've really been buzzing off him as he's absolutely fucking hilarious. Going into this game I was just hoping he wasn't going to do something to ruin that and make me go back to thinking he's just an arrogant, petulant little knobhead. I had visions of him scoring in front of the Kop and acting the twat. Thankfully his antics just made me embrace the madness even more. He is unquestionably an arrogant, petulant little knobhead, but he's funny as fuck. A child's brain in a man's body. The standing around looking as though he wanted to be anywhere but on the pitch, the two yellow cards that hurt his team, having to be ordered back to the dressing room by Mancini after he refused to leave the field, and then the coup de grace, attacking the dressing room door whilst Adam and Lucas were doing their Sky interview. The lad is nuts. Gloriously, wonderfully nuts.

The sending off didn't affect City too much as he was contributing nothing to their cause anyway. It did present Kenny with the opportunity to introduce Carroll however. Up until then, it was difficult to get him on because you have to be concerned about being over-run by City's midfield. Carroll being on the field means we more or less have to play two up top, and for that to happen we need to sacrifice a midfielder. Dirk made way, meaning Henderson moved out to the right hand side. We lost a bit of momentum for a little while after that, perhaps due to the formation change to accommodate Carroll, or maybe it was down to City trying to baton down the hatches. Either way, it wasn't until stoppage time that we really seriously threatened again. When we did, it almost brought the winning goal. Johnson had been more and more of an influence as the 2nd half wore on, and he clipped in a hopeful ball towards Carroll in the centre of the box. The striker did extremely well to not only hold off the defender and get his head to the ball, but to also direct it towards goal. Hart made a flying save to keep it out, and then also kept out Suarez's well struck follow up. Downing reached the loose ball ahead of the defender but couldn't keep his shot down and it ended up in the back of the Kop and with it went any hope we had of three points.

Disappointing that we couldn't win, but encouraging that we outplayed the best team in the country. It was a good team performance in which everybody played their part. Some played better than others, but I wouldn't be critical of anybody as I felt they all made a contribution and there were no passengers. Defensively we coped very well with the most potent attack in the country. Skrtel and Agger impressed again, but it was the midfield duo of Lucas and Adam who stood out for me. Adam has been playing very well for most of the season and has been great in recent weeks. He was class again, but he was eclipsed by Lucas who produced a monstrous display. These are the kind of games where Lucas really shines, at Anfield against the big boys is where he comes right into his own. I don't remember him losing a tackle and he also seemed to win every aerial duel too. He was all over the park pressuring City players and his passing was precise and crisp. Just a top class performance. The only blemish was late on when Dzeko got away from him down the left wing and almost created a goal for Silva (Reina did enough to hold him up and we ended up with three players on the line ready to clear the danger.). Even then, Lucas tried to do the right thing by fouling Dzeko. He tried to pull him back but couldn't get close enough, and he tried to hack him down but again he just couldn't get in range to do it. Aside from that, flawless.

We've played all five of the other sides likely to make up the top six at the end of the season (unless Newcastle last the pace, which I very much doubt they will). We outplayed City and United but could only draw. We outplayed Arsenal and Chelsea and beat them both, and it's only Spurs that have looked superior to us on the day. As ever, our problems are coming in the games that we are expected to win. Sort that out and we're in great shape. Days like this show we're headed in the right direction, but they count for nothing if we can't follow it up by beating Fulham next week. That's the challenge facing Kenny and the players now.

Premier League Round Up (26-27 November 2011)

There have been some terrific weekends of football so far this season in the Premier League. This wasn't one of them, and it was all a bit 'meh' to be honest. Of course there was the hilarious weekly episode of 'Mad Mario's World', but that's already been covered in the match report. Thankfully normal service will be resumed next week when City are playing someone other than us. No wait, he'll be suspended won't he? Shit. I wonder if I can appeal?

MOTD got off to the worst possible start on Saturday; Chelsea at Stamford Bridge, with Motson commentating. There's really nothing worse: A stadium full of knobs, a pitch full of scumbags and that bastard providing the commentary. The hysterical, high pitched yelling any time a Chelsea player had an attempt at goal seemed worse than ever this time. It was so ear piercing I contemplated muting the TV until the game had finished. But then I wouldn't know what the bumbling old fool was saying and I wouldn't be able to rip into him for your reading pleasure. So I took one for the team and endured it. Thinking about it, this might be the biggest sacrifice to mankind since God sent his son down to get nailed to a cross. Be interesting to know what Jesus would have done given a choice of the cross or 30 years listening to Motson every Saturday night. Tough call.

Mongo gave Chelsea an early lead, as 'Motty' predictably screeched: *"Who else but John Terry?"* Do the BBC put a clause in their commentator's contract that forces them to say that shit? Terry has scored 46 goals in 13 years, an average of under four goals a season. So I'm sure a lot of you are wondering, "why this 'Who else' crap every time he scores?" Luckily for you, I'm here to tell you why. It's because he's committed 376 despicable acts that have put him in the public spotlight in the 13 years he's been playing for Chelsea. That's an average of just under 29 a season, meaning any time he scores a goal it's usually at a time when he's in the middle of some sort of self inflicted scandal/controversy. Hence the "who else but John Terry" line, which is actually commentator speak for "for fucks sake, this vile specimen just can't keep out of the headlines, can he?"

If Motson had actually said that he'd have lost his job, obviously, but he may have gained my respect which I would say is surely more important. I could probably forgive the years of torture he's subjected me to if he did that. I say 'probably', because it's a lot to forgive really. I'm really not sure I'm that big a person if I'm truthful. I know this might come as a bit of a surprise to some of you, a shock even, but I'm probably not the most objective person in the world when it comes to John Motson. No really, I'm not. Even so, I don't think I'm being unreasonable when I say that he is definitely getting worse by the week. There's probably some of you reading this who think he's ok. To you people I would say this; Fuck off, you bad wrong uns.

Sturridge scored to make it 2-0 and Mata added another before half time, prompting Motson to plumb depths of inept shitness not seen on TV since John Barnes (bless his tight fitting little shorts and wondrous, muscular thighs that you just want to... never mind) was stinking it up as a frontman on Channel 5's footy coverage. "MATAAAAAAA!!!!! What a finish. Well I thought Mata should have been found earlier by Drogbaaarrrr, but no 'Mata' now. Ha ha!!" Laughing at his own shit puns now? The man is a fucking joke, except it's not funny because our licence fees are paying him to inflict this on us. I don't wish him any harm, I'm sure he's a nice enough fella in real life (maybe), I just wish him off my fucking television on a Saturday night. I don't know what gets to me the most. The high pitched hysterical screeching, the creepy little Chief Wiggum 'snort' laugh he does, or the weird slurping sound he makes when he's finished a sentence. Actually no, I do know what gets to me the most. It's the whole Meirelesssshhhhhhh and Villassshhhh Boassshhhh thing.

Speaking of 'Shitcoat Junior', what an odious little dweeb he is turning out to be. I reckon if I'd gone to school with him I'd have been taking his lunch money every day and giving him wedgies. And I was a shithouse in school, that's how much of a biff Villas Boas is. He looks like the kid who'd sit in the corner of the playground on his own arranging his pogs into alphabetical order whilst the rest of the lads were either playing footy, snogging birds or smoking, or in my case all three at the same time. Ok, ok, I'm exaggerating a little there, I never smoked. I bet half that Chelsea squad rip the piss out of him behind his back. The other half do it to his face. And Petr Cech, what's his game? The headgear was one thing, now he's got some kind of face guard with it. He's slowly but surely turning into an ice hockey netminder or whatever they call them. Have a word with yourself, ye big tart.

As for Wolves, they're shit. I was completely wrong about them earlier in the season, I bought into what Mick McCarthy was selling, when it turns out he was selling cow dung in pretty packaging. The packaging came off after three games and the stench has been unbearable ever since. Kevin Doyle was out injured and with nothing better to do he took to ripping into Suarez on twitter. What is it with these nomarks at West Midlands clubs taking potshots at our Luis? As we know, Luis' English isn't the best, so allow me to reply on his behalf. "At he's not a poor man's Shane Long, knobhead."

No longer unbeaten Newcastle were up next, making the trip to Old Trafford having lost for the first time a week earlier to the other manc gobshites. United are nowhere near as formidable as City right now though, and the Geordies returned to the North East with an unexpected point. The game was not without it's controversy though, as you'd expect any time United don't get their own way. Rooney hacked away at Colloccini without any kind of punishment, largely because the Argentine didn't make anything of it and immediately shook Rooney's hand. Surprisingly, Ben Arfa was the only player who seemed to take exception to it, pointing out that Wiggy should have been off. Had it been a Champions League game he probably would have been. As it was, he stayed on and created the opening goal when his shot was hacked away by Taylor but the ball cannoned into the net off Hernandez. Spawny bastards.

Usually that would signal the end for Newcastle. A brave effort, kept it tight for a while but ultimately take nothing from the game. They are made of sterner stuff these days it seems, although they got a nice little helping hand from a linesman. It was never a pen in a million years, but fuck it. About time a bad decision went against them, and how ironic was this after what happened against Sunderland when the linesman gave a pen and then thought better of it? After that it was like the Alamo, especially after 'Jonas' was stupidly sent off, but somehow the Toon held on. Ferguson predictably went mad afterwards, tearing into the ref and linesman. After the Sunderland debacle, I half jokingly suggested the officials changed their mind because of the inevitable repercussions they'd face. Well guess what, the ref and lino that gave the pen in this game apparently won't have a game next weekend. Whatever happened to that "Respect Campaign"?? Oh yeah, it started and ended when Mascherano got screwed at Old Trafford.

Next up was West Brom v Spurs. The Baggies took the lead with a nice header from Mulumbu, but a dive by Lennon earned Spurs a pen that

Adebayor missed but converted the rebound. West Brom had chances to regain the lead but late goals by Defoe and Adebayor gave Redknapp's side the points. My dislike for Spurs is growing by the week, I don't like them being good, I'm not used to it.

Arsenal were held to a draw at home to Fulham. Murphy and Riise combined to create the opening goal, which was bizarrely turned in by Vermailen. The Belgian made amends by getting the equaliser with his head after one of his trademark forward runs. Class player him, he's their Daniel Agger. Cultured footballer - check. Excellent defender - check. Left footed - check. Misses loads of games as his bones are made of chipsticks - check. Like I say, their Daniel Agger.

Not happy times up on Wearside. It's bad enough for them seeing Newcastle doing so well, but when you lose at home to Wigan it must be very hard to take. Steve Bruce got dog's abuse from the home crowd. "You fat Geordie bastard, get out of our club" Ouch. Bruce will deal with that though, he's a strong character and he'll just take the abuse on the chins. What makes it worse is they took the lead and were all over Wigan for most of the game. They should have won this easily, and yet not only did they lose, they allowed Franco Di Santo to get the winner (in fairness it was a chance not even he could miss). Just about as bad as it gets that is.

At least it's taken a bit of the spotlight of Steve Kean for a week. Not that he's arsed, who cares if the fans hate you if your bosses are giving you a new contract and a pay rise? His team went to struggling Stoke, but they got thumped unfortunately. This was a brutal game, as you'd expect. Not much football being played (apart from the talented Rochina who was superb in Rovers' losing effort), just lots of scrappy play and NZonzi doing his best to kill people. Can't say I'm shocked, I remember his attempt to DDT Lucas a couple of years ago (one for any Jake the Snake Roberts fans there). By the way, that noise you may have just heard was my irony detector exploding after hearing Stoke players and fans complaining about 'agricultural' challenges.

Everton were back in their regular late night spot, second to last on the MOTD playlist because no-one cares about their shitty win at shitty ten man Bolton. Wheater was sent off early doors, not sure if it was because of the shin high tackle or the horrendous touch that forced him into it. Either way, it was probably deserved. Mophead put the blues in front and the supersub Greek lad wrapped it up late on. Apparently Duncan Ferguson has been coaching him recently, but despite that the lad still seems to be doing ok. Early days yet, just wait til Drunken gets him down Matthew Street on the lash, then let's see how he does. Bolton are shite though, I hope they go down.

MOTD ended with Norwich - QPR. You have to be pretty offended when you're deemed less relevant than Everton and Bolton, but I guess both these sets of fans are used to the late night slot as until this season they'd be on the Football League highlights show which is on directly after MOTD. Norwich won, probably undeservedly so on the balance of play, and QPR's players have some proper dodgy tache's going on right now. They look like the Village People, maybe next 'Movember' they should go the whole hog and trade in the Blue and White hoops for a leather kit with silver studs in it? They seem to have a good team spirit there and they'll probably stay up based on the crapness of some other sides. Good luck to them, even Neil Warnock who was pretty funny in his post match interview. I don't mean the usual unintentional, 'let's all laugh at that dickhead' kind of funny either.

There were two games on Sunday, one of which was of course our draw with City. The other was Swansea v Villa. It finished 0-0, which is another point on the road to survival for Swansea, and another point on the road to their customary mid-table anonymity for Villa. If Aston Villa were an ice cream, they'd be vanilla. Not the nice, 'Cornish' kind of vanilla, I'm talking supermarket own brand vanilla. No strawberry sauce, no sprinkles, certainly no flake, and not even any Phil Babbs (crushed nuts). Just plain old boring vanilla. Aston Vanilla!!! Ha ha! See, that's how it's done Motson, if you're gonna laugh at your own gags, at least make them funny.

CHELSEA 0 LIVERPOOL 2

Competition - Carling Cup
Date - Tue 29 Nov 2011
Venue - Stamford Bridge
Scorer(s) – Maxi Rodriguez, Martin Kelly
Half Time - 0-0
Star Man – Craig Bellamy

Team: Reina; Kelly, Carragher, Coates, Enrique; Henderson, Lucas (Adam), Spearing, Maxi (Skrtel); Bellamy (Kuyt), Carroll:

We've now won as many games at Stamford Bridge this season as we have at Anfield. If Chelsea were a trophy, Kenny would be entitled to take them home and keep them.

Not in his trophy cabinet of course, they aren't worthy of that honour and besides, it's already full to the brim. I'm sure he could find room in the the cupboard under his sink, or maybe in his shed. The point is, Kenny owns Chelsea. This was a great performance, even better than the one a week or so ago. Villas Boas was even gracious enough to acknowledge how superior we were on the night. A far cry from the usual 'best team lost' nonsense spouted by his mentor. I may have to rethink my initial appraisal of 'AVB'.

We were better than Chelsea in every area of the pitch despite making seven changes from the City game and whatsmore we did it without Suarez. That's the most heartening aspect of it for me, as I wasn't sure we were capable of playing this well without our talismanic striker. The team selection was more or less what most people expected. There were always going to be a lot of changes, but some of the starters from the weekend would have to turn out too.

The question was which ones. One of Lucas and Adam was going to start alongside Spearing, and one of Kuyt, Henderson or Downing would have to play too due to the lack of other options. Kenny opted to start with Lucas and Henderson, whilst Enrique also retained his place.

The current squad depth is probably as good as we've seen. Carragher and Maxi returned to the side, Bellamy and Carroll started up front and people like Spearing and Kelly can come in without any significant drop off in the performance of the team. The one concern I had was Coates who's not played enough yet to earn any degree of trust. He did well at Stoke aside from one error that cost us a goal, and he also conceded a daft pen for the reserves last week. I was worried about him, I'm not going to pretend I wasn't. That worry seemed justified when he lunged in foolishly at Luiz early on. It looked a stonewall pen on first viewing, but a furious Phil Dowd was having none of it and immediately booked the Chelsea player for diving. Looking at the replays, he was right. Luiz left his leg in and played for the pen, but if Dowd had pointed to the spot I wouldn't be complaining about it. Most times that would be given, and regardless of the 'dive' Coates can't be lunging in like that. That moment aside though, Coates was top drawer. I'm not worried about him any more. He will probably continue to make the occasional bad decision, young defenders generally do, but he's no Gabriel Paletta that's for sure. Defensively we were terrific. The back four were brilliantly marshalled by Carragher and protected superbly by Lucas and Spearing.

Lucas was a human wrecking ball in that first half. He just kept bullying Chelsea players off the ball, especially Torres. Any time our former number nine got the ball, Lucas steamed into him and took it off him like some kind of unlikely playground bully. It was fucking boss to see. And if it wasn't Lucas doing it, it was Carragher, who caught Torres right in the chops in the first few minutes. Fernando must be getting used to it now, last year he had his clock cleaned by Agger. He's lost three times to us now too. If he isn't wondering what the hell he was thinking back in January, then he fucking should be. Even if Chelsea go on to achieve anything, he won't be playing much of a part of in it. The real shame of it all is that he'd probably be devastating in this team Kenny has put together. I thought Andy Carroll played well in this game (penalty miss aside, I'll get to that in a second), but the way we played would have been perfect for someone like Torres rather than someone with Carroll's style.

Carroll did everything I could expect of him, he worked hard, he held it up and brought team-mates into the game and defensively he helped out massively in his own box at set-pieces. How many chances did he have though? Not his fault, it's just that his strengths don't always match up well with what the team is doing. He didn't get much service from out wide, and without that he's not going to pose much of a threat. When the ball did come in from wide he was a handful. He should have been awarded a penalty when he went to attack a left wing cross and was shoved in the back by Bosingwa. Both hands in his back it was, but Dowd gave nothing. From another left wing cross he did win a penalty when Alex used his arm to clear the ball away as Carroll was about to head it. Again, Dowd wasn't giving it, and I'm not sure the linesman was either. I didn't see a handball at the time, but Carroll's reaction to it was so passionate it was obvious something had gone on. You can't fake that kind of reaction, and Carroll was going mad. Dowd didn't give it straight away, but got a message through his ear piece and pointed to the spot. Who gave that message though? Linesman or 4th official? Whoever it was, they were right as it was a shocking piece of play by Alex.

Carroll immediately grabbed the ball, and with no Charlie Adam to take it off him this time he had a free run at the pen. Was there anybody who didn't think it was going anywhere except straight up the middle as hard as he could? Most of the time that works, but only because keepers generally dive out of the way. Turnbull dived late which meant he was able to get his legs in the way. Sums up Carroll's Liverpool career so far, it just isn't happening. At least he had the confidence to take it I guess, but that's three pens we've missed now this season. Can't afford to do that.

The first half was pretty cagey, we played well but weren't creating too much. I'm not sure what role Bellamy was supposed to be playing, but not only was he playing very deep but he never seemed to be more than five yards away from the man in possession when we had the ball. He'd get a five yard pass, then give it to someone else and then go and get it again and so on. It wasn't what I expected from him, although there were also some of those trademark runs down the left where he looks for the overlap from Enrique. I'd have liked to have seen him further forward trying to take advantage of the fact three of their back four were on yellow cards, but this had to be a tactical plan. Keep the ball, take the sting out of Chelsea, attack when the opportunity is there but don't do anything daft. It was a controlled performance and we looked very assured, but we didn't create a great deal in the opening half.

Chelsea weren't doing much either and unlike us they looked very disjointed. They'd rested plenty of players too and they had a few youngsters in the side, but even so with the quality they had on the field I expected a bit more from them. The only moment of concern for us (penalty appeal aside) was a header by Lukaku that flashed wide. He probably shouldn't have even been on the field at that point, as moments earlier he'd gone over the top on Henderson. Could have been a leg breaker, but fortunately Jordan was able to come back on after treatment. To add insult to his injury, Dowd booked Bertrand for the foul and Lukaku escaped.

The second half was a completely different game. It was open more or less right from the start, and the game became very stretched which allowed Bellamy to really come into his own on the counter attack. Chelsea had a couple of decent moments early on too, most notably when Malouda's mis-hit shot looped up onto the bar and Coates blocked Luiz's follow up on the goal-line with his chest. It was end to end stuff at this point, they'd attack, it'd break down and we'd quickly counter. This kind of game doesn't suit Carroll as much though, and had Suarez been on the pitch I think we'd have torn Chelsea apart.

We didn't need Luis though as we scored two goals without him. The first was a beautiful move. Spearing switched the ball quickly to Henderson and with the full back having moved inside there was a nice gap for Henderson to send Bellamy scampering clear of the offside trap. He carried it forward and then delivered a perfect cross to Maxi on the back post who rolled it in with his left foot. That's what Maxi does, he has a habit of taking up positions that lead to him getting goals. Would Downing have been in that position? Maybe, I'd say probably not though as he's a different player to Maxi with different strengths and weaknesses. In a team that struggles for goals though, right now Maxi has to play more often than not, whether it's on the left or the right I don't really care, but he deserves his place. So too does Bellamy, who's made valuable contributions every time he's been on the pitch for any length of time this season. He made the first goal, and then made the second too. He attacked Chelsea down the left and won a free-kick, which he then whipped in perfectly onto the head of Kelly who claimed his first Liverpool goal. He's been on a bit of a tear lately has Kelly, I believe he scored a couple for England u21s a couple of weeks ago too. So he should, he's a big powerful lad and there's no reason he shouldn't be getting on the end of set-pieces. Johnson is going to have to stay right on the top of his game to keep Kelly out of the side.

Chelsea made a couple of changes, introducing Anelka and Mata, but it didn't 'Mata' ha ha (how d'ya like that Motson) They penned us back in the last 20 minutes, largely because we were happy to protect what we had and make sure we didn't throw it away. We also lost Lucas, which was a big blow as he was fantastic once again. The injury didn't look too bad initially. He was in some distress and limped off for treatment, but when he came back on he then crumpled in a heap and appeared to be in agony. I'm no doctor, but it looked like whatever injury he had was made worse by sending him back out there. He left on a stretcher and in a lot of pain. Fingers crossed it's not a long term injury, but in the short term we should be fine as Spearing is a more than capable replacement and he was terrific in this game too. I can't remember him misplacing a pass all night.

The longer it went the more possession Chelsea seemed to have, but the less threatening they looked. Carragher and Coates cleared virtually every ball that found it's way into the box, and we held out comfortably in the end. Once again, I can't fault any player. Everyone played well and made a valuable contribution. I don't think anyone stood out above the rest as there were so many excellent performances. The lads who played on Sunday showed great energy and performed brilliantly, and those who came into the side all gave Kenny something to think about ahead of the game at Fulham. Special mention has to go to Bellamy though. Seeing him in tears before the game during the tribute to Gary Speed was very moving, clearly this has been a really tough time for him but he put that to one side and produced a match winning performance for us. He made both goals and was involved in everything we did. He's fucking class Bellamy.

chapter six

December

FULHAM 1 LIVERPOOL 0

Competition - Premier League
Date - Mon 5 Dec 2011
Venue - Craven Cottage
Scorer(s) –
Half Time - 0-0
Star Man – Jose Enrique

Team: Reina; Johnson, Skrtel, Agger, Enrique; Henderson, Spearing, Adam; Bellamy (Kuyt), Carroll (Downing), Suarez:

I don't know why I'm even surprised anymore. We beat the good teams, and drop points against the rest. It's what we do, sadly, it's who we are. Did we deserve to lose this? No, not in a million years, just like we didn't deserve to lose at Stoke and we didn't deserve to drop points at home to Norwich, Sunderland and both manc teams.

I'm sick of the hard luck stories though, it's time we made our own luck. That said, the disgusting performance of referee Kevin Friend can't be overlooked, he played a massive part in this defeat and there are certain things he did that really need looking at by his superiors. Still, if we'd put our chances away then that cunt's antics would have been a minor footnote to a welcome three points.

Once again we played good football, we were the better side but we were wasteful in front of goal. It's gone on too long now to simply be a matter of bad luck. A lack of fortune has played a part of course, and once again we were denied twice by the woodwork. 12 times now in just 14 games, five more than any other team. It's more than that though, we have an obvious inability to convert chances and it's killing us. The approach play is superb, the final pass or shot is often anything but. This game highlighted all the good and bad things we've been seeing from the side all season. Nice passing football, Suarez being fouled all over the place and getting nothing from the ref, Adam pulling the strings in midfield, being denied by the woodwork, getting punished for any mistake we make at the back and failing to take any of the numerous good openings we create. Same old story. On the one occasion we did put the ball in the net it was incorrectly ruled out by the linesman. It was a close call and he got it wrong, but it's difficult for me to make too big a deal of that given some of the scandalous decisions made by the referee later on. With offside calls as close as that, you win some you lose some. We were never going to 'win' this one as we didn't get a decision of any sort all night.

A lot will be made of the sending off and also the incident involving Adam on the edge of the box. There were plenty of other examples of Mr Friend's bias though, especially the continued beating Fulham's defenders were allowed to dish out on Suarez without any kind of punishment. Getting way beyond a joke that now, it's happening every week. The worst decision of the entire game for me though was the booking of Craig Bellamy. That was a fucking disgrace that. Bellamy wins the ball with a strong challenge on Dempsey, who leaps up with a huge bee in his bonnet and goes at Bellamy. He gets right in his face screaming abuse, and he puts his forehead into Bellamy's face in an aggressive manner. Bellamy keeps his cool, looks at the ref to say 'what are you going to do about this', and the fucking inept cunt books both players. Scandalous. He needs reporting for that.

Not far behind it was the sending off of Spearing. I've read some comments suggesting it was a red card as he was 'out of control'. He was to a degree, well after he'd won the ball cleanly. But since when has that kind of tackle been a sending off? It needs clearing up, as if this actually is now a red card offence they need to let everybody in the game know, as every footballer I've seen comment on it on twitter reckoned it was a great tackle. If players are going to be sent off for this, shouldn't someone actually, ya know, tell them about it as they don't seem to realise? It's the kind of tackle that young English footballers are encouraged to make and I bet you anything you like we see worse go unpunished next week. Jay Spearing has been brought up with the mentality of going in hard but fair, and that's the kind of tackle that gets the crowd going. Being sent off for that is a joke as far as I'm concerned, unless it's going to be the same right across the board and anyone who does it gets a red card. It won't be though, and that's what's so annoying about this. It seemed to me that the ref couldn't fucking wait to do it. He was dying to send one of our lads off, and in my eyes the only crime Spearing is 'guilty' of - and I use that word very loosely - is of giving the twat the opportunity to do what he was itching to do.

It'd be easier to take if this was simply a case of a jobsworth ref handing out cards like confetti. It wasn't though, he was letting all kinds go all night. Senderos did enough to be sent off twice, and Hangeland got away with a couple of forearm smashes into the face of Suarez. The ref wasn't card happy, he was just biased. We should appeal the suspension, but we probably wont win. There's no way that ref will admit to any wrongdoing, and the panel won't over rule it either, although they did in Rodwell's case so I guess there's a precedent there. It's really unfortunate for Jay and couldn't have come at a worse time for him as he looks to show he can adequately fill in for Lucas. He was playing fairly well, moving the ball quickly and getting his foot in. Even though Fulham were finding space between our back four and midfield that's not just on him, it was more of a collective issue I felt. It's not like it was a case of one player dropping off and not being picked up, the way Fulham were playing they had two and occasionally three players trying to get into that space. We had some issues picking them all up, sometimes it would be Dembele and other times it was Dempsey, or even Ruiz.

Most of those problems had been in the first half and we looked more compact after half time. Fulham did pose a threat all game, as they would as they are a strong side at home and have some good attacking players, but I never felt particularly worried about the result until the sending off. I liked the 433 formation Kenny went with, it wasn't perfect and there are some things that need working out, but I applaud the effort to get Carroll, Suarez and Bellamy all on the pitch at the same time. It worked to a degree. We created chances and played some good incisive football, but we didn't put the ball in the back of the net. We went very close through a great effort by Henderson that hit the post, can't blame him for not scoring there he was just desperately unlucky. But the fact is we didn't put the ball in the net and it doesn't matter what formation you play with and what players you select, if you can't score you won't win games. It's not rocket science. Carroll was the main offender, although I'm loathe to have a go too much as he was unlucky with one of the two chances he had. The shot that went straight at the keeper from Suarez's cutback was a bit unfortunate. On another day that flies into the net, but it's endemic of what is happening with Carroll. He struck it flush, and if he'd not caught it as well it would have gone in. Someone like Darren Bent for example has made a career out of shinning, bobbling, deflecting, mis-kicking those kind of chances into the net. He's got the knack for putting the ball in the net, regardless of how scrappy and fortunate it may seem. Carroll hasn't got that, and even his good efforts don't seem to find their way in.

The other chance he missed, again from a great cutback by Suarez, wasn't good at all. He kicked it onto his own leg by the looks of it. I don't like saying it, as I do rate Carroll and I was buzzing when we signed him, but our biggest problem this season is we have a number 9 that can't score. That is putting more pressure on others to find the net, and with the exception of Suarez and Maxi (who can't even get a game most weeks) and I suppose Bellamy, no-one else is doing it.

We've scored fewer league goals than Blackburn, Bolton and Norwich, and a whopping 31 goals less than Manchester City. We've got the best defensive record even though we're far from being a defensive side. We're an attacking side that can't score, and it's killing us. It must be doing Kenny's head in, but it's looking increasingly likely that he's going to have to do something about it as it isn't going just sort itself out with the players we have. We needed Andy Carroll to be good, but he hasn't been. It's not that he's always been bad, but he just looks to be a bad fit for us and we're a bad fit for him too. Most areas of the team are functioning well, but we don't have a centre forward who is banging the goals in. If we did have, we'd be a lot higher in the table than we are because there's really not a lot wrong with us aside from that. I'm not worried about the direction we're headed, I'm enjoying watching us play, but the lack of a cutting edge is incredibly frustrating.

This was an enjoyable game until the referee decided to ruin it. It was end to end, both teams were getting the ball down and passing it, and there were numerous chances at both ends. There were three key incidents in the game, and the officials got all of them wrong for me. The sending off, the disallowed goal and the Adam incident. I keep hearing that Senderos fouled Adam outside the box, and I keep hearing people ripping into Adam for not playing in Bellamy. Personally I disagree on both counts. The foul may have started outside the box, but Senderos was still dragging Adam as he went into the area and the final contact was well inside. Not only a penalty, but it should have been a red card too as Adam had full control of the ball and his next act would have been a shot at goal from a great position. That brings me to the second point. Yeah, he could have rolled it to Bellamy, but he backed himself to beat Senderos knowing that if he did he would be in on goal, on his left side, with a great opportunity to score. Adam did beat Senderos, and he was hauled down. It seems like he's getting more criticism over this than Senderos or the ref! That's harsh for me, I don't have a problem with what Adam did at all. He just got cheated out of a goalscoring opportunity. If he wasn't fouled I'd have bet on him scoring from there. The goal we conceded was a bad one. Neither Johnson or Reina covered themselves in glory on it, but there was a certain inevitability about it at that point after all that had gone before.

Kenny shuffled his pack and sent on Downing and Kuyt for Bellamy and Carroll, and Downing was desperately unlucky not to draw us level with a great run and shot that Schwarzer tipped onto the post. If there was any doubt before then that this wasn't going to be our night, I think we all knew after that incident we may as well just pack up and go home.

I'm going for Enrique as the star man. Could easily have been Suarez or Adam, but the full back did well at both ends of the pitch and is just churning out good performances week in week out. He's been a great signing and looks to have solved a position that has been a problem for years. The result is a real setback as there's a little gap opening up now between us and 4th spot. Nothing to panic about just yet, but we can't keep dropping points to sides outside of the top seven. We've had a long unbeaten run and now we need to embark on another. A home game with QPR should be just what the doctor ordered, so why can I see us slipping up again?

Premier League Round Up (3-4 December 2011)

Tributes continued across the country for Gary Speed this weekend. It's been remarkable really as it's not just been a case of fans 'doing the decent thing' and observing a silence or applause etc because they have to, it's been really genuine and heartfelt. It doesn't matter if he played for a rival team, football fans have shown great respect to him and in some cases (such as our game at Chelsea in midweek) fans have even chanted his name.

It's rare that you find a player who commands that kind of total respect across the board. There's just one gripe I've got here and it's not specifically related to Gary Speed's case, it's about tributes in general. Maybe it's just me, but do we really have to see the club mascot lined up with the players around the centre circle whilst the silence/applause is taking place? I still cringe when I think of that big green dinosaur in an Arsenal shirt lined up with the players during a tribute to the 96 last season. No doubt there were many similar instances across the country this weekend, and it just seems to cheapen the whole thing.

There was a giant bear lined up with the Blackburn players at Ewood, I dunno, that just seems wrong. I mean, should Steve Kean really have to go to such lengths just to be able to pay his respects on the pitch without the fear of being jeered by the angry Rovers mob? I'm well on board the Steve Kean train now. I've sort of been rooting for him in a half arsed kind of a way, just because I want him to shove it right up the arses of those Rovers' fans who've been acting the twat with their giant P-45s and planes flying banners over the stadium on matchdays. It's amusing to me seeing them frothing at the mouth as he just tries to ignore it and do his job. I didn't really care one way or another though whether they won or lost. I'm right in his corner now though, I want him to succeed just to piss those fans off. And if he can't succeed, I want him to stay and take them down. Either is good for me, I just don't want them getting the satisfaction of him getting sacked, and if he does get sacked then I hope they lose every game after that. Blackburn have been playing ok since an awful start and haven't had the results they probably deserved. The players are clearly still with Kean, but they might think twice about showing it as publicly as the Yak did after his stunning first goal. He ran towards the bench where an overjoyed Kean raised both hands for a double high five. The Yak obliged, and the cheers of the home fans turned to loud booing. Surreal stuff. I was listening to it on the car radio at the time, but having seen it on MOTD it was even worse than I expected. Poor old Steve, his little face lit up like a kid on christmas morning when the Yak scored. His team were in front thanks to a brilliant goal by a player he signed, yet still the fans boo. The stadium announcer yells *"and the scorer of Rovers' first goal, YAKUBU!!!!!"* and it's greeted with silence. Mental.

Leroy Lita equalised with a nice header after a typical Swansea passing move. Some of those home fans may even have been inwardly happy when that went in, I mean if they boo when their team scores how are they going to feel when they concede? I don't actually know, it's a really unusual situation and I don't think they are helping matters. They were kicking off wanting Kean sacked and rightly or wrongly the Vencky's gave him a new contract. Clearly they aren't going to sack him, so them stamping their feet isn't going to achieve anything. The team is still playing for Kean and given the size of the club and the calibre of the squad, is he really doing THAT badly? Newsflash Rovers fans, Jack Walker is gone, you don't have King Kenny or the SaS anymore and you can't fill your ground. You're at the level of Bolton/Wigan and that's not down to Steve Kean.

Yakubu went on to complete a hat-trick to put Rovers 3-1 up, but Luke Moore got the nerves jangling for Kean by pulling one back for Swansea. The way things have been going for Blackburn they probably felt they were gonna blow it, but Joe Allen was sent off for the Swans and the Yak made it safe with a cooly converted penalty. Four goals in a Premier League game is nothing to be sniffed at. All 'fat' and 'old man' jokes aside, you've got to hand it to Yakubu. He knows where the goal is and he's been fantastic this season. For a fat middle aged man. As for Kean, I'm nailing my colours to his mast now, so to speak. I like him, I didn't used to, but he's won me over with how he's handled all the shit that's been thrown at him. Only a heart made of stone could fail to be moved by his little beaming little face every time Yakubu scored. You keep pluggin away son, 'fuck da haters' as they say in the 'hood.

Moving on, and Chelsea were looking to put their recent woes behind them and will have been delighted to have been facing someone other than Liverpool and Kenny Dalglish. They made the trip to one of Kenny's former clubs to face the Toon, who are in the middle of a brutal run of games that had just seen them visit both manc clubs. It ended with Chelsea winning 3-0 but it was far from as comfortable as the scoreline suggests. Sideshow Bob somehow escaped a red card when he hauled down Demba Ba after just four minutes. I don't know how a ref can give a foul but not send him off in that situation, it seemed pretty clear cut. Sturridge then won a penalty but Lampard's shot was superbly saved by Krul. Sturridge was running riot in the first half and Ryan Taylor couldn't deal with him. Ba was having just as much joy at the other end though. He hit the post with a header and forced a good save from Cech with a nice flick. Drogba's superb header put Chelsea in front, but Newcastle kept at it despite losing the influential Colloccini to injury. Drogba headed against his own bar, Mongo had to clear off the line and Shola Ameobi smacked a great shot against the bar as plucky Newcastle piled on the pressure. Chelsea had their chances too, but Krul once again caught the eye with some fine saves. Steven Taylor went off with a bad injury and that was just one setback too many for the Geordies as Chelsea took advantage with two late breakaway goals through Kalou and Sturridge. Lampard was subbed and spat his dummy. You know by now what I think about Villas Boas, and I made reference last week to how those players don't respect his authority. I'm specifically referring to the 'old guard' such as Terry and Lampard. To them, he's still the little fella who used to *"hand out the DVDs"* when they were winning titles under Mourinho. I liken it to Goodfellas with AVB in the role of Tommy and John Terry as Billy Bats.....

Scene: Newly appointed Chelsea boss Andras Villas Boas walks into the dressing room at Chelsea's training ground to meet the players and renew acquaintances with some old friends he hadn't seen since the days when he was but a lowly assistant to Jose Mourinho....

Terry: *"HO! I haven't seen you in years. Jesus Christ Almighty. You look terrific."*
AVB: *"Watch the suit."*
Terry: *"You little prick. I know you all my life. Don't get too big on me."*
AVB: *"Just don't bust my balls."*
Terry: *"If I was gonna bust your balls, I'd say, "Go get your DVD box."*
Terry (turns to Juan Mata): *"This kid was great. "AVB the DVD". He'd make DVDs like Steven fuckin' Spielberg. Excuse my language. He was the best."*
AVB: *"No more DVD's Johnny".*
Terry: *"What?"*
AVB: *"No more DVDs. I've been away a long time. They didn't tell you? I don't make DVD's anymore."*
Terry: *"What's got into you? I'm breaking your balls a little, that's all. I'm only kidding with you."*
AVB: *"You don't sound like it. There's people around."*
Terry: *"I'm kidding. I haven't seen you in a long time and you get fresh. I don't mean to offend you."*
AVB: *"I'm sorry, too."*
Terry: *"Now go home and get your DVD box."*
AVB: *"Motherfucking mutt!"*

The Canaries have not exactly been flying lately, but they've been doing well enough and have been picking up points here and there to find themselves in the top half of the table. They were only ever going to get a thumping at City however. Even so, they should have taken the lead when Morrison got away from Toure and Kompany but he over ran the ball. Aside from that it was all City. Aguero showed terrific footwork and awareness to put City in front, and a howler by Ruddy allowed Nasri to make it 2-0. Don't wanna keep banging the same drum, but I'm sick of seeing keepers who have worldies against us start throwing them in in the weeks that follow. Yaya Toure got in on the act to make it 3-0 but Morrison headed in a consolation for Norwich. Substitute Balotelli scored the kind of goal only he could, or more specifically, only he would. Any other player would have headed that in, Mad Mario just arrogantly flicked it in with his shoulder and then refused to even crack a smile. Never a dull moment is there? Glad to see that the FA listened to my appeal to quash his suspension and let him play. Adam Johnson rolled in a fifth and City look to me like they'll win this league by at least 15 points. The top sides might be able to take points off them, but they'll just blow away everyone else on this form.

Norwich have been doing way better than expected, as have the other newly promoted teams. One of them will hit a wall after Christmas though, just as the likes of Blackpool and Hull did. If I had to pick one of them, it would probably be Norwich although Swansea are showing signs of struggle at the moment. For what it's worth, I hope they both survive, QPR too.

One team who look nailed on to go down at the moment are Bolton. They never really had much of a chance at Spurs anyway, especially when they fell behind to an early Gareth Bale goal. They could certainly have done without the ludicrous sending off of Gary Cahill though. I'm staggered by that, there's just no way you can justify that decision. Sometimes refs get things badly wrong because they've not seen something clearly. You know why they gave the decision even if you can see they've dropped a bollock. This one though, there's just no explanation for it. Stuart Atwell, you should find another career mate. Tottenham twatted Bolton but the tramp was in inspired form in the Trotters' goal. He couldn't do anything about Spurs' second goal though, which was fantastic to be fair. Spurs should have had a pen after that when Assou Acotto was tripped by Davies (yet more ineptitude from Atwell), but then scored from a corner that should have been a goal kick. Defoe hit the post and 'Scruffy' continued to make saves as Bolton kept getting torn apart. Owen Coyle was understandably pissed off about the red card, but it's difficult to have any sympathy for a grown man who insists on wearing shorts and football socks pulled up to the knee when he's not actually playing football. He looks like he should have a carer. Managers wear suits, or tracksuits. That's how it is. Shorts are acceptable in pre-season, providing the socks are rolled down and not pulled all the way up of course. But in December? Sorry, that's as big a fashion faux pa as grown men who wear replica goalie shirts.

Wigan were looking to build on their unlikely win at Sunderland last week by picking up another three points at home to Arsenal. I doubt if even their most optimistic of supporters believed they'd get anything other than a good hiding here though. Legohead put the Gunners in front when his shot just went right through Al Habsy. Vermailen made it 2-0 with a header from a corner. You never see Arsenal score from corners, they're even worse than us in that department. Vermailen is the one player who seems capable of winning a header in the opposing box, he's just a good all round centre half him. Gervinho made it 3-0 after great play by Van Persie, and Walcott then teed up his skipper for his customary goal. Walcott is starting to look like the player people expected him to develop into, he seems to be creating or scoring every week now. Good win for Arsenal, but if there is one team that are taylor made for a bumming by the Wenger Boys, it's Wigan. They're doooooomed. Bet they take at least a point off us though.

The Mancs won at Villa. Not much to say other than it was entirely expected. They're not playing well and haven't been for months, but they have this irritating habit of just spawning 1-0 wins no matter how shite they play. They have spells like this every season, it does my head in. We seem to have to play well to win games, and even that isn't enough sometimes. They just turn up, do nothing and go home with a 1-0 win. Aside from their early season flourish, I'd say we've played better than them this season. Points wise they're pissing all over us though, and that's what counts at the end of the day. Hernandez was stretchered off early on, and he'll be a big miss for them. Speaking of big misses, what the fuck was that shot from Heskey??? Edge of the box, clear sight of goal, left foot strike. Throw in. Nice one Emile.

At Loftus Road QPR got off to a great start when Heidur Helguson gave them the lead against West Brom. He's crap, but he's doing for QPR what Andy Carroll isn't doing for us. Does that say more about Helguson or Carroll? SWP had a cracking goal wrongly disallowed for offside and Barton missed a great chance to make the game safe. West Brom had done nothing, they were distinctly second best but QPR got edgy the longer it stayed at just 1-0 and Shane Long equalised on the counter attack. Neil Warnock was predictably pissed off afterwards, I've got nothing against QPR but I like seeing bad decisions go against them solely because Warnock is great value when he's been hard done by. He might be a bit of a knob but he raised a very interesting point afterwards. He said he'd love to know how much it hurts officials when they see their mistakes on MOTD. I'd like to think it bothers them, but in most cases I bet it doesn't, especially with referees. Put it this way, I guarantee Kevin Friend doesn't feel as bad as Jay Spearing right now.

Onto Sunday's games now, and Sunderland went to Molyneux with no manager. Martin O'Neill watched from the stands having just agreed to take over from the sacked Steve Bruce. Sunderland fans had demanded Steve Bruce's head on a platter, but in the absence of one big enough to accommodate it they had to settle for him being made unemployed instead. This was a surprisingly good game with chances for both teams and some good football played. Kieran Richardson's brilliant strike gave Sunderland the lead, and he was booked for taking his shirt off. I didn't need this to tell me Kieran Richardson is a knobhead. That's long since been established. He revealed a vest that said 'I belong to Jesus'. Somewhere up there Jesus is holding his hands up and saying *"hey, that helmet is nothing to do with me".*

Wolves looked finished when Seb Larsson won a penalty with an outrageous swan dive, but justice was done when the keeper saved it. Larsson's punishment was twofold as Fletcher equalised 25 seconds later. Larsson looked mortified, and the phrase 'cheats never prosper' briefly sprung to mind. Then I remembered all the titles the Mancs have won and that cheats do indeed prosper, often. Larsson is just the unlucky one. Fletcher won it for Wolves with his second of the game. He's a good player and he makes a big difference to them. Apparently he's only 24, which is incredible as he looks at least ten years older than that. Is he the oldest looking mid-twenties footballer on the planet? Not whilst Scott Carson still has a job he isn't.

Sunday's other game saw Everton play host to Stoke. Tony Pulis' side have been crap this season following Europa League games, and they were pretty shit in this game too. They won it though, somehow. Roberth Huth's scrappy effort proving to be enough to see off the toothless blues. Good to see Everton lose, but unfortunate that it had to be Stoke to beat them. A bit like winning an all expenses paid, fortnight's holiday for two........ in Rochdale.

LIVERPOOL 1 QUEENS PARK RANGERS 0

Competition - Premier League
Date - Sat 10 Dec 2011
Venue - Anfield
Scorer(s) – Luis Suarez
Half Time - 0-0
Star Man – Charlie Adam

Team: Reina; Johnson, Skrtel, Agger, Enrique; Downing (Shelvey), Henderson, Adam, Maxi (Bellamy); Kuyt, Suarez:

Should never have been this close, but I'm not complaining as at least this time we got the right result. Outside of Manchester City and maybe Spurs, I'd say we're playing the best football in the country so far this season.

Unfortunately, like a Neville at the Playboy Mansion, we just can't fucking score. Our build up play is excellent, we're defending well, nobody is outplaying us, but we can't put the ball in the net. At least we managed to do it once against QPR, and that proved to be enough. Just. All it would have taken was a lucky bounce in our penalty area and they could have snatched a draw. It would have been incredibly harsh on us, but we've seen it happen before. The glass half empty view is that our poor finishing will cost us when the points are tallied up in May. The flip side of it is just imagine how good we'll be if we actually sort this shit out?

Other than the almost criminal profligacy in front of goal, I don't see a lot wrong with this team. In fact, that's actually the only thing I see wrong as every other aspect of our game is fucking boss. Unfortunately, being able to put the ball in the net is actually quite important when it comes to winning football matches. I'd be more worried if we weren't creating so many chances though. I keep saying it, but I love watching us play these days, the style of football we're playing on a weekly basis is the best I've seen since Roy Evans's side. It's great to watch, it's pass and move and we are going out and attacking in every game we play. I know I'm saying it every week, but there's really not a lot wrong with us. Certainly nothing that a goalscorer wouldn't solve.

The football played in the first half of this game was superb at times. Suarez, Maxi, Downing and Kuyt all linked up well and created numerous openings which, predictably, went begging. Downing was outstanding on the right, he seemed to realise early on he had the beating of the full back and he was much more assertive than we've seen before. He combined to good effect with Johnson several times, and could be worth a look in that position again, especially as it means Maxi can play on the other side. Maxi surely needs to play every week now? The bottom line is that when he's in the side things happen. He always looks like he'll get a goal, and could easily have had a hat-trick in this game. He has a better understanding with Suarez than anyone else in the squad too, with the possible exceptions of Kuyt and Bellamy. The style of football employed by Kenny is perfect for someone like Maxi, and he's thrived more than anybody since the King took charge. That's what makes it surprising that he's often left out of the side.

The Argentine was involved in most good things we saw in the first half and his clever movement off the ball saw him get in behind their back four a couple of times. The first time he opted to play it to Suarez instead of going himself. It seemed to take Luis a bit by surprise and he couldn't adjust his feet properly and screwed his shot horribly wide. The second time - after a lovely ball from Kuyt - he looked to have done everything right but the keeper got down to make a good save. There were other close calls for him too, most notably when he was just unable to get on the end of a Suarez cross that fizzed across the goalmouth. Suarez was running amoc, the QPR defenders couldn't deal with him but far too often the final shot or pass wasn't what it needed to be. He opted to shoot from virtually on the goal-line rather than cut it back to the waiting Kuyt. Another time he tried a shot from a tight angle that ended up going for a throw in, much to the frustration of Kuyt again. He was denied by the keeper after a nice run and through ball from Downing who also forced Cerny into a save after yet another good run.

As well as we played, that first half was as frustrating as hell once again. QPR offered nothing at all in attack and they were under the cosh for the entire half. Yet they went into the break level. Their fans were enjoying themselves, it's a long time since they've been able to go to places like

Anfield. That's probably why they are still stuck in an 80's timewarp, waving ten pound notes at 'the poor scousers'. Hey losers, 1987 called, it wants its taunt back. They also spent most of the first half ripping into our players. "Luis Suarez, he looks like a rat" as well as "Jonjo Shelvey, he looks like E.T." (to my shame I laughed at that one) and "Andy Carroll, he looks like a girl" (half the ground laughed at that, not me though, I was empathising with my flowing locked compadre).

We've been in this situation so many times this season. Level at half time after missing loads of chances. I'm sitting there thinking 'here we go again, same old story' when suddenly Journey's 'Don't stop believing' echoes out around the stadium as the team takes to the field again. Talk about a sign! "There's no way we're not gonna win now" I say to myself.

The second half starts, and a minute later the goal arrives. It was defo the song that did it, I'm gonna email DJ George and demand he plays that at half time every game from now on. Charlie Adam and Suarez played a part too I guess. Adam showed nice trickery on the left, and then produced a perfect ball in with his RIGHT foot that Suarez despatched into the net with ease. Not many lefties are capable of that kind of quality on their right side, but Adam has shown a few times he can use both feet. The ball in was so good it was difficult for Suarez to do anything but score.

Would this open the floodgates? Well one day it might, but not this day. Normal service was resumed after that as we missed chances and hit the woodwork twice. Played some great stuff again though. Probably the best move saw Adam break forward and find Suarez who then exchanged passes a couple of times with Maxi that ended with the midfielder having a shot saved by the keeper. Had that gone in it would have been a goal we'd have been talking about for a long time. Really exciting stuff. Maxi was then denied by a combination of keeper and post after more good work by Suarez and by this time nerves were beginning to creep in on the pitch and in the stands. QPR had done nothing at all but with 15 minutes left they were still in it and started to pile men forward. They didn't really look like scoring as we defended extremely well, but they got plenty of crosses into the box and forced some corners. When that is happening, it only takes one slip or lucky bounce to concede a goal, and that made for a nervous finale.

Anfield held it's collective breath when Faurlin went down after appearing to have been kicked in the chest by Skrtel. I didn't have a good view of it, but with Lee Mason in charge you have to fear the worst when anything like that happens. Thankfully he waved play on. Having since seen the replay, Faurlin definitely made a five course banquet of it but if that's outside the box it's a free kick every time. Mason COULD have given that, it would have been incredibly soft, but he could have given it and we caught a bit of a break there. Having said that, he could have given us one in the 1st half too when Suarez was being held in the box and tumbled over. Outside the box, you get a free kick nearly every time for that. Inside it, not so much. The Faurlin incident just shows the danger of not putting your chances away though, as on another day, and by that I mean if that twat Kevin Friend was refereeing, that would have been given.

There was time for us to hit the woodwork once again as Bellamy skinned the right back and squared towards Suarez only for Wright-Phillips to get there first and smash the ball against his own crossbar. Bellamy had been brought on for Maxi, a sensible decision that could have been made a little earlier I thought, given how high up the pitch QPR had started to play. Shelvey also got on, replacing Downing as Kenny went with five across the middle late on. We might see more of Shelvey in the next few weeks with Spearing being suspended. It's not going to be easy for either of them to get in the side given how well Adam and Henderson did as a pair and with Gerrard due back soon.

I thought Adam was the best player on the pitch, and Henderson was very good too in a slightly more understated way. As a pair they played well and bossed the middle of the park. For the visitors, Joey Barton was very quiet. He was rightly given a good reception by most of the home crowd, the work he did pushing the e-petition for the 96 deserved our thanks. He's not quite the villain a lot of us thought he was, but there is still that dickhead streak in him that he can't control. Trying to start a fight in the tunnel with Bellamy and making rat faces at Suarez isn't going to endear him to anyone at the football club, that's for sure. He's trying to clean up his act, but the snide little bastard in him keeps rearing it's ugly head.

Premier League Round Up (10-12 December 2011)

Coming off their humbling at the hands of 'FC Baselona' in midweek, the Mancs would have done well to hand pick a better opponent than Mick McCarthy's hapless Wolves. Not only are they in awful form, but aren't they the side who waved the white flag last season and rested their entire first choice side when they went to Old Trafford? Or did I imagine that?

Anyway, this was a gimme for United even though Wolves did put out their best team this time and had a go. United's midfield isn't the best but as long as they have the likes of Nani and Rooney they'll be able to beat up on teams like Wolves. Shrek finally got himself back on the scoresheet, bagging a double when he could easily have had six. Nani got two as well and they were very dangerous in wide areas. Fletcher pulled one back for Wolves with a great header. That kid clearly had the world's toughest paper round but it's stood him in good stead and is paying off now as he looks a very good player, as does Jarvis who had the beating of Smalling and surely won't be at Wolves for much longer. The likes of Sunderland, Villa or Everton (assuming they either sell someone or Bill finds some loose change down the back of his sofa) would seem a likely destination for Jarvis, especially if Wolves go down.

Ferguson was kicking off afterwards about how he can't understand the criticism his young players have been getting. The fuck is he on about? All I've heard all season is people creaming themselves over Jones, Smalling and Wellbeck. I'm sick of it in fact, as it's been excessive. *"Oooh look at Phil Jones sprint 30 yards and then lay the ball off, he's a real bargain even though he actually cost more than Luis Suarez" "oooh look how powerful he is"*. Sick of people fawning over him, the big dope. As for Wellbeck, I liked him better when he was in Red Dwarf. Don't mind Smalling though for some reason. I'm looking for a reason to dislike him but other than the shirt he wears and the company he keeps I'm struggling. Actually, what am I saying. The shirt he wears and the company he keeps is clearly reason enough. Gobshite.

Ferguson is talking shit as usual though. Roy Keane made some off the cuff remark in midweek and now all of a sudden it's a campaign against 'Fergie's newest Fledglings', despite the fact that pretty much everyone else has been lauding them. Tell you what though, no-one will dare say anything about those lads now regardless of how shite they may play. Except Roy Keane, who doesn't give a fuck.

Moving on, Newcastle have had a fun ride but like all good things (and by 'good things' I mean 'flukey runs') it had to come to an end. The injuries to Colloccini and Steven Taylor effectively nobbled them. Their squad is ridiculously thin, to the point that they had no other centre backs to put in and had to use two full backs in there. James Perch and Danny Simpson are going to struggle as a pair against any big frontmen and Norwich's strikers must have been licking their chops in anticipation of this one. Grant Holt got a rare start and he and Morrison were just too much for Newcastle to handle. Their physical presence was something the Geordies couldn't deal with and every cross that went into the Newcastle box looked like it would end up in a goal. The opener was harsh on Newcastle as it came from a corner that shouldn't have been. Demba Ba equalised just before half time, and the more I watch him the more impressed I am. He's actually really good, his movement is terrific and he's a great finisher.

Holt and Morrison both scored headers to give Norwich some breathing room but another brilliantly taken goal by Ba gave Newcastle hope, even though they'd been reduced to ten men by that stage after Gosling saw red. Another header from Holt sealed the points for Norwich. Newcastle would probably have won this game if they'd had their centre backs available, but they might have to get used to this unless they can bring someone in when the window opens. Given Mike Ashley's track record there's more chance they'll sell somebody.

Aston Vanilla picked up their first away win of the season with a 2-1 success at Bolton. They were good value for it too and should have won more convincingly. Mark Albrighton (who is the most 'brummie looking' brummie I've ever seen) opened the scoring and Petrov added a second before Klasnic gave Bolton hope with a typical poacher's finish. Does nothing else but he knows where the net is that lad. Bent missed three great chances for Villa and Bolton never really looked like getting back into it. They're really, really, shite. So much so that I feel I should maybe apologise to the word shite for associating it with Bolton. Whatever word 'shite' uses to refer to shite, that's what Bolton are.

It didn't take Owen Coyle long to realise Ngog is hopeless did it? He couldn't even get off the bench when they were a goal down at home. Not that I'm disagreeing, I'm just wondering how Coyle can see through Ngog so quickly yet still persists on selecting Paul Robinson at left back every week. I'm not sure a manager's stock has ever fallen as quickly as Coyle's has in the last 12 months. Wasn't long ago he was being linked with the Arsenal job. The only hope he has of landing a job with Arsenal now is if they're looking to hire an 'ugly George Clooney' kiss-a-gram for their Christmas Party.

Speaking of Arsenal, Saturday was their 125th anniversary and was therefore a big day for Gunners fans. So nice of the BBC to spoil it for them by assigning Motson to commentate on it. All the legends were on the pitch prior to kick off; Thierry Henry, Tony Adams, Charlie George, Bob Wilson, Lee Dixon, Dennis Bergkamp, Ian Wright, Christopher Wreh.... The club unveiled statues of Herbert Chapman, Adams and Henry, and in the spirit of the occasion Arsene Wenger included one at centre half in the shape of Per Mertesacker. Is it just me, or is that Gervinho a bit poo? He's one of those players who manages to somehow look like he's good whilst he's actually being shit. Nicklas Bendtner is another one like that, apart from the looking like he's good part, obviously. Everton were useless again. They defend in numbers and work hard, but up front they're about as much use as an ejector seat in a helicopter. Tim Cahill used to be an average midfield player who's only real contribution to the team was to score goals. Now he's a below average striker who makes no contribution to the team whatsoever as he no longer scores. Seriously, if he isn't scoring headers then what is the point of him? He's become the football equivalent of a betamax video.

Van Persie settled the game with another great finish as Motson went into trademark 'out of breath, hysterical screeching' goal celebration mode. Makes my skin crawl. If the season ended today, RVP would get my vote for player of the year. If I had a vote, which I don't, although I should, as if people like me had a vote then that fucking adulterous, sister in law shagging, country abandoning, walking carpet Ryan Giggs would never have had a sniff of winning it.

Swansea took on Fulham at the Liberty Stadium and karma had a big hand in proceedings. Clint Dempsey had acted the twat the other night against us but he was rewarded when the ball fell kindly to him to score the winner. Sadly, on that occasion karma wasn't instant, but it did get him eventually as he scored an oggy and missed a pen in this game. Swansea won 2-0, albeit a bit fortunately.

Wigan made the trip to the Hawthorns to take on Roy's Baggies. Neither are any good, but I expected West Brom to take the points because Wigan are so bad defensively, and they were made even worse by the return of the hapless Alcaraz who was back from his spitting related suspension. Fortunately for them he was forced off injured midway through the second half, so he wasn't around for the inevitable late West Brom onslaught and Wigan held out. It says a lot about the shitness of Hodgson's side that they somehow managed to get beat at home by Wigan. The last manager who lost at home to Wigan was sacked. That's not going to happen to Hodgson, but the goodwill he built up with the Albion faithful last season is evaporating fairly quickly if their forums are anything to go by. Moses was the match-winner for Roberto Martinez's side. He scored one and also won the penalty that settled the game. He's a good player, but his end product has been badly lacking up to now. If he starts adding goals to his game he won't be at Wigan long as he's very talented. Unlike Paul Scharner, who missed a great chance to equalise. The shit bastard. Hodgson's side have now conceded penalties in four consecutive home games prompting him to bemoan his luck. Here's a novel idea, how about tell your players not to commit stupid fouls in their own penalty area? And I didn't need 35 years of management experience to come up with that either.

Onto Sunday now. I didn't actually see MOTD2 this week. I have it set to automatically record, but when I went to watch it, it wasn't there. Interestingly, the X Factor results show had been recorded though. I suspect foul play, but the wife insists she knows nothing about it. She would say that though, wouldn't she. There'd have been hell to pay if I'd missed any games worth watching, but fortunately for her I'd watched the Spurs game on sky earlier in the day so the only game I missed was Sunderland's win over my mate Steve Kean's Blackburn. The missus escaped with a slap on the wrist and a warning not to let it happen again. I've since watched the highlights of the Sunderland game via the ESPN goals app on my phone. Cracking little invention that. The app I mean, not the phone, although that's a pretty good one too. Blackburn were a little unlucky on the day, even though Sunderland will feel they deserved the three points as they dominated the 2nd half.

The story of the game was Martin O'Neill taking charge of Sunderland for the first time. I heard on the radio that he was a boyhood Sunderland fan. *"Bullshit!"* I thought. Turns out it's actually true though. Who knew? I guess eventually someone was going to be telling the truth with all this 'boyhood fan' crap. Maybe Sunderland were winning titles when O'Neill was a kid growing up in Northern Ireland or something, but then that would make him about 120 years old? O'Neill has never lost his first game with any club he's been at, but this was a close call. Blackburn should have had an early penalty when the returning Titus Bramble brought down the Yak. The ref didn't give it, but Rovers went in front anyway when Vuckevic headed in a rebound. He's got 'Simon' on the back of his shirt. That's actually worse than any of the others on the twat list I think. Well, it's on a par with 'Bryan' Ruiz I guess, but Vuckevic doesn't have silky, shiny, beautiful hair that you just want to sniff, so he loses points for that. I honestly don't know how this slips through the net, are there no guidelines for this kind of thing? The whole 'Chicarito' thing is bad enough, but players just deciding to have their first name on their shirts, I don't know how that's even allowed. How long before we see 'John', 'Steve', 'Mark' etc on the back of shirts? It's ridiculous. The FA need to stop wasting time persecuting Luis Suarez and appealing international suspensions correctly handed out to thugs in wigs, and deal with the real problems affecting football in this country; ie piss poor referees who are ruining games, and attention seeking cunts who refuse to have their surnames on their shirts.

Blackburn went into a defensive shell in the 2nd half and Sunderland laid siege to their goal. Maybe Kean paid the penalty for being overly cautious, but he wasn't helped by injuries that meant he had to use all three substitutes very early in the game. What that meant was effectively playing with ten men as Yakubu is a passenger when his team is on the back foot. He doesn't hold the ball up, he doesn't show for the ball, he doesn't close anybody down. Hell, he doesn't even move. He's bad enough when he's in a slump, but that four goal performance last week means he'll be dining out on that for a few weeks yet. Literally, if that 'all you can eat' clause rumour has any truth in it, and with those dodgy owners Blackburn have anything is possible. Not having any more subs to call on meant Yakubu had to stay on and Rovers couldn't get out of their own half. Spectacular late strikes from Vaughan and Larsson gave the Mackems the points and left Rovers still languishing in the bottom three and all the fans in the stadium went home happy.

The other game on Sunday was dominated once again by shite refereeing. I'm not particularly arsed as it helps us and Spurs are doing my fucking head in these days, but this was some pretty shocking officiating and this season is worse than any I've known. So many games are being settled by crap referees. Stoke's first goal was well set up by Crouch, but he clearly used his arm to control the ball. It came via a long throw by Ryan Shotton. The second goal also came from a Shotton throw in, and you have to feel for poor Rory Delap. The one thing he's actually any good at and it looks like Stoke have found someone else who can do it too, only with the added bonus of actually being able to play football a little bit. Delap is now obsolete, he's Stoke's Tim Cahill.

Spurs were denied a blatant pen when Shawcross was clearly holding Kaboul from a corner. Whilst I'd concede that most sides do this kind of thing at set pieces, Stoke are notorious for it and this was a particularly obvious one. He didn't even try to disguise it. Kaboul was booked for complaining about it and would later be sent off for a soft foul. The sending off doesn't happen if the ref spots the hold by Shawcross. Spurs did get a pen that they probably shouldn't have when Modric went down after a kick by Whelan. There was some contact, albeit minimal as Whelan attempted to pull his foot back before he kicked him. It wasn't enough to bring Modric down though, and there was also a split second delay before he decided to fall. Morally it wasn't a penalty, but it's incredibly difficult for referees to know who's diving and who's genuinely been fouled. This was less of a pen than the one West Brom didn't get, and Modric was more worthy of a yellow card than Dorrans. Thing is, even after looking at replays there's still room for debate as to whether these incidents are penalties or not, so how can referees be expected to consistently get these right when they only get one look at it? Players are constantly trying to cheat, and as long as that is happening refs are going to get decisions like these wrong. Modric milked it, but it's asking a lot for a referee to be able to know that at first viewing. Adebayor tucked away the pen and Spurs piled forward trying to get the equaliser. I'm not sure how they didn't, chance after chance came and went, and Stoke really rode their luck. One shot was cleared off the line by the elbow of Shawcross. Clear pen and also a red card, but neither ref or linesman saw it. Spurs also had a goal ruled out for offside even though Adebayor was two yards onside. A lot of similarities in this defeat for Tottenham and the one we suffered at Stoke earlier in the season. Still, we're three points closer to Spurs so I'm not complaining. Well I suppose I am complaining a bit, but I'm happy they lost.

The final game of the 'weekend' was on Monday night where City travelled south to play Chelsea at Stamford Bridge. Balotelli put City in front within two minutes, and the way they started it looked like it might be another rout like we saw at Old Trafford. They were denied a stonewall pen when Silva was hacked down by Bosingwa, but Clattenberg was having none of it. Fishy this, as if he didn't give a pen he must have thought it was a dive, so why no yellow card? City have strength in depth all over the park, with one notable exception. Left back. Clichy isn't very good. Admittedly it took me a while to come to that conclusion, I used to think he was ace and to my shame I'd have signed him ahead of Enrique last summer given the choice. He's really average though, and it's only his pace that makes him that. Sturridge had the beating of him all night, and that's where Chelsea won this game. Meireles equalised and after that Chelsea were the better side. Yaya Toure should have been sent off, Meireles was lucky not to pick up two yellows for bad tackles, Kompany should have gone after hacking down the excellent Mata, but eventually Clattenberg had to get the red card out when Clichy gave him no choice. Mancini went back into last season's 'shithouse mode' and started taking off attackers and replacing them with defensive midfielders until Chelsea finally took the lead through a Lampard pen and he then had to try and get an attacker on to salvage something. They couldn't do it and their unbeaten record has gone up in smoke.

Chelsea are technically back in the title race as they only trail City by seven points now. They aren't really title contenders though are they? Not with that defence, and not with the uncertainty they have in the striking positions. Not to mention Lampard's pouting about being left out. They've also got a rat in the house apparently. 'Dressing room secrets' keep appearing in the press, the most amusing of which was a story that claimed Villas Boas had told players they should come and celebrate with him and the coaches when they score, to show that he has the backing of the team. Only problem, he doesn't have the backing of the team. I don't believe the story either, but someone clearly wants to make him look like a tit. 'AVB' had a go at Gary Neville this week too, which would usually have people from all corners of England lining up to agree. It says a lot about a person when they slag off Gary Neville and don't get any back up, not even from Liverpool or Man City fans. He accused Neville of being biased against Chelsea and seemed pretty offended. Listen Andre, I don't think Neville meant to cause any offence, if he wanted to do that he'd tell you to go get your fucking shinebox.

ASTON VILLA 0 LIVERPOOL 2

Competition - Premier League
Date - Sun 18 Dec 2011
Venue - Villa Park
Scorer(s) – Craig Bellamy, Martin Skrtel
Half Time - 0-2
Star Man – Martin Skrtel

Team: Reina; Johnson, Skrtel, Agger, Enrique; Henderson, Adam; Downing, Shelvey (Carragher), Bellamy (Kuyt); Suarez (Carroll):

I wrote after we beat West Brom that we won't pick up an easier three points away from home all season. I may have been wrong about that. This was ridiculously easy and was all over inside 15 minutes. Villa are so bad we even managed to score from a couple of corners, and that almost never happens. Apart from the two goals from set-pieces, this was more or less business as usual. There were missed chances, the now customary twice hitting the woodwork and the obligatory farcical booking for the persecuted Craig Bellamy.

Kenny sprung a bit of a surprise in his line up by opting for Jonjo Shelvey ahead of Maxi, whilst Andy Carroll was also left out once again. I doubt if many expected that choice, but Kenny loves Shelvey and tries to get him on the field as much as possible. The 19 year old played really well I thought, he certainly justified his selection and is worth another look. He hasn't scored for us yet, but he has goals in him and it's just a matter of time before he breaks his duck. He looked confident and sharp, and the spell on loan at Blackpool has probably done him a lot of good both in terms of fitness and self belief.

Shelvey was involved in the opening goal when he flicked Downing's corner goalwards. Suarez latched onto it and also flicked it, the keeper made a save and Bellamy had a tap in. A great start, and it got better not long after. Bellamy whipped in a beautiful corner and Skrtel rose highest to glance the ball into the far top corner. Great header to be fair, it's an area he's massively improved on this season as in the past he's always had a head like a ten bob coin.

We were in total control of the game, dominating possession and moving the ball around well. Villa were fucking hopeless though, this was hot vomit in a bag stuff from them. You take Agbonlahor and Bent out and there's really not a lot left is there? Heskey's performance was laughable. Just about the only thing he did was dive to win a free kick in the first half. Their fans just sat and watched in stunned silence for most of the game. Just about the only time they could be arsed doing anything was to boo Downing and chant 'there's only one greedy bastard'. Coz he left Villa for the money you know, nothing else. Certainly nothing to do with them being Aston Vanilla, a completely insignificant mid-table nobody that will never compete to win anything. They may not even be that anymore, as 'Big Eck' looks to be trying to turn them into Birmingham MkII. Won't be long before Bent, Agbonlahor and Albrighton are following Downing and Young out of the exit door.

Agger and Skrtel were untroubled throughout, and the full backs both played very well too, at both ends of the pitch. Reina had nothing to do aside from field a few routine shots from distance. We were just in control all over the park, and if anything it was a little too easy as we eased off noticeably in both halves. I'm not going to be critical after such a routine win and convincing performance, but we definitely left some goals out there on the field. It doesn't matter because we won, but had we really pushed for them we could have scored two or three more easily. We almost did anyway, even though we spent much of the game in 2nd gear. I'm not too bothered by that, we have a lot of games up over the festive period so not going flat out for ninety minutes in a game we have in the bag isn't a problem for me. There were times when it looked like we were just keeping the ball rather than trying to force the issue, and you could even hear Steve Clarke yelling from the touchline "keep the ball!! keep the ball!!" Even so, we still cut through Villa several times and should have added to the lead. Suarez was denied by both post and bar once more. He's personally hit the woodwork more than any other Premiership team has now apparently. He should have buried the first one that hit the bar, but the lob that hit the post was quality, although he had handled in the build up and was lucky to get away with that. That was just about the only decision that went our way all day. Peter Walton was terrible as usual, and his assistants weren't much better. Thankfully they didn't have any major decisions to make, but they got plenty of minor ones wrong. Bellamy was booked for absolutely nothing, he didn't even make a challenge or any kind of contact, the player just hit the deck. That's three games in a row he's been booked for fuck all, and he must be close to a suspension now. He's being refereed on reputation rather than behaviour right now. Having said that, yelling at the ref to 'fuck off' later on wasn't smart, given he was already on a booking. That's Craig though, he can't help himself, the lovable moaning little bastard. Imagine him at the breakfast table....

Craig: *"I can't wait for my sugar puffs today, I love sugar puffs I do."*
Mrs Craig: *"The supermarket were all out of sugar puffs luv, I got you some cheerios for a nice change though"*
Craig: *"Fuckin cheerios??? Cheerios? I should fucking send you cheerio darlin'. I want fuckin sugar puffs. The Honey Monster says 'what about the honey, mummy?' he doesn't say nothing about no fuckin cheerios does he?? Cheerios?? Fuck off. I guess I'll just have toast then."*
Mrs Craig: *"Oh... I err... I just had the last piece of bread....."*

Anyway.... Charlie Adam could have scored when he burst through the centre. He had Shelvey in space to his left, and Suarez to his right but he went on his own and his shot was deflected inches wide off the heel of a defender. I don't blame him for having a go himself, he was inside the box in a great position and it opened up for him. The way he strikes a ball I've got no problem with him not passing there, although I know plenty will disagree. I'm a striker though, no way am I passing in that situation. Shelvey went close with a nice left footed effort that was saved, whilst Johnson was also denied by the keeper after a spectacular effort. What's the deal with that Villa keeper anyway? Stone age looking fucker, he looks like he should be wielding a big club and hunting Mammoths.

During this spell we looked like we'd score every time we attacked. Villa weathered that storm, and we appeared to just get a bit bored and stopped attacking with as much intent. It would have been dangerous against anyone half decent, as all it takes is one goal late on to induce panic and before you know it you've dropped two points. To score though, you have to attack and Villa seemed happy enough to keep the 2-0. The only hairy moment was a deflected shot by Bannan that almost crept in the far post as Reina scampered across.

In the final 15 minutes Villa seemed happy to just keep passing the ball around their back four and in midfield. I couldn't believe what I was seeing, there was no urgency about them at all. We kept our shape very well and just sat there picking them off as soon as they tried to play a forward pass. Kenny had the luxury of making changes with an eye on the midweek game at Wigan. Suarez was given a rest and was replaced by Carroll, Shelvey made way for Carragher and Kuyt replaced Bellamy as we settled for what we had.

It was a difficult game for Carroll to come into as we were not bothered about attacking at this stage, we had a few counter attacks but mostly we'd stop and then pass the ball backwards and just play keepball. Hard for a striker of his style to shine in those circumstances, which are tailor made a for someone who will run with the ball and exploit the space. Not Carroll's game though that, obviously. As much as I'd like to have seen us put Villa to the sword, it's not particularly important as we got the three points and we've made up two on Chelsea and three on Arsenal this weekend. Defensively we have the best record in the league and not many teams will fancy running into us right now. We just need to keep it going, and try to become a bit more clinical. When I say 'a bit', I mean 'a lot'. All in all, a very satisfactory day and another good away win. Villa were terrible, but some credit has to go to us for making them even worse than they are. Hopefully we'll be saying the same about Wigan on Wednesday night, it's about time we went there and won.

Premier League Round Up (17-18 December 2011)

So we aren't the only side who'll beat the big boys then drop points to the shite then. Don't think too many people saw that Wigan equaliser coming, well Petr Cech didn't anyway, the big dopey looking bastard. Maybe if he wasn't wearing more headgear than Michael Myers he'd have had a better view of Rodallega's pea roller?

Fair play to Wigan, they deserved the point as they gave Chelsea problems throughout. Di Santo came off the bench for them, but how does that work? He's on loan from Chelsea isn't he? I didn't think that was allowed. Then again, if anyone knows how completely useless the lad is it's Chelsea, so why wouldn't they give their blessing for him to play? Smart move really. (Update: He's not on loan, Wigan actually bought him!!) Brilliant goal from Sturridge again, he's tearing it up at the moment. Needs to jib the dancing off though, the tit. Chelsea were actually down to ten men when they scored, as Lampard was off the field with what appeared at first glance to be blood dripping from his mouth. Turns out it was just ketchup from the cheeky big mac he was having. That's why he completely saw his arse when the cameraman tried to get in close. Understandable, no-one likes that kind of intrusion when they're eating.

Other observations. It's funny how my perception of Meireles has changed. Last year the tattoos and mad haircuts were kind of endearing. Now I just think they make him look like a cunt. Speaking of which, someone needs to tell Villas Boas to clear his throat before doing interviews, I'm getting really sick of his croaky voice. Kevin Friend was the 4th official. I hate his face.

Moving on, and I'm officially off the Steve Kean bandwagon. It's been a fun ride but I'm done now. He lost at home to Hodgson's West Brom, so he's on his own I'm afraid. I can't continue to have his back after this debacle. Blackburn's fans had agreed to stop the protests for their next two home games, probably because they thought that not even they could lose at home to the awful Baggies. So there was no organised protest, they just chanted 'Kean Out' or simply walked out instead. Can't blame them this time, they allowed Roy Hodgson to win an away game, and that almost NEVER happens. Morrison gave the Baggies the lead with a cracking volley but Scott Dann levelled when he buried Chris Samba's knock down. This was awful stuff though, nothing happening at either end and those fans who could be bothered to turn up looked bored off their tits. Neither side deserved to win, but in fairness Odemwingie's last minute strike was fit to win any game.

Bolton's woes continued with another defeat. Hardly a surprise, they're dog shit and Fulham are fairly useful at home. Dempsey scored from a Ruiz cross and then Ruiz and his lovely silky hair added a second with a beautiful little chip. That finish may have been even more exquisite than his hair, it was THAT good. I love goals like that, don't know why more strikers don't do it. It's not that difficult to do as once you get it up and over the keeper you've got the whole goal to aim for, it widens the target area significantly. I guess you've got to have big balls to try it though, as you look like a tit if it doesn't come off.

Wolves took the lead at home to Stoke as Hunt tucked away a pen after the once again impressive Jarvis had been felled by Woodgate. Jarvis was brilliant in the first half. He tied Woodgate in knots to such an extent that Pulis had to sub him before he was sent off. Stoke drew level with a deflected free-kick from Huth, and Crouch won it late on with a back post header. That's four wins on the spin for Stoke, I don't know how they've done it but they have and they've moved well away from the bottom dwellers now. Twats. Wolves are in trouble though, they're really not very good at all. Shame, as Mick McCarthy's post match interviews are one of the highlights of the weekend. Always entertaining, often funny, and I'd miss him if Wolves went down.

Everton just about salvaged a point at home to Norwich thanks to a late equaliser by Osman. Tim Cahill has now gone an entire year without scoring a Premiership goal. He's now as much use as a glass cricket bat. Everton had a player called Gay playing for them. Firstly, who the hell is he? Secondly, where did he come from? Thirdly, how come I've never seen him before? Lastly, how the hell is he keeping Royston Drenthe out of the side? The Dutchman is one of only a handful of decent players the blues have, and he's a bit of a character too, bringing his little kid out to do the post match interview with him. He's a bit of poor mans Balotelli really. He's 'Richard Blackwood' to Mario's 'Will Smith'. Norwich went in front with a brilliant goal by Grant Holt. It was the first time they'd got anywhere near the Everton goal as it had been one way traffic up to then. It was one way traffic afterwards too, until eventually Osman deflected substitute Drenthe's shot past the inspired John Ruddy. Everton were so desperate they even sent on that big giant Argentinian goon who's name I'm not even going to attempt to spell. He's awful, and he looks like what would happen if Carlos Tevez turned into the Incredible Hulk.

The wheels have really come off the Newcastle bandwagon now. They've taken just two points from their last available fifteen after being held at home by Swansea. They were unlucky to be fair, they created plenty of chances and hit the woodwork twice. They should have won and a few weeks ago they probably would have. To re-iterate what I said last week, Demba Ba is really good.

Onto Sunday now. The Mancs kicked things off at QPR and they were boosted by the return of a couple of key men. Hernandez was back on the bench and Howard Webb returned to the starting line up. Webb has often been a key man for United but he had a quiet afternoon. He wasn't really needed, this was a walk in the park for the Mancs against an over-matched QPR. His day will come again though I'm sure. Jonathon Pearce claimed in commentary that this was only the second time in three years that United had named an unchanged line up in the league. Remember all the 'Tinkerman' Ranieri and 'Rafa the Rotator' media jibes back in the day? I guess 'rotation' is fine when you're winning titles. Or if you're such a bullying cunt that everyone is too scared to say anything that might get them on your bad side. Everyone except Roy Keane that is, who clearly doesn't give a fuck. If you haven't read his thoughts on Ferguson from this weekend, google them as he nailed it. United went in front inside a minute. Valencia crossed and Rooney headed in after Luke Young completely missed the ball. You know what I hate about this time of year? Fucking manc christmas songs. The tedious 'feed the scousers' and the shitty '12 days of Cantona' are especially irksome. Boring, droning nasal sounding chimps.

Evans hit the bar after a howler by Cerny. *"The keeper who had such a great game at Liverpool last week got nowhere near that"* exclaimed Pearce as Liverpool fans across the country gave a knowing nod of the head before turning to their completely disinterested wives and saying *"You see, what have I been saying? Happens every week that does"*. Or is that just me? Cerny actually redeemed himself a little with a fantastic save afterwards, but I obviously ignored that one. Can't be losing face in front of the wife. The home side didn't learn their lesson from the opening goal and almost conceded another one right at the start of the second half. Mind you, they were down to ten men at that point as Gabiddon was still in the dressing room having stitches put in. Luckily Rooney's touch let him down. Looked like he took his eye off the ball, or maybe his fake fringe got in his eyes. QPR didn't make the most of the let off and not long after they were 2-0 down, allowing the ponderous Carrick to amble from the halfway line to the edge of the box and then score with a shot so weak the keeper could have threw his cap on it to save it. Wouldn't have let that in last week. Twat. Joey Barton was equally to blame, his sloppy pass gave the ball to Carrick in the first place and then he somehow failed to keep up with him. I immediately unfollowed him on twitter, that'll teach him, the knob. Speaking of knobs, how bad was Patrice Evra in this game? He got completely ruined by Mackie, it was hilarious. On a separate note, my desire to punch Alex Ferguson in the face grows by the week. I don't care that he's a pensioner, I want to hit him. Hard. If that makes me a bad person, that's a cross I'll have to bear. I'm not bearing it alone though am I?

What's going on with Jocky though, he's lost all perspective lately. He described this as United's *"best performance of the season"*. So better than the 8-2 against Arsenal then? He wasn't done there though. *"A lot of people including myself thought Rio Ferdinand was gone. Today he was back to his very very best, I don't know where it's come from but today instead of being on the back foot all afternoon he was totally on the front foot"*. Don't know where it's come from? I do, three words; Queens Park Rangers. Here's another three; Jay fucking Bothroyd. C'mon Jocky, you're better than this reactionary 'in the moment' bollocks.

That win put United back on top of the table, which is pretty bizarre when you consider how inferior they've been to City all season. They've kept getting wins despite not playing well and City's defeat at Chelsea last week opened the door for them to get back in. City could go back to the top if they overcame a tricky looking fixture against improving Arsenal. They did, but only just. I was really impressed with Arsenal, I thought they deserved something from the game and had City hanging on at the end. Van Persie had a goal wrongly ruled out for offside and they had plenty of other near misses too, as did City to be fair. It was a cracking game but thankfully City got the points, as it not only knocked United off the top but also allowed us to claw three points back on Arsenal. Mancini was asked afterwards whether the rumours of Balotelli dressing up as Santa and giving money out around the streets of Manchester were true. His reply was *"Mario is a fantastic player"* which merely added fuel to the rumour. Don't know if it's true or not, but it says everything about Balotelli that no-one would be shocked if it was.

Martin O'Neill took his new Sunderland side to White Hart Lane to take on Spurs. Cattermole and Bendtner were left on the bench after their breach of discipline in midweek. For those who don't know, they were nicked for vandalising cars outside St James' Park. On the one hand, you have to say they're complete fucking dickheads. On the other, let's be honest, two Sunderland players getting shitfaced and trashing cars outside Newcastle's ground is really fucking funny!

Predictably the Londoners won, they didn't play well but they didn't need to. Wes Brown's loose pass put Sunderland on the back foot and Pavlyuchenko made them pay. Brown is pissing me right off, he seems to be making cock ups every week. He's 'out-Titusing' Titus Bramble, and that takes some doing.

WIGAN ATHLETIC 0 LIVERPOOL 0

Competition - Premier League
Date - Wed 21 Dec 2011
Venue - DW Stadium
Scorer(s) –
Half Time - 0-0
Star Man – Jose Enrique

Team: Reina; Johnson, Skrtel, Agger, Enrique; Henderson, Adam; Downing, Maxi (Shelvey), Kuyt (Bellamy); Suarez:

What a thoroughly shitty couple of days that was. It's bad enough that we got shafted by the FA's Kangaroo Court on Tuesday, but 24 hours later we did it to ourselves with another display of absolute wastefulness. Kenny said afterwards he feels sorry for the players as they are playing well but just not finishing off their good work. I know what he means, but he's more charitable than me.

It wasn't sympathy I was feeling after this, it was annoyance. Just add this to the long list of games we 'should' have won. It's actually almost criminal that we didn't win this game as at one stage it looked like it would be a formality. The opening 15-20 minutes of it were surreal. I haven't seen us look more in control of a game for a long time. We were camped in their final third and they just couldn't get out. They just kept giving the ball back to us, it was like an attack v defence training session. Wigan were asking to be put to the sword, but unfortunately our sword is more akin to one of those foam ones you get for kids in 'Home Bargain' than it is Excalibur.

We created chances, as usual. And we wasted them, as usual. We let them off the hook and the longer the half wore on, the more belief Wigan started to get and they began to have a go back at us. The last 15 minutes of the half saw them give as good as they got, whereas before that we were all over them. It was similar after the break, we had them penned back but didn't make them pay and they grew in confidence, probably because they knew we wouldn't score even if we played until New Year's Day. It won't come as a surprise to read that we've got the lowest ratio of goals to shots in the league. Christ, we're so bad in front of goal we've even managed to miss four out of five penalties. Some going that, it's harder to do that than it is to score four out of five. It's undoing all the good work we're doing all over the rest of the field, and it's really, really, annoying. It's not as though it's the same player missing chances either, it's all of them. There's not one player who is reliable in front of goal, with the possible exception of Maxi. Worryingly, for the first time all season it started to look like the missed chances were affecting morale. We started the game with a swagger, but ended it looking pretty clueless and dejected. After the penalty miss, it started to look like the players stopped believing they would score. They started feeling sorry for themselves a bit. Al Habsy played well for Wigan, but I didn't think any of the saves he made were particularly special. Most keepers would have made them, it was just poor finishing on our part. Johnson, Kuyt, Suarez, Adam, Henderson, Shelvey, Bellamy and Skrtel were all wasteful. We can't even bemoan hitting the woodwork this time.

It's difficult to gauge how much of an impact the Suarez verdict had on the team. Obviously they are all completely behind their team-mate and they will have wanted to go out and put on a performance, hopefully with Suarez getting a goal. Maybe they were trying a little too hard, they certainly seemed to snatch at any chance that came their way. But then they've been doing that all season anyway, so how can you tell? Suarez started brightly enough and didn't seem to be letting things affect him. He was laughing and joking with Maxi and looked in good spirits. He got dogs abuse from the home crowd though, with chants of 'Cheat' and 'Racist bastard'. Thing is, this was only Wigan, there's only about 5,000 of the fuckers. It's going to be a lot worse at other grounds, in town's where people actually care about football. It's desperately unfair of course and he shouldn't be subjected to this kind of shite. Three middled aged, white, Englishmen, sitting in judgement on whether something a mixed race South American said in Spanish to an African born Frenchman is racist?? It's fucking ludicrous. Still, if it gives them some kind of moral high ground over that arsehole Sepp Blatter, who cares if a man's character is destroyed in the crossfire, eh? Cunts the fucking lot of them, from Evra to Ferguson to that panel to that parasite Gordon Taylor. Some people are talking as though Suarez has been judged by a jury of his peers in a criminal court of law. Those same ignorant cunts are condemning Kenny, LFC, the players and the fans for standing by him. Apparently we're 'condoning racism' as he's been 'found guilty'. Fuck that, I've got nothing but contempt for the FA and I'm certainly not going to accept Suarez is guilty simply on their say so. The whole process was a farce from start to finish and these pig ignorant bandwagon jumping wankers have no idea of the details of what went on, and whatsmore they don't care. They are assassinating a man's character based solely on the judgement of three FA appointed men, one of whom happens to be one of Ferguson's best mates. They aren't a jury at the Old Bailey, and their 'verdict' doesn't mean shit as far as I'm concerned.

I expect the abuse from rival fans who are going to use whatever leverage they have to try and wind up Suarez and put him off his game. We all do it, it's the tribal nature of football. When I see journalists who 'should' know better pontificating about this shit and having a go at Kenny for railing against what appears to be a clear injustice, that's a different story altogether. Some of the comments I've seen on twitter from journalists from such bastions of morality and equality as the Daily Mail and Daily Star are simply beyond contempt.

It's going to be difficult for Suarez, especially as not every referee will be as competent as the kid who did this game. Can't remember his name, which says a lot about his performance actually. If you don't know who the ref was, chances are he's done well. He didn't get everything right, but this was probably the least inept refereeing performance I've seen in one of our games this season. He's only in his mid-20's apparently, so there's plenty of time for Mike Riley & the FA to ruin him yet. He had two major decisions to make and he got them both right. Moses dived to try to win a penalty from Skrtel, but the ref was onto it. He should have booked Moses though and I'm not sure why he didn't. The other big decision was the penalty he did give. He was a good position to see it and Caldwell didn't even argue, he knew it was a stonewall pen. Part of me wanted Suarez to take it, it had been his brilliant overhead kick that won it and it would have been fitting for him to get on the scoresheet. He looked like he wanted it too, he pointed at himself as if to say "I'll have it" but it was probably sensible that he didn't take it. The pressure on him would have been immense, and the last pen he took was woeful. Kuyt had missed the last one he took as well, whereas Adam had scored at West Brom. So Adam was a sensible enough choice, but I don't know who'll take our next one. Hopefully Gerrard!

I knew when the pen didn't go in that we weren't going to score. It looked like the players did too. We didn't create too much after that, and some of the shots we attempted were awful. There was a hint of desperation about our play for the rest of the game. Kenny sent on Bellamy and Shelvey for Maxi and Kuyt but it didn't really make any difference. The game was getting away from us at the point and we'd gone right off the boil. Carroll also replaced Suarez for the final five minutes. Not sure what the point of that was. For one thing, why bring Suarez off when we needed a goal? It wasn't to give him a rest, as it was so late in the game that would be pointless. Also, Carroll needs a lot longer than five minutes if he's going to get to the pace of the game and have any kind of impact.

On the plus side, we defended well enough and another clean sheet is welcome. Unfortunately all the teams around us won and we lost two points on them despite having arguably the easiest fixture of the night. Bottom line is the players charged with the responsibility of getting goals just didn't deliver again. Maxi started the game brilliantly but faded terribly. Kuyt is in a really bad rut that he's showing no signs of coming out of. Suarez looked to be trying too hard and Downing was back in 'play safe' mode and basically did nothing other than cut infield and play five yard passes to Adam or Henderson. Adam had his worst game in ages, but I thought Henderson played well.

I'd have gone for him as the star man were it not for Enrique. He was terrific, it seems impossible for people to get the ball off him as he's so strong and composed. So many times it looked like he'd run into trouble only for him to just hold people off and emerge with the ball. Skrtel and Agger did well again, and Johnson was good going forward. He struggled to deal with Moses a few times though. He's a good player that kid, but he lacks end product. Wait, he'd fit right in at Anfield actually.....

chapter seven

Christmas & New Year

LIVERPOOL 1 BLACKBURN ROVERS 1

Competition - Premier League
Date - Mon 26 Dec 2011
Venue - Anfield
Scorer(s) – Maxi Rodriguez
Half Time - 0-1
Star Man – Stewart Downing

Team: Reina; Johnson, Skrtel, Agger, Enrique; Downing, Henderson, Adam (Gerrard), Maxi (Bellamy); Suarez, Carroll:

Whatever the football equivalent of Viagra is, can someone send a few dozen cases of it over to Melwood as there's been a mass breakout of 'brewers droop' this season. Maxi's been unaffected and is the only one still capable of getting it up but the rest of them have got a severe case of the Pele's, and not in the good way.

There's really not much left to say that hasn't been said over and over. We didn't learn anything new from this game and we really shouldn't be shocked by it. Disappointed, yes. Angry even, yes. Shocked, not at all. This was just more of the same, there's very little difference between performances, the only variable is how many times we manage to stick the ball in the net.

It went past the stage of being unlucky a good while ago, we're now well and truly in 'negligent' territory. How can we not win this game? It's inexcusable. Blackburn had just lost at home to West Brom and Bolton. THAT'S how bad they are. They should have been sent packing by four or five goals. Instead, not only did we allow them to escape with a point, we extended the christmas spirit to such a ridiculous extent we even scored their fucking goal for them. The surprising part is it actually found the target. I thought Adam was a little unfortunate as he just making a challenge on the near post and the ball could have gone anywhere. The real problem was in the conceding of the corner. That's on Agger, who was far too casual and tried to be too clever. Just put the ball in the fucking stands Daniel.

It's weird, but whenever we concede a corner in such needless circumstances I always feel we're going to concede from it. Had that corner come about in a more natural way I'd not have thought anything of it, but as soon as Agger gave that away I had a bad feeling about it. Thing is, shit like this happens from time to time and it shouldn't be the end of the world, especially against teams as bad as Blackburn. At any time you can make a mistake that leads to a goal, so you have to make sure you score enough for it not to be an issue. Unfortunately for us, we score so few goals that any mistake we make can and does usually end up costing us points. Whether it's conceding a daft corner, scoring an own goal or missing a penalty or a sitter. It's like we have to play an almost perfect game to pick up maximum points. One defensive lapse against Sunderland costs us two points. A missed pen at Wigan the other night costs us two. A goalkeeping error at Fulham cost us one. Carroll somehow hitting the bar from five yards against Swansea cost us two. I could go on and on. As I say, we don't have any margin for error because we score so few goals. I'm so fed up of seeing us dominate games and not win, it's fucking depressing. We didn't play particularly well today, but we were ok and on the balance of play we should have won by three or four. As usual though, we couldn't score. Well, not quite, as we managed one when Maxi once again showed the knack he has for being in the right place at the right time to head in a nice cross by Skrtel.

That goal came very early in the second half and there was plenty of time for us to go out and win it. It's damning that we couldn't do it. I suppose we should be grateful that we managed to get one and didn't lose. That's how bad we are in front of goal. Plenty of players missed chances, it's not all down to one man. Having said that, it's impossible not to focus on Andy Carroll. He's not a regular in the side so any time he is given a start he should see it as an opportunity to stake a claim. He's not doing it though, and he's done nothing to dispel the widespread belief that we play better when he isn't on the field. He had chances to score, but he didn't take any of them. They weren't sitters but at the risk of repeating myself we bought him to put these kind of chances away. We need him to be good, we need him to be banging in goals, and he's just not doing it. Had we signed Darren Bent instead of Carroll how many points better off would we be? Not that I'm a fan of Bent, and it's certainly a case of being wise after the event as if you'd given me a choice of Bent or Carroll last January I'd have taken Carroll and laughed at you for even suggesting Bent as a credible alternative. Right now though if Villa offered me a straight swap I'd snatch their hand off, and I may even be willing to throw in some cash to sweeten the deal.

It's not just down to Carroll, others are guilty of missing chances too, but when you're a 'number nine' and you cost £35m, then rightly or wrongly that brings certain expectations and those expectations aren't being met. Suarez actually missed more chances than Carroll and he's far from being exempt from any criticism, but he does so much more that he's built up enough credit to be given a bit of leeway. Carroll doesn't have any credit in the bank as he's shown so little to date. He's a centre forward, it's his job to score goals and he isn't doing it even when presentable chances are coming his way. It's that simple really. And what was that shiner all about? Hopefully we wont be reading anything about that in the redtops this week. Actually, they'll probably find a way to blame Suarez for it.

The only positive to come out of this was Gerrard being back on the field. There were some understandable signs of rustiness but also plenty of moments of absolute class. We need him back in the side, as along with Maxi he's just about the only one who is capable of converting chances. This goal shortage is killing us, it's preventing us from getting where we need to be and where - based on performances - we should be. It's becoming clear that the solution to it isn't within the current squad, we'll have to bring someone in. Hopefully we can do that soon otherwise there's plenty more where this came from.

Premier League Round Up (20-27 December 2011)

The holiday fixtures started with Wolves and Norwich playing out an entertaining 2-2 draw at Molyneux on the Tuesday before Chrimbo. Good point for Norwich, not so good for Wolves who are right in the thick of it at the bottom.

The shitness of the three Lancashire sides is the best hope Wolves have of safety, as they're really struggling. On paper they've got a much better side than the other clubs at the bottom, but as no nonsense Mick McCarthy will yell thee, 'gerrmmms plerrred on grass, not perrrper'

Tuesday also saw Bolton visit Blackburn in a relegation six pointer. Seems odd to say that at this early stage of the season, but both of these teams are in deep shit already. There was a serious lack of quality on show, but it made for compulsive viewing. It was the football equivalent of two twenty stone men doing the 100m hurdles. You don't know which one will stumble over the finish line first and you don't particularly care as you're watching solely to see them repeatedly falling flat on their fat faces. Car crash TV. Two awful teams, both completely desperate for points and a local rivalry thrown in. It made for an interesting spectacle, despite the lack of quality on show. Blackburn's fans had agreed to lay off Kean for two games, presumably as those two games were against West Brom and Bolton and they figured they may just win them and they'd look a bit daft kicking off after they've won. May as well save the protests for games they're actually gonna lose eh? Having lost to West Brom they'll have been kicking themselves for forgetting to bring their hilarious 'taxi for Kean' banners, so this time they had them at the ready just in case they were needed. They were.

That West Brom defeat really hurt Rovers and this was always going to be a nervy game for them because of that. They started it terribly and quickly went 2-0 down as the Gog set up the opener for Mark Davies and Reo-Coker doubled Bolton's lead. It was all too much for the Rovers fans, the

Kean protests were in full flow once again. I'm off his bandwagon now as I said last week but I can't help but feel a bit sorry for the guy, especially as his defence has been decimated by injuries of late. Still, you lose at home to Bolton and you're on your own I'm afraid. Bolton are so bad even we put three past them. The Yak did give Blackburn some hope with a typically cool finish and Samba should have equalised at the death but put his header wide. Bolton may have won this, but I wouldn't bet on them finishing above Blackburn come May as they stink.

Onto Wednesday, and Man City took on Stoke at the 'United Stadium'. Pulis went with six at the back with the rest sitting just in front of them. Six at the back?? Really?? He was even laughing afterwards, saying *"Man City are better than us"* and then referencing the money they've spent. He's right of course, but if you're going to just admit defeat before you even start, at least go down fighting like Norwich did. Just fuck off Stoke you boring cunts. This was like watching San Marino or Lietchenstein taking on Argentina. They got exactly what they deserved. Is it just me or does Adam Johnson score every time he plays? He'd be in my team every week, I think he's really good but there must be a reason no manager's ever pick him. Me, I'd take him over Nasri any day of the week and if he ever gets fed up of warming City's bench, our number 10 shirt is vacant....

Wilson Palacios on the other hand, is proper shit. He was good when he was at Wigan, he's been garbage ever since. I guess you could say he's the black Charles N'Zogbia. Wait, can I say that? If there's an eight week absence of round ups, then you know the FA have caught up with me. If that happens, I expect you to wear t-shirts in my support. Sergio Aguero against Robert Huth was the biggest mis-match since that Irish/American loser was put in the ring to face Iron Mike Tyson when he first came out of the clink. What was his name again? Peter something. *googles* Peter McNeeley, that's the chump. He had as much business being in that ring as Alcaraz has on a Premier League pitch. The lumbering Huth marking the fleet footed, nimble Aguero is in that ball park too. City won 3-0, it could easily have been ten. I wish it had been. Fuckin' Stoke.

As for the other Mancs, they battered Fulham and Phil Jones had his face re-arranged, so a good night all round for them. *"Justice for Evra"* they chanted. For once I'm in agreement with them, I'd love nothing better than to see that little fucking ballbag get the justice he deserves.

West Brom went to Newcastle fresh off the back of a rare away win at Blackburn. They managed another one at St James', which has to be a personal record for Roy doesn't it? He may have *'36 years of top level management experience'*, but does he have two consecutive away wins in that time? He does now, well done Roy, a magnificent achievement. It was a cracking game this one actually. The lively Odemwingie put the Baggies in front, but Demba Ba levelled matters with a great free-kick. Every week he shows something else. Is there any kind of goal this lad can't score? Headers, tap ins, right foot, left foot and now he's taking free-kicks too?

What a signing he's been. McAuley put West Brom back in front, and both teams hit the bar before another great strike from Ba made it all square again. That twat Scharner won it for West Brom late on after some superb play by Long and Odemwingie. Harsh on Newcastle though.

There was better luck for the other North East side as Sunderland won at QPR. Bendtner got the first and Sessignon added a brilliant second. I really like him, he's good to watch and he's direct and unpredictable. Helguson pulled one back for the home side, no surprise that it came with his head, although this wasn't from the usual salmon like leap, it just hit him on the head as he was falling over. They all count though I guess. He made the equaliser with one of those salmon leaps though, nodding it across for Mackie to find the net. Helguson really is absolutely amazing in the air, he's like Inspector Gadget, he must have springs in his boots or something. He's Tim Cahill before he went crap, only without the snideyness and shit goal celebration. Speaking of shit, Wes Brown won it for Sunderland, scoring in the right end for once.

Robin Van Persie FC won at Villa Park. RVP scored from the spot to equal a club record for goals in a calendar year. He's been the best player in 2011 by some distance, even though I obviously voted for Suarez in Sky's poll just to piss them off. Van Persie has been amazing though, and he's the only reason Arsenal are even competitive as without him they have nothing other than the inconsistent Walcott. Steven Ireland went off injured for Villa. I'd forgotten he was even still playing. He was good a few years ago, very good in fact. Now he's playing for Villa, the poor bastard. Villa Park is where once highly rated players who didn't quite live up to their potential go to die, or in Darren Bent's case to line their pockets. Sometimes they get lucky, like Stewart Downing, and there's still hope for Mark Albrighton who might be able to get out as that lad can play a bit. He equalised after poor play from Mertesacker, who is proper shit isn't he? The white Stepanovs if you like. Think I'm ok with that one aren't I? Yossi won it for Arsenal with a header from a corner, and the thuggish Alan Hutton was sent off for a typical rush of blood to the head. He's just a shit Danny Mills him. He's the kind of nasty fucker who used to end up at Everton, but that was back in the days when they could actually sign players.

The blues continue to defy the odds though as Moyes has them competitive once again despite not having a pot to piss in. They beat Swansea 1-0 thanks to a Leon Osman goal. Everton are just incredibly nondescript these days though aren't they? If they weren't our local rivals they wouldn't even be on my radar at all, they'd be even more Vanilla than Villa. There isn't even anything about them to particularly dislike anymore, they're just pretty irrelevant. There's no Alan Stubbs or David Weir, no Duncan Ferguson and not even a Thomas Gravesen. In fact, since Tim Cahill retired there's really not much about Everton to get the blood boiling. Phil Neville is about the closest thing they have, but then he's usually either scoring own goals or getting sent off whenever we play them so what's there to dislike, apart from his sibling? And even he's becoming less dislikeable by the week, the cunt.

Onto Boxing Day now. The Mancs have suddenly clicked into gear after a couple of months of crap form. The fuckers keep on winning even when they aren't playing well but now that they have found their feet again it's bad news for the rest of the league, especially cannon fodder like Wigan. That Wigan side had drawn with Chelsea and then with us. It says more about the inadequacies of us and Chelsea than it does about Wigan improving. They're still crap, and the Mancs have a habit of taking crap sides to the cleaners. Of course they were ably assisted by the referee. Phil Dowd's dismissal of Conor Sammon when the score was 1-0 was just.... well it was fucking typical. One final observation; Alcaraz is actually even worse than I've been saying he is. He must have some seriously incriminating photo's of either Roberto Martinez or Dave Whelan (or both, now there's an image) to not only be getting a game every week, but to also have the captain's armband?? We're not talking run of the mill photo's of a mistress or even a gay lover. We must be talking beastiality or something here, as this fella should not be earning a living playing football.

To make things even worse, City have started dropping points just as United are rediscovering their form. Failing to beat West Brom??? I didn't see that coming at all. Motson was commentating and wasn't bad. I didn't see that coming either, in fact that shocked me more than the result. There wasn't much of that screechy, over-hysterical nonsense and he was quite reserved actually for the most part. I've noticed that he seems to save his worst for when he's covering Chelsea. A 'rent boy' when he was younger perhaps? I reckon so. Probably a Chelsea fan too. Mancini had a little bit of a dig at West Brom afterwards, saying *"it's difficult to play when the other team has ten men behind the ball at home"*. Oh listen to fucking Pep Guardiola there. Cheeky bastard, until this season City were one of the most boring, negative, defensive sides in the league despite having spent 800 billion pounds on wingers and strikers. He spent most of last season playing five holding midfielders, and as soon as they went in front he'd be turning to David Platt and saying *"ok Moonface, get Patrick Vieira warmed up, we're taking off Carlos Tevez"*. He's only released the handbrake this season, so he's not in any position to be snide about the likes of West Brom who weren't actually THAT defensive, not in comparison to what Stoke did last week anyway.

Newcastle finally got back to winning ways, turning over Bolton at the Reebok. Just about deserved too, they were marginally better than Bolton. Admittedly that's like being marginally taller than Willie Carson and certainly nothing to get too excited about. Ben Arfa gave them the lead with a smart finish. *"Couldn't miss"* yelled the commentator. Couldn't miss? Not seen many Liverpool games then I take it. Andy Carroll missed the same kind of chance except he was about five yards closer in. Couldn't miss indeed. Demba Ba wrapped it up with yet another goal, his 14th of the season. He's almost managed as many as our entire squad combined. Pardew was ultra smug afterwards, he talks a good game does 'Pards'. He was even sharing his tactical insight with us, talking about his players getting *'between the lines'* no less. No mention of *'storming the castle'* and *'capturing the princess'* with his *'bravest, fastest warrior'* though. Disappointing.

Chelsea played host to their neighbours Fulham. Torres was given a rare start, whilst Fulham had some players I've never even heard of in their side. Stockdale in goal, Frei on the wing and Sa up front. I used to know all this shit, but that was back when it was acceptable to collect Panini stickers. I can't justify that anymore, except for World Cups obviously. Fulham had been spanked a few days earlier by the Mancs and Zamora and Johnson couldn't even make the bench for this one. Clearly Martin Jol doesn't fancy either of them. I could see Johnson back at Everton in a week or two (if they manage to sell someone first, obviously), and who knows where Zamora will end up. The likes of Sunderland and Newcastle should be looking at him I think. Zamora and Ba would be pretty handy. Mata put Chelsea in front but Dempsey equalised after good play by my boy 'Bryan'. Ashley Cole was beaten all ends up by the flamboyant Costa Rican. Defenders are always told to watch the ball and not the man, but with Ruiz it's so difficult as the temptation to fixate on his lovely hair is just too great. Cole was bamboozled by it, and so was Meireles who made the most half arsed attempt at blocking a cross I've seen since Abel Xavier was stinking it up in our right back berth.

The blueshite made the long trip up to the North East to face Sunderland. Not that I care about Evertonians being inconvenienced, but would it not have made more sense for them to be playing Bolton and for Newcastle to play Sunderland instead? Making fans travel so far on Boxing Day is stupid. The Mancs played Wigan, we had Blackburn, City didn't have to go too far either, so why send Everton all the way to the North East and Newcastle all the way to Bolton? It's not like the football authorities to do things that make no sense. Not like them at all, no sireebob. No matter, it ended all square but the big talking point was the award of a penalty for Everton. I'd heard about how bad this decision was before I saw it, firstly through irate text messages from my brother-in-law, and secondly via a lot of Liverpool fans either on twitter or on the forum. When I eventually saw it, and I can't believe I'm saying this, I thought Howard Webb got it right. Yes, Osman missed his kick and booted the floor and that's why he went down. But he only did that as Cattermole must have clipped his heel just as he was about to shoot. Osman isn't that hopeless that he'd just randomly boot the floor and not the ball, he isn't Tony Hibbert for Christ's sake. Wait, I've just seen the post match interviews and Osman must actually be that hopeless as Moyes categorically stated that it wasn't a penalty and Howard Webb got it wrong. I'm uneasy defending Webb, but I'm even more uneasy agreeing with Moyes. I'm sticking with my original assessment. PENAL-

TY!!!

The final Boxing Day game was Stoke at home to Villa. Is that the most uninspiring fixture you can think of not involving Everton? Boring, dull as fuck Stoke City and Aston Vanilla. Two teams playing for territory and hoping to nick something from a set piece. The only player on the field worth watching was Agbonlahor, he's always lively and capable of producing something. He provided the best moment of the game but this time it wasn't anything to do with his pace and trickery, it was him running over Mark Clattenberg. It was boss, not only did he just flatten him but he didn't even slow down afterwards, he just kept sprinting at full pelt after the ball whilst an embarrassed Clattenberg had to pick himself up and wipe the mud off his hands. Shawcross helped him out by picking up his pen and handing it to him but didn't even get so much as a 'thanks' from the ungrateful Clattenberg who didn't see the funny side at all and clearly had his ego bruised. That's the thing with some of these refs, they're just so fucking arrogant and full of their own self importance. Clattenberg is a prick, he's number three on the shitlist at the moment behind Kevin Friend and Lee Mason.

The day after Boxing Day saw Arsenal draw at home with Wolves. Arsenal and Chelsea are just as bad us aren't they? Dropping points in games they should be winning easily. They even took an early lead, so there's no excuse for this. I haven't seen much of this game but I did watch brief highlights of it on my phone. Gervinho scored, and I still can't work out if he's any good or not. I'm leaning towards him being not bad, but a step or even two below the kind of player Arsenal had when they were winning stuff. That theme is repeated throughout their entire team actually. Wolves equalised through Fletcher, and then had a lad sent off for what looked like a good tackle to me. They surrounded the ref and Roger Johnson was wagging his finger under his nose and yelling in his face. I await the FA charge for failing to control their players, even though the real problem was the scandalous red card given by the ref.

QPR drew at Swansea. Again, all I saw of this were the goals on my phone. Graham put the home side in front but Mackie equalised for Neil Warnock's men. Can't help but be a bit put out when I see the likes of Graham, Helguson, Morrison and Holt banging in goals whilst Carroll is doing fuck all. Still, I'd be a lot more put out if Torres was scoring too, so be grateful for small mercies I suppose.

So far I haven't made any mention of Spurs. They weren't on either of the Match of the Day's I watched, and it turns out that in both rounds of fixtures they played a day later than everyone else. I can't find any highlights on the ESPN Goals app on my phone, so I've now got to try and find highlights online somewhere as I don't even know who they played or what the score was. Spurs are just a royal pain in the arse.... Ok, turns out they drew 1-1 with Chelsea (I did actually know that, I'd just forgotten). I didn't watch the game at the time, but I did see some of the headlines the next day about 'Lionhearted' John Terry. Sickening hypocrisy. Spurs' second game of the holiday period saw them win 2-0 at Norwich. Gareth Bale scored both, he's just a top, top player him. Can't help but think he seems like a bad knobhead though. Admittedly that's based entirely on how he celebrates goals and nothing else, but you can tell a lot about a man by how he celebrates a goal I think. With a Suarez or Dalglish for example it's just pure unadulterated joy. Ergo, good guys. The flip side is Balotelli, who just looks like a moody, miserable, petulant child. That's because he is a moody, miserable, petulant child. A hugely entertaining one, but a moody, miserable petulant child nonetheless. The likes of Bale, Cahill, Sturridge and Adebayor….. knobheads. It's a foolproof scientific method.

LIVERPOOL 3 NEWCASTLE UNITED 1

Competition - Premier League
Date - Fri 30 Dec 2011
Venue - Anfield
Scorer(s) – Craig Bellamy (2), Steven Gerrard
Half Time - 1-1
Star Man – Steven Gerrard

Team: Reina; Johnson, Skrtel, Agger, Enrique; Henderson, Spearing, Adam (Gerrard); Downing, Carroll, Bellamy (Kuyt):

How 'bout that Steven Gerrard eh. He's a bit good isn't he? He had such a huge impact on this game that it actually reflects well on the rest of the squad that they've done pretty well without him. You sometimes forget how good he actually is as he's been out for so long.

Any team in the world would miss him, he's that special, but on the whole we've kept ticking along without him and Kenny and the squad deserve credit for that. Now he's back, we should be a much, much stronger side in the new year. This game was plodding along at 1-1, we were in control of it but were making hard work of breaking down an unambitious but well drilled Newcastle side. Then the skipper appears off the bench and suddenly everyone's game went up a notch or even two in some cases (Henderson springs to mind). The crowd came to life too, he completely transformed everything. The net result is we ended up with three goals to our name for the first time since we beat Bolton back in September. It should even have been four or five had Carroll been able to do what we bought him for. The header that hit the bar was unfortunate, the mis-control of a beautiful Gerrard pass was not. At least there were some flickers of life from him once Gerrard arrived, and that's something to cling to.

Aside from the Swansea game, this might just be the worst we've played at home all season. We were still comfortably the better side but we didn't match the standards we've set previously. Despite that, we not only got the win but we also scored three goals. Funny old game as they say.

I was disappointed with Newcastle's approach. I thought they'd come here and have a bit of a go as they're having a good season. Demba Ba is flying, but he was isolated for most of the game due to the lack of ambition Pardew showed. Surprising, as you can't 'capture the princess' unless you 'storm the castle' and support your 'bravest, fastest warrior' eh Alan? You of all people know that. We were missing Suarez and had been held to consecutive draws by Wigan and Blackburn. It was an ideal time to play us, but the Geordies didn't take the game to us at all, and they were time wasting from as early as the first few minutes. It was embarrassing. Tim Krul started wasting time about two minutes in, and it went on for the entire first half.

Kenny made two changes from Boxing Day, Bellamy replaced Maxi on the left and Spearing came in for Suarez as we went with a 433 formation. That meant Carroll leading the line against his former side, and this was the perfect chance for him to make his mark. I even stuck a fiver on him getting a hat-trick. I won't be making that mistake again, I don't know what I was thinking there. The first half was a bit crap. We weren't that bad, but we didn't look threatening enough and the tempo wasn't good. It was all a bit flat I thought, and the crowd were very quiet too aside from a small hardcore who did their best with little help. Newcastle's following seemed to enjoy themselves though. Carroll, Enrique, Bellamy, Downing and Henderson were all booed heartily for varying reasons. The 'Dalglish' chant from the Kop was also booed. They don't like many people do they? They were probably gutted Suarez wasn't playing, as they'd have slaughtered him too, the small time bastards. Still, had to laugh at them taunting Enrique with *"you're just a shit Ryan Taylor"*. Very good that, assuming they were joking of course. They may not have been, the words 'deluded' and 'Newcastle fans' do often go hand in hand, but I'd give them the benefit of the doubt on this one and say that it was pretty funny.

The Geordies took the lead with more or less their first attack. Taylor whipped in a cross from deep, Cabaye flicked it on and it went past Reina after appearing to strike Ba and then Agger. Ba was credited with the goal by DJ George but I assume it will go down as an oggy by Agger. I almost didn't even see it, I was distracted by the sight of a Newcastle player being hit in the face with the ball and immediately signalling to the bench he wanted to come off. I was just thinking *'what's that shithouse doing, he got hit by a football not a baseball bat, the big baby'* as I watched him make his way over to the sideline and then next thing I looked up and saw some pinball in the box and the ball in the net. It just compounded what had been a frustrating opening half for us up to that point. We'd had numerous occasions where we'd worked a good position out wide and got the ball into dangerous areas only to have no-one attacking it. That falls mostly on Carroll's shoulders, but it isn't just him. Even the goal we scored was slightly fortunate. Adam did really well to beat his man and drill a low cross into the danger area, but we didn't have anyone attacking it and Newcastle had plenty in there covering. It worked to our advantage this time as the ball was cleared only as far as Bellamy on the penalty spot and he found the corner with a powerful low shot. Really good finish it was.

It was a big relief not to be trailing at half time, and I expected us to come out firing in the second half. It didn't really happen and it was very difficult to build any kind of momentum, in part due to the amount of time Krul would take to get the ball back into play from goal-kicks. Aside from the goal, which was a fluke, we were very solid at the back again where Skrtel and Agger did a great job on the dangerous Ba (who was left completely on his own with no support). Spearing locked down the midfield area and was constantly chasing and harrying and getting his foot in. There was one incident after the break where he went in hard to win the ball in a similar manner to the tackle that saw him red carded at Fulham. Just as he did that night, he won the ball hard but fair, but this time the opposition player, Cabaye, went over the top of the ball and caught him on the shin. Speo immediately yelled out in pain and signalled to the bench he was in trouble, as a few of our players let the Newcastle midfielder know what they thought of his challenge. We didn't even get a free-kick, let a lone a red card for Cabaye. Makes you sick when you look at what happened the last time Jay went in for a 50-50. That was a red card but this doesn't even warrant a foul?? Thankfully his shin pads did their job and after some brief treatment he was able to continue. No doubt it'll be sore for a few days though. He can be well pleased with how he performed on his return to the side, I thought he was excellent.

We did create some chances but we didn't work the keeper enough. All eyes were on the bench and the skipper. Eventually he got the call, although I was surprised it was Adam who went off. Not that he'd played particularly well, but he'd been far more involved than Henderson who had been fairly anonymous and hadn't really done anything up to that point. That changed as soon as Gerrard came on. Henderson was very good after that, he got involved and he was running all over the place. He's one of numerous players who will benefit from playing alongside the captain. Downing, Carroll and Spearing all spring to mind, and even Suarez has hardly had the opportunity to link up with Gerrard.

Gerrard's quality was immediately on show in everything he did. He just does things that others can't. The pass to play in Carroll was something that no-one else at the club (with the possible exception of Adam) would have even seen, let alone been able to execute. Similarly the pinpoint cross that saw Carroll thunder a header against the bar. That's something

Carroll hasn't had anything like enough of since he's been here. For all his faults and all the valid criticisms there are of Carroll, it's a fact that most of the crosses that have come his way have not been in front of him for him to attack. Usually he's jumping from a standing start. Gerrard's delivery was early enough and good enough that it allowed Carroll an unobstructed run at it, and when that happens he's going to win it 90% of the time. Having won the header you can argue he should have scored.

Personally I just thought it was a bit unlucky, as he has been on several other occasions when his headers have hit the woodwork. It's just not happening for him, even when he does something well he can't catch a break. We have little choice but to stick with him and hope it turns around, as selling him in January isn't a realistic option, especially with Suarez's impending ban looming. One of the biggest concerns people have with Carroll is his apparent lack of game intelligence. It was therefore slightly encouraging seeing the minor role he played in the second goal. Agger's forward foray was brought to an illegal halt by Tiote, and as Bellamy lined up the free-kick Newcastle brought Simpson back onto the goal-line. Carroll saw that and immediately went and stood in front of the keeper to obscure his view, knowing he couldn't be offside. It worked perfectly, as Bellamy's powerful shot would probably have been saved had Carroll not affected the keeper by standing in his way. The ball clicked Simpson's chest on the way in, but there's no doubt it's Bellamy's goal. What was interesting about it was that Gerrard deferred to Bellamy and let him take the free-kick. That isn't something you see very often, but since he's returned to the club Bellamy's set-pieces have been terrific. He's the best dead ball option we have at the club in my opinion. I'm happy for him to take all our set-pieces.

Having fallen behind Newcastle now had to come out and play and they almost equalised immediately when Ba got in behind Agger and skillfully got the ball over Reina. As the ball rolled towards the empty net a goal seemed certain but then out of nowhere came Skrtel to miraculously hook the ball to safety. Great defending from a player who is having a terrific season. He might just be our player of the season so far, he's certainly in contention. Aside from that scare and the goal, Newcastle didn't threaten us at all. It would have been nice to see Bellamy complete a hat-trick, especially given the taunting he was getting from the Geordie fans. *"You're shit scared of Shearer"* they sang. Really? I doubt if Craig Bellamy is shit scared of anything, he's the very definition of 'small man syndrome'. He left the field with blood pouring from a cut above his eye after he was elbowed by Colloccini. He had some verbals with Krul on the way off, then ended up arguing with Pardew as he left the field. I love him, he's fucking boss.

Gerrard made the game safe when he collected a pass from Henderson and rolled the ball past Krul from a tight angle with his left foot. It looked easy but it really wasn't. Few players would have even been able to adjust their feet to take Henderson's pass in stride, let alone go on to finish like that. You'd think after the amount of time he's been out, and the seriousness of the injury problems he's had for so long that it'd take him some time to regain his form. Maybe I'm getting carried away, but he looked as sharp as ever to me. His touch was there, his pace was there, his awareness of what was going on around him was there. He looked like he'd never been away and he certainly didn't look like the injury had taken anything away from him. We just need to keep him fit and we'll be a much more efficient team and he'll help massively with our lack of goals. 2011 has been a good year for us on the whole, despite us not having our best player available for most of it. Hopefully 2012 will see him having an injury free run, as he really deserves it after what he's been through.

We end the year in pretty good shape, just two points off 4th spot despite all the stupid points we've thrown away. It will only take a slight improvement for us to turn those draws into wins, and because of that we go into 2012 full of hope. Now if we can just add a goalscorer in the next week or two....

MANCHESTER CITY 3 LIVERPOOL 0

Competition - Premier League
Date - Tue 3 Jan 2012
Venue - Etihad Stadium
Scorer(s) –
Half Time - 2-0
Star Man – Jay Spearing

Team: Reina; Johnson, Skrtel, Agger, Enrique; Henderson, Spearing (Maxi), Adam (Gerrard); Kuyt (Bellamy), Carroll, Downing:

Last year we lost this fixture 3-0 but the main talking point surrounded a South American who refused to play. This year, we lost 3-0 but the story was a South American who was refused the right to play. There's a world of difference between the cases of Mascherano and Suarez, but the net result was the same. It hurt the team. Badly.

City were very uninspiring, they didn't play well at all. They didn't need to. We dominated for long periods, but how much of that was down to City taking it easy? They won at a canter and not even going down to ten men gave them anything to worry about. Our chronic lack of quality in the final third made this far too easy for City, and to top it off we also decided to gift wrap a couple of goals for them too.

We were on a massive downer even before the game kicked off. The news that the club were not going to appeal the 8 game ban was perhaps unsurprising, as appealing to the same bunch of cunts who dished out the ban in the first place was never going to lead to anything good and anyone who thinks it would have is kidding themselves. He didn't get a fair go last time, they're hardly likely to admit that and if anything they were more likely to increase the punishment. I don't know if there were any other avenues we could have gone down in order to clear Suarez's name, presumably there weren't but I have no idea. Kenny's comments today suggest there may still be a twist to this story yet, but any further action won't prevent Suarez from sitting out eight games. More important than that is clearing his name anyway, and I hope we do have something up our sleeve on that score.

Rightly or wrongly (and there is a big split in the fanbase on this), LFC felt they had to accept the ban under protest and the decision they were faced with was when was the best time to let it start. By starting it with the City game we ensured he would be ready to return when we visit Old Trafford next month. If we beat Oldham and progress to the next round of the cup, he'll be able to return for Spurs a game earlier. Would we have been better served letting him play in this game? It's a difficult one, and there's no ideal solution to this. For all we know he may not have been in the right frame of mind to play in it. I'm not saying that's the case, I have no idea as to how Suarez is handling all this but if it was me I'd be struggling badly. Imagine if he'd scored the winner? On the one hand he'd be made up for helping his team, on the other he'd just helped his accuser move a little bit closer to another title winners medal. He must be feeling completely helpless right now, and it's surely no co-incidence that the goals have dried up since that charge was made against him. This is a horrible time for him and I hope he's not paying any attention to the absolute deluge of ill informed shite that's being spoken about him in various media. There's virtually no-one fighting his corner, not even pro-LFC pundits like Thommo and Jamie Redknapp. A lot of ill informed, sensationalist drivel being spouted by people you'd like to think ought to know better. Are Liverpool's PR people even attempting to get the message out as to how unjust that hearing was? TV, radio, papers, internet, there's so much crap being thrown at Suarez I wouldn't blame him if he just said 'fuck this country, I'm off'.

I hope it doesn't come to that, obviously, but it would be perfectly understandable if he did. He wouldn't be treated like this anywhere else in the world. I'd love to know what his thoughts are on the decision not to appeal. I'd like to think he sees the futility of appealing to the same body that stitched him up in the first place, and I hope he doesn't think he's been hung out to dry by LFC (a lot of fans are certainly thinking that way). I'd tell him to take his family back home to Uruguay for a few weeks, relax, recharge his batteries and try and put all this shit behind him. I'd also tell him to get himself prepared for that game at Old Trafford and to be ready to produce the performance of his life. That game is always poisonous anyway, but has taken on whole new levels of bad blood now. We need cool heads, but that won't be easy for anyone, least of all Suarez. The abuse he's going to get (on and off the field) will be unprecedented, but the way to react to it is to not react to it. He needs to ignore it, keep his mouth shut and play to the best of his ability. That will hurt them more than anything, and that's what he needs to keep telling himself during this time on the sidelines. They've won the battle, they haven't won the war. He'll get his chance to hit back at them in February. That's a long way off though and for now we have to do without him. We're obviously going to miss him and if we are relying on Andy Carroll to fill his shoes then we're in real trouble. Hopefully we have something planned in the transfer market, but I'm not holding my breath.

This game perfectly exposed the weaknesses we have in attack. It's not just on Carroll by any means as he's not being helped at all by those around him. They could make the same point about him in fairness. Carroll is not Luis Suarez, he can't play like him and shouldn't be expected to play like him. His failings are a collective thing, it isn't just his fault although he clearly has to do better. There's things he can do and things he can't do. What we need to do is put him a position to do the things he's good at and not ask him to do too much of the things he can't do. The service from wide areas in this game might actually be the worst I've ever seen. It was completely hopeless. It's not just one player either, it's all of them. Whether it's Adam's set pieces, or Downing, Enrique, Johnson, Kuyt or whoever in open play, the balls into the box were fucking shocking. They were either over everybody's head or they went straight to Vincent Kompany. He's a great defender, there's no doubt about that, but he can thank our piss poor crossing for his man of the match award tonight. Every ball into the box went to him, he was on the end of everything it seemed. Credit to him for making so many clearances, but at some point surely we have to start looking to miss him out? I'm far from blind to Carroll's failings, but under the circumstances I'm not sure what else he could have done in this game. He had a half chance when he flicked a Downing cross just past the far post. He had a header that went narrowly wide too, but again it was more of a half chance than anything. Aside from that, he knocked one down for Kuyt who's shot was blocked by Kompany, and he knocked one down for Adam who was fouled on the edge of the box (we completely wasted the free-kick). That showed he can be effective given a ball he has a chance to win and if we have runners off him. Too often he has neither, which merely highlights his limitations and the things he doesn't do. If you want to make the point that he's been a terrible signing, that he's not a Liverpool player etc you won't get an argument from me at the moment. But in the absence of Suarez he's all we have right now so let's at least give him a chance to be effective. He didn't have that chance in this game, he simply can't be effective if we play like that.

It sounds daft to say this as it was so early in the game, but for me the writing was on the wall when Downing went clean through and failed to score. He did everything right up until the final moment, and the pass from Henderson to play him through was class. You've simply got to score though, as chances like that aren't going to come around too often against a side as strong as City. Yeah, Joe Hart did well, he made himself big and blah blah blah. I don't care, Downing has to put that chance away and he didn't. It's been the story of our season, and the story of his season. I can live with the lack of assists, he can't convert his own crosses can he? The lack of goals is simply unacceptable though, he's had plenty of chances and taken none of them. This was the worst yet.

To compound things, City went in front not long after and it was completely self inflicted. Kuyt lost the ball cheaply from our throw in, and Aguero's shot squirmed under Reina. How long before we have to stop referring to 'rare' mistakes from Pepe? Not so rare anymore are they? Off the top of my head that's three goals so far this season I can think of that can be put down to him. There may be some I've forgotten too. If we weren't so fucking toothless at the other end it wouldn't matter. All keepers make mistakes but they only really hurt you consistently when you aren't scoring at the other end. He made some amends shortly after with a good tip over after Kompany had beaten Skrtel to a left wing corner, but ultimately it mattered little as they scored from the resulting corner from the opposite wing. Johnson didn't get tight enough to Yaya Toure and this time Reina could do nothing about it. Game over.

We dominated possession after that and up until the final third we played very well. Defensively we dealt with them comfortably enough, but they'd say the same about us. We didn't look like scoring and it was incredibly frustrating watching the poor decisions and poor execution any time we got near the box. Rank incompetence at times. It was crying out for Gerrard and Bellamy but there were no shortage of candidates to come off. Adam and Kuyt were the two most obvious ones to me, but you could make a case to sub any of the midfield or forwards aside from Spearing who did his job excellently and couldn't have done any more than he did. Adam and Kuyt were the two to get hooked but it didn't really change much. Bellamy was lively enough but the end product wasn't of the level required. Gerrard was fairly quiet and also seemed to be quite deep I thought. It was one of those nights where we were never going to score.

When we did get a glimmer of hope as City went down to ten men it was quickly extinguished as we gave away another stupid goal. From our own free kick near the City box we gave it away needlessly (Bellamy or Enrique I think?) and Yaya Toure ran clear before falling over as Skrtel ran alongside him. It was never a pen, Toure had over ran the ball and just tumbled, but I can see why the ref thought it was and I'm more annoyed at our own play than that error from the official.

Milner was only ever putting that penalty in one place, his entire body shape gave that away. Pepe dived the other way though, not that I'm surprised as I think the last time he saved a pen he still had hair. As for Barry's sending off, on their own merits both bookings looked somewhat harsh but he was persistently fouling and deserved what he got. The abuse he gave Spearing after catching him late was ridiculous too. Said it before and I'll say it again, but I really fucking hate Gareth Barry far more than I should. Twat.

At 3-0 down the only thing left was to try and grab a consolation goal, but we couldn't even do that. Joe Hart was equal to everything we threw at him, which in truth wasn't that much. Our attacking play was abysmal in that second half, which Downing the main culprit for me. He did ok in the first half aside from blowing that great chance at 0-0, but the longer it went on the more cowardly he became. He had chances to go at the full back, loads of chances in fact. And pretty much every time he shit out of doing it and looked to pass the responsibility to someone else, whether it was the supporting Johnson or one of his midfielders. Downing has talent, but he's frustrating as it just looks like he has no balls. Far too timid, he needs to start being assertive or this move he's waited his whole career for is going to turn sour.

We took a big step backwards in this game and I can't deny it hurt watching it. Some perspective is needed though and as much as this knocked the stuffing out of us, the reality is that overall we've been doing ok. This was certainly a step back, but City are better than us and we started the game without our two best attacking players. One of them isn't going to be available for a while but the other should be ready to start our upcoming games. As Dalglish said afterwards, hopefully we'll learn some lessons from this. The scoreline was very harsh, we lost through a goalkeeping error, a corner kick and a dubious penalty. We weren't outplayed or outmatched, but we weren't good enough in the final third and that's where we have to get better. The good thing is we don't have to wait long for a chance to put this straight and given a choice I'd prefer to win the cup game anyway. Not that that makes this defeat hurt any less, but beating City to get to Wembley is more important than this in my mind, as we've still got plenty of league games left to try to break into the top four. That's important, but it's been too long since we won a trophy and I'm desperate for us to put that right. Before we get another crack at City though we have another cup game to deal with. There's a big part of me would like to see us tell the FA they can fucking shove their cup up their arses and pull out of the competition, but I accept that's not the right way to go. No, we need to win the fucking thing and when we do we should send Suarez up to get the trophy, on his own.

Premier League Round Up (31 December 2011 - 4 January 2012)

What's funnier than a Manchester United defeat? Two Manchester United defeats! What's even funnier than that? A Manchester United defeat on Ferguson's birthday, after the sad bastards had got a choir on the pitch to sing to him. And what's even funnier than that? Steve Kean and Yakubu beating him.

Kean showed up at Old Trafford with two bottles of wine for Ferguson. When I heard that my first thought was *'I'm glad I got off his bandwagon when I did, the snivelling little arse licking rat'.* Shame on me, I should have had more faith in him as there was clearly method to his grovelling. Lull the old prick into a false sense of security by helping him get bladdered. Worked like a charm and Ferguson has clearly never heard the expression *'beware of geeks bearing gifts'.* Looking at United's starting line up was when the genius of Kean's plan hit me. Carrick and Jones at centre half. Valencia at right back. Rafael in centre midfield, De Gea in goal. Those two bottles of claret had served their purpose and then some.

"Rooney and Giggs get a rest" proclaimed the MOTD commentator. A rest eh? That's one way of describing it. Another way would be to say Rooney was dropped for turning up to training with a stinking hangover and fined 250k. He's a complete moron isn't he? Wayne, when people say 'hair of the dog' is a good cure for a hangover, they don't mean to get it stitched into your fucking head you thick twat. Dunno what Giggs needed a rest for but we'll probably read about it in the Sunday papers soon enough, unless he gets an injunction that actually works this time. Nani was playing though and he was sporting a ridiculous new haircut. Come on lad, the whole world already knows you're a complete helmet, you don't need to make it any more obvious.

Blackburn went in front when Mike Dean (scouse twat etc) awarded a penalty against Berbatov for a clear foul on Samba. Ferguson was having none of it of course. It wasn't even remotely contentious but it's still shocking whenever one is given against them (especially at home) and Ferguson always has a look of incredulity about him when it happens. He's always had a hard on for Dean too as he's one of the few officials not in his pocket. The Yak nonchalently buried the pen, as you'd expect, as there's an air of nonchalence about everything he does. There isn't a more laid back player in the Premier League than Yakubu. Cool as a cucumber. A portly, old, cucumber, but a cool one. God bless him, he's a massive inspiration to overweight, ageing gunslingers (some would say goalhangers) like myself. It got even better for him early in the 2nd half when he bundled past Carrick and then easily skipped past media darling Phil Jones to make it 2-0. No, that isn't a typo, the amazing Phil Jones was actually beaten by somebody. I know it's hard to believe, what with him being Roy Keane, Gary Pallister and Mark Hughes rolled into one and all that, but it actually happened.

A huge upset was suddenly looking like a possibility. Didn't last long though, as with an infuriating predictability United pulled one back within seconds and not long after they were level. Ah well, nice while it lasted wasn't it? But wait, where there's De Gea there's hope.... The error prone Spaniard had just gotten away with flapping at one corner, but the second time it happened he wasn't so lucky as Hanley bundled the ball into the net. United threw everything forward but couldn't find a breakthrough and Ferguson's birthday party was ruined. Funny as fuck. I want back on the Steve Kean bandwagon if there's room. At the final whistle he should have been dancing a jig of delight that a man of his limitations had managed to win at Old Trafford, but instead he was Mr Cool. He really, absolutely, vehemently believes that this is the kind of result he should be getting as he's 'Steve fucking Kean dammit'. I love that. Serious delusions of grandeur, but I find it endearing.

Saturday got even better with Chelsea losing at home to Villa. Motson was commentating, and as I pointed out in the last round up he was far more excitable than he is when covering games that don't involve Chelsea. Insufferable old goat. Chelsea had some fella in a white mask playing at right back. They also had a fella in a white hood at centr... no I'm not going there. Turns out the fella in the mask was Paolo Ferreira. Who knew? I thought he'd left years ago, where's he been all this time? Can we expect Celestine Babayaro to trot out next week, or Claude Makalele? He'd do a better job than Obi Mikel, but then so would Eddie Newton and John Bumstead. Chelsea went in front with a penalty from 'Drogbaaarrrr'. Villa equalised through Steven Ireland and Motson sounded gutted. Torres came off the bench and hit the crossbar. No goal for him though, meaning he finished 2011 with more league goals for Liverpool than Chelsea, the fucking chump. Villa continued to look dangerous on the break and eventually went in front through Petrov. A Lampard mistake then sent Ireland clear and he teed up Bent to make it 3-1. Typical Bent finish, he hit the keeper with it but it somehow found it's way in. No-one scores more scrappy, scruffy, fortunate goals than Bent. I don't know how he gets his goals, but he does get them. Somehow. Still shit though.

Spurs dropped points on Saturday too, away at Swansea. Van Der Vaart gave them the lead with a deflected effort on the stroke of half time, but Swansea came storming back in the second half and equalised through Sinclair. Swansea seem to be doing really well and I'm impressed every time I watch them. Look at the table though, they're not in great shape and could easily get sucked into the bottom three if they have a bad run. I hope not.

Van Persie FC beat QPR 1-0 at the Emirates. No prizes for guessing who scored. The most notable thing about this game was Neil Warnock's fucking awesome post match interview. The man is a comedy genius, being funny is all about timing and set up, and no-one does it better. He comes on, all smiles, and says *"I look at Van Persie and he's so clever isn't he? Deary me"* So far so good, Wenger had just been on eulogising about his flying Dutchman and now Warnock is paying his own tribute. But wait, what's this, it's a twist! *"Every ball in the air... he fouls the centre half and gets away with it. He gets away with absolute murder. I wish I could educate referees on free-kicks that he commits. We make it obvious when we go for a ball if it's a free-kick but Van Persie gets his arm up, he backs in, he fouls and looks at the referee and gets away with it. It's amazing how he does it. But he's a great player"*. It's an unpopular view but I think Neil Warnock is dead funny and I enjoy him being in the Premier League. So shoot me, I don't care.

Wigan went to Stoke in a game no-one other than those two sets of fans wanted to see. Wigan are pretty good to watch in fairness, but that's rendered meaningless as hardly anyone manages to look good against the cloggers of Stoke. Moses gave Wigan a deserved lead after good play by Rodallega, but Stoke levelled from the spot after Caldwell handled on the line. The defender was red carded for his troubles. Walters scored from the spot, which lets face it, is the only way he can score the shit bastard. Cameron Jerome then put the home side in front and it looked like a typical hard luck story for Wigan. Then out of nothing Wigan were awarded a pen after Shotton had a handful of Rodallega's shirt. Tony Pulis didn't think that was a pen. Strange that he had a different viewpoint when it was Carragher on Walters. Martinez sent on Watson to take the pen, which he promptly buried in the top corner. It takes some balls to come off the bench just to take a pen, fair play to him. Good point for Wigan, and fuck off Stoke.

Bolton and Wolves met in a relegation battle at the Reebok. Sam Ricketts' screamer broke the deadlock as Bolton's PA system belted out Depeche Mode's *"I just can't get enough"*. It was bad enough when they used to play *"I feel good"* but this is taking it a step too far, the smalltime bastards. Music after goals belongs in the lower leagues, which is handy as so do Bolton. Steven Fletcher levelled for Wolves, he's in a great run of goalscoring form at the moment and if Wolves stay up they'll mostly have him to thank for it.

Danny Ayala made his debut for Norwich and partnered another ex red, Zak Whitbread, at the heart of the Canaries defence as they took on Fulham. The Cottagers took the lead early doors through Sa. Norwich fought back well and Whitbread hit the bar whilst Morrison had one cleared off the line. Dempsey hit the bar for Fulham and the youngster Frei looked very lively throughout. Might be one to keep an eye on him. Naughton was next to be denied by the woodwork but Norwich eventually got the goal they deserved when Simeon Jackson headed home four minutes into stoppage time. 2011 has been some year for Norwich, credit to Paul Lambert and the amazing job he's done there. He might be the next big thing, or the next Owen Coyle. Time will tell I guess.

Onto New Year's Day now, and Sunderland managed to upset City with the very last kick of the game at the Stadium of Light. It was a pulsating game, Sunderland put up a great effort and there wasn't much between the sides. The goal was marginally offside but the lad took it very well. Pretty funny seeing City lose in this manner, just a pity that it's let United off the hook after they lost the day before.

West Brom v Everton was a stinker. I watched a fair bit of it live, and it was brutal stuff. No quality on show from two shithouse teams who both went out looking to not lose. Everton won it very late with a scrappy goal from Anichebe. He comes across as a really, really nice lad in interviews, yet he's a right horrible fecker on the field. The main thing people will take from the game was of course Roy's headbanging. It may have been the first day of 2012, but I doubt there'll be a funnier moment this year. Simply amazing.

Onto Bank Holiday Monday now and Arsenal were looking to bounce back against Fulham at the Cottage. They pummeled Martin Jol's side early on and took the lead through Koscielny. They were playing some lovely stuff but couldn't kill Fulham off. Djourou was sent off for a second yellow and Sidwell made them pay shortly after. Out of favour Zamora popped up in the last minute of stoppage time to win it for the home side. Wenger went off on one afterwards about the sending off, saying once Djourou got booked Fulham were trying to get him sent off at every opportunity after. He doesn't have a leg to stand on though. If Fulham were trying so hard to get him sent off why would he then put his arm on Zamora's shoulder and pull him back? Because a) he's shite and b) he's stupid. Wenger embarrassed himself a little, but that wasn't a shock was it?

As for the Fulham boss, Spurs fans used to sing about how they 'love Martin Jol'. So do I, he'sh a fucking shupershtar. One final point, my boy Bryan Ruiz; he's actually a quality footballer. I hadn't really noticed before as I couldn't see past the beautiful hair. There's definitely more to him than amazing locks though. He's a similar player to Dembele (also very good), but with better hair.

Chelsea went to Wolves and caught a huge break when Lampard was allowed to stay on after a shocking challenge on Adam Hammill. Mick McCarthy was seething, but it got worse when Hammill was then yellow carded for a nothing challenge on Cole, who himself escaped two or three blatant yellow cards for bad fouls. Hammill and his manager were pissing themselves laughing at the sheer ridiculousness of it. That's Peter Jones for you though, he's woeful yet he's nowhere near the worst. Ramires gave Chelsea the lead as the Portuguese speakers all made a beeline for their manager. Noticeable that the rest of the team never bothered. Lampard got a late winner from a Cole cross, which stinks considering neither of them should have even been on the field at that stage. Cruel on Wolves that.

Aston Vanilla were looking to build on their big win at Chelsea and a home game with Swansea was an ideal chance to do that. Ste Warnock's howler gifted the opening goal to Dyer though and it didn't get any better for Villa after that. Swansea were brilliant, they were all over Villa and eventually made it 2-0 through Routledge. Typical Villa, good enough to beat Chelsea, bad enough to lose to Swansea. They're so damn bland you'd never describe them as good, but they aren't ever bad enough to even be classed as bad. Alex McLeish is doing his best to change that though.

It was a bittersweet day for Joey Barton as QPR hosted Norwich. He put his side in front with an excellent finish but was later sent off in controversial circumstances. He went head to head with a Norwich player, who turned away holding his nose and then kept holding it for a good 30 seconds or so afterwards, even though he clearly wasn't caught. Neither ref nor linesman saw it, yet Barton was red carded. Presumably it was the 4th official then? They claimed it was the lino, but you can see on the replays he didn't give anything. Grant Holt's reaction when he saw the red card said it all for me, he was disgusted by it. Credit to him for that but maybe he should have a word with his team-mate as it was his over-reaction that caused the whole thing. Not the first time a Norwich player has done it this season either, just ask Ivan Klasnic. Having said that, Craig Bellamy will tell you what happens when you don't feign injury in those circumstances, when you stand there without reacting and waiting for the referee to do something about it. You get a yellow card. The fact that Barton's red card wasn't overturned by that shower of cunts at the FA is frankly ludicrous, but not surprising.

Pilkington equalised with a long range effort and then Morrison got the winner from Pilkington's cross late on. Neil Warnock produced another hilarious post match interview in which he caned Bradley Johnson for cheating, added that he wasn't surprised that Johnson would do that but then praised his acting skills. Great stuff again. He's a funny guy. Funny how? Like a clown, he amuses me.

Having secured a draw at Anfield and a win at Old Trafford, Steve Kean brought his blue and white army back to Ewood to face Stoke. They started brightly but fell behind to a great goal by Crouch. His 100th career goal, and he celebrated by making a '100' gesture using his fingers to make a '1' and an '0' and his mouth to make the middle '0'. Very clever, except he got them the wrong way round, the big loveable dope. Unless he was saying this was goal number 001 of course, which would be weird. I love Crouchy though, I'll always have a soft spot for him and fond memories of when 'Crouchamania ran wild' for a while. He added a second with another classy finish. Should have made a '101' gesture as he wouldn't have to worry about getting that backwards. Never mind. Goodwillie *sniggers* pulled one back for Rovers but despite piling on the pressure the equaliser wouldn't come. Fuckin' Stoke.

Poor old Kean also suffered the indignity of being knocked to the ground when Gamst-Pedersen accidentally ran into him and knocked him on his arse, much to the delight of the home crowd. Kean had a good laugh about it, and I can't help but want him to do well. I can't even remember why I'm not supposed to like him and why so many people seem to hate him. Something about how he stiffed Allardyce to get the job? Since when has screwing over Fat Sam been a bad thing? Did I miss a memo?

Sunderland's revival under Martin O'Neill continued as they battered Wigan at the DW Stadium. Wigan hit the post twice within the space of a few seconds and were the better side in the first half. They fell behind to a terrific Craig Gardner free-kick in first half stoppage time and never recovered. McLean made it 2-0 and even though Rodallega got them briefly back into it, Sessegnon and Vaughan wrapped it up for the Mackems.

Spurs beat West Brom 1-0 thanks to Defoe's second half strike. Spurs lost two more players to injury and their squad will really start to be stretched in the coming weeks. Nothing else to add here other than Billy Jones is the latest player to wear a hairband despite not having hair long enough to justify it. Tool.

Finally onto Wednesday night's action. If Carlsberg made midweek nights.... Everton get a goal from their keeper and still manage to lose at home to Bolton for whom a former Liverpool player scored, whilst the Mancs got tonked by the toon as wonderboy Phil Jones scored a hilarious oggy. As the 'Four Seasons' once sang, *'Oh what a night'*.

I'll start in the North East. De Gea was dropped after his clanger the previous weekend but Rooney was back after the Christmas ale finally worked it's way out of his system. Howard Webb was also recalled the starting line up after Mike Dean's shoddy display against Blackburn. Webb wasted no time in showing he's still United's man for the big occasion, turning down a clear penalty for Demba Ba after he was clumsily tripped by Ferdinand. Webb can't do it all himself though, he needs some help from his team-mates and he didn't get it in this game. Ba put Newcastle in front with the latest in a long line of class finishes. The more you watch it, the better it gets. Great finish. He ran United ragged, they couldn't cope with him and not even the 'new Duncan Edwards' could keep him under control. Cabaye made it 2-0 with an amazing free-kick and at this stage the Mancs had barely even threatened. They came to life after going two down though and Simpson had to clear off the line to deny Rooney, who was later subbed. The coup de grace came when 'SuperBoy' put through his own net in hilarious circumstances. Is this lad the most overhyped player in the Premier League right now? Never has one man been so praised for doing so little. I'm not saying he isn't any good, I think he is actually very good (but not at centre half, not yet anyway), but any little thing he does brings totally over the top praise. He makes a run and Jamie Redknapp creams in his tight fitting trousers and coos *"Oh just look how powerful he is!"* He plays a routine ten yard pass and Shearer is like *"What a pass that is"*. It seems everyone is buying into this shit and that's why this own goal was extra special. Interesting to see Ferguson throw Rooney under the bus afterwards in his interview, singling out a chance he missed in the first half as a big reason why they lost. All isn't well there, but we've seen this before and they usually sort things out. Those two are a match made in Hell, they'll work things out.

Meanwhile, over at the Pit the prodigal son returned. Evertonians have been waiting for Landon Donavan to come back to Goodison ever since he went back to LA last year. They've been counting the days, sending him love messages on twitter and convincing themselves he'll be the answer to all their prayers. I almost feel sorry for them. Almost. He's not the Messiah, he's just a very average boy. He couldn't even prevent them from losing at home to Bolton. BOLTON!!!! Moyes and Coyle shared a warm embrace before the game, both seemed genuinely delighted to see eachother. Moyes was no doubt thinking *'boy am I glad to see this loser and his awful team, should be an easy three points tonight.'* Coyle was no doubt thinking *'boy am I glad to see this loser and his awful team, should be an easy three points tonight'*. The Hobo was missing for Bolton, which meant hapless Adam Bogdan featured in goal for the first time since letting in 12 goals in half an hour against Chelsea a couple of months back. That last sentence may not be exactly accurate, it may have only been 11 goals. He was poo, that much is certainly accurate. It didn't get any better for the poor lad here either, beaten by a clearance from Howard that bounced over his head after picking up pace on the wind. A nightmare for any keeper. Howard didn't celebrate it, saying it happened to him a few years ago and it isn't nice. Classy touch, credit to him for that. Donavan's only contribution to the game was an outrageous dive to try to win a penalty. It's one of the worst I've seen all season, shocking stuff. I didn't think Everton's players did stuff like that, it's only da redshite that pull that kind of shit isn't it? Speaking of redshite, the Gog looked lively throughout and could have had a hat-trick. Howard denied him twice but it was third time lucky for Daveed who equalised with a classy finish. Gary Cahill then grabbed the winner for Bolton, although Baines almost levelled when his free-kick hit the bar.

Lots of statistical quirks to come out of this one. 'Cahill' was on the scoresheet at the Pit for the first time in over a year. Sadly for the blues it wasn't Tim. A 'Tim' was on the scoresheet for Everton for the first time in over a year, but sadly for Everton it was Howard and not Cahill. The keeper is apparently now Everton's joint second top goalscorer in the league this season. He also has more goals in 2012 than Liverpool and Manchester United combined, and more goals this season than Stewart Downing. Interestingly, another Tim, Tim Krul at Newcastle has more assists than Downing.

The funniest thing related to this game though was something I heard about on the BBC's live text updates of the game. *"Everton goal and wait for it, this is not a typo, Tim Howard the scorer"*. Underneath was a reply *"I know Howard wasn't a typo, but surely Ngog was?"* Ouch.

chapter eight

Evra

I don't pretend to know exactly what transpired between Luis Suarez and Patrice Evra. They are the only two people who know what went down that day. Everybody outside of LFC was quite happy to believe Evra's version because 'the FA said so', but Kenny Dalglish was steadfast in his support of his player. I'd back Kenny over an FA panel any day of the week, but still I wanted to find out as much about the case as I could and I wanted to know why the FA came to the conclusion that Evra's version was the more likely.

Having studied the report, I'm none the wiser as to how they came to the decision they did. If anything I'm completely at a loss as to how they could completely ruin a man's reputation without proof. Suarez has forever been branded a racist based on three fellas deciding that Evra's version of events was 'probably' the true version. There is not a single scrap of evidence to back that up, and having spent hours going over that report I'd argue that even if you were to judge it on the balance of probability (which should never happen on a case as serious as this), then Suarez's version is **STILL** the more credible and he should never have lost this case.

I apologise for the length of this, I have kept it as brief as I could but it's something I felt so strongly about I needed to get all of this down in writing for my own peace of mind as much as anything. It appears to be a huge injustice and it should never have been allowed to happen. As I've said, I don't know that Luis Suarez did not say the things Patrice Evra claims he did. I don't think he did, as there is nothing to suggest that to be the case other than the word of Patrice Evra, who's story changed several times and who has previous for this kind of thing. This whole thing has bothered me far more than maybe it should have, it's been on my mind for months, some days more than others but it has never been far from my thoughts. I kept putting myself in Suarez's shoes. Imagine if someone accused you of the things Suarez was accused of. Imagine if seemingly the whole world believed you did it even though there is not a single shred of proof. Had this gone to a court of law Suarez would have been cleared. Actually no, it would never have gotten that far to begin with as like I say, there is no evidence at all. Every time I saw some ignorant fuck slating Suarez on TV or on twitter, it bothered me. A lot. Every time I read a newspaper article about how he racially abused Evra, it bothered me. It still does. The injustice of it all played on my mind for months. I don't like that somebody can see his reputation completely savaged when there is no proof at all that he has done anything wrong. There appears to be a huge injustice here, and I don't think anything like enough was done to fight that injustice. Most of the country now think Luis Suarez is a racist scumbag. Many of them also think Kenny Dalglish is defending a racist scumbag. They also think the likes of you and me are condoning racism because we've supported Suarez. The most listened to daytime sports show in the UK put out on their twitter *"Suarez admitted kicking Evra because he's black. How can Kenny Dalglish defend that?"* That's completely false, Suarez admitted no such thing, in fact he denied it emphatically. But people who have no knowledge of the case see that tweet and assume it's the truth. It's harmful and damaging, and LFC should have been compiling a list of this stuff with an eye on taking legal action. Instead they just sat back and took it, whilst Suarez was ordered to keep his mouth shut about the whole thing.

Between December 2010 and December 2011, the FA's 'Independent' Regulatory Commission heard 473 cases. Only TWO ended in a not guilty verdict. TWO!!! That tells me that anyone who goes up before that panel has already been judged guilty, and has a hell of a job on their hands to reverse that. Our legal people came across as being so inept that Luis effectively turned up to a gun fight with a water pistol, yet I can't help but think the verdict would have been the same even if we'd had Rumpole of the Bailey, Kavanagh QC and the entire cast of LA Law as well as OJ Simpson's lawyer in our corner. The inconsistencies in Evra's evidence were glaring to say the least yet it was Suarez who was deemed to be the unreliable one. Manchester United and Evra clearly learned a lot from the last time they cried racism when Evra was found to be lying after an incident with a groundsman at Stamford Bridge. This time Evra rehearsed what he was going to say and was allowed/encouraged to arrange his evidence around the video footage. Suarez was asked to recount from memory what happened, and anything that didn't quite fit perfectly into the chain of events shown on the video was pounced on and used to discredit him. Evra's discrepencies - and there were many as I will highlight shortly - were ignored, as was any evidence given by people such as Kuyt, Comolli and even Hernandez if it contradicted that of Evra.

Highlighting all the holes in the FA's report could fill an entire book on it's own, so in order to keep things as brief as I possibly can I'm just going to look mainly at the evidence given by the two players and show how ridiculous it was that the FA tried (and sadly succeeded in most cases) to convince the world that Evra was more credible than Suarez.

I'll start with the coin toss at the start of the game, as that's as good a place as any:

The FA: *"Mr Marriner explained that he used a FIFA coin which is blue* *on one side and yellow on the other. He asked Mr Evra, as the visiting captain, to call the colour. Mr Marriner tossed the coin, it came down yellow, and he awarded it to Steven Gerrard who elected to stay in their current ends. Manchester United had kick off. Mr Evra remonstrated that he had called correctly but, Mr Marriner said, he had not. Mr Evra then spoke to Ryan Giggs about it, and Mr Marriner walked over to Mr Evra to assure him that he (Mr Marriner) had got it right. Mr Evra's evidence was that when such a coin was used, he always called yellow given that the alternative, blue, is a Manchester City colour, which he would never call. The toss came down yellow and so Mr Evra knew that he had won it. He particularly wanted to change ends at the start, he explained to the referee that he had called yellow, and why he had done so. Mr Evra was angry but the referee did not change his mind."*

So if we are to believe the referee then Evra either forgot what colour he chose or he lied about it. Either way it surely casts doubt on his credibility as a witness. It also seems strange that he sees blue as a Manchester City colour when it's the colour of the shirt he wears for his national team, when he's not leading a mutiny in a major tournament that is of course. It's interesting to note that he reacted far more to this than he did when he claims Suarez called him 'n***er' numerous times in the penalty area later on. Does this not seem highly dubious?? Ref says you were mistaken about a coin toss = flip your lid. Opponent calls you a n***er five times = No outward reaction. Hmmmm.

The FA: *"In the 58th minute of the game, Mr Suarez fouled Mr Evra between the edge of the Manchester United penalty area and the corner flag at the Kop end. It seemed to us to be a deliberate foul, and the referee awarded a free kick. The foul was committed by Mr Suarez kicking Mr Evra on his right knee. Mr Evra explained that he had previously had a bad problem in that knee. He remained on the ground receiving medical treatment for about one minute after the tackle."*

A deliberate foul?? Watch the video, it's a nothing challenge with minimal contact. A foul, certainly. Deliberate? Not a chance, and Evra's overreaction to it was ridiculous, as was him blowing kisses to the Paddock and then kissing the United crest on his shirt as he came off for treatment. For the FA to say this was a deliberate foul shows their agenda very early on in the report. As I said, their verdict had been made, this is now about trying to show why they made it.

5 minutes later...

The FA: *"Mr Evra faced up to Mr Suarez and kept walking towards him. This forced Mr Suarez to move backwards along the goal-line and, in fact,* *slightly behind the goal-line. All the while they were talking to each other. They reached a position approximately halfway along the goal line when Mr Kuyt, the Liverpool player stepped in between Mr Suarez and Mr Evra. Mr Kuyt had been standing in the middle of the six-yard box. Mr Kuyt faced up to Mr Evra and prodded him in the chest with his finger. Mr Evra pushed Mr Kuyt away in the chest with both hands."*

So, Evra is the aggressor and Suarez is trying to move away and isn't the one initiating any confrontation. For Evra to be making such a big deal over an innocuous foul says a lot about his mental state at this point too. A complete over-reaction.

The FA: *"Mr Evra and Mr Suarez are agreed that they spoke to each other in Spanish in the goalmouth. Mr Evra said that he is not exactly fluent in Spanish but that he can easily converse in Spanish. Mr Evra told us that he began the conversation by saying "Concha de tu hermana". Mr Evra's evidence was that this is a phrase used in Spanish like when you say "fucking hell" in English, but the literal translation is "your sister's pussy".*

He uses a phrase that is highly offensive in English but one that he claims means something different in Spanish. Language experts said the comment can either be used as a grave insult, or it can be a general curse word similar to saying 'son of a bitch'. The FA chose to accept he meant it in its less-offensive context, despite his aggressive demeanour. This is the exact opposite of how they interpreted Suarez's use of the word 'negro'. Their logic, because they were in an argument, Suarez must have meant it as an insult. One rule for one....

The FA: *"Mr Suarez said that he did not hear this first comment from Mr Evra but that he heard him whispering something. Mr Suarez told us that he then said "What did you say?" Mr Evra told us that he then said to Mr Suarez "Porque me diste un golpe", meaning "Why did you kick me?". The video footage shows that Mr Evra looked down at his knee then at Mr Suarez's face as he asked this question, which does support his evidence that he asked a question about being kicked in the knee. Mr Evra said that, when he asked that question, he was in shock and upset at having been kicked in the knee by Mr Suarez. Mr Suarez agrees that, at this point, Mr Evra asked him why he had kicked him, referring to the earlier foul. That is largely the end of the agreement between them as to what was said in the goalmouth."*

He was in shock about THAT challenge??? Really? The FA actually believe that? One of that panel is a former player and manager (and close friend of Alex Ferguson, co-incidentally), yet he saw the footage of that 'foul' and didn't laugh his cock off when he heard Evra say he was 'in shock' about it? Embarrassing.

We move onto the confrontation in the penalty area:

Evra's version: PE: "Why did you kick me?" LS: "Because you are black"
Suarez's version: PE: "Why did you kick me?" LS: "It was just a normal foul"

The FA: *"Mr Suarez said he shrugged his shoulders and put his arms out in a gesture to say that there was nothing serious about it. At this point on the video footage, Mr Suarez's face is obscured, but he does appear to shrug his shoulders."*

Even the wording of it shows you the bias in the report. It's as though they are reluctant to even admit that he shrugged his shoulders. What's all this 'appear to' crap. He did or he didn't. If you've seen the video you know that he did. The video shows Suarez shrugging and holding the palm of his hands up looking completely baffled by it and his body language appears defensive and conciliatory. Look at it and ask yourself what he is more likely to be saying; "I kicked you because you are black" or "It was just a normal foul"

Evra's version: PE: "Say it to me again, I'm going to punch you". LS: "I don't speak to blacks" PE: "Okay, now I think I'm going to punch you" LS: "Okay, blackie, blackie, blackie"
Suarez's version: PE: "Ok, you kicked me, I'm going to kick you" LS: "I told him to shut up and made a brief gesture with my left hand like a 'quacking' motion as if to say he was talking too much and should be quiet".

The video shows Suarez making a gesture with his hand, which again backs up his version. Also, does anyone actually believe he would say 'I don't talk to blacks' and then say 'blackie blackie blackie' in a crowded goalmouth? (actually it would have been 'negro negro negro' but the point stands) And if he did, how come NOBODY heard it?? NOBODY!!! Even though David De Gea amongst others was stood right next to them. And what relevance would the 'quacking' gesture have in that context?

The FA: *"Mr Evra said that as Mr Suarez was speaking he reached out to touch Mr Evra's arm, gesturing at his skin. Mr Evra said that Mr Suarez was drawing attention to the colour of Mr Evra's skin. In cross-examination, Mr Evra said that at the time he did not realise that Mr Suarez had pinched his arm. He was more focussed on his lips and what he was say-*

ing. Mr Evra only realised that Mr Suarez had touched his arm in this way when he saw the video footage later."

Drawing attention to the colour of his skin by pinching him?? Please!! Who does that??? Nobody, that's who. It's a ludicrous and desperate suggestion. I've seen the video of this, and Suarez clearly reached out and pinched him on the arm, yet Evra claims he didn't notice until he saw the video! Really?? Someone is stood in front of you and pinches your arm and you don't notice? The FA don't find that even the slightest bit dubious? I would suggest that had Evra admitted noticing the pinch it would make Suarez's 'don't touch me South American' accusation a lot more plausible. By saying he didn't notice he makes it easier to then deny saying 'don't touch me South American'. After all, why would you say 'don't touch me' if you didn't realise you'd been touched?

Suarez says *"Evra did not back off and Dirk Kuyt was approaching us to stand between us. At this point I touched PE's left arm in a pinching type movement. This all happened very quickly. I was trying to defuse the situation and was trying to intimate to Evra that he was not untouchable by reference to his question about the foul. Under no circumstances was this action intended to be offensive and most certainly not racially offensive. It was not in any way a reference to the colour of PE's skin."*

This was used by United's lawyer against Suarez to make him look less credible. The way the statement was worded implied that the pinch was part of an attempt to defuse the situation which is clearly a ridiculous suggestion. Under cross examination Suarez said that he'd been trying to calm things down by saying it was just a normal foul and for Evra to be quiet. He then admitted that the pinch was done in response to Evra saying he was going to kick him, it was to show that he was not untouchable and it was not done to defuse the situation. He said he was trying to defuse the situation and then he pinched him, not that the pinch was part of his attempt to calm things down. When you read the statement it can actually be taken that way, it's just not very clearly worded. The FA seized on this and made a big thing of it, even though LFC's lawyer admitted it was due to 'bad drafting' by them and was not what Suarez actually meant. Unprofessional on the LFC legal team's part, but by no means a big deal. Still, it gave the FA something they could use to question Suarez's reliability as a witness. Any inconsistency with Evra is ignored, anything they can use on Suarez is pounced on. It's a recurring theme.

The FA: *"Mr Suarez said that at no point did he use the word 'negro' during the exchange with Mr Evra in the goalmouth."*

If he had done, surely there'd have been a visible reaction from Evra?

After all, this is a man with a well known short fuse who had earlier gone nuts because he lost the coin toss. If you actually watch the footage, Evra is relatively calm throughout the whole exchange. He doesn't lose the plot until he gets booked after an altercation with Kuyt. Whilst the alleged racism is happening he's completely in control of himself and at one point is even half smiling as he talks with Suarez. Not the reaction you'd expect of somebody who believes he is repeatedly being called 'n***er'

The FA: *"The referee called them over to him. Mr Suarez said something to Mr Evra, then started to walk away. There is a clear reaction by Mr Evra to Mr Suarez's comment. This is apparent in two ways. First, there is a facial reaction by Mr Evra, akin to a look of surprise. Secondly, whilst looking at the referee, Mr Evra points to Mr Suarez, first with his forefinger then with his thumb. Mr Evra walks towards the referee and says something while pointing back at Mr Suarez."*

The FA: *"Mr Evra's evidence was that while he was walking towards the referee he said "ref, ref, he just called me a fucking black". He said that he did not know whether the referee heard his comment. The referee said something like "Calm down, Patrice, the game has been brilliant, stop the pushing between you and Suarez, the game is going well."*

So, there's no visible reaction previously to anything said or even when Suarez pinched him. Then, suddenly Suarez says something that causes him to visibly react. So, with that in mind, whos version makes more sense now? Surely Suarez's account, as this is the point where he admits saying "Por que negro?". Evra reacted to the 'negro' comment with shock, which seems strange if - as he'd claimed - he'd been subjected to it five times previously. It would be a natural reaction if it had been the first time the word had been used however. What's even more puzzling is that Evra doesn't even say in his testimony what Suarez said to make him look so shocked. Given that at this stage he was apparently under the impression he'd been called 'n***er' five times (remember it was only much later that he supposedly realised that 'negro' did not mean 'n***er'), what could Suarez possibly have said that would suddenly cause him to look shocked, and more importantly, why did he not feel the need to mention it? This is your 'impressive' witness? Really?

The FA: *"Mr Suarez's evidence was that simultaneously with the blowing of the whistle, Mr Evra said to him "Don't touch me, South American". Mr Suarez took this to be a reference to his touching Mr Evra's arm on the goal-line a few moments earlier. Mr Suarez said that he turned to Mr Evra and said "Por que, negro?". He said that he used the word 'negro' at this point in the way that he did when he was growing up in Uruguay, that is as a friendly form of address to people seen as black or brown-skinned or* *even just black-haired. He said that he used it in the same way that he did when he spoke to Glen Johnson, the black Liverpool player. He said in no way was the use of the word 'negro' intended to be offensive or to be racially offensive. It was intended as an attempt at conciliation.*

So, Suarez admits using the word but claims it was done in a conciliatory manner. That may or may not be true, only Suarez knows. You can perhaps argue that whatever the context it was used, he shouldn't be using that word on an English football field, but you cannot state that it was used in an insulting manner as the language experts stated that it can be used in a positive or negative way. Much like Evra's "Concha de tu hermana", except in this case the FA were not giving any benefit of the doubt.

The FA: *"After he had spoken to them, Mr Evra and Mr Suarez walked away from the referee in the direction of the goalmouth. They walked side by side. Mr Suarez stretched out his left arm, and put his left hand on the back of Mr Evra's head. Mr Evra immediately and firmly pushed Mr Suarez's arm away. The referee called them back and spoke to them again. He spoke first to Mr Suarez. The referee clasped Mr Suarez's two arms down by his side, and spoke to him. He then spoke briefly to Mr Evra. Mr Evra made a comment as he and Mr Suarez walked away. Mr Suarez can then be seen making a comment to Mr Evra"*

Mr Evra's evidence on this incident was as follows. As he and Mr Suarez walked away from the referee, Mr Suarez put his hand on Mr Evra's head. Mr Evra pushed his hand away as he did not want Mr Suarez to touch him. The referee must have seen this as he called them over and told them to calm down. The referee told Mr Suarez not to touch Mr Evra as Mr Evra was saying he did not want Mr Suarez to touch him. As they walked away Mr Suarez said something to Mr Evra but he did not remember what he said to him or what Mr Evra said to Mr Suarez.

Evra doesn't remember what Suarez said to him or what he said to Suarez.

Mr Suarez's account was as follows. The referee called the players to him the first time. Mr Suarez did not understand what the referee was saying but he gained the impression that what he was doing was to say that they should each say sorry to each other and get on with the game. As they walked away from the referee, Mr Suarez took his advice and patted Mr Evra on the back of the head. According to Mr Suarez, this was "a friendly gesture designed to be conciliatory" but Mr Evra reacted adversely to it and quite violently pushed his arm away. At that point the referee called them both back again to him, spoke to them again and, Mr Suarez believed, delivered the same message about getting on with the game. There was no more conversation between Mr Evra and Mr Suarez for the rest of the game. It will be noted that Mr Suarez makes no mention of the players talking to each other as they walk away from the referee for the second time.

Suarez doesn't mention the conversation either. Given that neither bothered to state what was said, presumably it wasn't important. Suarez claims the touching of the head was done in a conciliatory way. That's how it looked at the time and on the video. Only Suarez knows what his intent was, for everybody else there's simply no way of knowing. The FA decided it was done to further wind up Evra, despite them having no evidence to back that up. Their logic for this was because they had been arguing Suarez must have not only meant 'negro' in an insulting manner, but the seemingly apologetic 'let's just forget it' tap on the head was also meant to provoke. So, apparently, if you are in an argument with somebody at no point is it feasible for either of you to attempt to end it by saying 'ok let's forget this and move on mate'. I wonder if they even know how ridiculous they sound? Only Suarez knows what his intent was, and the FA's interpretation of it is flawed and appears pre-judged.

The FA: *"The corner came to nothing and the ball went out of play with Manchester United being awarded a goal kick. As the players moved upfield, there was an exchange between Mr Evra and Mr Kuyt. The referee called Mr Evra over and gave him a yellow card. Mr Giggs spoke to the referee about the caution and then spoke to Mr Evra."*

"The evidence of Mr Marriner about this incident was as follows. In the 65th minute of the game, he had to issue a caution to Mr Evra after he saw him push Mr Kuyt in the chest following a coming together. Mr Evra was clearly upset and mentioned that he was being called "black". Mr Marriner did not hear whether Mr Evra said who was calling him 'black' and he did not understand what Mr Evra was referring to at the time. Mr Evra made no other comment to the referee."

The referee says he 'did not understand what Evra was referring to' and that he did not hear Evra accuse any individual of anything. His words. If he did not understand what he was referring to or who he was accusing, how can he say that Evra said he was being called black? Answer; he didn't say that, the FA did based on what Evra told them and Marriner is accepting it based on what Evra has stated since. It's right there in the above paragraph. The ref didn't hear what Evra said to him, he may accept after the fact that Evra did say he'd been called black, but at the time he didn't know what Evra was talking about. He said it himself.

The FA: *"Mr Evra described the booking in the following way. Mr Kuyt told him to stop diving so Mr Evra pushed him away. The referee called Mr Evra over to book him. Mr Evra asked the referee why he was booking him* *and the referee said it was because he had pushed Mr Kuyt. When he was being booked, Mr Evra told the referee again that he had been called black. Mr Evra added that after booking him, the referee spoke to Ryan Giggs. Mr Giggs then asked Mr Evra what was wrong and Mr Evra told him that he had been called black. Mr Giggs told Mr Evra to calm down and not get sent off.*

"Mr Giggs said that he was reasonably close to the referee and after he had shown Mr Evra the yellow card, Mr Giggs approached the referee and asked him why he had booked Mr Evra. The referee said to Mr Giggs "just calm Patrice down". It was obvious to Mr Giggs from looking at Mr Evra that he was upset. He said that Mr Evra did not seem quite with it, you might call it red mist. Mr Giggs said to Mr Evra "what's happened?". Mr Evra replied "he called me black". Mr Giggs assumed that Mr Evra was speaking about Mr Kuyt since he had just been booked for some kind of tussle with Mr Kuyt. Mr Giggs said to Mr Evra "did the ref hear it?", to which Mr Evra replied "I don't think so". Mr Giggs then told Mr Evra to calm down and not get himself sent off."

"Mr Kuyt gave a slightly different version from Mr Marriner, Mr Evra and Mr Giggs. He said that after the goal kick he was close to Mr Evra and said "Come on, let's move on, let's keep going with the game" and touched Mr Evra just on the arm. According to Mr Kuyt, Mr Evra reacted aggressively and smashed his arm away and at that point, the referee having seen the incident, called Mr Evra to him and booked him. Mr Kuyt said that he was very close to Mr Evra and the referee at this time. He said he was "absolutely certain" that he heard Mr Evra say that the referee was only booking him because he was black."

The FA: *"We found the evidence of Mr Marriner on this point to be credible and plausible. He recalled Mr Evra telling him that he was being called black. This is consistent with Mr Evra's evidence of what he told Mr Marriner at that time, and also with Mr Giggs' evidence of what Mr Evra said to him shortly afterwards. In light of this, we reject Mr Kuyt's evidence that Mr Evra said that the referee was only booking him because he was black, however certain Mr Kuyt was that he heard it. Moreover, it would make no sense in the circumstances for Mr Evra to accuse the referee of only booking him because he was black. Not only had Mr Evra pushed Mr Kuyt away, which he is likely to have realised had led to his booking, but his concern at that stage was that he had been called black (bearing in mind that, at the very least, Mr Suarez admits having called Mr Evra 'negro' by this stage of the game).*

Marriner has already said he didn't know what Evra was on about, now he's saying he recalled Evra telling him he was called black. Sorry, not having that. He's heard something involving the word 'black' and he's now going along with Evra's version of events here when he clearly doesn't know for sure what was said to him. If he was made aware that someone had been racially abusing Evra, why did he not do anything about it? He admitted he didn't know what was said, whereas Kuyt said he was 'absolutely certain' Evra said he was being booked because he's black. So, the FA are accusing Dirk of lying too, based on 'it would make no sense'. This despite Giggs admitting Evra did not seem 'quite with it' and had seen the 'red mist'. Come on. And if we are going down the 'it would make no sense' route, then I give you "I don't talk to blacks" from a player of mixed race with a black grandfather. Or how about a man who speaks Spanish but claims he didn't know what the word 'negro' meant. Now THAT makes no sense.

The FA: *"Mr Evra said in evidence that some of the other players could see that he was upset and asked him what was wrong. He said that Mr Suarez had called him a n***er and said that he had kicked him because of that. Mr Evra said that he told the other players that Mr Suarez had said "porque tu eres negro". We note that Mr Evra did not say in his own evidence that he had told his team-mates that Mr Suarez had said he would not speak to him because he was black. However, we accept that Mr Evra did say this to his teammates after the match because that is what all four of them say in their statements and their evidence has been accepted in full by Mr Suarez. It is possible that Mr Evra also told them that Mr Suarez had said he had kicked him "porque tu eres negro", and this was not recalled by the players.*

So, there's an inconsistency here. Evra's evidence is completely different to that of his team-mates (I haven't included their statements to save space) but the FA are fine with this. It's possible that Evra said it but all four of his team-mates did not recall it? Hahaha this would be funny if it wasn't such an incredible injustice. I love how they keep stressing through the report that Mr Suarez accepted this evidence in full as though it somehow validates the information as being beyond reproach. This is based on conversations that took place in Manchester United's dressing room. Of course Suarez is going to accept it as how the hell would he know what was and wasn't said, he wasn't there!!

The FA: *"Sir Alex said that as he was speaking to David De Gea, Mr Evra approached him. He said "Boss, Suarez called me a n***er." It was obvious to Sir Alex that Mr Evra was upset and angry. Sir Alex was shocked and asked Mr Evra what he wanted to do about it. Sir Alex told him that he should report it to the referee and asked Mr Evra if he wanted to do that. Mr Evra said that he did. Sir Alex and Mr Evra went to the referee's room. Sir Alex went in first, followed by Mr Evra. Sir Alex told Mr*

*Marriner that they had a complaint to make. Sir Alex told him "Evra has been called a n***er by one of the Liverpool players." Sir Alex then motioned for Mr Evra to tell the referee what had been said. The referee told Phil Dowd, the fourth official who was also in the room, to take notes of what was said. Mr Evra then told the referee what had been said to him on the pitch and left the room. The referee told Sir Alex that he (the referee) would need to speak to Liverpool officials about the complaint. Mr Evra said that he told the referee that Mr Suarez had called him a n***er. Mr Evra, speaking in English, then told Mr Marriner that during a coming together in the penalty area in the second half of the match, Mr Suarez said to Mr Evra, "I don't talk to you because you n***ers". Mr Marriner told Sir Alex and Mr Evra that he would include the incident in his report. He also told them that he needed to speak to the Liverpool manager, Kenny Dalglish, in order to seek Mr Suarez's version of events.*

The FA: *"Mr Dalglish said, "hasn't he done this before?". This was the evidence to us of Mr Dowd, which was also accepted by Mr Suarez. Mr Dowd remembered this as it caused him to consciously stop and think whether he was aware of any previous allegation involving Mr Evra. Mr Marriner's evidence as to Mr Dalglish's explanation of what happened was as follows: "Dalglish said to me that Suarez had told him that he had said to Evra 'you are black', having been taunted by Evra with the comment 'you are South American'. Mr Dalglish's evidence of his explanation was in the following terms: "I said to the Referee that LS had told me (meaning in the general discussion to which Damien Comolli was a party as well) that he had referred to PE being negro (black) and that PE had referred to LS as "South American"."*

*Mr Comolli in his evidence said that he relayed to the referee what he thought Mr Suarez had said to Mr Evra, and Mr Dowd made a note of it. He told us that he explained to the referee that the context in which the word 'negro' was used was not in any way namecalling or an insult. He said that he felt something had been lost in translation in the way in which Mr Evra had interpreted the remark and had taken offence when none was intended. Mr Comolli confirmed to Mr Marriner that at no point had Mr Suarez said the word "n***ers"*

So, Luis Suarez's version of events has not changed at any point since the initial accusation was made. There is a discrepancy in terms of what Comolli thought he said ('tues Negro' as opposed to 'por que negro'). This was explained later by Comolli who put it down to an error on his part. It was also explained by a Uruguayan language professor who pointed out that the words Comolli used are not even proper Spanish, let alone the South American version spoken by Suarez). This discrepancy isn't particularly important unless you happen to be on an FA panel looking to justify a guilty verdict. As it turns out, this was one of the main things they used to hang Suarez, even though it is easily explained away.

The real issue here, and the point that should have stood out the most to the FA is that Evra made no reference at this point to 'I kicked you because you are a n***er' or 'ok n***er n***er n***er'. The accusation was that Suarez had called him it ONCE, this is confirmed in the referees report. Why would he not have told the referee that it happened numerous times, and why did the FA not find this to be extremely odd? Another discrepancy relating to this part of the story is that Ferguson was reportedly overheard by an LFC employee saying to the officials "Suarez called Evra a 'n***er' five times'. Yet neither Evra, Ferguson nor the referee mention this. Nevertheless, the FA chose to believe the word of the LFC employee because that would give Evra's claims of multiple abuse more credibility. Ferguson denies saying it and even Evra himself didn't even make that claim at this stage, so why are the FA taking the word of an LFC employee who claims to have heard something when Evra and Ferguson both deny it? Seems they'll believe LFC employees when it suits them, and not when it doesn't (Suarez, Comolli and Kuyt).

Evra then did an interview with French TV in which he said: *"There will be an investigation, there is the video. You can even see clearly on his lips what he told me at least ten times."*

The FA: *"Mr Comolli made reference to Mr Evra's Canal+ interview. He said that a few hours after the game, he received telephone calls from Canal+ who said that Mr Evra had been to see them in the tunnel after the game and said "I want to talk on TV. I want to report my record because I've been abused racially by Suarez ten times". The television representatives asked Mr Comolli if he was aware of this and he said "Yes, I am aware of what happened after the game, because Ferguson went to the changing room saying he's been abused five times". Mr Comolli told us that he said he was not aware about ten times, he was aware about five times." (this is based on what the LFC employee said he heard from Ferguson)"*

The FA: *"Mr Evra told us that he did not mean this in the literal sense, it was just a way of talking. In French, he said, it is common to say something like 'more than 10 times' but for you not to mean that it was actually over 10 times. It was just a figure of speech. When Mr Comolli gave evidence, he was asked whether that evidence from Mr Evra about the phrase ten times accorded with Mr Comolli's knowledge as a Frenchman of the French language and French behaviour. His answer was: not in these circumstances. He said that if his daughter asked him for a toy for Christmas and she says it five, six, seven times, he might say "You already told me ten* *times". But, in those circumstances (referring to Mr Evra giving an interview after the game), nobody in the French language will say that (ie ten times) because it's too important. You have to be precise in what you say."*

The FA chose to accept Evra's version of this, even though Comolli's clearly makes far more sense. Not only that, later in the report they claim that Comolli had confirmed Evra's statement that this is just a figure of speech in France, when as you can see, he actually refuted it!

The FA: *"Mr Suarez's account of his admitted use of the word 'negro' changed several times. He seemed unsure of when the admitted use took place and what triggered it. His account seemed to change in an attempt to fit in with the video evidence."*

So Evra's evidence ties in nicely with the video footage but Suarez's didn't. And of course that had nothing to do with the FA sitting down with Evra and going through the video with him as he gave his statement, whilst sitting in a room with no TV and asking Suarez 'so what happened then?' It's staggering and it should not have been allowed to happen. They've gotten away with it though as they answer to no-one, and the media - or LFC - haven't bothered taking them to task about any of it afterwards.

The FA: *"Mr Haughan (an LFC Employee) said that when he overheard Sir Alex Ferguson complain to the referee after the match, he heard him say that Mr Suarez had called Mr Evra a n***er 'five times'. If that is true, it is probable that Mr Evra was the source for Sir Alex's figure. Mr Evra said in his evidence to us that he had been called 'negro' five times. Thus, it might appear that Mr Haughan's evidence supports Mr Evra's evidence that the word was used five times in the goalmouth. In a supplemental statement, Sir Alex said that he thought he may have told the referee that Mr Evra had been called the word several times, but did not recall having said specifically that it was five times and thinks it unlikely he would have done so. Mr Evra did not mention in his evidence any specific number that he told Sir Alex at the time. Nonetheless, Mr Haughan does remember Sir Alex saying five times. This is the sort of detail that Mr Haughan might remember given the unusual circumstances in which he overheard the complaint and the fact that Mr Haughan reported what he had heard to the Liverpool management. In our judgment, this lent some weight to the credibility of Mr Evra's evidence that Mr Suarez used the word five times in the goalmouth."*

THIS is how they concluded Suarez said the word five times? Because a Liverpool employee thinks he heard Ferguson claim that Suarez said something five times?? Let's assume this is true (even though Evra and Ferguson deny it). So Evra tells Ferguson, who repeats the allegation.

How does that make it even remotely more credible? It still came from Evra. He could have told a million people the same thing and they could have told a million more people. But it's still Evra's word against Suarez. The FA know that, but they are using any little thing they can to try and support their verdict and make Suarez's guilt look more 'probable'. That's why certain things are mentioned in more detail whilst other more important things are glossed over. Such as how Evra goes from ONE accusation of the word 'n***er' to the referee after the game to five accusations of the word 'negro' when he met the FA five days later. That's a pretty damn significant fact, but it's barely even given a mention. In fact, isn't mentioned, I've worked that out myself from reading the report. It's so transparent what they've done here, and it's disgusting.

The FA: *"Mr Evra's evidence was that, in response to his question 'Why did you kick me?', Mr Suarez replied "Porque tu eres negro". Mr Evra said that at the time Mr Suarez made that comment, he (Mr Evra) understood it to mean "Because you are a n***er". He now says that he believes the words used by Mr Suarez mean "Because you are black".*

Leaving aside the laughable assertion that Evra can speak Spanish well enough to understand and recite exactly what he claims Suarez said, yet claims he thought 'negro' meant 'n***er', let's look at the phrase he claims Suarez used. "Porque tu eres negro" That is European Spanish, not South American Spanish. A language professor from Montevideo who works at Brown University in America posted a lengthy response to this on the forums of lfctv. I'm not going to quote it all, but here's a few snippets: *"It is clear to me that the Spanish language reported by Evra is inconsistent with Luis Suárez's way of speaking Spanish. I am surprised nobody (and especially, the Liverpool lawyers) raised this point. The key is that Evra makes Suárez appear to be using forms of Spanish Suárez just wouldn't use. Suárez cannot speak as Evra reported him speaking. And that strongly suggests that Evra made the whole thing up."*

The jist of it is that if Suarez were to say 'Because you are black' he would not say "Porque tu eres negro", he would have said "porque sos negro" He went into great detail as to how there is no way Suarez could have said what Evra claimed, as it's effectively a completely different language to that which Luis uses. He also dismissed Commolli's knowledge of Spanish, saying *"it is clear Mr Comolli can barely understand what he himself is trying to say in Spanish. I say this because "tues" is no Spanish word. And "tues negro" cannot be translated at all—let alone into what the FA says it means. It's simply not a Spanish expression, so it cannot be "translated". Comolli's recollection from his chat with Suárez just after the match is unreliable. The language is so ridiculously wrong it makes me laugh."*

Yet the FA used Comolli's evidence as one of their main justifications for casting doubt on Suarez's version of events. But then there's a recurring theme through all of this. Ignore anything that puts Evra's version into question, and pounce on anything that goes against what Suarez has said. It's apparent all the way through the report, there are numerous examples. They use Commolli's dodgy Spanish interpretation of what he thought Suarez told him, but dismiss his evidence that contradicted Evra's claim that 'at least ten times' is just a figure of speech in France and not meant to be taken literally. The did similar with Kuyt. They put great credence on what he 'initially thought' Suarez told him in Dutch but dismissed it when he said he was 'absolutely certain' that Evra accused the referee of booking him for being black. On the one occasion they dismissed the evidence of Evra and Ferguson, it was because the LFC employee's evidence suited their verdict better!

Look at what they said about the pinch....

The FA: *"Mr Suarez's action is difficult to interpret; it looks like a pinch, intended perhaps to annoy or provoke. The experts were not aware of any River Plate-specific meaning attached to this gesture. It was by no means clear to the experts that this was a reference to skin colour, but it might have been. In the experience of Peter Wade, in Colombia people may touch their own forearms to indicate their own skin colour or when issues of skin colour are being discussed or when they are indicating that skin colour was at issue in some incident, the gesture is usually to rub the forearm with the forefinger; the gesture is not used on someone else. In the context of all the previous usages of "negro" and "negros", however, it is very possible that this gesture was a way of highlighting Mr Evra's skin colour and would therefore constitute a racially offensive gesture".*

So even though there is nothing whatsoever to suggest this was a reference to skin colour, the FA decide 'it might have been'. They then decide that because of all the previous uses of the word 'negro' (which Suarez denies and there is no proof of) it is 'very possible' that the gesture was a way of highlighting skin colour. Come on, really?? That's the best you can do?

How about the FA withholding information from LFC??

The FA: *"As a result of a question raised by the Commission during the course of the hearing, it transpired that the FA had interviewed Mr Evra on 20 October, and that this interview had been recorded. No transcript had been made. The tapes should have been, but were not, included in the schedule of unused material. Upon enquiring into this omission, it also emerged that the FA was in possession of some brief notes of interviews,* *which also should have been, but were not, included in the schedule of unused material. When this came to light, Mr Greaney properly offered to provide copies of the tapes and other notes to Mr Suarez and his advisers. This development took place before Mr Evra had started to give evidence. In the circumstances, the Commission directed that this additional unused material should be disclosed forthwith to Mr McCormick; that Mr McCormick should have an adequate opportunity to review the material, including listening to the tapes, to take instructions from Mr Suarez on any matters arising from this additional material, and to review his planned cross-examination of Mr Evra in the light of it."*

So Evra was interviewed a few days after the match and had the benefit of video. Suarez was interviewed 18 days after the match and although he had watched the Sky footage beforehand, he was not allowed to use the video during the interview. Why? Evra's interview transcript was not made available until a day before the hearing. Why?

Based on all of these discrepancies, inaccuracies and general inconsistencies and changing of story, how did the FA go from this (after the hearing where the Chelsea groundsman was cleared of racially abusing Evra):

"We find Mr Evra's description exaggerated... There was no good reason for Mr Evra to have run over and barged Mr Griffin as he did. It was unnecessarily and gratuitously aggressive of Mr Evra... Mr Evra's suggestion that he was concerned about Mr Strudwick's safety is farfetched. They were two grown men having an apparently strong verbal disagreement but no more than that. The clear implication by Mr Evra that Mr Griffin's pitchfork gave some reason for concern about Mr Strudwick's safety is ridiculous...We find Mr Evra's account exaggerated and unreliable. It is an attempt to justify a physical intervention by him which cannot reasonably be justified..."

to this:

"We found Mr Evra to be an impressive witness. He gave his evidence to us in a calm, composed and clear manner. Mr Evra also demonstrated a measure of balance in his evidence. For example, he was prepared to make a number of concessions before us. Prior to 15 October 2011, Mr Evra and Mr Suarez had played against each other when Mr Evra was playing for Manchester United and in a France v Uruguay match. They had no relationship outside football, and Mr Evra had experienced no problems with Mr Suarez on the pitch before this match. We considered it improbable that Mr Evra would act in such a dishonest way in order to damage the reputation of a fellow professional whose footballing skills he admires, with whom he had had no previous run-ins, and who he does not think is a

racist."

Wow. He made a number of concessions such as telling them that:

1) France had played Uruguay before
2) He had no relationship with Suarez outside football
3) He had experienced no problems with Suarez before this match.

These are concessions that went in his favour to show he is credible? Read that again people, as frankly it defies belief. And just what exactly does Evra's opinion on Suarez's footballing ability have to do with anything? If he made the same claim about Tony Hibbert would he be more likely to be making it up because nobody other David Moyes admires Hibbert's 'footballing skills'? What a ridiculous thing for them to say. Finally, why is Evra saying he does not think Suarez is a racist? If I were black and somebody kicked me and told me that was their reason for it, and then followed it up by saying they don't speak to blacks, I'm pretty sure I'd consider them a big fat racist. In fact I'd say that is actually the very definition of what a racist is. So why were Evra and the FA at great pains to say how they do not believe Suarez is racist? I find that very odd. Much like the whole verdict actually. Odd, and disgusting.

chapter nine

January

LIVERPOOL 5 OLDHAM ATHLETIC 1

Competition - FA Cup 3rd Rd
Date - Fri 6 Jan 2012
Venue - Anfield
Scorer(s) – Bellamy, Gerrard (pen), Shelvey, Carroll, Downing
Half Time - 2-1
Star Man – Craig Bellamy

Team: Reina; Kelly, Carragher, Coates, Aurelio (Flanagan); Shelvey, Spearing, Gerrard, Maxi; Kuyt (Carroll), Bellamy (Downing):

There was a game tonight you know. We won 5-1, not that anyone but us seems to care. What should have been a really enjoyable night was tarnished by one unsavoury incident, so I may as well get that out of the way first.

As of yet we don't know for certain what happened, I just know I came out of the ground worrying about what may have taken place and the fall-out it would cause and that worry was sadly justified. It was pretty obvious at the time that Tom Adeyemi felt he had been racially abused. You simply don't react like that from regular insults. You can argue that you shouldn't react like that from any insult, but that's besides the point. I understand those who feel that crying over being called a name is excessive, but personally I felt bad for the kid, especially when his every touch afterwards was booed by the crowd. I'd say that most of those booing had no idea what had gone on, but that won't cut any ice with anyone outside of LFC. We're the club that supports racism don't you know.

If the lad in the Kop has shouted racist abuse at him then he'll get what's coming to him and rightly so. If it's a case of a misunderstanding ('manc' as opposed to 'black'??) then I'm sure there were enough witnesses to be able to determine what was shouted. Not that it will change the general football public's perception of what happened, the damage has been done now irrespective of the outcome of the police investigation. (Update: The case was thrown out, he did indeed say 'manc' and not 'black'). Quite why anyone felt the need to shout ANY abuse at a young lad they've never even heard of in a game that had been played in a good spirit and in which we led 3-1 is beyond me. If you can get that worked up against Oldham when your team is cruising then you have a problem, regardless of whether the abuse was of a racist nature or not. It shouldn't have happened, and it did spoil what was an otherwise enjoyable evening. Maybe spoil isn't the right word actually, but the shine was certainly taken off it. Putting that to one side and simply looking at the football, this was a good night. Not a great one as we didn't play particularly well for long periods, but it was a good one as we ended it well and scored five goals. More significantly, Andy Carroll got a much needed goal, Stewart Downing did likewise and Jonjo Shelvey also notched his first senior goal for the club. Craig Bellamy was electric and Gerrard completed 90 minutes. Hell, we were even treated to a rare sighting of the lesser spotted Fabio Aurelio. All in all, a lot to feel good about.

It didn't start particularly well though. I thought Oldham were quite impressive in the first half. Even before they scored they'd had a few promising situations and looked quite dangerous. Coates looked nervy and Aurelio was understandably rusty and Oldham's right winger clearly fancied it against him. Their opening goal was a screamer and the lad who scored it (Simpson??) will be able to tell that to his grandkids. Not many score goals as good as that at the Kop end. That woke us up, as prior to that we'd been very sloppy. We hit back fairly quickly, Shelvey's shot deflecting off Bellamy on it's way in. We had the lead before half time, Maxi was bundled over and Gerrard's spot kick just about found it's way in via the woodwork. The lead flattered us a bit, but when you face a lower league team at home you generally find that you can wear them down the longer the game goes. What you don't want is for them to have something to be clinging onto as that's when it's difficult. If they are chasing the game they run out of steam a lot quicker.

We needed the third goal to kill it, and we eventually got it through Shelvey. Good finish from the lad and he showed some good things I thought, mostly in the second period when he moved into the middle. He'd been on the right in the 1st half and didn't look particularly effective. Kenny's switch at half time helped everybody though. He went from 442 to 433 with Bellamy switched to the right wing and Shelvey tucked inside with Gerrard and Spearing. We looked much better and Bellamy ran their full back ragged. Oldham were defending too high up the field and they left Bellamy one on one far too often. All we had to do was play it into the space and let him chase it. He did time and again, and delivered some wicked low crosses into the six yard box. Most of them went unconverted and Bellamy was beginning to look more than a little pissed off about it, so Shelvey's goal came at a good time.

Craig was eventually withdrawn as a precaution with the City game in mind, but he'd done more than enough at that point to pick up the star man award. Downing replaced him and he looked very lively. Flanagan had earlier come on for Aurelio and he too played very well. He got forward often and was involved in the final two goals. With two minutes left Kenny sent on Andy Carroll. I didn't see the point, and said to the fella next to me I'd be pissed off if I was Carroll. Who knows, maybe he was pissed off about it but I imagine he wasn't when he came off the field with a goal to his name. It was a good goal too, Flanagan laid the ball inside to him and set off looking for a return pass. Had the pass come he was clean through, but Carroll opted to hit it first time and leathered it past the keeper from 25 yards. His relief was plain to see, and he seemed to have a bit of a spring in his step afterwards. He was closing defenders down and when the ball was out wide he had his arm up gesturing for the cross to come in. Little things that he should be doing anyway of course, but he just seemed to be a bit more into it. It's a pity therefore that he didn't take the great chance that came his way just after. Downing did well to cut inside the full back and put the ball right onto Carroll's head, but he failed to direct his header properly and the ball sailed into the Kop. Had that gone in it would have been a real boost to the big man's confidence ahead of the games we have coming up against City.

Would have been nice for Downing to finally claim an assist too. At least he's finally gotten himself a goal now, and a well taken one it was too. Once more Flanagan was heavily involved as he cut inside and drilled a shot goalwards that was parried by the keeper. Downing followed up at the back post and did very well to keep his shot down and find the back of the net, much to his delight.

Nice for us to finally rack up some goals and good that some of those goals fell to players who really needed them. Not everyone covered themselves in glory, I thought Dirk struggled and wasn't impressed with Coates either. It's difficult for the young defender, as he needs games to get used to English football and also for his sharpness but we can't give him any games except in the cups. A loan to somewhere like Swansea or Wolves would probably do him a lot of good but he may be needed here if anything happens to one of the other centre backs. Difficult situation really. Bellamy was comfortably the best player on the pitch, but others played well too. Notably Spearing, Shelvey and Kelly, as well as Flanagan who was class in the brief time he was on. Gerrard played within himself a little I thought, but having gotten through the full game he'll now surely be ready to take on City next week.

The past couple of weeks have been an absolute nightmare for the club as we've been pilloried by everybody. It's like that scene from Airplane where all and sundry are lining up to smack the woman in the face. Everyone is taking a shot at us right now. It's become so ridiculous that we even had to listen to Oldham fans accusing us of being 'a town full of racists'. Yes, that would the same Oldham that was the scene for race riots and has had all kinds of problems of that nature. That's how bad things have gotten since the FA hung Suarez out to dry. It's not going to stop any time soon either, so the best thing we can do is win games as nothing will piss them off more. Next week is the ideal place to stick it up everyone.

MANCHESTER CITY 0 LIVERPOOL 1

Competition - Carling Cup
Date - Wed 11 Jan 2012
Venue - Etihad Stadium
Scorer(s) – Steven Gerrard (pen)
Half Time - 0-1
Star Man – Daniel Agger

Team: Reina; Kelly, Skrtel, Agger, Johnson; Downing (Enrique), Gerrard, Spearing (Adam), Henderson, Bellamy (Carragher); Carroll:

So far so good, but as Lenny Kravitz famously sang, *"baby it ain't over til it's over"*. Securing a win in the 1st leg has put us in a tremendous position to reach our first domestic cup final in six years, but there's still plenty of work to be done as City will surely be better in the 2nd leg? They offered very little in this game as we completely stifled them and had answers for everything they tried to do. It was a defensive masterclass, a European away performance if you like.

The first half was brilliant, the second was resilient. The only moment of real danger in the entire game was caused by our own mistake (Kelly's shocking back pass) and aside from that City looked completely lacking in ideas and invention. City never lose at home so this was a fantastic result, especially without Suarez. In summary, I'm delighted at the win, I was very impressed by the first half and I was somewhat baffled by the second half. I'm not complaining about it as we got the win and I doubt if there is a Liverpool fan anywhere that wouldn't have been delighted with a 1-0 win beforehand. I was surprised by how we approached it though. The last time I remember us playing like this was in Turin against Juve in 2005, and even then we did attempt to attack when we could (and Baros or Cisse would have given us far more than Carroll in this game). This was more like Barcelona in 2001. Had we been up against City's strongest side it would have been more understandable, but honestly, that side that City put out last night are not much better than us and personally I don't think we needed to go so defensive against them.

The injury to Spearing may have contributed to that as when he was on the field we were well on top and completely controlling the midfield. He'd been very impressive and the balance to our side looked good. From the opening seconds of the game we took control and City were on the back foot. The absence of their two best centre halves offered encouragement to Carroll and at the other end they looked very disjointed with Aguero leading the line and Balotelli looking disinterested. They were also badly missing midfield powerhouse Yaya Toure. We just looked much better than them all over the park. Carroll should have opened the scoring early on when he rolled the awful Savic and went clean through on goal. His low shot was saved by Joe Hart. It was eerily similar to what happened last week when Downing was in the same situation. Joe Hart is class and he's difficult to beat, but I'd like to think someone is telling our players that when they are faced with that situation, just dink the frigging ball over him as he goes low EVERY time. He spreads himself wide and gets his angles right, meaning it's very difficult to get the ball either side of him. You might get lucky and the ball might find it's way through him (this is known as the Djibril Cisse approach to finishing), but generally you are going to struggle to put the ball past him. It's easier said that done I know, but the way to beat him is to wait til he spreads himself out and then just chip it over him into the empty net. Andy Carroll is never going to do that though is he? Gerrard might, so let's hope the next one on one we have with Hart falls to the skipper.

Whereas Downing's miss last week proved costly, Carroll's didn't. This time we didn't concede straight afterwards, in fact we continued to create openings and Hart continued to thwart us. He saved well from Gerrard's curler, and then he made a stunning stop to deny Agger after the defender had touched on Downing's excellent volley. We were pounding City at this point but Hart was proving to be unbeatable. Fortunately for us, cancelling out the brilliance of Hart was the shiteness of Savic. What a train wreck of a player he is. He looked a bag of nerves and the foul on Agger for the penalty summed up his performance. Great credit to Agger though, how many players would have brought that ball down on their chest as opposed to just trying a speculative header? Not many. Classy play from the Dane. Blatant pen but with Lee Mason in charge you can never take anything for granted. Thankfully not even he could deny us this one, and the skipper buried it in the bottom corner. Tell you what though, look at how close Hart was to saving what was basically an unsaveable pen. Hart is the biggest obstacle in our path to Wembley as the chances are we will need to score at least once more to go through and beating him has proved damn near impossible in the previous three games.

We'd had a dream start and City looked a bit shellshocked. Both full backs were charging forward, Henderson was making runs into the box and Gerrard and Speo were dominating the middle of the park. I don't even remember seeing Aguero in the opening half an hour and the only time Balotelli was involved was when he was making a spectacle of himself. Adam Johnson wasn't getting a sniff either as Glen Johnson was doing a good job on him. Was that why he got the nod over Enrique maybe? The City winger cuts inside onto his left foot all the time, was Enrique left out because Kenny wanted a right footed player marking Johnson? We've seen it before when Arbeloa did such a wonderful job on Messi. I thought it was strange that Enrique didn't start, but Glen was excellent and Adam Johnson did nothing.

It was all going great until Spearing felt a tweak in his hammy. He walked off the field so it doesn't look like it was a serious problem, let's hope not anyway as he's got a very important part to play as in the absence of Lucas we have no-one else to fill that role. Jay has been playing really well and he's vital to the balance of that three man midfield. I like Adam, but he's a different player to Speo and it definitely impacted how we played. Hopefully he'll be back for the 2nd leg as we clearly missed him when he went off. Having said that, the second half approach can't possibly be just down to not having Spearing. City bringing on Nasri for the hopeless Balotelli also played a part as they went from playing with ten men to having a full compliment again. It also gave them an extra body in midfield which helped them keep the ball much, much better.

The key change for me was simply that we set out to keep what we had and we just stopped attacking. Maybe Kenny felt we'd be too wide open without Spearing sitting in there so he decided to shut up shop, but my guess is we'd have taken that approach with or without Jay. Carroll became increasingly isolated and offered nothing at all. Not his fault, he's not got the pace to offer an option in behind the defence and we didn't get anybody close enough to him for him to be able to hold it up effectively. He was poor in the first half and for that I blame him (he had one decent header that went just wide but aside from that his play was often sloppy), but the second half was simply impossible for him. I keep saying that there's things he can do and things he can't do. In the second half we were asking him to do the things he can't do. He never stood a chance. If you sit as deep as we did when you have a lone striker like Carroll, you don't pose any kind of threat whatsoever. There's no out ball as he won't get anything hit over the top and when it was played up to him City just waited for him to bring it down and then took it off him.

Bellamy and Downing were so deep they didn't get close enough to Carroll to play off him and both were eventually brought off as they were really not needed to play the kind of game we were playing. The substitutions showed exactly what our mindset was. Enrique for Downing, Carragher for Bellamy. For a while it looked like Johnson had no idea where he was supposed to be playing. He didn't seem to know if he was playing a holding midfield role or if he was a third centre back. Eventually he moved to right wing back and Kelly went central, which is what I thought would have happened as soon as Enrique came on. It wasn't pretty during that period of uncertainty. We ended the game with six defenders, three central midfielders and Carroll. I didn't like it as I don't think the players City had on the field were worthy of that kind of approach, but it was effective as City didn't score and we came away with a fantastic result.

Maybe if we'd continued to play how we'd started the game we'd have this tie won already, or maybe City would have come back to equalise or win. There's no way of knowing but it's irrelevant as we won the game. I highly doubt we'll play the same way at home, even if we are protecting a lead. Kenny was part of a team that had plenty of these kind of performances when they were winning European Cups. It wasn't pretty to watch at times but it got the job done on many occasions. You have to be delighted at going to City and beating them 1-0. How we achieved it isn't important and if we go on to lift the trophy then the end more than justifies the means. If we'd conceded I'd have been seriously pissed off, but we didn't and a 1-0 win is a great result. City just looked really disheartened by the end. They couldn't find a way through and the only hope they had was nicking something from a set-piece. Richards had their best effort when he beat Agger to a corner but his header was stopped superbly by Reina at close range. That could so easily have gone in though and that's the concern I have about the 2nd leg. We're in a great position but still have a lot of work to do as the lead we have can be wiped out by one set-piece or defensive lapse like the one that saw Kelly pass the ball straight to Aguero. Pepe did a good job of holding him up and forcing him into a difficult shot, but it shows how precarious a one goal lead is. We need to score again, possibly even more than once depending on how that 2nd leg goes.

I'd much rather be in our position than City's though. We're at home, we have a 1-0 lead, they will still be missing key players and you can be sure the atmosphere at Anfield will be nothing like that at the Etihad. Seriously, what's the deal there? This was a semi-final and not only could they not sell all their tickets, but there was barely a peep out of the ones who bothered to show up. I know City have bigger fish to fry than the league cup, but still, you're Manchester City!! When did you become so successful that you are blazé about a league cup semi final against a North West rival? One FA Cup win and they think they're Real fucking Madrid. Anfield will be absolutely bouncing for that second leg and I can't wait. Star man is Agger, who was excellent at the back alongside the equally impressive Skrtel, but who also won the penalty that settled the game. Honourable mention to Glen Johnson who was also very good aside from one late lapse that could easily have led to him being sent off. Given what happened to Kompany last Sunday and how everyone has been talking about this week, is he fucking mad putting in a challenge like that??? Lee Mason usually doesn't need any encouragement to send our players off, and had he produced a red card for that there'd have been no complaints from me. Personally I wouldn't have sent him off and I wouldn't have sent Kompany off either (both won the ball with little actual risk to the opponent), but that is the kind of tackle that referees have been told should result in a red card as FIFA want to eradicate that kind of tackle. We got away with one there, no question about it.

The funny thing was that you could tell the City fans had been waiting for something like that all game. They'd got a little excited a couple of times previously when it looked like a player may have been about to go in with two feet, and they went nuts at Johnson's challenge. Mancini had a moan about it afterwards too. He had a point, but given his imaginary card waiving at Skrtel last week in a game they had comfortably won, he can fuck right off. A point that Gerrard made to him in no uncertain terms after the game as the Italian was conducting a radio interview.

LIVERPOOL 0 STOKE CITY 0

Competition - Premier League
Date - Sat 14 Jan 2012
Venue - Anfield
Scorer(s) –
Half Time - 0-0
Star Man – Glen Johnson

Team: Reina; Skrtel, Carragher, Coates; Johnson, Gerrard, Adam, Enrique; Downing (Carroll), Henderson (Bellamy); Kuyt:

Shite team selection, shite tactics, shite opposition, shite performance. Just shite. Three centre backs against a team who left the immobile Crouch completely isolated and showed no attacking intent? Really? Kuyt as a lone frontman supported by goal machines Downing and Henderson? Seriously? That front three between them have the same amount of league goals as Tim Howard. TIM HOWARD!!!!

Andy Carroll was Stoke's best defender when he finally got on and Howard Webb is a vile cheating scumbag who should never be allowed anywhere near Liverpool games due to his obvious bias. He should be locked up for his performance today, but he's not the only one.

Think that just about covers it. Apologies for being so brief, but having had to sit through this turgid crap for ninety minutes I'm not going to spend another couple of hours writing about it and I daresay you probably don't fancy reading about it much either. Abysmal, dire, cowardly, toothless, inept, whatever negative adjective you can think of probably applies to this. The only positive is that we didn't lose, but for that to have happened Stoke would have needed to come out of their own half, and that was never going to happen was it. Still, I'm not going to criticise them for doing precisely what we did to Manchester City in the second half the other night.

Star man was Glen Johnson as he was just about the only player who looked like he might be able to do something to break them down. When you're most dangerous attacker is your right back, you know you got problems.

Premier League Round Up (14-16 January 2012)

Tottenham could have gone joint top on Saturday. They've been on a bit of a tear since losing their opening two games and found themselves right on the coat tails of both manc teams. They beat the blueshite in midweek and it was at that point I finally resigned myself to finishing beneath them. They're just better than us, I don't want to accept it but unfortunately it's the truth. They score goals, we don't. They win games, we draw them. Until that changes they'll be better than us.

The real question is are they better than United and City though? A home game against Wolves was the perfect opportunity for them to prove that they are genuine contenders and they couldn't have picked a worse time to suddenly remember that they are Tottenham fucking Hotspur. Spurs are who we thought they were. I really hope I'm wrong as they're unquestionably the lesser of three evils and it would certainly be good for football if they somehow managed to win the title. I just think it's inevitable that old 'Spurs DNA' will kick in and stop them.

This was a such a great chance for them to make a real statement, and the statement they made was *"Hey everyone, don't let the league table fool you, we're still Spurs!!"* Wolves took the lead through Fletcher, his 9th goal of the season means by my calculations he has the same as Kuyt, Carroll, Maxi, Downing, Bellamy and Henderson combined. Think about that for a second. Not more than a second, as it'll ruin your day.

Adebayor had a goal ruled out for offside. It was the wrong decision and Bale's shot was going in anyway before he tried to steal it so it was botch job all round. I'm not gonna condemn Adebayor for that, as being a ruthless, single minded, 'goals pay the rent' kind of striker myself I actually admire it. Goalpoachers union and all that. In my eyes Craig Johnston scored twice in the 1986 FA Cup Final, as he got Rushy's shot before it had crossed the line. No-one acknowledges it, but that was Skippy's goal all day that, and in his shoes I'd have done exactly the same. Besides, no-one wants to see any more of Gareth Bale's shitty goal celebrations so Adabayor should probably be commended for what he tried to do. It should be a wake up call for Bale though, as is there anything that says *'you're a massive twat'* more than people preferring to see an Adebayor celebration than yours? Modric equalised and Spurs piled on the pressure but couldn't score again. Frustrating, as even though some of their players get right on my tits I'd much rather see Redknapp's side crowned champions than either of the two alternatives. So with that in mind, this was a shitty result. Spurs will be Spurs I suppose.

Given that the Mancs were at home to Bolton those two points were always going to prove costly for 'Arry's boys. The Mancs had lost their two previous league games but the hapless Trotters were never going to make be able to make it three, especially as they were in the process of selling pretty much the only good player they had to Chelsea. United could even afford the luxury of missing a pen. Bogdan made a brilliant stop from Shrek's spot kick that had been awarded after Knight had clumsily brought down Wellbeck. The words 'clumsy' and 'Zat Knight' go together like fish and chips, salt and pepper and Howard Webb and manc. How was that not a red card though? Wellbeck was about eight yards out with just the keeper to beat. Peter Walton is a terrible referee. I know I say it all the time, I'm even boring myself now but these refs have to be the worst group I've ever seen, there actually isn't a good one amongst them, only varying degrees of shit. Phil Dowd might actually be the least shit, THAT'S how bad they are. Scholes marked his Old Trafford comeback by grabbing the opening goal, meaning he already has more goals than Downing and Kuyt even though he was retired up until a week ago. Embarrassing that. They could probably wheel Remi Moses out and he'd outscore our lot within a few weeks as well. The Gog had a chance to equalise but his shot was so high it collided with Jaap Stam's Euro 2000 penalty that is still orbiting the earth. Ah, good old Jaap Stam. I hated him, but not as much as my mum did. Every time he appeared on the telly she'd scowl and remark that he looked like a Nazi SS Officer. She really, really hated him, it was something to behold actually. Remember the chant we had for him? *"We hate Jaap Stam he's an ugly man, can't pull a bird even in the Grafton. He's got no hair he's a baldy twat. Fuck off, Jaap Stam"* Boss that, we need more of those kind of chants. Not enough originality these days. Anyway, where was I? Oh yeah, Ngog. He's just awful, truly awful. Still has more goals than Kuyt and Downing and the same as Carroll though. That should shame Kuyt and Downing even more than being outscored by Tim Howard. Wellbeck made it 2-0 before a typical Carrick pea roller wrapped things up. No way will Bolton stay up, they stink.

Blackburn might though. They were involved in the best game of the day as they dug deep with ten men to beat Fulham at a half empty Ewood Park. A ref I've never seen before produced a red card for Yakubu early on. I wasn't happy about this for a couple of reasons. Firstly, I'm back on the Steve Kean bandwagon as you know, so I don't want to see his top goalscorer being sent off. Secondly, it gave my arl fella the chance to say *"I told you so"*. I'll explain; this was a virtually identical challenge to the one by Savic on Agger that led to our penalty last week which my dad is adamant should have been a red card. I said it was more of a yellow but he was having none of it, insisting it would have been a red had it happened anywhere else on the pitch. As much as it sticks in the throat to admit it, he's got a point hasn't he? To get a red card for an offence in the box is nigh on impossible unless it involves handball on the goal-line. I reckon you could take a baseball bat to someone's knees and the ref would just point to the spot and produce a yellow card. Unless the baseball bat was being wielded by Robert Huth or Ryan Shawcross, the knee belonged to Andy Carroll and the ref was Howard fucking Webb. In which case it would obviously be play on or a free-kick to Stoke and a big 'fuck you' grin at the Kop.

Still, I didn't think the foul on Agger was a red card no matter where on the field it took place, so I'm sat watching MOTD when the Yak is sent packing and I'm thinking *"ah for fucks sake I hope he isn't watching this as I'll never hear the end of it."* The lack of any *"See, I told you didn't I?"* so far tells me he hasn't seen it yet, thankfully. Anyway, it didn't look good for Rovers who have already been struggling at home. Could it be that going down to ten men allowed them to play more like the away side with a little less pressure perhaps? Kean said afterwards the crowd were brilliant, but that's the measure of the man isn't it? They hurl abuse at him, he throws platitudes at them. There's being the bigger man, and then there's being Steve Kean. He's a fucking giant, that's what he is. He's like Gulliver and Ewood

Park is his Lilliput. Pedersen put them in front just before half time with a nice free-kick and David Dunn doubled their lead just after the break. Duff pulled one back against his former team but a smooth finish by Formica (I know I know) made it safe for the home side. Pleased for my guy Keano, especially as his captain cried off 'sick' before handing in a transfer request two days later. If Samba leaves then whoever buys him will be getting a good player, but as captain you'd hope he had a damn good reason for missing this game. Otherwise he's a bit of a twat.

Speaking of twats, Chelsea just about overcame Sunderland at Stamford Bridge. Lampard got the game's only goal when the ball bounced back off the bar, hit him in the gut and went in, the spawny get. The funny thing about it was that it was almost a goal of the season from Torres as it was his scissor kick that hit the bar before finding it's way in via the ample sized frame of Lampard. Torres didn't even celebrate, he looked gutted, the selfish bastard. I must admit he looked sharp though, sadly. After one nice turn and shot that went just wide the commentator pointed out *"Lampard standing in front of him might have impeded his view of the goal"* His view of the goal?? Impeded his view of the sun more like, the fat fuck. Torres also had two good penalty shouts turned down and to make things even worse for him he was wrongly booked for diving. Hahaha. Here's a curious stat, he's actually scored the same amount of league goals this season (two) as his former understudy (Ngog) and also his replacement at Anfield (Carroll). Between the three of them they've still scored less than Grant Holt, Danny Graham, Ivan Klasnic and Heidur Helguson.

Sunderland should have had a pen when Bendtner was flattened by Cole, McLean missed an open goal after good work by Larsson, Gardner missed a great chance in the last minute and Bendtner then squandered a one on one in stoppage time as Chelsea just about held out. That Chelsea defence is horrific though. Gary Cahill may have thought he had it bad at Bolton, but wait til he has to play alongside the likes of Sideshow Bob, Mongo and Unibrow Bosingwa. He'll be earning every penny of that reported 100k a week he's getting. For Sunderland, Sessegnon was very good once again. I do enjoy watching him.

Moving on, and Norwich went to the Hawthorns and stunned the Baggies by hitting a late winner in a 2-1 success. Surman put them in front against the run of play when he volleyed in a right wing cross. Most of their goals come from headers, but virtually all of them come from crosses. Given the fantastic service from the flanks he'd be getting, Andy Carroll would probably score, oh I don't know, maybe five goals a season if he went there. Long equalised from the spot after a horrific lunge by former red Danny Ayala. As clear a red card as you'll see, it was a horrible, dangerous challenge that would have been a sending off anywhere else on the field but as my arl fella says you get away with virtually anything if it's in the penalty area. Don't tell him I said that though. I know he won't be reading this as he knows as much about the internet as John Terry knows about fidelity. By that

I mean he's heard of it, he knows it's something that is a big part of other people's daily lives but it's a completely alien concept to him. Norwich grabbed a late winner when Holt broke down the left and crossed for Morrison to head home. Typical Norwich goal. Morrison has eight goals now, whilst Holt has seven. That's just nine less than our whole team has managed all season. Makes you sick doesn't it? I know, I know, I'm boring myself again now with this crap but that Stoke game hit me hard. Real hard.

Everton gave Darron Gibson a debut in a 1-1 draw at Villa Park. He might just be the most anonymous Manchester United player of all time. Put your hand up if you think you would recognise him if he walked past you on the street. If you've got your hand up, you either watch far too much football or you're Irish. Or maybe both. If you're not Irish and you have your hand up, you're a liar, and as an aside you should probably put your hand down as chances are you look like a tit, especially if you're reading this in work or on a bus. Gibson is a complete nomark, so much so that a lot of United fans wouldn't even recognise him. Those that would probably had his face on their dartboard or had a Gibson doll they stuck pins in or something. This is the player who was driven off twitter by Mancs within a couple of hours as he was getting blitzed with messages telling him how shit he is and how he should fuck off. His departure to Everton was announced on United's face-book page and received 6,000 likes in about ten minutes. He's about as pop-ular with mancunians as soap and contraception. The only reason he ended up at Everton is because Martin O'Neill shut down the North East retirement home where washed up Mancs had been going to wind down what's left of their careers. Luckily for Gibson, the Merseyside branch of it has re-opened. Goodison used to be the number one destination for United rejects, it's just that recently they've been completely skint and couldn't accept any new res-idents. Gibson follows in the footsteps of the likes of Norman Whiteside, Mark Hughes, Tim Howard, Andrei Kanchelskis, John O'Kane, Phil Neville, Jesper Blomqvist and Louis Saha.

Darren Bent gave Villa the lead with a scuffed finish, he kicked it into the ground but it bounced up and into the roof of the net. It really is astonishing how many of his goals look shit/lucky. I've done some extensive research on this; He's scored 145 career goals to date. Of those, 45 have been penalties, 97 have been scuffed/shinned/bobbled/deflected and one went in off a beach ball. The other two were cracking finishes though to be fair to him. Anichebe levelled for the blues who had earlier been unlucky not to get a penalty when Saha was mugged by the useless Hutton. Cahill drew a blank again, so at least that's one player not outscoring Kuyt and Downing. Not yet anyway. By the way, what's going on with Ste Warnock lately? He's been having an absolutely torrid time of it. Every week he's getting ruined on MOTD by some crap winger. He almost scored a ridiculous own goal and needed a great save from Given to spare his blushes. Must be the Villa effect, it gradually wears you down if you don't get out.

Onto Sunday, and another brilliant day for Swansea who toppled Arsenal at the Liberty Stadium. They really are pretty good aren't they? The football they play is absolutely fantastic for a team of their resources and along with Norwich and maybe Newcastle (I feel dirty saying that) they might be the best coached team in the league. They're punching well above their weight and good luck to them. What made this even more impressive was the way they did it. They fell behind on four minutes to the latest stunning Van Persie goal. Another great finish from him and a nightmare start for the home side. They kept playing their football though and drew level when Dyer won a penalty after he was tripped in the box by Ramsay. Looked a bit of a harsh one to me, but Sinclair converted the kick, his fourth successful pen of the season. Dyer made it 2-1 when the impressive Joe Allen nipped in to set him up after catching Arsenal fannying about in midfield. The Swans were well on top and looking like they'd get a third but then they got caught cold when Walcott beat the offside trap and equalised. Arsenal will have expected to go on and win the game but they didn't get a chance to capitalise on it as Swansea hit back immediately with a terrific finish from Graham. They struggled to score goals early on in the season but they look like they've solved that now and Graham has done very well in recent weeks. We've been linked with a move for Sinclair this week. I'm not overly keen as I think we need to be aiming higher than that. Tell you what though, hypothetically if you could swap Kuyt, Downing, Carroll and Henderson for Dyer, Sinclair, Graham and Allen, would you do it? I can't say I would but I'd not find it THAT easy to turn down either. That's more due to the ineffectiveness of our four than the Swansea lads being anything special. Back in August I'd have laughed at the mere suggestion of it. It's not so funny now. As for Arsenal, they are basically the opposite of us. They can score but can't defend. We can defend but can't score. If you took the best qualities of both sides and combined them, you'd be looking at a championship winning team. As it is, you're looking at two also rans who are battling it out with another one, Chelsea, for fourth place.

Should Newcastle also be in that discussion? They beat QPR on Sunday and went above us in the table once again. Once we overtook them the other week I didn't see any way this would happen. It has though, and whatsmore they did it without Demba Ba who was at the African Nations and Cabaye who went off injured after a bad challenge by Derry. Leon Best's well taken goal proved to be the difference between the two sides, it was his 4th of the season. That's more than... ok ok I'll stop now. I'm sure you get the picture. Pardew said of the tackle on Cabaye; *"Yohan was really upset with it"*. Oh was he now? Well fuck him, his lunge at Speo was far worse than that. You live by the sword, you die by the sword, and you don't fucking cry about it afterwards.

This is the first round up I've written since QPR sacked Neil Warnock. I'm still not over that, Warnock's post match interviews have been a highlight of the season for me and I can't believe they binned him off. And for Mark Hughes?!?!? Hope they go down now the fucking killjoys. Hughes might have a better managerial CV (I say might as I'm not sure he has you know) but his after match interviews pale into comparison I'm afraid, he's a right boring bastard. I just don't care about anything he has to say, and I miss Neil Warnock already. If Wolves ever sack Mick McCarthy I might just stop watching MOTD completely, especially if they keep giving airtime to that slapdick Jason Roberts.

Onto Monday night's game and City just about edged out Wigan thanks to Dzeko's header. Wigan had chances through James McArthur and James McCarthy. Does anyone else reckon they signed James McArthur because he sounds like James McCarthy and because McCarthy is ace they thought 'what the hell, it's worth a shot'? No? Just me then. What an absolute bell-whiff that Mancini is turning out to be. Last week he was slagging Rooney off for trying to get Kompany sent off even though a week before he'd been giving it the imaginary card routine after Skrtel conceded a dubious pen. They were about to go 3-0 up, and he's doing that?? Gerrard tore a strip off him but the lesson wasn't learned as here he was again with his card waving on the touchline after Figueroa had handled on halfway. Rooney was all over it on his twitter, *"Was Manchini asking for red card???"* Much as I feel queasy about it, I'm siding with Rooney on this. 'Manchini' is indeed a cheeky bastard who needs to shut his mouth. He even said Suárez should apologise to Evra. Read the report have you Roberto? No, I didn't think so. Tit. Keep your nose out of our business, or Luis might just bite it off. I'm really getting sick of all these Mancs now. I can't stand the idea of either of them winning the title to be honest. If only we weren't so impotent in front of goal. And if only Spurs weren't Spurs.

BOLTON WANDERERS 3 LIVERPOOL 1

Competition - Premier League
Date - Sat 21 Jan 2012
Venue - The Reebok Stadium
Scorer(s) – Craig Bellamy
Half Time - 2-1
Star Man – Craig Bellamy

Team: Reina; Johnson, Skrtel, Agger, Enrique; Henderson, Gerrard, Adam (Kuyt), Maxi (Downing); Bellamy, Carroll:

And I thought last week was bad. This went way beyond the disappointment of the Stoke game, it was completely inexcusable. Unlike last week, this couldn't be explained away by a bizarre team selection and questionable tactics, or opponents who were quite content to park the bus. No, this is completely down to players who failed to perform and who were both outfought and outplayed by the worst team in the Premier League.

Look at Bolton's home record prior to this, the worst in all four divisions.

They're absolutely shite, but we made them look good and they deservedly beat us. No wonder Dalglish threw his players under the bus afterwards. He never does that, he always defends them as long as they've tried their best and for him to react like that should give that dressing room an almighty wake up call. He had every right to be pissed off. The problem is that when he says some of them won't play for the club again if they repeat that performance, presumably he's including some players he bought himself and paid a lot of money for. That wouldn't sit well with the owners and I imagine the players know that. It's an idle threat and isn't fooling anyone. I doubt if some of them are worried about being shipped out anyway, they get paid no matter what. In Andy Carroll's case he'd probably be relieved if we fucked him off as he doesn't appear to have any stomach for the fight he's in to prove himself.

Kenny is far from blameless for some of the failings we've shown this season (for example last week was more on him than the players) but for me this one sits squarely on the shoulders of a team who seemed to think all they had to do to win this game was show up. The complacency and casual approach was apparent right from the opening seconds of the game, we were just incredibly lax and sloppy in everything we did. It was like watching a preseason friendly. The full backs typified it. Glen Johnson's first involvement was to attempt a ten yard pass to Henderson that missed by miles and went straight out of play for a throw in. That set the tone and he didn't get any better after that, he was absolutely shocking. This was the old Glen Johnson, the one that looked like he needed a rocket up his arse as he was so laid back. In the 2nd half he got megged by Petrov and couldn't even be arsed sprinting back, he was running at three quarter speed. I'd have subbed him on the spot for that.

On the other flank, Enrique looked half asleep early on and made one really shocking error that he was lucky to get away with. All afternoon Chris Eagles gave him a chasing. That's Chris Eagles, not Cristiano Ronaldo. Chris Eagles, the 'David Beckham of the Championship' who has always looked like the Premier League was too big a step up for him. Enrique should be fucking ashamed of this performance, as should almost all of his team-mates. There was one notable exception. Craig Bellamy stood head and shoulders above everyone else in red, which is kind of fitting given that he actually is a head on shoulders. The no-necked Welshman is the only one who needn't feel embarrassed by his showing. He was lively, he was fiery and he can look in the mirror and know that he did everything he could. Nobody else can say that. I guess you can MAYBE add Agger to that too as he wasn't terrible and at least looked like he was trying. The rest should be sending back their weekly pay as they've stolen a wage this week. And the club should be using it to refund the expenses of the 5,000 reds who witnessed this embarrassment. There's getting beat, and there's getting beat like this.

For the most part this season I've been pleased with how we've played, if not always with the results. Bad finishing is the main reason we aren't closer to the top sides and generally I'd say we're moving in the right direction despite the huge question marks over some of the spending. This was one almighty big bump in the road though. The jury is out on whether some of these players are good enough, but even taking that into account there was still no excuse for this. That team is more than good enough to beat Bolton. The reason they didn't is that Bolton wanted it more than they did. You can point to the midfield being unbalanced with no natural holding player, but does that really excuse those who were in there from not tracking runners? Maybe Kenny could have moved Bellamy wide and Henderson inside to counter their extra man, but chances are that would have just given us three players ball watching instead of two and we'd have had nothing up front. Neither Adam nor Gerrard wanted to do any of the dirty work, they just wanted to get on the ball and go forward. Mind you, whenever Adam tried to help out he'd usually give away a free-kick. It almost goes without saying we are badly missing Lucas and Spearing, but we should still be able to beat Bolton without them. It's no excuse. Gerrard is capable of playing a holding role and has enough experience to be able to take command of that situation. I expect much more from him than this. As for Adam, he's been shite for a few weeks now after having a really good spell prior to that. His dip in form co-incided with Lucas' absence. There's a fair chance the two things are linked.

We fell behind on four minutes via a terrible goal from our point of view. Mark Davies was allowed to run right through the middle unchallenged and poked the ball into the bottom corner. Skrtel was mostly to blame, but others could have done better too. They made it 2-0 with an equally bad goal. Maxi let Reo-Coker run off him and Eagles was allowed to dribble into the penalty area before finding Reo-Coker who just about put it past Reina.

We were just shite all over the park. Bellamy was the only thing we had going for us, he was a big threat but he couldn't do it all on his own. He gave us some brief hope when he latched onto a Carroll flick and burst past the ponderous Zat Knight to finish smartly. That should have set us up for a second half onslaught but we gave away another bad goal just after the break and we were never coming back from that. We struggle to score goals and now we needed to find the net twice more just to salvage a point. Never gonna happen was it?

We had plenty of the ball but Bolton looked just as likely to increase their lead as we did to reduce it. Kenny sent on Kuyt and Downing to try and rescue something but the game had gone at that stage. They haven't managed a league goal between them all season so it was hardly a surprise that they made fuck all difference. Agger hit the bar with a good long range effort and we wasted several promising situations, either with a bad final ball or a poor shot.

Andy Carroll at times resembled a fan who had won a competition to play with his heroes. Or like when some actor/singer/celebrity gets to play with the pro's in someone's testimonial. Sometimes he doesn't even look a footballer at all. By sometimes, I mean pretty much any time he has the ball at his feet. How can a professional footballer who trains every day and has done since he was a little kid let the ball hit him on the shin and bounce ten yards off him or just fall over the ball as often as Carroll does???? I've cut him more slack than most because I was always hugely impressed with him at Newcastle, but he really needs to start showing something soon as it's reached the point where there can be no defence of him at all anymore. He's as weak as a fucking kitten these days too, he regularly gets outmuscled and spends so much time on his arse he's bringing back memories of Heskey on his bad days (at least Heskey had some good days). Carroll was a monster at Newcastle, a physically imposing, dominant number nine. He comes here and the sports science people are sneering about how they can't believe Newcastle never had him lifting any weights and "just you wait until you see how strong he'll be after we get him on a programme to boost his upper body strength". Worked a treat that hasn't it? He's somehow lost strength and now he can't run either. Good job team, well done.

I probably shouldn't single him out as he wasn't even our worst player. Not even close. At least with the others it can be put down to complacency or just not being at the races. This was standard fare from Carroll, it's what we've come to expect. In fact, you could even say this was one of his better recent performances as at least he managed to do a couple of decent things in amongst the shite. His latest fresh air shot from Downing's cross summed him up. You can almost read Downing's mind when it happens; *"Is it any wonder I can't get a fucking assist?"*

These players always talk about how they enjoy playing for Kenny and how much they respect him. Well they need to start fucking showing it again as this was a slap to his face. His signings aren't looking great (I realise that's being extremely kind), he's had a few questionable team selections and his league record since he got the manager's job on a permanent basis doesn't make for good reading. The knives are out for him already, twitter is an abomination after any bad LFC result and this is why initially I didn't want him to get the job - the fear of what would happen if it went wrong. Not much did go wrong initially, the back end of last season was great and everyone was buzzing. He brought the kids into the team, we began playing with a freedom and expression that had been missing in many a year, and everyone was smiling. The players were loving it, the fans were loving it, and so was Kenny, that big old grin was a feature of last season but it's been mostly absent in recent weeks. Maybe that was because there was no real pressure back then. League position wasn't important as the season had already been written off. It was easy to bring in Flanagan and Robinson and have Coady on the bench and Sterling in the squad because there was no real expectation.

This year it's different, there is an expectation to at least make a serious challenge for fourth and to hopefully win a cup. The kids are nowhere near the first team - Flanagan was overlooked in favour of forgotten man Fabio Aurelio for the Oldham game - and the players now seemed weighed down by the pressure to get results. Literally in the case of Kuyt, who looks like he's carrying a big old sack of spuds on his back now as he lumbers around. The goals flowed last season, they've dried up this year. However, it's still early days (the manager's first full season) and for the most part we are trying to play in the right way. We're in a bad spell right now and we're desperately missing Suarez, but it's far from a full blown crisis. Had the likes of Carroll, Kuyt and others converted even a fraction of the clear chances we've created this season then this result wouldn't have been such a big deal. It would have been seen as a bad day at the office, just one of those days. All teams have them, even our great sides of the past could throw in the odd stinker that took everyone by surprise (I remember Coventry putting five past us in the 80's, I think Terry Gibson may have even scored four of them). The reason this is so unacceptable is because we've drawn seven out of ten home games and therefore can't afford to take a day off like this one.

A top four finish is up in the air despite the major flaws of our rivals for fourth spot. As bad as this result was, we didn't lose any ground on Arsenal and only lost one point to Chelsea. Those two are arguably as flawed as we are, albeit in different ways. Whoever gets fourth will be the side who puts together a run to end the season. Losing Suarez has hurt us badly and it was compounded by also losing Lucas and Spearing too (the red card and then the injury have meant he's hardly been available since Lucas went down). Had the likes of Carroll, Downing, Adam and Kuyt performed to the level expected we'd have been able to cope but they haven't. There's still plenty of football left to play though.

Suarez can't return quickly enough, but we've got two huge games coming now without him. A lot of those who lined up at the Reebok don't deserve to keep their place for the semi final against City, but unfortunately we don't have too many alternatives. I'd like to see Shelvey brought into the side instead of either Henderson or Adam as at least he offers a goal threat and some creativity. Henderson runs around a lot and he's got a decent touch, but I have to say had Shelvey been given the same playing time Henderson has had I'm pretty sure he'd have contributed a whole lot more, in an attacking sense at least. I'm by no means sold on Shelvey but he's not afraid to try things and seems to have a confidence in himself that others would really benefit from. For me he needs to be on the pitch now as he offers something different. Aside from him, the only other options available seem to be in defensive areas unfortunately.

Even the kids aren't pushing for places this year. Coady, Wisdom, Morgan, Sterling, Suso, Silva.... all the lads who looked so promising last season for the u18s seem to have taken a step backwards this year. The reserve league is crap but they should be performing better than they have. None of them are knocking on the door right now. That means Kenny has persisted with the misfiring and out of form attacking players who've been letting us down so badly for weeks. Kuyt, Downing, Carroll.... it's time they did something to justify the massive salaries they're collecting, as this season they've mostly been stealing a wage up to now.

Of course, Kenny is responsible for buying two of them so isn't immune from blame either, but I'd suggest that even those who didn't want us to sign Carroll or Downing expected them to play better than they have. They may not be good enough, but they're a damn sight better than they have shown so far and it's time they delivered. We've got two massive games coming up now and hopefully that will bring out the best in the team. It usually does, as over the years we seem to have morphed into a side that will beat the top teams and lose to the shite ones. Having dropped points to the likes of Wigan, Blackburn, Stoke and Bolton in recent weeks, we really need performances against both manc teams this week as our entire season is on the line now. Fail to win either of these games, and there's very little left to play for. Failure against Man City this week simply isn't an option. The crowd will be up for it, the players better had be too. They aren't as bad as the last two performances suggest, but they need to go out and prove it.

Premier League Round Up (21-22 January 2012)

Another weekend of terrific Premier League footy completely ruined for me again by Liverpool. I'd been looking forward to Sunday's games but after the loss at the Reebok that was me done for the weekend. When we win I can't wait to watch MOTD and 'Super Sunday'. We lose and I'm like 'ah just fuck off football'. So you've got Sky+ to thank for this round up as after the Bolton debacle my house was a footy free zone for the rest of the weekend.

No surprise though that when I tuned into SkySports News on Monday morning everyone was talking about Mario Balotelli. He can say *'Why Always Me?'* as much as he likes, but there's a reason it's always him, its because he's an absolute fucking headcase. He's so easy to wind up it's comical and any team he comes up against should be in his ear trying to get him sent off as it's like shooting fish in a barrel.

This was apparently a great game (I've only seen brief highlights), the second half was pulsating stuff and yet all people are talking about is Mad Mario trying to stomp on Scott Parker's head. Of all the people he could have chosen to stamp on, Parker is probably the worst as he's the current media golden boy. Everyone down south seems to love him these days don't they? I think that's why I've recently re-discovered my old dislike of him. I used to think he was a twat back in the days when he wore girl's clips in his hair and then signed for Chelsea. After that he started to grow on me until every hack and pundit started worshipping at the altar of 'Saint Scotty' and now he does my fucking head in again, the 1940's looking div. That being said, stamping on his head is a tad extreme and I can't be condoning that shit at all. Balotelli will get banned for that and deservedly so. I can't actually believe the amount of people who've tried to say it was unintentional. Come on, it was as glaringly obvious as David

Platt's massive face. Lescott should have been sent off too after a snidey forearm smash on Kaboul. Being an England international he'll escape FA punishment but Balotelli doesn't have that luxury.

It was cruel on Spurs as Balotelli then went on to win and convert the stoppage time penalty that settled the game. Even more cruel given that Defoe had missed a glorious chance to win it seconds earlier after a lightning break by Bale. Spurs showed great character to come back from 2-0 down and were so close to winning the game that you can't help bit be impressed with what they did. And yet they lost, because they're Tottenham Hotspur, the pretty football playing, southern softies. Until they can prove otherwise, that's who they are I'm afraid. Still, at least they're now widely regarded as being better than Arsenal. For long suffering Spurs fans that's a bit of a big deal.

The Gunners are in decline and Spurs are on the up. You have to wonder what the future holds for Arsenal and for Wenger. Like Spurs, they also lost a close game to some manc bastards, but unlike Spurs they can't really take much encouragement from the game. The Arsenal of a few years ago would have ran rings round this United team, but the side they have now is probably worse than the one Wenger inherited. The reaction towards the manager when he brought off the impressive Oxlade-Chamberlain to send on the disinterested Arshavin suggests maybe Wenger's time there is drawing to a close. It's also significant seeing how friendly Ferguson is towards him these days. He's like that when he doesn't see you as a threat anymore, a few years ago he wouldn't have given Wenger the steam off his piss. Now he's all hugs and smiles. Says it all.

The crowd went mental when he brought the kid off but more worryingly for Arsenal was surely the reaction of Van Persie, who shouted *'Noooooo'* with a pained expression on his face when he saw the board with the numbers go up. Was he disappointed at who was going off, or who was coming on? Maybe both. Arshavin is a fucking joke these days. Hard to believe this is the same little fucking gnome who scored four at Anfield and 'shushed' us as we applauded him. The only people he needs to be shushing these days are the Arsenal fans calling him fit to burn and booing the shit out of his worthless short arse. If ever there was a player playing for a move it's him. Wouldn't surprise me if he was back in Russia before this transfer window closes, either with a move back to his former club or by Wenger sending him to the salt mines in Siberia. Is Siberia still classed as Russia? So difficult to keep track of these things since Rocky Balboa's *"If I can change, you can change, everybody can change"* speech ended the cold war and all those insignificant little countries got their independence.

Getting back on track, Van Persie had earlier missed a sitter but found the net after being set up by Oxlade-Chamberlain and he was clearly pissed off to see the youngster subbed almost immediately after. The last thing Arsenal need is RVP becoming unsettled as without him they've got nothing, nothing I tells ya! United won it late on when Valencia - who'd opened the scoring in the first half - got the better of the half arsed Arshavin and teed up Welbeck for an easy finish. A lot of unhappy campers at the Emirates at the moment, including the captain by the looks of this.

Onto Saturday's games now, and Robbie Keane scored twice for Villa as they won at Wolves. I'll get crucified for saying this but I'd have taken him on loan in a fucking heartbeat. I know he wasn't good when he was here last time, I know he's been worse since he left, but I also know that until Suarez comes back he'd be far more likely to get us a goal than Carroll and Kuyt. In one game he's got more than Kuyt and matched Carroll's league total of the last six months. IN ONE FRIGGING GAME!! Of course we should be aiming higher, and hopefully we have plans to get someone in. If that's the case then great. If we aren't getting anybody and plan on waiting until the summer before signing a striker then personally I'd rather have had Keane in the squad for a couple of months if the alternative is sticking with what we have. Maybe that's just me. Villa are already three points better off because they took him.

They went in front thanks to a penalty that Bent won and converted. Kightly equalised and Edwards then put Wolves in front. Keane scored a cracker to get Villa back on level terms and made a point of not celebrating against his former team. He's a class act like that. Unfortunately for him he's had so many clubs that he never gets to celebrate against anybody anymore. Karl Henry was sent off for a stupid kick out at Albrighton, who flopped around on the floor like a cod on the deck of a trawler. Embarrassing that from the kid, I hope he's ashamed of himself when he sees it. Henry is a clogger who deserves all he gets though. Keane won it with another fantastic strike but the result was a little harsh on Mick McCarthy's side who dropped into the bottom three.

There was an amazing game at Craven Cottage between Fulham and Newcastle. The Geordies led 1-0 at half time through Danny Guthrie's thunderous left footed shot. Always liked Guthrie when he was here, tidy little player and it's good seeing him doing well. Fantastic goal with his weaker foot too. Fulham were given a dubious pen early in the 2nd half which was converted by another former red, SuperDan. It was outside the box, but it's Lee Mason so anything can happen. That decision changed the entire game as Fulham pounded the Toon from that moment on. Dempsey bundled in the second and quickly added another as Newcaste's defence began to defend like you'd expect from a Newcastle defence. Another dubious pen presented Zamora with the chance to make it four goals in 16 minutes for the home side, which he did. Ben Arfa pulled one back with a nice individual effort before Dempsey wrapped up his hat-trick and sealed a 5-2 win for the Cottagers. Can't laugh at Newcastle too much though, they still sit above us in the table.

QPR moved out of the bottom three with a win over Wigan but they were made to work for it. Roberto Martinez's side had the better of the early exchanges and missed two great chances. James McCarthy's stupid handball in the box gave QPR a pen that was converted by Helguson and Buszaky's brilliant free-kick doubled their lead just before the break. QPR are another of those sides who wheel out players each week I've never seen before. Not as bad as Norwich, but then who is? And who is Buszaky?? Never heard of him, never seen him before, but he looked boss. He scored one great goal and almost had two more. Begs the question, why was Neil Warnock not picking him? Maybe BBC can ask him and show his response on next weeks MOTD instead of inflicting dullards like Hughes, Hodgson, Moyes and Villas Boas upon us.

Rodallega got Wigan back into it with a terrific free-kick and Al Habsy saved a pen from Helguson (justice there as it was a ridiculous decision). Tommy Smith's belter made the game safe for QPR and Wigan look doomed. Even when they play well they usually lose. Can't help but like how Martinez handles himself every week though. Classy guy, and probably the most positive outlook of any manager in the league. He never seems to get flustered no matter how bad the result has been or how dire the situation is.

West Brom travelled to Stoke for a game few expected them to get anything from. Stoke don't tend to lose at home much, especially not to struggling sides, and their record against West Brom is brilliant. Morrison gave the visitors the lead and could have had four or five as he peppered the goal with long range efforts. Stoke didn't do much at all, but they were awarded a dodgy pen for a questionable foul on that prick Walters. Most of his pens seem to be driven up the middle and Ben Foster must have been doing his homework as he was prepared for it and made the stop. Stoke had been second best throughout but got an undeserved equaliser five minutes from time when Jerome headed in Pennant's free-kick. It looked like they'd secured a point they didn't deserve but in stoppage time Walters conceded a free-kick and Dorrans somehow got it through a crowd of players to beat Sorensen. Hahaha fuck off Stoke.

Sunderland beat Swansea at the Stadium of Light. Sessegnon's briliant strike put the Mackems in front and Gardner scored a peach too. Loads of cracking goals on Saturday but Sessegnon's would probably get my vote as the pick of the bunch.

No goals at Carrow Road though, where Torres drew yet another blank and was subbed in favour of Lukaku. AVB has had his hair cut and looks even more like a young Roy Hodgson now. Norwich played well and deserved their point. As depressing a thought as it is, Grant Holt is actually better than Andy Carroll isn't he?

Finally, there was a ying and yang thang going on over at the Pit. A good willie scored for Rovers, a bad cunt scored for Everton. That was Tim Cahill's first goal in over 12 months but it shouldn't have stood as Fellaini had handled, the big cheating dope. Goodwillie *sniggers* levelled when he charged down Cahill's clearance after Howard had flapped at a high ball. Rovers' goal led a charmed life late on as Everton piled on the pressure. All Everton seemed to have were set pieces and crosses towards Fellaini. It wasn't pretty and it wasn't even particularly effective. Had that fucking traitor Chris Samba been playing I doubt Everton would have posed any threat at all. I was talking to an Evertonian mate on Saturday. He goes to most home games but had to work and couldn't make this one. He was made up he didn't have to go as he reckons it's like watching paint dry. Big problems at Goodison. Moyes has just sold that crap Russian winger for a big loss, and plans on using the £2.5m to buy a centre back..... and a striker. Fuck me, where's he shopping? Poundstretcher? Maybe United have got some more shite they'd like to get rid of? Still, at least he's trying to strengthen I suppose, which is more than we seem to be doing.

Steve Kean was chirpy afterwards, as he always is. Moyes was dour afterwards, as he always is. HD doesn't do Moyesy any favours though does it? He's got wrinkles on his wrinkes and he's so pale he looks like rigor mortis is setting in. Like a zombie that's spent too long in the bath.

LIVERPOOL 2 MANCHESTER CITY 2

Competition - Carling Cup
Date - Wed 25 Jan 2012
Venue - Anfield
Scorer(s) – Steven Gerrard (pen), Craig Bellamy
Half Time - 1-1
Star Man – Craig Bellamy

Team: Reina; Johnson, Skrtel, Agger, Enrique; Kuyt (Carroll), Gerrard, Adam, Downing; Henderson; Bellamy (Kelly):

We needed a reaction and we got one. This was everything the Bolton game wasn't. Everyone in red did themselves, the club and their manager proud with a display full of energy, desire and quality. Craig Bellamy maintained the high level of performance he'd displayed at the Reebok Stadium, but this time he wasn't alone and he had every one of his team-mates matching his commitment.

Once again City had Joe Hart to thank for keeping the game close but not even he could stem the red tide on an electric night at Anfield. It's been too long since we were at Wembley and it's fitting that Kenny has got us back there. It was moving seeing how emotional he was afterwards, I'm more pleased for him than anyone else. We have to go on and finish the job now though and Cardiff will be a tough game as the smaller sides never get turned over in finals, they always give a good account of themselves and make it difficult. We've got experience of that having needed penalties to beat Birmingham in 2001. We'll cross that bridge when we come to it though, for now I'm just going to enjoy the moment.

There were two key tactical decisions that gave us the edge in this game I felt. Looking at the team beforehand, I imagine a lot of people thought it would be Dirk through the middle with Downing and Bellamy wide. Or maybe it would be Dirk and Bellamy up top with Henderson on the right. I don't think many expected to see Bellamy as the lone frontman but it couldn't have worked any better as it's a long time since we had that kind of movement, work rate, tenacity, intelligence and searing pace in the centre forward position. He was fucking brilliant.

The other move Kenny made that really paid off was having Gerrard sacrifice his normal attacking game to sit deeper and protect the defence. That was the biggest worry I had about this game, our midfield were exposed badly against Bolton because we were too open and didn't have anyone doing the dirty work, the kind of stuff Lucas had been doing so well. If Eagles, Reo-Coker and Mark Davies could have that much joy, what would the likes of Silva and Nasri do to us? The answer was very little. Gerrard was terrific in an unspectacular but vital role. Kenny definitely won the tactical battle with Mancini this time. The Italian went in with three centre halves against one forward only for that one forward to run all three of them ragged. Micah Richards is an absolute fucking beast, but as good a centre half as he is I'm sure the likes of Enrique and Downing were much happier seeing him back there than marauding forward from right back. Downing clearly fancied it against Zaballetta and he had a very good game. Mancini had to scrap that formation at half time, but even after sending on Aguero for Savic they weren't particularly threatening despite having lots of the ball. They were fortunate to go into the break at 1-1 as they only had one shot in the entire half, a 25 yard screamer from De Jong that found the top corner. At the other end we'd have several good openings and had clearly been the better side.

We started brightly and should have taken the lead when a bad clearance from Kolorov landed perfectly for Enrique. He controlled and then prodded a low shot towards the corner but Hart stuck out a leg and blocked it. Downing then sliced the rebound horribly wide. Hart makes so many saves with his feet, and we've found him to be an almost impenetrable barrier this season. A deflected Charlie Adam shot that went in off Lescott and a Steven Gerrard penalty was all we had to show for 180 minutes good work. I wrote after the first leg that Hart was still the biggest obstacle we had to overcome to reach Wembley and when he saved from Enrique I just thought 'here we go again'. He made another stop to deny Adam and then denied Bellamy after he'd skinned the hapless Savic. We also forced several corners and were clearly on top. Then, out of nothing, we were behind. The elusive Silva broke forward, cut inside and squared to De Jong who curled one in leaving Reina with no chance. Typical of our luck, De Jong scores about as often as Rob Jones. Hell of a strike but he couldn't do that again if he tried it a hundred more times.

It was important to get level before half time and thankfully we did. Once again, it needed a penalty to beat Joe Hart although Agger's initial shot may have done so had it not been blocked by the hand of Richards. City can complain all they like, but what is the referee supposed to do in that situation? He's stood a few yards away as a player flings himself in front of a shot with both his arms raised above his head and the ball hits him on the hand. How can he not give a penalty for that? He'd have been rightly slaughtered if he didn't give that. Richards argued that the ball had struck his knee and then bounced up onto his hand therefore it was unintentional. That doesn't wash, his spread himself as wide as he could, he looked like a goalkeeper the way he made himself as big as possible. He didn't try to block it with his knee, that was just where it hit him and was more luck than good judgement. It could just as easily have hit him straight on the hand. I can understand City's players feeling a little hard done by, but if that was at the other end they'd have gone fucking mad if they didn't get the pen. They think they should have had one earlier for a foul by Adam on Dzeko. At the time no-one appealed for it, and it was only when I got home and heard that Mancini had been crying about it that I realised there'd been anything contentious about it. If it had been given I'd have said it was extremely soft, but technically Dzeko did get the ball first and Adam kicked him a split second later. No-one appealed for it because it wasn't clear that Adam had caught him and because Dzeko wasn't going anywhere. It's only after you look at replays that there's even a case for it. Whereas the entire stadium saw Richards' handball.

Both decisions could have gone either way, but anyone who thinks City's penalty claim was more legitimate than the one we got is either mental, biased or Alan Smith or Roberto Mancini. The City manager is an absolute fucking tit isn't he? He could take a few lessons in class and humility from his goalkeeper. I really want to not like Joe Hart as I'm sick of him making save after save against us. But the lad always warmly applauds the Kop and he handled this defeat with a maturity and dignity that Mancini could only dream of. I'll be happy for Hart if he gets a title winners medal. His manager? Not so much.

But back to the game. I felt good at half time, I felt that we'd played very well and restricted City to one long range shot that unfortunately went in. Tactically we'd been spot on, and performance wise we were looking good too. Downing was having his best game for a while, Bellamy was terrific and Kuyt was busy. This is exactly the kind of game that usually brings out the best in Dirk and this was his best game of the season by a mile. The 2nd half in particular he was tremendous. As were the rest of the side. Bellamy led the way and the rest followed. We attacked in numbers and defended resolutely when we needed to. City couldn't get near to threatening Pepe's goal, but once again Hart was working overtime. Within minutes of the restart Bellamy got away down the right, his cross was cleared to Kuyt who drilled the ball goalwards. Hart could only parry it but fortunately for City it didn't fall to the lurking Downing.

Next it was Skrtel's turn to be thwarted by Hart. The keeper's poor punch dropped kindly for the reds' defender and his toe poke looked destined for the top corner but, predictably, Hart somehow managed to keep it out. Magnificent save that. I was cursing him at the time like, just as I was shortly after when he denied Downing at the back post following more great work by Kuyt. We were playing some fantastic stuff at this stage, Bellamy and Kuyt were getting a lot of joy down the left of City's backline but we couldn't find a way past Joe fucking Hart. I said to the fella next to me that City would get one chance and score, and lo and behold they did.

The problem originated when Johnson was caught upfield when an attack broke down. As soon as it happened I feared the worst, but then Gerrard dropped in to cover for him and even when the ball was played out to Kolorov I thought we'd be ok, after all, the skipper was back there and we've seen in the past he's a brilliant right back. I expected him to cut out the cross but Kolorov did superbly to not only beat Gerrard but put in an unbelievably good ball that was converted at the back post by Dzeko. Hard to take from our point of view, it was a real kick in the balls. Have to hand it to City though, that was just clinical as fuck. It needed a show of character now, and we got it. No-one typified it more than Bellamy and Kuyt. Bellamy never stopped running and chasing lost causes, he didn't give their defenders a minutes peace and that kind of thing fires up the crowd. The fans were tremendous, and this was one of those nights where team and crowd feed off eachother. When that happens, we can be unstoppable. We've defied the odds so many times on nights like this, and City became the latest victims.

The winning goal came seconds after a move had broken down due to a misunderstanding between Johnson and Henderson. They both blamed eachother and for a second Henderson's head looked to have gone done. Over came Dirk yelling and screaming, 'fucking come on!!!' and clapping his hands. Two or three times he yelled it. Next thing he collects the ball, holds off Lescott and finds Bellamy in the box. He rolled it to Johnson who took everyone by surprise by immediately knocking it back to Bellamy who steadied himself and rolled the ball past Hart. I haven't enjoyed a goal this much in years. Anfield was absolutely bouncing and we could almost smell Wembley now. Despite having plenty of the ball City didn't look like getting another goal. There were a couple of nervy moments, Adam Johnson's shot was comfortably saved by Reina and Agger had to make a terrific block in his own six yard box, but generally we looked very comfortable. An exhausted Bellamy went off to a thunderous ovation, Martin Kelly replacing him as we put on an extra defender to see the game out. Carroll then replaced Kuyt in stoppage time.

There were joyous scenes at the final whistle, not least from Kenny who was clearly very emotional. It's been a while since our last cup final and personally I couldn't care less if it's 'only' the League Cup. It's a trophy, it's a day out at Wembley and ultimately that's what it's all about. Finishing fourth might be more important in some ways but there's no big day out and no trophy at the end of it. And there sure as hell isn't an open top bus parade through the city for it (not even the blues did that, and if anyone was likely to it was them). This was a great night and it was something we needed after a couple of bad results in the league. Hopefully this will get us back on track again and sets us up nicely for another massive game on Saturday. The atmosphere was fantastic against City, but it will be something completely different against their neighbours this weekend. The City game was about football, about winning and getting to Wembley. It was nothing personal. Saturday is personal. Very fucking personal. More of the same please Redmen, let's do these bastards.

LIVERPOOL 2 MANCHESTER UNITED 1

Competition - FA Cup
Date - Sat 28 Jan 2012
Venue - Anfield
Scorer(s) – Daniel Agger, Dirk Kuyt
Half Time - 1-1
Star Man – Martin Skrtel

Team: Reina; Kelly, Skrtel, Agger, Enrique; Carragher (Adam), Gerrard (Bellamy), Henderson; Downing, Carroll, Maxi (Kuyt):

The reaction of Luis Suarez in the stands said it all; this meant even more than usual. It was payback for the lies, the false allegations, the stitch up, the eight match ban and the unjust stain placed on a man's character. Whatsmore, in a delicious twist of fate, it was a lapse in concentration from Patrice Evra that allowed Dirk Kuyt to dump United out of the FA Cup with a dramatic late winner in front of a jubilant Kop. Suarez celebrated as wildly as any of the fans inside Anfield, victory just doesn't get much sweeter than this. Days like this are what being a football fan is all about.

It's been quite a week. Seven days ago we were at our lowest ebb of the season, humiliated by the worst team in the league and facing two huge games that could make or break our season. We had needed to play very well to overcome City, not so much to put out United. We defended well and for all their possession we never really looked in any danger, but we were limited in attack and a bit pedestrian at times. We looked tired and a bit flat. Not that anyone cares, the result was the only thing that mattered and we got it. That's three competitions Ferguson has been dumped out of this season already. It's the worst Manchester United side I've seen in many a year, yet somehow they are still involved in the title race. They aren't involved in the FA Cup though, Dirk has seen to that. It was only his second goal of a disappointing season, but what a time to get it. Once again, he delivered on the big occasion as he so often has.

All the hype beforehand was about Evra and the reception he would get and all the talk afterwards also centred on that. For me it was nothing. In terms of the volume, intensity and persistence of the booing I actually thought Gary Neville had it worse when he came here in 2006. Evra got booed and there were chants of 'there's only one lying bastard'. Big deal, nothing to get worked up about. The repeated chanting from the away end was far worse but nothing is being said about that. The treatment Evra got was pretty tame really, we made our point but there was nothing excessive and I'm sure the mistake he made for the goal upset him far more than anything he had endure from the crowd. Of course most of the media completely missed the point of the booing. They are either stupid or deliberately ignoring the reasons we are unhappy with Evra. He isn't being booed for being racially abused, he's being booed because we don't believe his claims. Your Olly Holt's of this world can preach and moralise all they like about how this might put people off reporting racial abuse in the future but I'd say that's bollocks. If someone is racially abused they aren't going to think 'oh I better keep quiet about this as I don't want to get booed'. I'd like to think maybe it will stop someone lying about it as I believe Evra did, but that's unlikely isn't it? It's only booing, it's not much of a deterrent really unless you're a bit of a shithouse.

If Evra had told the truth from the start and simply said 'Suarez referred to me as 'negro' and I don't think that is acceptable' then none of the ensuing shitstorm would have happened. Suarez could have explained that he meant no offence and it's a term that is used in a non-offensive way where he comes from. A cultural misunderstanding that both sides could learn from, shake hands and move on with no harm done. Instead, Evra lied and changed his story numerous times. On the field he claims he told the referee and Ryan Giggs that Suarez called him 'black'. In the dressing room he'd changed it from black to 'Suarez called me a 'n***er' (on one occasion). He then told French TV he'd been called 'n***er' ten times. At this stage how could Suarez possibly apologise for anything as it would have looked like an admission of guilt that he'd called him something far worse than he actually did.

By the time he met the FA five days later he'd settled on 'negro' and claimed the reason he'd initially thought it was 'n***er' was because he thought that's what 'negro' meant in Spanish. That's what he claimed and that's what the FA believed. This despite him claiming to be able to speak Spanish and claiming to have understood everything else that Suarez had said in Spanish. No-one heard any of these alleged comments, none of the numerous TV cameras trained on the pair were able to pick anything up, and the video footage backs up Suarez's account far more than the far fetched version of events conjured up by Evra. So no, we were not booing Evra because he was the victim of racist abuse, we were booing him because we don't believe his claims that Suarez said to him *"I kicked you because you are black"* and *"I don't talk to blacks"*. We think Suarez has unfairly been branded a racist on the basis of what we believe to be Evra's lies. So yes, damn fucking right we booed the little bastard and we'll do it again. In fact we'll boo him every time we have to face him and we'll make no apologies for it. If some people don't like it, tough shit. But enough of that fucking dog. Let's talk football.

This was a pretty tame affair and one of the most low key clashes between the sides in some time. The Evra thing definitely had an effect on both teams, neither of whom seemed to want to tackle anybody. The team selections also contributed to the lack of action, both sides going with negative line ups featuring a lone striker. United were without the likes of Rooney, Nani and Young which obviously limited Ferguson's attacking options. Then again, he left two of them on the bench last time they came to Anfield so there's no guarantee he'd have selected them anyway. Kenny was also a bit restricted, as there was obviously no Suarez and Bellamy was never going to start this one having already played twice in the previous seven days. Caroll up front with Downing and Maxi supporting from out wide wasn't very surprising, but Carragher in midfield certainly was. In theory, I can see why Kenny would do that. The lack of midfield protection for the back four has been an issue on and off all season, but with Lucas out for the year and Spearing not deemed ready for a return yet, it made some degree of sense to bring Carra into the side against a side who are very good at exploiting the kind of gaps we've been leaving. Depending on how you look at it, you could say that it worked up to a point as United didn't really create much at all whilst Carragher was on the field. Unfortunately neither did we, we were static in midfield and didn't get on the ball at all. We found it hard to keep possession and the likes of Scholes, Carrick and Giggs saw an awful lot of the ball in the first half. It was only when Kenny made changes in the second half that we took control of the midfield and began to look threatening. The City game and the short space of recovery time afterwards almost certainly played a part in how we approached this game, both in selection and tactics.

However, whilst at the time it was worrying seeing United knocking the ball around virtually uncontested at times, in the cold light of day when you analyse it pretty much all of their possession was in front of us and they rarely managed to get in behind. Perhaps that was part of the plan? For all the arse kissing of Paul Scholes, what did he actually do? He had a lot of the ball and was given plenty of space to knock it around and look good, but it was never in areas where could hurt us. He'd exchange a couple of passes with Giggs or Carrick etc and then float a little ball out to one of the full backs who's path would be blocked and it would go back in the middle for Scholes to do it again. It was frustrating for the fans as at the time it looked like we were getting a bit of a chasing, but looking back on it I don't think we were. I'm not suggesting we simply let them have the ball, as that would be doing them a dis-service. I do think we were set up to make sure they didn't get in behind us, and barring a couple of exceptions they didn't. Perhaps Kenny didn't think we had the legs to play a high tempo pressing game like we'd done against City? Having Carroll up front rather than Bellamy certainly makes it more difficult to play like that. Kuyt is an important part in that too but after his efforts on Wednesday night he was another who was rested. And would the amount of games he's played since returning from a long lay off catch up with Gerrard? He didn't look particularly fresh all day and was subbed with 15 minutes to go after feeling a twinge.

The more I think about it, the more I think United's territorial dominance was because we reluctantly surrendered ground high up the pitch to make sure they couldn't find any space in our final third, and for the most part it worked. It was definitely to the detriment of our own game and poor Andy Carroll was badly isolated for long spells. United were the better side in the first half but in terms of chances there was very little in it.

Maxi forced a decent save from De Gea and the lively Valencia hit the post for United. Giggs shot straight at Reina and Gerrard blazed wide from the edge of the box. Tit for tat. We went in front when De Gea decided that wrestling with Carroll was a better option than catching the ball and Agger rose highest to head it into the unguarded net. You could see early on it was our intention to try and unsettle De Gea from crosses. Instead of the usual corner routine where it looks as though he's trying to bum Skrtel before peeling away when the kick comes in, we had Carroll stand right in front of the keeper. Everyone can see that De Gea is a flapper on set pieces, and it made sense to exploit it. I don't think we did it anywhere near enough actually.

Aside from the Valencia shot that hit the post United didn't look threatening at all, but as we've seen so many times down the years they only need one chance and you've got to constantly be on your guard against them. We weren't, as a terrible mistake from Enrique allowed Rafael to get to the byline and cross for the onrushing Park to lash a shot past Reina. Great cross and great finish. Shouldn't have been allowed to happen though, and Enrique needs his arse kicking as he's been getting increasingly sloppy by the week recently. He started off brilliantly, but recently he's been holding onto the ball far too long which is just not how we play. The ball needs to be moved quickly, but at times Enrique seems more concerned with showing off how strong he is and how he can hold people off than he is with playing a quick pass to a team-mate. It isn't a big deal as it's easily addressed, but it's been winding me up a bit recently. Defensively he's generally been outstanding, but the mistake he made here is something that must never be repeated.

He almost cost us a goal a week ago at Bolton by doing virtually the exact same thing. Instead of just playing it simple he backed himself to be able to cut back inside and use his strength to hold the player off. For the second week in a row, it backfired. Clubs do their homework and I'm sure coaches have been looking at him and telling their players to pressure him as he takes chances. He got away with it at Bolton, but the chances of being punished by United are far greater and you could only admire the ruthless efficiency of how they made us pay. They made it look simple, but how many times have we seen our players in similar positions this season and how many of those have led to goals?

Don't get me wrong, Enrique is a really good full back and he's been a great signing so far, he's just maybe not quite as good as he thinks he is. There's nothing wrong with putting the ball out for a throw in sometimes, if he learns that instead of trying to be too clever then he'll be an even better player. In fairness to him he recovered well from that mistake and didn't let it affect him. Of all the players on the field, he probably had the most difficult task as Valencia is in great form and he's a real handful. He had his moments, but Enrique stuck to his task well and kept him relatively quiet.

On the other side Kelly was having a great battle with Giggs. Kelly was all over him like a sister-in-law on heat and it was fascinating to watch. Giggs actually looked really sharp but Kelly stuck to his task superbly and pretty much locked down that side of the field. He didn't attack much but he was very solid defensively which is the number one priority in games like this. Downing played his part too in tracking back and making sure Evra posed no threat.

Both teams were cancelling eachother out and it wasn't like a typical Liverpool-United game at all. The first tackle I can remember was in the second half when Maxi went in with two feet. I haven't seen any replays of it, at the time I thought it wasn't particularly dangerous but you always worry these days when someone goes in like that. There was a weird kind of pause around the ground when it happened, and the players seemed to stop as well as everyone looked at Mark Halsey. I think he gave a free-kick, but I don't remember exactly. I know Maxi was brought off immediately, but that was happening regardless of the tackle.

Maxi and Carra were replaced by Adam and Kuyt, and shortly afterwards Bellamy came on for Gerrard. The skipper had felt a twinge apparently, which is not surprising given this was his third game in seven days and he's not long back from almost a very long lay off. Hopefully it was just a precaution and he won't be sidelined again. I'd be more surprised if he didn't feel the odd twinge really, as he was out a long time. The changes definitely helped us and United's changes seemed to hinder them. By sending on Hernandez for Scholes they relinquished the control they'd had in midfield and the Mexican goalhanger was fairly anonymous. Goals are basically the only thing he brings to the table, he's a modern day Solskjaer. That's not a criticism, I'd love that kind of player here as it's just what we need.

The flow of the game definitely changed in the final 20 minutes. Adam was able to get on the ball and Bellamy was coming deep to find space and start attacks too, usually down the left flank where Downing and Enrique were becoming more of a factor the longer the game went on. We had a good penalty shout when Enrique's intended pass to Carroll was intercepted by Smalling who then slipped and handled the ball as he hit the floor. It was completely unintentional but he stopped the ball from reaching Carroll, who had to then stop his run and go back to retrieve the ball. His shot was blocked and he appealed furiously to Mark Halsey for the pen. I was appealing for it too as I had a great view of it from where I sit. In fairness to Halsey I'm not sure he could have possibly seen whether it was handled or not from where he was, and even if he did see it there's no guarantee he'd deem it worthy of a penalty. The Main Stand linesman should have seen it, but then again maybe he did and just didn't see it as a penalty? Some you get, some you don't. This could have gone either way and Halsey got most things right on the day. Having said that, this might just have been the easiest Liverpool v Manchester United game to referee in a long time. I just hope the league game in a couple of weeks passes off with as little refereeing intervention as this, but I won't hold my breath. There wasn't much in the way of chances for either side and the game looked to be heading for a bore draw and a replay at Old Trafford that we really didn't want. United would have been made up with that, although they were still trying to win the game and were more adventurous than they've been in recent league games here. Then out of nothing we took the lead again. As Evra stood watching, Pepe's long clearance was flicked on by Carroll perfectly into the path of Kuyt and he drilled a low shot past De Gea. In all honesty it wasn't even a good finish, it was straight at the keeper and if it had been Joe Hart in goal he'd have saved it with his foot and we'd all be cursing Dirk. De Gea isn't Joe Hart though, he's more like Tony Hart.

Carroll almost made the game safe with a towering header that hit the post from Enrique's deep hanging cross. Kuyt was inches away from converting the rebound too. It's a pity for Carroll that it didn't go in, he played well and deserved a goal. Even when he does everything right it just isn't happening for him, how many times has he seen great headers come back off the bar or force a wonder save from a keeper? It was a difficult game for him as often he didn't have people around him when the ball was played up to him. Still, he held the ball up much better than he has previously and he had a fire in his belly that hasn't always been there. He was yelling at Downing for a good 30 seconds after the winger cut the ball back to Adam rather than hang one up for Carroll. Downing kept pointing to Adam to say he did the right thing in picking him out, which is probably true. I liked that Carroll was angry about it though. Too often the ball is just floated at him instead of hung up in an area where he can attack it. I wouldn't say his performance was anything special, but he did play well and he did most things that you would expect from him. Too often he hasn't done that, but this was a step in the right direction and it is a real shame he didn't get the goal as it would have boosted his confidence no end. Despite having major doubts, by and large the fans are still in his corner, even the most basic lay off or piece of control is greeted by applause as everyone wants him to do well. Hopefully this is something for him to build on, but one swallow doesn't make a summer and all that.

It's often said that a week is a long time in football, and the last seven days are proof of that. Compare the emotions of a week ago with how we're feeling now? It shouldn't be seen as a surprise that we've seen off both manc teams after losing to Bolton. We've been doing this all season. Drop stupid points against shite and then go and win at Chelsea or Arsenal. The last couple of games have been great, we played superbly against City and we showed great battling qualities and determination against United. Hopefully we won't go and spoil it by losing at Wolves. Still, even if that happened at least we know Suarez will be back afterwards. How boss is it gonna be seeing him run out against Spurs next week?

WOLVERHAMPTON WANDERERS 0 LIVERPOOL 3

Competition - Premier League
Date - Tue 31 Jan 2012
Venue - Molyneux
Scorer(s) – Andy Carroll, Craig Bellamy, Dirk Kuyt
Half Time - 0-0
Star Man – Jose Enrique

Team: Reina; Johnson, Skrtel, Agger (Carragher), Enrique; Spearing, Henderson (Shelvey), Adam; Kuyt, Carroll, Bellamy (Aurelio):

A great result as this fixture had letdown written all over it prior to kick off. We've made a habit of coming off big wins by shitting the bed against the bottom feeders of this league and after emerging unscathed from two huge cup games against the top two sides in the country, would anyone have been surprised if Wolves had turned us over, or at the very least managed to hold us to a draw?

I certainly wouldn't have, my fingers have been burned plenty already this season. In the end though this was very comfortable and it was an excellent performance. The list of positives is lengthy. We did it without Gerrard. Carroll built on his encouraging display at the weekend with an even better display capped by a goal. Kuyt chipped in with another goal giving him two in two after a huge drought. Spearing was back from injury and was very impressive. We kept a clean sheet. Adam was back to the form he'd been showing at the back end of 2011. Enrique bounced back from some below par displays with a fantastic performance. Chelsea dropped two points. And most significantly, this was the last game that Suarez had to sit out.

Of course you can temper some of that by pointing out that Wolves were really fucking grim. I accept that, they were unquestionably hopeless, but so are Bolton, Blackburn, Wigan etc and they all took points off us. Wolves are bad and we put them to the sword. That in itself is a positive for me, as it's something we've been unable to do far too often this season. Even at half time this game was in the balance because we'd not made our superiority count. We've been there so many times before, but this time we took our chances in the second half and went home with the three points.

The first half was great to watch actually, it was end to end stuff with chances for both teams. It wasn't like watching a first half, the game was so stretched at times it looked like what you see in the closing stages. Wolves had two great chances to score. One when Edwards got in behind but put his shot too close to Reina, and another when Kightly played a one two with Fletcher and shot just wide. Fletcher also had a header from a corner that went just over, although I reckon Pepe had that covered. They played alright in the 1st half though. As for us, we had our moments but were a bit wasteful, both in terms of finishing and final ball. Agger's header was well saved by Hennesey, Bellamy had a couple of chances he didn't take, Kuyt was unable to convert from close range after a Carroll knockdown and we had two very good penalty shouts ignored by a mancunian referee who also booked two of our players in a half in which we committed just three fouls. The two non-penalties were a joke. The first was a foul on Johnson which may have been outside the box, it was certainly debatable as to where the foul took place but we didn't even get a free-kick.

We got into a lot of very good positions and I thought we played pretty well. We needed to be more clinical in the final third, and in the second half we were. It took just seven minutes for the goal to come, and it started in our own box when Carroll won a towering header to set up a counter. Bellamy chased a long ball and won a throw in, took it quickly to Adam who whipped in a cross to the far post where Carroll arrived to apply the finish. Encouraging, as one of the main criticisms of Carroll has been that he hasn't busted a gut to get in the box when we attack. He has been doing that much more recently, and this time he got his reward. Bellamy added a second when he ran from halfway as the Wolves defence backed off and he curled a low shot past Hennesey. The keeper should have done better and the defending was laughable. I used to rate that Roger Johnson, but I was wrong. He's absolutely fucking shite. We were in complete control now and Dirk added a third with a brilliantly executed goal on the counter. Enrique was the instigator, making an interception in his own box and then surging past Frimpong. A raking crossfield pass found Kuyt as four Liverpool players advanced on the box. Kuyt rolled it to Adam, who had Carroll and Bellamy to his left but opted to roll it back to Kuyt who's first time shot went through the keeper. It was great football, and even though I thought the keeper should have saved it, it would be churlish to dwell on that. Keepers have played blinders against us for most for the season and even though Hennesey made some good saves it was refreshing to see a couple of avoidable goals go in for once. Coming off the back of De Gea's generosity at the weekend, maybe things are turning around for us now?

Carroll's performance is probably the most significant thing to come from the game. He wasn't brilliant, but he played well and there is definitely signs of improvement there. The biggest thing for me was you could almost see him grow in confidence, especially after the goal. Some of his touches were very good, one in particular when he brought the ball down and embarrassed Johnson with a smart turn before running 30 yards and having a shot. The shot was crap, but that's not really relevant, next time it could just as easily burst the net. His shooting is the least of my concerns. It was just good to see him look like he had belief in himself and what he was trying to do. A lot of the good things he does go to waste because we haven't mastered how to make the most of what he does. How many times do you see him knock crosses down into good areas only for us to have no-one following it up? If our players start to anticipate his knock downs and get in positions to capitalise, it will make Carroll look far more effective. He's got a long way to go but at least it looks like he's heading in the right direction now.

The win puts us above Arsenal and Newcastle (for 24 hours at least) and within touching distance of Chelsea in 4th place. Losing Suarez has undoubtedly cost us points but it hasn't been completely catastrophic and we've not lost much ground. Having him back for the run in will hopefully see us kick on and really put some pressure on Chelsea now. They're not very good, they'll drop points and they still have to come to Anfield. It's up to us to make sure there is no repeat of what happened at Bolton, and plenty of repeats of what we did at Wolves.

Premier League Round Up (31 January - 1 February 2012)

Must admit when I heard the Mancs had won thanks to two penalties the first thing I wondered was which one of Howard Webb or Mark Clattenberg was the referee. Turns out it was neither, and having seen the highlights United can feel aggrieved at not having at least one more penalty given, if not more.

This game wasn't about the Mancs getting favourable decisions at home, it was about Stoke finally paying the price for repeatedly fouling in the box. Truth is, if referees were actually any good Stoke would be conceding two or three pens every week, the dirty clogging bastards. No-one fouls in the box more than these turds, yet they are rarely punished for it. Can't do it at Old Trafford though, everyone knows that. Fuckin' Stoke.

Meanwhile, Everton's title hopes were boosted as they beat City 1-0 at the Pit. Confused? I'll explain. Evertonians are hoping Manchester United win the title and this result boosted those hopes. Make sense now? Darron Gibson scored the only goal of the game with a deflected shot, maybe that will be enough to stop United fans abusing him for a while. City could have had a penalty when the ball hit Phil Neville on the arm, but overall they didn't really do enough to deserve anything from the game given the huge gulf in talent between the two sides. Everton had Hibbert and centre half and that big shit Argie goon up front for God's sake.

The game had to be stopped for a while as a man chained himself to the goalpost at the Park End. BBC reported that he was protesting about Louis Saha moving to Spurs. Hahahah no chance, not unless the fella was a Spurs fan. Most blues I know are happy to see him go, the underachieving bastard. Turns out the pitch invader was actually a red protesting to some airline about his daughter getting the sack or something like that. These pictures were shown all around the world and his face was seen by millions. When something like this happens, I always think of the poor family who must be completely mortified by what he's done and the shame and embarrassment he's brought upon them. I mean, the whole world now knows that he paid to go and watch Everton, that's the kind of stigma that stays with a family for years. He lessened the embarrassment slightly by chaining himself to a post and getting himself arrested, but still… paying to watch Everton when you aren't a blue?

The scenes at full time were hilarious. I've seen teams celebrate trophies with less vigour than this. My late grandad used to say you can always tell when Everton have had a big win as their fans come crawling out of the woodwork. People who you had no idea were blues are suddenly walking round in their Everton shirts all proud as punch. He was a wise man my grandad. It doesn't happen too often as big wins for them are pretty rare these days, but when they have one it's like turning over a stone in your garden and seeing all the woodlice and earwigs scuttling out. The morning after they beat City I dropped my daugher off at school like I do every morning. The temperature was minus two, and all the parents outside the school were suitably attired for such baltic conditions. All except one fella who strolled past me wearing shorts. SHORTS!!! It was minus two degrees! It made no sense, until I saw the Everton crest on them and it all fell into place as my grandad's words echoed in my head. I'd seen the guy before, but never noticed him wearing any Everton swag until that day. It's pretty funny really, he must have been desperate to show off his colours after their 'huge' win, but presumably the only item of Everton gear he could find were these shorts.

Imagine the scene in his house that morning:

Evertonian guy: *"Ey love, have you seen my Everton hat?"*
Evertonian guy's wife: *"What Everton hat?"*
Evertonian guy: *"You know, the wooly one I bought after we beat United in the 2009 FA Cup semi's"*
Evertonian guy's wife: *"You mean the one you only wore once and then stuffed to back of the wardrobe after you lost the final because it brought you bad luck?"*
Evertonian guy: *"Yeah, that one"*
Evertonian guy's wife: *"I gave it to the charity shop"*
Evertonian guy: *"You did what?? I wanna show off my colours today, the blue boys had a big win last you know!"*
Evertonian guy's wife: *"Have a look at the back of the sock draw, I think there's a pair of training shorts you bought after you beat Liverpool that*

time in the FA Cup. Remember, when that young Gosling boy scored. You said he was going to be the next Trevor Steven. Whatever happened to him?"
Evertonian guy: *"Never mind Dan fucking Gosling, it's minus two and you want me to wear fucking shorts??? Fucks sake."*

United's best chance of winning another title is Roberto Mancini. He's a complete fraud. He won titles at Inter because all the competition had been caught bribing refs and were being punished. That still rankles with me actually. Punishing Italian's for providing cash and hookers to referees is patently unfair. May as well punish them for eating pasta or riding scooters. It's what they do, who they are. How can you punish a select few when all of them are doing it? They should punish those who don't do it for being un-Italian. It's every Italian's birthright to be able to offer referees money and prostitutes in return for favourable decisions, and because everyone does it that means it actually evens itself out and no-one gains an unfair advantage because they **all** gain an unfair advantage. It's actually quite clever when you think about it. I'd much prefer the Italian model to the English one, where only one club gets favours from official and they don't even have to shell out on brasses and bribes to get it. Forza Italia!!

Anyway, to get back on track. For me Mancini is not a good manager at all but he's had a transfer budget that eclipses the fast food spending of the USA which makes it virtually impossible not to have some degree of success. He wears a nice coat and a smart scarf and looks very dapper on the sidelines and he's conned plenty of people into thinking he's the business. He's not, and if City win the title (which they should) it's in spite of him and his moonfaced assistant, not because of them. Half the managers in the Premier League could lead that squad to the title, and most would do it with a smile on their face and not come across as the world's biggest arsehole in every TV interview. Seriously, is there a worse interview in the Premier League right now than Mancini? Boring, miserable, pouting hypocritical shitbag with his long pauses between answers, his protruding bottom lip and his refusal to look people in the eyes. I actually hate him now I think. Not Alex Ferguson hate, where I'd like to just punch him in the face as hard as I could, but I'd definitely like to dismissively slap him across the face backhanded with a leather glove. There's very few managers whose interviews are worth watching, but none are more uninspiring than Mancini, and I include Roy Hodgson in that.

Chelsea were extremely fortunate to escape with a point from their trip to Swansea. Scott Sinclair opened the scoring against his old club and showed a lot of class by not celebrating. And therein lies the key to why he didn't make it at Chelsea, you can't go around acting like a classy human being and be a success at the Bridge. Ashley Cole has never had to concern himself with such things of course, completely classless bastard that he is. He was sent off in this game for losing his head and diving into stupid tackles. Remember when he used to be good? Seems like a long time ago now. Actually that's because it IS a long time ago. Just when it looked like Swansea would hold out for a famous victory, 'Unibrow' popped up with a spawny deflected equaliser deep into stoppage time. Heartbreaking for the home side, but they continue to impress with their style of play and they've been the biggest success story of the season so far for me. Few gave them a chance of surviving back in the summer, I know I didn't. They haven't survived yet and could always get sucked into a dogfight, but on what they've shown so far they are much, much better than those below them and they're arguably better than some of those above them too. Finally, no goal for Torres again. I can take extra pleasure in that this week because Carroll scored. *"He told us his heart was never red, Torres, Torres. He went to Chelsea and shit the bed Torres, Torres. He said he'd joined a massive club but now he's a 50 million sub Fernando Torres scored less goals than that alehouse blueshite twat Jon Walters"* Last line still needs a little work maybe.

Tottenham won again. Bale and Modric were on fire and Wigan were completely over matched. Not much more to say, it was easy for Spurs and not a particularly *taxing* evening for Harry Redknapp. Wigan are so bad even 'Arry's dog could have picked the side for this. *Bung* another three points onto Spurs' tally for the season.

Onto Wednesday, and Arsenal dropped two more points after being held to a goalless draw at Bolton. RVP hit the bar twice but Arsenal are really floundering at the moment. There was a thriller at Vanilla as QPR went into a 2-0 lead before the home side came storming back in the 2nd half. A nice finish by Djibs put QPR in front, it's great to have the Lord of Frodsham back in the Premier League. Good luck to him, he'll need it as QPR have been struggling of late.

Speaking of struggling, I've mentioned before how every time I watch MOTD lately Ste Warnock seems to be having a torrid time. This was his worst moment yet, heading past his own keeper to put QPR 2-0 up. The Villa fans booed the shit out of him afterwards. The scoreline hadn't reflected the game as Villa were generally on top and they made it count after the break as Bent and Nzogbia scored to earn them a point. Nzogbia has been a massive disappointment and I think this was actually his first goal of the season. I'm surprised by his struggles as he looked class at Wigan and I thought he'd do very well for Villa. He may still do, but up to now he's not been good. You know, I still can't believe Villa gave the manager's job to the man who got their neighbours relegated, it's mad when you think about it. Imagine if Everton were relegated and we hired their manager. You just wouldn't do that, it's mental. A Life Presidency maybe, or season tickets for life and maybe name a suite after him, but making him manager?? Crazy. You know McLeish is never going to achieve anything at Villa, although in fairness who possibly could? It's Aston Villa, not good, not shit, just Villa. Destined to forever hang around the middle of the table and never do anything good or bad. No wonder their fans are most miserable bunch of fuckers you could ever meet.

Speaking of miserable fans, poor old Blackburn lost at home to Newcastle. Just when you think they might be putting something together and could drag themselves out of the bottom three, they find a way to lose a game they'd have fancied their chances of winning. Newcastle without Demba Ba and Cabaye are not a side that will be feared by anybody and Rovers have been showing some real signs of life recently. I had this down as a home win but an own goal and a missed penalty condemned Steve Kean's side to defeat. Alien head Obertan rubbed salt in the wounds with a second goal on the break in stoppage time.

Fulham drew 1-1 at home with WBA. Clint Dempsey is Fulham's Van Persie, no-one else seems to be able to score consistently and now that they've sold Zamora they better hope nothing happens to Dempsey. Tchoi equalised for the Baggies. That's the first time I think I've ever seen him do anything worthwhile, he's useless that lad.

Sunderland battered Norwich at the Stadium of Light. Fraizer Campbell got the first with a great goal, proving the sun does indeed shine on a dog's arse somedays. My boy Sessegnon made it 2-0 and an oggy by the unfortunate Danny Ayala wrapped up the win. O'Neill has transformed the Mackems, they're on a great run since he went there. Loads of people hate O'Neill but I must admit I've always quite liked the fella. I enjoy him as a pundit, his interviews are usually interesting and he's had results wherever he's been. He gets saddled with this 'long ball merchant' tag but Sunderland are playing some good stuff at the moment. Of course that may change when he puts his own stamp on the side and signs Emile Heskey and coaxes John Hartson out of retirement this summer, but at the moment they're good to watch.

Norwich wore their away kit for some reason. They don't actually need an away kit as no-one else in the league wears canary yellow, the closest would be the gold of Wolves. I don't like it when a team wears their away kit through choice rather than necessity as I'm convinced it brings bad luck. I don't have any stats to back that up, but if I could find any I'd bet that teams who opt to wear their change strip when there's no need have a 100% loss record in those games. Even if I'm wrong, why take the chance? It's the football equivalent of walking under a ladder when there's plenty of room to go around it. Why risk it if you don't have to?? With that in mind, Norwich got what was coming to them.

chapter ten

February

LIVERPOOL 0 TOTTENHAM HOTSPUR 0

Competition - Premier League
Date - Mon 6 Feb 2012
Venue - Anfield
Scorer(s) –
Half Time - 0-0
Star Man – Martin Skrtel

Team: Reina; Kelly, Skrtel, Agger, Johnson; Gerrard, Spearing, Adam; Kuyt (Suarez), Carroll, Bellamy (Downing):

Eight home draws from twelve home games now. This was probably as frustrating as any, although looking at the bigger picture a point against Spurs is far more palatable than drawing with Sunderland, Norwich, Blackburn etc. In recent meetings with Tottenham we've been distinctly second best but this time it was the Londoners on the back foot for most of the game. I guess that's progress of sorts.

Former red Brad Friedel wasn't stretched too much but he was certainly busier than Pepe Reina and Spurs were reliant on outstanding defensive performances from King, Dawson and Parker to keep them in this game. Overall we played well, dominated the game and should have won it. Carroll and Suarez both wasted great chances late on although Spurs will point to the Bale opportunity when he was denied by Reina and say they could have won it too. That would have been the most unjust outcome since… well since Suarez was screwed over by Evra and the FA.

There was only one side really trying to win the game in the end, Spurs were more than happy to hold on for a point but I don't think they set out that way, it's just how the game panned out. They probably fancied their chances prior to kick off as they've had our number recently. This was a very tough game for them though. We played well and did a good job of stifling their key attacking players. We put them on the back foot and in the second half we pinned them back and made them defend, which they did superbly to be fair. Both sides can take something from this game, but Spurs will have been far happier with the point than us.

This is a game we've had circled in our calendar ever since Suarez was banned. It was his long awaited comeback game, and the big question was whether he'd come straight back into the side or not. Fitness wouldn't have been a major issue as he's not been injured and has therefore been training like everybody else. The main considerations would probably have been the opposition and the form of Andy Carroll. The last couple of games have seen a marked upturn in the form of the big number nine. He scored at Wolves and deserved the chance to build on that by starting this game. Leaving him out and putting Suarez straight back in would have been unfair and counter productive. Carroll needs a run of games now, he's starting to look something like the player we thought we were getting a year ago and it makes sense to roll with him to see how far his improvement can take him.

So, could Suarez come in alongside Carroll? That's where the opposition come into it. Playing 442 against Spurs wouldn't have been a good idea in my opinion. Their midfield has dominated ours in recent encounters, so we needed an extra body in there to combat that. Suarez could have played to the right or left of Carroll in place of either Kuyt or Bellamy, but Spurs are dangerous out wide with Bale who switches flanks regularly. Both Bellamy and Kuyt are more suited to helping out the full back than Luis is. So, it would have been difficult to put Suarez straight back in because of these factors and Kenny might have felt it was best to just ease him back in anyway.

He started on the bench, with the rest of the side being pretty much as you'd expect it to be. Enrique was missing through injury so Kelly started at right back with Johnson moving over to the left. Not a problem, they're both good players. Spearing and Gerrard were shoe ins for the midfield, the only decision to be made was whether Adam or Henderson joined them. Kenny went with Adam and I thought the Scot had a very good game. I wouldn't be the least bit surprised if Henderson got the nod at the weekend but it wouldn't be a reflection on Adam's performance, it's just horses for course and maybe Henderson's extra mobility and running power could be useful at Old Trafford.

I like Charlie Adam though, and I don't understand a lot of the criticism he's had. More often than not I think he's played pretty well, he's had some bad games too but overall he's generally been good. Yet you can sense the dissatisfaction in sections of the crowd any time he makes a mistake. Hell, it's there even when he doesn't make a mistake. There was a moment early on when he received the ball in midfield and played it back to Skrtel first time rather than taking a touch and turning with it. There was a huge groan around the stadium but had Gerrard or even Spearing done that it wouldn't have happened. There was no groaning after that, largely because he very rarely gave possession away and he did a good job closing people down without conceding the kind of fouls he is sometimes prone to. Our midfield functioned efficiently, they kept the ball moving and protected the defence well. Last season Modric completely ran the game at Anfield, this time he didn't. He was still very good and he's virtually impossible to get the ball off (he's a lot like David Silva in the way he can just change direction and glide away from people trying to get close to him), but for all his silky touches his impact on the game was minimal. Adam and Spearing in particular deserve credit for that, they got through a hell of a lot of work.

It was a fascinating game I thought. Not a great game by any means, but it was absorbing. Both defences were tremendous and the second half especially was on a knife edge. Would we be able to make our pressure tell or would we get hit with a sucker punch? The game was in the balance right up until the end and whilst it was frustrating that we couldn't find the breakthrough, the reality is that Spurs are currently better than us so it's not a bad result. It looks worse than it is because of all the stupid points we've squandered in previous games, but taken on it's own merit there was plenty to be pleased about in this game.

We were just about the better side in the first half, and we were by far the better side in the second. The only major criticism I have is the lack of quality service from out wide. Dirk was absolutely brutal until he was put out of his misery late on, Bellamy got very little change out of the excellent Kyle Walker and neither full back did much in the way of delivering crosses (with one notable exception from Kelly in the 2nd half that Carroll should have buried). That meant Carroll was again feeding on scraps, so it's to his credit that he still managed to put in a very good performance. In fact, I'd even go as far to say was his best display since he came here. He should have scored in the second half, but that blemish aside he was pretty much faultless throughout and did everything right.

Last year in this fixture Carroll couldn't win anything in the air and was completely dominated by King and Dawson. We played too many long balls on the night and it wasn't a good team performance, but Carroll was bullied by those two. This couldn't have been any more different. This was the Newcastle Andy Carroll. He won everything, whether it be flick ons, knock downs or simply bringing the ball down and laying it off. He closed defenders down with a purpose too (usually it's more of a token gesture but now he looks like he means it), and he's starting to look like the player I was so impressed with when he was at Newcastle. He even looked a yard quicker I thought. Has to be down to confidence that, he no longer looks like he has the weight of the world on his shoulders and he is winning the crowd over. Not that the crowd have ever really left him. For all his struggles the matchday crowd has been very supportive of him, which makes the Charlie Adam thing even more strange to me. If only he had a cross or two to attack eh? Time and again we had the ball out wide but either didn't deliver it or put a ball in that he had no chance of getting anywhere near. You can see the frustration in him, he's constantly berating the wide men and telling them to just hang one up there for him to attack. I've got no problem with him doing that when he's playing like this, in fact I applaud him for it. His head seems more into the game now, he's playing like someone who wants to be here and prove himself. It's just a pity he didn't take the chance that came his way as regardless of how he plays, he needs goals if he's going to prove himself.

Our best effort of the 1st half was a 20 yarder from Spearing that went just wide. Friedel then saved with his feet to keep out a Glen Johnson effort and we wasted two free-kicks from the edge of the box. At the other end, Adebayor was well shackled by Skrtel and Agger and Bale was invisible in the first half. It's not often you see a chimp upstaged by a simple cat, but it's fair to say that the feline intruder had more of a lasting impact on the first half than Bale.

Statistically I believe we are the most difficult side to create chances against. I'm sure I read that somewhere anyway, and the eye test certainly backs that up. We don't give up many chances and Spurs found it very difficult to break us down. Most teams do, which is what made the Bolton debacle so shocking. Equally, statistics also show that we're the most wasteful side in terms of chance conversion. The eye test backs that up too. This wasn't a game of many chances, but we had two great ones in the second half and wasted both. Carroll's shot over the bar from eight yards was really poor, it may have been on his weaker foot but that's still no excuse for not at least hitting the target. Suarez's miss was arguably even worse, heading Gerrard's pinpoint free-kick straight into the arms of Friedel when it would have been a certain goal had he put it just a yard either side of him. They were the only clear openings we created even though we were camped in their half for long spells. Kelly forced Friedel into a save with a shot from the edge of the box, and there were other half chances that were snuffed out, usually by King or Parker getting their bodies in the way.

The only chance Tottenham had all night was a breakaway by Bale. He looked about three yards offside to me but the flag stayed down and he ran clear on goal. Pepe did well to stand up and then make a good save, but Bale should have buried that. He's a great player but he's an annoying twat too isn't he? I haven't seen the replays but it looked like he dived to try and get Agger in trouble. Agger told him what he thought of him and Bale then shoved him in the chest and was booked. The ref didn't give Bale a free-kick, so presumably he thought it was a dive. Why no yellow card for that then? He's lucky he wasn't booked for the dive and then sent off for the shove. He also pissed off the fans (and Kenny) when he went down screaming after a hefty challenge by Skrtel. It was a great tackle, he won the ball cleanly but appeared to catch Bale with his follow through. The ref didn't even give a foul initially, it was seconds later when he decided to blow the whistle because Bale was rolling round like he'd been shot and their players were going mad.

A furious Skrtel was booked, the crowd went ballistic as Bale hobbled off only to return a few seconds later. He may have been hurt, I don't know, but there was no way he wasn't coming back on and after his earlier antics the crowd weren't giving him the benefit of the doubt. He's getting a reputation for this sort of thing sadly. Scott Parker is another that could have been sent off, the World War II looking gobshite. He was booked in the 1st half for a foul on Gerrard and got away with a couple more later on. Anyone so much as breathes on him though and he's giving it the full beans, writhing in agony and rolling around the floor. He's another who loves a bit of playacting. He looked like he'd broken his leg early in the second half as he rolled around in agony. Seconds later, miraculously he was fine. He also milked that Suarez kick for all it was worth too. Being kicked in the stomach like that doesn't actually hurt much at all, but look at Parker's reaction. Embarrassing.

He's the new golden boy though is 'Scotty', the London press love him, he's a proper salt of the earth, London lad, oozing that good old 'British Bulldog' spirit. I bet he loves his dear old mum too does 'Scotty'. That being said, I don't know what the hell Luis was doing. I don't think he deliberately booted him as that would be stupid beyond belief, even though I accept it must be incredibly tempting to take a swing at good old 'Scotty'. I've seen the replays though and it doesn't look good at all. Kenny said Luis didn't see him, but it's not like Parker just came out of nowhere is it? He was stood in front of him the whole time, even if you're looking at the ball there's no way you can't see Parker stood there.

Initially I was furious with the ref for booking Suarez, but that was before I saw the replay. If he'd wanted to be a dickhead about it he could easily have sent him off and I doubt anyone outside of ourselves would have had a go at the ref for it. So the yellow card was fair enough, even though it was hilarious seeing Bellamy race twenty yards to complain about it. Parker made another predictably swift recovery, but to his credit he didn't make anything of the challenge when asked by Sky afterwards, so that's something I suppose. There are plenty who would have done. I dunno, maybe I've got such a downer on Parker because I wanted us to sign him and we didn't.

The closing stages of the game were incredibly frustrating. We were piling on the pressure and Carroll and Suarez were both looking threatening. They linked up well a few times too, something we've not seen a great deal of to this point. Unfortunately, any time we got near the Spurs goal the referee seemed to spot some sort of infringement and awarded them a free-kick, much to the anger of the Kop. For 80 minutes Michael Oliver had generally done ok I thought, but I don't know what he was doing late on. Friedel comes charging out into a ruck of players, punches the ball and then collides with Skrtel. Ref awards a free-kick. What's Skrtel supposed to do, vanish into thin air? Carroll knocks one down for Suarez, he turns and has a shot that hits King (possibly on the arm, I couldn't really tell) and bounces back and hits Luis on the hand. Ref gives a free-kick. It did hit his hand, but if that's the other way around and the ball rebounds of Suarez onto King's hand, he doesn't give a pen for that in a million years, and nor should he. A lot easier to punish a striker with a free-kick than a defender with a penalty though isn't it? Finally, the ball is played into Carroll who controls on his chest and the whistle is blown again. I don't even know what that was for, presumably it was either handball or backing in, either way it looked ridiculous from where I was sat. The crowd were going ballistic at this stage, it just appeared that the ref was doing everything he could to stop us scoring. Has he not watched us this season, does he not realise we're perfectly capable of messing things up ourselves?

The final whistle was greeted with boos, but they were for the referee and not directed at the team who generally played very well. The only player who I felt didn't perform was Dirk. Nothing he attempted came off and it was one of those days for him. A pity, as he's been much better of late. I was leaning towards

Carroll for the star man award but that missed chance blotted his copybook a little so I'm going for Skrtel instead. He's been our most consistent player all season and he was tremendous again in this game. Agger was very good too, and aside from some poor crossing Johnson impressed on the left. Gerrard started off brilliantly but seemed to tire in the second half, whilst both Adam and Spearing did their jobs to a good standard.

We should have won but once again our inability to score has proved costly. We're still only four points behind fourth spot although we've lost ground on both Newcastle and Arsenal this weekend and we have a very difficult fixture coming up next. It's a game where the pressure is off us to an extent though. We're already in a cup final, we knocked them out of the FA Cup and we aren't chasing the title. Yes, we need to win to keep up in the race for fourth place, but generally there is a lot more pressure on them to win this game as a defeat has bigger repercussions for them than us. They'll be desperate to win this because of the FA Cup defeat and the Suarez factor and that puts extra pressure on them.

We can go there and just throw everything at them and hopefully we will. They're vulnerable if you attack them and I'd love to see Kenny go in with Suarez, Carroll and Bellamy and really try and get after them. They've got issues at the back and in the goalkeeper position, and Andy Carroll in this form could cause them all kinds of problems. Bellamy will relish it too. The one worry is that Suarez may be a little bit too keen to make his mark, and if he were to boot any of their players like he did Parker I dread to think what would happen. A red card would be the least of his worries, especially if it were Evra he kicked. Can the FA authorise firing squads? That's what Ferguson would be calling for. I'm sure Suarez can handle whatever their fans throw at him but he may be targeted by some of their players and he needs to be very careful. That said, I can't fucking wait for this one! Come on redmen, let's do these manc bastards!!

Premier League Round Up (4-5 February 2012)

RVPFC kicked off the weekend's action at home to Blackburn. They led courtesy of two tap ins from you know who either side of an excellent Gamst-Pedersen free-kick. Oxlade-Chamberlain made it 3-1 and then Givet was sent off for a two footed tackle on you know who. After that the floodgates opened in the 2nd half and Steve Kean's side crashed to a 7-1 defeat with you know who claiming yet another hat-trick.

If you let Arsenal play they're capable of cutting through anybody, and Blackburn certainly let them play. I'm off Kean's bandwagon again now. We needed a favour from him here and instead not only did his side's meek surrender allow Arsenal to leapfrog us in the table, they also let them build up their goal difference which was inferior to ours before this game. All that support I've given him and THIS is how he repays me? Fucking ingrate.

QPR flew out of the traps against struggling Wolves. In the first 10 minutes they could have had three or four but had to settle for a solitary Bobby Zamora goal. Wolves were on the ropes and Mick McCarthy's job was almost certainly on the line at this point. The game turned on its head after 14 minutes when Cisse was sent off after retaliating to a bad challenge by Roger Johnson. I hated this decision, even if by 'the letter of the law' Clattenburg probably did what he had to. That law stinks though. *"He raised his hand so he had to go"* they say, and none of us even argue anymore. When did that happen? When did we just accept this kind of crap? By we I mean fans, players, clubs, everyone in football. FIFA pass down some bullshit new edict and no-one bats an eyelid. It's a joke that a player can be sent off for what Cisse did and no-one even thinks it's wrong. An absolute fucking joke. It's been happening for years though and it's become ingrained in our collective mentality. Instead of saying how ridiculous it is that something so soft is deemed 'violent conduct' and worthy of a three game suspension, we all trot out the *'well if you raise your hands you're asking for trouble'* mantra. To listen to the BBC commentator you'd have sworn Cisse had just murdered Johnson's wife and kids.

It's a passionate game, people do things in the heat of the moment and as long as they don't actually assault someone then just give them a yellow card, tell them to settle down and get on with the frigging game. This *'you can't raise your hands'* nonsense might just be the thing I hate most about modern footy. Apart from ticket prices, players wages, the sudden emergence of Chelsea and Man City as 'big clubs' just because some filthy rich tit was looking for a new plaything, Alex Ferguson, nicknames on the back of shirts, semi finals at Wembley, Patrice Evra, John Terry, 90% of the sporting press and a shit load of other things. But leaving all those aside, I really hate this *'raise your hands it's a red card'* crap too.

Cisse's red card cost his team three points and he'll get banned for three games on top of this, and for what? For putting his hand on Johnson's throat for a second or two. A thick wooly gloved hand at that, which is hardly gonna hurt anyone is it. It's bullshit, this is footy not fucking snooker. I'll concede he was stupid to do it but in some ways it's understandable. He's had two horrific injuries in his career and the challenge from Johnson was really dangerous. Commit a reckless, dangerous foul that could put a player's career in jeopardy = yellow card. Get pissed off about it and put your hand on someone's throat = red card. What kind of fucked up logic is that? Djibs should have just chinned him as chances are the punishment wouldn't have been any more severe than the one he'll get anyway. Like they say, *"May as well be hung like a sheep than a lamb"* or something. I'm not suggesting football should go as far as Ice Hockey and just stand back and let players scrap (although I can't deny there is a certain appeal in that), but it's clearly gone way too far the other way.

Cisse's departure allowed McCarthy to be more adventurous. He needed to be, as there were rumours that Steve Morgan was livid at the performance he saw from Wolves against us last week. Big Mick must be feeling the pressure, and defeat to ten man QPR may have finished him off. So he came out swinging. On came Ebanks-Blake and Doyle, and Wolves went on to win the game with goals from Jarvis and Doyle. Harsh on QPR, but apart from Djibs I can't think of a single reason why I wouldn't want them to lose every week now that they've appointed 'Sparky'. And I still haven't forgiven them - or Luton - for their plastic pitch back in the 80s.

Wolves are still in trouble and wouldn't have gotten anything from this game without Cisse's departure, but the three points will be all that matter for the beleaguered McCarthy. Doyle will feel he's proved a point too, as he's been on the bench a lot recently. Had to laugh at his reaction when he scored though, yelling into a camera behind the goal. Yeah Kev, slight problem with that, it wasn't a TV camera it was just a photographer. I believe this is what today's youngsters like to call an 'EPIC FAIL!!'.

Sunderland won again. Like Wolves they were given a helping hand by a referee, the red card for Huth was a joke. Actually it was more of a disgrace than a joke, although I laughed my head off when I saw it so I guess 'joke' is still appropriate. It was a staggeringly bad decision though. Huth completely pulled out of the tackle and the only contact made with the Sunderland player was his knee being kicked by the lad's follow through. Not that I've any sympathy for Huth, fuck him the big dirty yard dog, and fuck Stoke too. The game was played in a snowstorm, and I saw a clip of Jermaine Pennant where he had snow in his 'fro. It was spookily like looking at Morgan Freeman in Driving Miss Daisy. Except obviously no-one is gonna hire Jermaine to be their chauffeur, y'know, with the jail time for drink driving and all that. O'Neill has got the Mackems flying now though. They were awful under Bruce, but they look a completely different side now. James McLean scored again, he looks useful.

Man City bounced back from defeat at Everton with a comfortable win at home to Fulham. Mike Dean awarded them an early pen after the latest dive by Adam Johnson. He more or less even admitted it afterwards too. He doesn't seem like the sharpest knife in the draw him, as thick as two Agbonlahors I'd say. Brain definitely in his boots. Aguero buried the pen for his 18th goal of the season. Baird put through his own net when trying to block a Johnson shot to double City's advantage and Dzeko made it 3-0 with a tap in after Aguero had ruined Senderos for the umpteenth time. Couple of points here. Dzeko; I still can't work out if he's really good or really shit. He's mostly shit but occasionally does amazing things that cloud the issue. I'm leaning towards shit but it won't take much for me to change my mind. My other point, Aguero against Senderos was a complete mismatch. It's bordering on unfair actually, maybe some kind of handicap system needs to be introduced for when Aguero lines up against a Huth or a Senderos. Make him wear his boots on the wrong feet or play with a patch over one eye or something. Anything to make it a bit more fair. The same policy could also be enforced on any defender who gets to mark Fernando Torres.

Swansea won at West Brom despite falling behind to Marc-Antoine Fortune's goal ten minutes after the break. They were level within a minute when the impressive Gilfi Sigurdsson sidefooted home, and a couple of minutes later the Icelandic midfielder had teed up Danny Graham for the winner. West Brom's home form is terrible, but they've done well on their travels. Strangely it's the exact opposite of Hodgson's Fulham who couldn't win away but were really strong at home. Then of course there was his Liverpool side that was equally bad at home and away. Hmmm, if there's a pattern there then whoever gets him next should be unstoppable. The natives are getting restless at both Black Country clubs at the moment. Who'll get the push first, Roy or Mick? They play eachother next week so we might not have to wait long to find out.

Norwich had a fairly routine win over Bolton despite losing both centre halves to injury in the first half. Fortunately you don't really need centre halves when you're only up against 'the Gog'. Surman and Pilkington got the goals in a 2-0 win for the Canaries. Norwich are proper old school, they're basically a throwback to their teams of the late 80s/early 90s. Almost all of their players are British and fairly nondescript, they've not gone down the highly paid foreigner route that virtually every other team has, but somehow they've made it work. For Robert Fleck, Ruel Fox, Mark Bowen and Jeremy Goss read Grant Holt, Wes Hoolahan, Russell Martin and Anthony Pilkington. They're headed for a top half finish, which would be a remarkable achievement given where they were a couple of years ago.

Moving on, and the blues had a big win in midweek against the league leaders in case you somehow missed it. *"One of the best wins since I've been here"* proclaimed Moyes. He must be very easily pleased. Still, that win over City wasn't enough to get them off the graveyard shift on MOTD this weekend. I love it when they're on last as you can almost hear the collective gnashing of teeth from the blue third of the city. Difficult to argue with the decision of the BBC producers though, as Wigan 1 Everton 1 was memorable only for the comical mistake by Howard that resulted in the latest Phil Neville oggy. Wigan should have made the game safe shortly after but Moses ignored two much better placed team-mates in favour of going on his own. He ended up desperately shooting straight at a defender and the chance was gone. If I was his manager I'd have subbed him on the spot for that, the greedy little bastard. He's the reason they didn't get three points and this kind of decision making is the reason someone with his undoubted talent is playing for Wigan and not a top six club.

Anichebe came off the bench to earn Everton a point, not that hardly anyone will have seen it as the only people still watching MOTD at this point are Evertonians, Wigan fans and divvies like me who have decided to write about it. Moyes hailed Steven Pienaar afterwards: *"He was our best player. He was involved in lots of bits where we looked as if we were on the verge of making things happen"*. As I said, easily pleased.

Onto Sunday, and Newcastle had their Senegal strike pairing available for the first time. Both scored as the Toon overcame Aston Vanilla 2-1 at St James' Park. Can't help but think people are getting a bit carried away about Pappis Cisse though. He's already been crowned King of Newcastle by virtue of being handed the coveted number nine shirt up there and scoring on his debut. The Geordies don't need much encouragement to crown a new messiah, but the BBC commentator really should know better. It's one game, far too early to be comparing him with Jackie Milburn, Malcolm McDonald, Alan Shearer and er Andy Carroll...

What about Villa though. Not a happy ship is it? Steven Ireland was subbed at half time for allegedly telling McLeish to *"fuck off"* in the tunnel. N'Zogbia tweeted after the game that for the first time in his life he isn't enjoying playing football. The tweet was later deleted but I always think what's point of deleting it when tens of thousands of people have seen it anyway? It's like walking into your bosses office and taking a shit on his desk whilst he sits there looking at you, then cleaning it up as though it never happened. Just because it's gone doesn't change the fact you laid a smelly brownie on your bosses desk. N'Zogbia actually created Villa's goal and is finally showing signs of getting into form, so it was an odd time for McLeish to be calling him out. Robbie Keane scored again, a nice goal too as he laid the ball off and then showed good movement to get on the end of the cross. He even got to celebrate too, as Newcastle are one of only a handful of clubs he didn't follow as a kid and then go on to play for. Double win for 'Keano' there. McLeish's post game interview was telling. He pointed out at great length how hard Gutierrez (Newcastle's left winger) worked for his team, the clear implication being that his left winger, N'Zogbia, doesn't do that. I expect Villa fans would argue that if it was hard work he wanted maybe he should have bought Gutierrez instead? N'Zogbia is who he is, and McLeish tried to sign him for Birmingham and did sign him for Villa. He knew what he was getting, so he can't start complaining when he finds a steaming turd on his desk.

The biggest game of the weekend was of course at Stamford Bridge, where Chelsea took on Howard Webb's Manchester United. They looked like they were going to turn them over too, leading 3-0 before Webb inspired his team to a trademark comeback. Chelsea had taken the lead when Sturridge's cross was deflected onto Johnny Evans by De Gea and the ball bounced into the net. I guess you could say he was.... 'Johnny on the spot'. Ha! See what I did there? Mata made it 2-0 seconds after the restart with a great volley from a Torres cross and then Sideshow Bob's header was deflected off Ferdinand to make it 3-0. Speaking of Ferdinand, he was booed throughout by the Chelsea crowd. Now am I missing something here, or is he being booed simply for being the brother of Anton? Chelsea fans have made it clear what they think of Anton Ferdinand, their *"We know what you are"* chant showed exactly what they think of him. Again though, am I missing something, or is their beef with Anton simply that he was allegedly racially abused by their captain? We were slated for booing Evra, but that's a completely different situation. Evra claimed Suarez racially abused him, there were no witnesses to it and no video evidence to support his claim. Evra reported Suarez and basically, we feel he's a lying twat so we booed him. Unless I've missed something, Anton Ferdinand did not report Terry as he didn't hear anything at the time. He has not made any allegations at all, he's just a lad that either has or hasn't been racially abused. Either way, he hasn't done anything wrong, has he? And what exactly is it that Chelsea fans 'know he is'? And does that mean Rio is one too? So many questions, so few answers.

I'm trying not to be too judgemental here as the rest of the country didn't have a clue what our beef was with Evra and just thought we were condoning racism just to support our player. We had good reason to react the way we did but virtually nobody knew what those reasons were as the press didn't report them. So I'm wondering what the deal is with Chelsea and Ferdinand. Do they have a good reason for their anger towards the two Ferdinands? If there's any Chelsea fan reading this, let us know why Rio was booed and exactly what it is that you 'know Anton is' as I'd love to know. Especially as the entire world knows exactly what John Terry is, regardless of whether he did or didn't racially abuse Anton Ferdinand. By the way, how weird was it seeing Torres being 'blessed' by Luiz before the game? What's that all about, it just smacks of desperation now. He'll try anything to get back among the goals won't he, the loser. What's next, a little voodoo temple next to his locker in the dressing room like the big Dominican guy in Major League who couldn't hit curve balls?

Webb had a half chance early on to give United the lead when Young took a tumble in the box. It wasn't an easy chance to take in fairness to the official as it was never a penalty in a million years. Not that that has stopped him in the past of course, but generally the worst of those decisions have come in the safe surroundings of Old Trafford. He let another opportunity slip when Cahill clearly fouled Wellbeck. It was just outside the box but it was a blatant foul. Webb could have got away with giving a pen or he could have just given a free kick and possibly sent Cahill off. He chose to ignore it much to his manager's disapproval. You have to wonder what was said at half time as Webb came out much more like his old self. Chelsea's two quickfire goals after the break had put them in a seemingly unassailable position, but you can never write off Howard Webb and his Manchester United team-mates. Evra and Sturridge ran side by side into the box, Sturridge tried to make a play for the ball and Evra craftily put his right foot in the way and took a tumble. Webb made no mistake this time, pointing to the spot and then looking on as Rooney buried the pen.

The momentum had shifted but Chelsea were still two goals up and in good shape. Not for long. Wellbeck moved away from the ball so he could step on Ivanovic and then fall over. Webb and Rooney did the rest, they're becoming a lethal pairing those two. Wellbeck and Evra both essentially did the same thing, Evra just made his look more convincing. Neither were penalties. Once it got to 3-2 there was no way Chelsea were going to be able to survive and slack marking allowed Hernandez to head in the equaliser. Cech's goalkeeping left a lot to be desired too, he just looked like an immobile old man. In a silly hat.

Villas Boas's post match interview was interesting and astonishingly I found myself supporting him. The interviewer was trying to get him to have a go at his defenders for being caught out by Hernandez's movement for the equaliser. *"Will you be asking Sir Alex the same kind of question?"* he responded. Go ed lad!! *"We've already spoken to him"* they said. What they didn't tell him was that the line of questioning for Ferguson was nothing like what they asked him. I reckon he knew that though, he might a bit wet behind the ears in management terms but he's clearly a bright guy and knew exactly what was happening here. The BBC wouldn't fucking dare ask Ferguson anything remotely difficult. If they had any balls they'd get Hansen there to interview the purple nosed, reprehensible twat. Speaking of the devil, rather than field questions about his own team's shit defending he was allowed to go off on one about the officiating. The only manager in the game who is allowed to do that after a game in which his side were awarded two bullshit penalties. It seems he also wanted a red card for Cahill and was annoyed that the linesman didn't flag for the foul. *"That linesman has given a penalty kick against us from 40 yards away last year against Liverpool, this year against Arsenal - and he can't see that? He is all too happy to flag at Old Trafford for penalty kicks."* I didn't even know what he was talking about initially, we didn't get a pen at Old Trafford last year did we? After some research, it appears he's talking about September 2010 when Torres was clearly fouled by Evans in full view of the linesman (who for the record was no more than 20 yards away).

Unsurprisingly, the FA didn't have a problem with those comments. Now imagine if any other manager in the country had said that. Whatever did happen to that 'Respect' campaign by the way? Don't expect to see that fella running the line at any United games in future either, Ferguson and his mate Howard will see to that.

MANCHESTER UNITED 2 LIVERPOOL 1

Competition - Premier League
Date - Sat 11 Feb 2012
Venue - Old Trafford
Scorer(s) – Luis Suarez
Half Time - 0-0
Star Man – Daniel Agger

Team: Reina; Johnson, Skrtel, Agger, Enrique; Gerrard, Spearing (Carroll), Henderson; Kuyt (Adam), Suarez, Downing (Bellamy):

We've had worse days at Old Trafford, but this was still pretty hard to stomach and it will sting for a little while. After all that's gone on this was a game we daren't lose, but we did lose it and deservedly so. We just didn't show up, it was a shocking performance and even though most of the focus will be about non-football related stuff, that shouldn't distract from how poorly we performed. We played the occasion, not the game, and we paid the price for it.

The media can hype up the whole handshake farce, the tunnel bust ups and the post match comments all they like, it's our non-performance that bothers me more than anything.

I didn't like the team selection but I liked the way we performed even less. We were completely second best and seeing those two old timers running rings around us in the middle of the park was really tough to sit through. Our midfield was crap, the widemen were worse and the full backs were garbage. Skrtel and Agger were the only ones to come out of this with any credit (Reina too I guess), the rest ranged between awful and mediocre. We were fortunate to go in level at half time, but the ensuing tunnel shenanigans seemed to affect our concentration as we let in two soft goals in a five minute period after half time. We were never coming back from that, and everybody knew it. I was surprised we even pulled one back to be perfectly honest. Nice that it was Suarez who scored it, but it was somewhat flukey and not down to good play on our part. The only other time we even went close to scoring was a shot from distance by Johnson that De Gea made look much more difficult than it actually was. Johnson had gone closest in the 1st half too, but overall I thought he was shite and didn't make the most of the acres of space he was afforded as Giggs tucked infield. He struggled defensively too and I have no idea where he was going on that first goal. Watch the replay, he's got position on Rooney but actually runs away from the ball whilst Rooney runs towards it.

The second goal was on Spearing who got caught on the ball by the impressive Valencia. I don't think Enrique helped the situation by playing it to him in such a tight space, but still, Jay has to do better than that. That Rooney goal ended the contest as we struggle to score goals at the best of times and it was going to take a miracle to get two back at Old Trafford. It looked more likely at this stage that they would add to the lead before we would reduce it, and they had chances before they appeared to settle for what they had and began trying to just play keepball. Suarez's goal gave us some faint hope and we did improve after the introduction of Carroll and Bellamy, but it was still fairly routine for United and De Gea had a piss easy afternoon. That's the most frustrating thing for me, that lad is dodgy as fuck, especially on crosses. Yet we barely tested him at all. I didn't agree with Carroll being left out as not only has he started to look decent of late, but he'd have strongly fancied himself against the likes of Evans and the washed up Ferdinand. Leaving him out when he's finally getting some confidence just seems counter productive to me. And quite why Downing got the nod over Bellamy is anyone's guess. Craig Bellamy is a big game player who thrives on the pressure occasions like this bring. Stewart Downing is the complete opposite, he disappeared as soon as the whistle blew to start the game. I can't say he was noticeably bad, as I didn't even notice him until he got booked for mistiming a tackle on Rafael. He was invisible and there's no excuse for an experienced international player to have such little impact on a game. Risible stuff, I was furious with him as this was just a cowardly performance. We needed players who wanted to take the game by the scruff of the neck and win their individual battles.

Instead we got Downing doing his Mr Passive act once more and not testing Rafael even once. Henderson wasn't much better but at least he looked like he wasn't scared of receiving the ball. I understood why Henderson got the nod over Adam (I even suggested it would happen in my Spurs report the other day), but in hindsight Adam should have played. Presumably Henderson, Kuyt and Downing were all selected because of what they could do without the ball rather than with it, as we'd have been far more threatening with Adam, Carroll and Bellamy in there. It was just a bad day all round, poor selection, even worse performance and yet more negative headlines and bad publicity that won't be going away anytime soon.

The day may have turned out differently had Phil Dowd penalised Ferdinand just before half time for the incident with Suarez. I'd say it was probably a foul based on the fact that both players seemed to play the ball at virtually the same moment, but Ferdinand was tackling from behind and went through Suarez to get it. You could also argue that it was his second movement that brought Suarez down after the striker had ridden the initial contact and was through on goal. It was far from clear cut though and even after numerous replays it's difficult to make a conclusive judgement of it, and that's before you even get into interpretation. There's no way I can have a go at Dowd for that as it was such a close call and unless he has a clear view of it and is completely sure what happened, he can't give it. Suarez was understandably furious and lost his cool for the first time. When the half time whistle went seconds later he booted the ball away in frustration and there's many a ref who'd have taken action against him. I have to say I thought Dowd was brilliant on the day. I can't think of too many decisions he got wrong, but more importantly he didn't allow the occasion to get to him and showed a lot of common sense. He was fully aware of the tension surrounding the fixture and how things could easily get out of hand, and he did everything he could to ensure it didn't. Instead of booking Suarez, he just told him to cool it. At the end when Evra was inciting trouble by celebrating right in front of Suarez, he got himself over there and dragged Evra away and told him to pack it in. So whilst he could have sent Ferdinand off for that challenge, I don't have any complaint about it and I actually have nothing but praise for Dowd on the day. Might be the first time I've written that, and may well be the last. Credit where it's due though, this could have got seriously out of hand with a different referee in charge.

As for the whole handshake fiasco, it's not as clear cut as is being reported for me (never is though, is it?). Did Suarez snub Evra? Well firstly let me say that if he did I wouldn't blame him as in his shoes there's no way I'd want to shake hands with Evra. What most people seem to be failing to understand is that Suarez completely denies saying most of the things Evra accused him of saying. That the FA decided to believe Evra over Suarez proves nothing but does add to the sense of injustice felt by Suarez. Evra accused him of saying that he *"kicked him because he is black"* and that he *"does not talk to blacks"*. Suarez vehemently denies saying either of those things. Now, if you did not say such things but had been branded a racist and suspended for 8 games because people chose to believe the word of your accuser, would you shake hands with that person? I wouldn't, it would have taken all the willpower I could muster not to fucking lamp him. That being said, Suarez had presumably told Kenny that he would shake Evra's hand (Kenny said during the week that Luis would shake all the United players hands) and by not doing so he put his manager in an awful position. Kenny was visibly shocked when he was informed after the game that Suarez had not shook Evra's hand. So whilst I wouldn't blame Suarez if he chose not to go through with it, if he'd told Kenny he would do it then he should have.

However, I'm far from convinced that the non-handshake was a result of Suarez 'snubbing' Evra. Luis had his hand out, he did not pull away from it. Evra appears to pull his hand back slightly before then moving it back as Suarez is on his way past. Watch how Evra shakes the hands of the other LFC players but then changes his movement when Suarez approaches. There's clear hesitation there. He then kicks off when Suarez continues on to De Gea and grabs his arm aggressively and makes a big scene. He had no right to do that, regardless of whether Suarez snubbed him or if it was just a misunderstanding. As I see it, there's three possible explanations for what happened:

1) Suarez decided to go back on what he told Kenny he would do and simply ignored Evra.
2) Evra feigned to pull away knowing Suarez wouldn't be able to do anything and then he made a big deal about being snubbed to once again portray Suarez as the bad guy.
3) There was a hesitation as to who should grab the other's hand, and neither did it. Both were wary of eachother and whether they were going to be snubbed, so neither made the first move to actually initiate the handshake and before you knew it Suarez had walked past and all hell broke loose.

I don't know which of these is accurate, nobody does apart from the two participants. Everyone has an opinion on it, but there's no way anyone can be conclusively sure about what went down. If I had to place them in order of most likely to least likely I'd say 3,2,1, but that's based on 'probability' which proves nothing unless you're an FA Kangaroo Court. In short, I don't know what actually happened but I'd certainly like to hear Suarez's version of events.

What I do know is that these things happen in a split second and even the slightest hesitation is enough to throw the whole thing off. If Suarez thought Evra was not offering his hand he's hardly going to just stand there like a dickhead. Some will argue that's precisely what he should have done, therefore forcing Evra into a decision. If Evra didn't accept his hand, at least Suarez could say he tried. They may also argue that when Evra grabbed him he could have rectified the misunderstanding and shook his hand then and explained he initially thought Evra didn't want to and he meant no offence.

I'm not going to condemn him for not doing that as I highly doubt I'd have done it in his position, especially if I thought he'd pulled his hand away.

Once again Suarez will be portrayed as the villain, even though once again it was Evra who completely lost his head and saw the red mist. Within seconds of the game starting he tried to do Suarez and ended up almost breaking Ferdinand's neck after Luis saw him coming and took evasive action (if we'd gone on to win the game this might have gone down as one of the funniest things I've ever seen). He then caused murder in the tunnel at half time when he went after Suarez and according to the Sky reporter on the scene had to be prevented from entering the LFC dressing room by Skrtel, which then almost started a mass brawl. Skrtel should have let him in and then closed the door behind him. Then finally there was his over the top celebrations at the final whistle, dancing and whipping the crowd up right in front of Suarez. Through all of this, Suarez didn't react to anything. Yet he'll be getting caned from all sides now because of the whole handshake farce whilst Evra will be portrayed as some kind of fucking conquering hero. It's sickening, and I'll be avoiding Sky and all the papers for at least a week. I'm not subjecting myself to the endless stream of shite that's going to be churned out. Scumbags like Jason Roberts and Gordon Taylor will be getting plenty of airtime over the next day or two.

The owners will no doubt be disturbed to see the club being dragged through the mud yet again, there were some suggestions they weren't happy about Kenny's remark after the Spurs game about how Suarez should never have been banned in the first place, and after the manager said earlier in the week that Suarez would shake Evra's hand I'm sure they'll be wanting an explanation for the latest shitstorm we've become embroiled in. All because of a stupid fucking handshake.

Those pre-match handshakes need to be fucked off completely, they're a total waste of time and it's become a pantomime now. *"Will Wayne Bridge shake John Terry's hand?" "Will Anton Ferdinand shake Terry's hand?" "Will Evra shake Suarez's hand?"* Who gives a shit? Everybody it seems. It's a joke, this fucking stupid pre-match ritual is getting more attention than the actual game. It's a morbid curiosity we have. Be honest, most us watched that Chelsea/City game to see what would happen with Terry and Bridge, and millions of neutrals will have tuned in to see what happened here. The storylines behind the matches seem to mean more than the actual games themselves, it's like the fucking WWE these days. The thing is, why should you HAVE to shake hands with everybody from the other team? If you don't like somebody why should you be forced to shake their hand? Let's face it, Evra didn't want to shake hands with Suarez, and Suarez didn't want to shake hands with Evra. They both agreed to do it for the benefit of other people, not themselves. They were put in a position were it was expected of them, just to satisfy some bullshit pre-match etiquette and to give some false impression that everything is cool now. Why? It should be completely optional who a person shakes hands with, and them two shaking hands wouldn't have changed anything in terms of what they feel about eachother. When the game finishes you can shake hands with whoever you choose, and refuse to shake hands with whoever you choose. Scrap this fucking charade as it's more trouble than it's worth. Ferdinand didn't shake Suarez's hand but fuck all will be said about that. Surprisingly I found myself agreeing with Rooney afterwards when he refused to rise to the bait dangled in front of him by Sky and just said something along the lines of *"It's between those two whether they shake hands or not, the rest of us need to just be professional about it."* Pity his manager didn't show the same level of decorum, the reprehensible piece of filth. There's a lot I could say about Ferguson and his comments but I'm not going to. It wouldn't do me or TLW any credit so it's better to keep it to myself. I'll be interested to hear what Kenny has to say in response though, that's for sure. When that will be is anyone's guess. He swerved the post-match press conference (for the best as nothing good was ever going to come of that) and they don't usually do one before FA Cup games so it might be a while before Kenny speaks.

Star man is Agger, he shades it from Skrtel purely based on the reports coming out of Denmark that he told Ferdinand he wanted to fight him outside. Maybe next time we can arrange that instead of the charade of shaking hands and pretending to respect eachother. Just let them all fight it out in the centre circle and be done with it, we've got the WWE style storylines, may as well go the whole hog and get the steel cage set up for next time. What I'd give to see Agger and Skrtel in a tag match with Ferdinand and Evra. Or Ferguson in a buried alive caskett match.

Premier League Round Up (11-12 February 2012)

The weekend's football viewing started and finished at Old Trafford for me. After that I didn't see another ball kicked in anger until this afternoon (Thursday) when I finally got round to watching the two MOTD's I'd sky plussed. I actually had good reason for the delay as I had to get the fanzine ready to go to print by Wednesday, but to tell the truth after what went down in Manchester at Saturday lunch time it was a relief to be able to just avoid it all like a Uruguayan swerving a Frenchman's handshake. I didn't even know some of the scores until today.

One game I did know the result of was Spurs v Newcastle as I was getting regular joyous texts throughout that game from my brother-in-law who, predictably, was as happy as a Manc in shit. Newcastle losing was good from an LFC point of view too, not that I was taking any particular pleasure from it at the time as obviously I wasn't in the greatest of moods. I'm sure he eventually realised that, what with every gleeful text he sent being met with a reply about the physical harm I'd like to inflict on Ferguson, Evra, Geoff Shreeves, et al. I think I may have killed his buzz as eventually he just stopped texting. I should probably apologise to him now I think about it....

Great result for Spurs though, they're still in with an outside chance of the title but you just know that any time they get within touching distance they'll fuck it up. They are still Spurs after all. For now though they are far back enough to be playing without much pressure, and when you take that pressure out of the equation Spurs look as good as anybody. They were 2-0 up inside six minutes against the Toon. Hair Bear Bunch got the first and Saha got the second. The former blue got another soon after, meaning he scored as many in 20 minutes for Spurs as he had in six months for Everton. Kranjcar made it 4-0 before the break but luckily for Pardew's men Spurs eased off a bit in the 2nd period, only adding one more to their tally when Adebayor eventually got the goal he deserved.

I was spectacularly wrong about Adebayor. Back at the start of the season when he was turning it on I said he'd fizzle out and wouldn't be arsed after he'd been there a few months. That's usually been the case but not this time, he's still producing and has been class all season to be fair to him. Great bit of business that was. The day was all about Redknapp though. *"Keep Harry Hotspur"* read one banner. Who's Harry Hotspur then? Actually, imagine being called Harry Hotspur, it's be ace. You couldn't fail to be a success in life with a name like Harry Hotspur. That's a winner's name that is. A proper comic strip footy hero's name. I bet he'd have had quite a rivalry with Roy of the Rovers back in the day. Little known fact - I once owned a pair of Roy Race football boots when I was a kid. I did ask for the full Melchester Rovers kit too but Santa let me down and got me a Scotland kit instead, the fuckin' arlarse. If I were to wear a full Scotland kit today I'd obviously look like a bad wrong un' (the only thing worse than a grown man wearing a full footy kit is a grown man wearing any kind of goalie shirt, the ones with elbow pads are the worst) but there's a good chance I'd get a call up to their squad, that's how far they've fallen since the days of Dalglish, Souness, Strachan, Sharp etc. But getting back on track, *"You're Spurs and you know you are"* they chanted to 'Arry. Yeah we'll see about that if England come calling. I can picture it now, car slows down, window opens, microphone shoved in face... *"T'riffic honour.... fantastic opportunity... proud Englishman... couldn't turn my country down... Spurs will always be in my heart ..."* etc etc etc

(Update: I've since been informed that there was indeed an actual 'Harry Hotspur'. You'll have to pardon my ignorance, the only experience I have of Shakespeare is using their fishing gear)

Next up on MOTD was our game and 'handshakegate' so naturally I fast forwarded that shit. But wait, what's this? BBC using Sky's interview with Kenny? What's that all about then? Curiosity got the better of me so rewound it back to make sure my eyes weren't deceiving me. They weren't. It seems Kenny had spoken to BBC afterwards but said he'd only talk about the game, nothing else. So the shit stirring feckers must have asked Sky for special permission to use Kenny's interview with them. Didn't see them doing that when

Ferguson went three years or whatever it was without speaking to them. Bang out of order that. Fucking rats.

Which brings me nicely onto… Everton 2 Chelsea 0. The wheels have really come off Chelsea's wagon this season, they're a bit shit now. The excellent Pienaar put the blues in front and that big Argie lump wrapped it up in the 2nd half. There's no finesse about him at all, he's basically a less refined Shefqi Kuqi. Where did Moyes find him, a Buenos Aires building site? The weight room in a Santa Fe prison maybe? Defensively Chelsea are simply horrendous, it's funny to watch them. I love watching David Luiz trying to defend, it's just great entertainment. How did he ever end up playing centre half? Who first put him there, and did they do it for a bet? Why does AVB keep playing him there? This fascinates me as it's probably the position on the field he's the least suited to. It's the equivalent of playing Tony Hibbert as a 'false nine'. Still, it gives Jocky plenty to talk about every week. Curiously, Villas Boas has become less and less irritating as the season has gone on. He's under a lot of pressure and that usually brings out the worst in people, but fair do's, he's not bothering me anything like I thought he would do after some of his early season shenanigans. The jury is still out though and I definitely don't trust him. He could flick the gobshite switch at any point I reckon, but I can't deny I'm warming to him just a little bit.

Sunderland were unlucky to lose to Arsenal at the Stadium of Light. At least that's what I was led to believe by my brother-in-law, who was then far from impressed with how MOTD presented it. The usual text arrived late Saturday night... *"MOTD wankers. Big eared crisp munching cunt"* Having watched it today, I'm not sure exactly what his beef with Lineker is but that's football fans for you, we all think the world is out to get our team. McLean put them in front, capitalising after Mertesacker was picked off by a sniper in the crowd. Not easy hitting a moving target, but when it moves as slow as the German it's a lot easier I guess. He was stretchered off, hopefully it's not as bad as it looked. Ramsey levelled for the Gunners within five minutes and Henry got the winner with seconds remaining when he converted a great cross by the Russian gnome. Henry's back off to America now but I'll admit it's actually been nice having him back in the Premier League again as he's been a truly great player. Great for the Arsenal fans to have had another chance to see him scoring goals for them. Class act.

The Canaries travelled to South Wales to take on the Swans in the 'battle of the birds'. I really fancied Swansea to win this but they lost out in a cracking game that probably should have ended in a draw as neither deserved to lose. Graham put Swansea in front with a tidy finish following a typically slick passing move. Holt equalised for Norwich in bizarre circumstances. Everyone thought the ball was going out but Elliot Ward didn't give it up and hooked it back into the danger area where Holt bundled it in. Chances then came at both ends but Norwich took the lead when Pilkington's shot took a wicked deflection to leave Vorm helpless. Holt made it 3-1 with an impressive finish, his 11th goal of the season before Graham set up a grandstand finish by converting a late penalty. Swansea piled on the pressure, Graham shot just wide and Ruddy had to make a great save to ensure Paul Lambert's team went home with maximum points.

Dunno if I've mentioned this before, but it seems like every week Norwich send out some random player I've never seen before. Just who in the blue hell is Elliot Ward? What position does he play and where has he been all season? I thought the same thing about Simeon Jackson a few weeks ago. David Fox was another. Before him, Elliot Bennett. Before that, Bradley Johnson and Russell Martin. I still don't know what positions any of these boys play. There'll be another next week no doubt. Do they have a conveyor belt that churns out nomarks?

Relegation six pointer at Ewood Park as Mark Hughes took his new side to the home of one of his old ones. The Yak was back from suspension and looked as hungry as ever. He put Rovers in front with a smart turn and finish from the edge of the box. Quick feet for a fat guy, defenders don't expect someone that size to be that nimble. He reminds me of me, aside from the nimble part. Nzonzi doubled Blackburn's lead and my boy Junior Hoilett made it 3-0 at half time with a deflected strike. Dreamland for Steve Kean, as for once he could have a relaxing second half. Fat chance. The Yak hit the bar with a terrific chip but then Mackie pulled one back for QPR who then laid siege to Paul Robinson's goal for the final 20 minutes. Mackie's brilliant strike in the last minute will have had hearts a fluttering on the Blackburn bench but they held on for a valuable three points to move out of the relegation places.

That wasn't the only relegation six pointer taking place in Lancashire on Saturday. Kevin Davies was back for Bolton as they played host to a Wigan side who for some reason recalled the absymal Alcaraz. 'The black Di Santo' was up front for Bolton, 'the white Ngog' led the line for Wigan. Caldwell powered in a header from a corner to put the visitors in front and the Bolton fans started voicing their displeasure, booing the shit out of anyone who made a mistake. That meant a lot of booing, as Bolton are fucking woeful. Still can't believe they beat us.... Owen Coyle's side levelled out of the blue when the ball hit a confused Ngog on the back and fell perfectly for Mark Davies to lash it home (note to any stat virgins reading: That is classed as an 'assist' by Ngog, therefore showing once again that stats are for losers and you can make them prove any point you like, no matter how ridiculous. It's still one more than Downing though).

Wigan always looked more dangerous however, and McArthur won it for them when a Moses shot was parried into his path for a tap in. Moses ran Bolton ragged but his decision making is generally shocking. Even the goal, he had two players waiting for a tap in and he chose to shoot. So exciting, but so wasteful. Wigan are still bottom but they are only a point behind Bolton now. Difficult to say who is worse, but I'm leaning towards Bolton.

The final game on Saturday saw Fulham see off Stoke. Pogrebnyak's cracking finish broke the deadlock and Dempsey's screamer hit the bar but went in off the back of the unlucky Sorensen. Shawcross pulled one back with a towering header from Pennant's corner but Fulham held on. Tony Pulis was bitching about a bad tackle by Pogrebnyak and a lack of consistency from referees. He's right, but it's a bit like Simon Cowell complaining about how shit the charts are these days, or how TV on a Saturday evening ain't what it used to be. Shut up Pulis, and fuck off Stoke. Martin Jol is boss, I could listen to him talk for hours, the big cool Dutch bastard.

Onto Sunday now, Wolves went into the Black Country derby on a run of wretched home form. West Brom went into it on a run of excellent away form. Even so, I don't think anyone saw this coming. Odemwingie gave the Baggies the lead with a deflected effort late in the first half but they could have easily been 3-0 up at that point as they'd battered Wolves. Fletcher levelled on the stroke of half time with a goal Wolves didn't really deserve and that should have given them the momentum going into the second half. They came out brightly and Fletcher went close again but then they made a meal of clearing a corner and Olsson's shot somehow squirmed through Hennessey's grasp. Fletcher and Johnson went desperately close to levelling but once again they failed to deal with a corner and Odemwingie made it 3-1 from close range. That's when Wolves completely capitulated. Wolves old boy Keith Andrews added a fourth before Odemwingie completed his hat-trick to make it 5-1. Dreamland for the Hodge, the stuff of nightmares for Big Mick. He apologised for the performance afterwards, but it wasn't enough to keep his job as Steve Morgan wielded the axe a couple of days later. Or maybe it was his wife, you can never be sure with old Steve, can you? Sad for Big Mick, even more sad for me as this comes hot on the heels of Neil Warnock getting the push. Wolves will no doubt go down the QPR route of bringing in some boring, cliche spouting bastard in to replace him, meaning MOTD has just got even duller. Big Martin Jol is all I have left now.

Moving on, and Man City went to Villa Park knowing they needed a win to return to the top of the table. They got it, but it was a close call with Lescott's late header just about seeing off a plucky Villa side. *"Man City winning ugly"* they said as they showed a slo mo of Lescott celebrating. Bit unfair that, especially when it's in HD. Even a Bryan Ruiz would struggle to look anything but ugly whilst being shown in slow motion, pulling tongues with his face all scrunched up as he shook his head in glorious High Definition. Imagine how his hair would look though. Truly majestic. *swoons*

There was an unfamiliar face on Villa's bench next to McLeish. Kevin McDonald, who won the double with us in 85/86, is assistant manager at Villa these days. You'd never recognise him though, the years haven't been kind to Kev at all. Whereas the likes of Jocky, Big Jan, Brucie, Whelan, Rushy and the King just look like older versions of their younger selves, McDonald looks like some random old geezer and nothing remotely like his panini sticker. Sadly it's due to an untreatable condition known in medical circles as 'Mike Phelan Syndrome.'

LIVERPOOL 6 BRIGHTON & HOVE ALBION 1

Competition - FA Cup
Date - Sun 19 Feb 2012
Venue - Anfield
Scorer(s) – Martin Skrtel, 3 O.G.s, Andy Carroll, Luis Suarez
Half Time - 2-1
Star Man – Martin Skrtel

Team: Reina; Johnson, Carragher, Skrtel, Enrique; Henderson (Kuyt), Gerrard, Adam (Shelvey): Suarez, Carroll, Downing (Maxi):

The magic of the FA Cup eh? 13 goals in three home games so far. That's actually just one less than we've managed in a dozen Premier League games in L4. Of course it helps when the opposition are rattling them in for you, and it's fair to say we had more breaks in this game than we've had in those 12 league games combined. We could even afford the luxury of yet another missed pen, at least this time the game wasn't in the balance when we failed from the spot.

This was the ideal preparation for next weekend's League Cup Final. Brighton made it easy for us by being so wide open at the back and by sticking to their footballing principles throughout. Cardiff will present a much sterner test but we go into that game with Suarez and Carroll amongst the goals and finally in tandem with Steven Gerrard. Apparently this was the first time all three had started together. That means that we've never seen those three and Bellamy at the same time, as the Welshman was absent from this game with a slight knock. Just shows what we've been missing.

Carroll's form has taken a significant upturn since Gerrard returned to the line up (not saying that's the reason for it, but it hasn't hurt him that's for sure) and he's now looking like the player we thought we were getting when we broke the bank to get him from Newcastle. He scored one and then made one for Suarez, and once again he showed a great hunger and desire for the game. He's getting there, and it's great to see. I'd all but written him off a few weeks ago but he's completely turned things around recently. I thought the finish for his goal was brilliant, that wasn't an easy chance to take and I half expected the ball to end up in the back row of the Kop when he swung his left boot at it. He showed great technique to keep the ball down and steer it into the corner, and the towering header back across goal to tee up Suarez was terrific to see as well. I'm really enjoying watching Carroll play these last few weeks, long may it continue. Well in big man, keep it going.

The most important thing for him now is to develop a partnership with Suarez. That's proved to be difficult so far for a number of reasons. The first being Carroll's mostly poor form. In addition to that though both players have missed a fair amount of games for differing reasons, and that's drastically reduced the amount of playing time they've had together in the 12 months they've both been at the club. Another issue has been the system.

Kenny has sometimes found it difficult to accommodate both of them as it generally means playing 442, and often when we've done that it hasn't worked as we've been outnumbered in midfield. Bringing in the extra midfielder means one of the forwards has to either sit on the bench or play out wide. In the previous game Carroll was on the bench, this time Suarez started the game on the right of a front three. It didn't really work and we ended up moving Henderson out to the right flank and going 442. It's a problem for Kenny, no question about it. Against Brighton it didn't really matter, Gerrard and Adam bossed the middle of the park and didn't need an extra body in there with them. That allowed Suarez to play off Carroll and the end result was an avalanche of goals.

The first of which came with only a few minutes gone, Skrtel heading in a left wing corner by the skipper. Skrtel's been immense this season and the fact he's added goals to his armoury now is a much welcome bonus too. We didn't build on it though, we seemed to get complacent and were lacking in urgency. It took a Brighton equaliser to snap us out of it. Good goal it was too, although from our point of view it was one that should have been avoided. The strike from Lua-Lua was excellent, but our wall was pretty shoddy.

Suarez had struggled in the early stages, his touch wasn't as assured as we've come to expect and he was spending most of his time on the right hand side. As the half wore on he started to find his feet and he was extremely unlucky not to score when he dribbled his way into the box and beat the keeper only to see the right back get round on the cover to clear the danger. More magic from Suarez led to the second goal. The keeper flapped at a corner and as the ball dropped down Suarez showed terrific technique to pull it down and send a shot goalwards. The keeper saved with his feet, Johnson headed it back towards goal and a Brighton defender lashed it against his own player (Bridcutt) who could only watch as the ball rebounded into the net. Exactly what we needed before half time, and there were shades of the Oldham game about this first half, the only major difference being Oldham scored first. Just like the Oldham game, the floodgates opened after the break. Poor old Brighton had no answer to the movement of the likes of Suarez, Gerrard and Downing. Yes, Downing. He was very good and bounced back well from his non-show at Old Trafford. Not that a good display against a Championship side makes up for what went before, but he did play well and finally managed an assist when he picked out Carroll for his goal. He did well against Oldham too, but given that he's an experienced international player you'd expect him to be able to produce this level of performance against better opposition too.

Another Bridcutt own goal saw us go 4-1 up. Henderson broke out of defence and burst forward. He lofted a pass in the direction of Gerrard but it looked like it would be dealt with by Navarro. The bouncing ball made it difficult for the former reds' reserve who grew up in the shadow of the Kop, and Gerrard was able to outmuscle him and get a shot away. The keeper saved, Gerrard latched onto the rebound and from a tight angle he hit the ball against Bridcutt who could do nothing to prevent it bouncing into the net. Those two oggies had been unfortunate for Brighton, the poor lad could do nothing about either of them, but now he was on a hat-trick (even though DJ George had announced Johnson and Gerrard as the scorers. Gotta love George, if an opposing player were to ping one past his own keeper from 30 yards, George would just credit whichever LFC player was nearest to him). Amazingly our next goal was also courtesy of a Brighton defender, although thankfully Bridcutt was spared the hat-trick.

This one wasn't unlucky either, it was just hilarious. A left wing cross didn't find Carroll and Dunk had time and space to do whatever he liked. He could have headed it away, he could have chested back to the keeper or he could have brought it down and then leathered it upfield. He chose to take it on the chest, then try and juggle it on his knee and ended up carrying it over his own goal line. I didn't catch it but I believe George credited Fernando Torres with the goal as the poor bastard needs all the help he can get.

The only thing missing now was a goal for Suarez. It's what everyone wanted, especially Kenny. When the three subs were all preparing to come on, I was just hoping that the front two would stay on as this was a great chance for them to fill their boots and work on their partnership. I was made up when Kenny left them on, I thought that was great management. The same with the penalty. Adam and Kuyt were having a discussion over who would take it, and you could see Carroll was more than a little interested too. Suarez was hanging around the penalty spot looking hopeful, and then he spotted Kenny on the touchline holding up seven fingers. Suarez quickly directed Kuyt and Adam's attentions towards Kenny and then grabbed the ball. His penalty was awful and it was an easy save for the keeper, but that's not really important. The big picture here was Kenny making a statement. Any rumours that may have been flying around about a possible rift between Dalglish and Suarez after the handshake debacle were quoshed in that moment. In terms of man-management, what a great move by Kenny. We were 5-1 up so it didn't matter whether he scored or not, the important thing here was the statement of support for his player.

Everyone wanted Suarez to score, and credit to his strike partner for teeing him up a few minutes later when he could easily have gone himself. Enrique stood a ball up at the back post for Carroll just as he had against the Mancs in the last round. That time Carroll went for goal himself and hit the woodwork. This time he only had eyes for Suarez, nodding the ball back across to give his partner a tap in. I loved seeing that, it was nice for Suarez to get his goal but I was made up with Carroll's part in it.

We need Andy Carroll to be the player we thought we were getting when we signed him. We desperately need it, and if he'd been that player we'd be much higher up the table. He's starting to show signs that he's becoming that player, and if he and Suarez can get something going together then we're in business. There's a lot of football left to be played this season and the big lad is coming into form at just the right time. The key is whether we can find a way to shoehorn all of our best attacking players into the side at once in a system that will be effective. Carroll, Suarez, Gerrard and Bellamy will give anybody problems, but how do you accommodate all four without being caught short in the middle of the park against the better sides? That's what Kenny and Steve Clarke need to figure out, if they can then those four could wreak some havoc.

Overall this was a really enjoyable cup tie. Loads of goals, played in a good spirit, some good banter between the fans and even the streaker at the end was funny. I usually hate that crap, but at least this fella waited until stoppage time when the game was all but over. It was pretty funny, especially as he left his shoes and socks on. The funniest part was seeing how uncomfortable Carra looked having to hug him as he made his way off the field. Wonder what the streaker was saying to him? My guess would be *"I've lost my cat, you haven't seen one running around here have you?"*

Here we go gathering cups in... February

CARDIFF CITY 2 LIVERPOOL 2 (2-3 ON PENS)

Competition - Carling Cup Final
Date - Sun 26 Feb 2012
Venue - Wembley Stadium
Scorer(s) – Martin Skrtel, Dirk Kuyt
Half Time - 1-0
Star Man – Stewart Downing

Team: Reina; Johnson, Skrtel, Agger (Carragher), Enrique; Henderson (Bellamy), Gerrard, Adam, Downing; Suarez, Carroll (Kuyt):

Back in 2001 it was *"Wine for my men, we ride at dawn" "On my signal unleash hell" and "What we do in life echoes in eternity"*. After this latest epic it was another 'Gladiator' quote that came to mind; *"Are you not entertained? Are you not entertained?"* No-one does finals like us. No-one. We don't do boring finals, we don't even do average finals, we only do classics.

In fact we should be just given a bye to every final from now on just to make sure we're in it. We could be playing Barcelona or Boston United and it wouldn't matter, it's going right down to the wire and everyone is getting their money's worth. The last boring final we were in was against the Mancs in 1996 and that was clearly their fault given that every one we've been in since has been edge of the seat stuff. Fuckin' Mancs.

Of course we shouldn't be cutting things so fine against Cardiff, but this is what we do isn't it? Just ask Birmingham and West Ham. It's not important how you win a final, just that you win. A week earlier we'd put six past a Championship side and this game was probably just as one sided. On another day we'd have scored six again, but then it wouldn't have been a final would it? Poor decision making in the final third combined with sloppy finishing by the reds and heroic defending from Cardiff ensured this was another classic final. Ultimately the best team won but they could have had no complaints if they hadn't. It could have been so different. Kenny Miller missed a sitter late on that would have won it for Cardiff, we needlessly sat back after going 2-1 up and were virtually begging them to equalise, we then missed two penalties yet still won a shoot out even though our keeper didn't make a single save. This was so close to being an embarrassing defeat and Cardiff must be kicking themselves.

They beat themselves in that penalty shoot out by failing to hit the target with three of their kicks. None of it matters now, the trophy is in our cabinet and the record books will show that the 2012 League Cup was won by Liverpool. It won't say that Cardiff should have won it through Miller at the end, or that they bottled it in the shoot out. It will simply say that Liverpool won it, and when it comes to finals that's the only thing that matters. Most people will have forgotten about the chance Marlon Harewood had late on in the 2006 FA Cup Final, or which West Ham players missed in the shoot out. They only remember who won and they remember Gerrard's Superman act that day. It's even become known as the 'Gerrard Final'. In years to come what will we remember from this day? There was no outstanding individual performer in the mould of Gerrard against West Ham, but what I'll remember most about this game is Dirk's contribution. It won't ever be known as the 'Kuyt Final', but his impact on the outcome of this game was massive. Fittingly so, he's delivered in so many big games down the years but has no medals to show for any of it. Until now. He arrived at the club not long after our last trophy meaning he's our longest serving player yet to win something. It was therefore fitting that he played a key role in this success. The energy he brought off the bench in extra time, the goal he scored, the cool head he showed from the spot and just his general attitude in geeing up his team-mates and keeping everyone believing. He was the first one over to Gerrard and Adam after they missed, he was the first one over to Downing and Johnson when they scored. As far as team-mates go, you'd struggle to find a better one than Dirk and I can't think of a more deserving trophy winner than him.

It's brilliant for Kenny too, he was at the heart of so many great days at the old Wembley and it's fitting that he led us to our first trophy at the new one. I'm pleased for the likes of Skrtel and Agger to finally win a trophy with us too, as well as the new lads. Now they've experienced what it feels like winning trophies for Liverpool and celebrating in front of the fans, hopefully it will spur them on to more, starting with the FA Cup which we have as good a chance as anyone of winning. Hopefully we won't be as wasteful against Stoke as we were in this game. So many chances came and went, whilst there were countless times the wrong option was chosen. When it needed a shot we saw a pass, when it needed a pass, we'd see someone shoot. Incredibly frustrating stuff, especially as the approach play was pretty good and we completely dominated virtually the entire game.

Maybe it would have turned out differently had Johnson's brilliant early effort been an inch or two lower. When that came back off the underside of the bar my first thought was that this might not be our day, especially when Gerrard blasted the rebound high over the bar. It deserved a goal as it was a terrific break and a superb shot from the full back. No surprise to see the woodwork denying us though is it, we should be used to it by now. Downing was having a lot of success down the left, which shouldn't really come as a surprise given how he has performed previously against lower league opposition. He probably took one look at the silver haired full back he was up against and thought 'if I can't make an impact today I may as well give up'. I'm half joking, but Downing's form does often seem to depend on whether he believes he has the beating of the full back. When he starts well he usually has a good game. When he doesn't start well he ends up going missing and taking the safe option far too often.

The same criticism can usually be levelled at Henderson on the other side, he's another who plays it 'safe' too often. Unlike Downing though, this wasn't a good day for him. The game generally passed him by and he did did virtually nothing of note before he was subbed early in the second half. The only things I remember Henderson doing - or more specifically not doing - was whiffing at a great cross by Downing (Gerrard then blasted it over the bar again, which summed up his day) and twice refusing to shoot when it opened up for him. That happened seconds before Cardiff took the lead, and whilst I'm in no way blaming that goal on Henderson, it did piss me off at the time. He was in a great position to get a shot away but spurned it twice and played the ball wide. The cross came in, it came to nothing and Cardiff went up the other end scored. Of course he could have shot and it could have been blocked and they could have gone down the field and scored anyway. As I say, I'm not pinning the goal on him at all but I just felt he didn't want to take responsibility and as usual went for the 'safe' option. It's a cup final, you have to seize the moment, not pass the buck.

I didn't think he should have been starting the game, but equally I'd have been amazed if he didn't. He was always going to be picked even though Bellamy, Kuyt, Spearing and Maxi were all more deserving based on what they've done this season. I'm not writing him off or saying get rid of him, I'm saying I don't think he's shown enough to warrant a regular place in the team.

Anyway, Cardiff went in front against the run of play but it wasn't a complete shock as they've had a couple of promising situations previous that didn't come to anything. The goal highlighted the one area of concern I had going into the game; the gap between our defence and midfield. They found space far too easily, there was a huge gap between our centre midfielders and defence meaning Agger had to come out and press the man with the ball

(Miller I think). When he did that it left a gap behind him for Joe Mason to run into and roll a shot past Reina. The goal stunned one half of the stadium and delighted the other. Cardiff's fans went nuts whilst we stood there wondering what the hell was going on. The game continued in the same vein up until the break. Us on top, lots of possession, plenty of good situations but nothing at the end of it. Adam fizzed a shot inches wide and Agger headed straight at the keeper when he really should have scored.

The second half was much the same. Suarez had been very subdued in the first half but came more into it after the break. He had a shot across goal that was parried by the keeper, but Carroll had been guilty of ball watching and hadn't moved in to anticipate it. Both strikers were involved in the equaliser though, Carroll getting his head to Adam's corner and directing it towards Suarez, who's flicked header hit the inside of the post. Just as everyone was thinking 'here we go again' Martin Skrtel arrived on the scene with a deft first touch and a cool finish through a crowd of players. He did really well actually, he made it look easy but a lot of centre halves would have just swung at it and hoped for the best. He took that like a striker, and he's becoming more of a goal threat every week now.

He nearly scored again not long afterwards, forcing a save from the keeper with another well struck effort. Downing was also denied by a full length save from Heaton as the reds piled on the pressure but couldn't get the winner.

Agger was forced off late on with an injury, meaning Carragher got to play in another final. Nice reward for him, he played in most of the games to get us to Wembley, but a pity for Agger and hopefully he won't be out for too long. Cardiff weren't threatening us at all as they'd pretty much stopped even trying to get men forward and were desperately holding on. Set pieces were the only way they were going to hurt us as in open play they were unable to do anything and looked out on their feet. However, even teams that are completely under the cosh tend to get at least one good chance at some stage, and Cardiff had a glorious one that Miller put narrowly over the bar. He has to score that, and that miss was more significant than any of the penalties they failed to convert in the shoot out. We dodged a bullet there, no doubt about it.

Extra time followed the same pattern the rest of the game had. Attack v defence. The tiring Carroll was replaced by Kuyt as Kenny used his final substitution, and the Dutchman's fresh legs and energy gave us an important lift and extra attacking impetus. Carroll had not really been in the game, but he did little wrong either. He won the flick ons he needed to win, when the ball was played into his feet he laid it off to team-mates and was generally neat and tidy in his work. He won plenty of headers in his own box from Cardiff set pieces too, and I wouldn't say he had a bad game. He was pretty quiet though and it was the right thing to do taking him off. It could even have happened sooner really, Dirk was unlucky not to get more playing time I thought.

Eventually we managed to break the deadlock, as Kuyt's awful shot was cleared straight back to him and he lashed the rebound home. He took the shot so early that it caught the keeper by surprise and found the bottom corner. Dirk went mad, so did the fans behind the goal and it looked like the Cup was in the bag. Unfortunately we then sat back and got into the mindset of just protecting what we had. I don't think it was a conscious decision by anyone, it just happened. Little things start happening that you wouldn't normally see. An example of it was Johnson was under a high ball under no pressure. Had we not been up 2-1 he'd have brought that ball down every time and then carried it forward. He didn't even look, he just knocked it into the stands. I'm not singling him out, it's not like he was the reason we sat back and encouraged them to come at us. Overall I thought Johnson was outstanding actually, third only to Downing and Skrtel for me. It was symptomatic of the mindset we were in after finally getting in front though. We weren't keeping the ball anymore either. Chances to counter attack were squandered by poor decision making and suddenly Cardiff began to force set pieces and they were able to get their big men forward. We were inviting trouble and we got it. It needed a fantastic goal-line clearance from Kuyt to prevent them scoring from a right wing corner, but the warning wasn't heeded and 30 seconds later they scored from an almost identical situation. You could argue there was a foul on Kuyt as the lad appeared to haul him down before he scored, but really we brought this on ourselves.

Credit to Cardiff's players, they were completely out on their feet and had been hanging on grimly for pens. Dirk's goal should have finished them off but they dug in, found some reserves of energy and threw everything they had at us and got their reward. I didn't fancy us on pens at all. Our record in shootouts is second to none, but there are a couple of reasons I wasn't confident this time. Firstly, we've missed so many pens this season that it's a struggle picking five takers that I'd trust. Secondly, Pepe doesn't save pens any more. He won the 2006 shoot out for us, and I think he's saved just one penalty since (it may be more, I've not checked). I felt a little bit better when I saw the pens would be taken down our end, but I still feared the worst. Gerrard stepped up first and struck a decent pen, but the keeper made a hell of a save. Uh-oh, the worst possible start. As the players all stood on the halfway line, Dirk broke ranks to go and comfort his skipper.

Miller looked to have done everything right with his pen, he sent Pepe the wrong way and the ball was flying towards the corner. It was a little too close to the corner as it struck the post. Massive let off for us, and surely Adam would take advantage of it? He's one of the few I would have trusted, but he missed by a mile. Couldn't believe that. Dirk once again had words for his team-mate, the big fucking hero. The Cardiff lad buried his kick to put them 1-0 up, and Dirk simply had to score really as I don't think we could have recovered from another failure. His pen was just fucking brilliant, he's got bollocks like medicine balls has Dirk. He's missed one this season, but if I needed someone to score a penalty with my life on the line, I'd pick Kuyt over anybody.

The pressure was back on Cardiff and their next taker went the same way as Miller by hitting the woodwork. Up next, Stewart Downing. Now the biggest criticism levelled at Downing has been that he lacks the bottle to play for LFC. It's been a valid criticism I reckon as at times that has appeared to be the case. He went a long way to proving otherwise here though, firstly by having the balls to be one of the five takers, and secondly to keep his nerve and score with the pressure on him. The strange thing is when he stepped up I was convinced he'd bury it. Don't know why, but I was. I knew Whittingham would score for Cardiff too, he was the one player for them I'd have put good money on scoring. Great penalty, and it was all down to the final taker from both sides now. Who would ours be? Prior to the shoot out starting I'd have expected one of either Suarez, Bellamy or Carragher to be in the five. There was no way Suarez would have been on the fifth one though, so I knew it wouldn't be him. Bellamy probably wouldn't have been a wise choice either considering the added pressures on him due to his links to Cardiff. So I half expected to see Carra coming forward. I certainly didn't think it would be Johnson, and I'll be honest, I wasn't confident at all. Fantastic pen that though, unsaveable. Massive credit to him for that.

The pressure on Anthony Gerrard was huge now and I knew he wasn't going to score, I think everyone knew. I thought Reina would make a save though, the law of averages would suggest that he'd save one of them surely, and what better time to do it? Had it been on target he may well have got it, he went the right way and seemed to get right over to the corner of the goal, but the ball rolled wide and once again we'd pulled one out of the fire on penalties. Unbelievable.

Huge relief, not just for winning this particular game, but also for ending the six year trophyless run. It was important to stop that rot, we've seen with the title how easily six years can become ten years and ten can become fifteen and fifteen can become twenty etc. We've got that monkey off our back now and there is definitely shades of 2001 about what is happening now. The main difference is we have no UEFA Cup to go for this time, but we could still win both domestic cups and then clinch a Champions League place on the final day as we did back then.

It's easy to just focus on this one particular game and be critical of how we struggled to overcome a side a division below us, but it's important not to forget how we got here in the first place. On the road in every round, wins at places like Stoke, Chelsea and Manchester City.... this was a fine achievement regardless of how we won it in the end. It's also important not to overlook the part played by some players who didn't get on the field against Cardiff. I'm thinking about Maxi and Martin Kelly who both scored at Chelsea, Jay Spearing who was superb in numerous games prior to the final, Sebastian Coates who also impressed at Stamford Bridge, and of course Lucas who was struck down with a season ending injury whilst helping us beat Chelsea (a game in which he was fucking awesome). Hopefully everyone who appeared in the earlier rounds of the competition will be rewarded with a medal, including Raul Meireles for his late cameo at Exeter. I'd like to see him get one but only on the condition he is made to wear it to training just so Fernando 'I've got more chance of winning medals at Chelsea' Torres has to look at it every day. As for us, we're back on the trophy trail and we're two games away from another final. If we get there, hold onto your seats as it will surely be another wild ride. After all, it's what we do.

Premier League Round Up (25-26 February 2012)

Whilst we were lording it up at Wembley and bringing home yet more silverware for our already bulging trophy cabinet, those less fortunate than ourselves - I like to call them 'peasants' - had to get on with the weekly grind of mundane, boring old Premier League games.

No walking down Wembley way for them. No dramatic penalty shoot outs, no weekend long partying in the Big Smoke, no victory celebrations and no trophies. Just routine league games for all the peasants. All except poor old Everton. Have to feel for our neighbours, this weekend was supposed to be their cup final but it had to be postponed because we were in an actual, real one. The cancelled derby fixture meant Moyes & co had the weekend off but at least Kenwright put his time to good use, securing a return to his former role in Coronation Street. I don't think it's possible to add anything to make that sentence any funnier than it already is, so I'm not even going to try.

Anyway, with the exception of the two Merseyside clubs, it was a full fixture list this weekend. The most intriguing game of the day was up on Tyneside where Newcastle were taking on a Wolves side being managed for the first time by Terry Connor. Having been reportedly turned down by a whole host of people Steve Morgan eventually had to give the job to Mick McCarthy's loyal number two, but no-one seemed particularly happy about it, except Connor and possibly the players who seem to like him. That might count for a lot over the coming weeks. I'll be honest, I didn't even know his name until this weekend. Obviously I knew him as 'TC' as like all good number two's he has his initials on his coat and he was always on the telly as he never seemed to leave McCarthy's side. He's still wearing the coat but presumably he'll trade that in for a smart suit once he gets his feet under the table. He should call Pardew's tailor, the Newcastle boss is always immaculately turned out. You can't pull birds if you're a scruff I guess.

This was a difficult first game for Connor. He knew he'd got the job by default and he probably knows everyone is expecting him to fail. A trip to Newcastle isn't the easiest start in the world as their front two are a handful for anybody. Interesting then that the first thing he did was drop Roger Johnson. Even looking at them from afar I'm sure I've mentioned how poor Johnson has been this season, but McCarthy probably felt he had to stick with him as he paid a lot of money for him. Connor didn't have that dilemma and wasted no time in binning his captain, although he may have been regretting it when they quickly went 2-0 down after goals by Cisse and Gutierrez. Whatever Connor said at half time worked a treat as Wolves came storming back into it after the break. Jarvis pulled one back with a deflected shot and Doyle scored a scrappy equaliser and this was a good point for them. Not bad for us either, I had Newcastle down as a certain three points so we've kind of made up two points on them this weekend. Connor came across well in his interview afterwards, he seems like a good guy and I'm rooting for him. Not as much as I'm rooting for Steve Kean, obviously, but I wish him well.

Speaking of Kean, his team got dicked at Man City, which is great as obviously it hurts Man United. Balotelli opened the scoring and then revealed a t-shirt with a message telling his girlfriend he loves her. To quote Phil Leotardo from the Soprano's, *"My estimation of him as a man..... just fucking plummeted"*. Aguero made it 2-0 and substitute Dzeko wrapped it up with a header from a typically pinpoint Kolorov cross. Blackburn had less than 500 fans in the stadium, which is understandable given how far they had to travel. Oh... Fuckin' part timers, they don't deserve Steve Kean. Actually they probably do, but he certainly doesn't deserve them.

Sunderland got absolutely murdered at West Brom. Didn't see that coming at all, West Brom are shite at home and Sunderland have been flying lately. It finished 4-0 but it could have been double figures as the Mackems were beaten like a red headed step son. Odemwingie's recent good form continued with a hat-trick and after an iffy start Hodgson's side have had some great results of late. I don't think Paul Scharner has been playing much lately, maybe that explains it.

Meanwhile, crisis club Chelsea were in dire need of a win and couldn't have wished for a better opponent than Bolton. Motson was commentating, and I reckon the twat only bothers working these days if he's allowed to do his beloved Chelsea. I haven't noticed him for weeks, it's been great. Then here he is, not only back on MOTD but doing a Chelsea game. He's bad enough whoever he's covering, but he cranks the cunt factor up several notches when he's doing Chelsea. 90% of the games he does these days seem to involve them. As if I needed any more reason to hate the fucker. He doesn't even try to hide his bias. Chelsea attack and he can barely contain his hysteria. Opposition attack and he sounds like he's announcing somebody's death. *"The owner is here today, what does that tell us?"* Er, it tells us fuck all as he's at quite a lot of games you overly dramatic sensationalist twat. Chelsea won at a canter, Bolton are so bad they couldn't even score against a back four that had David Luiz in it. The Brazilian actually scored a cracker to put Chelsea in front, but then he can do that as he's a superb footballer, he just can't defend. Drogba and Lampard wrapped up a comfortable and much needed win for AVB, although there was no demented seal clapping routine from Abramovich as the goals went in, which doesn't bode well for the young manager who may have to take his shine box somewhere else if they can't overturn Napoli's 1st leg advantage.

Not a good day for Torres again. Left on the bench, he came on and once again did nothing. He was singled out by Shearer on MOTD too, who compared his work rate and desire unfavourably with Mario Balotelli. An inferior work rate to Balotelli? Even I'd be insulted by that. It's up there with having worse facial hair than Gary Neville or being a worse husband and brother than Ryan Giggs. How much further can Torres fall? A lot, hopefully.

Fulham went to QPR in what seemed to be a bit of a grudge match. The two managers apparently don't get on and this was a bit of a niggly game at times. Fulham were the more accomplished side and went in front with a brilliant goal by Pogrebnyak who collected a superb back heel from Dembele and went round the keeper without actually touching the ball. Just shimmied a couple of times and the keeper bought it, leaving him with a tap in. Two cracking goals in his first two games for the Russian, and Fulham have some decent attacking talent despite selling Zamora a few weeks back.

QPR lacked discipline and were reduced to ten men when Diakite saw red for two bookable offences. The first was a lunge on my boy 'Bryan'. The Mali international just kept fouling people all the time and was eventually dismissed just past the half hour mark after another lunge at Ruiz. Nasty stuff, a clear case of hair envy which although understandable is certainly not excusable. Is it just me or do QPR end up playing with ten men every week? I'd like to see 'Useless' take them down, the smug twat. He took exception to Jol trying to pat him on the head afterwards as they shook hands. He said he thought Jol was trying to patronise him, Jol politely told BBC that the QPR boss is a 'winner' but also said he thinks maybe Hughes doesn't like him. How can anyone not like Martin Jol? It takes a special type of twat to not like Martin Jol, and Mark Hughes unquestionably fits that bill. He probably hates Santa Claus too, the miserable, dour bastard. Hughes was a fucking lowlife as a player and he's still a lowlife now. The difference is, he was a great player but he is far from being a great manager. So listen 'Sparky', next time Martin Jol wants to pat you on the head, be a good little boy and let him do it. Knob.

Wigan played host to Aston Villa, for whom Robbie Keane was playing his last game before returning to LA Galaxy. It was a dreadful game, the most notable thing to happen was Bent picked up a serious injury and could be out for the season. That's seriously bad news for Villa, especially with Keane no longer there. It was an innocuous looking incident too.

There was no contact at all but Bent tried to jump out of the way and landed awkwardly. Typical Darren Bent, even his injuries are scruffy efforts. The offender was Alcaraz, and the incident summed him up too, trying to kick the player and missing by a mile. He can't even do that right, the shit bastard. Interesting fact. Villa have one less point at this stage of the season than Birmingham had last year when McLeish took them down. Villa fans are worried, they needn't be. They've still got big Emile. LOLZ!

Onto Sunday's games, and Norwich embarrassed themselves against the Mancs by giving up goals to two pensioners. Come on Norwich, it's the Premier League not the fucking Masters. Shocking stuff, if this is how they deal with old timers we should wheel out Gary Mac and John Barnes when we go to Carrow Road. By the way, remember what I said last time about Norwich sending out a player every week I've never seen before? They did it again. Ladies and Gentlemen, I give you 'Wilbraham'. Don't know his first name, but he's the latest off that nomark conveyor belt they have in Norfolk.

Stoke had lost four in a row but got back to winning ways against Swansea. May have been different had Scott Sinclair not wasted a great early chance when he put the ball so high over the bar it cleared the stadium. Stoke took the lead from a set piece. I know, I was shocked too. Even more shocking, Crouch added a second from a long throw. Love Crouch, hate Stoke. Pulis said afterwards *"We work very hard on set pieces and on closing down."* No shit. In other revelations, Barcelona work on short passing and keeping the ball, Gareth Bale works very hard on diving and QPR don't spend much time working on how to tackle cleanly.

The biggest game of the day, well the biggest game that didn't have a trophy at the end of it obviously, was at the Emirates. Arsenal went into it on a really low ebb after two bad defeats in Europe and the FA Cup, whilst Spurs were in good form and were still harbouring faint title hopes. Therefore it was no surprise to see Redknapp's side flying out of the traps. Saha found a huge gap through the middle of the Arsenal defence and his awful shot deflected over the head of Szczesny. Bad luck for Arsenal but that's what happens when you're struggling. The Gunners came back well and they were all over Spurs but Gareth Bale's latest dive fooled Mike Dein and Adebayor scored from the spot. What happened after that was crazy. Arsenal just leathered Spurs everywhere. Sagna pulled one back and then a brilliant goal by Van Persie got them level before half time. What a player he is. Spurs fell apart after that, they were all over the place at the back and Rosicky's first goal in a year put Wenger's side in front early in the second half. Walcott then took advantage of great play by Van Persie to make it 4-2 and later put the icing on the cake with another tidy finish to complete the rout.

Scott Parker saw red late on with a stupid foul that earned him his second yellow and means he's suspended for their next game, which is against the Mancs. 5-2 down, only a minute or two left, that's just fucking reckless and irresponsible. Still, if you want to be England captain you need to be a scumbag and this probably sealed the deal for 'Saint Scotty'. That and the fact he's a war hero who flew a Spitfire in the Battle of Britain. As for Arsenal, I guess their fans will go back to 'In Arsene We Trust' again now. Until their next defeat anyway.

chapter eleven

March

LIVERPOOL 1 ARSENAL 2

Competition - Premier League
Date - Sat 3 Mar 2012
Venue - Anfield
Scorer(s) – Laurent Koscielny O.G.
Half Time - 1-1
Star Man – Luis Suarez

Team: Reina; Kelly, Carragher, Skrtel, Enrique; Henderson, Spearing (Carroll), Adam, Downing (Bellamy): Suarez, Kuyt:

From the ecstasy of winning a cup at Wembley to the agony of a stoppage time defeat six days later. That's the rollercoaster ride we sign up for as football fans I guess. Losing a big game right at the end is always hard to stomach, but it's ten times worse when it's a game where you have played well enough to win comfortably. In some ways it's better to see your team get battered, at least you can let off steam by slaughtering them. When you play this well and lose it's difficult to know what to feel. I was just stunned after this one.

It's not unreasonable to say we haven't got what we deserved from the vast majority of home games this season, but this one really took the piss. If it wasn't so heartbreaking it would be funny. Considering how well we played I'd have been gutted with a draw, so to come away with nothing was absolutely sickening. I feel sorry for the players but then at the same time I think they only have themselves to blame. Yet again. This hard luck story actually started on the opening day against Sunderland and eight months later the same shit is still happening. Missed chances. Check. Hit woodwork (often more than once). Check. Fail to convert penalty. Check. Opposition keeper plays blinder. Check. Concede goal from rare attack. Check. It's happened so many times, particularly at Anfield, but this was the most glaring example yet. Bad luck played a part, unquestionably, but when it's happening so frequently there comes a point where you have to stop blaming luck, and we passed that point months ago. The harsh truth is that we're just extremely wasteful. Even games we win often tend to be much closer then they should be (last week at Wembley being a case in point).

Realistically, we should have been three or four goals better than Arsenal given how superior we were. To say we let them off the hook just doesn't do it justice. Some would say we were robbed, but is it robbery when we effectively opened the door, invited them in for a cup of tea whilst handing them the keys to the safe before finally giving them a hand packing their car with our swag? Arsenal won't have been able to believe their luck.

We played excellent football and completely dominated this game. There are times when you take consolation or encouragement in that, but I don't think this is one of those times. On reflection, how we played counts for absolutely nothing. This was a six pointer and a game we badly needed to win to stay in contention for a top four spot. That's all but gone now. Ten points behind the worst Arsenal side I've seen in years, we need to be more concerned about the likes of Norwich and West fucking Brom behind us. That's the shocking reality we are facing now. It shouldn't be that way, we should be much higher in the table based on performances. I wouldn't say we're in a false position as we are where we are, but I would say we're better than anyone outside of the top three. It's all 'coulda woulda shoulda' though isn't it? Bottom line, we've not put the points on the board to prove it. That's mainly down to how terrible we are in front of goal. Off the top of my head I can only think of four games in which we've been second best. Spurs away, Bolton away and away at both manc teams. We didn't deserve to beat Stoke or Swansea at home but aside from that we've been the better side in virtually every game we've played.

Far too often however we don't make that superiority count, and this might be the most glaring example of it yet. Chance after chance went begging, and maybe it was just me but even in the first half I got the feeling it was going to be 'one of those days'. I didn't think we'd get kicked in the nuts late on like that, but I'd more or less resigned myself to yet another home draw. Martin Kelly's missed sitter in front of the Kop was the moment I completely gave up any hope of three points, but that vibe was definitely in the air when we hit the woodwork twice and missed a penalty in a dominant first half. It's unfortunate to hit the post two more times (how many is it now this season?), but at the time I felt Suarez should have scored and it was a bad miss. Having seen the replay it wasn't as easy as I initially thought as there were two defenders back there meaning there wasn't much of a gap between them and the post. Kuyt's was really unlucky though, he did everything right and on another day that finds the corner. Maybe we used up all our luck last weekend when Kenny Miller missed that great chance at the end, or when Cardiff missed three penalties. Speaking of missed penalties, just how many are we going to miss this season? Are we on for some sort of record now? If we can't even rely on Kuyt to score from the spot then we're fucked. He's missed two now, so have Suarez and Adam, Carroll has missed one and so has Gerrard (actually he may have missed two, I'm not sure). This was a very un-Dirk like penalty, and to make it worse he also failed to convert the rebound. We'd been well on top and a goal then would have been just rewards for how we'd started. It looked a stonewall pen to me at the time although replays show Suarez played for it. Still a penalty though.

Suarez was fantastic at times in the first half, he just seemed to be megging defenders at will. The move that led to the penalty was class, it was superb play between Suarez and Kuyt and was reminiscent of how well the pair linked up last season. Reminded me of the Man United game actually when they ran riot. Kuyt's not had too many chances to play up front with Suarez this season but the understanding they had is clearly still there.

The missed pen was a real downer but thankfully we didn't have time to dwell on it as we scored not long after. It was a sweeping move that began when Spearing's clever pass picked out Downing in space in the centre. He played a first time ball out to Henderson who charged down the right wing and drilled in a low cross towards Suarez that Koscielny diverted into his own net. Just rewards for our play, but a little disconcerting that once again we needed an opponent to put the ball in the net for us. 'Own goal' might even be our top scorer this season now? Definitely up there, that's for sure. It was almost 2-0 a couple of minutes later. Another fine move saw Adam surge away down the left leaving Arteta in his wake. He carried the ball to the edge of the box and picked out Kuyt in the centre who immediately shifted it on to Henderson. His shot was parried well by Szczesny but only into the path of Suarez who sidefooted it against the post. Not the sitter I initially thought it was, but a chance you really have to take in games against the better sides.

I hesitate to call Arsenal one of the better sides as honestly I'm not impressed by them at all. They do somehow sit fourth in the table though, which is kind of my point. You can explain why they are where they are in three words. Robin. Van. Persie. Without him I don't even think they'd even be in the top half. No team relies on one man as much as the Gunners rely on him, they've got nothing without him. He's carried them all season and he basically won this game on his own, yet again. He drew Arsenal level when he headed in Sagna's fine cross. It's galling seeing the opposition score such a simple looking goal when we have to work so hard for anything we get. Carragher was actually marking Van Persie quite tightly but he couldn't get goal-side of him to prevent the header. I thought Reina could have come for the cross but ended up rooted to his line doing nothing. For every ten chances we create we might get a goal if we're lucky. I'm fairly certain that opposing sides must have a ridiculous goals per chance ratio against us. Arsenal scored twice from four chances in this game. Cardiff did similar last week. Does my fucking head in.

You know what else does my head in? Players staying down to stop the game and waste time. Arsenal really pushed the boundaries of this, especially in the first half. It was like watching Porto a few years ago. Several times their players stayed down to stop our attacks and take the sting out of the game when it was clear to everyone that there was fuck all wrong with them. Rosicky was the worst, he went down after a great challenge by Spearing and was about to get up when he saw us on the attack, so he sat down again forcing us to put the ball out. Arteta did it too, as did Sagna and Vermailen. Actually hang on, an Arsenal player has just hit the floor again now so I'll have to put the report on hold whilst he gets treatment......

two minutes later

So.... we bounced back well from their goal and Suarez almost conjured up a goal of the season contender when he wriggled his way past several defenders and prodded a shot goalwards only for Szczesny to dive full length and palm it behind for a corner. Skrtel then put a free header over the bar from the corner kick. We looked pretty threatening from corners at times but were unable to convert any of them. Carroll may have helped in that area but given how well Kuyt linked up with Suarez I can't really complain about that selection.

I have to admit that when I heard the line up it killed my pre-match buzz completely. I didn't like it at all, but to be fair the likes of Kuyt and Henderson justified their selections. Henderson needed a bounce back game after his no-show at Wembley and he was much improved, I have no complaints about his performance. He was much more effective than he has been in most of his other appearances on the right. Kuyt was arguably our best player (penalty miss aside) and Spearing had a tidy game in the middle of the park too. Whether he'd have started had Gerrard been available who knows, he probably should do though and I hope he keeps his place now as we look more balanced in the middle when he plays.

As for Gerrard, I'm seething about that situation. Blame Pearce and England all you like, but Gerrard needs to take a long look at himself over this too. Pearce is a selfish twat for selecting him to start a meaningless friendly three days after he'd played for TWO FUCKING HOURS in a physically and emotionally draining cup final on a strength sapping pitch, but what was stopping Gerrard from pulling out? It was totally irresponsible for him to play in that game as far as I'm concerned. Given how long he's been out injured, how he's picked up a few little niggles since he's been back and how he has been unable to play three games in a week (last time he did it he had to be rested away at Wolves), just what the fuck is he doing agreeing to start a game for England coming off the back of a cup final that went to extra time, and knowing we had such a massively important game against Arsenal three days later? Seriously Steven, have a fucking word with yourself as that's not on. Even if it had been a qualifier I'd have been upset about it, but a fucking friendly under a caretaker manager? Like I say, irresponsible. I love the guy, but this was a game that we really needed him.

Anyway, moving on.... We had another great chance to regain the lead when Adam did very well to get to the byline and drill a great ball across to a sliding Kuyt who's shot rolled across goal. It seemed to be headed for the net until it struck the far post and was hacked to safety. I was up celebrating that one, couldn't believe it didn't go in. I think that's when that sinking feeling really started to kick in for me. Sometimes you just know it's not going to go your way, you still have some hope that you're wrong as there's plenty of time left, but with each missed chance after that the feeling grows. The moment that finally convinced me we weren't winning this game was when Kelly missed an absolute sitter after a great cross from Kuyt. Chances like that usually come back to haunt you, and it did. You have to score that, I don't care if you're a striker, a defender, a goalkeeper or a fucking fan, four yards out with an empty net, you have to score.

There were other chances we should have made more of too, the best of which fell to Downing who got in behind Sagna and just needed to roll it square to Suarez for a tap in. He put it too close to the keeper and the chance was gone. Really sloppy that was, but it's typical of this team in the final third. Things like that have plagued us this season, it's not just the missed chances, it's the failure to make the most of great situations through a bad final pass or just awful decision making. The problem Kenny had was that we were playing really well and were so much on top that it must have been tempting to just leave things as they were and hope the goal would eventually come. You want to get Bellamy on, and maybe Carroll too, but who do you take off? Downing was the first to make way, a little unfortunate for him as he did alright without ever really giving Sagna too many problems. I'd have probably took Adam off and moved Henderson inside, as Adam didn't wasn't having a good second half (thought he did well in the first half though).

Bellamy coming on didn't really improve us, perhaps not surprising given how late he came on and how little time he had to make an impact. He never really got into the game and we actually looked better when Downing was out there. Kuyt continued to look lively and had one fantastic run into the box but his cut back didn't find a red shirt and Arsenal cleared. Just really frustrating, and the game looked to be petering out into our ninth home draw of the season. The board went up to signal eight minutes stoppage time (Arteta was stretchered off after a long delay), but we were never going to score now regardless of how long was added on. Arsenal never looked likely to either, they'd only had one chance in the entire half (when Gibbs got in behind a sleeping Kelly and Walcott forced Reina to save with his feet). Out of nothing though Song lofted a ball over Carragher and Van Persie drilled a volley past Reina's near post. Again, both centre back and keeper maybe could have done better, and Kelly isn't blameless either as RVP had pulled onto him before running in behind Carragher, but against the vast majority of other strikers we'd have gotten away with it. Look at last week, a similar thing happened where Miller got in behind one of our defenders (Skrtel I think?) but put his shot over the bar so no harm done. Van Persie isn't Kenny Miller though, and he made us pay. Carragher and Skrtel kept him very quiet on the whole yet he's still come away with two goals. He's just everything we aren't, he's a lethal cold blooded ruthless killer in front of goal. He's almost scored as many goals on his own as our whole fucking team has.

This result is really hard to take, especially when you look at the league table. We're only four points ahead of Roy Hodgson now. That's not good enough, obviously, and our results in the league have been really disappointing. Maybe I'm kidding myself, but for me we're miles better than the league table suggests. I don't think there's too much wrong with us, it needs tweaking a little rather than overhauling. Performances are usually pretty good, but we aren't scoring enough goals and it's killing us. It's been killing us all season and it's still killing us now. I don't know what the answer is, certainly a lethal striker would help but it isn't just down to the forwards is it? Kelly missed an absolute fucking sitter in this game, I don't care if he is a defender that's a chance you have to bury. Other players have been just as guilty in previous games, so it's not just the frontmen. Henderson and Downing have one league goal between them this season whilst Spearing and Lucas don't have any. You have to wonder where the goals are going to come from? Performances suggest we're not far away, it's rare that anyone outplays us but if you can't score you're going to find it very difficult to win consistently.

Given our impotency in front of goal, it's virtually impossible to see us getting 4th place now. I have no doubt Arsenal will continue to drop points, and I knew Chelsea would lose at West Brom this weekend as they've got big problems. Newcastle will drop points as well, but it won't matter because we won't score enough goals to be able to make a run. It's incredibly frustrating as Arsenal and Chelsea haven't been this vulnerable in years, yet we haven't taken advantage. We just have to hope we can score enough goals in the FA Cup to hopefully win a second trophy. If we were to do that, missing out on the top four wouldn't feel half as bad. The league table doesn't paint a pretty picture and our home record is shocking. The eye test tells a different story for me though. I'm frustrated at the results, but not overly disheartened by the performances and overall I still think we're heading in the right direction (just not as quickly as we should be). Put it this way, if Robin Van Persie and his 25 league goals were in this Liverpool side, where about in the table do you think we'd be? We wouldn't be looking up at Chelsea, Arsenal and Newcastle that's for sure. That's the challenge facing Dalglish and Comolli this summer, they need to find us a 'Van Persie', someone who doesn't need ten chances before he can score a goal. Easier said than done of course, as every club out there is looking for goalscorers and barring an amazing turn of events it doesn't look like we'll be able to tempt anyone with Champions League Football.

Premier League Round Up (3-4 March 2012)

Another defeat for crisis club Chelsea proved to be the final straw for Roman Abramovich, who reluctantly told AVB to pack up his shinebox and get out of town. Chelsea probably should have won the game at the Hawthorns, they had enough chances to do it comfortably.

Sturridge had a rare off day in front of goal and Lampard missed a sitter at the end. Not that he'll be arsed, if he'd scored that maybe the manager he's been undermining all season would have survived another week. Abramovich paid £13m to get Villas Boas nine months ago and now he has to pay him a further £9m as a golden handshake. That's on top of the money he had to pay Ancelotti and the £75m he spunked on Torres and Luiz a year ago. Somehow the expression 'more money than sense' doesn't quite seem damning enough for this helmet does it? He's such a gormless looking bastard he'd have more money than sense if he only had ten bob to his name. For someone like him to end up with THAT much money boggles the mind. How does someone that intellectually challenged end up with so much dough? Russia must be one fucked up country. At least over here the only way stupid people become rich is by winning the lottery or marrying the Queen.

Villas Boas had been compared by some (ok, by 'some' I mean 'me') to a young Roy Hodgson, especially in the hair department, and in a cruel twist of fate it was Roy Hodgson who put the final nail in his coffin. I don't think anyone was surprised that Chelsea lost at West Brom and Abramovich would argue that in itself is enough justification for getting rid. Another way of looking at it is if you spend so much to get the fella and you're convinced he's your guy, then you have to let him do it his way even if it means getting rid of any dissenting senior players. Not that I give a shit as to the rights and wrongs of it, I just enjoy seeing them in disarray. Apparently AVB had been working so hard that he's even been sleeping at the training ground recently. That could just as easily have been to stop Mongo and Cashley shitting in his draw and writing 'virgin' with tipex on his stapler and hole punch. To those who've been there a long time, he was still the office junior who used to hand out the DVD's when Mourinho was there.

I've joked about it, but it's actually true, it's been obvious for months. This was in one of the papers the day after he got the bullet:

"In the dressing-room the players grew tired of his timekeeping, fed up of him monitoring their arrival some days from the balcony of his first-floor office. Some started a game among themselves, flying into the car park as the seconds counted down to the scheduled arrival time. They would jump out of their cars with moments to spare, winding up the manager by acknowledging him with a sarcastic wave as they headed in to change."

Horrible, spoilt, arrogant wankers. You don't need to be Einstein to work out who the culprits are either. Put it this way, I can't see the likes of Meireles, Luiz, Torres, Mata, Ramires etc carrying on like that. Terry, Lampard and Cole would be near the top of any list of suspects, probably Sturridge too as he seems like a bit of a dickhead as well. Admittedly, I'm basing that solely on his goal celebrations, but as I've said before they reveal a lot about a man's character. Based on celebrations alone, I can say with a 97% degree of certainty that Sturridge would be the type to pull that kind of stunt in the car park.

It's actually become the impossible job, and the only reason I can see for taking it now is to make a quick buck. Go in there, make some money, fall foul of the dressing room mafia, get the push and enjoy the payoff. Swansea boss Brendan Rodgers was asked if he'd be interested and said: *"I'm trying to build my career, not destroy it"*. He used to be on the staff at Chelsea, so that quote is pretty damning. AVB hasn't destroyed his career though, he was only there five minutes and his success at Porto is still fresh enough in people's memories for him not to have been tainted too much by the stench of John Terry & co. So I don't feel sorry for him, in fact I'd swap places with him in a heartbeat. I'm fairly certain I could have done an equally underwhelming job at Chelsea and alienated Terry & chums, but could he have written about it as humorously as me? Doubt it. I've got better hair too, although I concede his ability to grow facial hair pisses all over mine (I get large bald spots, much to my chagrin) and he's a snappier dresser. Then again, if you give me a £9m golden handshake I daresay I'd be able to give Pep Guardiola a run for his money in the style department. In my defence it's not so easy to look dapper when you shop in Primark and Asda.

The money Villas Boas got for nine months work was pretty obscene, but then you can argue that any fundamentally decent person that has to go into work every day and deal with some of the vermin at that club deserves to be well compensated. His reputation won't have been harmed too much, he's financially set for life and he'll go and find another job where he doesn't have to deal with pondlife like Terry, Cole, Lampard etc as well as a remedial owner who thinks he knows more than the manager. Chances are wherever AVB ends up next he won't have a £50m striker go 22 games without a goal either. And just what the hell is going on with Fernando's barnet these days? He starting to look like that rough old bird Phil Mitchell is knocking off in Eastenders. Shirley is it? Chelsea could do worse than sound out Phil about a swap deal, Torres is more feminine looking than his bird and could she really do worse than 22 games without scoring even once? *"Bonnet de douche, everyone's a winner"*.

I'm glad AVB has gone, as in recent weeks I've been struggling to maintain the dislike I'd developed for him early in the season when he was being an obnoxious arse in his post game interviews and telling us all how proud we should be to have John Terry captaining our country. Usually when results go south, managers tend to become more arsey and lash out at anyone and everyone as the pressure mounts. I didn't see that with Villas Boas, he handled himself with a dignity I didn't see coming. The way he fielded the questions after this game was admirable I thought. He actually seems like a decent guy, and for that reason alone I'm glad he's no longer associated with that club. Much like his predecessor, he's just not enough of a cunt to fit in at Stamford Bridge. It's a pity Roberto Mancini is at City as he's a perfect fit for Chelsea.

On a separate note, David Luiz is great. He might be the most entertaining player in the league right now, it's side splittingly funny watching him try to defend. Remember how we took the piss when Mourinho would send Robert Huth up front? That's how I feel when I see Luiz line up at centre half. I can't wait to see what stunts he pulls next. My favourite one is when he turns his back and jumps in the air when he thinks someone is going to shoot, only for them to just stroll past him. I see Motson was commentating on them again. It really does seem like this weapon doesn't cover any other team these days doesn't it? Fitting really, everything else about Chelsea screams out 'OBNOXIOUS CUNT!!' so why not the commentator? Once again he got over-excited at every Chelsea chance and was generally underwhelmed when chances came at the other end. Scumbag.

Moving on, and Manchester City had an easy looking home game against Bolton. It was routine without being particularly impressive as they ran out 2-0 winners. Balotelli was apparently seen in a lap dancing bar in Liverpool the night before this game. Didn't seem to have any adverse affect as he scored and looked lively throughout. Maybe we can ask him to take Suarez and Carroll with him next time? Roberto Martinez came up against his former club as Wigan entertained Swansea at the DW Stadium. Funny how things turn out really, few would have blamed Martinez for swapping South Wales for Lancashire at the time. He had an emotional attachment to Wigan but not only that, they appeared to be a club with better prospects. He's generally perceived to have done a decent job there under the circumstances, and yet they went into this game ten points behind the Swans. Shows what an amazing rise it's been for Swansea, as their prospects look a shitload better than Wigan's. This was a decent game with chances at both ends. Sigurdsson's fine curling effort on the stroke of half time gave Swansea the lead and he then doubled their lead with a 25 yard free-kick. Dyer was harshly red carded for a nothing tackle on Gomes, you see far worse challenges than that in every game (not least the North East derby which I'll get to in due course).

Struggling Villa went to Ewood Park to face Blackburn minus Bent and Keane. They did have Agbonlahor back and he was supported by Albrighton and N'Zogbia, and the French winger put them in front early on with a good finish. That's not actually that bad a front three if they are all on form. The half time whistle was greeted by boos from the home fans but Steve Kean's men responded well in the second half and eventually equalised through Dunn with five minutes left. Kean gave himself a pat on the back afterwards, pointing out that there were harsh words said by him in the dressing room at half time, and that his substitutions made a big difference too. He's what's known as an 'irrational confidence guy'. He really believes he's the fucking man. *"I'm Steve Fucking Keane dammit"*.

Everton overcame their 'cup final disappointment' from the week before by getting a draw at QPR. Drenthe gave them the lead with a typically fierce long range drive. He turned from hero to villain by conceding the free-kick that led to Zamora's equaliser. Taraabt hit the post and Buzaki missed an open goal as QPR blew a great chance to pick up three points. There was a squirrel on the pitch. It made more of an impact on the game than the other rodent involved, Tony Hibbert.

Norwich wore their away kit again and predictably lost to Stoke. I've said it before, it's bad mojo wearing your away kit when you don't need to and Norwich deserve all they get for not heeding this lesson. Etherington won it for Stoke with 20 minutes to go. I see Huth has got a Scott Parker 1940's throwback snide part going on these days. They were once team-mates at Chelsea, yet fought on opposite sides in World War 2. Small world eh?

Onto Sunday, and just as Mancini said they would, Manchester United went to Spurs and won. I don't see why people made such a big deal of the City manager's comments. It's not mind games, it's science. Tottenham don't beat Manchester United, everyone knows that. Why? Because they are Spurs, that's why. This game was ridiculous, Spurs were by far the better side and had plenty of chances. Yet they lost 3-1. Typical Tottenham. Typical United. The Mancs continue to defy logic by racking up all these wins. Just look at the team on paper, it's the weakest they've had in years but they keep winning, the despicable bastards. My arl fella always says that the Mancs are at their most dangerous the minute before half time and the minute before full time. It's true, the amount of goals they get during those periods is sickening. Spurs dominated the first half, had a goal harshly disallowed, missed other chances and then BANG, seconds before half time Shrek heads in from a corner. No surprise to see him fit and well after missing the England game in midweek. Slag him off all you like, but he knew his club had an important game this weekend so he put that first. Pity certain others didn't do likewise. *cough* Gerrard *cough*

Poor old Terry Connor came back down to earth with a bump as Wolves got thumped 5-0 at Fulham. Pogrebnyak is fucking awesome, he's just a beast. He scores goals with both feet and his head, his touch is superb and I have to ask, why the fuck did we not get him in on loan? Look at the technique he's shown on all of his goals, he looks a natural goalscorer and Fulham have been rewarded for taking a chance on him. They've got some really good attacking players in him, Dembele, Dempsey and Ruiz. Even Andy Johnson looks to be playing well now and Fulham are a real handful at the moment. Staying with the Cottagers, he may not have been playing in this game but I was horrified to see in the midweek international between Wales and Costa Rica that my boy 'Bryan' has cut his hair. Players have been handed eight game bans for lesser crimes than that. Shocking behaviour.

Last but not least for this week, the North East derby was a predictably tasty affair. Newcastle had caused a bit of a stir on Saturday morning by calling a press conference with the promise of big news. Turns out it was just Tim Krul and Coloccini signing new contracts. You're calling a press conference for that? Really?? What a letdown. Still, it's a step in the right direction for them, at least it wasn't on the St James' Park pitch with Jim White 'whoopin and holerin' to a crowd of thousands this time. They're basically Everton in black and white stripes.

Lee Cattermole is a headcase. Booked after 40 seconds for clattering Tiote, he set the tone for a mad opening to the game. Tiote was lucky to not get booked for taking his revenge just after (amongst a series of other fouls), and then McLean sparked a bout of hand bags by going through Simpson. Ba went in the book just after for hacking down Gardner, and then Williamson was booked for shirt pulling in the box. That resulted in a pen which Bendtner buried to put the Mackems 1-0 up. Ba then smacked a header against the crossbar and McLean missed a great chance for Sunderland.

Someone was always going to get sent off, but you'd have got good odds on it being Sessegnon. He can have no complaints, he threw his arm backwards into the face of Tiote, but the over-reaction from the Newcastle man was cringeworthy. That incident changed the game as it was all Newcastle after that. Fraizer Campbell's daft challenge on Ba resulted in a penalty. Campbell might be the most unlikely England call up in history, I mean it's not as though the other fifty or so English strikers who are all better than him were unavailable is it? Did Pearce have money on it? That's the only explanation that makes any sense. Anyway, Ba's pen was saved but Ameobi eventually levelled in stoppage time and Cattermole was sent off after the final whistle for giving Mike Dean grief as they left the field. Pardew got in O'Neill's grid after the goal, and his post match interview made my skin crawl, as he spoke of how 'angry' he was at all the tackles that had been flying in (and he gritted his teeth together as he said it just to show that he was, y'know, ANGRY!!). Hey, faint hearts aren't going to storm the castle and capture the princess, know what I mean, Alan?

SUNDERLAND 1 LIVERPOOL 0

Competition - Premier League
Date - Sat 10 Mar 2012
Venue - Stadium of Light
Scorer(s) –
Half Time - 0-0
Star Man – Jay Spearing

Team: Reina; Kelly, Skrtel, Coates, Enrique; Henderson (Downing), Spearing, Adam (Gerrard), Bellamy (Carroll); Kuyt, Suarez:

If you can't win when you play well, what chance do you have when you perform as woefully as this? Last week's defeat to Arsenal was hard to take, this was just hard to watch. It was dire, utterly demoralising stuff. It may be even worse than the shameful display at Bolton, as at least we created the occasional chance in that game.

This was just soul destroying, we were wasteful in possession and clueless in the final third. I don't remember their keeper even making a save in the 90 minutes. We deserved to get beat although Sunderland didn't deserve to win, if that makes sense? They were almost as bad as us and not even a draw would have been a fair result as for me both teams deserved to lose. It wasn't a game for the neutrals that's for sure.

One of the supposed benefits of not being in Europe is that you can play a settled team as you're only playing once a week and players don't need to be rested as much. It hasn't worked out like that though has it? We're no nearer to knowing our best side now than we were back in August. Our team is anything but settled and there appears to be no pattern to team selection from week to week. Players are selected when they are playing badly (Carroll, Henderson, Adam, Downing etc), and often find themselves left out after a good game (Bellamy, Downing, Carroll). A few weeks ago I thought we were onto something and were ready to make a run at 4th. It hasn't happened, we've had no consistency in selection and we've gotten ourselves into a position where we now have to be more concerned about Everton, Sunderland, West Brom and Norwich than we are about reeling in those above us. In 2012 we've won once, drawn twice and lost five in the league. Appalling stuff. Of those defeats, only the Arsenal one was undeserved. Good results in the cups have meant that the league form has kind of slipped under the radar a bit. I have to admit it wasn't until today I realised our league results in 2012 had been so bad. I've generally stayed positive through our numerous setbacks this season because for me the results don't tell the whole the story. If you judge it solely on the league table and results, things look as grim as they've been in a long time. The eye test paints a different picture though, more often than not we've played good football and there's not been too much wrong that better finishing wouldn't fix. It's easy to not get too down hearted at results when the team is playing well, you just have to hope that eventually you get the breaks and start to get the results you deserve. After a performance like this however, it's much, much more difficult.

To keep things in perspective though, every team has days like this, even the top sides. Look at Spurs for example, the wheels have come off them in a big way recently, yet a few weeks ago they were being talked up as serious challengers for the title. They've lost three on the bounce and are now trying to hold off Arsenal for 3rd place. The same Arsenal who let in eight goals at Old Trafford and who have had numerous abysmal results themselves this season. As I say, every team has days like we had at Sunderland and in fairness we've not had many of these kind of shocking performances. We've had far less this season than we've had in the last few years in fact, but we've also had less wins, especially at home. That's why when you have a day like this it seems like the sky is falling in.

This performance was wretched, completely unacceptable, but it seems much worse because of all the points we've dropped in games we should have won. A week ago we produced arguably our best league performance of the season even though we lost. We've had plenty of disappointing results, but the terrible performances have been pretty rare. Hopefully that remains the case as we can't afford a repeat of what happened at the Stadium of Light. A couple of wins and good performances in the next week and the hope will return and we can still salvage plenty from the season. That's what has to happen, we simply cannot follow up that Sunderland display with anything other than three points in the derby and progression to the FA Cup semi final. Players need to play better, but Kenny has to sort it out as well as he's not covered himself in glory recently. His selection policy has been baffling at times, none more so than in this game. Gerrard was fit and desperate to play, but he was held back for the derby. Carragher has been out of the side due to the form of Agger and Skrtel, he comes back for one game and then finds himself back on the sidelines as Coates is brought in out of nowhere. Why? Did Kenny just think this was a game where he could afford to give Coates a run out, or was Carragher dropped? If Coates keeps his place for the derby, then clearly Carra has been dropped. I doubt that's the case though and my money is on him starting against Everton.

It's the same with Downing. He's had his struggles this season but had recently picked things up and seemed to be growing in confidence. Like Carragher and Gerrard, I'd say Downing is nailed on to start the derby and would have done regardless of what happened at Sunderland. It looks to me like maybe Kenny prioritised the Everton game over the Sunderland one. That's disappointing as it suggests we've given up on trying to finish as high up the table as possible. Even if that's not the case, we don't have a settled side do we? We still have Henderson playing on the right, which continues to baffle and infuriate in equal measures. Occasionally he'll do alright there, like last week against Arsenal. More often than not he offers very little. Bellamy, Carroll, Kuyt and Downing never know if they're starting from one week to the next. In fairness, only Bellamy has performed well enough to have any right to be aggrieved at being left out, but I do have some sympathy for Carroll and to a lesser extent Downing that when they do play well they often find themselves left on the bench for the next game. A few weeks ago Carroll was finally putting in some encouraging performances and looked like he might be finally turning the corner. He's been left out of the last three league games. How is he ever going to get into any kind of run of form? I just don't get it, I can understand not picking him when he was crap, but surely the minute he starts to show something you'd want to try and let him build on that? He has a quiet game against Cardiff and straight away he's back on the bench. He'll come in for a game or two, may even score, and he'll be back on the bench again. He cost us £35m for God's sake, you have to give him every chance to succeed and we simply aren't doing that. Play him every game and let's see if he's worth keeping around, if he isn't then sell him. But at least give him a proper run to see if he can hack it.

The team selection didn't give us the best chance of winning this game and neither did the use of substitutes. It's always Bellamy that comes off isn't it? Granted, he'd been quiet in the second half, but he still had more right being on the field than Kuyt or Henderson. On that subject, the under-use of Maxi Rodriguez this season is as mystifying as the over-use of Henderson. We were offering nothing at all in the final third, it was pitiful stuff. The only time we threatened was when Suarez took matters into his own hands and decided to try and beat three defenders himself. He almost did a couple of times, but in the end his levels dropped to that of those around him and in the second half he was as disappointing as the rest.

I'm struggling to actually write about the game itself, as fuck all happened. I watched it online and it was so bad I kept hoping the stream would die and put me out of my misery. I'm told Match of the Day managed to get three minutes highlights out of it. What did they do, put the goal on a three minute loop? Skrtel's foul on Bendtner was just about the only other 'highlight' worth seeing. Even the goal was shite. Campbell was allowed too much time to turn and his shot hit the post, bounced of Reina's head, hit the post again and fell perfectly for Bendtner who was following it up. A goal fitting to settle such a wretched game.

The moment it went in I knew it was game over. It had that feel about it, there was just no way we were coming back as we didn't have it in us, it couldn't have been more apparent. Kenny eventually sent on Gerrard and Carroll for Adam and Bellamy. Adam could have no complaints, he had an absolute nightmare and could barely complete a pass, especially in the second half where you could see his team-mates frustration with him growing with every bad decision he made. His set-pieces were garbage too. I thought Bellamy should have been left on as he's more likely to get a goal than anybody else we have. Instead, he made way whilst Jordan 'one goal' Henderson stayed on. Bizarre. We never threatened a come-back and the keeper didn't have to even make a save of any kind. Suarez scuffed a volley wide after working an opening with Henderson, and Kuyt didn't connect with a header after a great pull back from Gerrard. That was as close as we came, it was truly pathetic. Henderson was belatedly hooked in favour of Downing, but it made little difference.

It appears we've now put all our eggs in the FA Cup basket. That's all well and good if we win it, if that happens I doubt many will care if we finish 5th or 7th. Anything below that is seriously unacceptable but is a very distinct possibility now. I had hoped that winning a cup would relieve any pressure on the squad and allow them to just go shit or bust for a top four spot knowing that failure to secure it isn't the end of the world. Hasn't worked out like that though. We're looking like Spurs from a few years back when they couldn't win a game after they lifted the League Cup. Birmingham did it last year too. We need to get our shit together fast, we're one defeat away from slipping below Everton in the table. That would be the same Everton who've spent virtually fuck all in two years whilst we've spunked over £100m on players. It's embarrassing to see us in this situation and defeat in the derby doesn't even bear thinking about.

LIVERPOOL 3 EVERTON 0

Competition - Premier League
Date - Tue 13 Mar 2012
Venue - Anfield
Scorer(s) – Steven Gerrard (3)
Half Time - 1-0
Star Man – Steven Gerrard

Team: Reina; Kelly, Skrtel, Carragher, Enrique; Henderson (Kuyt), Spearing, Gerrard, Downing; Carroll, Suarez:

This was going to be their moment. Unbeaten in nine games whilst we'd won just one league game in 2012, they'd chipped away at our lead and found themselves in a position where victory at Anfield would see them leapfrog us in the table. What better way for David Moyes to celebrate his ten year anniversary than with his first victory at Anfield? They genuinely fancied their chances, and why shouldn't they? Thankfully, and fittingly, Steven Gerrard bitch slapped them back to reality and hopefully they won't get this close to us again for a long time.

I'm buzzing off this, it was fucking boss. Seeing all the TLW lads after the game too, they were the same, far more so than usual. I think it was because most of us went into this game fearing the worst, I certainly did. I've had a bad feeling about it ever since the final whistle went at the

Stadium of Light. We'd been abysmal at Sunderland and went into this on the back of three straight defeats in the league, whilst Everton had beaten City, Chelsea and Spurs in recent weeks. There seemed a very realistic chance they would end the evening sitting above us in the table, and I don't mind admitting I had a very bad feeling about this game. Turns out I was worried over nothing, it was extremely comfortable and we ran out easy winners. It could and should have been even more convincing, but I'm not greedy, I'll take the 3-0. I'm absolutely made up for Gerrard, this will have meant a hell of a lot to him. I wouldn't say he owed us one after missing the Arsenal game due to his England exploits (he's built up enough credit down the years that he certainly doesn't 'owe' us anything), but he will have been desperate to do well as it's been far too long since he made the blues pay for the distasteful chants they subject him to every derby game.

He's lived the Kopite dream, scoring goals for the reds in cup finals and lifting trophies as skipper. Now he's scored a derby hat-trick, with the third goal coming in front of the Kop. The celebration was class, sucking his thumb and then pointing to himself and saying 'mine'. The message was clear, 'the baby is mine you fucking meffs'. It was almost as much of a 'fuck you' to the Evertonians as the hat-trick itself. Almost, but not quite. This is another nice memory for him to add to the vast collection. Hopefully there's plenty more to come, on this form it seems likely. He was brilliant, it was a remarkable performance really given that he was playing centre mid in a 442. We came to expect this kind of rampaging display when he was playing off Torres in the 4231, but it's rare you see a central midfielder do what Gerrard did in this game. He scored three and it would have been four but for a great save by Howard early on. His touch as he collected Suarez's pass was unreal, no other player on the pitch could have done that. It was a stunning piece of skill and took unbelievable technique to pull off. He couldn't get much power on his shot as the ball was under his feet a little, but it was going in the bottom corner and Howard did well to keep it out. Henderson looked certain to bury the rebound but Rodwell came from nowhere to make a fantastic block.

Howard made another good save shortly after when Suarez ran onto Carroll's flick but his snapshot was a nice height for the keeper to parry it. The link up between Carroll and Suarez is improving all the time. Carroll is winning pretty much everything in the air and Suarez is now running off him and getting onto the flicks. It's coming along nicely and the partnership is definitely beginning to click. They play a lot closer to eachother now and Suarez knows what he needs to do when Carroll challenges for the ball. I watched them hug just before kick off and Carroll was animatedly talking and gesturing to Suarez about what they needed to do. There have been encouraging signs from those two since Suarez returned from his ban, which makes it all the more infuriating that Carroll has been on the bench for the last three league games. I appreciate it can be difficult pairing them against good sides who pack the midfield, it's just frustrating to see Carroll on the bench when he's hit some form.

The way Everton set up played into our hands I thought. They played 442 for the most part (Anichebe spent some time on the left early on but they changed it pretty quickly and moved him up front) and that is why Gerrard was able to get forward as much as he did. He and Spearing were both fantastic, but had they been up against an extra man in there it would have definitely restricted the skipper. I don't think there'll be too many sides play as open against us as Everton did, and that's the problem we face. Clearly we need Gerrard on the field with Carroll and Suarez. This is the first time it's happened in the league, which is incredible. Find a way to get them on the field and wreak havoc, we've got nothing to lose now.

The blues only real chance of the 1st half came when Henderson dawdled on the ball and was robbed. They had a four v three break but Pienaar's pass was cut out by the once again hugely impressive Skrtel. Henderson struggled badly in the first half, not much went right for him at all and he was the only player in red not at the races. Everyone else was right at it and it was a good half of football, but there was a lot of groaning coming from the stands directed towards Henderson. Having watched a replay of the entire game I'd concede that Henderson wasn't as terrible as I thought at the time but he was clearly the weakest link. He did play some nice passes and was involved in two of the goals, so it was far from all bad.

The blues looked to have weathered our early storm and were actually having their best spell of the game when we took the lead. It was a great goal too, it started in our own box when Enrique did well to make an interception and play the ball up to Suarez. He laid it off first time to Downing who carried it forward before giving it back to Suarez who played an instant ball to Henderson and then collected the return pass. Kelly had gone steaming forward and Suarez tried to pick him out but the ball brushed Gerrard's knee on the way through. Kelly still got there and shot straight at Howard, and his follow up was also blocked by the keeper. The loose ball fell to Gerrard on the edge of the box, and he curled the ball over Howard and the covering defenders into the net. Kelly was inches away from making it 2-0 when he powered onto a cute pass from Henderson and drilled a shot across Howard but just past the far post. Kelly was awesome, especially in the first half, his best performance of the season by some distance. He was in beast mode and was just bullying people, fantastic to see.

Gerrard grabbed his second not long after the break. Kelly won the ball, Henderson released Suarez and he megged Distin in the box before stepping aside as Gerrard came in to leather the ball past Howard into the roof of the Kop net. Kelly went close again when he just failed to get a touch onto Downing's brilliant cross, and Gerrard was almost sent clear by

Suarez but Distin got over to cover. That move started with a raking 60 yard pass by Carroll to Downing. The big man was turning on the style now, and more great play from him sent Suarez clean through seconds later. The finish was horrible, as Luis tried to take the shot early with the outside of his right boot. Great stuff by Carroll though.

Everton had actually responded pretty well to going two down, they knocked the ball around quite nicely without ever really threatening Reina. Baines and Fellaini were prominent, but the lack of a decent striker was glaringly obvious. Anichebe is shit, always has been always will be. He's big and strong and can pose problems based on that, but he's shite. As for the big goon alongside him, I've said it before but he's basically an Argentine Shefki Kuqi. Everton have as much trouble scoring goals as we do, and it was asking a lot for them to come back from 2-0 down. Still, I couldn't relax until around the 88 minute mark when I figured there was no way they would score twice. I'd been pretty nervous despite how comfortable we were looking, I'm not exactly sure why but I guess it's because we've been kicked in the teeth so many times this season I was half expecting it to happen again. The closest they came was a Rodwell shot that Enrique cleared off the line, and another Rodwell shot that went well wide. How over-rated is he by the way?

I thought we were superb for most of the game. So many great performances all over the park. The back four were all terrific, Spearing did his job to perfection and allowed Gerrard to bomb forward at will, whilst the front two dovetailed nicely and gave the blues more than they could handle. There was a hilarious moment involving Suarez and Baines right by where I sit. They clashed at a throw in, and it looked like Baines had a little kick out at Suarez who wasn't happy. Suarez then collected the ball and megged Baines. It came to nothing, but Suarez wanted to let Baines know about it and was shouting 'Hey!' 'Hey!' trying to get his attention. The full back wouldn't turn around and look at him, he knew. Baines pissed me right off just after that when play was stopped due to an injury to Pienaar. When the ref blew up, we actually had a two against one on our right flank with Kuyt and Kelly. That was annoying, but for Baines to then knock the ball out for a throw in our half, a throw which they pressured to try and win the ball back, that wasn't cool. Just give it back to the keeper like everyone else would, you fucking hobbit.

Gerrard's hat-trick just topped off a great night. Drenthe fell over and presented him with possession. He carried it forward, played it to Suarez and then took the return pass and put a left foot shot into the roof of the net. Great credit to Suarez, a lot of strikers in that situation would have just gone themselves, after all the game was virtually over and our forwards have found goals hard to come by. To set up the skipper for his hat-trick showed what a great team-mate he is.

Other observations. I have to say, Phil Dowd was outstanding once again, with the only blemish being the bizarre booking of Enrique late on.

What was that for? For upsetting Hibbert and causing him to spit his dummy and petulantly kick the ball at him (and predictably miss the target!)? Leighton Baines is really good and should be playing for a better side than the blues. Royston Drenthe is basically just a blag Balotelli. His cameo was hilarious. Then there's Fellaini and his fucking elbows. Spearing caught one in the first half after dispossessing him, Carroll took a right then a left in the space of about half a second after the break, it's ridiculous. He's good at making it look accidental though, you have to give him that. Tim Howard can fuck off as well. Applauded by the Kop at the start of the second half, he didn't even have the good grace to acknowledge it.

We needed a performance after three straight defeats, and it sets us up nicely for the FA Cup game with Stoke at the weekend. The last time we faced Stoke we went with Kuyt as a lone striker. Predictably, it ended 0-0. Hopefully we'll see a much more positive line up and result this time.

Premier League Round Up (10-12 March 2012)

I had a dilemma this week. Do I write this before or after the derby? Given the frame of mind I was in after the steaming turd we dropped on the Stadium of the Light pitch I felt it was probably best to wait an extra day or two. It was a gamble, as had we lost the derby I'd have been in no mental state to be writing about frog eyes Moyes leapfrogging us in the table, Manchester City bottling it and allowing United to return to the top of the table and Chelsea and Arsenal both winning.

Thankfully we didn't lose and that makes what happened at the weekend slightly less stomach turning now. It was still a bastard of a weekend though wasn't it? Not one result went in our favour, although 'Useless' took a step closer to relegation and my guy Steve Kean took another small step towards safety so on a personal note at least it wasn't a complete write off. Actually, is Kean still my guy or did I jump off his bandwagon again? Difficult to keep track, I'm pretty fickle.

Anyway, there was no shortage of controversy as QPR travelled to Bolton in a relegation six pointer. Zamora hit the bar following a great ball by the returning Djibril Cisse. Djibs was sporting a yellow mohawk as well as matching sideburns. Will he ever grow out of it, or will he still be pulling this kind of shit when he's in his 60s? I hope he never changes, the mad bastard. Scouser Clint Hill opened the scoring for QPR, well, kind of. His header was two foot over the line but no-one saw it. The lino had a few bodies in his way and couldn't see, and the ref wasn't in position to give it either. I find it hard to blame them too much, but then maybe that's because I like seeing 'Sparky' pissed off and want the cheating manc bore relegated? Pratley ensured Bolton took full advantage of the let off by heading past Paddy Kenny to put the Trotters in front, but Cisse equalised with an untypically neat finish. He was actually offside, not that Hughes mentioned that of course, he was too busy bitching about the goal that they didn't get. Klasnic won it for Bolton with three minutes left.

Quality finish, but then that's what he does. Bit of a lazy bastard who doesn't do much else, but he's a lethal finisher. Amazes me that he doesn't start every week. What do you value more as a manager, hard work or goals? You'd like both but if you have to choose, what do you value more? You don't see Blackburn leaving Yakubu on the bench. Steve Kean > Owen Coyle. That's how the kids say it these days isn't it? I hope I got that right, I'm never sure which way the arrow is meant to point. To be clear, I'm saying Kean is better than Coyle. Not sure whether to feel sorry for Clint Hill or not, depends if he's a good red like Ryan Taylor or bitter blue like that Jon Walters prick. If someone can find that out and let me know so I know if sympathy or ridicule is required that would be great. Bad result for Rangers, but on the plus side the Lord of Frodsham looked in great form and his partnership with Zamora is QPR's best hope of survival.

Meanwhile, staying at the bottom and Wolves are in deep, deep shit. 'TC' had his first home game since taking over from Mick McCarthy. Roger Johnson was on the bench after turning up to training bladdered earlier in the week. Not the first time he's done something like that, I'm pretty sure he's been shitfaced in most of the games he's played since joining them last summer. He's the number one reason McCarthy was sacked. He was their marquee summer signing but he's been a disaster. Wolves really needed to win this game against fellow strugglers Blackburn, but that was never going to happen. For me, Blackburn were always going to win this game as they are nearly always competitive whereas Wolves have generally been anything but. If you had to back one of them to survive, it would be Kean's boys all day. My boy Junior Hoilett stole the show with two goals, the second of which was a corker with his left foot. Jarvis was the only Wolves player who looked like doing anything, as usual. The Wolves fans turned on their chairman, former LFC shareholder Steve Morgan. A banner saying *'Scouse Mafia out'* was unveiled in the stands. Scouse Mafia? What the fuck are they talking about? Morgan is hardly Curtis Warren now, is he? The fella doesn't even wear the trousers in his own home, his wife calls the shots, just ask David Moores. If you can wake him up of course. Scouse Mafia?? Hahahaha, he's as 'mafia' as Bill Kenwright.

Which leads me seamlessly onto Everton beating Spurs at Goodison in the week David Moyes celebrated ten years in charge at the Pit. In that time they've won precisely fuck all. His greatest achievement was finishing above the reds once, in a season when we took our eye off the ball because we were pre-occupied with, y'know, winning the European Cup. Despite the lack of success, Kenwright still describes Moyes as one of the 'world's best'. Then again, he still thinks Everton are a big club. He's a dreamer is Bill. A dreamer, and a cock. Jelavic got the only goal of the game with an impressive finish after good play by Osman to set him up. Spurs webbed them everywhere in the second half but couldn't score. Everton did what they have been so good at. They played 451, were difficult to beat and held on desperately to the goal they scored. Makes it all the more baffling that they came to Anfield wide open and tried to take us on at our own game. Few decent results and suddenly Moyes is getting delusions of grandeur. Sally Webster from Coronation Street was in the crowd. Bill putting his little rollerdeck of celebrity contacts to good use again. Bit of a drop off from Stallone to Sally Webster though. Presumably Ken Barlow was busy. Who's next Bill, Schmeichel the dog? (Yes, I know he's dead but you think that's gonna stop Kenwright?).

Moving on, and I was relieved to see Motson was kept away from Chelsea this week (he ruined the Wolves game instead). Mind you, Johnathon Pearce is turning into Motson junior. Another hysterical, loud, irritating goon. But at least he's not Motson, and you can't under-estimate that. Chelsea just about did enough to overcome Stoke, but were helped greatly by the rank stupidity of Ricardo Fuller who got himself sent off for stamping on Ivanovic. Absolutely fucking insane, unforgivable, irresponsible behaviour. I mean why would you stamp on Ivanovic when you can do it to John Terry? The dickhead deserved two red cards if you ask me. Speaking of Mongo, he hit the bar with a header from a corner but went nuts that the ref didn't penalise Shawcross for holding him. He was right too, but Stoke do this constantly and always get away with it. Do refs actually watch MOTD, and if they do how have they not got onto this by now? I'd be giving six penalties a game against the crabs if I was a ref. Fuckin' Stoke. Ivanovic hit the bar too, whilst Stoke barely got out of their own half (just for a change). Eventually the deadlock was broken when Mata picked out Drogba and he took it in stride, rounded the keeper and scored his 100th Premier League goal. He's been an embarrassment at times with the playacting and cheating, but what a fucking player he's been. I'll be glad to see the back of him when he eventually goes, but he's been a great, great player.

Moving on, and in form Fulham made the trip to the Midlands to take on Aston Villa. Judging by the highlights, this game was almost as bad as what we served up with Sunderland. Danny Murphy got his face smashed up by Steven Ireland's elbow, Albrighton hit the bar as did Damien Duff and then some kid I've never heard of won it for Villa right at the end after a howler by Schwarzer. Going back to the Murphy thing, remember the crackdown about ten years ago when refs were handing out red cards all over the shop for any elbow to the face, accidental or not? The novelty seems to have worn off recently, they're more concerned with booking people for taking off their shirts these days. Steven Ireland was actually laughing about it. Murphy wasn't, his face was so messed up he could have passed himself off as a Rooney.

Onto Sunday, and how predictable was all that? United have been unimpressive for much of the season, they've been embarrassed in Europe and knocked out of two domestic cups which would back up my view that this is one of the worst sides they've had in several years. Yet somehow they've kept winning in the league and City haven't been able to shake them despite looking a far more dominant and impressive side all season. This was always going to happen, City would have a bad day and suddenly find themselves knocked off top spot by a United side who've not been pulling up any trees but have relentlessly kept churning out narrow wins. Was anyone even surprised City lost at the weekend? Swansea are a good side, they've been the feel good story of the season for many. They've given all the top sides a game and were unlucky to lose against United recently. They did lose though, and therein lies the difference between City and United. United have kept winning regardless of how they've played. City have mostly been playing great and winning, but whenever their standards have slipped they've dropped points. Swansea could even afford the luxury of a missed penalty, as Scott Sinclair's weak spot kick was saved by Joe Hart. The keeper pysched him out, repeatedly yelling at him that he wasn't going to score. Sinclair completely bottled it, a bit like City actually. The pressure appeared to be getting to Mancini's men as they were arguing amongst themselves and never looked settled. How long before they panic and recall Tevez to the side? Richards had a goal controversially ruled out in the last minute for offside. He was offside, but it was really, really close. Sian Massey is the only lino who's name anybody knows. Keys and Gray have made her famous and she's been involved in numerous big decisions such as this one. And from what I can remember she's been right every time. Eventually she'll make a mistake, and when she does no doubt it will be because *'birds have no business running the line at a footy match'*. Whilst I admit to having some understandable concerns that there may be dishes being left unwashed and ironing not being done whilst she's off doing 'mens work', the fact is she's pretty fucking good and unquestionably better than the vast array of deadbeats I've seen running the line in front of the Main Stand this season.

I've now resigned myself to United winning the league again, as City just don't appear to have what it takes to go the distance. They're clearly the best team in the country but chances are they're gonna bottle it and United's mentality will probably see them through. As sickening as it initially felt hearing that United had gone top again, my instinctive reaction when I saw that knobhead City fan crying was to piss myself laughing and mock the pathetic little shitkicker. So rather than fretting over Ferguson adding another title to his collection, I'm just going to resign myself to it and then regardless of who wins the title it's going to be funny laughing at whichever manc team misses out. That weeping City fan is almost reason enough to want to see them fail, it was that ridiculous. What a fucking loser.

On the subject of losers, Roy Hodgson was clearly the happiest loser of the weekend, as it made his buddy 'Sir Alex' happy. Rooney diverted in a shot from Hernandez to give United the lead. West Brom should have have had a penalty when Evra clumsily tripped Odemwingie in the box. He got away with it though, which has been a recurring theme this season. He's like OJ fucking Simpson isn't he? Wellbeck missed an open goal and then Olsson was sent off for a second yellow card. He deserved that one, but the first yellow was softer than Pele without his pills. The latest in a long line of Ashley Young dives gave United a penalty which Rooney converted to make the game safe. Hodgson was livid on the touchline, and rightly so. The anger didn't last long though, the shithouse. By the time he faced the cameras after the game he'd gone back into 'don't upset Sir Alex' mode. *"I don't think Evra intended to foul him"* What the fucks that got to do with anything you arse licking snivelling little turd? *"When Rooney scored that excellent goal to put them 1-0 in the lead, meaning that we had to come out and then find a goal from somewhere it was always going to be an uphill task"*. Seriously, who fucking talks like that after a loss at Old Trafford in which you've been shafted by a few decisions? Roy Hodgson, that's who. Embarrassing, cringeworthy and fucking cowardly.

Finally, and I can't stress this enough, I really, really fucking hate Ashley Young. I hate his face. I hate the way he runs. I hate his diving. I hate the way he seems to tip toe around the field without putting any weight down. He could run across the beach without leaving a footprint, or across a wooden floor in tap shoes without making a sound. I hate him, the massive, massive twat. If I had a hit list (which I don't, in case there's any coppers reading this), he'd be on it, sandwiched in between Evra and Rooney.

The 'Super Sunday' game this weekend was Norwich entertaining Wigan. Can Sky be sued under the trade descriptions act for that? Surely it's more of a 'So what Sunday' or 'Mediocre Monday'? There was no way I was sitting through 90 minutes of it, but I did watch the highlights and it wasn't a bad game from the looks of it. Norwich scored first through a tidy Wes Hoolahan volley. Wigan played well though and almost hit back through Rodallega who went close three times before the break. McCarthy was also denied by Ruddy as Wigan piled on the pressure and eventually Moses went clear and deservedly earned them a point. Good result for Wigan, less so for Norwich who could have gotten themselves within one point of us had they won. Does that say more about us or them?

One more game to cover, Arsenal's win over Newcastle on Monday night. Robin Van Persie scored again. Surely it's time for a name change now? Let's face it, Robin is a bit of a shit name if we're being honest. It screams out 'SIDEKICK'. It was fine when he was wingman to Thierry Henry, but he's outgrown it now he's the big cheese. Batman Van Persie actually has a good ring to it, he should probably go with that.

It's better for us that Arsenal got that late winner, as we've got more chance of overhauling Newcastle than we have of catching the Gunners. That makes me a sad panda, but I'm just keepin' it real, yo.

LIVERPOOL 2 STOKE CITY 1

Competition - FA Cup
Date - Sun 18 Mar 2012
Venue - Anfield
Scorer(s) – Luis Suarez, Stewart Downing
Half Time - 2-1
Star Man – Jay Spearing

Team: Reina; Kelly (Coates), Carragher, Skrtel, Enrique; Maxi (Kuyt), Gerrard, Spearing, Downing; Suarez (Henderson), Carroll:

Not pretty but job done. It's incredibly difficult for anyone to ever look good against Stoke, they're a horrible, niggly, cynical, dirty alehouse team who make it virtually impossible for teams to play football against them. This was a war of attrition but we came through it. I don't care how we looked performance wise, it was all about reaching the semi final and we did it. There's little point analysing a performance against Stoke, they'd even manage to make Barcelona look disjointed.

After performing so well in the derby it was encouraging to see Kenny more or less stick to the same team. The only change was one that I was actually really happy to see, Henderson making way for Maxi. The Argentine has been massively under-used this season so it was nice seeing him back on the field, although you could argue Stoke are not exactly the ideal opposition for a small, ball playing midfielder like Maxi. The first half wasn't good. We didn't really get going as it was so stop start, and the referee didn't help matters by being typically fucking clueless. His assistants were actually worse, which takes a unique brand of shitness given how shocking the ref was. Not that I was surprised, Kevin Friend is an absolute twat. You'd have to watch a hell of a lot of football to see a worse refereeing display than he turned it at Fulham earlier this season when he sent Spearing off. He did his best to top it but I'd say he fell just short.

Things had been going well for us initially, Suarez opened the scoring with a terrific strike after linking up with his boy Maxi. It's really important getting the first goal against Stoke, as if they get their noses in front they can be very difficult to break down. Score first though and they have to come out of their shell a bit and it makes it much easier. In theory anyway, it kind of falls down a bit if you only hold onto the lead for three minutes.

Friend & friends more than played their part in the equaliser. The initial corner that was given was dubious, but everyone in the ground then saw that no Liverpool player touched the ball as it travelled across the face of goal. Well, everyone except Friend and the Centenary side lino who awarded another corner. It was ridiculous, but I turned to my arl fella and said *"they'll probably score from this now"*. It's amazing how often it happens.

You concede a corner either through a stupid mistake or an incorrect call by the officials, and it results in a goal. I haven't seen any replays of the goal, at the time I just saw Crouch with a completely free header. Carroll was picking him up from set-pieces so I assume he lost him on this one. I've heard people say Reina was fouled, but there's no way I could see that from where I was sat. Reina was booked for arguing about it, I assumed he was arguing about the award of a corner but maybe he was complaining about being impeded. I'm not convinced, I simply can't imagine Stoke doing anything illegal from a set-piece, it's just not in their make up....

Gerrard also had a right go at the ref, and continued to do so throughout the first half as a series of bizarre decisions went against us. The most disturbing was when Suarez tried to cut inside Huth but the ball struck the defender on the leg and went towards the Kop end. Huth tried to retrieve it whilst shielding Suarez but he fell over, yet linesman and referee both gave a goal-kick. It was incredible. Carragher stayed behind at half time to remonstrate with the officials about Stoke's goal, you could see him pointing to the corner flag and it was obvious what his complaint was. Not that there's any point, it's too late to change his mind and he seems like the type of referee who would be even more inclined to favour the other side the more you complain about it. Known in the business as 'doing a Steve Bennett'.

We'd not looked good in that first half, we'd had a few promising moves but weren't getting enough from out wide. Maxi wasn't involved much and Downing didn't look particularly comfortable playing in front of Kelly. He's done ok at times on the right when Johnson has been there, but I'm not sure him and Kelly have played much together and they were pretty ineffective I thought. Suarez and Carroll didn't have great service and Stoke made it very difficult for us in the final third. It's just very difficult to look good against them, we always used to find it hard against Wimbledon back in the day too, and that was when we had a great team. Stoke are the modern day answer to the Crazy Gang and they excel in making good teams look ugly and disjointed. They play for set-pieces, they constantly foul and time waste and disrupt the flow of the game, and they're very good at it. It's actually seemed easier playing them at the Britannia than at Anfield this season, as they just completely park the bus when they go away. They're hardly gung ho at home either like, but we have seemed to find it a little easier to get the ball down and play at their place. We've played them four times this season, and we played much better football in the two away games even though we lost one of them.

The second half was better but we never managed to really get going and didn't come anywhere near to the level we'd shown against the blues a few days earlier. Thankfully we did enough, Downing's fine strike proving decisive. It was a good goal, he was heavily involved in the build up and his finish was excellent. We've waited a long time to see him do that, but he's been playing better of late and hopefully he'll continue to grow between now and the end of the season. A lot of it is confidence with him, technique wise he's very good, he just needs to start asserting himself more. Stoke put us under pressure in the final ten minutes, but it's worth mentioning that Reina didn't actually have to make a save other than to come out and catch a few long throw ins. Not that Stoke's keeper was much busier. I can't think of a save he had to make either. Suarez worked a good opening for himself and then hit one of the worst shots you'll ever see. Kelly almost went clean through after a great ball from Kuyt but Shawcross came from nowhere to make a fine block. Kelly was injured in the challenge and never recovered, he was eventually forced off late on and replaced by Coates. Suarez went off at the same time, I have no idea what happened to him but it looked like something occurred off the ball and he hobbled off. I've been told that Huth stood on his foot. Could have been an accident as he's a clumsy big bastard. Could have been deliberate as, well, he plays for Stoke.

I thought we defended brilliantly aside from that one first half blemish that saw them score. Carragher and Skrtel were faultless, both did their jobs superbly and we held on fairly comfortably despite Stoke having far more of the ball late on than you'd expect. We sat back a bit more than I thought necessary, but there were no real scares and we deservedly went through to a semi final against either Everton or Sunderland. I don't care who we play, we should beat either side if we perform to the levels we have for most of the season and our finishing doesn't let us down. The important thing now is to put this on the back burner and try and pick up maximum points in the league between now and the semi final. And thankfully we've seen the last of Stoke for one season, the horrible bus parking alehouse bastards.

Premier League Round Up (17-21 March 2012)

Bit of a disjointed week this one. With seven Premier League sides involved in FA Cup ties at the weekend, there were only two league games on the Saturday and a further two on the Sunday as well as a few midweek match ups.

First up on Saturday was Fulham entertaining Swansea at Craven Cottage. Martin Jol's side are generally solid at home and hadn't lost a Saturday league game all season. Swansea have been better at home than they have away, so this result was a bit of an eye opener to say the least. Swansea are just class though aren't they? What's not to like about them? Well there's that shitty droning *'Land of my fathers'* song, I hate that. That's a small beef though, and football wise there's nothing to dislike. They don't have any knobheads playing for them, their manager seems like a good guy and they play football that's more pleasing on the eye than any other team in the land. Sigurdsson headed them in front when Sinclair teed him up from a Routledge cross. He added a second after playing a one two with Routledge and you have to say he's been a fantastic signing. He's added goals to a team that was struggling to put the ball in the net despite all their great approach play. Joe Allen then made it 3-0 with a tame shot that Mark Schwarzer somehow let past him. He usually reserves that kind of shitness for games against Manchester United, the fucking loser.

As for Fulham, the 'Samson effect' continued for Bryan Ruiz as he was replaced by Damien Duff after another disappointing outing. This is why I won't cut my hair, I'm petrified if I do I'll go from just being a bit shit to becoming Fernando Torres (hey, it's gonna take more than two scruffy goals against a Championship side to make me stop the Torres gags). Comparisons are being made with Swansea and Barcelona. Obviously the standard of player is much lower (although Leon Britton is clearly the 'Xavi of the Valleys'), but the philosophy is basically the same. Short passing, everyone comfortable on the ball and press the shit out of the other team when you don't have it. It's early days but Brendan Rodgers really seems like the real deal doesn't he? If I was him I'd be sending DVD's of their games to the Nou Camp and seeing if I could get a couple of their best youngsters over on loan for next season.

The other game on Saturday was at the DW Stadium as West Brom made the trip to Wigan. We're coming to that stage of the season where Wigan usually start picking up points, but that won't be easy when they have the awful Di Santo leading the line. The sooner Rodallega is back the better for them. Di Santo ballooned one shot over early on, then saw a better effort tipped over by the keeper, completely whiffed at a cross and then didn't get enough on a header. Boyce and McCarthy both hit the bar as Wigan dominated but couldn't score. You watch, they'll have one chance at Anfield this weekend and they'll score. It'll probably be Di Santo too! They eventually did find the net when Moses' cross wasn't cleared and McArthur scored from close range. That sparked West Brom into life and Scharner headed in an equaliser against his old team from a corner, the fucking Judas. After the game he said "*You can see why they are bottom. They can't score and they always concede*". It's true of course, but still.... What a dick.

Mulumbu then lost the plot after a nothing foul by McArthur. He jumped up and put his hands in McArthur's face, then grabbed the throat of Boyce right in front of the referee who gave him a yellow card. Meanwhile, in a mansion somewhere in Frodsham a Lord of the Manor yelled 'sacré bleu' as he shook his bleached blonde head in bewilderment. Mulumbu committed the same offence as Cisse did against Wolves the other week, except he did it TWICE and he didn't even have the excuse of reacting to a dangerous tackle like Djibs did. I've made my feelings known on the whole *'if you raise your hands you have to go'* nonsense, but Mulumbu's reaction was largely unprovoked and I'd have sent him off for acting the twat. Other observations, Beausejour played really well on the left and looked like the player who'd impressed so much for Chile in the last World Cup. Don't know why he flopped at Birmingham, but he's a good footballer. Actually that will be why he flopped at Birmingham. Finally, Keith Andrews looks like Gareth Barry with Aids.

Onto Sunday, and the Mancs couldn't have had an easier fixture to bounce back from their latest European humiliation. When they got knocked out of the Champions League they bounced back with a 4-1 win at home to Wolves. Having been bummed senseless in the Europa League by a brilliant Bilbao side the last thing they needed was to face anyone half decent. Fortunately for them they had Wolves. On current form Terry Connor's side are the worst team in the league. I was rooting for Connor initially, but if they are to have any chance of staying up they need a proper manager, quickly. The poor guy is in way over his head. Having been a number two for so long you'd think the one thing he'd be good at would be coaching and organisation, yet they defend set pieces about as well as we take penalties. They're so bad they even allowed Johnny Evans to score. Zubar was then sent off for two reckless tackles. The first was a bad foul on Rooney, the second was a staggeringly stupid challenge on Wellbeck. This is one of the many reasons I could never be a manager (not knowing enough about the game being the most obvious one). How do you react when one of your players does that? I'd flip my lid completely, probably take a swing at him and end up getting my arse kicked into the middle of next week as I can't fight my way out of a wet paper bag. United inevitably ran riot against the ten men, Valencia made it 2-0, Wellbeck scored and Hernandez got two, the second of which came from a brilliant move. I have a confession to make. I really like Antonio Valencia, he's quality and I'd love him in our side. The game raised a lot of questions for me though, the biggest of which being; Will Rio Ferdinand EVER grow into that face of his? Saggier than an old mans ballbag it is.

Norwich went to Newcastle, wore their green kit again, and lost. Again. They'll never learn. Papis Cisse scored the only goal of the game, a superb finish from a Gutierrez cross. Not a great result for us, or was it? Should we be looking up at Newcastle or over our shoulders at Norwich?

Tuesday night saw Sunderland travel to my main man Steve Kean's Blackburn. Another of my guys, Junior Hoilett, grabbed the first goal in a 2-0 win that put some daylight between Rovers and the bottom three. Yakubu (who else?) got the other one. Knows where the goal is doesn't he? Knows where the chippy is too. Man after my own heart. Rovers are a couple of wins away from probably being safe now. When that happens, maybe Kean will stage a sit in protest to sack those fans and get some proper supporters in? Or perhaps he'll hire a plane to fly over Ewood with that banner of him giving them the middle finger.

Onto Wednesday, Man City simply had to beat Chelsea. I asked last week 'how long before desperation sees them recall Carlos Tevez?' The answer was 'not long at all'. He was back on the bench and came on to play a crucial role in Nasri's winner as City won it with a late comeback after falling behind to a Gary Cahill goal. Aguero scored City's other goal from the spot after Mike Dean awarded a penalty for a handball by Essien. Dean wasn't on Ferguson's Christmas card list before that, he'll be lucky if he referees another game now. Torres played well, didn't score, and saw his arse when he was substituted. Mongo was left on the bench, no doubt putting his time to good use coming up with new and innovative ways to get rid of the latest pretender to his throne. Watch your back, Roberto.

The wheels continue to come off the Spurs wagon, they just about managed a draw at home to a Stoke side in which the Mighty Salif was given a rare start. He needed to be at his dominant best as he was partnered by the woeful Palacios. Stoke went in front from a set piece, but Spurs really should have been out of sight by then as they'd had plenty of chances. The outstanding Bale hit the bar with a great effort and it was his brilliant cross that set up Van Der Vaart's stoppage time equaliser. Is it just me or did Spurs go shit when they signed Saha? Curiously, his departure from Goodison also co-incided with Everton going on a great run. Finally, and I can't stress this enough, Jon Walters is absolutely shit. And a twat.

Arsenal leapfrogged Spurs after winning a controversial game at the Pit. They started like a runaway train. Ramsay missed a sitter, Vermailen put them in front and Tim Howard needed to make a good save to keep out Van Persie. The blues thought they'd equalised through Drenthe but the linesman's flag cut short their celebrations. Hilariously, he was at least two yards onside. Can we find a way to clone Sian Massey, as to a man the rest of these lino's are complete dogshit. Early impressions of Everton new boy Jelavic is that he loves a dive and he's slower than me. I was talking to a blue last night and he said they love Jelavic already because *"he looks like Kanchelskis"*. Nil Satis Nisi Optimum baby. *"Hey, hey, get into them"* hissed an agitated Moyes from the touchline. That's some proper 'school of science' shit right there folks. Honestly, I haven't seen Moyes that fired up since Leighton Baines stole his 'precious' and threw it into a volcano.

Finally, someone really needs to have a word with Fellaini about that head of his. If he wants to look like a tit that's his own choice, but when it starts hampering his performance that's when his manager needs to step in. He had a free header that just sunk into his hair and looped harmlessly to the keeper. It's like heading a ball with a sofa cushion strapped to your head or hitting a tee shot with the big furry head cover still on your driver. When being tall and good in the air is just about the only thing you've got going for you, why would you handicap yourself like that?

QUEENS PARK RANGERS 3 LIVERPOOL 2

Competition - Premier League
Date - Wed 21 Mar 2012
Venue - Loftus Road
Scorer(s) – Sebastian Coates, Dirk Kuyt
Half Time - 0-1
Star Man – Stewart Downing

Team: Reina; Kelly (Coates), Carragher, Skrtel, Enrique; Gerrard, Spearing, Adam (Henderson); Downing, Suarez (Carroll), Kuyt:

I'm struggling to remember a time when I was more angry after a loss. Let's not sugarcoat this, QPR are an absolutely fucking woeful football team and were made to look so for most of this game. They were so bad you could make a legitimate case for criticising our players for taking so long to build up a two goal advantage.

We should have been 3-0 up inside the opening quarter of an hour, but as usual we couldn't turn our superiority into goals. No matter, by the 72 minute mark we'd given ourselves a two goal and were cruising to three points. Then we gave away a stupid goal from a corner, and it was all downhill from there. Once they'd pulled one back, you could tell a second was coming. We'd been caught with our pants down and the momentum had shifted completely in the home side's favour. An equaliser was inevitable, you could see it coming a mile off and when they got the second with five minutes plus stoppage still to play, I was more worried about them scoring than I was hopeful about us getting one. They didn't even have to work for it, Enrique gift wrapped the winner for them with more or less the last kick of the game.

I'm struggling to even find the words, I'm so pissed off. This should just never happen, the players need a massive kick up the arse for how they switched off after going 2-0 up. Newsflash lads, you're not fucking good enough to be complacent, just look at the league table. This is just so far from being acceptable that.. well I can't even come up with anything to describe just how far from being acceptable it is. Come up with an analogy for the most unacceptable thing you can come up with, and this was worse. It would be bad enough if this had happened against a good side, but QPR??? We missed chances, as usual, but even worse than that was the amount of times we failed to take advantage of great situations. I want to see Hughes take QPR down, and we've just handed them a lifeline they didn't deserve. A good side would have absolutely murdered QPR, they were wide open all night. We're not a good side though. Oh don't get me wrong, we often do a great impersonation of one as we dominate most games we play in. Good sides have killer instinct though, we most certainly don't. We're like a boxer who dances around the ring landing pretty little jabs and nice combinations but who doesn't really hurt his opponent. And all the while, the opponent is biding his time waiting for chance to deliver the knockout punch. In boxing terms, we're not big punchers and we've got a weak chin.

I think it's about time I addressed the huge elephant in the room. Nobody wants to say it, but when was the last time our goalkeeper saved anything? The majority of goals we've been conceding may not be directly attributable to Reina, but he's paid a huge amount of money to make saves yet he never fucking does. He's got this reputation as one of the world's top keepers, but he's barely made a good save of note all season. Week after week we see keepers making great saves against us. Week after week our keeper saves fuck all. We've all seen the stats about our poor conversion rate. That's used as a stick to beat the attacking players with, and justifiably so. But what about the stats at the other end? We give up fewer chances than almost anybody, yet the percentage of those chances that end up in the net is amongst the highest in the league. Is that not reflective of the goalkeeper? Surely it has to be to some extent.

I don't need stats to tell me this though, I can see it with my own eyes. Joe Hart made more great saves in the four games he played against us than Reina has made all season. Be honest, how many great saves can you remember from Reina this season? It's not that he's making howlers, that's not the problem. Yes he's been directly at fault for a few goals, but not enough to be worried by as you can look at every keeper in the league and there'll be goals that he should have done better with. That doesn't bother me, it's the fact he hardly ever makes a save. For me, a top goalkeeper is someone who you hate playing against as you know you'll have to do your damndest to beat the fucker. A top goalkeeper is a difference maker. Pepe Reina has not been a difference maker for some time, even though none of us want to admit it. How many saves has he made this season where you've thought 'he had no right to stop that?' You can look at each of the goals from this game in isolation and the blame lies more with individuals other than Reina. Henderson for the first, Skrtel the second and Enrique the third. It's the same for most of the goals we concede. But great goalkeepers make saves, they bail their team-mates out when they've made a mistake, they frustrate the other team by stopping shots you don't think they will be able to stop. Pepe Reina isn't doing that, it seems almost every shot on target against us ends up in the net. He's the goalkeeping equivalent of our attackers if you like. Being a great goalkeeper isn't just about not making big mistakes, you have to make some saves once in a while too, just like the forwards have to score more goals than they have been doing.

It may seem like I'm blaming him for this defeat. Far from it, this is a collective thing and I'm not pinning it on the goalkeeper. He's not being made the scapegoat, this defeat wasn't his fault and there's plenty of other reasons as to why we're underachieving so much this season. He is a factor though. It's been on my mind for weeks, months even. This was the straw that broke the camel's back I guess. None of the goals were his mistakes, but for me a top goalkeeper saves at least one of them (Hart may have even saved all three, he's saved very similar efforts in games against us). Hell, even a very good goalkeeper would be saving one of them, it's not like any of them were worldies. Pepe needs to step it up big time, as he's been outperformed by most of the keepers we've faced this season, whether it's Vorm, Ruddy, Hart, Al Habsy, Szczesny or whoever you care to name. I've made a similar point about our attacking players and how their goal tally's are inferior to players at the likes of Swansea, Blackburn, Norwich, Newcastle etc. The same applies to Reina, he's not performing anywhere near the level we should expect, the level that rightly earned him his reputation as one of the best keepers around. The attacking players need to start putting the ball in the net, and Reina needs to start making saves again.

Most of what happens between both goalmouths is good but it's bordering on criminal now how many times we've lost or drawn games that we were by far the better side. We were so superior to QPR it was embarrassing at times but we've ended up losing a game that was so one sided for 75 minutes it's not even funny. We could beat Wigan 10-0 on Saturday (don't laugh) and it won't make up for this. Those three points were ours and we simply gave them away. We're not going to get anywhere near Chelsea or Arsenal, and Newcastle can probably breathe easy now too I reckon. That's embarrassing. We've won one cup, and hopefully we'll win another. Even if that happens, the players should be looking at the league table, seeing themselves below Newcastle and they should be absolutely fucking ashamed of themselves.

Kenny isn't blameless, I didn't like the starting line up and I liked the three substitutions even less. Coates scored a stunning goal but why not put Flanagan on instead of shunting Carragher out to right back? When Adam went off I'd have preferred to see Carroll or even Shelvey than Henderson, and whilst I didn't like to see Suarez brought off either there may have been an injury there as he'd been limping just before. Regardless of team selection or substitutions, the players have to carry the can for what happened in the closing stages of this game. It wasn't anything Dalglish did that caused us to lose. They had the game won, they were in complete control and they blew it. They folded under pressure and there is a definitely lack of mental toughness in this squad. They can't kill teams off, and they often bottle it when defending leads.

It's not all doom and gloom, we've played some great football this season and we've shown in the cups and in some of the more difficult league games what a good side we can be on our day (even if we haven't won all of those games). I still feel pretty good about the big picture and I'd be a lot more concerned if we were producing performances like the Sunderland one on a regular basis. We aren't, those are thankfully rare, we're mostly playing well even if the results don't always show it. We desperately need to develop a ruthless streak, a winning mentality throughout the entire club, but how do you do that?

I don't know, I just hope Kenny does.

LIVERPOOL 1 WIGAN ATHLETIC 2

Competition - Premier League
Date - Sat 24 Mar 2012
Venue - Anfield
Scorer(s) – Luis Suarez
Half Time - 0-1
Star Man – Jon Flanagan

Team: Reina; Flanagan, Carragher, Skrtel, Enrique; Henderson (Carroll), Spearing, Gerrard; Kuyt (Sterling), Suarez, Downing (Shelvey):

I wasn't even angry after this. I was just massively deflated not to mention more than a little fearful about the immediate future. Is this as bad as it's going to get, or can we fall even further? Two defeats in a week against sides in the bottom three is absolutely shambolic, and I suppose we should be glad we don't have to play Wolves any time soon. Kenny blamed this one on 'tiredness'.

That's one way of looking at it I suppose. Another is that they've got the deckchairs out and are only arsed about the cups. I'm not sure either one is completely accurate, but there are elements of both in what we're seeing at the moment I'd say. Were they tired after playing three games in six days? Probably. Did they have the desire to fight through that tiredness and get the job done? No, they never.

I can't completely dismiss Kenny's explanation for the loss, even as I watched this horror show unfold I could see tiredness was a factor. We started both halves playing at a high tempo and pressing the ball, hunting in packs to win back possession and put them under the cosh. It lasted all of about ten minutes, then we completely stopped doing it. Fatigue may have been the main reason for that, but as I said, the desire to fight through that tiredness and summon up that extra bit of effort to get the job done just wasn't there. And if they are tired then is that not a damning indictment on the fitness of the squad? Put it this way, imagine how much worse off we'd be if we'd been having to deal with the demands of European football this season. We'd probably be in the relegation zone, but no doubt still in Europe as, y'know, we find the energy from somewhere when it's a cup game.

Look how many games Stoke have played this season, yet they were able to hold Man City to a draw despite playing their third game in six days. If we can't perform against Wigan because the players are 'tired', then someone isn't doing their job properly. Yes Sports Science team, I'm looking at you. Again. This performance was so bad that it can't JUST be put down to heavy legs. Application, or lack of, is surely an issue as well. I wouldn't go as far as to say the team didn't try, as I don't think the group of players we have here are capable of going out and deliberately going through the motions. I do think that sub-consciously they're not as motivated as they should be. I mean, would we have lost this game had it been in the FA Cup? Not a chance in my opinion. The bottom line is that Wigan wanted this game more than we did. They needed it more than we did. Just as QPR did the other night. The players don't want to lose games, they don't want to play badly, but the evidence of 2012 points to them only being able to get themselves completely up for the games in the cup (as well as the 'glamour' league games like the derby and Arsenal). There's an obvious issue with quality too, we have often failed to win when we've played well but any time we've not performed we've almost always dropped points. This team can't win ugly, they can't grind out a result on the days when the performance level drops. You're not going to play well every week, and there will be times when you're tired, but good teams find a way to win anyway. Have we done that even once this season?

Admittedly we've got some players missing at the moment, but I can't honestly offer that up as explanation for this debacle. Wigan were missing Hugo Rodallega who's arguably their best player. They also lost Victor Moses in the first half, who is probably their next best player. So no, injuries aren't an excuse as the side we put on the field should have been good enough to do the job. There's just something about Wigan though, we always find it hard against them. No-one else does, as let's face it they're fucking crap. Can't defend, can't attack. Play nice football, but shite at both ends of the pitch (a bit like us some would say), that's why they are in relegation battles every year. If Wigan were a top four side we'd no doubt beat them every year. We're abysmal against the relegation sides though, it's the same every season. Last season we lost to Blackpool twice and also to West Ham. We dropped points to Birmingham as well. This year we've lost to Bolton, QPR and Wigan already and been held to a draw at home by Blackburn, who will probably beat us at Ewood Park in a few weeks.

I wasn't looking forward to this game at all after what happened at QPR. I was even less enthused when I saw the starting line up. Henderson and Kuyt both starting and no Andy Carroll again. Fucking great. I'm not a big believer in stats as generally I find they can be misleading as they don't take numerous factors into account. I saw one on twitter about Carroll that did catch my eye though. In his last seven starts we've won five and drawn two (we beat Cardiff on pens but including that as a win would be what's known as 'padding the stats'). In the last seven he's been left out we've drawn two and lost five. Interesting I thought. Of course it doesn't take into account the quality of opposition in those games but it does fly in the face of popular opinion that we play better football without him. It was undeniably true for a good while, but is it still the case now? Not for me, not anymore.

Not that all our problems will be solved just by starting Andy Carroll, I'm not suggesting that at all as there are so many things going wrong right now that it's difficult to even know where to start. I don't see the point in not picking him though, not unless the decision has already been made to sell him in the summer. And even if it has, I'd still be playing him anyway as he's unquestionably in better form than he's been in at any time since he came here. His transfer value isn't going to drop by picking him, hell, it may even increase. I keep saying it, but if Kenny thought Carroll was worth paying £35m for he should back his judgement and just fucking let the lad have a run of games to try and get into top form. It's not as though anyone else is playing well enough to keep him out.

As for Henderson, he keeps getting games regardless of how poor he is. He was hooked at half time against Wigan and was lucky to last that long. I'll be honest, I'd have subbed him immediately after he shit out of taking a shot from the edge of the box when it opened up for him. Everyone around me went mad when he did that, and rightly so. It's becoming a regular occurrence, I mentioned a similar incident in the League Cup final. There seems to be two schools of thought on Henderson. One is that he's desperately average and will never be a Liverpool player as long as he's got a hole in his arse. The other is that he's a young lad with loads of potential who'll prove all the doubters wrong and become class in a couple of years, just as Lucas did. I sit somewhere in between the two, leaning slightly more towards the first point of view to be honest. Just because Lucas came good after a dodgy start in which many wrote him off doesn't mean Henderson will. Lucas is actually the exception rather than the rule. I wouldn't write Henderson off because I do think technically he's pretty sound and by all accounts the lad has a tremendous work ethic and trains as hard as anybody to improve his game. What worries me is the lack of balls. He just seems scared to try and express himself. I compare him with Jonjo Shelvey, and I'd take Shelvey all day at the moment as he isn't scared. I'm not even a big Shelvey fan, but that lad has swagger, he has confidence in his own ability to the extent that he probably thinks he's much better than he is. That's not always a bad thing. Shelvey came on against Wigan and was demanding the ball off everybody. He wanted to get on the ball, to make things happen and to drive the team forward. He believes in himself. When Henderson gets the ball he just looks like he wants rid of it as soon as possible in case he loses it.

It's probably unfair to single him out, he was just the worst of a bad bunch. Gerrard was arguably even more disappointing because unlike Henderson, there are actually expectations on Gerrard to perform. He was nowhere near his usual standard, and the tiredness excuse looked to apply to him as much as anyone. Way below par from the captain, although he did set up Suarez for our only goal.

I thought Suarez was shite too, maybe he's another who was a bit 'leggy'? He fell over quite a lot, he gave the ball away quite a lot, and he complained a lot. He also scored so deserves credit for that, even if he later blotted his copybook by using his arm to put the ball over the line when it appeared to be going in anyway. He was booked for it, harshly I think as it didn't look intentional to me but if he had stayed away from it Skrtel's header looked to be on it's way in anyway. Mason was right to disallow it, much as I hate to admit it as he's battling it out with Kevin Friend for the 'biggest cunt with a whistle who's name isn't Howard Webb' award. Had that goal stood we'd have probably gone on to win the game as we'd started the second half very well and had Wigan on the ropes. From that moment on though we just seemed to lose all belief and all life was sapped from our performance. The flurry of effort we'd seen immediately after half time fizzled out and Wigan were very comfortable after that. They did nothing in attack, they only had two shots in the entire game but both of them ended up in the net.

The first of those was a first half penalty which at the time I had absolutely no idea what it had been awarded for. I saw Carragher head the ball up in the air and then Moses send a weak header straight at Reina. Next thing I knew a penalty had been awarded and Moses was flat out on the floor and the physio was sprinting on. Whatever had happened I assumed it was the correct decision as neither the players nor crowd seemed overly upset with the refs call. Having seen the replay of it, Mason was right to give the penalty as it was a clear foul by Skrtel. Why he'd go in with his foot raised so high in the penalty area I don't know, he's always been prone to reckless, rash challenges but this season he has cut right down on them to his great credit. A rare rush of blood to the head, but he's been our best player this season and even in this game I thought he played very well, that one lapse aside.

Pepe guessed correctly but the pen was right in the corner and he just couldn't get there. Un-saveable. Wigan's first attack and they scored, fucking typical eh? We'd had a few half chances and had started the game well but quickly faded. The same thing happened in the second half too, which does lend more weight to the whole 'tiredness' thing, or more specifically the whole 'not fit enough' thing.

The lack of quality in our attacking play was difficult to watch, and it was clear from around midway through the second half that we weren't going to score again. The arrival of Raheem Sterling was greeted with a huge roar. That's how desperate we've become, we were looking to a 17 year old making his first team bow to come on and save us. Not an ideal situation for him to come into, but needs must. He was only in the squad due to all the injuries, but we may as well keep him in there now for the rest of the season, or at least until Bellamy returns. He's a useful option to have on the bench as unlike most our other attacking players, he can actually run. He did alright when he came on, he was lively and didn't look overawed, he even managed to get a shot on target which is more than most of the others managed. Wigan were never troubled though and the boos at full time were not pleasant but entirely expected. You can't follow up a loss away at a bottom three side with a loss at home to another bottom three side. It's unacceptable and if people want to boo to show their disapproval I'm not going to tell them they're wrong, even if I wouldn't do it myself.

We've completely fucked up our league season now. The best we can hope for is 7th again, and right now you wouldn't want to put any money on us even achieving that. There's teams breathing down our neck now, including the blues who have once again drawn within two points of us, as have Sunderland. Swansea and Norwich are also just one win away from catching us whilst Stoke are only a further point back and probably laughing their heads off at Kenny's claims of 'tiredness'.

Winning the FA Cup to go along with the League Cup would represent an excellent season, but we really can't be finishing any lower than 7th (which in itself is bad enough) and if the players need any extra motivation to get through those games when they're feeling a little bit jaded, then maybe we should pin a giant league table to the dressing room wall at Melwood and make them look at it every day.

Premier League Round Up (24-26 March 2012)

Whilst Liverpool were continuing to do their bit for Sport Relief by donating another three points to those desperately in need, the sides at the bottom who were not so fortunate as to be facing the reds were having to fend for themselves.

Two of those, Bolton and Blackburn, met at the Reebok stadium on Saturday. It was always going to be tough for Rovers to go there and get anything due to the 'Muamba factor', it was the worst possible time for anyone to play Bolton. Still, it could have been different but for a controversial refereeing decision when the score was 0-0. Junior Hoilett (my boy) had a great shout for a penalty waved away by Andre Marriner, and shortly after David Wheater headed Bolton in front. I have to confess I always liked Wheater when he was at Boro, I thought he was going to become a very good player but something must have gone wrong somewhere along the line as he's playing for Bolton for a reason. Either that or he's never been any good, which would make my judgement so questionable I should apply for a scouting job at LFC. Wheater hadn't scored for them prior to this game, but having broke his duck he then scored again seven minutes later to make it 2-0. Nzonzi headed in a long throw from from Pedersen to set the Bolton nerves jangling but Owen Coyle's men held on for a huge three points that have sucked Blackburn back into the relegation mix. They have two massive advantages over the other strugglers however. Firstly they have Steve Kean, and secondly they've got a game against us coming up soon.

Meanwhile, bouyed by a huge win over Chelsea in midweek, Manchester City travelled to the Britannia Stadium to face Stoke. Mancini's men were boosted by the news that the Mighty Salif was ruled out for the home side due to a spot of hamstring trouble. Another former LFC man was playing though and he produced the best goal of the season so far. Absolutely stunning strike from the big fella, evoking memories of when Crouchamania ran wild for us. I'll always have a soft spot for Crouchy, he's like the ex-girlfriend you really liked but didn't treat too well as you always thought you could probably do better. You dumped her and she ended up with some inoffensive nerd who was punching well above his weight because he had come into money. You felt bad for her, but couldn't help feeling just a tad smug as you knew that she knew she'd 'settled'. She'd peaked with you and it was all downhill from there. Then all of a sudden everything changed as the nerd's money ran out and she got with someone who was maybe as good looking and had better prospects than you. Pity is overtaken by resentment and you start thinking maybe you'd like her back. Did you make a mistake in jibbing her off? Then normal order is restored again as the good looking guy with the prospects dumps her having found someone better and she winds up with some steroid fuelled meathead who's only goal in life is to get bladdered and get into fights every weekend. You realise you don't actually want her back but still, this is not the kind of fella you want to see her with. Erm, yeah, so, what a strike eh?

Thankfully City hit back when Yaya Toure took full advantage of the Diao sized hole in the middle of the park to equalise with a long range effort that took a slight deflection, but neither side could find a winner and a draw was probably a fair result. Other notes from this game; David Silva was on the receiving end of a typical Stoke challenge, Dean Whitehead almost taking the little Spaniard's head off with a careless elbow. A bloodied Silva had to wear a big bandage on his head for the remainder of the game. Didn't stop the Stoke fans booing him though. Neanderthals. For some reason David Platt replaced Mancini for the post match TV interviews. There was no warning, no *'if you don't want to see his giant egghead look away now'* message, nothing. Just this huge moon-face suddenly filling my entire TV screen. Scared the crap out of me, I haven't jumped like that since the first time I saw the head fall out of the boat in 'Jaws'. I'm still shaking now as I type. I don't even know what Platt had to say for himself, I was that shaken up. Having said that, even when he's interviewed on the radio I struggle to take it in as his voice is so monotone and dull. You know the priest in Father Ted who no-one can listen to because he has *'an incredibly boring voice'*? That's David Platt that is. There were no surprises from the Stoke camp in the post interviews, it was all very predictable; Tony Pulis yet again complaining about a penalty his side didn't get. *sigh* He might have had a point if he didn't manage Stoke, a team that gets away with more fouls in the box than any side not managed by Alex Ferguson and playing home games at Old Trafford.

Moving on, and Motson was assigned to Arsenal v Villa this week. I'll concede that he's definitely slightly more bearable when he's not screeching about Chelsea. *"Has the penny finally dropped with the BBC programmers?"* some of you are probably asking? Well no, you idiots, obviously it hasn't as the prick is still working. Moving him away from Chelsea games is but the tiniest of steps in the right direction. Getting him off our TV altogether would be a bigger step and having him framed for a crime he didn't commit and thrown in jail would be one glorious, giant leap for mankind. I could probably settle for just having him removed from MOTD though. Anyway, Arsenal were good value for their win and Villa were crap once again. Gibbs was lively early on and opened the scoring after 16 minutes with a shot that Shay Given should have done better with. Walcott made it 2-0 after the latest brilliant defence splitting ball from Song (very under-rated player him). 'Legohead' added a third in stoppage with a cracking free-kick as the Gunners recorded their seventh win in a row. Still think it's the worst Arsenal side I've seen in years, but they've hit a run of form at the right time whilst those around them are choking like Greg Norman in the final round of a Major. They may even finish third unless Spurs manage to forget that they are Spurs and get back to being whoever it was they were before they remembered they are Spurs.

Speaking of Spurs, they went to Stamford Bridge in the early kick off on Saturday. It was a game both teams badly needed to win and that goalless draw wasn't really any use to either. Tottenham should have won the game, they had the better opportunities but didn't take them. Van Der Vaart missed the only chance of the first half and Adebayor had one cleared off the line by Cahill in the second, whilst Bale hit the bar and was denied by a good save by Cech right at the death. The only winners from this game were Arsenal. Chelsea's usual lack of sportsmanship came to the fore again as Kaboul went down with a knee injury and the Spurs players were virtually pleading with Chelsea to put the ball out. They refused, carried on attacking until eventually Bale had to deliberately foul Ramires just to allow his stricken team-mate to receive treatment. Mata hit the post with the free-kick, there'd have been murder if it had gone in though. Hilariously, David Luiz stuck out a foot to try and get the rebound and diverted it away from the incoming Drogba who was in yards of space and would have had a tap in. Drogba flung himself to the floor, arms outstretched like some extra from one of the Rambo movies. He may have even appealed for a penalty as he crashed to the turf, he's that shameless you can't rule anything out.

Moving on, and QPR went to Sunderland looking to build on the three points gifted to them by us in midweek. They're absolute fucking dog dirt though and they won't come up against sides as generous as us very often.

Sunderland wiped the floor with them and Cisse got himself sent off again to compound Mark Hughes' misery. Bendtner headed Sunderland in front before Djibs went in two footed under the ref's nose. It wasn't malicious, but his tackling is about as effective as his left foot and he knew as soon as he'd done it he was in trouble. McClean and Sessegnon added to the Mackems lead but Taiwo grabbed a consolation goal for Rangers with a superb free-kick. If we'd have seen QPR off as we should have they'd be in really deep shit now and Sunderland would not be within two points of us either. Then again, if Gary Neville's aunty had bollocks she'd be his uncle. Or his brother. Or should that be his dad? Doesn't matter, the point is that it's all ifs and buts.

Norwich continue to impress, not only with their ability to win games but also how they keep wheeling out these chumps no-one has ever heard of, some dude called Simon Lappin being the latest. As with most of his team-mates I have absolutely no idea what position he plays. I know their keeper, the strikers and the centre halves, the rest of them are a mystery even Scooby Doo and the gang would struggle with. *"Hey Fred, let's take off the mask of the right winger and see who he is" ..... "Oh look it's... erm... nope sorry I haven't got a scooby dooby doooo"*

Jarvis gave Wolves the lead against the run of play but yet another impressive finish by Grant Holt drew the Canaries level within a minute or so and he then made it 2-1 from the penalty spot. There was to be no hat-trick though, two quick yellow cards saw him sent for an early bath. The ten men held on comfortably enough and Paul Lambert is giving Brendan Rodgers and Alan Pardew a real fight for that manager of the year award.

Speaking of Rodgers, Evertonians made the journey from North to South Wales to take on his in form Swansea side. With the FA Cup replay coming up this week I didn't give the blues much of a chance in this one so it was something of a shock when I heard the score. Baines broke the deadlock with a trademark free-kick and Jelavic wrapped it up late on to give the blues the Welsh bragging rights. The bad news is the result put Everton within two points of us again. The good news is Swansea would have gone level with us had they won. Actually there is no good news there at all is there? It's bad news and slightly less bad news. Depressing stuff.

Onto Sunday, and Newcastle went to West Brom looking to draw level on points with 5th placed Chelsea. They did it at a canter and had this game won before half time. West Brom look to have the deckchairs out now having secured their survival for another year. Papis Ciise scored again - this time after just five minutes - to give the Geordies the lead and six minutes later Ben Arfa doubled their advantage with a fantastic goal on the counter attack. Cisse scored his second after another wonderful move as Pardew's side made the points safe with just 35 minutes gone. Shane Long pulled one back after Williamson and Krul got into a right old mess, but Newcastle were always on top and West Brom had no answer to Ben Arfa who ran riot. 3-1 flattered the home side. There was a minute's applause before the game for a Baggies legend who passed away this week, and the West Brom players and management all wore black armbands in his memory. Hilariously, Hodgson tore his off and threw it on the ground in a fit of pique after Newcastle's third goal. He quickly realised and picked it up, but the damage was done and he had to apologise. Bizarre really, I can understand lashing out in frustration, but what I don't get is how that frustration translates to *'I know, I'm gonna rip this black armband off and lash it on the floor'*. Kick an advertising board or punch a wall or something. Hell, even rub your face like a madman if you like, but don't be throwing a black armband on the floor, you disrespectful crank. There's talk that Roy is next in line for the England job if 'Arry turns it down. That's a fantastic idea and could would definitely end well. By 'well' I mean 'badly' if you're an England fan, and 'hilariously' if you aren't. Even a top manager like Capello couldn't turn that ship around, I doubt if anyone could make a success of it given the expectation to talent ratio. The pressure it brings is unique and many a man has folded under it. Steve McLaren and his umbrella are small potatoes in comparison to the kind of shit Roy could pull, as he's got a bit of a temper on him hasn't he? Picture the scene, 'Remembrance Sunday' at Wembley, England go 3-0 down before half time and a furious Hodgson rips the poppy off his blazer, wipes his arse with it before repeatedly punching himself in the face over and over. Hodgson for England you say? Make it so.

One more game to cover, but I've got very little to say about it. The Mancs beat Fulham 1-0. They didn't play well but they won, again. Fulham should have had a penalty right at the end, but the ref completely bottled it, again. Understandable, if you're a young ref starting out the last thing you want to do is upset the 'Head of Referees' and end up being blackballed from taking charge of any big games in the future. And that's not even taking into account what Mike Riley thinks...

Finally, I noticed there were a lot of players this weekend wearing pink boots. Most of those players were a bit shit. Not surprising, there's always some kind of new fashion fad that crap players all get on, the kind of shite that you just don't get good players wearing. Pink boots, lime green boots, those banana yellow boots, Everton shirts....

chapter twelve

April

NEWCASTLE UNITED 2 LIVERPOOL 0

Competition - Premier League
Date - Sun 1 Apr 2012
Venue - St James' Park
Scorer(s) –
Half Time - 1-0
Star Man – Jonjo Shelvey

Team: Reina; Flanagan, Skrtel, Carragher, Enrique; Gerrard, Spearing, Shelvey (Downing); Bellamy (Henderson), Carroll (Kuyt), Suarez:

There was no doubting who the April Fools were at St James Park as the reds produced a joke of a performance that had the Geordies pissing themselves at our expense. It's a new low being taunted by Newcastle fans as they're supposed to be the butt of everyone else's jokes. Not any more it seems, now it's our turn to be mocked. If these players have any sense of fucking pride whatsoever they'll be ashamed of the embarrassment they've heaped on the club and their manager so far in 2012.

Newcastle fans don't like Kenny Dalglish and they took great pleasure in mocking him and laughing at him. Carroll, Bellamy and Enrique also had the piss taken out of them but they were in a position to do something about it and failed. Kenny Dalglish being ridiculed by Newcastle fans was just horrible to witness. Of course as the man at the top he takes the responsibility for results and performances and much of the criticism that will come his way is justified. Still, it's infuriating seeing the spineless, half arsed manner the team are surrendering these league games now. Six defeats from seven, with each one seeming to get worse than the last. Where's their professional pride?

Once again, this was really painful to watch. As usual we started well, predictably missed a couple of glorious chances, hit the woodwork and also had a couple of good penalty shouts turned down. Even more predictable was how we conceded from the first chance our opponent created and then didn't have the balls to bounce back from it. They shouldn't be this bad, they were playing well in the first part of the season even if results didn't always show it. Now results have finally started to reflect the performances and unfortunately neither are any good.

Skrtel and Carroll both had clear chances to give us an early lead but both put their headers over the bar. Carroll's wasn't easy in fairness as he was being punched in the head by Krul and there wasn't much room to get the ball up and down. Still, I'm not really in the mood to be 'fair' to him after the ridiculous incident before that which saw him booked when he should have scored. Contrary to popular opinion, I don't think he dived. It looked to me like the ball got stuck under his feet and as he dragged his foot back to retrieve it his body carried on moving and he just toppled over like a big fucking tree. I almost wish he had dived as that would be less embarrassing. As for the two penalty shouts, one was a blatant shove/hold on Carroll by Williamson from a corner and the other was a clear handball on the line by Simpson. The one on Carroll was a foul but it's the kind of decision you never get as refs always seem to let them go. If they ever start to give them then Stoke will be relegated with a record low points tally and we'll probably have to chop Skrtel's hands off or make him wear boxing gloves. The Simpson one however should not only have been a penalty it should also have been a red card, which would have clearly changed the whole complexion of the game. Unfortunately the ref couldn't see it as there were too many bodies in the way, and the linesman was just fucking useless all day. He couldn't see a fist if it was headed straight for his face, a theory I'd be more than happy to put to the test.

There's no question bad officiating played a part in this defeat but I really don't want to use that as an excuse because the players don't deserve any excuses to be made for them. Six defeats out of seven? 11 points behind Newcastle? Below Everton in the table? No, there should be no excuses offered on their behalf and bad decisions or not they got what they deserved from this game. Nothing. The way it unfolded was typical of our season. Newcastle hadn't done much early on and we'd been dominant without making it count. Then out of nothing Ben Arfa creates space for himself and plants a perfect cross onto the head of Cisse who places his header right in the far corner giving Reina no chance. There's no point dissecting the goal and looking to apportion blame. Sometimes teams will produce moments of quality that catch you out. Skrtel's positioning wasn't bad, he was an inch away from getting his head on the ball but the cross was simply too good, as was the finish. I can live with us conceding the odd goal like that as shit happens, but unfortunately our own impotence in front of goal means every time we concede it's probably going to cost us points. If you're a good side you should be able to concede and still win games. This weekend Spurs conceded one to Swansea and won, Chelsea let in two at Villa and also claimed maximum points whilst Man City contrived to let in three at home to Sunderland yet still avoided defeat. Not us though, we concede and we're fucked. We just can't come back, the lack of goals in this team is frightening.

It says everything about our current predicament that as soon as we fell behind I thought it was game over as I didn't think for a second we had it in us to come back. As a team we are now mentally weak and generally lacking in bottle. You could almost see the confidence visibly drain from them after going behind. Not for the first time this season either. There's an acceptance from too many players that the game is lost and the lack of fight when we are behind is completely unacceptable. The bright start we'd made fizzled out into nothing as soon as we went behind and after that Newcastle were generally very comfortable. The second goal was a joke, it should never have stood as Cisse was several yards offside. I don't care if it hit somebody else on the way through to him, the ball was played in his direction and he was miles off. He wasn't 'passive' as the ball went straight to him and he fucking scored!! I'm not having all this 'second phase of attack' bollocks either. It's not like he was trying to get back onside, nowhere near the ball and not looking to gain an advantage when it was played. The ball was played towards him, it reached him and he scored. It took a slight touch off someone before it got to him as Flanagan challenged Ben Arfa but if that isn't offside we may as well just scrap the law altogether and let players stand wherever they like.

It was an unfortunate way to concede but they always looked more likely scorers than us and had previously hit the post through Williamson. As toothless as we are, at 1-0 we always had a chance as even we can occasionally manage one goal. At 2-0 however we were finished. That doesn't excuse how some of them were just strolling around waiting for the final whistle. It doesn't excuse the lack of discipline we witnessed (not just from Reina either). It doesn't excuse Aurelio laughing with Doni on the bench. Did any of you feel like laughing as you watched this? I felt more like crying, but then I haven't been paid thousands of pounds a week to sit on a treatment table for most of the last five years. I get that he probably isn't arsed about us losing to Newcastle and being 8th in the league, he hardly ever plays and probably doesn't feel a part of things. I understand that, really I do. It's not going to ruin his weekend and he's probably not given it a second thought since. So yeah, I accept that he isn't going to hurt as much as we do and don't expect him to, but still, act like a professional and at least put on a pretence of giving a fuck as when the fans are hurting the last thing they want to see is some millionaire footballer sat there laughing whilst their team is losing it's sixth game out of seven.

Maybe I'm being a bit of a meathead fan about all this, but I didn't like seeing Carroll and Enrique all smiley and pally with the Newcastle players in the tunnel before the game either. I know they're your mates, but leave that shit out and get your game faces on as this is a serious situation we're in. Do these players realise just how fucking embarrassing it is for us to sit below Newcastle and Everton in the table? I don't think some of them do you know. Reina clearly does, his frustration was there for all to see as he totally over-reacted to a trip by Perch. The red card was inevitable, as is the three match ban that will follow. Perch embarrassed himself as contact was minimal to say the least, but this referee was always going to produce a red card and Reina was incredibly stupid for doing what he did. There was clearly a lot of pent up frustration in his actions, but doing what he did only made a bad situation even worse. Hopefully Doni doesn't make any costly errors and Reina will have an FA Cup final to look forward to when he's served his punishment.

Some would suggest it's a pity a few more of them can't be given a three game ban, but then who would you bring in to replace them? The subs bench at St James' didn't exactly inspire confidence. A mate text me midway through the second half furious at the lack of changes. I saw his point, we were doing nothing and were completely devoid of ideas, confidence and effort. Usually I'd be the first to call for substitutions, but this time it wouldn't have bothered me if Kenny had left it as it was for the entire ninety as none of those on the bench were going to come on and change this game around. In fact, Downing, Henderson and Kuyt coming on probably made us even weaker. Shelvey was the first one to get hooked when I'd suggest you can make a strong case that he was our best player up to that point. Bellamy going off didn't bother me, he was poor and his fitness needs to be looked after as he's been out a few weeks. As for Carroll, personally I'd have left him on if only to deprive the Geordies of the opportunity to mock him as he was subbed. He stormed off down the tunnel and wasn't happy. Hopefully his anger was directed at himself for falling over when clean through on goal and not at Dalglish for bringing him off, although I doubt it.

We're a right mess at the moment. We seem to play a different system with different personnel every week and it's not doing anyone any good. The players don't seem to know what they're supposed to be doing and don't have the strength of character to just grind out results when things aren't going their way. At least earlier in the season when we were losing and drawing games we were generally playing well and putting in maximum effort. The arse has fallen out of us in a big way since the turn of the year though. Kenny has to take responsibility as he signed several of these under-performing players. He also trains the squad and sends them out to play to his instructions and tactics. He won't try and shy away from that and he's still defending the players publicly even though many of them don't deserve it. He's coming under mounting criticism, plenty of it justified, but he's not being helped in the slightest by the players. If they try their best and fall short through a lack of quality that's on the manager. If they fall short through a lack of effort it's on them as well. Right now it's both that seems to be the problem, so the blame lies with everybody connected with it.

They all need to pull their fingers out and start winning some games. Kenny needs to get a grip of them and let them know that anyone not pulling their weight can forget about playing in the FA Cup and he needs to get his own house in order in terms of the shape of the team and how they are approaching games. Maybe they all think winning the FA Cup will make all this ok, and up to a point they'd be right. What if they lose that semi to Everton though? It's entirely possible, probable even, given how both sides have played since the last derby. The idea of losing to them at Wembley is almost unthinkable, but then so was falling below them in the league and yet here we are. Things are bad right now but they could easily get worse. It's up to everyone at the club to pull together and make sure it doesn't. I made the analogy the other week of us being the boxer with no knockout punch and a glass jaw. Here's another boxing analogy; We're now on the canvas and have two choices. Either get back on our feet and come up swinging or stay down and be counted out. I believe we'll come up swinging, but I wouldn't bet my house on it.

Premier League Round Up (31 March - 2 April 2012)

There've been some bad weekends this season, especially since the turn of the year, but this was by far the worst yet. Everton leapfrogged us in the league table, Newcastle went 11 points clear of us, 'Useless' saw his QPR side edge three points closer to safety, Man City's recent choke act plumbed new depths as they've now started dropping points at home, and finally their neighbours tightened their grip on the title and in the process sent my boy Steve Kean tailspinning back into the relegation dog fight. Oh, and the fly on top of the turd sandwich? Torres finally scored. You could say it was a complete Ibrahimovic of a weekend. A stinking, steaming, rancid pile of Zlatan.

Sunderland couldn't have looked much more inept against the blues in the FA Cup quarter final last week. They'd been absolutely dire in what was their biggest game of the season, but four days later they turned it on in what was essentially a 'dead rubber' league game for them. They're unlikely to finish much higher or lower than they are now, but you'd have thought they were in a relegation battle given how hard they fought at City. Our players could learn a lot from them actually. Not the embarrassing themselves in the cup against Everton part, obviously. They took the lead against City through Larsson and even after being pegged back by a Balotelli penalty they kept at it, finding themselves 3-1 up with five minutes left to play following fine goals by Bendtner and another from Larsson. City threw everything at them in the closing stages and got back on level terms through goals from Balotelli and Kolorov but the Black Cats dug in and held out for a point.

This game saw all the aspects of Balotelli's character that make him so fascinating to watch. A nonchalent penalty, a terrific goal, and of course the mad moments that you're almost guaranteed whenever he takes to the field. One minute he's acting as peacemaker when Dzeko lost his rag and was trying to batter Phil Bardsley. Mario was doing that pointing at his own head gesture telling Dzeko to 'think' about what he was doing. Amazing, but no doubt the irony would be lost on the mad bastard. Next thing City have a free kick on the edge of the box and he's kicking off at Kolorov because he wanted to take it. Kompany had to drag him away and even then he wasn't having it. He pissed on a lot of chips the other week when he did that interview with Noel Gallagher and dismissed almost all of the mad stories we've heard about him as being bullshit, but he's still the most entertaining player in the Premier League, and not because of his ability.

Disappointing to see loads of City fans getting off when the score was 3-1. Mancini's men had won something like 20 home games on the bounce and they almost came back to win this one too but just ran out of time. They're in their first title race since the days when Henry VIII was going through wives like Abramovich goes through managers (albeit with a different kind of 'severance' involved, although if he was back in Russia you know Roman would be chopping off heads instead of writing cheques for £10m), and here they are walking out on their team when their support is needed most. Pricks like that don't deserve a title.

Moving on, and Di Matteo went with a 4231 formation to finally try and get Torres firing, and it worked, sort of. He should have scored twice in the first half but fluffed both chances. Fortunately for him Sturridge was on hand to turn in the rebound on one of them to put Chelsea 1-0 up at half time. Ivanovic bundled in a second from a corner but Villa came storming back with late goals from Collins and Lehaj slid in at the back post to make it 2-2. Never heard of that fella, he's an American international apparently. Not sure where he's been hiding all season, but Villa are a little bit 'Norwich' on that score. McLeish's side were level for just three minutes, Ivanovic once again bundling one in from a corner. This time it hit him on the head as he was running into the six yard box. Deep into stoppage time Sturridge led a breakaway and Torres drove a shot home for his first league goal since September. Hopefully he has to wait as long for his next one, although I doubt it. Knob.

It says a lot about how bad Wolves have become that I actually expected Bolton to beat them. I don't think I've tipped them to win a game all season but I knew they'd win at Molyneux as Wolves are incapable of beating anybody right now. Hell, even we went to their place and won, one of only TWO league wins for us in 2012. Bolton stink, they've got Championship level players throughout their side and that's where I still think they're headed. Position for position Wolves are superior, but they've got themselves stuck in a huge rut they can't get out of. They've even started fighting amongst themselves now, as Hennessey and Johnson squared up to eachother. Johnson was probably bevvied, so at least he has an excuse but the keeper should know better. Kightley broke the deadlock with a fine strike from 20 yards but Bolton quickly hit back with a contentious penalty when former Wolves man Mark Davies was felled in the box by Johnson. There was minimal contact, but there WAS contact and it would be difficult for the ref to give anything else. Petrov scored, Wolves' fragile confidence was shot to pieces and Bolton were soon in front when Alonso tapped in after Ngog's header had came back off the bar. Substitute Kevin Davies scored a fine third and although Jarvis got one back for the home side Bolton hung on for a huge three points and, remarkably, their third win on the bounce.

Arsenal had won seven on the spin but that run came to a shuddering halt at Loftus Road. Taraabt's first league goal of the season set QPR on their way and it was a great finish too. At Championship level he's fantastic, but it seems like he's in over his head in the top flight. Hopefully next season Rangers will back in the second tier and he can strut his stuff again. Walcott equalised, Van Persie should have added a second and then Diakite put the home side back in front. It was a lead they would hold onto without too much difficulty as Van Persie had an off day and when that happens there's really not much else there. It was an upset, but I'd argue it was less surprising than the Gunners' seven game win streak.

The battle to survive is really hotting up as aside from Wolves, all the teams at the bottom are putting wins on the board. It's the time of year when Wigan start to get hot and it's happening again as they won their second game in a row, seeing off Stoke relatively comfortably. They started well and Di Santo went clean through early on but there's no prizes for guessing the outcome. Failure. He's proper crap that boy. Beausejour then missed an absolute sitter and Wigan were denied a clear penalty when Whitehead handled. Don't expect Pulis to remember that though next time he's crying about not getting decisions. Fuckin scruff. Alcaraz put Wigan in front with a bullet header. Here's a thought, let him swap positions with Di Santo. He's a crap defender who can finish, Di Santo is a crap striker who can't finish. Who cares if Di Santo can defend or not, he can't be any worse than Alcaraz and at least by doing this they might get a goal or two from their centre forward for a change. Moses wrapped it up late on when he robbed the useless Wilkinson (he's a poor mans Tony Hibbert, which is just about as insulting as it's possible to be to anyone without bringing their mother into it) and showed good composure to go past the keeper and score.

Meanwhile, the blues had a piss easy win over Hodgson's West Brom at the Pit. The Baggies have completely mailed it in now, they're safe and they're on their summer holidays already by the looks of it. They were terrible. Osman hit a deflected opener and then a surprisingly good strike by Anichebe wrapped it up, proving once again that the sun does indeed shine even on a dog's arse somedays (I've used that before, but it's a class expression). West Brom were a shambles and Odemwingie and Foster went head to head as tempers flared. The striker threw his head in on the keeper, which begs the question; should he have been sent off? Is it any different just because it's a team-mate? Actually it had probably more to do with the reaction of Foster than them being on the same side. We've seen it a few times this season. Bellamy stood his ground against Fulham so Dempsey got away with it. Klasnic saw red after a Norwich player hit the deck like a sack of shite early in the season, and then there's what happened with Perch and Reina. There's definitely a pattern there. Make a meal of it and it will be a red card, act in an honest manner and it's a yellow. Is it any wonder players are acting like such shithouses?

Moving on, and Norwich did it again. Some lad called Ryan Bennett this time. Surely they must be running out of players now? They lost 2-1 at Fulham this week, thankfully, or else they'd be another team on the verge of overtaking us. Dempsey's tap in put Fulham in front after a Ruiz shot was only parried by Ruddy. Ruiz looks like his hair is starting to grow back at a decent rate, which has also sparked an improvement in form. Tellin' yer, the two factors are not unrelated. Duff made it 2-0 with just 13 minutes gone when he beat the offside trap and finished neatly. It almost got worse for Norwich as Dempsey hit the post and then former reds' reserve Alex Kacaniklic saw a brilliant effort tipped onto the bar by Ruddy. Nice to see him getting an opportunity to play, he's a good lad from a nice family, I used to talk to his dad a fair bit when Alex was playing at the Academy.

Aaron Wilbraham gave Norwich hope with a late goal but they couldn't find an equaliser and went home empty handed. Wilbraham has cruelly been dubbed 'Wilbrahimovic' by Norwich fans. They mean it as a compliment but I fail to see how that's anything other than insulting. I speak from experience here as I've been on the receiving end of something similar in the past when some bird in town told me I looked like Ruud Van Nistelrooy. *"You cheeky bitch"* I replied, much to her shock. Turns out she was actually hitting on me and meant it as a compliment as she thought he was *"really handsome"*. Just as that unfortunate young woman didn't mean to offend me, the Norwich fans obviously don't mean any disrespect to Wilbraham, they're just gravely misguided in thinking flat track bully Zlatan is a great striker and not a big gormless show pony who never shows up to big games (at least any big game I've ever seen him in, and there must have been at least 20 down the years). He's as 'great' as Van Nistelrooy is 'handsome'. The only comparison to be made between me and the horsefaced former manc goalpoacher is the uncanny ability to be in the right place at the right time and put the ball in the back of the net.

*note: I may be overstating my goalscoring prowess just a smidge, but there's little doubt that I'm closer to RVN's level of footballing ability than he is to my level of handsomeness.

Onto Sunday now, Swansea went to Spurs and gave a good account of themselves again. The first half was all Spurs though, Van Der Vaart's beautifully controlled finish set them on their way and they squandered numerous other chances before the break. It was noticeable that they pressed Swansea high up the pitch and didn't give them any time on the ball. Swansea will pass it around even in their own penalty area and if you pressure them you can force mistakes. It's virtually impossible to do it for ninety minutes though and in the second half Swansea found more space to play and it was a much more even contest after that. Friedel made a wonderful save to keep out a piledriver by Sigurdsson who was once again impressive. He scored again too, as Swansea levelled midway through the 2nd half. Two late towering headers by Adebayor secured the points for Spurs who took advantage of Arsenal's defeat to regain third spot.

The final game saw Manchester United grab two goals in the final ten minutes to eventually see off plucky Blackburn on Monday night. Nothing to add to that other than Blackburn have been sucked right back into it and United are still absolute cunts who's fans sing more about us than they do about themselves.

LIVERPOOL 1 ASTON VILLA 1

Competition - Premier League
Date - Sat 7 Apr 2012
Venue - Anfield
Scorer(s) – Luis Suarez
Half Time - 0-1
Star Man – Martin Skrtel

Team: Doni; Flanagan, Carragher, Skrtel, Enrique (Agger): Shelvey (Carroll), Henderson; Kuyt, Suarez, Downing (Bellamy):

Well the good news is we didn't lose. The bad news is we failed to beat a depleted Aston Villa side containing numerous players I'd never even heard of. Not for the first time the result didn't reflect the performance but that's because we don't score goals and if you don't score goals you don't win games. It's that simple.

We had enough chances to win it, but yet again we failed to take them. That's two wins from 13 league games in 2012 now. I wouldn't bet on us making it three from 14 at Ewood Park on Tuesday night either. It's a sign of how far we've fallen of late that I'm trying to take some small crumbs of comfort in a performance that in all honesty never really rose above 'not bad'. It's difficult to even do that when you consider how awful the opposition were. Villa aren't a good side even when they've all their best players available, and I don't think I'm going overboard in saying that the team they sent out at Anfield wouldn't look out of place in the Championship.

With that in mind, the very least I'd expect is for us to be the better side, which we clearly were. It would have been nice for us to turn that superiority into three points, but it seems like we've almost forgotten how to win now. There's a massive crisis of confidence in the players that surely stems from their inability to score goals and the constant pressure they are playing under as a result of that. It doesn't appear to make any difference what combination of players Dalglish puts out either. We seem to get the same failings regardless of who is in the side. There's no magic solution, no player we can introduce to solve our goalscoring problems, we've just got to muddle through and hope things pick up. Ideally you'd want Kenny to stick with the same group of players and keep picking them instead of changing two or three every game. It's difficult to do that when so few of them are doing enough to justify their selection.

After the Newcastle game there were any number of players who could have been dropped. As it turned out, only three lost their starting places as Spearing, Bellamy and Carroll all dropped to the bench with Henderson, Downing and Kuyt returning to the side. God knows who'll start the next game, as how many could have cause for complaint if they didn't? With Carroll and Kuyt it's a case of picking your poison. I'd choose Carroll but it's not a clear cut decision as neither of them can score, both are regularly missing good chances and it's looking increasingly likely neither will be here next season. Dirk missed an open goal from two and a half yards out in the first half and blocked a goal bound shot by Agger in the second. It's been that kind of season for him. As for Carroll, he came off the bench and had a good headed chance that he put straight at the keeper. Not a sitter but that's the kind of chance that is meant to be his bread and butter and the reason he was signed. It's uncanny how so many of our games have followed such a similar pattern as this one. We hit the woodwork, we have penalty appeals turned down, we concede from any chance the opposition creates and we waste numerous good openings. It's been happening all season and this was just the latest in a long line of these frustrating, disappointing days.

The first good chance we created came very early on when Downing ran onto a ball and immediately knocked it into the space behind Hutton and flew past him with a pace and purpose we've seen all too infrequently this season. He left the full back for dead and whipped in a fantastic early cross that was begging to be converted. Suarez couldn't get there but Kuyt arrived at the back post and sent the ball goalwards. Given blocked it but Kuyt thought it had gone over the line. Whether it did or not I don't know, but neither ref or linesman gave it so it's irrelevant. It's incidents like this that make a mockery of the whole 'assists' stat in my opinion. Downing has no assists in the league but he's put in a shitload of crosses, some of them crap of course but several of which have been beauties. None have been converted but that's not his fault, he can't convert the chances he creates for others. This was a fantastic piece of wing play that deserved a goal at the end of it. Unfortunately it came to nothing and no-one will remember it in a week or two. It looks bad that our £20m winger has no assists in the league yet, but I'm far more concerned with the big fat zero he's sitting on for goals scored. He can't get on the end of his own crosses or do anything about the poor finishing of others but there's no excuse for him having fewer league goals than Tim Howard.

Suarez had two penalty shouts turned down in the first half. First when his cross struck the arm of a defender from point blank range (not a pen for me), and secondly when he appeared to be clipped by Hutton as he played a one two with Kuyt. Probably went down too easily but he was caught by the full back.

This is the ref that didn't give Fulham that last minute pen at Old Trafford when Murphy was bundled over from behind however. If he'd given this one there'd have been plenty of questions asked by fans of Fulham and Manchester City as this wasn't as clear a pen as Murphy's one. The expression two wrongs don't make a right seems apt in this case. Michael Oliver did his level best to not give us anything. Suarez was later booked for diving when once again there was contact, and Oliver turned down another penalty appeal when Lichaj handled after Kuyt had chested the ball past him. We'd probably have missed any penalty we'd gotten anyway, so I can't get too worked up over it. Even allowing for the referee we should still be able to beat this awful Villa side. Typically they scored with their only decent attack of the game. Shelvey's header to Flanagan was a little short but the full back hesitated as the ball bounced and Ste Warnock surged in to win it before whipping in a great ball that Doni flapped at. Villa retrieved it and the ball was worked back to Herd on the edge of the box and his fine shot beat Doni all ends up. They didn't even bother trying to attack after that, Heskey went into a holding midfield role and Agbonlahor cut an increasingly isolated figure up front. Carragher and Skrtel dealt with his threat very well but it can't have been easy for the pacey front-man when he had no support at all. The goal gave them something to cling to and it piled the pressure onto a Liverpool team that has been struggling badly, especially at Anfield. We toiled away but there was precious little inspiration there. Kuyt squandered the best chance of the half when he couldn't convert a cross-shot from Gerrard that came at him quickly. He was so close to goal that it was more difficult to miss than score but he blazed it high over the bar. That came after a rare bit of good play from the otherwise subdued Suarez, who also wasted a good chance of his own when he hit a left foot shot straight at Given instead of finding one of the corners.

The second half saw an improvement in our play and we put Villa under quite a bit of pressure in spells. Gerrard began the half playing on the right as Kuyt was moved up top with Suarez. If there's one thing the captain being out there gives us, it's quality delivery. One delicious cross found the head of Suarez who's effort struck the inside of the post before it was palmed away from on the goal-line by Given. Great cross, fine header, desperately unlucky. I'd love to know how many times we've hit the woodwork this season now, and I'd also be curious to know how many times Suarez has been denied by post or bar. I'd guess Suarez alone must be close to 15 by now, it's ridiculous how unlucky he's been at times. Even the goal we scored came after we'd been denied by the bar. Gerrard whipped in another great ball that Agger did brilliantly to reach at the far post and head goalwards. It bounced down off the bar but luckily enough this time the loose ball fell to a red shirt and Suarez headed it over the line. It had been coming as we'd been piling on the pressure.

Kenny had made changes and Villa were hanging on, offering no threat of their own and just hoping to see out time. Downing and Shelvey were replaced by Bellamy and Carroll, meaning Gerrard went back into the centre alongside the quietly efficient Henderson. Agger was sent on to replace the struggling

Enrique and the changes did give us a lift. There was more than enough time for us to go on and get a winner, but expecting us to score more than one goal in a game was asking too much. It's rare were do that these days. We had a couple of opportunities, Carroll headed another great Gerrard cross straight at Given and Kuyt got in the way of a shot from Agger that was going in.

Having seen their lead wiped out Villa began to show a little more ambition and tried to catch us on the counter when possible. We were throwing so many men forward there was always the chance we'd leave the back door open but thankfully we dealt with any attempted counter. They had a penalty shout of their own when Agger appeared to trip their substitute, but Oliver waved it away and booked the Villa player for diving. Looked harsh to me, but at least Oliver was consistent in his bad calls.

It's difficult to describe anything from this as a 'positive'. It's more a case of being 'less negative'. By that I mean we didn't play especially well, but we weren't as bad as we have been. There was some improvement on the Wigan and Newcastle games for example, but was that simply because Villa didn't play as well as those sides and had less to play for? Individually I thought most of the players did ok without being outstanding. Certainly they were better than against Newcastle and showed more determination than they did at St James'. It's all such a struggle though isn't it? Because we don't score enough goals we're constantly playing under massive pressure, and any goal conceded is likely to cost us points. It's difficult to play under those circumstances but until we can find a way to put the ball in the net consistently it's how it's going to be.

BLACKBURN ROVERS 2 LIVERPOOL 3

Competition - Premier League
Date - Tue 10 Apr 2012
Venue - Ewood Park
Scorer(s) – Maxi Rodriguez (2), Andy Carroll
Half Time - 1-2
Star Man – Andy Carroll

Team: Doni; Flanagan (Jones), Coates, Skrtel, Johnson (Agger); Spearing, Henderson; Bellamy, Shelvey, Maxi (Enrique); Carroll:

Phew. It's nice to be able to write about a win for a change. Normally three points against Blackburn would be seen as par for the course, nothing to get too excited about. There's been nothing 'normal' about this season however, and the manner of victory and the circumstances under which was achieved made this a result and performance to be proud of.

Everything that had been sadly missing in recent weeks was there in spades at Ewood; character, resilience, desire, mental toughness, and crucially, goals. Had it not been for the unfortunate incident that saw the desperately unlucky

Doni sent off and ruled out of a Wembley showpiece game against the blues, we may have ran riot in this game. We were certainly threatening to as the likes of Shelvey, Maxi, Bellamy and Carroll started the game like a runaway train. Doni's red card forced a major reshuffle that resulted in Shelvey having to play deeper and that made it much more difficult for us, and in particular for Carroll who was left to plough a lone furrow.

I doubt if anyone expected us to start as quickly as we did. The starting line up didn't fill me with confidence as Gerrard and Suarez were both left out of it with an eye on the cup semi final. The good news was the return of Johnson and it's always nice to see Maxi in the side as the odds of us finding the net are greatly increased by his presence. His lack of gametime is one of the biggest mysteries of the season. He thrived more than anybody under Dalglish last season and he's played his part this season too in the limited opportunities he's had. Yet he's had to sit and watch from the bench for most of the year whilst the likes of Downing and Henderson have managed just one goal between them and the side in general has been desperately short of goals. Maxi hit two hat-tricks towards the back end of last season and ended up with ten league goals in total. In his limited opportunities this season he's still found the net frequently, with six goals in twelve starts in all competitions and an impressive four in just six league starts. How does he not start more often? He doesn't do anything special to get his goals either, just uses his football brain to get himself into positions where he will have a chance of scoring. Too many of our players don't know how to do that. His first goal was a tap in, but look at the ground he covered to get into position and also the way he held his run to give Bellamy the opening for the cross (which he delivered perfectly). There's no way in a million years Downing would have been in that position.

The goal also owed much to a stunning ball out of defence by Skrtel that released Bellamy. Admittedly, Blackburn's defending left a lot to be desired but we took full advantage of that for a change. Carroll had also done well in his own penalty area to win the ball and show good composure to roll it to Skrtel. The second goal was all about Shelvey. He won the ball cleverly in his own half from Dunn and then set off towards goal unchallenged. He reached the edge of the box, made a yard for himself and shot low towards the far corner. Robinson could only palm the ball out and as Carroll challenged the centre half the ball popped up for Maxi to volley in at the back post. He made the chance look easier than it was, but he's got good technique and a cool head.

At 2-0 up so early in the game and with our confidence suddenly flooding back it was looking like we may fill our boots. The one concern was that Flanagan was having a really bad time of it. He'd been booked for pulling down his man after he'd been caught in possession, and almost picked up a second yellow when he was a fraction late to a loose ball and sent Olsson sprawling. It could easily have been a sending off but the referee to his credit recognised it for what it was, a young lad who'd shown his inexperience by trying to win a ball he thought he could get and arriving a split second too late. Skipper for the evening Skrtel was called over to tell the young full back to watch himself. Unfortunately Flanagan's evening would soon be ended prematurely by a red card, but not to himself. His badly underhit backpass sent Hoillett clear and he was brought down by Doni, leaving the referee no choice but to send him off. Flanagan was immediately replaced by sub keeper Brad Jones who remarkably saved Yakubu's weak penalty. Everyone knows what Jones has been through recently, and it was a touching moment seeing him point skywards.

Hard not to feel a little sorry for Doni though, and it was good seeing Reina go to the dressing room to check on him before reporting back to the rest of the lads on the bench who were all clearly concerned. Not sure if he is definitely ruled out of the semi final as I heard something about if we appeal it by a certain time he'd be eligible to play in that game but may face an extra game punishment if he loses the appeal. Given that Reina would be back then we've really got nothing to lose if that is indeed the case. Whether or not Doni is a better option than Jones is another question. I don't trust either if I'm honest.

The penalty save was a great boost to us, had we conceded a goal immediately after going a man down it would have been a massive setback. We needed to get to half time at 2-0 but slack marking from a free-kick allowed Yakubu to atone for his penalty miss and blow the game wide open again with a simple header. Not sure who was responsible for picking him up, looked like either Carroll or Johnson. Someone fell asleep though as how can you not notice a 20 stone, middle aged man lurking in your penalty area?? Despite that setback we generally looked quite comfortable even with ten men and led at half time. The cutting edge we'd shown early on was no longer there, understandably, with Shelvey having to drop into midfield to replace Henderson who had been pressed into emergency duty at right back. We never attempted to sit back and hold what we had though, the second half saw us continue to press for goals and we did create some decent openings. Carroll headed wide at full stretch following a brilliant Bellamy corner, and Bellamy could have done better when Carroll's header sent him scampering goalwards. Unfortunately a poor touch allowed a defender to get back and concede a corner.

Jones didn't have much to do, he made a few routine saves from shots that were straight at him and he was looking composed and confident. Then out of nothing he had a triple brainfart. First, he took too long to clear the ball and Yakubu charged it down. Second, he flapped at the ball as it dropped from the sky underneath the crossbar. Third, he pushed Yakubu as they went for the loose ball. A penalty was inevitable, even though the Yak clearly did his usual 'dying swan' routine as he crashed to the floor like he'd been hit by a truck. Given what had happened to Reina and Doni, I'm sure everyone's heart was in their mouth for a second until the referee - correctly - produced a yellow card. Yakubu was going away from the goal and headed towards Coates. It was not a clear goalscoring opportunity as Yakubu would have still had to beat Jones even if he reached the ball before the defender. Correct decision.

Yakubu's penalty was even worse than the first one but this time Jones had dived the other way. 2-2 and the much needed three points we looked to be heading towards was suddenly looking like it would be just the one, assuming we could hold on that is.

As the game wore on however, we seemed to get stronger. Whereas in recent weeks the desire to dig in and fight for the result has been sadly lacking, this time the players could not be faulted in that regard. The setback of going a man down seemed to galvanise them into a great effort. They played for eachother, they worked hard, they showed a desire to win the game that has been missing far too often in 2012. Even had Carroll not headed that late winner I'd have been praising the effort and commitment shown by the side. It was fitting that they did go on to win the game however as it was no more than they deserved.

Blackburn can complain all they like about the winning goal, for me they don't have a leg to stand on. Hanley tangled with Skrtel and both were as guilty as the other. Hanley held Skrtel down, and when Skrtel got up he pushed off on the Blackburn player. The officials were right to ignore it, and there was no question of offside either as even if you take Hanley out of the equation Agger was onside when he flicked on Coates pass and Carroll was on when he hurled himself forward to head past Robinson in front of a delirious away end. It was a huge goal for us and one that will hopefully prove to be a watershed moment in our season. Nothing has gone right recently. The only luck we've had has been bad and in truth we've not done enough for ourselves to deserve a change in fortune either. This was different, we forced this result through sheer determination.

Carroll was a fitting matchwinner too, he worked tirelessly at both ends of the pitch and his use of the ball was good throughout. He's had numerous performances of a similar nature in recent months but generally the goals have not been there to cap them. Given the way things have gone for him this season he'll probably find himself on the bench on Saturday. Good performances have often been rewarded with a spell on the sidelines, but he's done well against Everton this season and I hope he retains his place at Wembley. Ditto Maxi. Bellamy is another who I'd love to see starting at the weekend, but having played the full game here the chances are he'll be on the bench as he's very rarely started two games in a week. A pity as his pace was a big factor in this victory, he gave us a great outlet ball and we're a better side when he's in it. It was funny as he was in the refs ear all night, and when the ref got tired of listening to him he went over and bent the fourth officials ear when there was a stoppage in play.

In his defence, the thing that riled him initially was the free-kick that led to Blackburn's first goal. It was given for a handball against him when the ball struck his arm from point blank range. He felt his arm was by his side and he couldn't do anything about it. He's hilarious though, when a decision goes against him he'll approach the other player involved for support and then try and get them to tell the ref, as if that's going to make any difference.

The thing that really wound him up however was a yellow card for diving when he was kicked on the knee by Bradley Orr. He spoke to Orr who clearly agreed that he did catch him, so Bellamy then attempted to drag him over to the ref to explain. Bellamy has been labelled many things in his career, plenty of them deserved and most of them he's taken on the chin. 'Cheat' is not something he'll accept though and he was extremely upset at being booked for a dive and the implication that brings. That's what he was saying to the fourth official, you could see him say something about *'he's effectively calling me a cheat'*. I love Bellamy though, he's fucking boss.

Two players that deserve special mention are Henderson and Shelvey. Henderson's energy levels as he bombed up and down that right flank were hugely impressive. He defended well but he was surging forward and actually taking people on. He showed more assertiveness in this game than I've seen from him all season, his energy really helped us cope with being a man down. As for Shelvey, he was good throughout and it's just unfortunate that he had to play in a more disciplined role after the sending off as he was running the game from that position between midfield and attack.

This was a huge result for us, as we couldn't afford to lose any more ground on Everton in the table (not to mention the sides who are creeping up behind us) and we also desperately needed the win for morale as it's been such a wretched run we've been on. In terms of Saturday's game it doesn't mean anything, just as Everton's impressive win over Sunderland the day before doesn't have any bearing on what will happen at Wembley. Even so, I'd rather be going into it on the back of a win than another defeat, and Carroll's late winner has given everyone a much needed lift.

Roll on Saturday then I guess....

Premier League Easter Round Up (6-11 April 2012)

Things are hotting up at both ends of the table after an incident packed Easter programme. Manchester City looked to have blown the title at the weekend only to be handed an unlikely lifeline by Wigan a few days later, who risked the wrath of their owner Dave Whelan by upsetting Alex Ferguson's side to give City a glimmer of hope.

The holiday fixtures got underway on Good Friday with Newcastle travelling to the Valleys to take on Swansea. Two more fantastic finishes from Papis Cisse gave the Geordies another win as they continue to confound doubters like me and stay in the hunt for a top four spot. Incidentally, for those who were worried, James Perch played in the game despite the broken face he suffered at the hands, or should I say head, of that thug Pepe Reina. What a hero Perch is, a modern day Gerry Byrne. His family must be so proud. Wait did I say 'proud'? Obviously I meant 'ashamed and embarrassed.'

Wolves travelled to Stoke and took the lead with a flukey goal by Kightley before they were undone by two set pieces. I doubt if there was anything more predictable than that in any of the Easter fixtures. Interesting stat: 98.6% of Stoke's goals come from set plays. Crouchy's belter the other week accounts for the other 1.4%. Ok, I made that up but there's a 93.1% chance that I'm correct. Yeah, I made that one up too, but the point still stands, Stoke can only score from set pieces because aside from Peter Crouch there is zero skill and talent in their squad, but they are all big bastards. Combine that with that fact that Wolves defend set pieces about as well as they make managerial appointments and there was only ever going to be one outcome here. It was cruel on Terry Connor though, as neither of the free-kicks that led to Stoke's goals should have been given. Said it before and I'll say it again, Stoke get the benefit of more refereeing decisions than any team in the league that is not managed by a purple nosed tyrant. For the record, Huth scored the first and Crouch bagged the second with a great header. Oh yeah, and Jon Walters missed from two yards out, the hapless, bitter blue, good for nothing yard dog.

Little known fact, Stoke's Academy actually has a stretching machine that they put kids on, and any kid who doesn't reach six foot tall by the age of 16 is cut loose. Unless they can throw the ball further than most players can kick it that is, in which case they're given ten year contracts. The Stoke Academy is unlike any other in the sporting world. The closest thing there's ever been to it would probably be a Roman 'Ludis', the training facility in which Gladiators honed their skills back in the days of Spartacus. Only the toughest survive Stoke's Academy and it's barbaric training methods, but many of those who've not made the grade have gone on to achieve success in other fields, including the WWE and MMA where the skills they learned in Stoke can be put to good use.

Moving on, Fulham went to Bolton and won comfortably. Dempsey's terrific free kick set them on their way, and the American then headed in a second. Riise's strong run and cross made the third for former Real Madrid midfielder Diarra to bag his first goal for Fulham and leave Bolton in deep trouble. This was a fixture they'd have been looking at getting something from, so to lose it 3-0 is damaging to say the least. Fortunately for them all the other sides at the bottom lost too, including Blackburn who were embarrassingly turned over by West Brom at the Hawthorns. An oggy from one of the Olsson twins and further strikes by Fortune and Ridgewell made it a miserable day for Steve Kean's side, and it got worse when Modeste (who the hell is he by the way and when did they sign him?) was sent off for kicking out at Billy Jones. Nice to see Jones not make anything of it other than to shrug his shoulders at the ref as if to say *'did you see that, ref?'*. The ref did indeed see it and Modeste was suitably punished. Hopefully James Perch saw how Jones handled the incident and was suitably embarrassed, although I doubt it, the shameless shitbag.

Speaking of shitbags, Motson was at Stamford Bridge commentating on his beloved Chelsea again as they shafted Wigan with the help of the officials. I don't know what sickened me more, Motson's hysterics or the way Wigan got completely screwed over. Both Chelsea goals were offside, the first one in particular was the kind of call a linesman should never get wrong, it was unforgivable. Wigan played well and scored a great goal through Diame. You know, every time I see him he looks a player, but he can't be that good because he isn't even first choice at Wigan (he missed a couple of bad sitters recently too which probably hasn't helped his cause). It's a bit like Diaby at Arsenal, who looks class every time I watch him but isn't a regular starter and apparently is a bit of a whipping boy for the Arsenal crowd. I think Diame's good but I'm probably wrong.

Everton made the long trip to Norwich and took the lead through Jelavic. Howson equalised, Jelavic scored again and finally Grant Holt ensured it would be honours even with a cool finish. He's had a great season has Holt, but I find talk of him getting an England call up to be hilarious if I'm honest. By that, I mean I'll piss myself if he gets picked, not that I don't think it will happen. Worse strikers than Holt have had call ups before *cough* Michael Ricketts *cough* What the hell was Andre Marriner doing for Everton's second goal though? Pienaar was crouched down over the ball ensuring Norwich players couldn't get it unless they booted fuck out of him in the process. They didn't do that, Norwich aren't that kind of team, but they should have done as a) Pienaar deserves a kicking and b) it ended up costing them as they stood around waiting for a whistle that never arrived. Hate to say it but Jelavic has been a steal for the blues hasn't he? His movement in the box is great, he always seems to be able to find space and he's got a cool head when he gets a chance too. Kenny and Comolli apparently looked long and hard at him but decided against bringing him in. I wasn't arsed at the time, but I can't say I feel the same now as he's looking like a natural goalscorer, which is exactly what we've been missing. He was cheap too. Perhaps it's missing out on the likes of Jelavic and Cisse that did for Commolli?

Tottenham and Sunderland played out a dull goalless draw at the Stadium of Light, although Spurs did narrowly win the battle of unsuccessful 'handball' penalty appeals 7-6. Amazing how Spurs have completely capitulated in the last couple of months, their run isn't much better than the one we've been on and they're looking like they're going to blow the top four spot that seemed a formality not so long ago. You can't fight genetics, and as I keep saying failure is in Spurs' DNA.

Onto Sunday, and it was all about the top of the table as both manc teams were in action. United had the easier fixture, at home to QPR. Ferguson's record against teams managed by his former players is staggeringly one sided and Mark Hughes was never leaving Old Trafford with anything other than a defeat and a few condescending platitudes about his team from his old master. United were given a helping hand early on by the official (I know, shocking isn't it) who awarded a penalty when a clearly offside

Ashley Young produced his latest ridiculous piece of cheating to win a penalty that was converted by Shrek. To rub salt in QPR's wounds, defender Shaun Derry was sent off for the 'foul' too. Hilariously, Ferguson downplayed the incident and suggested that the decision hurt United as they relaxed too much against ten men and would have been better off facing eleven. Scumbag, does he think we were all born yesterday? Whatsmore, the FA disgracefully turned down the appeal for Derry's suspension. But there's nothing dodgy about English football, nosiree. Nothing at all. I'm putting this out there; Ashley Young is by far and away the biggest diver in the Premier League. No-one is even close to his level of constant cheating, yet fuck all is ever said about him. His manager had the brass neck to label Suarez a diver, yet Rooney, Nani and Young are as bad as anything you'll see anywhere in Europe. And is it a co-incidence that Ronaldo has cut right down on the diving since he escaped from the clutches of that sour faced, evil old bastard? No, it's not, as my twin Van Nistelrooy did the same after he left.

United's victory added to the pressure on City and sadly they wilted under it at the Emirates. In fairness Arsenal were superb and absolutely battered Mancini's side. It's amazing that the scoreline was so close really as City got their arses handed to them. Balotelli continues to amaze with his stupidity. He somehow got away with a disgusting tackle on Song when he deliberately went in studs up onto the Arsenal man's knee. The usually card happy Martin Atkinson somehow missed it, but he would soon make up for it as the City striker was then booked for a far more innocuous challenge on Sagna and eventually collected the inevitable red card in stoppage time. I keep saying it, but he's great isn't he? There's never a dull moment with him. You know the best thing about him though? He's someone else's problem. He won't be City's problem for much longer it seems, as Mancini's patience finally snapped as he said he won't pick him again this season and will probably sell him. The decision should be taken out of his hands and City should be saying 'ciao' to both of them in the summer. There were a few tasty challenges going in, and not just from mad Mario either. Koscielny was booked for a bad one on Barry, which is a little unfair as if it were up to me such an act would be rewarded with an instant O.B.E. Kicking Gareth Barry would be an Olympic sport if I ruled the world, the fat arsed crab. In fact that's what I'd name the event; *"Fat Arsed Crab Kicking."* Arsenal hit the woodwork three times and missed so many chances it was like watching Liverpool. The worst of them saw Vermailen and Benayoun both fail to convert from a yard out. It was remarkable, and you can imagine the furious reaction of any United fans watching. Obviously I include Evertonians in that, so I suppose it was fitting that Mikel Arteta grabbed the games' only goal with four minutes left. You can take the lad out of Goodison, but you can't take the Manc out of the Evertonian.

There were five fixtures on Easter Monday. Spurs' wretched form continued as they lost at home to Norwich. That's bad enough in itself, but it gets worse. Norwich were wearing their green away kit and still managed to win the game! That's how shit are Spurs right now. Pilkington put Norwich in front with his 8th of the season. Eight goals from a wide midfield berth. All of our wide players other than Maxi and Bellamy should look at that and feel suitably ashamed. Defoe equalised for Spurs with a composed finish. 16 goals in 20 starts for him apparently. I'm not his biggest fan but that's an impressive tally by anyone's standards. Well, anyone who's name isn't Messi, Ronaldo or Maxi. Norwich were furious about that goal as they should have been awarded a pen at the other end when King pulled back Holt. Looked pretty blatant too. Johnson missed a sitter after being teed up by Holt and they were denied another clear pen when 'Wilbrahimovic' was barged over by Adebayor. So many bad refereeing decisions over the Easter period. Bale smashed one against the bar and Assou-Ekotto forced a brilliant save from Ruddy as chances came at both ends. It could have gone either way but some chap called Elliott Bennett eventually won it for the Canaries with a fine strike 20 minutes from time. Have I mentioned him before or is he another new one? I've now lost track of all these jobbers they keep sending out each week. I thought Bennett was a defender but maybe I had him confused with Barnett. There was another Bennett who played last week, but his name was Ryan and I think he's a defender too. They've got another Elliot too I think. So who in the blue hell is Elliott Bennett??

Bolton travelled to St James' Park with Kevin Davies as a lone striker. Clear sign of their intent there, but the longer it went the more adventurous they got. Newcastle were awful but Bolton let them off the hook by failing to convert a couple of great chances. Ben Arfa broke the deadlock with a great individual goal late on, but Bolton's defending for it was abysmal. More awful defending allowed Ameobi to run through and tee up Cisse for his 10th goal since arriving in January. It's a good job for the Geordies that Cisse has been such a revelation, as Demba Ba has been missing in action lately. May as well start calling himself Demba Heskey. One final observation on this, is Owen Coyle the only person in the world who calls it the 'Barclays Premier League'? Is he on Barclays' payroll? Why does he do it? What will he do if someone else takes over the sponsorship? Probably won't matter as he'll be in the Championship anyway, but nevertheless it's getting on my tits and I wish he'd pack it in.

Chelsea were given a very generous penalty to set them on their way against Fulham but they were pegged back late on after yet another goal by Clint Dempsey, his 22nd of the season. I'm not buying into his hype though, he's a good player having a purple patch but he's not top drawer. You know how I know that? Pink boots, that's how.

Over at the Pit Everton spanked Sunderland 4-0 with all the goals coming in the second half. This despite resting a load of players ahead of their cup final this weekend. Yes, I said final, it's not a typo. Sunderland's record against Moyes is truly horrific, it's right up there in shitness with Moyes' record at Anfield.

Aston Villa v Stoke was not exactly one for the neutrals, or the purists for that matter. It was Villa's lowest gate of the season, which is completely understandable. They watch Villa coz they have to, but asking them to watch Stoke as well is a step too far. The only surprising thing to come from this game was the opening goal from the young lad Weimann, which was class and deserved to grace a far better fixture than this shitfest. Yet again a referee failed to penalise Stoke for WWE style grappling in their own box when defending a corner. There was one ridiculous incident where that deadbeat Walters suplexed Chris Herd whilst James Collins was being placed in a bearhug by Shawcross. Both offences went unpunished and I'm now convinced that referees don't watch MOTD, as there's no way Stoke would still be getting away with this shit on a weekly basis if they did.

Stoke's equaliser came from.... wait for it.... a set piece! Huth heading in Pennant's right wing free-kick. He had two hands on the shoulders of Collins yet once again they got away with it. If I knew how and I was sad enough to do it, I'd compile a video montage of all their fouls in the box from set pieces that have gone unpunished. It's be longer than the extended version of the Lord of the Rings Trilogy, and probably a little more gruesome too (the Stoke crowd doing a more than passable impersonation of the Orc army). I don't know how, and I'm not quite that sad yet, so Tony Pulis can breathe easy. For now anyway, I can't rule it out completely in the future however. Fuckin' Stoke.

Last but not least, Wednesday's games. With Blackburn and Bolton both losing QPR had a great chance to capitalise and did so with a vital win over Swansea at Loftus Road. The game meant more to the home side and it showed. Scott Sinclair missed a sitter when he failed to get a touch on the ball from a yard out. He was wearing pink boots, Nothing says 'decent player who thinks he's far better than he actually is' than a pair of pink boots. Honestly, I'm right about this. Have a look around the league and you'll see. I might even compile a list next week to prove it. A player who wouldn't be seen dead in pink, orange or lime green boots, Joey Barton, put QPR in front with a good finish in 1st half stoppage time. I take it he's not being booed by the home crowd now? Fickle bastards. Jamie Mackie added a second in some style although he was slightly offside when he received the ball. He's pretty good him, not 'pretty good' in a 'we should sign him' kind of way, I just mean he's pretty good and always seems to make a positive impact for his team when he plays. One more time for clarity: I AM NOT SAYING SIGN JAMIE MACKIE. Buszaky bagged a spectacular third and Barton went close to a brilliant fourth as QPR battered Brendan Rodgers' side. I wonder if Swansea have been found out a little recently? The way they play has been one of the highlights of the season, but recently teams have stopped them from doing their thing. I hope it's just a dip and they haven't been rumbled. It could just be that they've eased off a little knowing they've secured their place in the Premier League for next season. ('Barclays Premier League, surely?' - Owen Coyle)

No such problems for Wolves, complacency is the one thing they need not worry about. Shitness would be top of their concerns. Stupidity would be second on the list. A home game with Arsenal was going to be extremely tough for them, but Arsenal have often been found wanting in this type of game so there was some hope. Bassong's sending off inside the opening ten minutes put paid to that though, the moron. Van Persie scored the most nonchalent penalty of the season and Walcott and Benayoun also got on the scoresheet as the Gunners continue to look like they'll nab third spot. Just shows how bad this league is that the worst Arsenal side in many a year look like finishing third.

Dave Whelan had dismissed reports that Martinez was on his way in the summer, claiming he'd do everything possible to keep the Spanish boss. That was before he went and beat Whelan's beloved United. He'll be in the doghouse now for sure. Great credit to Wigan though, they overcame the customary awful refereeing decision they always get when they face the Mancs and went on to win the game. The goal they had disallowed in the first half was a joke. There was fuck all wrong with it, De Gea is a bad fanny isn't he? He made no attempt to get past Caldwell to get the ball, just stood there like a fucking dummy waiting for the ref to bail him out, which he did. Poor old Moses didn't know it had been disallowed and was giving it the beans, as was the stadium PA guy who was playing their shitty goal celebration music. Embarrassing. Maloney settled the game with a cracker, although it came from a corner that never was. The ball was nowhere near Phil Jones, who was livid at the decision and was throwing his arms up like Kevin the teenager. Mouthbreathing gimp. Johnny Evans should have been sent off for a second yellow but Dowd bottled it, and United were later denied a penalty when Figueroa got himself in a tangle and handled a cross. Astonishing that wasn't given, usually refs (and linesmen) can't wait to give those. Maybe they saw a half time replay of the goal they'd disallowed and wanted to even it up? No way would they have let it go at Old Trafford though. Ferguson was full of praise for Wigan afterwards and was fairly magnanimous about it all for a change. Easy to be like that with a five point lead, I guarantee he won't be like that if they lose again and their lead is whittled down. Hopefully we'll see if I'm right.

City took full advantage of United's slip up, laying a beat down on West Brom at the Etihad. Aguero got things under way with a cracker after just six minutes. He grabbed another early in the second half and Tevez and Silva got on the scoresheet too as City ran riot. Poor old Roy, no doubt he'll have felt the need to apologise to *'his friend Sir Alex'* after this one. Mancini said afterwards that the title race is 'finished' and he's just concerned with City ending the season well. He then claimed he didn't know United had lost as he didn't even know they were playing. Fucking crank, if they don't win the title it's his fault they've blown it. Him and that dickhead Tevez. And Balotelli, obviously.

LIVERPOOL 2 EVERTON 1

Competition - FA Cup
Date - Sat 14 Apr 2012
Venue - Wembley Stadium
Scorer(s) – Luis Suarez, Andy Carroll
Half Time - 0-1
Star Man – Andy Carroll

Team: Jones; Johnson, Skrtel, Carragher, Agger; Henderson (Maxi), Gerrard, Spearing, Downing (Bellamy); Suarez, Carroll:

I believe the great Titi Camara said it best on twitter: *"I sorry everton we always win"* Does that rival Nick Barmby's *"I want to play for Liverpool"* as the 'six worst words in the English language' in the eyes of poor old Bill Kenwright? You'd have to ask Bill, that's if you can find him. He seemed to go AWOL after Carroll's late winner and hasn't been seen on our screens since. You couldn't keep him off the TV before that, ESPN seemed to have their own 'Kenwright Cam' running throughout the game.

I felt somewhat cheated not being able to see him blubbering at full time, but at least he had no shortage of 'Luvvy' pals present to console him. I imagine Dame Judy Dench in particular will have been a tower of strength for him. Even in a year when we've had our worst run of results in over 50 years we've still beaten them twice in the league and just for good measure handed them a heartbreaking loss in an FA Cup semi final at Wembley. They may actually end the season above us in the table, but there's no trophy for that and just like the last time it happened back in 2005 there'll be silverware in the reds cabinet and none in theirs. Is it any wonder they hate us so much? As much as I am revelling in the heartache this result will have caused Kenwright and Moyes, all piss taking aside I do feel sympathy for the average Evertonian.

It was fitting that we faced them on the anniversary weekend of Hillsborough, they were there for us and shared in our grief back then and although relations have soured between the two sets of fans since, they were there for us once more and came out of this fixture with a lot of credit. It may not have been holding hands and singing 'Merseyside' along Wembley Way, but it was a day for the city to be proud of. You could have heard a pin drop during the minute's silence and it was heart warming to see so many blues holding up 'Don't buy the S*n' posters to the cameras at every opportunity. Like many of you I have blue friends and family members and I take no pleasure in their disappointment. I'm delighted we won obviously, but I won't be rubbing it in when I see them (and hopefully they're not reading this report!). Losing a semi final is horrible (slightly less so since it no longer denies teams a trip to Wembley) and losing one to your fiercest rivals is unthinkable. I feel for those blues I know personally, as most of them are sound. Kenwright and Moyes? That's a whole different kettle of fish, I'll never tire of seeing their sad little heartbroken faces as their hopes and dreams were shattered once again.

The pressure on both teams going into this game was monumental. Defeat for us would have put Kenny under immense pressure. In a week in which Damien Comolli had been canned - in part due to the disappointing results of the players brought in by him and Kenny - the last thing Dalglish needed was a Wembley defeat to an Everton side that had recently overtaken us in the league. We've been on a terrible run but the cup results had compensated for that somewhat. Win this and the poor league form could continue to be swept under the carpet. Lose this and… well let's put it this way, there'd be a lot of people at the club fearing they'd be going the same way as Comolli. As for the blues, there was more pressure on them to win this game than there has been in many a year. A club that thrives on going into derbies as the plucky underdog with nothing to lose, the little man with the chip on his shoulder trying to stand up to the big bad neighbourhood bully, this time they went into it with expectations they don't usually have. Above us in the table, on a great run of form and facing a Liverpool side that has been struggling desperately and suffering from a confidence crisis, a lot of people expected them to win this game. Everton (and specifically Moyes) don't like being in that position going into a derby as they just don't know how to handle it. Remember a few years ago when Gerrard was sent off early in a derby game at Anfield? Suddenly the onus was on the blues to go out and win the game, and they froze like a rabbit in the headlights. A similar thing happened at Wembley, as they went in at half time a goal to the good and with a great chance of winning the game. I can imagine them sitting around in the dressing room thinking "Oh my God, we could actually win this!!". They came out for the second half and played scared, desperately hoping to protect what they had instead of trying to go out and win the game. Say what you want about Liverpool, but when it's all on the line and the pressure is at it's most intense, we've usually found a way to come through it and get the job done. Add this one to the ever lengthening list. We put ourselves in a hole at half time, a mess completely of our own making, but the second half saw the players dig themselves out of it with a display of determination and character that could have seen them win by three or four goals in the end.

Kenny's starting line up wasn't met with universal approval but I have to say if I'd been picking the side I'd have had 10 of the 11 he went with. The one choice I disagreed with was Henderson over Maxi. I don't know what the Argentine has to do to earn a place in the side, but clearly scoring two in the previous game isn't enough. Maybe he'll have to score three? He's done it before, twice in fact. 14 goals from his last 20 starts is an impressive return, but it's not enough to get the nod over Henderson. Baffling.

The other bone of contention was Agger starting at left back. That didn't surprise me at all, it made perfect sense as Enrique's form has been so suspect since the turn of the year I wouldn't have taken a chance on him in this game either. You could argue that it backfired as Agger and Carragher were both guilty of hesitation that cost us a goal, but that one moment aside the defence played well overall and Brad Jones had very little to do. The goal was an awful one to give away. There was no danger as the ball bounced between Carragher and Agger. It looks like Agger feigns to clear the ball with his right foot but hesitates and decides to leave it to Carragher. Carra is waiting for Agger to launch it, and eventually he panics and hits an off balance clearance straight at Cahill. The ricochet fell fortunately to Jelavic who buried it. He was offside, but it was such a close one and it happened so fast that it's difficult to blame the linesman too much for that. The two defenders were more to blame than the linesman, someone has to take the decision to clear the ball but it's one of those unfortunate things that happen occasionally. It was the kind of awkward hesitation like when you're walking down the road and someone is walking toward you. You step to one side to avoid them as they step the same way. You step back the other way, and so do they and before you know it you're in an embarrassing dance and apologising sheepishly. That's what happened to Agger and Carragher, and it couldn't have happened on a worse stage.

Everton had done little to deserve their lead, and whilst we weren't playing particularly well we'd still had the better openings and not looked in any real trouble. The first chance of the game fell to Spearing when he couldn't keep his shot down after good approach play by Johnson and Carroll. Earlier we'd been denied a great opportunity when Gerrard's attempted through ball to a free and clear Suarez was well intercepted by the head of Howard Webb. Skrtel had a half chance too, his shot was saved after Carroll had nodded the ball down to him. The goal knocked us back a bit and the rest of the first half was pretty poor. Henderson being moved to the left wing didn't exactly help matters and made Maxi's exclusion even more infuriating. I don't think Henderson could have done much more than he did to be fair to him, it's just not his position. It's like playing Spearing up front or Maxi centre half.

Suarez spent much of the first half in an annoying feud with Heitinga. The Dutchman kept blocking his path by standing in his way when he was trying to close down the keeper or latch onto a Carroll flick. Suarez got increasingly frustrated about it and things got heated between the pair as half time approached. Eventually Suarez ended up doing some kind of MMA style takedown on the defender. That kind of distraction is only going to benefit Everton and Heitinga will have been delighted at the effect he had on our dangerman in that first 45 minutes as Suarez was a complete non-factor. Everton had the lead at the break but I'm not having it that they'd done enough to deserve it or had played particularly well. The only difference between the sides was one terrible moment of hesitation in our defence. That aside, Jones didn't have to make a save and neither did Howard. Neither side performed in the first half and the occasion looked like it had gotten to both teams.

The second half was a different story. Suarez forgot about his ongoing arguments with Heitinga and Webb and we dominated from start to finish, although there was one major similarity with the first half in that it took a defensive howler for a breakthrough to be made. We'd started the half brilliantly and had the blues pinned back in their own half. Carroll was guilty of an incredible miss when he headed wide after brilliant work by Downing on the right. He buried his face in his shirt but to his credit he didn't let his head go down after it and he gave the blues all they could handle and then some. At Newcastle he was known for getting smashed on Jager Bombs and Newcy Brown, now he just sinks bitters a couple of times a year.

Downing had the beating of Baines and another good run and cross from him saw Suarez completely miss his kick. We had four players in the box for that attack, including Glen Johnson. We were dominating but as always, you wonder whether a goal is going to come as we've had so much trouble putting the ball in the net this season. Fortunately Distin was there to give us a helping hand. The blues are complaining about a foul on Cahill in the build up to the goal. I've watched it several times and don't see any foul, just a coming together of players. They've always got to have something to moan about after derby defeats, but that's really clutching at straws if it's the best they can come up with. Carroll flicked the ball into space for Suarez to chase, Distin got there first and should have played it down the line with his stronger foot. Instead he tried a backpass on his weak foot and left it well short. Suarez was onto it immediately, as Distin put his head in his hands and walked off the pitch. As Howard came out Suarez took the shot early with the outside of his right foot and rolled the ball into the net. Worth noting that Carroll had made a great run into the box and was square of Suarez and would have had a tap in had Suarez chosen to pass to him. Carroll has not always made those kind of runs, which is why I mention it as it was good to see.

The big fella was inches away from making it 2-1 when he showed good footwork on the edge of the box to create space for a shot that flashed just wide. He was then denied by Suarez as his shot struck his strike partner. We were causing Everton plenty of problems and were dominating possession. Spearing and Gerrard were bossing the midfield, although the skipper was having to play a much more disciplined role than he had when bagging a hat-trick at Anfield the other week. Kenny shuffled his pack by sending on Maxi for Henderson and then Bellamy for Downing. I thought both changes were made at a good time and helped the team. Downing wasn't happy, once again muttering his disapproval as he saw his number go up. He'd played quite well and got a few good crosses in, but he really has no cause for complaint as it was the ideal time to get Bellamy on and so it proved. Straight away he was into the action, Carroll flicking the ball on for him to run in behind Osman. He was pulled back but didn't go down and eventually won a corner. Predictably he let both referee and linesman know of his disapproval of their failure to spot the offence. From the corner the ball wasn't cleared properly and Gerrard was clattered by Coleman. It should have been a second yellow card but Webb went for leniency and Coleman survived. It mattered not, as

Bellamy whipped in a beautiful cross and Carroll held off the attention of Fellaini to head the ball past Howard. No more than he deserved, his all round play was very good and Everton really struggled to deal with him once again. Fitting that 'Wor Horse' was the matchwinner on Grand National day. This has been a huge week for Carroll's Liverpool career. He's been playing well for several months but the goals haven't come and he's missed chances.

Whilst his general play in terms of holding up the ball, winning flick ons and defending set pieces in his own box has been generally very good of late, he hasn't been doing a significant part of his job - putting the ball in the back of the net. All the dirty work he's been doing for the team is great and all, but without goals it's not enough. We need him to be Fernando Llorente, not Emile Heskey. In his defence he hasn't been helped by frequently being left out or substituted and not having a lengthy run in the side. This week may prove to be a turning point for his Liverpool career and hopefully he can go on to establish himself here. And even if he doesn't, he'll always be remembered for this game at least.

Everton's goose was cooked at 2-1, they had nothing left and we really should have made it safe by scoring a couple more. Maxi missed a sitter when he hit the post following great set up play from Suarez, and Suarez himself was denied by Howard after Gerrard played him in. Everton pumped a few long balls into the box to try and put pressure on Jones, but he did what he had to do very well. He punched a couple away, and then in the last minute he came out and caught a high ball under pressure. That's a killer whenever that happens, it halts any momentum the opposition is trying to build and allows you to waste precious seconds as you push up the field waiting for the keeper's clearance. His team-mates certainly appreciated it.

The final whistle saw Carroll mobbed by team-mates, whilst Brad Jones was also getting some love, especially from a delighted Pepe Reina. An emotional Carragher sank to the floor in relief, whilst at the other end a distraught Distin was busy apologising to the Evertonians. Those who were still there at that point anyway, not that I blame any blue who got off at full time as the last thing you want to see is your rivals celebrating on the pitch.

I felt for Distin, he seems like a good pro and that mistake will live with him for the rest of his life. Also have to say that Phil Neville was the epitome of class in his post match interviews. Moyes claimed before the game that the whole country wanted Everton to win. Probably true, much the same way they wanted Chesterfield to beat Boro a few years ago, or for Wycombe to beat us back in 2001. With that in mind, I guess that means you let the whole country down then, doesn't it, loser? Poor old Moyesy, Kenny has won more in one season back in charge than Moyes has in his entire life. ***"David Moyes, a winner in every sense of the word"*** proclaimed the ESPN commentator. Yeah, in every sense except the actual, y'know, winning part. David Moyes is a survivor, Kenny Dalglish is a winner, he has the medals to prove it. Fingers crossed he'll have one more to add to the collection in a few weeks.

Premier League Round Up (14-16 April 2012)

With four Premier League sides in FA Cup action it wasn't a full fixture list this weekend. On the plus side that meant nobody had to watch Stoke. I believe that's what Charlie Sheen would describe as *'winning'*. Despite the reduced number of games there was plenty of significant action at both ends of the table as City went goal crazy at Carrow Road, Ashley Young's cheating shafted his former team-mates and Blackburn and QPR found themselves being sucked ever closer to the relegation trap door.

Carlos Tevez had an eventful afternoon at Norwich, bagging a hat-trick but also getting booked for diving. Replays showed it was a clear foul and that Tevez did absolutely nothing wrong. Didn't stop that fucktard Andy Burton from Sky asking him *"Did you dive?"* afterwards. Sky really need to to drop that chump before somebody else drops him, and drops him hard. It's only a matter of time, he'll ask the wrong stupid question to the wrong person at the wrong time, and BANG! Down he'll go. It will be glorious. The 'interview' itself was fantastic, Tevez just stood there just long enough to ask *"I'm man of the match, yes?"* before grabbing the champagne and leaving. He's got his critics has Tevez, and rightly so, but that's the way to deal with that sloppy turd Burton. Do Sky not realise there's a reason why people like Tevez and Dalglish just want to walk away from him and can't be arsed indulging him and his rude, inappropriate line of questioning? Much is made of how Kenny deals with the media, but he's completely different with BBC and ESPN than he is with Sky. Why is that? Andy 'the Transfer Gimp' Burton that's why. Tevez's extended beach holiday could turn out to be the difference between City winning the title and just falling short. You look at what he's doing now and then think back to all those points City dropped whilst he was away, and he really could have made all the difference to them, the stupid, selfish little troll. That advisor of his Kia whatshisface really needs stringing up, the shit-stirring parasite. Tevez's first goal was stunning, as was Aguero's strike that made it 2-0 after a back heel from Tevez had teed him up. Surman pulled one back for Norwich - they had actually played quite well up to that point - but then City pulled away from them as their Argentine strike duo tore the Canaries apart. Tevez headed the third, Aguero hit a brilliant fourth before Tevez completed his hat-trick and did a Bellamy style golf club celebration. What's that about then, did he twat Riise with a nine iron as well? Turns out it was a response to all those who've slagged him off for playing golf when he should have been helping his team try to win the title. Yeah, I mean how dare anyone take exception to him taking a six month golfing break in the middle of the season. He just doesn't get it, does he? Balotelli may be as mad as a march hare that's eaten a box of frogs, but at least he didn't take six months off in the middle of the season. Admittedly he didn't need to as if you tot up his various suspensions he probably missed as much time as Tevez, but you get my point. Adam Johnson and Aguero both hit the woodwork before Johnson eventually made it 6-1 with a well crafted goal in stoppage time. Can't help thinking it's too little too late though.

Moving on, and just what the hell has happened to Blackburn lately? They were virtually safe a few weeks ago, but then Wigan and QPR started winning games and Rovers embarked on a losing streak at the worst possible time. This drubbing at Swansea was their fifth defeat on the bounce and it's put them right in the shit now. Sigurdsson scored yet again. A brilliant left footed curler having earlier gone close with a right footed piledriver. Two good feet, scores goals, great engine, looks a player him. Turns out he's only on loan too, I thought they'd bought him from Reading until I saw his interview after this game when he was going on about having a couple of years left on his contract at Hoffenheim. After the impact he's had on the Premier League it's safe to assume that bigger clubs than Swansea will be in for him this summer, but maybe he's happy there? He's certainly a good fit for them, but a lot of clubs could use a midfielder who will get into double figures every season, including us.

Nathan Dyer then made it 2-0, and that reminded me that I have a fantasy team and he's in it. I'd completely forgotten about it and haven't checked it since September, but given that I've got Downing in there (0 goals and 0 assists) and I forgot to drop Suarez during his suspension I'm not holding out too much hope. I lost interest, neglected my duties and basically just left my team rudderless, fending for themselves without a manager. A bit like Steve Morgan did at Wolves really. Scott Dann's own goal compounded Rovers' misery and their complacency looks like it might see them relegated. *"What have they got to be complacent about?"* I hear you ask. Well I'll tell you, although I would have thought it was fairly obvious. Steve Kean, that's what. Those players thought they'd survive just because they have Kean in the manager's seat. Unfortunately, Kean, genius though he is, can't get on the pitch and do it for them. So pull your fucking fingers out Blackburn, having an iconic figure on the sidelines doesn't give you a divine right to stay in the league you bunch of deadbeats. Sort your shit out as you're making my boy look bad.

At least QPR lost as well, going down 1-0 at the Hawthorns courtesy of a fine strike by Graham Dorrans. Bobby Zamora missed a hatful of chances for QPR and Shane Long should have scored at the end but sliced his shot wide. Long was brilliant early on in the season but he's done fuck all for months now. As for QPR, if they go down then the two red cards picked up by Cisse will have been a huge factor in that as he's been class when he's played and they've really missed him. Replacing Warnock with Hughes wasn't smart either.

Meanwhile, Sunderland had another goalless draw at home, this time against lowly Wolves. This was pure unadulterated crap, Sunderland were terrible and barely deserved their point. I did notice that Nicklas Bendtner finally succumbed to the inevitable. I'm surprised he held out this long and I give him credit for that, but it was only ever going to be a matter of time before he reverted to type. In life you can't pretend to be something you're not, you can only live a lie for so long before you eventually embrace who you really are. Who is Nicklas Bendtner? He's the pink boot poster boy, baby. Nothing screams out *"Not as good as he thinks he is"* like a pair of pink boots, and no-one fits the description *"Not as good as he thinks he is"* like Nicklas Bendtner.

Wolves left out Matt Jarvis for some reason. He's been just about the only bright spot they've had for weeks now, so they leave him on the bench. Crazy. It's almost like they want to go down isn't it? Terry Connor seemed pleased with his point afterwards: *"We've been building towards that kind of performance"* he said. Strewth, he actually thought this was good? The poor fella, he's probably counting the days until he can fade into the background as a number two again, as this run in the big chair has turned into a nightmare. It's a shame as he seems a thoroughly decent guy. You have to say though, Wolves sacking Mick McCarthy without having any replacement lined up is the worst decision made by a football club since Leeds let Peter Ridsdale loose with their chequebook and he came back with the world's most expensive fish tank for his office and Seth Johnson on a 35k a week contract.

Onto Sunday and Aston Villa travelled to Old Trafford for their annual bumming. They had no chance to start with as the side they put out was incredibly weak and inexperienced, but United still resorted to foul means to win the game. I refer you to this line from last week's round up: *"I'm putting this out there; Ashley Young is by far and away the biggest diver in the Premier League. No-one is even close to his level of constant cheating"*. Now I'm not the kind of guy to say *'I told you so'*, but if I was the kind of guy to say *'I told you so'* then I'd have to say, *'I told you so'*. Admittedly, it's not like I discovered how to split the atom, I was merely highlighting the obvious, but let me have my moment here as it's not often I'm this right about anything. Almost everyone can see what a deceitful little shit he is, unfortunately the only ones who can't all happen to be Premier League referees. (ahem that's 'Barclays' Premier League referees - Owen Coyle). That he'd stoop so low as to do this against his old team-mates (who are not yet safe from relegation let's not forget) says a lot about him, the absolute lowlife. Wellbeck then made it 2-0 following horrific play by Villa's two centre backs who both dummied the ball instead of clearing it. Villa's woes continued as Kieran Clark was forced off with a nasty head injury. He left the field looking dazed and confused and was replaced by Emile Heskey, who entered the field looking dazed and confused. Rooney made it 3-0 with a deflected shot and Nani added another late on. The celebratory backflip was decent but needs some work to match the one Young produced to win that penalty against QPR last week. Ferguson admitted afterwards that Young had *'gone down easily'* for the penalty but then blamed the Villa defender for not staying on his feet. He's got a point, except for the not staying on his feet part as the defender didn't go to ground at all, he stood there with both feet firmly planted. So actually he doesn't have a point at all, he's just a massively hypocritical old cuntaxe.

Villa fans chanted *"Stand up for the 96"*. The manc response? *"Always the victim, it's never your fault"*. That's not a Hillsborough song though, honest it's not. It's just a co-incidence that they happened to sing it in response to Villa fans paying their respects to the 96. You know the worst thing about that song? It's most of the stadium singing it. It's as though they think they've got a free pass to sing about Hillsborough now as they play the 'get out of jail free card' and claim that's not what the song is about. Well it fucking is when they sing it. They know it. We know it. They just won't admit it.

Finally, Monday Night Football at the Emirates. Wow. How about those Wigan boys, eh? Winning at Arsenal to round off a five game run in which they've also won at Anfield and beaten United and Stoke as well. The one blemish was a defeat at Chelsea, and they should have won that game too but for a linesman who allowed Chelsea two offside goals. What Wigan have done in the last few weeks is astonishing and they deserve all the credit in the world, especially considering they've done it with Franco Di Santo leading the line and Alcaraz in their back three. In fairness Di Santo managed to score at the Emirates and for once it wasn't deflected. Well, technically I suppose it was as it went in off the keeper, but beggars can't be choosers. It changes nothing, you can put a dog in an oven but that doesn't make it a biscuit. He's still crap. Alcaraz on the other hand is vastly improved on the liability he was in the first half of the season. He's been much better of late, well I assume he has as I've barely noticed him and that has to be a good thing given how a few months ago he stood out like a dick on a cake. As for Arsenal, if Van Persie doesn't deliver there's just not that much left is there? Song is very good and Walcott has his moments, but other than that.... RVP is unquestionably my player of the season, but what a spolit, petulant little shithead he is. His reaction towards Caldwell's attempted handshake was arrogant and classless, not to mention incredibly camp. Don't know where he gets that lack of grace from, I mean it's not as though his manager would ever.... Oh wait, yes he would. In fact he's made a habit of it down the years. Wenger's refusal to shake Martinez's hand afterwards, presumably because he didn't like Wigan's time wasting tactics, was sad, petty and typical. What did he expect Wigan to do? They're going to do anything they can to survive and besides, his team had 82 minutes to turn this game around and failed. Everything he said about time wasting and how referees are not dealing with it properly is 100% spot on, I've been saying the same kind of thing for years (especially the ridiculous rule that lets keepers take goal kicks the opposite side to where the ball went out) and I don't blame him for being frustrated as Wigan did clearly take the piss. You can't blame them for doing that given their situation though. Blame the ref by all means, refuse to shake his hand if you feel that strongly about it, but don't blame Martinez. A classic case of "hatin' the playa, when he should be hatin' the game", yo. Not shaking Roberto Martinez's hand just makes Wenger look like a wanker. As does wearing an Arsenal sleeping bag with the bottom cut off and trying to pass it off as a coat.

Pink boot hall of shame: Scott Sinclair, Anthony Modeste, Jerome Thomas, Mark Antoine-Fortune, Peter Odemwingie, James McLean, Nicklas Bendtner, Steven Fletcher, Ronald Zubar, Steven Ireland, Gaby Agbonlahor, Yossi Benayoun (why Yossi, why?).

LIVERPOOL 0 WEST BROMWICH ALBION 1

Competition - Premier League
Date - Sun 22 Apr 2012
Venue - Anfield
Scorer(s) –
Half Time - 0-0
Star Man – Jordan Henderson

Team: Reina; Johnson, Skrtel, Agger, Enrique; Kuyt (Bellamy), Henderson, Spearing (Shelvey), Maxi (Downing): Suarez, Carroll:

***"This will be one of those days when everything we hit goes in"* I declared before the game. I wasn't far off, as substitute the word 'everything' with 'nothing' and you have a perfect summation of our latest disappointing home result. It's hard to believe this can keep happening, and yet it somehow does. In the league anyway, we have no such problems in the cup which makes it all the more baffling.**

We've apparently hit the woodwork 31 times now this season. That in itself is an astonishing statistic, but even more remarkable is that only one of those was in the cups. That goes a long way to explaining why we've won one cup and are in the final of the other, whilst in the league we're dogshit. As shocking a defeat as this was, there was also a sad inevitability about it. Having missed loads of chances and seen two efforts come back off the woodwork yet again, was anyone even surprised when we gifted West Brom a goal they clearly didn't deserve? The most disappointing aspect of it all was that we offered nothing after going behind. Prior to that we'd played well and torn West Brom apart. After the goal we had no shape and just looked desperate. It's understandable I suppose, the players were probably wondering how the hell this keeps happening and just what they have to do to score. I'm not even mad at them, they tried their best but it just isn't happening. We just can't put the ball in the net. Is it bad luck? Is it something we aren't doing in training? Are the players just not good enough? Is it a mental thing? Did someone break a mirror over a black cat's head at Melwood whilst walking under a ladder? It's probably all of the above, well maybe not the cat thing but the rest all applies to some extent.

We don't have enough players in the side capable of scoring goals on a regular basis, that's patently obvious. It's also obvious that it shouldn't be THIS chronic a problem. As I watched this unfold in front of me, I came to the conclusion that this season is just a complete anomaly and it can't end soon enough. We'll never hit the woodwork this many times again, we'll never miss as many penalties again. I just hope we can get that FA Cup in the trophy cabinet and then consign this league campaign to the dustbin where it belongs.

I started to get that sinking feeling when Kuyt missed a great early chance. That's just symptomatic of the season that one missed chance has me thinking *'here we go again, one of those days'*. I mean, really, one missed chance early on shouldn't be causing these kind of negative thoughts should they? It also crossed my mind as to whether the players are also thinking this too? Probably not after Kuyt's miss, but when we didn't score after a ridiculous goalmouth scramble midway through the second half, they wouldn't be human if they weren't thinking 'fuck this, we're never gonna score'. West Brom's goal then merely rubbed their noses in it.

It's difficult to criticise anyone too much after this. I didn't think anybody played badly and whilst the finger can be pointed at Johnson (and to a lesser extent Reina) for West Brom's goal, it's a little unfair as really you should be allowed to give away the occasional bad goal without it costing points. For us that isn't the case. Every goal conceded leads to a defeat or if we're lucky, a draw. Unless it's in the cup of course, we usually come back and win then. It was a bad mistake by Johnson, no question about it, but that goal should have been no more than a consolation for Roy Hodgson's side as we should have been out of sight at that stage. In fairness to the Baggies, they didn't come and put everybody behind the ball and 'do a Stoke'. I wouldn't say they were over adventurous either, but they always looked like they had a goal in them as their front two are both pacy and hard working.

Despite us dominating the first half, Reina did have to make two saves before the break (one of which was top drawer), but the longer the game went the further back we pushed them and the worse their time wasting began to get. With an hour or so gone they'd have been overjoyed with a point as they were under the cosh so badly. They had one good chance after the break and they took it. We had half a dozen and took none, much like the first half. As usual, creating chances wasn't a problem. Kuyt's early miss came after Carroll had closed down a defender and won the ball for Suarez who put it on a plate for the Dutchman. Suarez then played a great 1-2 with Johnson, surged into the box and put a perfect ball across the face of goal that was begging to be converted. Only Agger attacked it and he couldn't get there. Everyone else was hanging back doing nothing, including Carroll who was near the penalty spot. You're a centre forward Andy, fucking get in the danger area. Carroll is doing a lot of things very well at the moment, but he isn't a natural goalscorer and too often he's caught on his heels when the ball is being played into the danger area. I don't think that's a fault that can't be fixed though, he just has to be a bit more aware of what's going on and hopefully that will improve over time. I thought he played very well again, he was involved in a lot of our best chances and he linked well with his team-mates throughout. A great flick by him then set Suarez racing towards the box, he cut inside but his shot was superbly blocked by an Albion defender.

It was all Liverpool at this point, but then out of nothing the Baggies almost took the lead. A long ball was played up towards Shane Long who was being covered by Agger. As the ball was in the air I noticed a West Brom player charging through the middle and it was obvious if Long won the header we'd be in trouble. He did win it, and Billy Jones was clean through on Reina who made a terrific instinctive save with his left hand. Suarez then headed onto the roof of the net after being picked out by Enrique and Spearing flashed a shot just wide from 25 yards. Agger then brought a save out of Foster when he did well to turn in the box but he went near post instead of far and it was an easy save for the keeper. At the other end Reina had to make another save too, this time with his chest from close range. The referee wasn't giving us much, and Suarez in particular was especially irate at the official after he was clearly bundled over from behind on the edge of the box only for the referee to wave play on. That was a ridiculous decision. He also waved away penalty appeals when Maxi took a tumble. Haven't seen any replays of it but at the time I thought it was never a pen and that Maxi had clearly gone looking for it. Apparently replays showed there was contact, but that doesn't automatically mean it's a penalty and it looked to me like Maxi was going nowhere and was always looking for the penalty.

The second half was all us up until they scored. Wave after wave of attacks at the Kop end goal came to nothing as the Baggies' goal led a charmed life. Johnson lifted a ball into Suarez who took it on his chest and then played another great ball across face of goal. Once more Agger was the only one who attacked it and once more he couldn't quite get there. Next, a great move ended with Carroll laying it back to Henderson on the edge of the box. He struck the ball beautifully only to see it smack the bar. That was difficult enough to take, but the rebound hit Foster and looked certain to bounce back into the net. We've seen that kind of goal so often, but somehow it rebounded away from goal. They nearly always go in, but our luck was out yet again. Suarez then skinned a defender on touchline, beat another and then ignored Maxi and Carroll in the centre and shot over. Carroll was livid, rightly so I thought at the time. Looking at a replay of it though it wasn't as clear cut as there is a defender between Suarez and his team-mates which made the pass a lot more difficult. The decision to shoot isn't the problem, it's the fact he ballooned it.

Henderson curled a shot inches wide after again being teed up Carroll, and the big number nine put a couple of headers over from decent crosses. I thought we could have had a penalty when Agger looked he was shoved as he went for a header. The ball struck his hand and he was booked, but for me the only reason he handled was because he'd been shoved and wasn't in control of his movement as a result of it. We continued to lay siege to Ben Foster's goal, and Kuyt was next to be denied by the woodwork when he collected a pass from Suarez and drilled a low shot across the goal onto the base of the far post. By now the entire stadium were getting that De Ja Vu feeling. Worse was to come. Suarez once again burst into the box collecting a great layoff from Kuyt. His cross came off Foster and looped into the air. An off balance Carroll missed his kick but did well to then play it back to Spearing who looked as though he'd scored his first senior goal until it was cleared off the line. Maxi's latched onto it and tried to cross for Suarez but the ball was eventually smothered to safety. Definitely one of those days.

Kuyt was replaced by Bellamy and Maxi made way for Downing as Kenny looked for the breakthrough. Next thing Glen Johnson took an unnecessary risk and Odemwingie was running clear on goal. We all knew what was coming next. His shot was crap but Reina had anticipated the ball going to his left and had all his weight on that side and was therefore unable to adjust and make what should have been an easy save. 0-1.

Our response wasn't good. Kenny took off Spearing and sent on Shelvey. That meant we lost all shape and there was a huge void in the middle of the park. Not Shelvey's fault, both he and Henderson were trying to get forward as we were desperate and it showed. We resorted to lumping it at an isolated Carroll and he stopped being as effective as it was too predictable. The only time we threatened after falling behind was when Bellamy had a shot parried and Carroll's follow up struck Olsson on the knee and went to safety. It's soul destroying seeing us losing so often and had we not beaten the blues at Wembley last week this would have been a real sickener.

Having a cup final to look forward to eases the pain a fair bit, but the sooner we see the back of this freak of a season the better.

Premier League Round Up (21-22 April 2012)

Another eventful weekend as teams at the bottom continue to win and most of those at the top don't. The title race was blown wide open, one team was relegated but everyone else down at the bottom are still fighting for their lives and picking up points, whilst the battle for the Champions League spots is really heating up too.

We're not involved in any of it though and our game with West Brom was described on MOTD as 'a mid table clash'. *"Cheeky bastards"* I initially thought, before I realised it wasn't a dig it was just a fact. Thank God for the FA Cup eh?

Newcastle's amazing season continued with a home win over Stoke that catapulted them into the top four just three points behind 3rd placed Arsenal with a game in hand. The perennially shite Jon Walters ballooned a great chance over the bar early on for Stoke but after that it was one way traffic. Great play by Ben Arfa made the opening goal as his cross was headed against the bar by Cisse and Cabaye put the rebound in. Cisse made it 2-0 with another good finish after a great pass by man of the match Cabaye. The French midfielder's second goal of the game made it 3-0 in the second half with a curler from the edge of the box. Newcastle did something in this game that virtually nobody does; they managed to look good whilst playing against Stoke's cloggers. Fair play to them, I think I'd like to see them make the top four as they deserve it more than any of the other contenders, and more to the point I want to see two of the other three missing out (ideally Chelsea and Arsenal). I hope Newcastle get third actually, irrespective of the disdain I have for that slimeball Pardew and the moronic fans who have bizarrely labelled Andy Carroll as some kind of Judas. Do they still hate Fat Mike Ashley and his 'cockney mafia', or is he 'alreet like' now?

That there's even a chance of Newcastle getting third says a lot about how Spurs have imploded. They lost yet again, this time at QPR. I've mocked Spurs regularly about them being chokers, but even I never dreamed they'd fuck things up as badly as they have. Unbelievable really. Taarabt's floated free-kick gave QPR the lead and for the first time Brad Friedel actually looked like the 40 year old man he is. The free-kick wasn't even any good, it seemed like it was in slow motion. Fortunately for QPR Brad's dive was in super slo-mo and he got nowhere near it. Still, it should never have been a foul in the first place and Mark Clattenburg had a bit of a 'mare. He later sent off Taarabt for a second yellow card for kicking the ball away. It looked ridiculously harsh, and Clattenberg initially didn't even realise he'd already booked him. When the penny eventually dropped he produced a red card and yet again Rangers were down to ten men. It's just a pity this one didn't prove costly as it's always fun seeing Mark Hughes upset. By the way, is there a more pointless footballer in the league than Giovani Dos Santos? What purpose does he serve? It seems like he's been at Spurs longer than Ledley King, but he never plays. They loan him out, he comes back. They loan him out, he comes back. They can't find someone to loan him to, so he sits on the bench and plays the odd cup game and has a cameo every now and then in the league if the good players are unavailable. He's a complete waster. The Mexican Aquilani.

Since Capello quit England, Tottenham's form has gone down the pan and their top four hopes are disappearing around the U-bend. I don't really understand why Redknapp being linked with the England job should cause the Spurs players to lose the plot like this, but then I'm not a footballer and have never been in that situation. It's definitely not a co-incidence though is it?

Meanwhile, Arsenal played out a goalless draw with Chelsea reserves at the Emirates. Van Persie and Koscielny both hit the woodwork as Arsenal dominated. RVP could have had five in this game but his finishing has been off a bit recently. Earlier in the season everything he hit went in, but it was inevitable his scoring rate would slow down eventually. And if he's not doing it who else will? Answer, no-one, that's who. As for Chelsea, they were terrible and Torres was anonymous. He was so irrelevant that he didn't touch the ball even once during MOTD's highlights of the game. I saw him throwing his arms around a bit and bitching at team-mates, but not touching the ball. Like 2010 all over again, only in a blue shirt not a red one.

Moving on, and there was a massive win for Blackburn at home to Norwich. Yakubu hit the post with the least graceful looking overhead kick you'll ever see. Play had to be stopped whilst the groundsman came on to fill in the two crators his arse cheeks made in the goalmouth. Formica volleyed Rovers in front after an inviting cross by Pedersen and my boy Junior Hoilett made it 2-0 with a trademark goal, cutting in from the left and curling a shot into the top corner. He'll be playing in the Premier League next season, regardless of whether Blackburn are or not. Norwich continued their tradition of sending out another random jobber. This one was slightly different in that he was a familiar face, albeit not one we've seen in a Norwich shirt since the early weeks of the season. James Vaughan, the elbow throwing dirty blueshite. I'd forgotten he was even at Norwich. His only contribution to this game was to completely miss his kick in front of goal and later get subbed. He was wearing pink boots too, the loser.

With Blackburn and QPR both winning, Bolton's home game with Swansea took on added importance for them. Swansea haven't been doing great recently so this was a game that the Trotters will have seen as a great chance to pick up a vital three points. They got off to a terrible start when Scott Sinclair cut in from the left and whipped a shot into the top corner, but Chris Eagles quickly got them back on level terms. Petrov went close with a free-kick but was denied by a fantastic save by Vorm. Graham should have scored when Sigurdsson played him in and then Sigurdsson himself saw a close range effort blocked by Wheater. Graham then curled a shot inches wide and hit the bar with another effort as Swansea dominated. Bolton were second best but Eagles almost won it for them at the end only his shot went just the wrong side of the post. Sigurdsson was impressive again, the more I see of him the more I think he looks a class act. If he fancies a move to Anfield I've got a shirt here with his name on it waiting for him. Not literally, it's just a figure of speech. I don't do shirts with names on, not since that impulse buy after we played Lazio in 2002. I mean how was I supposed to know he wasn't actually the 'new Zidane'? Had my fingers burned that day, never again though.

In form Wigan went to Fulham and took the lead through Emerson Boyce. It didn't last long though, Pogrebnyak returning to the side with a well taken goal to equalise a minute later. The Russian then hit the bar and would later hit the post. We should definitely sign him, he'd fit right in here. Fulham won it in the last minute with a header from Senderos. Cruel on Wigan but Fulham deserved the points. As a sidenote, Fulham must have by far the worst club badge in the league, it's absolutely shit. Did they actually pay someone to design that? Truly pathetic.

You'll rarely find a more obvious 0-0 for your coupon than Aston Villa playing host to former boss Martin O'Neill's Sunderland. Sunderland have been firing more blanks than the A-Team whilst Villa are just, well, they're pitiful. I can't even call them Aston Vanilla anymore as they're not even plain old run of the mill under McLeish, they're just bottom feeders now. This had 0-0 written all over it. Bentdner missed one sitter, had another cleared off the line and also had a good goal incorrectly ruled out for offside. It's hard to have any sympathy for him though, he just seems like such a massive weapon. Everything about him is crap. His face is crap. His hair is crap. His pink boots are crap. Hell, even his tattoos are crap, they look like they were drawn on by an 8 year old. If he wasn't so crap I'd probably hate him as he doesn't even have the humility and self awareness to know that he's crap, he thinks he's King Dick. He's the Danish Ibrahimovich.

As for Villa, they're fortunate the season is coming to a close and games are running out, as if there were another half dozen games left they'd definitely go down as they're in freefall. McLeish did the same to Birmingham last year, and it's genuinely puzzling how he landed the Villa job. It wasn't so long ago that Randy Lerner was being held up as an example of how not all foreign owners are conniving schysters. Then he fell out with O'Neill and appointed McLeish and his best players all left. He may not be a Shyster, but his standards aren't exactly high are they? His other team is the Cleveland Browns in the NFL, a perennial struggler and the butt of a lot of jokes over there. He's effectively turned Villa into the Premier League's answer to the Browns. What pleasure does someone like Lerner get from his teams? They stink every year and there's never any chance that they won't. I hope he buys Everton next.

Onto Sunday, and how amusing was it to see what unfolded at Old Trafford? Whilst any kind of positive result for the blues isn't great for us, a draw was clearly the best outcome from my perspective. I had it all worked out, a draw would seriously damage United's title chances whilst leaving the door wide open for us to leapfrog the blues by seeing off West Brom at Anfield. The only problem I could foresee was Everton's natural inclination to drop their trousers and bend over for Ferguson. Turns out their desire to finish above us is stronger than their desire to see United win another title. Who knew? Certainly not United who were taken completely by surprise by this unprecedented resistance from Moyes' men. From an LFC perspective this was a great result and everything was going according to plan until we lost to West fucking Brom.

In his programme notes Ferguson claimed the media *'had a field day'* over the Ashley Young penalty incident last week. A field day? You want to talk about field days? How about the way Luis Suarez was hammered for months because of the various falsehoods peddled to the press and the FA by you and your shithouse captain? Field day? Count yourself lucky it wasn't a 'field six months' like what Suarez had to deal with, you odious old skidmark. Ferguson also reckoned he'd *'had a word'* with Young about it. I'm sure he did, something along the lines of *"great job son, you've done well but we need to take you out of the firing line for a bit until the heat is off. Take a seat on the bench and let Nani take over."* Benching Young and bringing in Nani. Like an alcy pouring his stash of whiskey down the sink and then cracking open a bottle of rum. What's the point? Young is the whiskey, Nani is the bottle of rum which makes Ferguson... well you get the picture. Everton surprisingly took the game to the Mancs from the off. Jelavic and Osman both had chances before the Croat superbly headed the blues into the lead. Hate to admit it but I quite like him you know, his movement off the ball is ace and he's a lethal finisher.

Predictably, Rooney equalised just before half time. After the break Wellbeck made it 2-1 and then laid on the third for Nani. It looked all over but then Screech volleyed in a cross from Hibbert to briefly make it interesting until Rooney combined with Wellbeck and then restored the two goal cushion a couple of minutes later. Job done, Everton had once again done a fine impersonation of a side that hadn't actually gone to Old Trafford with the intent of rolling over, but we all knew the score, we've seen it so often. Aside from beating us, the thing that gives the blues the most pleasure is United's success and the hurt that causes Liverpudlians. Hell, they've even chanted "UNITED" at derby games. But as much as they revel in United's glory, beating us is just about more important to them. They've tried and failed three times this season but despite their inferiority in head to head clashes, our goalscoring problems have put the Blues in with a great shout of finishing above us in the table. That's the X Factor that United didn't take into account. Everton shocked United by actually fighting back. It was the last thing Ferguson and his players expected and they were completely caught cold. The playground bully ended up with a bloody nose after the kid he'd been giving wedgies to for years finally plucked up the courage to hit back and boot him him in the balls. Jelavic made it 'squeaky bum time' with another cool finish and as United went into full blown panic mode Pienaar amazingly equalised after some class play by Fellaini in the United box. Rooney's face was a picture after that went in. Traitorous little bastard, he plays for a side that chants about hating scousers in EVERY game they play and yet he regularly kisses their badge. He's a disgrace to his home city and if United end up not winning the title it would be beautifully ironic that it was the club he shit on that may have put the biggest dent in those hopes, especially if it counts for nothing and we end up finishing above Everton anyway.

It goes without saying that I don't want to finish below the blues, and yet I do have a morbid curiosity as to what they'd do if they did end up pipping us to 7th. Remember the DVD they brought out last time they ended the season in that spot? *"The Magnificent 7th"*. What's that in Latin? Maybe they can incorporate it onto their crest as that old mantra of theirs is clearly way past it's sell by date. *"Nothing but the best will do, but obviously we'll bring a DVD out if we finish seventh as let's face it, that's magnificent."* It may even be worth finishing below them just to see if they release *"The Magnificent 7th Ride Again"*.

United's loss in the early game meant that City knew victory at Wolves would put them right back in the hunt. Wolves needed to win to avoid the drop but that was never going to happen as they went into freefall months ago and aren't capable of beating anybody, let alone the best team in the country. City didn't even play that well but Wolves are so bad it didn't matter. Mancini's men started well enough, Aguero went close twice and Nasri missed a great chance too. Aguero eventually scored just before the half hour mark but City then eased off and needed Joe Hart to keep them in front when he kept out Fletcher's header. Nasri made the game safe when he collected a pass from Tevez and made it 2-0. City will go top again if they beat United next Monday whilst Wolves are now officially down.

It was impossible not to feel for Terry Connor afterwards. The poor fella was on the verge of tears, although in fairness he's been like that in most interviews. He always looks like he's shitting himself in front of the cameras, and I just feel bad for the guy as he was thrown in at the deep end and sadly he drowned. Steve Morgan is to blame for Wolves relegation though, not Terry Connor and not Mick McCarthy. Had McCarthy seen out the season and they'd gone down then it would be on him, but McCarthy may have saved them if he'd been given the chance. He's done it before. We'll never know though because Morgan sacked him without a clue what to do next. I look at what Morgan has done to Wolves this year and thank my lucky stars he never got his hands on LFC.

NORWICH CITY 0 LIVERPOOL 3

Competition - Premier League
Date - Sat 28 Apr 2012
Venue - Carrow Road
Scorer(s) – Luis Suarez (3)
Half Time - 0-2
Star Man – Luis Suarez

Team: Reina; Johnson, Carragher, Agger, Enrique; Shelvey, Henderson; Downing, Gerrard (Coates), Bellamy; Suarez (Kuyt):

You could say this has been a long time coming. The performance wasn't much different from how we've played for most of the season. Plenty of the ball, chances created, denied by the woodwork, the main difference this time was the comfortable margin of victory, which was a result of Luis Suarez finding the net instead of the post, the keeper or the stands.

There's been much discussion as to whether this is the best hat-trick ever scored by a Liverpool player. In terms of the quality of all three goals, it certainly takes some beating. Each finish was better than the last. The first sublime, the last ridiculous. This could have happened numerous times this season and I'm certain Suarez will never have a year like this again. So many chances missed, so many times denied by the woodwork, so many games missed through an unjust suspension. He has 11 league goals to his name but it could and should be double that. I'm certain next year it will be. Even in this game he missed the easiest chance he had. It didn't matter, as he buried three others, two of which he had no right to score and a third that more often than not he wouldn't take. Aside from the goals, he was electric and the Norwich defence just couldn't contain him. They resorted to crude fouls out of sheer desperation. Bennett and Ward will never face a more difficult opponent than Suarez in this form.

Having said that, they were ultimately responsible for their own downfall, as all three goals were a result of their defenders either being caught in possession or losing out in challenges they were favourite to win. The first goal owed much to the desire of Gerrard, who pressurised the defender and won the ball before dinking it into the path of Suarez. The striker was through on goal but was on his left foot and Ruddy was coming out to narrow the angle. Not an easy chance but the shot was unerring and found the corner of the net to set us on our way. A crisp strike and a great finish, but one that he would soon eclipse with his second of the game. A short pass put Norwich defender Bennett in a bit of trouble as he was closed down by Suarez but he still should have cleaned everything out. Instead he was robbed by Suarez who had acres of space to run into, but he was the furthest player upfield and had no support (he had the awareness to have a quick look to see that before going alone). He advanced into the box but the angle wasn't favourable. The only way place he could beat Ruddy was in the far corner, but given the angle and how far out he was, it would have to be a shot of extreme power. And it was. It was an amazing strike from an amazing player. Simply stunning. We were completely on top and in total control of the game. Defensively we were untroubled, as Carragher and Agger were rock solid and neither full back was tested by a Norwich side that couldn't get anything going in the absence of top scorer Grant Holt. Henderson, Shelvey and Gerrard controlled possession and provided us with a fluid base to attack from. Mostly it was the outstanding Gerrard furthest forward in support of Suarez, but Shelvey regularly got himself up there too and should have scored at least once in the second half.

There was a feeling of deja vu about this game, it was starting to look like the QPR game from the other week. 2-0 up and totally dominant, but missing chances to kill the game off completely. Shelvey was unfortunate to hit the bar with a header and then somehow missed from virtually on the goalline after a great ball by Enrique (in Jonjo's defence the ball appeared to strike a divot just before it reached him). Downing saw a good effort saved and Suarez wastefully chipped over the bar when he should have scored. I was getting pissed off at this point. The likelihood of us seeing a repeat of what happened at Loftus Road was remote, that wasn't what was bothering me. It was the inability to turn our superiority into goals that was annoying me. The two goals would almost certainly be enough to secure the points, but really we should have been 5-0 up. Both our goals had come from Norwich mistakes, and we can't rely on that happening every week. Even in victory, the failings in front of goal that we have seen all season were still there. For once it didn't prove costly as Suarez had his shooting boots on, demonstrated perfectly by the amazing strike that sealed his hat-trick. Without taking anything away from the brilliance of the goal, it has to be pointed out that once again it came from a Norwich mistake. Johnson's clearance out of defence went straight to Ward who once more failed to deal with it and was robbed by Suarez. The beauty of this goal is the little look up he has as soon as he wins possession. Knowing that Ruddy was well off his line he didn't need to look again, he kept his head down and struck through the ball, sending it flying over Ruddy's head into the net. The ideal way to complete a hat-trick, and it's lucky for Suarez that it found the net as Gerrard was in acres of space to his left screaming for the ball. When Luis hit the shot you can see Gerrard throw his head back in disgust, ready to launch into him for not passing. If I remember rightly, he did exactly the same when Xabi scored from inside his own half against Luton. Amusingly, he admitted on live TV afterwards *"it was just on the tip of my tongue to give him a bollocking but then he does that!"*

With the game won Kenny wisely got Suarez and Gerrard out of there. No point taking any risks, and if it were my decision both of them would have their feet up in the stands on Tuesday night against Fulham. We want to win the game and it's important that we don't finish below the blues, but with the cup final a few days away I don't want to see any key players involved against Fulham. Everyone who played against Norwich did their cup final selection chances no harm at all. Kenny certainly has plenty to think about this week. A slight injury to Carroll meant he wasn't involved, and that couldn't have come at a worse time for him. His absence meant we saw Gerrard playing much closer to Suarez than usual, and the results were impressive.

Given the way Chelsea set up in midfield it might be difficult to go with Carroll and Suarez, and Gerrard's performance in an advanced role may see Carroll miss out at Wembley. Ideally I'd want to see all three playing, but it's a problem fitting them all into a system that would not be over ran by Chelsea's three man midfield.

Skrtel was rested for this one and will hopefully not play on Tuesday either. He's a certain starter at Wembley, as is Agger. In the semi final Agger played left back at the expense of Enrique, whose form hasn't been good since the turn of the year. He played well at Carrow Road though. So too did Carragher, he had a fine game once he stopped continually trying to play the ball over the head of their left back in a futile attempt to get Downing into the game. He played far too many long balls in the first half but corrected the issue after the break and defensively he was excellent throughout, typified by a fantastic block to deny Vaughan late on. Henderson had another tidy game in the centre of the park and he clearly looks happier there than out wide. It wouldn't be a surprise to see him back on the right hand side at Wembley though would it?

Overall, everyone played well and we were comfortable winners, even if Norwich did contribute greatly to their own downfall. They've been a nice little story this season, most expected them to go down but not only have they survived but they've done so comfortably. I was pleased for them as they've always been an inoffensive club and it was nice seeing them confound the odds. Fuck all that now though. *"Always the victim it's never your fault"* they chanted for what seemed like most of the first half. When they weren't chanting that they were abusing Suarez. What the fuck is that all about? Why the hostility towards us? Smalltime, carrot munching fucks. This 'victim' shite goes beyond 'banter' and the sooner opposing fans realise it the better. There are certain fans you expect that from, Norwich are not amongst them. At least, they weren't until this weekend. Maybe the rest of the league are too fucking stupid to know that it's a manc chant and it's a cowardly dig at Hillsborough. The Mancs can claim it's not all they like, but we all know it is. As to whether Norwich fans knew, I'm guessing they didn't and hopefully the response of *'Justice for the 96'* from the travelling Kop drove the message home as it seemed to stop after that. The Mancs chanting it is one thing, it's expected from them, but now it seems everyone is jumping on it and it's getting out of hand. They've done the same with that Suarez *'you know what you are'* nonsense. Yeah he knows what he is, and so do we. He's fucking brilliant, that's what he is. Those Norwich yokels know it too after the way he single handedly tore them a new one. I look forward to seeing him do the same to Chelsea this weekend. Come on redmen, let's fucking do these disrespectful, Hillsborough mocking, plastic flag waving, bus parking cunts.

chapter thirteen

Holy Comolli!!

I wasn't sorry to see Damien Comolli go, but I wouldn't say I was thrilled about it either. I've got nothing against the fella, I just don't know if he is any good at what he does, or what exactly it was that he was supposed to do. As fans I don't think any of us do, we're not privvy to the ins and outs of it all and we can only make guesses based on what we see, read and hear.

Comolli was meant to be the man in charge of transfer strategy, but there's little evidence to suggest he was calling any shots in that area. It looks like he just went out and signed the players Kenny wanted him to. On the face of it, it appears he had the title and the responsibility, but not the power that usually goes with it in other countries or in the equivalent position in US Sports.

Kenny claims (on and off the record) that no player was brought in that he did not want. Whilst he doesn't really have any other choice than to say that, I'm fairly sure it's the truth, certainly in terms of those brought in last summer. The Suarez and Carroll deals are more complicated because Kenny was only caretaker boss at the time. He'd been in the job only a few weeks, there was no way of knowing how it would pan out and how long he'd be in charge. There's no way he'd have been given the authority to sanction those deals, although his opinion will surely have been sought. We'd been scouting Suarez well before Comolli arrived (pretty sure I remember reading that Kenny himself had been to watch him at Ajax) but the Andy Carroll signing came right out of the blue. I don't doubt that Kenny was happy to have Carroll at the club, but from an FSG perspective you'd have to assume they held Comolli accountable for the fee we paid as you aren't going to leave a decision as big as that to a caretaker manager who at that point in time you had no intention of giving the job to on a permanent basis.

Last summer was different, as it seems like Comolli just went out with Kenny's shopping list and the owners cheque book and brought back the players the manager wanted. He is not culpable for the players who came in but he is for the fees paid to get them here, as essentially that's his responsibility regardless of whether Dalglish felt they were worth it or not. Whilst I wouldn't exonerate Kenny entirely for the fees paid, ultimately it was Comolli's call whether to pay it or not. If he felt they were not worth what we were paying then presumably he had the authority to say no, and clearly in the owners eyes he didn't do that.

The statement from the club made reference to him not being the right person to 'implement their strategy' which is funny because that's the exact reason he was hired in the first place. He was supposedly someone who shared their philosophy and appeared to be the ideal person to 'implement their strategy'. Go back to when FSG bought the club. They knew nothing whatsoever about what they were getting into. They didn't have a clue about English football and needed somebody in position who did. They required someone who could look at all aspects of the club and report back to them about what needed doing and how to do it. They needed to know how strong the first team squad was, whether the manager was any good, the quality of the youth players coming through etc and who could come up with a strategy on how to improve things moving forward. Not only did they not have a clue about any of that stuff, they had no clue who they should hire to tell them.

That's where Comolli came in, at the recommendation of Billy Beane, a baseball mate of Henry and Werner's and someone who knew Comolli well. Beane is the fella who came up with the whole 'Moneyball' concept. I was going to just skip over that and didn't want to get too bogged down in what 'Moneyball' is but it's pretty relevant to Comolli's situation, so bear with me for a bit. Without going into the specifics too much, essentially 'Moneyball' was a strategy that Beane came up with to make his team - the Oakland Athletics - competitive against teams that spend vastly more than they were capable of spending. In his words; *"Our club would be like a Blackpool or Wigan. We can't do the same things like the Yankees or the Red Sox - like Wigan can't do the same things as Manchester United - so you have to do something different"* That 'something different' was to analyse players by statistics. Nothing new there, baseball has always been stats based, but Beane gave more emphasis to aspects of the game that were deemed by others as not being that important. Now, pretty much everyone in baseball uses Beane's approach, meaning he is no longer as successful. The secret is out, not least because he allowed it to be made into a book and then a movie starring Brad Pitt!

The specifics of it aren't relevant to us, the main point is that Comolli is a stat geek too, he read the 'Moneyball' book and became friends with Beane who recommended him to FSG. Whilst the players we signed last summer were those that Kenny wanted, it's interesting to note that Adam, Downing and Henderson were all in the top eight when it came to chances created in the Premier League last season. That could go a long way to explaining why Comolli was right on board with Kenny's choices. They'll have looked far better on his spreadsheet than they have done on the pitch. The reality of the situation is that stats are far more relevant to baseball than they are to football. Downing is right up near the top of that list again (even if none of those chances have been converted), but would anyone say he's been anything other than a big disappointment this season?

Still, the statistics side is only a part of the 'moneyball' philosophy. I don't pretend to be an expert on it, I haven't read the book, haven't seen the movie and I've only got a passing interest in baseball. I have read up on it a little for the purposes of researching this chapter, and found more quotes from Beane that are quite interesting; *"Younger players are cost-effective. They may cost more to acquire, but their wages are lower. With an older player you may be paying for past performance, whereas with a younger player you are paying for future performance. It is like stock. Young players are attractive because they are cheaper and offer more value. They may not be as good, but if they perform at a certain level it makes more sense financially. There is a misconception that you never pay much for anybody, that is not true at all. You want to make sure you are getting more value than you are paying. That may come in the form of a very expensive player it may come in the form of a very young player, but it is not about being cheap or not spending money. It is about getting the most out of your dollar, or pound."*

Pretty simple stuff, and that's the kind of thing every well run sports team should be doing anyway, regardless of whether they're into 'Moneyball' or not. You buy young players before they've reached their potential, so therefore they should be cheaper than buying somebody who has already reached the top level and is an established star. Common sense. If you buy younger players at a low value, that value increases as they mature and their game improves. Again, common sense. You only buy big if it's a low risk move and you're sure you'll get value for money, and if you're taking a punt on a youngster with potential you get them cheap and hope they develop. It's not rocket science.

If that's the strategy that FSG are trying to implement, then it's easy to see why they are unhappy with what's happened as half of the players we've brought in don't match that criteria at all. We paid big money for Carroll and Henderson and if we sold them today we'd make big losses on both. With young players you're supposed to buy them before their value skyrockets and then make a return on your investment should they move on. Not sign them at a price they'll struggle to ever live up to. Then you have Downing. He doesn't have youth on his side as he's a player who is supposedly in his prime. Therefore his value is going to be at it's highest right now, which it was as he was Villa's player of the season and they didn't want to lose him. We had to pay top dollar to get him. That's fine, as long as you get the production you need. Whilst I don't think Downing has been as bad as some suggest, he has been disappointing and has certainly not provided value for money. He was never going to be John Barnes, but the problem is he hasn't even been Stewart Downing most of the time. If we sold him this summer there'd be no shortage of takers but we'd only get £12-14m for him.

Charlie Adam is what he is. A £6m squad player who unfortunately had to play more regularly than intended because of Gerrard's injury problems. No real issue with that signing, we'd get at least get our money back if he left, probably a bit more. Enrique the same, the way he started he looked like the signing of the season, but since the turn of the year he's been all over the place. Despite his recent wobbles, given what we paid for him I don't think there's much cause for complaint. Sebastian Coates is one that does fit in with the 'strategy', a young player with potential who was signed for a reasonable fee. If he goes on to become the player we hope he will, he could easily treble his value. If he doesn't pan out, he's young enough and highly rated enough that we'd get a fair few quid back on him. I'd expect to see more transfers of this nature moving forward, and less - and by less I mean 'none' - of the Carroll / Henderson type deals.

The one unqualified success is Suarez. We paid a lot for him but we'd probably double it if we sold him now. You're not going to strike gold on every deal like we did with Suarez, but Carroll, Downing and Henderson set us back over £70m when their true value is around half that. The likes of Chelsea, United and City can just write that off and move onto the next multi million pound deal (and regularly do), but we're not in that position. We have to be accountable for our spending, and presumably Comolli had to sell these deals to the owners to get them to sign off on them. Whatever he told them clearly doesn't look too good to them right now. FSG are big believers in the whole 'Moneyball' thing, that's why Comolli was appointed as he was supposedly a disciple of it. If he wasn't in with Beane there's no way FSG would have hired him, as what they knew about football you could write on a gnat's nutsack. Beane knew a little about it though, and he nudged them in Comolli's direction. FSG appointed him on the strength of that and an impressive CV that showed he had worked at both Spurs and Arsenal and overseen some impressive signings (although I daresay his CV is unlikely to list the bad ones or reveal how much of a part he played in the good ones!).

When they hired him they may have thought they were getting the football equivalent of Theo Epstein, the impressive young General Manager who helped the Boston Red Sox end their 86 year wait for a Championship and followed it up with another one three years later. Like Epstein, Comolli loves his stats, his spreadsheets and his databases and was heavily influenced by Beane's ideas (Epstein was also sacked by FSG, leaving behind a slew of expensive signings that 'the Sox' will struggle to get anything back on). The big difference - apart from stats not playing as big a part in football as baseball - was that a Director of Football is not as vital to a team's success as a GM is in baseball, and he wields nothing like the same kind of power. In English football, the manager is by far and away the most important man at the club and success or failure depends largely on how capable the manager is. In baseball, the team manager is given a squad of players and told to get on with it. He doesn't decide who comes or goes, and he answers directly to the GM. He doesn't have the kind of clout that a football manager in England has. I'm not sure FSG were fully appreciative of that cultural difference when they appointed Comolli, or whether are even now for that matter.

Had Comolli commanded that kind of power then perhaps we'd have seen things done a lot differently. That's never going to happen though, not in England and certainly not at Liverpool. The 'Director of Football' thing just isn't in our culture, it's basically a fancy title for a chief scout as the manager will choose which players he wants at the club. In fairness, Comolli never claimed it to be otherwise, he always maintained that he would bring a list of players to the manager who would then say who he liked and didn't like and they'd take it from there. I suspect that's not how FSG would like it done in an ideal world, everything I've heard from people who've had dealings with them suggests they want the same kind of structure in place here that works so well in American sports and also in some European leagues.

That means a Comolli type figure in charge, with a young coach reporting directly to him and working with whatever players he is given. That's their vision, but unfortunately for them Roy Hodgson screwed that up by not being able to see out the season. They wanted to just limp through until the end of the year and then dump Hodgson allowing Comolli to go and get a young, vibrant coach to come in and get us back on track. Didier Deschamps was a name that was often mentioned, and had Hodgson not made his position completely untenable then who knows how things would have played out?

Kenny getting the job on a temporary basis was always going to be risky from FSG's point of view, as if he did well it would cause them to have to scrap any plans on appointing a younger coach and having Comolli as the senior figure at the club. Kenny's status would make that impossible, if he was the manager he'd have the power. He's Kenny Dalglish after all. The upturn in results - and more crucially performances - at the back end of last season meant that FSG had no choice but to give him the job. It wasn't what they'd planned but they had to roll with the punches. Comolli's power was now seriously diluted. Even if he'd wanted to (and there's no suggestion that he did), he couldn't have gone out and signed whoever he liked, forcing players on Kenny that he didn't want. The second it got out that Comolli was buying the players and Kenny had no say, the fans would have gone mental.

It looks to me like he went too much the other way, not that I'd criticise him for that. He did everything he could to help the manager, a fact that Kenny has stated several times. I don't know if he's any good at spotting players or not, but by all accounts he is a nice fella, a charming, softly spoken guy who talks a good game. That's probably what got him the job here to begin with. That and the recommendation from Mr Beane.

In recent months FSG have been doing some fact finding and speaking to lots of people involved in football at different levels, gathering as much information as possible about various aspects of the game. Brian Barwick was brought in to review the TV channel amongst other things whilst they've also been talking to David Dein (who even attended a couple of our games recently) and that may have played a part in Comolli's downfall as the Frenchman worked for Dein at Arsenal. Whilst his sacking came as a shock to most of us, Comolli himself had suspected the writing was on the wall for a couple of weeks. He had travelled to the states to meet the owners at the start of April and reportedly told people on his return that he feared for his future at the club. When FSG came over in the week of the cup semi, Comolli was summoned to another meeting and was fired.

At that meeting in the US, Comolli had been asked by the owners to explain the disappointing league form and what he planned on doing to fix it next year. Whatever Comolli's solution was, it obviously didn't impress Henry and Werner. They were reportedly unhappy at reports that Kuyt has a £1m release clause in his contract. Understandably so. Why would you agree to a clause like that when he'd surely command a fee of at least £5m? The part Comolli played in the Suarez affair won't have done him any favours either, he was trying to help but in the end the cack-handed way he went about it only served to help the FA in their stitch up. His statement was one of the key pieces of evidence in the FA's judgement against Suarez. I have sympathy for him, he's basically a glorified scout, he's not equipped to deal with a situation like that and was caught cold by it. Others were more to blame than him in the Suarez case (it wasn't Comolli who hired Lionel fucking Hutz to defend Suarez), but it was another black mark against his name in the eyes of the owners.

I'm speculating here, but I suspect that FSG had been hearing some negative feedback from people they were speaking to and when they sat down with Comolli perhaps his responses confirmed the fears they had about him. It has to be seen as a shot across the bows for Kenny too as presumably when Comolli was asked about how he planned to make things better, the answers he gave will have been part of a plan that he and Kenny had put together. In addition to that, it's been reported that amongst the concerns FSG had was the lack of game time for Maxi and the plan to allow Kuyt to leave in the summer. If Maxi is on the bench and Kuyt is surplus to requirements, that's down to Kenny, no-one else. If Comolli were to over rule the manager on those kind of issues, then you really have a problem as the club cannot function properly. Comolli may have been the fall guy but it has also put Kenny right in the firing line now. Whatever plans he and Comolli had for the summer on how to get us back competing for a top four spot clearly didn't impress the owners. Comolli has gone, but then he was much easier to get shut of than Kenny would be, especially if the King ends the season with two trophies in the cabinet.

The fans aren't going to be bothered about Comolli being fired, but Kenny is a different kettle of fish. The owners know that and it's a problem for them, especially if they do plan on simply replacing Comolli with a like for like 'Director of Football'. If they do that, then who makes the calls on transfers? For me Kenny deserves to keep his job, that's not even a question. You don't sack a manager after his first season in which he's won one trophy and may well add another one to it. However, clearly whatever money is made available this summer has to be spent a lot more shrewdly than we've seen in the last 18 months (you can actually go back a lot longer than that but what happened before Dalglish is irrelevant to this current situation). A debate can be had as to whether some of the players that have been brought in are even good enough to be here, but there is no debate at all as to whether the owners got value for their money. They didn't. It doesn't even warrant a discussion as it's irrefutable.

I'm sure the owners have looked at Newcastle and wondered how we missed some of those players, and more specifically why we can't go out and find similar bargains as they are clearly out there. What Newcastle have done is actually a lot closer to the strategy I expected from FSG than what we have seen, and that's probably what they were referring to in that statement. Of course Newcastle have signed some duds too. Sylvain Marveux, remember him? You should do, he's a player that Comolli was pushing hard for us to sign and who even sat in the directors box at Anfield for one of our home games last season. Huge alarm bells were ringing about him as he had a history of injuries and it was a big relief when we didn't push the deal through. He went to Newcastle, and has predictably spent most of the season on the sidelines through injury. That Comolli would even have entertained the thought of bringing him in was worrying. Newcastle also signed Obertan from the Mancs. He's crap but he only cost them £2m, and if you like stats, here's one for you; Obertan has contributed one league goal, the same as Henderson and one more than Downing. Just saying like.

Nobody has a perfect record when it comes to transfers, but if we'd done as well last summer as Newcastle did then Comolli would still be in a job and there'd be no question marks over Kenny. We're not going to have the same kind of funds this summer that we had last time. As a rule of thumb, £20m plus sales each summer should be enough for us to be competitive and pushing for the top four. Because of how far we'd fallen, last summer was an exception in that we clearly needed a high number of players. Money was spent, but we are still short in certain areas because the money wasn't spent particularly well. Why would the owners make another £50m available this summer when there's little to suggest they'd get value for it? They obviously no longer trusted the judgement of Comolli and presumably Dalglish. With that in mind, should they trust Kenny to identify the players we buy, or will he have to defer to whoever comes in to replace Comolli? And if they do take that responsibility away from the manager and the players who come in are not up to scratch, would it be fair to blame Dalglish for that? And if not, then what, do they sack the Director of Football again? Mind you, they've got to find one first. And this time Billy Beane can keep his nose out.

chapter fourteen

May

LIVERPOOL 0 FULHAM 1

Competition - Premier League
Date - Tue 1 May 2012
Venue - Anfield
Scorer(s) –
Half Time - 0-1
Star Man – Alexander Doni

Team: Doni; Kelly, Skrtel, Coates, Aurelio (Enrique); Spearing, Henderson (Downing); Kuyt (Sterling), Shelvey, Maxi; Carroll:

Well that was a complete waste of time. Half the squad were sat in the stands and the rest of them looked like they wished they were too. It almost felt like the players who played in this game treated it like some kind of punishment, as much like the crowd they really looked like they'd rather be somewhere else.

This was bad, really bad in fact, but it wasn't particularly surprising. There's no point getting worked up over it, the decision to leave Gerrard, Suarez and Bellamy at home was the correct one as far as I'm concerned, but it didn't leave us with much to work with. The attacking burden fell on the shoulders of Carroll, Maxi, Kuyt and Shelvey. All have their attributes and all can look good when surrounded with better players. Essentially, they're the supporting cast, with Gerrard and Suarez (and to a lesser extent Bellamy) being the star turns. With none of the star turns involved, we were relying on the supporting cast to step up and they were simply incapable of doing it. None of them are 'difference makers' on their own. Throw in the fact that half the team appeared to be sulking because their selection suggests they won't be starting the cup final and it made for a wretched evening. It's not that there was no effort, but there was no passion and no belief. Most of this team are not going to be starting on Saturday but there was always the possibility that an outstanding performance from someone may have changed Kenny's mind. Not one of them gave the manager anything to think about and I imagine he knows exactly what his starting eleven at Wembley will be.

Fulham had never won at Anfield before, but it was obvious from early on that they'd never have a better opportunity. They included three former

Liverpool players in their starting line up, and two of them combined for the first goal. Riise's cross should have been turned in Alex Kacaniklic but he scuffed his shot and the ball hit Skrtel on the chest and went past the helpless Doni. Unlucky for Skrtel as he could do nothing about it, but Fulham were looking menacing every time they attacked. Probably because they did it with pace, something we could only dream of with the players we had on the field. Everything we did was slow and laboured, there was no incisiveness about anything, especially out wide where Maxi and Kuyt would always have to stop and go backwards because they didn't have the legs to run the full back. Pogrebnyak almost made it 2-0 when Fulham sliced through the middle of our backline with ease but Doni kept him out with a decent save. It wouldn't be the only time he needed to do that. Our midfield was terrible in the first half, Spearing wasn't at the races at all and was either giving the ball away or falling over. He improved a lot in the second half in fairness, whilst his partner Henderson was equally as bad before the break and was subbed at half time. I'd like to think he was hooked for his poor display, but let's be honest, he was being rested for Saturday wasn't he?

Carroll and Shelvey actually did alright in the first half. Carroll won most of his headers and did as much as could be expected, whilst Shelvey was the only one to really try and threaten Schwarzer's goal. He had one shot cleared off the line by Haageland and also flashed another shot across the face of goal after being sent clear by Carroll. He's the classic example of someone who can offer something to the side when he's with the better players, but it's asking a lot to expect him to lead the charge as he's just not at that level.

At half time I would have said Carroll was our best performer up to that point, but he was shite in the second half. He wasn't alone. Kuyt was abysmal throughout, really bad. I'd have subbed him at half time and put Raheem Sterling on, but instead Kenny replaced Henderson with Downing. Let's be honest, how many of this team actually wanted to be out there and how many would rather have been sat in the stands with the good players? At least the game would have meant something to Sterling, he wouldn't have seen it as being a chore. Whatsmore, the kid can do something than nobody else in that forward line could. He can run and he can take people on. He would have also woken the crowd up too, this was as bad an atmosphere as I can ever remember, but it's hardly surprising. Sterling excites people, and it pissed me off that we had to wait until 15 from minutes from time for him to get his chance. He did alright when he came on, he put in two brilliant crosses and won us a free-kick just outside the box. If he'd had longer who knows what he might have done. He certainly couldn't have contributed less than his more experienced team-mates.

We barely created anything second half, it was dire. Carroll had a couple of openings but didn't threaten the keeper and Maxi almost got through before he was denied by a last ditch challenge by Haageland. Fulham had the better chances and should have won by more than just the one goal really. Substitute Frey hit the post and Dempsey was twice denied by the excellent Doni, who was the only one to come out of this with any credit. There's really not much more to say about it. It was brutal, our league position is brutal, but Saturday is all that counts right now. If we win that game then the league woes can be swept under the carpet in the euphoria of two cup wins. This defeat to Fulham will be forgotten as the important thing was that we were allowed to rest our key players.

If we don't win at Wembley however, everything takes on a whole different slant and there's going to be plenty of flak flying around as not only are we likely to finish below the blues, but we're now level on points with Fulham and only three ahead of West Brom. Defeat on Saturday is simply not an option.

Premier League Round Up (28 April - 2 May 2012)

Newcastle travelled to Wigan on the back of six straight wins but got off to a nightmare start and just never recovered. Wigan are full of confidence at the moment and they blitzed the Geordies with a quickfire double from Moses to go 2-0 up inside a quarter of hour.

Maloney then made it 3-0 when he latched onto a brilliant ball by Di Santo (yes, I did just write that) and then... and I can't believe what I'm about to say... Di Santo made it 4-0 with a glorious chip from 25 yards. Fittingly he followed it up with one of the worst celebrations of the season. Centre forwards are not supposed to celebrate like idiots as scoring goals is meant to be fairly routine, it's what they do. At least it's what they're supposed to do. Di Santo was celebrating like a full back that scores maybe once or twice a season and sees goalscoring as kind of a novelty. Probably because it IS a novelty, but even so, you're a striker, son. Act like you've been there before. Pappis Cisse hit both post and bar and even on a day when he didn't score managed to look shit hot. His strike partner Demba Ba on the other hand just looked shit. It's worth mentioning too that he was wearing gloves. Gloves!! We're almost in May and he's wearing gloves! That's pretty pathetic, much like his goalscoring record since he got back from the African Nations.

Swansea took just 25 seconds to go in front against relegated Wolves when someone called Orlandi headed in. Never seen or heard of him before. Joe Allen made it 2-0 four minutes later with a shot that took a wicked deflection off Stearman and left the keeper totally wrongfooted. Motson described it thus: *"that might just have clipped Richard Stearman when Allen released the shot..."* Gee, d'ya think? He then sees the replay and adds *"yes, it just scrapes the boot of Richard Stearman"*. My God, I fucking hate him. *"Just scraped the boot"*? Allen was going across the keeper, Stearman tried to block the shot and diverted it to the other side of the goal. Come on BBC, we pay our licence fee for this shit? Sack him, you know it makes sense. You know, each week I tell myself I need to lay off Motson, because - and I'm honestly not trying to be a twat here - he's getting on a bit and he could keel over at any time. I'd feel bad if I ripped into him and then the next day something terrible happened as I'd look like a right snidey bastard. I know I'd probably regret some of the things I've written about him so each week I tell myself to ignore him, don't let him get to me. Then he goes and says something incredibly stupid like that and I just can't help myself.

Anyway, Dyer added a third with just 15 minutes gone after good play by Orlandi again but Fletcher pulled one back with an absolutely brilliant header. Hell of a goal that, he shouldn't be playing in the Championship next season as he's a good player. Danny Graham restored Swansea's three goal cushion with his 13th goal of the season and poor old Terry Connor must have been wanting the ground to open up and swallow him until Jarvis gave them a lifeline with a goal before the break. Wolves completed a remarkable comeback as Edwards ran through the centre to make it 4-3 and Jarvis then equalised with his second of the game. Credit to Wolves for not just rolling over, but Swansea really blew it. If they defend like this next weekend at Old Trafford they might let in ten, which would put a big dent in City's advantage in terms of goal difference. Get your shit together Swansea. That Sigurdsson is boss though, the more I see of him the more I like him.

Bolton travelled up to the North East to face out of form Sunderland. Kevin Davies was back in the side and he bagged the game's opening goal when he coolly volleyed in at the back post from Petrov's cross. Bendtner equalised with Sunderland's first goal since September. That may be a slight exaggeration, it may actually be October. James McLean took advantage of some shithousery in the Bolton wall to blast a free-kick through them and into the net. He's ditched the pink boots now and looks much better for it. Presumably he saw how much of a goon Bendtner looks in his and came to his senses. Bolton were obviously desperate for a goal as every point could prove crucial. Captain fantastic Kevin Davies came up with the goods when he headed in a cross from Ricketts to keep their survival hopes intact. You'd think Sunderland would know what to expect from Davies, after all O'Neill tried to sign him back in January, so it's not like it's a secret. I mean Kevin Davies isn't a 'Secret Footballer' or anything. Oh wait…

Swiftly moving on before I get into trouble, Everton trounced Fulham at the Pit. Jelavic set them on their way with a pen after Pogrebnyak had handled the ball in an attempt to protect his face, the big baby. Ivan Drago he ain't. It appears his belly is as yellow as the boots he was wearing. He's paid tens of thousands of pounds a week, the least he can do is take a ball to the face to help his team out. Disgusting stuff that. Fellaini headed the blues into a 2-0 lead but Damien Duff's piss poor attempt to clear on the goal-line was almost as risible as Pogrebnyak's earlier cowardice. An offside Jelavic made it 3-0 as once again there was a hideous attempt at a goal-line clearance from a Fulham defender, and Cahill wrapped it up with a good finish from a Pienaar chip.

Crouchy (the big leg) gave Stoke an early lead against Arsenal at the Brittannia with a cracking header only for Van Persie to equalise with a simple finish after a brilliant ball by Rosicky. Stoke were once again the beneficiaries of some helpful refereeing. Shawcross used both hands to block a shot from Vermailen as he stood on the edge of the box. Possibly a penalty but a free-kick at the very least, yet strangely nothing was given. Then Yossi was bundled over from behind as he ran into the box, but once again the ref ignored it. It's fortunate for the rest of the league that Stoke are shite, because given the amount of decisions that go in their favour if they were even half decent they'd be top four every season. Even right at the end Whitehead was running the ball out of defence and just flopped on it under no contact from anybody. The ref gave him a free-kick and it was all too much for Wenger to take who flipped his lid and was throwing his arms around like one of those inflatable arm waving men they have at car show rooms. My good friend google tells me the official name for those things is "whacky waving inflatable arm flailing tube man". Bit of a mouthful that, should just call them 'Wengers' for short. All the Stoke fans behind the bench then mimicked him and seemed very pleased with themselves. *"Oh look at us, aren't we dead funny"*. About as funny as piles. Stoke home games are like the Jeremy Kyle show on steroids, the fucking mutants. They booed Aaron Ramsay throughout the game. His crime? Having his leg broken a couple of years ago by a typically 'robust' challenge by Shawcross. As I said, mutants.

Struggling Villa made the trip across the Midlands to face Hodgson's Baggies. It was 0-0 but it wasn't without incident. Villa should have had a pen when Brunt handled, but then somehow both referee and linesman failed to spot a clear deliberate handball by Hutton to deflect a goal-bound header from Mulumbu onto the bar. Shocking stuff that. They also missed one by Olsson who blocked Herd's shot with his arm. Not a good day for Clattenberg & co, but not untypical either as he's amongst the worst of an awful bunch. Villa's best chance of survival is hoping the teams below them don't win as they're not going to be putting many points on the board themselves. Looking at the fixtures that QPR, Bolton and Blackburn have left, Villa should probably be ok to carry on being insignificant for at least another year.

Onto Sunday, and QPR made the short trip to Stamford Bridge to face neighbours Chelsea. Once again John Terry was spared the potential flashpoint that the pre-match handshakes could bring. I don't disagree with that, I do wonder how come Suarez and Evra weren't afforded the same consideration. Still, at least the Premier League didn't ask us to form a guard of honour for United players like they asked QPR to do for Chelsea. Unbelievable that, I'm not sure who's worse, the Premier League or the FA. Actually that's not true, the Premier League are idiots, but at least they are honest idiots. Chelsea fans booed Anton Ferdinand throughout and once again I'm left wondering exactly what it is he's meant to have done? Anyone?

Sturridge gave Chelsea the lead with a great strike after just 47 seconds. Mongo ("Who else" you may cry given his midweek misdemeanour at the Nou Camp) headed in a second when he climbed all over Clint Hill and got his giant fod on the end of a Lampard corner. His mock humble, apologetic celebration isn't fooling anyone, the selfish prick. Well, it probably fooled Chelsea fans but that's not difficult. QPR's heads went after that and they capitulated. Torres ended up with a hat-trick as Chelsea fans chanted *'he scores when he wants'*. Fucking divs. There's a lot I could say about that right now but I'm not going to tempt fate ahead of the Cup Final. Malouda added a sixth before Djibs bagged a late consolation. Never nice seeing Chelsea win, but the pain is eased when it's Mark Hughes getting his arse handed to him in the opposing dug out.

It looks like a straight fight between QPR and Bolton to avoid that third relegation spot after Blackburn's meek and embarrassing surrender at Spurs. It was only 2-0 but it was one of the most one sided games of the season, in fact it may have been one of the most one sided top flight games ever. Rovers didn't manage a single shot either on or off target, which takes some doing. They did somehow win one corner though, so fair play to them for that. Van Der Vaart scored the first and Kyle Walker's brilliant free-kick sealed the victory for Spurs who badly needed these points. Rovers look like their goose is cooked now. Even if they win both their remaining games it may not be enough to save them. Ever the optimist, Steve Kean said they need to beat Wigan and then *'charge on'* to beat Chelsea on the last day. I'd love to see it, but I'm beginning to worry that my faith in Kean may have been a tad misplaced.

Onto Monday and 'the biggest game in Premier League history'. * throws up in mouth * With it being a big game at an away ground, Ferguson reverted to type and dragged Park Ji Sung out of cold storage for the occasion. You can set your watch by it, Park only ever gets wheeled out when they're playing someone decent, you won't see him for months and then United have a big game and there he is. I'd actually forgotten he still played for them. I forgot he was playing in this game too after about ten minutes as he was completely invisible until he got hooked in the second half. Ferguson's team selection was laughable, had any other Premier League boss done that they'd have been caned for it. Their starting midfield had a combined age of 604 or something. Giggs starting ahead of Valencia? Haha. Mancini was probably delighted with that, I wish they'd left Valencia on the bench when we played them, he's fucking boss. United went there for a point and hoping maybe they could nick something on the break. I've said it all season but City are a far superior side than United. Unfortunately for them they've struggled to win games when they've not been at their best, that's not a problem that affects United who've not played well large chunks of the season. Ferguson knows they aren't as good as City though which is why he went into shithouse mode for this one. They didn't manage a single shot on target even after they got desperate and sent on the attacking players that would have started the game if Ferguson hadn't shit his pants. Kompany was outstanding, and his performance was even more impressive considering he picked up an early booking for a nothing challenge on Rooney who typically made a five course banquet out of it. Someone's got to fill the void left by Ashley Young I suppose. Rooney's just a little rat. He's everything that Kompany isn't. The City captain is a great player but seems like a really classy guy too. Him and Joe Hart are a credit to their club and United have no-one to compare to those two. Their so-called great leaders are vermin, the likes of Ferdinand, Giggs and Rooney. Pond life. Scholes is the closest thing they've got to anyone that possesses any semblance of class, but then he threw a punch at Xabi Alonso which is like glassing Mother Theresa, so fuck him too, fanta pants.

The game itself wasn't great, United's negativity saw to that. Kompany's goal came at a great time though. Once again you have to look at how easily De Gea got boxed out from a corner and wasn't in the right position. Things got heated in the second half and the two managers had to be separated by the fourth official after Ferguson lost the plot when De Jong fouled Wellbeck. For him to accuse anyone of harrassing officials almost defies belief. But then you realise that it's Ferguson, this is what he does and nothing is surprising anymore when it comes from this rancid, hateful old ballbag. In a week where an Italian coach made the headlines for diving on one of his own players who'd shot his mouth off after being subbed, I can't help but think City appointed the wrong Italian. Fiorentina's Delio Rossi would have broken Ferguson's neck for that kind of disrespect. With any luck his next job will be in England and he'll prove me right. Unfortunately Mancini isn't made up that way. He reminds me of that old joke about Italian World War II tanks. He's got five gears, one forward and four reverse. The longer the game went, the more he went into reverse. He replaced Tevez with De Jong, he didn't smack Ferguson despite extreme provocation and then he sent Richards on for Silva. City held on fairly comfortably so Mancini will argue he got it spot on. He's such a negative bastard though, he couldn't wait to get all his defensive subs on and if United had managed to get an equaliser the blame would have been squarely on his shoulders. I don't like him, I don't rate him, but it will be ace if he ends the season as the manager of the champions, because that means United end up empty handed.

The pressure seems to have been getting to United lately. It's not something you expect but they've definitely been getting twitchy in the last few weeks. I'd say that Ferguson's decision making and touchline behaviour suggest he's losing the plot, but that can't be true as he's the 'master of the mind games' isn't he? Rooney is another, he's been there and done it but you'd never have guessed looking at this. He was shite and ended up completely losing it with his team mates at the end. The ref was also getting both barrels from him all night. Much is being made of him not having any bookings in the league this season, but that's not quite as impressive a stat when you see him shouting *"Ref? Ref? You fucking twat!"* and getting away with it. That shit don't fly in European football, it's only Premier League refs who don't have the stones to deal with him.

As a footnote, there were 5 mins stoppage time at the end of this. I don't remember any significant stoppages and don't recall the physio being on. Yet they get 5 minutes? Why? I believe refs are supposed to add 30 seconds for every substitution but they very rarely do. There were six changes so even allowing for that it's only three minutes. It's immaterial as United didn't score, but what if they had done? It wouldn't be the first time and it won't be the last. It needs addressing. The next night we played Fulham and they had the physio on twice for lengthy stoppages. There were also five substitutions. How many minutes stoppage time? Four, that's how many. Not that it mattered, we could have played forty and we wouldn't have scored. I just don't like that the rest of the league has to play to a different set of rules to Ferguson.

Whilst we were stinking it up against Fulham, Everton were picking up a difficult point at Stoke. An own goal from Crouchy (the big dope) gave them the lead but substitute Cameron Jerome equalised. Shame they both couldn't lose really.

Onto Wednesday, and Bolton are still in trouble after losing 4-1 at home to Spurs. Fabrice Muamba attended the game and was in tears at the reception he got. Bollocks to him, he burnt his bridges with me when he sold his story to the S*n despite them running that photograph of him when there was every chance he might not have pulled through. I'm glad he's ok and all, but he's a tool. A cracker from Modric put Spurs in front, Reo-Coker equalised but three goals in nine second half minutes from Van Der Vaart and Adebayor (2) gave Spurs the win and kept them in fourth place. Funny how they've started winning again since it emerged 'Arry would be staying after all.

Newcastle bounced back in style from their weekend whooping at Bolton, going to Stamford Bridge and winning 2-0 thanks to two wonder goals by Papiss Cisse. The first goal was brilliant, the second goal just incredible. The Chelsea defenders just turned away after he'd hit it thinking it was going miles wide, the next thing it was flying into the net past a flailing Cech. An amazing strike, and a rival for Crouch and Suarez for goal of the season.

LIVERPOOL 1 CHELSEA 2

Competition - FA Cup Final
Date - Sat 5 May 2012
Venue - Wembley Stadium
Scorer(s) – Andy Carroll
Half Time - 0-1
Star Man – Andy Carroll

Team: Reina; Johnson, Skrtel, Agger, Enrique; Bellamy (Kuyt), Henderson, Gerrard, Spearing (Carroll), Downing; Suarez:

If 1996 is remembered as 'the white suits final', for an hour this one was shaping up to be the 'white flag final'. Andy Carroll's arrival changed that and sparked a spirited fightback that saw us go within an ant's pube of finding an equaliser.

Whether or not Carroll's header was over the line or not doesn't matter now, it wasn't given and not even countless replays from various angles have provided conclusive proof to say that it should have been. No, I'm far more concerned about the complete no-show we witnessed until Carroll arrived and put the team on his back in a valiant effort that just fell short.

It's just so disappointing to lose like this, and even more disappointing that it was to them of all teams. Them winning hurts almost as much as us losing. Chelsea didn't have to work for their victory, we virtually handed it to them. That's difficult to take regardless of the opposition, but it's worse when it's those lowlifes. I don't think they were better than us on the day, but they didn't contribute to their own downfall the way we did and tactically they'll feel they got it spot on until Carroll's arrival changed the landscape with half an hour to go. After that they dug in, rode their luck a bit and saw it through.

Unfortunately our worst fears became reality as the Premier League version of Liverpool turned up when we needed the cup version. By the time the cup side showed up we were 2-0 down against a well drilled team that had managed to keep Barcelona out with ten men for the entire second half in the Nou Camp a couple of weeks ago. They had eleven men this time, and we're no Barcelona. Chelsea went into 'park the bus' mode again and although we put them under a lot of pressure they just about withstood it and we were left to reflect on what might have been. It's difficult to pinpoint exactly what went wrong in that first hour or so. Obviously with the benefit of hindsight Carroll should have started, but that alone doesn't explain just how awful we were. It was shocking stuff, there was nothing there at all. It was 1996 all over again, two teams more concerned about cancelling out the other and not really showing any ambition of their own. Chelsea weren't any great shakes, but then they had the gift of an early goal to protect and the onus wasn't on them to force the issue. This was an FA Cup Final, our biggest game of the season and the last chance to salvage something from what now has to be seen as an appalling campaign. How could we produce such a lifeless, insipid display? Clearly it's not an issue with effort, nobody is going to give less than 100% in such a showpiece game, so it has to be mentality. Too many players looked overawed by the occasion, which in turn affected those who wouldn't have been overawed, specifically Gerrard and Suarez. Luis was ridiculously isolated in the first half and found himself surrounded by two or three Chelsea defenders on the rare occasions we managed to get the ball to him. As for Gerrard, initially I couldn't work out why he was playing so deep. I'd assumed the reason Carroll didn't start was because we wanted Gerrard as close to Suarez as possible whilst still giving us an extra midfielder to match Chelsea's three when we didn't have the ball. He ended up miles away from Suarez though, probably due to him having to babysit Henderson and Spearing who were both having 'mares.

We couldn't get our big players into the game because the rest of the side froze and because tactically we didn't get it right. The opening goal was a culmination of three mistakes, each worse than the one before. Spearing lost the ball in the Chelsea half and it was played swiftly to the strong running Ramires on the right. It looked like Enrique should have dealt with it but he got his angles all wrong, Ramires was too quick for him and ran clear. Despite those errors, the goal should still have been prevented. I've written before about how great goalkeepers make saves that help out team-mates who have made mistakes. Pepe used to do that, as he used to be a great goalkeeper. Overall this season he hasn't even been a good one and you could probably argue he hasn't even been an average one. His slump is alarming and his attempt at keeping out Ramires' shot was borderline negligible. It was poor on so many levels. Firstly, positioning. Why didn't he come off his line to make it more difficult? You just don't stand on your goal-line when someone is bearing down on you, it was incredible to see that from such an experienced keeper. Maybe the chip Ramires scored against Barca was on Reina's mind, but I'd rather he was challenged to try and do that again than for Pepe to just stand on his line and let him score at the near post. Secondly, look at his balance. Keepers are supposed to be on their toes, ready to spring into action to make a save. He's flat footed and almost falling over, having once again started to shift his weight to one side only for the ball to go the other way. How many times is that now? Too many. Thirdly, what's with the weak hand? Even after the errors in positioning and balance, he STILL should have kept out what was a pretty crap effort from Ramirez. You got your hand to it, so fucking keep it out. There's just no excuse for it, he didn't even look like a goalkeeper, you could have grabbed anyone out of the crowd to do what he did and seeing him then bollock Enrique didn't sit well with me at all. Save the fucking shot and then shout at whoever you like, I don't care. You embarrass yourself as badly as that then you've got some front trying to put it on someone else.

Reina was all over the papers on the morning of the game admitting his form hasn't been good this season. I'm happy that he's accepting of that and isn't shying away from it, but I'd be even happier if he hadn't given a demonstration of it on such a big stage. Most of his problems seem to be down to a complete breakdown in technique, which makes me wonder just what the fuck our goalkeeping coach is doing to him. It's not that he's making poor decisions, handling errors or flapping at crosses, the kind of 'normal' mistakes that will affect even the best keepers occasionally. He's just not making many saves and he's letting shots in that shouldn't be going in, and it's mostly down to poor technique in my opinion.

When you break it all down to it's bare bones, essentially the most significant difference between us and Chelsea on the day was the two goalkeepers. Reina couldn't keep out a simple effort from Ramires whilst Cech made that miraculous stop in the second half to prevent Carroll making it 2-2. For all the discussion about Kenny's tactics and team selection, or the merits of Spearing, Henderson, Downing etc - and those discussions are certainly valid - if you swap the two keepers then we win the game. That's simplifying things a great deal I know, and you could just as easily say if we'd turned up for the first hour then we'd have won the game, or maybe if Carroll had started we'd have won the game. It's all 'if' 'if' 'if' though. The facts are we didn't turn up for the first hour, we didn't start with Andy Carroll and we have Pepe Reina and not Petr Cech. We also have FA Cup losers medals, and all of those facts are not unrelated.

Downing was pathetic in the first half, not because he was doing a lot wrong but because he was just cowardly once again. He's an international player in the prime of his career. He's got plenty of ability but he's got no balls. If the team is playing well he's fine, if we're struggling he just doesn't bring anything to the table. This reminded me of his non-performance at Old Trafford. Top players take it on themselves to make things happen, they take responsibility. It's about having a winners mentality and sadly Downing just hasn't got that. It's not a question of ability, he's got that although a lot of people may disagree. When things are going well you can see his talent, he's got good control, pace, sound technique and a sweet left foot. His right foot isn't bad either, I've seen him put plenty of good crosses in with his right foot. Unfortunately talent isn't everything, you need that mental strength and I just don't think he has it. Instead of taking the initiative, he becomes passive and looks for other people to do it. I've got no doubt that he's got the talent to be playing for Liverpool, I have huge doubts about whether he has the mentality. It was depressing watching him and Enrique in that first half. They were like the chuckle brothers, neither taking any responsibility. 'To me to you, to me to you' and then one of them would lose it. I blame Downing more as he's supposed to be the one to make things happen, not just pass the buck and hope someone else does it instead.

The right flank was not much better, despite the best efforts of Glen Johnson. Bellamy started out there but didn't get in the game and was often so far infield that Johnson had no option ahead of him when he had the ball.

This was Bellamy's worst outing of the season and couldn't have come at a worse time. Johnson was one of only three players for me who performed before the break (Agger and Skrtel being the other two), but he had very little support from Bellamy and then Henderson when he was switched over there. The one chance we had in the first half came from a great run by Johnson, his cross was half cleared and Bellamy's shot was blocked by Ivanovic (Cech seemed to have it covered anyway).

Whilst hindsight suggests Carroll should have started, I can't be too critical of that because I wouldn't have picked him either. Don't get me wrong, I want to see him and Suarez paired together as much as possible - and against most sides I'd have no hesitation in doing it - but Chelsea pack the midfield and going in with just Gerrard and Spearing/Henderson didn't look like a good plan to me. I think a lot of people felt that way, and the team Kenny picked is exactly the one I expected him to, especially based on who was rested for the Fulham game. Like most people, I had no issue with it but I'd say it was obvious to everyone (except Kenny) that it needed changing at half time. That was the main topic of conversation as a few of us met up for a half time chat. It couldn't continue, Carroll was going to be brought on at some point so why wait? Just do it now.

We'd been so bad in that first half that any number of players could have been brought off. The likes of Maxi and Shelvey couldn't have been worse then Henderson, Spearing or Downing, Bellamy could have had no complaints if he'd made way for Kuyt and you could even have made a case for getting Carragher on for Enrique and moving Agger to left back as Enrique's performance in the first half was piss poor. Hell, I wouldn't have even objected to Doni coming on for Reina! But for all of the poor individual performances the most glaring thing that needed addressing was getting some support for Suarez. If we did that it would hopefully make everybody else better as a result. Whilst I wouldn't make excuses for how poor the players were in the first half, the formation wasn't helping as the ball wasn't sticking up front. Leaving Carroll out was supposed to make us stronger in midfield and allow Gerrard to play higher up the pitch as he'd done to great effect last week at Norwich. It just never happened, we were weak in midfield and we didn't support Suarez. May as well get Carroll on, we'd be a man down in midfield but at least we'd give them something to worry about and maybe get our best player a bit of support. It obviously wasn't going to get any better with the same players on the field and even though Kenny usually waits ten or fifteen minutes into the second half to change it, this wasn't a time to be doing that. Our season was on the line and it was no time for caution. We needed action now, there was just no point in waiting and I was seriously pissed off when I took my seat for the second half and saw that no changes had been made. And guess what, we began the second half exactly how we'd ended the first. Who'd have thought eh? If the change had been made when it should have then who knows, but it wasn't and it didn't take long for us to go 2-0 down.

Lampard got away from Spearing far too easily and found Drogba in the box. There didn't appear to be any huge danger as Skrtel was in close attendance, but Drogba got his shot away and it went through the legs of Skrtel and trickled into the far corner. Two shots on target, two goals. Typical. (for the record, I'm not pointing the finger at Reina for this one). The game was really threatening to get away from us at that point. We were disjointed, timid, basically just shite all over the park. With the game almost lost, we belatedly saw the introduction of Carroll. He would eventually change the momentum of the game completely, but before he did Chelsea were threatening to put themselves out of sight. Gaps were appearing all over the place every time we lost the ball and they had several good opportunities to hit us on the break. They didn't make the most of them and then almost out of nothing we were back in the game. An attack down our left hand side looked to have broken down, but Downing made a great challenge on Unibrow Bosingwa as he attempted to clear, and the loose ball found it's way to Carroll. Initially it looked like he'd delayed his shot too long as he turned 'Mongo' inside out, but credit to Carroll he was in full control of what he was doing and it was a brilliant finish. The more I watch it the better it gets, that was footwork that Peter Crouch would be proud of. Game on now.

Chelsea went into a defensive shell and our tails were suddenly up. Carroll was on fire, he was winning everything and bullying Terry and Ivanovic. He had them rattled and now that he had someone up there to share the load Suarez suddenly came into it. The rest of the game was one way traffic, players who had been struggling badly now wanted the ball and looked confident. The transformation in Downing and Enrique from first half to second highlights this as well as anything. They not only looked like footballers in the second half, they actually looked like they had some semblance of an understanding too. Like I say, Downing can be effective when the team is playing well and I thought he had a good second half. The part he played in the goal probably boosted his spirits too. From the moment Carroll's shot hit the net, the whole team suddenly looked more confident and got the bit between their teeth. Suarez was menacing, the full backs were bombing forward, the widemen were linking up with them and the midfielders were backing up the play and dominating possession. And when Chelsea did manage to get the ball out to Drogba, usually Skrtel or Agger dealt with it and got us moving again.

The last half hour of the game was tremendous, we couldn't ask for much more than that and we were unlucky not to take the game into extra time. Had we done so I'm convinced we'd have won as Chelsea didn't seem to have much left in that second half. The Cech 'save' from Carroll's header is what decided the game. If a goal is given, I'm sure we would have gone on to win the game, possibly even in normal time. You could say a linesman's call has decided the game, but you can't say whether he got it right or wrong. Having studied the replays I'd say the ball did just about cross the line, but there's no way the linesman could be sure either way. How could he be, even I'm not sure either way and that's after the benefit of a load of replays. Of course it would have been nice if he'd just given us the benefit of the doubt, but he can't give it unless he's sure and how can you be sure when something happens so fast and is so close? Chelsea got lucky with a goal-line decision at a critical point in the semi final against Spurs, and they got lucky again here. I don't blame Carroll, it was a good attempt and 99 times out of 100 it's a goal. You have to give Cech great credit for the stop, he's not the keeper he was back in 2005 but he rolled back the years with that save, it was a fantastic effort regardless of whether it had crossed the line or not. We had other chances, but none as clear cut as that and Chelsea held firm, meaning Torres got to collect another medal he'd done fuck all to earn. Well done Fernando, you've become the new Josemi.

The way we ended the game does not make up for what went before I'm afraid, especially given the diabolical league results this season. After effectively just writing off the Fulham game a few days earlier it's unacceptable to see us shit the bed like this. It's easy to forgive the Fulham defeat (not to mention all of those that went before it) if we go on to win the cup. Not so easy when we play the way we did for an hour.

Carroll was superb, Agger and Skrtel were both very good, Johnson and Suarez (once he got some help up there) were ok and everyone else should be looking at themselves today thinking they didn't do enough. After the season we've had in the league, they owed it to the fans to put on a performance and they failed to deliver. The fans were a credit to the club as usual, they deserved a better performance than this but at the same time you can't win them all and over the years we've been very fortunate to witness some great victories in finals.

Much is being made of us booing the national anthem. Not sure why, this happens at every cup final we're in so I don't know why suddenly people are surprised. Admittedly there was more booing this time than usual, but we always sing YNWA over God Save the Queen and have done since 1989. The booing will have been intensified because it was Chelsea and they love that whole patriotic shite. That's their anthem, not mine. There's also an element of sticking it to the FA and the 'establishment'. The rest of the country don't seem to understand, but a lot of Liverpool fans don't see themselves as English and that anthem simply means nothing to many of us. I can see why some aren't happy about the booing, perhaps it would have been better to not boo and just sing YNWA over it. I understand that viewpoint but I can't say I'm particularly bothered. The idea of sitting there and joining with Chelsea fans singing anything is pie in the sky. Let them have 'God Save the Queen', their shitty plastic fans, that loser Suggs, toad faced slimeball David Mellor, unfunny cunt David Baddiel, their degenerate captain and that fucking birdie song shite they come out to.

When it's all said and done, I'd much rather lose as a Liverpool fan than win supporting Chelsea.

Premier League Round Up (5-7 May 2012)

Only one Premier League game on Saturday due to a cup final that shan't be mentioned again. Hell of a game it was too, as Norwich went to the Emirates and came away with a highly creditable 3-3 draw.

Yossi started the ball rolling for the Gunners with a great goal after 70 seconds. Hoolahan equalised when Szczesny went all 'Pepe Reina' and fumbled the ball in at his near post. Grant Holt's deflected shot then looped over the Gunners keeper to give Norwich the lead and it got worse for Arsenal when Sagna bizarrely broke his leg whilst trying to control the ball. Turns out he'd been stepped on seconds earlier by Bradley Johnson and that had done the damage. When he got to his feet and stretched for the ball his leg just cracked and now he'll miss the Euro's. It's the second time this season he's broken that leg, which is obviously really unfortunate for the lad. He has since been quoted in the French press claiming Johnson did it deliberately, which is all just a bit 'Arsenalish' really isn't it? Jackson and Hoolahan both wasted great chances to make it 3-1 and Norwich also should have a had a pen when Koscielny grappled Martin to the floor at a set piece. Not something you usually see from Arsenal, but they played Stoke last week and you know what they say, if you lay down with dogs you get fleas.

Van Persie equalised with his 29th league goal of the season. It came via Song lifting a ball over the defence into his path for the umpteenth time this season. 'Umpteenth' is actually a great word, I'm gonna use it more often. Goal number 30 of the season soon followed as Arsenal regained the lead with 10 minutes left, but their leaky defence would cost them once more as Morrison went through to finish very nicely to level things up again. There was major controversy right at the end Van Persie when looked certain to complete his hat-trick from close range but was shoved in the back by the full back. As clear a pen as you'll see but it wasn't given. Wenger wasn't happy, saying: *"Here the whole season we have got zero penalties. It is absolutely amazing, because you see other clubs who have got 10."* They actually have three, not zero, but presumably Arsene 'didn't see them'.

That surprise slip up from the Gunners gave Newcastle even more incentive ahead of their game with Man City, as a win over the title challengers would have put them 3rd in the table. Before the game they unveiled a statue of Bobby Robson. How come these statues rarely look like the actual people? This one is particularly bad, which is a shame as everyone loves Bobby Robson. City were good value for the win even though they left it later than most of us would have liked. The spine of that team is just so good. Joe Hart went long periods just watching but any time he had to make a save he was there. Kompany was immense again and kept Cisse fairly quiet even though he still had his moments. And

Yaya Toure is just a fucking beast. A vastly overpaid one, but a beast nonetheless. He scored a cracker to put them 1-0 up, and then fell over when clear through after going around Krul. Poor Andy Carroll got slaughtered for 'diving' when that happened to him the other week. Newcastle pressed to try and get an equaliser but City looked so threatening on the break and it wasn't a surprise when they wrapped it up late on when a brilliant counter attack ended with Toure finishing in some style again. The title is almost theirs now, but wouldn't it just be so Manchester City of them to somehow blow it next week against the manager they sacked?

Despite losing to City, the Geordies could still finish third if results go their way next week. That says as much about the failings of the rest of us as it does of how well they've done. Even so, and as much as I hate admitting this, Pardew should probably be manager of the year. Who knows, maybe one day he'll have his own statue outside St James like 'Wor Bobby'. At least they won't need to commission whoever it was that fucked up the Robson statue to do it, as I'm sure 'Pards' will just let them have a replica of the one he has in his hallway at home. Alright, I don't actually know for sure that Pardew has a statue of himself at home, but if I had to choose somebody that would have one he'd be pretty damn high on the list, probably nestled in between Jose Mourinho and Glenn Hoddle, the smug fuck.

City's win in the North East meant that United really needed to run up a cricket score at home to Swansea. Had they done that they would still have been in with a chance of the title even if City beat QPR next week. Given that it was not a game for cowardly tactics, Ferguson put Park Ji Sung back into stasis and also left old man Giggs out. Swansea gave as good as they got until they conceded to a Scholes flick. They wobbled a bit for a while and when they let another in before half time it was threatening to get a bit edgy. The Swans let in four to hapless Wolves last week, but one thing in their favour is it's difficult to score against them when you don't have the ball and they keep it as well as any team in the league. It ended 2-0 and if City win by one goal next week then United need to beat Sunderland by nine. With Wes Brown, Phil Bardsley, Kieran Richardson and John O'Shea possibly making up their back four I'm taking nothing for granted.

From the top end of the table to the bottom now, and Bolton had a very winnable game at home to West Brom. What effect would the Hodgson thing have on the Baggies, who had nothing to play for anyway? Not much as it turns out, they were the better side in the first half but went a goal down to a Petrov penalty and despite having chances to draw level they ended up conceding another after a freakish own goal. The scoreline didn't reflect the play, but Bolton looked on their way to a huge three points until with 15 minutes left Brunt pulled a goal back and then it was panic stations for the home side. West Brom threw everything at them late on and in stoppage time Morrison equalised. Devastating for Bolton but if they can win their final game at Stoke they should be ok as QPR would need to win at City .

With that in mind, QPR went into their game with Stoke knowing that they really needed to win or it was probably all over for them. Stoke named four strikers in their side. Well, three plus Jon Walters, who is more bricklayer than footballer. One of them, Cameron Jerome, missed a glorious chance early on and after that it was mostly the home side on the offensive. QPR certainly had the better of it but Joey Barton failed to score from about 38 efforts on goal. Maybe think about passing once in a while, Joey? Just a thought. Just when it looked like time had run out for them, up popped substitute Djibril Cisse to score in the last minute. Crouch went close to an equaliser but QPR held on and given what happened at Bolton this was a huge result for them, but it still doesn't really change much as if Bolton win next week QPR must cause a huge upset at City. Stranger things have happened, I mean Franco Di Santo scored last week so anything is possible.

Moving on, and Spurs travelled to Villa knowing that a victory would put them right back in the hunt for 3rd place. Given the horrifying possibility of Chelsea winning the Champions League, getting 3rd has suddenly become huge for Tottenham, Arsenal and Newcastle. Redknapp's side have been limping towards the finish line for months but they've managed to win a few games of late and Villa is a team everybody should be beating right now. The Londoners fell behind when Ciaran Clark's shot was deflected past Friedel, who in truth didn't seem to make much of an effort to keep it out. It got worse for Spurs when Danny Rose was sent off for a bad challenge on Hutton. Definite red card but if ever a player deserved to be on the end of a challenge like that it's Hutton. Actually it's John Terry. Or maybe Didier Drogba. Or Lee Cattermole. Hutton makes the list though, for sure. Spurs got back into the game when they were awarded a pen after Dunne recklessly brought down Sandro. Adebayor made no mistake from the spot and although Tottenham pressed for a winner they had to settle for a point. Villa are safe now, so let me say a big sarcastic *"well done"* to 'Big Eck', the only manager in the league that might be more unpopular with his own support than Steve Kean.

Clint Dempsey scored again. A brilliant 25 yard free-kick to put Fulham 1-0 up at home to Sunderland. Bardsley leathered one in from 25 yards to bring the Mackems level but straight from the kick off Dembele put Fulham ahead again with the help of a deflection. Dempsey also had a good effort headed off the line by Colback and Campbell missed a sitter after a good knock down by Bendtner. Can I just point out again that Fraiser Campbell was capped by England this season. Whatever people think of Hodgson he will really have to go some to beat that one.

Everton went to relegated Wolves looking to extend their lead over us to six points. Jelavic had a goal wrongly ruled out for offside and put another effort wide when well placed. Good player but I hate his face and his hair and I'm sure I've seen him somewhere before. Did he used to play Zelda in the Terrahawks? Hilariously, Terry Connor once again looked close to tears as he faced the TV cameras. He claimed there have been some *"positive changes"* and *"good signs from the lads"*. He was in charge for 12 games and they won none of them!! Yet he sees positive changes and good signs?? Can't help thinking of 'Comical Ali' and his *"Tanks? What tanks?"* routine as the US army rolled into town behind him. Pretty disgusting that Wolves put him into this situation, they've made a decent fella look like a complete fool.

Finally onto Monday night. Blackburn are down after losing at home to Wigan who are now safe despite looking dead and buried not so long ago. Alcaraz got the only goal of the game, so I guess you could say there was no 'escape from Alcaraz' for Steve Kean. *tumbleweed* Oh come on, that's pretty damn good that is. Tough crowd.

Rovers were so desperate they resorted to sending on a chicken to play on left wing. That's not gonna work, just ask Kenny, he's been doing that for most of the season. Either that or someone misunderstood the meaning of the 'Feed the Yak' chant. You gotta love that he was first on the scene to grab the chicken. Al Habsy tried to help but quickly backed off when he saw the menacing look in the Yak's eyes. None of the Rovers players wanted any part of it, they've seen at close quarters what happens if you get between Yakubu and his food. The only thing that could have made the scene any funnier was if he'd been carrying a knife and fork and wearing a napkin, Wile E. Coyote style.

Interesting stat; The Blackburn chicken had as many Premier League goals and assists in it's brief cameo that ours has had in almost an entire season, and theirs didn't cost £20m. Rovers had just 39% possession in a home game they needed to win to stay up. Understandable if you're playing Barcelona or Swansea, but Wigan? That's some sorry shit right there. Up until a few weeks ago they were looking ok, then the arse fell out of them. So now not only have they been relegated, but the fans are not even going to have the consolation of seeing Kean and the owners leave, as according to the chrome domed Scot: *"Every time I have spoken to them they have told me categorically that they are in it for the long term. They feel emotionally bonded with the club. They want to get the club back to the level it should be at and beyond as soon as possible. They are obviously disappointed, but agree we must now look forward. I am here for the long term. These are challenging times for the club and the owners, but I believe Venky's are 100 per cent the right owners. I am not going anywhere and neither are the owners."*

Ha! Whaddya know, turns out the Blackburn fans were right all along, Steve Kean IS just a stooge for the worst owners in the league and he did indeed get them relegated. My bad.

LIVERPOOL 4 CHELSEA 1

Competition - Premier League
Date - Tue 8 May 2012
Venue - Anfield
Scorer(s) – Essien O.G. Henderson, Agger, Shelvey
Half Time - 3-0
Star Man – Andy Carroll

Team: Reina; Johnson, Carragher, Skrtel, Agger; Downing (Sterling), Henderson, Shelvey, Maxi (Kuyt); Suarez, Carroll:

We really needed this. It doesn't make up for the disappointment of Wembley or the staggeringly poor home record but it was nice all the same. Everyone had smiles on their faces coming out of Anfield, and I'm still smiling as I write this the day after.

The performance was fantastic from players and crowd and, bizarrely, this was the most fun I've had at the game in ages. It was just nice seeing us playing well and actually getting the goals the performance deserved for once. And I'm not gonna lie, seeing John Terry being made to look like a Sunday league clogger wasn't bad either. "Mongo no like big man with pony tail or little man with big teeth".

The great thing about it was that there was no feeling sorry for ourselves after losing the cup final. The crowd were as up for this as they've been for any league game all season and the players did their bit too. After the season we've had you'd expect everyone to be down in the dumps, but it wasn't like that at all. Seriously, if you didn't know the result from Saturday you'd have assumed that we'd won based on the two sets of fans at Anfield. Loads of empty seats in the Chelsea end, and a fired up, hugely supportive home crowd. Like I said the other day, I'd rather lose as a Liverpool fan than win supporting Chelsea.

Kenny had his name chanted throughout the game and no-one was on the player's backs either. That's not just because of the scoreline, the atmosphere was lively right from the off. Andy Carroll's all action display also helped raise the noise levels and right now his stock amongst the crowd is sky rocketing. He had great support even when things were going badly, but now that he's hit form there's every chance he could become idolised if he can sustain this level of play.

The scoreline would suggest this was our best performance of the season, and in terms of all round football it probably was as this time the goals were there to reflect our dominance. We've produced similar displays on numerous other occasions only to come away with a draw or even worse. It's unfortunate that it took until the last home game for us to get that big win, but I'm not going to let that kill my buzz. It provided some form of closure after losing to them at Wembley. Yes, they left out a lot of players and the game was fairly meaningless especially in comparison to an FA Cup final.

But still, I'm glad we got the chance to get it out of our system so quickly and so emphatically. It should really have been an even bigger margin of victory as once again we struck the woodwork twice (one from a penalty that saw us set the record for the most spot kick misses in a season), but this time it didn't matter. The woodwork actually came to our aid a couple of times too, which never seems to happen. That Torres was one of the players denied by it made this even sweeter. There have been games where virtually everything has gone wrong, but this was one where almost everything went right. About fucking time our luck changed. Shame it took until the second to last game of the season!

In the immediate aftermath of the Wembley defeat I have to admit I was really, really dreading this fixture. Yet by the day of the game I was genuinely looking forward to it. The main reason for sudden enthusiasm was Andy Carroll. Having had time to reflect on the carnage he caused in Chelsea's backline at the weekend I couldn't wait to see if he could do it again, this time from the start. I was buzzing about what we saw from him at Wembley and an awful season could take on a more positive light if Carroll could continue in the form he's been in recently. By that I don't mean it salvages anything from a disappointing campaign, but it would certainly provide hope that things might be better next year.

Well he did more than continue that form, he actually improved upon it. Chelsea just couldn't handle him and he was the leading light in an all round team performance that matched anything we've produced all season. He led from the front and everyone else followed his lead, including the fans who were loving it. The ovation he got for chasing a ball down at the Kop end to prevent a goal-kick was spine tingling. It seemed like everyone was on their feet applauding for ages after that. He must have felt ten foot tall. At times he looked ten foot tall, as he soared above Terry and Ivanovic time and time again. Those two are no shrinking violets but they got their arses handed to them repeatedly, both in the air and on the ground. It wasn't just Carroll either. He dominated them physically, but Suarez was just making them look stupid with one nutmeg after another. He was mesmerising at times, and between them our front two megged Mongo three times in the opening twenty minutes. Brilliant stuff. Having Carroll there to occupy the centre halves allows Suarez to go roaming about, just looking to get on the ball so he can do his thing. As a pairing they've been steadily improving since the turn of the year and there's definitely something there for us to build on next season if Carroll can maintain the level he's at now. I'm loving watching them develop, both individually and as a partnership, and it's a shame the season is ending just as Carroll has hit top gear.

It wasn't just about those two however, everybody performed to a high level and the two young midfielders deserve a pat on the back for how they played. Both got on the scoresheet and both looked impressive. This was easily Henderson's best game and I'm struggling to think of a single mistake he made. My only fear coming into the game was whether those two could live with Chelsea's more experienced midfield trio. Romeu is only a young lad too, but Ramires and Essien present a tough match up for even the most experienced of midfielders, let alone two lads aged 20 and 21. They were terrific though, and not just because they both scored. I'm not kidding myself, I know Chelsea have bigger fish to fry and left a lot of key players out, but it was still a strong line up and those who were selected seemed pretty up for it to me. A little too up for it in fact. Ivanovic, Ferreira, Mongo and Essien were all booked in the first half, but Ivanovic and Essien could easily have seen red. Essien's horrific two footed lunge from behind on Carroll was a clear red card offence, and for the same referee who sent Spearing off at Fulham to only produce a yellow for that is a little bit galling. Chelsea's players did not want to lose this game and many of them were trying to show they are worth a place in the Champions League final. Cech may have made a difference though, and leaving him out was a little stupid I'd say. Generally, I thought they were up for it but were just well beaten on the night.

No-one in blue was more up for it than Torres. You could see just how desperate he was to score and to play well. He did more chasing in this game than he did in his last six months in a red shirt. He wanted it badly, but not as badly as Carragher & co wanted to shut him out. Aside from one flash of brilliance that saw him smash a shot against the bar at the Kop end, he didn't get a sniff. Carragher and Skrtel were outstanding and both full backs also performed excellently. Any time Torres got the ball our players swarmed around him. It wasn't just the fans that badly wanted him shut down, our defenders wanted no part of him coming back and scoring against us either. Torres really got it in the neck from the fans and at full time he couldn't get off the field quick enough, the fucking baby. The lowest ebb had to have been the 'She fell over' chant after he'd slipped over in front of the Kop. Not the return he hoped for, that's for damn sure.

But as well as we played things could have been different had Ivanovic's free header from a Malouda corner found the net instead of the post early on. Three of our defenders collided and fell to the ground leaving him unchallenged six yards out. This gormless looking dope scored twice in one game against us in Europe a few years back from similar situations, but this time his luck was out. All season those have been going in against us, we've not been able to catch many breaks at all so it was nice to see fortune favour us for a change. It came against the run of play, we'd started brightly and were on top, but how many times have we seen that this season? It's fair to say that our opening goal had an element of fortune about it too, although perhaps not as much as people may think. Surely I'm not the only one that thinks Suarez deliberately played that ball off Essien? When you look at it, he didn't have any other option as there was no angle to take on a shot and the path to cut the ball back to Maxi was blocked. I reckon he knew what he was doing there, it was the high percentage play under the circumstances. The run that led to it was vintage Suarez too. Despite Romeu trying to foul him as he weaved his way down the right wing, he managed to retain his balance and drive towards the box. Over came Mongo and… whoops… through the legs and he was bearing down on goal. For someone who doesn't have blistering pace, Suarez is amazing when it comes to going past players. It's a rare gift he has, especially when it comes to megging people. There's so many pointless stats and most of them mean nothing to me. They didn't do Damien Comolli much good did they? That said, I'd love to see stats for how many nutmegs Luis averages per game. I'd set the over/under at three. Terry was having a bad time of it regardless of which striker he was trying to mark and his evening would get worse when he did the splits as he tried to cut out a Maxi through ball intended for Henderson. Between the three nutmegs and doing the splits, it was clear that Terry was having trouble keeping his legs shut with so many scousers around. Can't imagine where he gets that from.

Aaaaanyway, Hendo was clean through on goal with just the keeper to beat. Last time that happened he made a right pig's arse of it at Stoke. This time the finish was as cool as you like, just bent it around the keeper into the bottom corner. Great stuff. Agger made it 3-0 when he headed in after Carroll had towered over Mongo at the back post to put the ball back into the danger area. We had other chances in the first half too. Carroll curled one over from 25 yards after a brilliant lay off from a stretching Suarez. Luis had earlier dragged one wide after his first meg on Terry and he also forced a tip over from Turnbull with a clever chip after a Downing corner. Maxi had a chance following a typically slick one-two with Suarez after another towering Carroll flick had set us on the attack, and Carroll himself was denied by Turnbull after running clear onto a poor header by Terry. Carroll's first touch and control on the run was unrecognisable from the player he was a few months ago, but he's clearly fitter and a lot more confident these days. This is the lad who looked so good at Newcastle.

There were other chances too. Downing hit the bar with a brilliant effort and earlier he should have been played in by Suarez only for the striker to overhit the pass after Carroll's closing down had forced a Chelsea error. It was brilliant stuff, the tempo was high and we were pressing Chelsea in their own half and forcing mistakes. It was starting with Carroll who was defending from the front and not letting them settle. He chased, he harried and he was tackling back too. When your centre forward is doing that and everyone else follows suit, it makes you very difficult to play against and it gets the crowd involved. Chelsea just didn't know how to deal with him, and Ivanovic ended up resorting to desperate measures when he elbowed him in the throat as 'the divine ponytail' prepared to attack a Henderson cross. Not even Kevin Friend could fail to spot that, and he rightly awarded the penalty. Ivanovic got a yellow but it could have been a red. Had the elbow been a few inches higher it surely would have been.

With no recognised penalty taker on the field Downing took the responsibility. He'd produced arguably his best half as a Liverpool player and a goal would have been just reward. He'd missed his previous two pens in the league apparently but he slotted for us in the League Cup shootout and he was unlucky not to score this time, his shot hitting the foot of the post having sent the keeper the wrong way. I felt bad for him, he's desperate to get that first league goal as it must be a real weight on his shoulders, much like the 'no assists' stat. I really hope he can rectify both at Swansea this weekend as he won't want to have those two fat zero's on his record.

That was the last action of an amazing first half. It's funny because I'd said to a few people beforehand I thought we were going to win 6-0 so I was pretty smug at the half. I'd have been a lot smugger (is that even a word?) had Downing put that pen away, but the way Carroll and Suarez were playing - not to mention Terry's performance - I was still fairly confident of being proved right. Admittedly I've predicted similar scorelines before most home games this season (most recently West Brom when I was convinced we'd get five), but that's not the point. Half time came at the right moment for Chelsea and the wrong moment for us. It's always difficult just picking up the pace straight away when you've performed so well before the break, and the second half began in fairly low key fashion. Chelsea had more of the ball than they'd had previously and we didn't appear to be pressing as much, instead preferring to stay in position and just contain them. The intensity had gone out of the game and it suited them more than us.

Chelsea pulled a goal back from a set-piece when Ramires bundled the ball home with his chest. It wasn't great from Reina but I have some sympathy with him on this one. If he stays where he is and Ramires doesn't make contact, the ball goes in and everyone points the finger at the keeper. So he moves to his right, Ramires does get a touch and the ball is in the net and people are pointing at the keeper. He probably should have done better, but I didn't think it was that bad, certainly not in comparison to some he's let in. It was certainly not as bad as the howler made by his opposite number shortly afterwards. Turnbull's poor clearance went straight to the one man in the Liverpool side he'd least want it to fall to. Shelvey strikes a ball as cleanly as anybody at the club with the possible exception of Gerrard. I've been watching him warm up at half time in a lot of games this season, and he just pings the ball from one side of the field to other effortlessly and with pinpoint accuracy. It may have been an empty net but there was still a fair bit of work to do as the half volley had to be struck with plenty of pace to prevent Turnbull getting back to make a save and it's easy to sky those. Jonjo made it look incredibly easy. Not a bad way to open your Premier League account.

That goal ensured there'd be no unlikely Chelsea fightback and the rest of the game was all Liverpool aside from one glorious chance for Lukaku that brought a fine reaction stop from a fired up Reina. After making the stop he kicked the post and pumped his fists, probably thinking the same thing most of the fans were; "Finally!!". Carroll should have done better when he miskicked from a stunning early cross from Johnson. The one blot on his copybook that, aside from that his performance was close to perfect. Nice to see him and Suarez both left on for the entire game too. Kuyt and Sterling were always going to be brought on in this game, and rightly so, but it would have been very disappointing to see either striker make way. The two widemen were the logical choices, particularly Maxi as it allowed him to get the ovation he deserved on his final game at Anfield. It was a little sad seeing him waving to the fans on his way off, he'll be missed as not only is he a quality player but he's a fantastic professional and all round good guy. He was replaced by Kuyt, who may also have been making his last appearance at Anfield. That one isn't as clear cut though, we'll have to see what happens there. Sterling replaced Downing and within seconds had a glorious chance to make a name for himself. Carroll once again towered above Ivanovic and flicked the ball on to Suarez, who in turn flicked it on into the path of the youngster. It was presentable chance and one that he may well have buried on his right foot. Unfortunately his left foot isn't great and the ball flew into the Kop. There are a lot of similarities between Sterling and Michael Owen at the same age. A weak left foot is one of them, but Owen worked on that and his heading and improved markedly within a few years. Heading probably isn't as important to Sterling as he's not likely to be a central striker like Owen was, but if he can work on his left foot then he'll be virtually unstoppable when you ally that to his searing pace and trickery.

Henderson had a shot deflected narrowly wide after being teed up by Suarez. Yet again, the key to the move was a great flick by Carroll into the path of his strike partner. They really are starting to combine well. Carroll wins virtually every aerial duel these days and Suarez is now anticipating it and running off him into space. It bodes very well for next season. Suarez then should have done better after some lovely interplay between him and Kuyt, and finally Agger headed just wide after a brilliant right wing cross by Carroll. He's shown a few times this season that his crossing is seriously good. It's a pity he can't get on the end of his own deliveries as he'd fill his boots I reckon.

There was a late incident involving Suarez and Ivanovic when they tangled by the corner flag as the defender tried to shepherd the ball out of play. He initially seemed to swing an arm at Suarez but missed, and then Suarez tried to get around him and caught him with his arm. Looked like nothing to me and Suarez was extremely apologetic as soon as it happened. Ivanovic made a meal of it and wouldn't get up, and in the end Carroll went over and tried to pull Suarez away but Luis was having none of it. The only time they weren't on the same page all night, but I loved Carroll's attitude. Basically it was 'just fucking leave him there the shithouse'.

The Kop taunted Chelsea with chants about Bayern Munich, the pick of which was *"Bayern Munich, they'll win it five it times"*. Let's hope they do, can't be having these scumbags getting their grubby little chav hands on our trophy. This feels like it's turning into the longest report of the season so I'm going to wrap it up by saying that whilst it's often said that the league table doesn't lie, I'd suggest that it's seriously stretching the truth right now. We may be 8th and will hopefully climb to 7th after the final day, but if the season were to start again I'd expect us to be right in amongst that battle for the top three or four. My logic is thus: Things have happened this season that will surely never happen again. Hitting the woodwork close to 40 times. Missing a record number of penalties. The Suarez suspension. Being without our first choice midfield pairing for virtually the entire season (Lucas and Gerrard played less than a handful of games together). Suarez missing so many chances. A world class goalkeeper forgetting how to save shots. Downing failing to register a single goal or assist.

Clearly this season has been unacceptable, but I'd argue that things are certainly not quite as bad as the results alone would suggest. We've got some major flaws and there's a lot of work to be done, but we have plenty to build on including a centre back pairing that's as good as anything out there and a strike partnership that is belatedly showing the potential to be the same. We've displayed on many occasions the kind of football we can play and but for some of the freak circumstances listed above that will surely not be repeated we'd be in a much better position. That all sounds a little bit 'Evertonian' I know, but I think it's a valid explanation at least, if not an excuse.

In closing, whilst Kenny is far from blameless and has made numerous mistakes (and I admit I've got major concerns about him in the transfer market), I really hope he's given another year to see where he can take us, but it seems very much up in the air right now. I highly doubt that the Swansea game will have any bearing on whatever decision the owners make, but it would be nice to finish off with a win anyway and hopefully Carroll and Suarez can pick up where they left off against Mongo and the other knuckledragger, Ivanovic.

SWANSEA CITY 1 LIVERPOOL 0

Competition - Premier League
Date - Sun 13 May 2012
Venue - The Liberty Stadium
Scorer(s) –
Half Time - 0-0
Star Man – Alexander Doni

Team: Doni; Kelly, Carragher, Agger, Johnson; Downing (Kuyt), Shelvey, Henderson, Maxi (Bellamy); Suarez, Carroll:

So much for going out with a bang. We barely managed a whimper. After the promise and cause for optimism the 4-1 win over Chelsea in midweek provided, Mr Hyde showed up at the Liberty Stadium and we ended the season with yet another lacklustre defeat. Over the course of 38 games we managed to lose as many as we won. I don't even know the last time that happened.

This was your typical 'meaningless' end of season fixture and it showed.

No pressure on either side other than playing for their own professional pride, and that usually means a stroll in the May sunshine. To say we were just going through the motions would be overly harsh, yet more often than not there is an obvious lack of intensity in these last day games when there's not much at stake, especially when we're away from home.

Whilst the prize money for league positions means a lot to those in the boardroom, players don't give a shit about that kind of thing. I doubt there's been too many dressing room rallying calls down the years along the lines of *"Come on lads, win this today and the club will get another 750k"*. Swansea wanted to round off a fine season with a home win and for us there was the incentive of trying to finish above the blues. I suspect that meant far more to the likes of me and you than to a lot of those players however. Everton's comfortable win over Newcastle put paid to any chance of that happening anyway, but the players will not have been aware of the score at Goodison so their lack of urgency cannot be put down to that. Not that this was especially terrible, it just wasn't very good and not a nice way to end the season. It leaves a bit of a stink really, particularly as it may turn out to be Kenny's last game in charge. If it is then this sure as hell wasn't a fitting way to go out. We probably shouldn't have lost as we did enough to merit a point, but we know as well as anyone that you don't always get what you deserve, especially if you can't take your chances. It won't surprise anybody that we didn't take our chances in this game. In fairness we didn't actually create that many and for a side that generally needs more clear openings than most to put the ball in the net, that's always going to lead to trouble.

The best efforts we had were almost all from Andy Carroll. In a disappointing first half from the reds he had a shot from 25 yards that he dragged wide when he probably should have played Suarez in. He also had an effort deflected just over the bar after being fed by Maxi following good pressing by Kelly to force a Swansea mistake. Aside from that, we didn't offer too much before the break and had Doni to thank for not being behind. He was playing because Reina had the mumps. He made one error when he picked up a backpass from Carroll but other than that he was excellent and made two very good saves to deny Sigurdsson and an even better one to foil Dyer. The backpass thing was weird, Carroll looked to be playing it to Carragher but put way too much on it and Carra allowed it to go through to Doni who picked it up. Difficult one for the ref and I'm not even sure of the exact rule. Is it a backpass if it was played to a defender who then chose to leave it? I dunno, I'd have given the free-kick too though. Carragher did well to come out of the wall and block the shot so it was immaterial in the end.

Swansea were clearly the better side in the first half, but after the break we came into it more and had the better chances. Carroll brought a good save out of Vorm with a brilliant overhead kick and he then should have done better with a right foot shot after being set up by Kuyt. It was a weak finish and Vorm saved easily. Doni had a much quieter time of it after the break but had no chance with the winning goal that came five minutes from time as Routledge crossed for Graham to smash the ball home from ten yards. Agger went close to an equaliser when he looped a header just over the bar, but it wasn't to be.

What happens next is the million dollar question. Like most fans, I hope Kenny gets another year. In part because he's Kenny Dalglish, but also because as I've said before, next season couldn't possibly be as bad as this one. Whilst so many bad results can't just be blamed on bad luck, there's no denying it played a part. There are some mitigating circumstances for what has happened this season, but that's easy for me to say as a fan. I expect the owners will view it differently.

Kenny wasn't their guy, he wasn't the man they ideally wanted to take the club forward. To say he was forced on them would be going too far, but in an ideal world they would not have made him the long term successor to Hodgson. He stepped in at a time when the club desperately needed him and he did so well that they were left with little choice but to keep him on beyond the initial period they intended. Dalglish earned a shot at it but now he has to convince them as to why he should be given more time. Even if he can persuade them that the poor league showing is in no small part down to certain freak occurrences unlikely to ever be repeated, there's still the issue of how the money was spent last year and whether they trust him to wisely spend whatever is made available this summer. Had he been someone who they had gone out and headhunted, the man they saw as the long term choice then it would be much easier to persuade them as they'd be more inclined to give him the benefit of the doubt. As it is, I worry he could be in real trouble. I hope I'm wrong.

Premier League Round Up (13 May 2012)

The Manchester United end of season DVD is out next week. It's called *"Gone in 60 seconds"*. Boom! How does your own medicine taste Ferguson? Those 'noisy neighbours' just laid a big old steaming turd on your front lawn, egged your windows and they slashed your tires.

Some would suggest it's pretty sad taking so much pleasure in the failure of your rivals when your own team has so many issues of their own. Well some can go and stick it where the monkey stuck the nuts. If you didn't enjoy seeing what happened to Ferguson & co on Sunday then you're either a United fan or an Evertonian. It doesn't make our season any better, but it prevented it being worse and it was seriously funny how it all unfolded. Everyone expected City to beat QPR and win the title and United fans will have been resigned to that before the games kicked off. Losing the title to City was going hurt them no matter what, but it's the hope that kills you, and going into their game at Sunderland there was little hope amongst United fans and that makes it much easier to accept your fate. It's when hope returns that things get complicated. When City somehow turned a 1-0 lead into a 2-1 deficit and still trailed as the game went into stoppage time, those United fans who'd travelled to the Stadium of Light suddenly had hope oozing out of every stinking mancunian pore. Seeing those hopes suddenly shattered into a million pieces put a smile on the faces of football fans all over the nation. Except at Goodison of course, where QPR's goals had been greeted with cheers by the home crowd. No, I'm not joking.

Michael Owen was back on the bench for United. He hasn't been seen or heard from for months, but when there's a chance of getting a picture taken with a trophy he's all over that shit like Tiger Woods on a Hooters waitress. Chester's very own Josemi. Other than the inclusion of Owen, United were at full strength as Ferguson once again called on his big game comfort blanket. No, not Park Ji Sung, the other one - Howard Webb. United took an early lead through Rooney, but just have a look at Michael Turner's defending for it; absolutely risible stuff. I'd have expected it from a Brown, O'Shea, Bardsley or any of those other ex United gimps, but what's Turner's excuse? For all the good Turner's been to them they'd have been better off signing Hooch instead. Predictably Sunderland weren't offering much and unfortunately the one chance they did create in the first half fell to the wrong man. Fraiser Campbell may be a striker, but he's also a) shite and b) a former Manchester United player. No surprise he ballooned his volley wide, the deadbeat.

Meanwhile at Eastlands, City began nervously and weren't helped by Yaya Toure doing his hamstring in the 1st half. He stayed on for a bit even though he could barely run. He played a part in the opening goal for Zabaleta but had to go off shorty after. A big loss, but still, it was only QPR so they'd be alright, wouldn't they?

Back at the Stadium of Light, and Sunderland's fans heard the news and rubbed the Mancs' noses in it, chanting *"1-0 to the City boys"*. Warms the heart the way everyone hates United. Well, almost everyone. Anyway, half time in both games and everything is going to plan as City had the lead, but early in the 2nd half came a glimmer of hope for United as Lescott's howler sent Cisse clear and he finished in typical Djibs style. Blast it hard towards the keeper and hope for the best. The ball was close to Joe Hart but had enough power that he couldn't save it. QPR's equaliser sent the United fans crazy at Sunderland. I love watching this now because we know that this story has a happy ending, but at the time it wasn't much fun.

The drama hadn't even started at that point though. Enter Joey Barton. Just what can you say about this loon other than he's a massive helmet? Give the devil his due though, what he did against City was absolutely fucking hilarious. Much like Balotelli, the best thing about Barton is he's someone else's problem. Better than that, he's someone else's captain!!

What kind of fucktard makes Joey Barton captain? Fucktard's like Neil Warnock and Mark Hughes, that's who. I'm not sure I've ever seen anything as crazy as this outside of South American or Italian footy. Cantona jumping in the crowd set the bar pretty high, but given the stakes involved in this game and the numerous offences committed in such a short space of time, I'd say Barton has cleared that bar like a Charlie Adam penalty. In his defence it should be pointed out that he didn't start it. Tevez did take a sly swing at him first, but Barton being Barton he just had to react and he elbowed him in the face. Got him good too, right under the chin. The linesman's flag went up straight away and as soon as that happened it was obvious he was in big trouble. Barton kept repeating *"he punched me in the face first"* which was true, but unfortunately for him the linesman didn't see that and Tevez escaped punishment.

What happened next was just fucking ace. Just look at his snarling face as he knees Aguero in the back, it's side splittingly funny. Then, in perhaps the most stupid act of all he tried to throw the head in on Kompany. He missed, fortunately for him. Kompany didn't even flinch, real hardmen don't need to throw their weight around, they just give you 'the look'. Had he chosen to do so, Kompany could have put his fist clean through Barton's face and out the other side of his head. And he'd still probably be banned for less games than what Joey will be for his catalogue of offences. The Tevez elbow, the Aguero knee and the Kompany head butt adds up to three red card offences already and a nine game ban, but he was just getting started. Lescott and then Richards tried to escort him from the pitch, but then.... what's this... out of left field it's Mad Mario wanting a piece of the action!! You couldn't make this shit up! Barton ducked away from Richards to try and get to Balotelli but there were too many people in the way. Wonder what Balotelli's beef was? That someone was 'outlooning' him maybe? Gotta love Balotelli finding a way to get involved even though he wasn't even on the pitch at that point. Forget David Haye and Derek Chisora, that fraud Frank Warren should be promoting this instead of scripting out of ring brawls to sell tickets for a fight between two bums that no-one cares about. Balotelli v Barton wouldn't even need promoting, it would sell itself.

The two hilarious things about Barton are that not only is he an ill disciplined, head the ball that can go off at any moment at the slightest provocation, but he will tweet about it afterwards. Be honest, when he was leaving the field how many of you immediately thought; *"aye aye, his twitter account will be lively tonight"*? It was the first thing I thought of, and he didn't disappoint. He even went as far as to say that his *'head hadn't gone at any point'* and he knew exactly what he was doing, he was just trying to provoke a City player into getting a red to even it up. Funny that the only one he nearly succeeded with was Balotelli who wasn't even playing! That confession might be treated even more seriously by the FA than the acts of violence themselves. What a complete crank. Still, his war of words with the MOTD team was pretty damn funny...

*"Shearers still on my case. I know I f*cked up Alan, thanks for stating the obvious. Whilst were both stating the obvious about each other, can I just say for the record what a great player u were. Well better than me but I have better hair (which is not hard), wear well better shirts on TV and have a personality (something u lack)."*

"I really don't like that prick, in fact I honestly despise him. I'd take it off Hansen and @GaryLineker but not from that bell, same fella that stamped on Neil Lennon then threatened FA if they banned him that he would retire from international football. No sorry, not having him, never have. Selfish, boring man him. He can do one."

I'm sure there are many people in the game who have similar views on Shearer, but there isn't a single one of them who would air those views like Barton did (maybe Bellamy if he ever brings out a book!). He really just does not give a fuck does he? 1.5m people follow him on twitter, 1.4m of them probably think he's a complete arsehole. But he's an entertaining arsehole, which is why he has 1.5m followers on twitter. For the record, I'm not one of them, I unfollowed him ages ago as I've got no interest in this Nietzsche fella he buzzes off, and I fucking hate the Smiths. As the night wore on, it emerged that he wouldn't *'take it off @garylineker'* after all, as when the jug eared crisp muncher (© my brother-in-law) got involved Barton let him have it with both barrels too...

Lineker: *Hear @Joey7Barton had a dig at Shearer. Is this an attempt, I wonder, to deflect from the obvious and deserved criticisms coming his way?*
Barton: *no deflections here mate. Think the fact about 100m people seen it will see to that. Just don't like how he gets personal...*
Lineker: *Still raging then? Still kicking out? And still, presumably, misunderstood? But only by yourself I suspect.*

Aaaaaand we're off.....

"do u wanna go there publicly "Mr Squeaky Clean" ? Think u should have a look in that vast closet of skeltons before u respond. I know a lot about THAT side to u the people don't and won't bat an eye lid at exposing u. So mind ur manners Squeaky. Now back under your stone you odious little toad."

You know the only thing that could have made this whole situation more entertaining? If Balotelli was on twitter and he'd gotten involved as well. QPR would be better off sacking Barton as had things gone differently at the Britannia Stadium they would have been relegated and he'd have been a big reason why. Some captain eh? Vincent Kompany is a captain, Joey Barton is a knob. They'd save money on his wages and it's not like he'll command much of a transfer fee if they find anyone stupid enough to buy him. Get rid.

City absolutely bombarded the QPR goal immediately after Barton's dismissal. Chance after chance came and went but then out of nothing they got done on a breakaway as Traore (who replaced Cisse after Barton's dismissal) crossed for Mackie to head past Hart. Typical bottling City everybody thought. And typical spawny United. City's fans just sat there in stunned silence feeling sorry for themselves. The atmosphere was shocking considering they were trying to win their first title in 44 years. Fear just seemed to grip the whole stadium and it was looking like United's title. As much as the thought of that distressed me, I still had to piss myself laughing at the City fan booting fuck out of his seat and others crying like new born babies. Get a grip, losers. Even worse, some of them left at 2-1 down. Probably the finest hour in the club's history, and some of them weren't there to see it because they'd left before the end. Shocking behaviour.

The fourth official signaled five minutes of added time and City had looked to have run out of ideas. Balotelli had played a pass straight into touch, Dzeko had a shot that was so wide it went for a throw in and Clichy put a cross straight over the crossbar and out for a goalkick. They'd completely lost the plot, but then with two minutes of the five gone Dzeko headed in from a corner, and two minutes later Aguero scored the most dramatic goal since Michael Tho... the most dramatic goal in many years.

The real beauty of it was that United's game had already finished and they were just standing around waiting for confirmation that they were champions. The looks on their faces when news filtered through of Aguero's goal was just priceless. Phil Jones looks gormless at the best of times, but he managed to crank up the gorm factor by about a thousand when the score came through. He's a bad gurning bastard him isn't he? My mate Terry calls him a *'Warrington faced cunt'* and try as I might I just can't top that. (apologies to anyone from Warrington reading this!)

Hearing Ferguson complain about City's game still going on after theirs had finished just added to the hilarity of it all. They had just the three minutes added time (because they were winning!) whereas City had five (mainly because it took that nutjob Barton about that long to leave the pitch). What did he want the ref to do, call for time at the same moment as Howard Webb? If that was the case then Webb would have blew up the second he heard QPR had equalised.

City fans must be in dreamland right now. Not only have they won their first title for 44 years, but they beat their hated neighbours to do it. And not only did they pip their hated neighbours to the title, but they did it by coming from eight points behind and sealed the deal with two goals in

'Fergie time'. It's difficult to see how they can ever eclipse that, no matter what success they go on to achieve in the future.

As a final footnote to this, City had to apologise for a banner that was held up by Tevez at the back of the bus on their victory parade the day after. *"RIP Fergie"* it said, in reference to him saying that *"Manchester City will never win the title in my lifetime"*. What exactly are they apologising for, the big shithouses. It was funny and very clever, which means it obviously had nothing to do with that dimwit Tevez. Amusingly, #RIPFergie was trending on twitter afterwards, which meant you had half of Merseyside ready to crack open the bubbly, and most of America freaking out as they thought the delightful 'Fergie' from the Black Eyed Peas had come to an untimely end. Disappointment for Kopites, relief for fans of the Black Eyed Peas and mixed emotions for me as I like both. What? Yeah, I said it, I like the Black Eyed Peas, not as much as I like Lady Gaga but I like 'em and if that makes me uncool then that's a cross I'll have to bear. I'll bear it whilst listening to some poptastic tunes though.

To the bottom of the table now, and QPR's late capitulation meant that Bolton would have stayed up had they won at Stoke. They probably should have but fell foul of the dodgy refereeing that Tony Pulis' men benefit from virtually every frigging week. The first goal was disgusting really. That dog Walters miscontrolled a cross, the keeper caught it and Walters just barged into him and the ball ended up in the net. Only Stoke would be allowed to get a way with that, it's a joke and I feel sorry for Bolton. Seriously, how can you give that, it's ludicrous. They came back well from that setback and took the lead thanks to two flukey goals from Mark Davies and his namesake Kevin, but a contentious pen after a Crouch tumble allowed Walters to score his second and condemned the Trotters to the drop.

Interestingly, once QPR knew they were safe their fans were actually willing City to score and celebrated wildly when Aguero's shot hit the net. Sunderland's fans cheered when they heard the score too. No cheers at Goodison though. I've got no love for Bolton and don't really care that they were relegated, I didn't like how it happened though, that shit just wasn't right and besides, I really wanted QPR to go instead, if only because of 'Sparky'. Is that the worst nickname in football? 'Big Eck' gives it a run for it's money, but 'Sparky' is worse for me as it's actually impossible to call someone 'Sparky' without sounding like you're patronising them. It's the kind of thing an American soccermom would say to a little kid: *"Hey good job today 'Sparky!'"*, usually followed by a pat on the head. Wait, that probably explains the whole Martin Jol/Hughes bust up the other week. *"Hey bad luck Shparky, let me just pat you on the head in a condeshending manner"*. '*Sparky*'. Pffft. May as well call himself '*Champ*' or '*Sport*'. Arrogant wanker, hopefully next year he'll get what's coming to him. Final observation on this. Jonathon Pearce actually said *'nice touch for a big man'* after some deft control by Crouch. Hey

Jonathon, 2004 called, it wants it's tired old cliché back.

Moving on, Arsenal went to West Brom looking to secure third spot. A howler from Fulop presented Yossi with a gift after just four minutes but a clearly offside Shane Long equalised shortly after and then a good strike from Dorrans put them in front. Fulop was at fault again when he failed to keep out a shot by Santos and he completed his hat-trick of assists when he punched the ball towards his own net allowing Koscielny a tap in. Not his finest hour and Ben Foster's value to the Baggies skyrocketed without him even playing. Add an extra nought to your contract demands lad if that's their alternative. Strewth.

The Arsenal celebrations at full time were a little over the top for me. The fans, players and Wenger were all giving it the big un. Bit embarrassing that, it wasn't so long ago Arsenal used to be winning stuff. Celebrating Champions League qualification is a bit small time, especially for a team like Arsenal that qualifies every year.

Speaking of people with a penchant for embarrassing celebrations, Adebayor scored inside two minutes as Spurs beat Fulham at White Hart Lane. No cringeworthy celebration this time, but he didn't need that to embarrass himself as he appeared to be sporting some kind of dead animal on his head. A squirrel possibly? Motson used the phrase *"quick feet for such a big man"* to describe the goal. Hey Motty, Jonathon Pearce called, he said stop stealing his lines and go and fuck yourself, you hysterical, whiney old goat. Ok, it wasn't Jonathon Pearce, it was me. Still, the point stands. The lively Dembele went close twice for Fulham before Defoe doubled Spurs' lead with a typical poachers goal. Spurs finished fourth and are now relying on Bayern to beat Chelsea to make the CL. Does anyone other than Chelsea fans want them to win that game? Evertonians probably, just because they know it will piss us off.

With Spurs and Arsenal both winning, it didn't matter what Newcastle did at Goodison. Good job too, as they got their arses handed to them. Pienaar's deflected shot put the blues in front and Jelavic doubled their advantage soon after with another good finish. Heitinga made it 3-0 before Hibbert finally found the net after 11 years of trying with a neat header in front of the Park End. Unfortunately for him it was in his own goal. Cahill was given a red card at the end of the game for grabbing Cabaye by the throat. I'm not going to condemn anyone for grabbing that snide by the throat, he's a dirty bastard on the sly him. There is some suggestion Cabaye had pushed over a ballboy and that's what Cahill took exception to. If that's the case I hope his suspension is overturned. Yes, that's right, I did just take Tim Cahill's side. In my defence it's a lot easier not hating him when he's only scoring three goals a season. Keep it up Timmy lad.

Wigan v Wolves was one of the few games that had absolutely nothing riding on it. Jarvis opened the scoring with a cracker but Di Santo equalised with a feeble shot that the keeper could have stopped by throwing his cap on it, if he had one, which unfortunately for Wolves he didn't. Still, he could have, y'know, dived for it or something. Just an idea like. Emerson Boyce then bagged a brace before Fletcher pulled one back and it ended 3-2 to Wigan. Jarvis, Fletcher and Doyle should not be playing in the Championship next season, but will Wolves allow all three to leave? Doubtful. Still, at least Ebanks-Blake will be back in his comfort zone. He'll probably score 30 goals next season.

Norwich beat Villa 2-0 thanks to goals by Holt and Jackson. McLeish said afterwards he sees no reason why he won't be in charge at Villa next season. The next day he was sacked, so there's one reason.

Chelsea's reserves took on relegated Blackburn in another game that mattered little to anyone, including the two teams involved. Torres was left out in favour of Lukaku. So he can't even get in a second string side these days? Still, if they win in Munich no doubt he'll be gegging right in at the front of the team photo. He's like a Spanish Michael Owen, in more ways than one. Mongo bagged the first goal of the game, Meireles made it 2-0 and although Yakubu pulled one back Chelsea held on for the win. Steve Kean was typically cheery and upbeat afterwards, probably oblivious to the storm that was about to blow in the next day when a video was released of him calling Allardyce a *'fucking crook'* and predicting a top ten finish and League Cup win for Rovers. He also claimed to have single handedly discovered Phil Jones and plucked him from the youth team when everyone else at the club thought he was crap. Now he's being sued by Fat Sam amidst growing calls for him to be sacked and a petition containing over five thousand signatures from Rovers fans had been sent to the Venkys demanding his dismissal. Just when I thought he couldn't possibly be any more dumber, he goes and does something like this.......and totally redeems himself!! I tried to distance myself from Kean last week but after watching the video, who am I kidding, he's still my boy!

chapter fifteen

Game of Thrones

So the season ends and the King is removed from his throne. Not exactly a surprise - he was in trouble from the moment the owners got rid of Comolli. Maybe winning the FA Cup would have granted him a stay of execution (Ian Ayre claimed that it wouldn't but how can you sack a man who'd won two of the three competitions he entered?) but ultimately Kenny paid the price for an 8th place finish and his signings not providing 'bang' for the owners' 'buck'. Spending as much money as he did and then finishing below Everton and Newcastle was always going to leave him vulnerable, especially given that he wasn't the owners' ideal choice to begin with.

Had he been a bright young coach they'd head hunted themselves, maybe he'd have been given the benefit of the doubt and could have survived. He wasn't though; he was a compromise they'd had to make, and a few days after we'd lost to Swansea on the final day of the season it was announced that the second reign of 'King Kenny' was over.

There was understandable outrage from supporters when the decision was made. That was always going to be the case, as despite the poor league results there was plenty of evidence to suggest that the 8th placed finish was something of an anomaly and if anyone was going to be cut extra slack by the fans it was Kenny Dalglish. Had performances been as poor as the results I'm sure the majority of fans would have reluctantly gone along with the decision to replace him, but the fact is for the most part they hadn't been. Many of the dropped points came in games that we had dominated. It wouldn't take much to turn those draws and defeats into victories, and from that perspective we weren't too far away from being very competitive. For Kenny not to be given the chance to put it right rankled with many, and FSG came under a lot of fire on the LFC forums. That criticism escalated as it became clear there was no-one lined up to step in and it appeared that there was no real plan in place. John W Henry and Tom Werner know very little about football - that's not meant as an insult, it's merely a statement of fact - and having already sacked Comolli, the man they had brought in to assist them in making football decisions, questions were naturally being asked about who was now advising them: 1) who are they to sack Kenny Dalglish? and, 2) how could they be trusted to get the next appointment right?

I shared those fears about whether they knew what they were doing about who was advising them, but not the outrage at Kenny's departure. I was disappointed and more than a little sad about it, but not especially angry. I'd have much preferred he'd been given another year but I'd be lying if I said I was spitting feathers that he didn't get it. My concern was more to do with their capability to bring the right man in to replace Kenny than the actual decision to let him go. I felt sadness and was certainly going to miss not having him around any more, but I wasn't angry because I'd been preparing for it ever since we lost the FA Cup final. Beating Chelsea was the only way he was going to be given another year and even then it would have been done reluctantly, if at all.

The owners wanted to go in another direction with a younger coach; it's what they intended to do from the first day they walked through the door. I understood the logic in that but couldn't see anybody at the club who'd be qualified to identify who that man should be. I still don't, but FSG have been assuring people that they are being advised by some of the 'biggest and most respected names' in world football. They won't say who, understandably, although Johann Cruyff is surely one of them given the numerous links in the press with him towards the back end of the season (he was linked with DoF job which suggests that someone found out he was talking to us, put two and two together and came up with five). That would help to explain how close Roberto Martinez came to getting the job too. Martinez has close ties with the Cruyff family and is big pals with Cruyff's son Jordi. Cruyff was a wonderful player, he was a successful manager and he's been involved in the game in various capacities. His opinion is certainly worth seeking out if you're someone with a limited knowledge of the game, but who are these other 'biggest names in football' who FSG have been talking to? Who knows, but being a big name in football isn't always a guarantee of sound judgement.

Take Pele for instance. The world's greatest ever player in the eyes of many, yet this is a fella who included El Hadji Diouf in his list of the '100 greatest living footballers' whilst leaving out Steven Gerrard, Rivelino and Jairzinho amongst others. He also recently claimed that Messi isn't as good as Neymar. Then you have good old crazy Diego. Would you want him advising anybody on who our new manager should be? He'd probably put himself forward for the job, which would certainly have ended in tears but would have been a hell of a fun ride while it lasted. I'm not suggesting that FSG were consulting with Pele and Maradona. My point is that we have no idea who helped them come to the decision to sack Dalglish and who advised them throughout the process of finding his successor. That is a little alarming to me and clearly was to others.

The backlash from fans was fierce, with some making comparisons between FSG and our previous 'custodians'. The lack of knowledge and understanding of both the game of football and Liverpool Football Club itself was certainly something shared by old and new owners and obviously they shared the same nationality, but for me that's where the comparisons ended. Like Hicks and Gillett, FSG naturally want to make money out of LFC, but unlike those two parasites I don't believe they are looking to run the club into the ground to do so. I would question whether they know what they are doing, but not their motives for doing it. The easiest thing in the world for them would have been to keep Kenny Dalglish. It would be cheaper than having to pay him off, then pay compensation to another club to get their manager and then have to back the new boss with cash as he reshaped the team to suit his own style of play. It would also have been the safe option in terms of an easy ride for them. They knew replacing Dalglish would be an unpopular move. There was no fan movement to oust Dalglish, his name was still chanted right up until the end and it was rare to find anyone calling for his head. Indeed, the list of reasons to keep him may well have been longer than the list not to; it all depends on who was making the list doesn't it?

My list was definitely stacked on the side of keeping him. The way I looked at it, there's no way we'd have as bad a season in the league next year. As I've already written, too many freak occurrences affected us this season, things that would never, ever be repeated. We're not going to hit the woodwork as many times - it may even take us three years to match the tally we racked up this season. We're not going to miss as many penalties again either, and there was strong evidence late in the campaign that Andy Carroll has now found his feet and is ready to make the impact that we hoped when we signed him. Fingers crossed we won't ever have to go through anything like the Suarez/Evra debacle again, and when you take all that into account (as well as the injury to Lucas) there's every chance that next season would have been much better. That's not the heart ruling the head; I'm basing that entirely on logic. It's not like we played badly and looked a poor side for most of the season. Generally we played well. Arsenal finished third but I'm not prepared to accept they're better than us, and I'm certainly not going to say we're inferior to Newcastle and Everton. You can say I'm kidding myself and the table doesn't lie, maybe that's true. But my argument would be that if we were to replay last season all over again we wouldn't finish behind those sides. Chelsea are a different kettle of fish. You can make a good argument that like us they badly underachieved in the league and I'd make the same point on Spurs who looked very good until the wheels came off when the whole 'Arry for England' thing started. My point is that I believe there's no way we wouldn't have significantly improved next season and no reason we couldn't have been strong contenders for the top four.

The owners may well have even felt the same. I don't know. What I do know is that if they wanted to replace Kenny (and clearly they did) they would never have a better opportunity to do it than after a season in which we finished in 8th place. Had they given him another year and we'd finished, say, 5th and really close to the Champions League places, what then? Dalglish would legitimately be able to argue that progress was being made and that he deserved more time. No, if they wanted to bring their own man in this was the perfect opportunity to do it. Finishing 8th will have been high on any list of 'reasons to make a change', but it may not have been top. Failure in the transfer market is perhaps the biggest knock on Dalglish as that is inextricably linked to the poor league placing. You can make excuses for why we finished 8th, but there are no excuses for the lack of value for money FSG have seen from their investment in players. Assuming they plan on making a decent transfer kitty available this summer it's difficult to condemn them if they didn't trust Kenny to spend it wisely. Hand on heart, as much as I wanted him to stay I'd be lying if I said I wouldn't have been worried about how he'd spend this summer's budget. I doubt FSG will throw money at it every year, so it's imperative that we don't have a repeat of last summer. Comolli lost his job in large part due to that, and it probably did for Kenny too.

I guess what I'm saying is that had it been up to the overwhelming majority of fans (myself included) Kenny would have got another year, but I can understand why the owners felt differently. As long standing supporters we have an emotional attachment to Kenny Dalglish that few other sets of fans have for anybody. Who else has done for their club the things Kenny Dalglish has done for his? No-one, that's who. There's a reason he's known as 'the King', and it's not because he does a mean Elvis impression. He's probably the club's greatest ever player, unquestionably the club's greatest ever servant and ambassador and in the eyes of the supporters he holds a status that no-one else is close to matching. No-one is bigger than Liverpool Football Club, but no-one comes as close to it as Kenneth Mathieson Dalglish MBE.

John W Henry and Tom Werner don't have that emotional attachment and reverence towards him however. Sentiment simply doesn't come into it for them as they don't have the history with Kenny that we do. They speak warmly of him and I'm sure they hold him in high regard, but unlike us they wouldn't have been thinking *"we have to give him another year, he is Kenny fucking Dalglish"*. Perhaps that's not such a bad thing, only time will tell on that. At least now they can be judged properly as this is finally their club with their people running it. Kenny was their appointment, but he wasn't part of their vision. Now they'll stand or fall by their own decisions.

Whilst I could reluctantly understand their decision to part company with Dalglish, what happened after that was far more difficult to comprehend. If they'd known for some time they were going to replace Kenny (and it's fairly obvious they had) then surely they'd already have his successor lined up and ready to go? The last thing I wanted to see was for them to sack Kenny and then have to start a 'process' to find his replacement. Even Parry and Moores didn't fall into that trap. When they decided Houllier had to go (after a defeat to Portsmouth in the FA Cup) they sent a delegation over to Spain to speak with Benitez to see if he'd be interested in taking over in the summer. That was in February. By the time they pulled the trigger on Ged at the end of the season they already had their man in place, although it couldn't be announced straight away as there was the small matter of clearing it with Valencia first, which they hadn't done! Of course that's not strictly playing by the book, but it's what everybody does and it's the only sensible course of action as the last thing you want is to sack a manager and then find yourself being rejected by those you approach to replace him. Before you know it you're down to number six or seven on your list; someone you don't really want but have to take as you're under pressure to make an appointment and can't come up with anybody better. See Alex McLeish at Villa for example.

FSG seemingly didn't go down that sensible road that Parry and Moores took back in 2004, unless they and Brendan Rodgers have pulled the wool over everybody's eyes of course and this whole 'manager search' and 'interview process' was a big sham. They initially had a list of around twelve managers they wanted to speak to. That was worrying, especially given some of the names reportedly on that 'dirty dozen'. Even more worrying was that the first name we were made aware of was *gulp* Roberto Martinez. In FSG's defence, that was down to motormouth Dave Whelan, who got straight on the phone to Sky minutes after agreeing to LFC's request to speak with his young manager. Still, you sack Kenny Dalglish one day and then approach Roberto Martinez the next, and the fans are understandably going to hit the roof. I wasn't particularly concerned that Martinez was going to be our next manager - I didn't think for a second he would be (not at that point anyway) - but it bothered me that he was even being considered, especially as it appeared that he was the first person FSG wanted to speak to. This may not have been the case as they could have been tapping u… I mean chatting to various people well before that without anybody knowing about it. But if that was the case why would you even consider Martinez? Wigan were bottom of the league in March before a great run of form saw them climb the table and survive comfortably. It seemed that Martinez was being judged on that late run of form rather than his whole body of work. Let's not forget that they were bottom for a reason. I'm just thankful that Terry Connor didn't turn Wolves around or God knows what may have happened!

Martinez seems like a nice, personable fella who demands his teams play attractive football. I'm sure he's a decent enough coach and may well go on to be a very good manager but at this stage in his career what had he done to even merit an interview for the Liverpool job? Admittedly the 3-4-3 system he changed to late in the season proved a masterstroke and kept them up, but why did it take so long for him to change to that formation if he knew it was so good? Seems to me like he sort of stumbled on it as a last throw of the dice. Of all the names rumoured to be on the list of 12, Martinez ranked next to bottom in my eyes. Who was bottom? Alan fucking Pardew, that's who. There was probably no substance to rumours

FSG wanted to speak to him, but then again if Martinez was on the shortlist then why wouldn't Pardew be?

The day after Whelan dropped his Martinez bombshell on us, Brendan Rodgers announced that he had declined an interview. It was reported by some that he didn't want the job, which was not strictly true as it would later transpire. What he didn't want was to disrespect Swansea and upset their fans by going to interview for a job with eleven other candidates, especially when some people at the club appeared to be briefing the press that Jurgen Klopp and Pep Guardiola were top of their list. I didn't blame him - it made perfect sense. Then Ajax boss Frank De Boer also ruled himself out of the running whilst Klopp said he was flattered at interest in him from English clubs but had no intention of leaving Dortmund, so that was him crossed off the list too. They were dropping like flies now. Villas Boas had been extremely keen but then found out that LFC had gone to Chelsea to get the lowdown on him and apparently saw his arse over it. He had been lined up for an interview but told Ian Ayre not to bother flying out to meet him as he was no longer interested. I sort of see his point. It's not like anyone at Chelsea is going to give him a glowing reference as how stupid would they look if he went to one of their rivals and was a success? Of all the candidates who hadn't already ruled themselves out AVB would have been my preferred choice, assuming Guardiola wasn't interested of course (it appeared he wasn't as he said he planned on taking a few months off before even considering another job). Villas Boas should never have gone to Chelsea but I guess the opportunity - not to mention the money - was too good to turn down. I can't hold what happened at Chelsea against him. I know I took the piss out of him relentlessly when he was there but the Goodfellas 'Spitshine Tommy' comparison actually has a lot of basis in reality. He was never going to gain the respect of that dressing room, certainly not from the moment he dropped Lampard and upset the old guard. Just a pity he didn't do a 'Billy Bats' on John Terry really isn't it? Would have done the world a huge favour.

Potentially AVB could become a great manager and although it would been a big risk I'd have been ok with it if we had appointed him. We didn't though, and it was looking increasingly likely we'd be giving the job to Martinez, especially when he was photographed out strolling with John W Henry in Miami Beach. In fact, according to Dave Whelan we'd already offered it to him. That has since been emphatically denied by various people at LFC, from Steven Gerrard to Ian Ayre, but at that time the Wigan chairman was posting hourly updates on the whereabouts of his manager, what he was having for breakfast, who he was eating it with, what they were having… it was becoming ridiculous. It wasn't the fault of Martinez, but I found myself holding it against him anyway. Could he not just pick up the phone and tell the busy old bastard to give it a rest?

Then I got a text message off a mate saying he knows someone at Paddy Power and they were panicking after a load of money was thrown on

Rodgers getting the job. This kind of thing always happens and doesn't usually mean much; if anything it usually means to completely disregard it. There'd been loads of money lumped on AVB and then on Benitez, and there was even a flurry of bets for Harry Redknapp after a rumour swept through Merseyside that FSG wanted a 'Harry and Jamie' father and son management team. I'm not kidding, that actually happened. On that note, if anyone reading this bet on 'Team Redknapp' taking charge, I've got some magic beans for sale if you're interested.

The difference in the betting patterns this time was that the money was coming from Rodgers' home town, and some of the bets were pretty significant. Something was afoot. His odds were slashed and a couple of days later the papers were reporting that it was a straight choice now between him and Martinez. If that's the choice, to me it's no choice at all - it's the Ulsterman all the way. I like Rodgers a lot, as you'll have gathered from my regular praise for Swansea in these pages. However, if you'd said to me at the end of the season that we were going to sack Dalglish and replace him with Rodgers, I would have been far from happy about it. Not because I don't rate Rodgers, but because I don't think he's done enough yet to deserve a crack at the Liverpool job. Certainly not at the expense of Kenny Dalglish. However, the landscape had changed now with Kenny already gone and the owners dead set on appointing a bright young coach. The lack of any real credible alternative meant I was warming to the idea of Rodgers, especially the more and more I read up on him. Swansea eventually gave us permission to talk to him (like we hadn't already!) and a day later he was being unveiled at a press conference.

And what a press conference it was. If I had a tenner for every time I've seen or heard people using the word 'impressive' about Rodgers following his first appearance as Liverpool boss, I wouldn't be writing this book as I'd be enjoying early retirement in the Bahamas. He was impressive though wasn't he? I mean that really is the first word that comes to mind to describe him. Impressive. His coaching credentials are as good as anybody's, he's studied the game all over Europe and his Swansea side were very pleasing on the eye. More than that though, they were effective. Sure you can pick holes in it - they didn't score that many goals and a lot of their possession was in their own half - but surely that has a lot to do with the quality of players at Rodgers' disposal? Many of those lads are Championship level players at best, the same as Norwich who also punched well above their weight under an impressive young coach. I'd go as far as to say they were the two most well organised sides we faced last season. You could see that everyone knew exactly what they were supposed to be doing and there was a clear pattern of play. We couldn't beat Swansea in two attempts and we only beat Norwich due to a combination of Suarez's brilliance and some defensive errors on their part. With better players at his disposal, in theory Rodgers' system of play should be even more effective.

Obviously we need some strengthening in certain areas but there's no reason why the players we already have can't adapt to his style and system. After all, it's not like we've been playing hoofball for the last 18 months. Kenny had us playing pass and move so there shouldn't be that big a transition when we have the ball. The most intriguing aspect will be how we adapt to the pressing game employed by the new boss. It's very much based on what Barcelona do and if he can pull that off we'll be very difficult to play against. We Liverpool fans love our soundbites and the one Rodgers delivered on his first day about *"wanting to make coming to Anfield the longest 90 minutes of an opponent's life"* is certainly banner material. How will he do that? Well I'm no coaching expert, far from it, but I've read up a lot on how Rodgers likes to play and discovered some interesting things. For example, when his side loses the ball, he sets the target that they must win it back within six seconds or six passes. That takes a lot of energy, which is why his sides then rest when they have the ball, which explains the amount of possession in their own half. That's why they'll knock it about in little triangles at the back as it allows players further up the field to catch a breather. The idea is when you have the ball you keep it and when they have it you win it back quickly and then keep it some more. Obviously you also have to do something creative with it, but it's more about building attacks patiently and working the right opening. As I say, very much Barcelona based and FSG's idea is for the club to develop a way of playing, an identity if you like, that doesn't change even when the coach does.

In theory it all sounds very encouraging, especially as we already have in place people who helped shape the Barcelona youth system in Rodolfo Borrell and Pep Segura. But I'm reluctant to completely buy into the hype just yet as we haven't even played a game and besides, for me the most important thing with any manager isn't their coaching, man-management, how they handle the press or whatever. The one thing that tops everything is whether they are any good in the transfer market. You can get away with costly mistakes at some clubs, but we aren't one of those clubs; not anymore. We are in a fortunate position in comparison to a lot of teams in that we can compete at the high(ish) end of the market (as long as we aren't going up against the likes of City or Chelsea obviously), but we can't afford to get it wrong again. Rodgers has to spend well as if he doesn't it won't really matter how good he is at everything else, bad signings will make the job impossible. We have nothing to base an opinion on as to whether he will be any good in the transfer market or not. What he did at Swansea is largely irrelevant as he won't be shopping at Lidl anymore. It won't be Harrods either unfortunately; three years without Champions League football and a succession of expensive mistakes mean he'll mostly be shopping at Marks & Spencers with maybe the odd pick up from Harrod's bargain bin if we're lucky (Real Madrid cast offs usually represent good value). He's not had that luxury before so it will be fascinating to see what he does.

It's also interesting to note that it will be Rodgers having the final say on signings and he won't be working under a Director of Football, as that most certainly isn't what FSG originally planned. They were dead set on bringing in a replacement for Comolli, and it's well documented they wanted Louis Van Gaal in the role. Rodgers even mentioned him by name when he told the press he had refused to work under the Dutchman as he won't work in that kind of set up. He also claims he told FSG; *"If you want to have a sporting director, get him in and then pick your manager. But if you do I won't be the manager."* It's funny really: here you have the rookie manager of Swansea telling Liverpool FC *"it's him or me"* about a guy that has won pretty much everything there is to win and is one of the most well respected figures in the game. The remarkable thing is, he didn't come across as being out of order or arrogant in saying it! He's got that kind of authority about him even though he's only been a top flight manager for one season. Rodgers made such an impression on the club that they agreed to scrap the Van Gaal plan as they didn't want to lose him. Easy to see why, as from watching him talk I reckon if you spent five minutes in his company he'd have you believing he was the second coming of Shankly and Paisley rolled into one. I'm not saying he is, obviously, nor that he'd make any such wild claims of self grandeur; it's just that he has a certain aura and quiet authority about him. Speaking fluent Spanish (and Italian) should also help and I'm sure Suarez in particular will appreciate that. If his team-talks are anything like his press conferences then those players will believe anything is possible. I'm trying to take a step back from it as on paper this is a massive gamble by FSG, but it's difficult not to just jump right on board the Rodgers bandwagon as he's just so… I hate to say it… impressive.

Of course it could go tits up and he could be a massive flop. There's certainly a large element of risk that could happen just as there is with any appointment. Rodgers is almost completely unproven as a manager and FSG could really end up with egg on their faces just as Chelsea did when they appointed Villas Boas. The young Portuguese boss is a good comparison as there are a number of similarities between the two. Both spent time working under Mourinho and like the Real Madrid boss are multilingual. Also both have devoted their lives to coaching having not had any worthwhile playing career to speak of and both are very young in management terms. Their coaching credentials are impeccable, but managing is different to coaching as AVB found out when he re-entered that poisonous Chelsea dressing room he'd previously worked in as a junior coach under Mourinho. Rodgers won't have to deal with that thankfully, and that may have been a big reason why he ruled himself out of the running to succeed the sacked Villas Boas at the Bridge, saying *"I want to build my career, not destroy it"*. Interesting comment that, especially as he accepted Liverpool's offer just a few months later. Clearly it wasn't about wanting to stay at Swansea, more about not wanting to work for Chelsea again. After what happened to AVB it's understandable.

The risk of failure is probably higher for Rodgers than it would have been with a lot of other candidates, especially people like Capello and Van Gaal who were rumoured to be interested, but the potential ceiling is also a lot higher too which is probably what landed him the job. In US Sports terminology, Rodgers would be described as having *'massive upside'*. He's someone who could possibly become the next great manager or he may turn out to be the next Owen Coyle. I feel the same about Lambert; I could see him managing a top club one day but you never know do you? You take the wrong job at the wrong time, have a bad time of it and your reputation never recovers. It wasn't long ago Coyle was being tipped to replace Wenger at Arsenal. His stock has plummeted since. Will he ever be spoken that highly of again? Doubtful.

Big clubs in England don't generally make these kind of appointments. It's usually the tried and trusted experienced managers who get the nod. That makes it difficult for the bright young managers to get a chance to prove themselves, and from that point of view FSG deserve some credit as whether it turns out to be the right or wrong move it certainly took balls to do what they did. Chelsea bucked the trend with AVB and it backfired but they got away with it as Di Matteo came in and fluked the European Cup. If the Rodgers appointment goes wrong FSG will rightly be slaughtered for it, but if he turns out to be the man they think he is then they should be applauded for their bravery. Whatever happens, at least we can now hold them accountable either way and that's how it should be. As for Kenny, it would be nice to see him back at the club in some capacity, but understandable if he feels it isn't for him. He waited a long time to get back in the manager's seat. He had unfinished business and ultimately whatever anyone else says for me his return was a successful one as he put silverware in the cabinet, just as he's always done. Coming back for a second go at it didn't harm his legacy; it enhanced it. He went through some trying times with the Suarez/Evra thing, and the lowpoint of the season for me was him being cornered on Sky after the 'handshake' debacle. That should never have happened: someone failed miserably in their job by not informing him what had took place. He went out to face a barrage of questions about an incident he didn't even know had happened. It was uncomfortable to watch and even more uncomfortable when the club made him - and Suarez - apologise the next day to appease angry sponsors. Seeing a great man put through that didn't sit well with me at all, but he came through it with dignity as he always does and whilst some were hinting at a rift between him and his star striker, a few days later he was leaping off the bench and demanding his players step aside and let Suarez take a penalty. *"Rift? What rift?"* That's the kind of man he is: someone who players love playing for and who only ever has the club's best interests at heart. He's a rarity in football these days. It's become a dirty business, ruined by money and rife with snakes and lowlifes. Kenny may well be better off out of it; hopefully he'll enjoy his retirement knowing that he helped the club out in it's hour of need and put the smiles back on peoples faces.

That just about covers it I think as we prepare to get back on the LFC roller coaster as a new season approaches. It's a time of uncertainty: we have a new, young manager who could just as easily turn to be a huge flop as a roaring success. We'll have new players coming in too, whilst some old players may even return from their loan spells to see if they can salvage a future at the club under a new boss (wouldn't hold my breath on that but you never know). There's a lot of question marks going into next season; we're a club that has finished 7th, 6th and 8th in successive seasons and a number of players as well as the rookie manager have it all to prove. Yet when it all kicks off in August I'll have somehow convinced myself we're in for a great season. That pre-season optimism bug has a lot to answer for...

"It has been an honour and a privilege to have had the chance to come back to Liverpool Football Club as manager. I want to put on record my heartfelt gratitude to Liverpool's fans, who have always given me and the club their unwavering support. Without them neither the Club nor I would have achieved anything."

Kenny Dalglish, May 2012

Also from the author

Dave Usher is the editor of *'The Liverpool Way'* fanzine and popular website of the same name. You can read more of his thoughts throughout the course of the 2012-13 season in the printed fanzine as well as online via the website.

web www.liverpoolway.co.uk

fanzine www.liverpoolway.co.uk/shop/

twitter @theliverpoolway

You can also find *'The Liverpool Way'* on Facebook, Sulia and don't forget to check out the regular podcasts on itunes.

20422240R00236

Printed in Great Britain
by Amazon